THE ELITE

THE ELITE

First edition, a de luxe, leather bound and numbered edition (0001-1500)
published in 1984. ISBN 0 620 07420 5.

Second edition, a standard hardcover edition,
published in 1984. ISBN 0 620 07421 3.

Third edition, published in 1985.
ISBN 0 620 07421 3.

Softcover edition, published in 1985.
ISBN 0 620 08517 7.

Cartography by Dave Arkwright, SAS.

Cover photograph, Paddy O'Reilly.

Typesetting and reproduction, Wissink Associates, Durban.

Black and white photographs, Adcolour, Durban.

Design, Pete Cole, SAS.

Printed and bound in South Africa by Interpak Natal, Pietermaritzburg.

Published in South Africa by the Three Knights Publishing,
Transkei, PO Box 483, Amanzimtoti 4125. Telephone (031) 933827.

© The Three Knights, 1984.

THE ELITE

The story of the

RHODESIAN

SPECIAL AIR SERVICE

Best wishes,
Barbara Cole

Barbara Cole

Three Knights

*Dedicated to all Rhodesian Special Air Service men
who died during operations*

also

To Captain Mac McIntosh, Bronze Cross of Rhodesia

and

Staff Sergeant Dave Berry, Bronze Cross of Rhodesia

Another time, another place

*It was the best of times,
it was the worst of times
—Dickens*

Acknowledgements

The author wishes to thank everyone who helped compile this book. The list is too long to publish, but special mention goes to SAS members, SB and CIO officers, the Commander of the Selous Scouts, Lieutenant-Colonel Ron Reid-Daly and to the Durban branch of the SAS Association of South Africa.

Picture Credits

The author thanks the following people for the use of their photographs:

Pete Allan, Steve Baletta, Imre Baka, Lee Berry, Iain Bowen, Charlie Buchan, Pete Cole, Carol Doughty, Jappie du Toit, Ken Harvey, Alan Hider, Mike Longuet-Higgins, Stu Hulley-Miller, Rob Johnstone, Bob Jones, Steve Kluzniak, Karl Lutz, Cpl *Lucy*, Bob McKenna, Scotty McCormack, Irene McIntosh, Vernon McLuckie, Paddy O'Reilly, Dave O'Mulligan, Dave Padbury, Ron Reid-Daly, Mike Rich, Brian Robinson, Wayne Ross-Smith, Keith Samler, Dale Scott, Dave Scott-Donalan, Rich Stannard, Colin Willis, The Rhodesian Ministry of Information, unknown photographers and those who wish to remain anonymous.

Cartoon Credits:

Geneva: Vic McKenzie, *The Sunday Mail.*
Nkomo: *SB official.*
General Walls's Last Stand: Meintjes, *The Herald.*
Hagar: *King Features.*

Contents

Maps

Foreword

The Rhodesian Special Air Service, one of the most formidable fighting forces in the world, operated almost exclusively across the border during the long bitter bush war, undertaking deep-penetration missions against insurgents being harboured inside neighbouring Mozambique and Zambia.

There were missions into Botswana too, and at one stage, they were operating without benefit of passport in all three neighbouring black territories at the same time.

Long before the war escalated and the whole region became their batttlefield, secret clandestine missions across the border were undertaken by Special Air Service operators. Later, when the situation intensified, they were responsible for some of the most audacious and highly sensitive missions of the war.

Yet little is known of this highly-professional Special Force unit, which had its beginnings in the days of the Malayan Emergency, and like its parent unit, the British SAS, boasted the coveted and very apt motto, Who Dares Wins.

Even before the men of the elite, carefully-selected Special Air Service mounted their most daring tasks far from home, the then Minister of Defence, Mr Jack Howman said: "My only regret is that the exploits of the SAS cannot yet be disclosed to the public so that they can share my pride in full."

Fought against the magic and madness of a changing Africa, against almost insuperable odds, against two terrorist armies who were aided and abetted by the armies of their host nations and backed by Russia and China, two of the world's superpowers, the role of the Special Air Service was unique. The Commander of Combined Operations, Lieutenant-General Peter Walls, while reluctant to single out any one unit, was to acknowledge this after the war.

It is this unique story that the writer set out to discover, and this book – the first ever released to fully detail the secret exploits of the elite Regiment – has been based on rare interviews with the very people involved in the SAS's many and varied operations, the heroes of an era. Some of their exploits may seem far-fetched, even impossible, but then, truth is often stranger than fiction.

It is a history of high-adventure and daring, courage and humanism, be it driving through the streets of a neighbouring city, walking bold as brass down those of another, knocking out trains, bridges and vital installations or swooping out of the morning skies, then with the ability to hit hard and fast, attacking and taking their leave, the devastation complete, the mission accomplished. Nowhere was out of reach or safe from SAS attack and no target too big.

The writer takes the reader from the early days in the Western Desert to the formation of the Rhodesian SAS for service in Malaya, then back to Africa where the action spans the days of the Federation . . . the UDI era . . . and finally the decolonisation of Rhodesia by the British in 1980.

The SAS was not in the habit of giving out medals for what was no more than expected from its operators. Outstanding deeds of gallantry were honoured however, and one SAS operator and one former officer, were the only two soldiers in the security forces to have been awarded the country's highest military honour, the Grand Cross of Valour, equivalent to the Victoria Cross and the American Congressional Medal of Honour. Both held the Silver Cross of Rhodesia and one also had the Bronze Cross, making him the only holder of the "hat-trick" and thus the most decorated member of the security forces.

Paying tribute to the Rhodesian Special Air Service, Lieutenant-Colonel Ron Reid-Daly, the legendary and extraordinary founding commander of the Selous Scouts – and himself a former SAS man – had this to say: "It was a thoroughly professional unit which, in my opinion, more than lived up to the standards set by the British SAS."

In addition to the interviews given to the author by SAS men and those in other branches of the security forces, information has also been gleaned from top secret documents smuggled out of Zimbabwe, intelligence and aerial photographic interpretation reports, logs, maps, SB films, citations, private scrapbooks and the memories of hundreds of contributors.

As this is a history of a Rhodesian military unit, ZANU/ZANLA and ZAPU/ZIPRA are referred to as terrorists or terrs, for that is what they were called at that particular time from the Rhodesian viewpoint, and while it is accepted that not all readers will see them in this context, such terminology is used for reasons of historical accuracy.

About the Author . . .

While it is unusual for a woman to write a military history, this is not the first time a woman has written about the SAS. Virginia Cowles wrote the much-acclaimed *Phantom Major,* the story of the SAS founder, David Stirling and the SAS's beginnings in the Western Desert.

Barbara Cole has worked on newspapers and magazines in Britain, Rhodesia and South Africa, specialising in court work and human interest affairs. She was a High Court reporter for the *Rhodesia Herald* at the start of Operation *Hurricane* and in that capacity saw many an insurgent, albeit from the safety of the Press bench.

Barbara was the news editor on the controversial *Zimbabwe Times* during the interesting days of change in 1978 and later worked for the publications department of the Rhodesian Ministry of Information, helping to distribute those dreaded wartime communiques:

"Combined Operations Headquarters regrets to announce . . . "

She gave up her career with a South African publishing company to concentrate on researching and compiling the history of the Rhodesian SAS, one of the most interesting and fascinating stories to come out of the Rhodesian bush war. It took several years and despite many hurdles, Barbara was able to track down some hundreds of SAS men now dispersed in many countries around the world and get them to tell their tales. The fact that secrecy is a way of life with SAS men, makes this all the more remarkable.

The Heritage

As they waited in the silent darkness all eyes were fixed on the enemy headquarters. At last came the "Good luck" from the overall commander. The young Rhodesian selected to lead the attack against the headquarters, mumbled something in reply, gathered his men and headed off in the direction pointed out to him by the guide.

They stepped over a low wire, crossed a large open patch, then scaled another low fence. The young officer thought it a peculiar arrangement. Then the penny dropped. Surely he had not led his men through a minefield? Then he saw a notice. It was easy to translate . . . *Beware Mines.*

Somehow, they had crossed it without mishap. The problem of how to get back would have to be sorted out later. There was going to be a lot of action in the next hour and Lieutenant Ken Harvey reckoned that an inflexible plan would be doomed to failure. He was not to know it at the time, but there were no mines there. It was merely a hoax.

Still, there was no time to congratulate themselves on their good fortune. They arrived on the large expanse of lawn in front of their target. Harvey dropped off his gunners with orders to shoot anyone who appeared at any of the windows or who came out of any of the doors.

"Not the front door – we'll be using that ourselves," he reminded his men in a whisper.

Young and inexperienced though he was, Harvey, 19, was about to lead his small party of nine men into battle deep in enemy-held territory. The opposition would be numerically superior but Harvey and his men were banking on the element of surprise giving them the advantage.

They set up their bazooka in front of the door but soon learned it had a failure. As they gathered around to find out the cause, they suddenly heard the unmistakable crunching of boots on the gravel road and the sound of deep gutteral voices.

Obviously they must not be caught red-handed messing about with their defective weapon, so Harvey got everyone to lay flat in the shadows on the lawn. He then ran to the gate by the road.

From his hiding place behind the masonry pier, he could see four sentries marching up the road a few paces from him.

Harvey did not hesitate.

He stepped into the road and the silence of the night was shattered as four shots rang out. All four men dropped dead at Harvey's feet, killed at point blank range.

There had been no time for finesse and it was essential that they be killed immediately. But those few shots would have alerted the whole neighbourhood and the raiders would have to act quickly if they wanted to achieve the best results. Besides, Harvey could not have wounded enemy lying in the road while he stormed their headquarters.

As soon as the shots rang out, his men reacted immediately and charged across the lawns to the main door. By the time Harvey got there, they were busy shooting their way in.

The opposition were shooting at them from the windows, but the partisan Bren gunners they had brought along for the purpose were doing a fine job and taking a good toll, thereby easing the attacker's job.

One man was wounded in the leg... then Harvey gave the lock a final burst and they pushed the door. They threw in a few grenades and ran into the dark interior.

There were scuffling noises and then the bullets really started to fly. The din of the battle was deafening in such a confined space.

Holding his torch at arm's length so as not to attract fire to himself, Harvey switched it on to enable him to see the lie of the land. He had a quick look around and the firing increased. The enemy could see him so he dived under the table, torch still on. As he went to ground, his sergeant, who was close behind him, opened up and killed the main offender.

They rushed the spiral staircase but the enemy were firing over the ballustrade from above and it was impossible to get past the hail of bullets... they just did not have enough men for that sort of thing. As if to finalise that thought, someone rolled a hand-grenade down and it went off between three of the strike force. One man was badly wounded and Harvey ordered him to be taken outside.

Outside meanwhile, the overall commander, Roy Farran, who had taken along the unit's Highland piper, got him to play *"Highland Laddie"* just to let the enemy know that they were contending with more than a partisan raid... and as Harvey pressed home his attack on the operational headquarters and a second group prepared to storm another enemy position nearby, the defiant skirl of bagpipes rang out across the countryside.

When the enemy began firing at them, Farran, undaunted by such distractions, pushed the piper into a convenient slit-trench and he continued to play from a sitting position. At the second target, the attackers charged the enemy stronghold, cheering when they heard the pipes.

Over at the main target – the German 51st Corps Operational Headquarters at Albineat, Italy – the ground floor had soon been taken and no enemy remained alive. The German Chief of Staff, Colonel Lemelson, was also accounted for during the furious room-to-room fighting.

Outside, the Bren gunners were continuing their work and many Germans were killed when they tried to shoot from the windows, or as they ran out of the back doors.

As it was impossible to take the house with their limited force and in the twenty minutes allowed, Harvey decided to raze the building to the ground.

They started a fire on the ground floor and helped it get a good start with some explosive they had taken along. They added some furniture to keep it going and made their exit as many valuable German maps and documents went up in smoke.

They kept the Germans confined to the upstairs floor until the fire was well ablaze. Despite the accurate and determined Bren gun fire, the Germans were lobbing grenades on to the lawn, and Harvey and his men had to run the gauntlet as they dragged their wounded with them.

By now, the whole area was in a state of alarm and Germans on the road where Harvey had killed the sentries were firing towards the house.

The small band of raiders were fully silhouetted against the red glow of the blazing building and how they managed to get out of the headquarters' confines without suffering further casualties remains a mystery.

They kept up their relentless fire from outside as more and more of the trapped enemy tried to get out of the house.

Harvey gathered his men together, assessed the position and looked at his watch. Hell! he thought, they had been there 15 minutes longer than planned. The troops involved in the other aspects of the operation would already be on their way back to the safety of their mountain hide-out.

As the strike force got thinner on the ground, the Germans would be rushing about unhindered – and there were Harvey and Co still in the middle of the hornets' nest.

He decided to head in the opposite direction to that which they would ultimately take. He aimed to outsmart the enemy, who were likely to try and cut them off on the direct route back into the mountains.

They were extremely tired and inflicting extra distance on his men was not an easy decision, particularly as he did not know what further demands they would have to make on their stamina before they reached the comparative safety of their mountain sanctuary.

They skirted the area, walked straight through an enemy post unchallenged and cut the telephone wires. One wire turned out to be a power line and Harvey got a severe shock for his pains.

Harvey and his party joined up with the remainder of the force, quickly exchanged news and were soon on the march again. The other attack had been a success but they had lost men.

They had to get as much distance between themselves and the scene of the action in the shortest possible time. By the time they reached the safety of base, they had marched continuously for twenty-two-and-a-half hours.

The objective of their mission had been to cause panic and confusion and they had certainly done that. What's more, the enemy now knew that they were not safe, no matter how far they were from the front line.

It had of course, been a Special Air Service operation, carried out by bold, swift, resourceful men; operators whose daring and courage have, together with that of others who followed afterwards, contributed to the legendary SAS's special image and mystique.

The operation – codenamed *Tombola* – was the Special Air Service's last and most ambitious Second World War mission. The war was all but drawing to a close in Europe when No 3 Squadron of the 2nd SAS Regiment was flown to Italy for guerilla operations behind the German Gothic Lines, the last enemy defensive position in the Apennines.

Operation *Tombola* differed in many respects from former SAS operations in that rather than adopt the usual hit-and-run tactics against the Germans, Commander Roy Farran and his men joined forces with the Italian partisans, set up a base in the inaccessible valleys of the Apennines and together formed an offensive force to attack the German supply lines.

Roy Farran was later awarded the American Legion of Merit, and his citation said that the SAS's operations against enemy rear units had materially assisted the attack of the United States Fourth Corps and contributed significantly to the success of the Fifteenth Army Group.

The successful attack on the German Headquarters was a major contribution to the Allied cause, and Rhodesian Ken Harvey was awarded the Distinguished Service

Order for leading the attack. It was considerable achievement. DSOs are generally awarded to officers holding the rank of a least lieutenant-colonel, not to humble lieutenants.

Harvey's citation told how he had inspired his little band of men with great courage, gallantry and complete disregard for his personal safety.

"Throughout this action, Harvey was remarkable for his gallantry and cool, clear-thinking decisions. The damage he did to the whole German Army from Bologna to Massa was grievous. His behaviour inspired his men to follow anywhere an officer they love and trust."

Yet the attack on the German HQ was only one of the young Rhodesian's successes. In view of his good showing on the headquarters, Harvey – ultimately to become Honorary Colonel of the Rhodesian SAS – was tasked to command an independent mission . . . an attack on Highway 12, an important German route and a difficult target.

Overall commander Roy Farran conceded Harvey was young to lead the mission, but he had a good sergeant behind him and besides that, his enthusiasm was unbounded.

Harvey's partisan guide, unsuitably attired in a bowler hat, led the ambush group which included the piper, to the highway. The area was thick with enemy troops and they cautiously made their way towards the road.

Suddenly there was a long burst of machinegun fire. The ambushers had been ambushed by the Germans. The piper received a nick in his elbow and the guide had his bowler hat knocked off.

Somehow, as they all fell flat and rolled for cover, the guide picked up his bowler hat, replaced it and disappeared down the hillside into the night. He would reappear a few days later complete with battle scar – and bowler hat – to tell the most hair-raising story.

Harvey and his men immediately returned fire, killing two enemy before rapidly extricating themselves from the position.

Next time, they fared much better.

They found a new position on the inside of a large "U" in the road and took up their places in the long grass about fifty paces from the road and well in the loop.

Within half an hour, they heard the rumble of transport and were to discover later it was part of a German division withdrawing from the front to take up new positions.

Everyone was itching to start shooting as the convoy rolled ever closer to them, but Harvey had other plans. When the vehicles were well strung out and had surrounded his forces on all three sides of them, he gave the command to fire.

They opened up with everything they had – and with great effect, too. They were rewarded for holding their fire when the enemy on each side of the "U" began firing at fellow Germans on the other side, each group thinking the other was the enemy.

They were credited with completely destroying two trucks and three horse-drawn carts, and inflicting injuries on more than 100 enemy soldiers.

When the Germans began firing at each other, Harvey ordered his men to withdraw but stayed on for a further 15 minutes by himself, fascinated by the chaos he had started and which soon developed into quite a battle.

However, he did not tempt fate too much. They were firing directly above him and some of the enemy might discover their mistake, and decide to devote their attentions to the real culprits.

Next day, as a direct result of that action and the ensuing pandemonium, 158 Germans surrendered.

It was now April, 1945. The war in Europe had virtually run its course and the enemy was hurriedly withdrawing under pressure from the American Fifth Army. The SAS men were soon to be feted by the local population who were beside themselves with the joy of liberation. The roads swam with the transport of the advancing Army and the amount of destroyed enemy transport paid tribute to the Air Force and the guns of the Fifth Army.

Spasmodic firing could be heard in a nearby village and was attributed to a fanatic sniper; perhaps it was the odd partisan having his last fling.

After seven strenuous weeks deep behind enemy lines, food and sleep were now foremost in the minds of the SAS men. They returned to Florence, tired, wet and cold but thankful. They went straight to their headquarters, fell on the floor and slept. The operation was over and the prospect of leave lay ahead . . .

* * *

The Beginning

The Special Air Service all started with an ingenious plan to help defeat the German Army at a time when Britain was very much on the defensive.

A British Army unit, known as Layforce, was tasked to operate along the North African coast, where it could land on enemy beaches and move up to wreck German airfields and lines of communications. The only snag was that the plan relied entirely on the Navy to get them to the coast, and, as there were no ships to spare, it seemed certain Layforce would have to be disbanded.

A subaltern, David Stirling felt that just because the Navy could not ferry them there, that was no reason to abandon the raids. Surely troops could be dropped into the target by parachute instead?

But parachuting was still in its infancy and to further complicate matters, there was neither parachute expert nor the necessary equipment in the Mediterranean area.

Then, Stirling's fellow officer Jock Lewis laid his hands on fifty parachutes which had mistakenly and fortuitously been unloaded in Alexandria. He obtained permission to experiment with them and Stirling joined the trials.

Lewis, Stirling and two others rigged up their own static lines in an ancient Valencia aircraft by fastening them to the chair seats of the plane. Then the four men, none of them a trained parachutist, leapt out of the plane.

Only Stirling was unlucky. His parachute caught on the tail and ripped holes in the canopy. He smashed into rocky ground so hard and injured his back so severely that both legs were temporarily paralysed.

Undeterred, he used the time spent in hospital to plot a scheme for special operations in the Western Desert to hit the Germans in the heart of their own territory.

He argued that it was not necessary to use large groups for in-depth penetration operations behind enemy lines, where, because of the great numbers involved, the element of surprise was often lost. What was needed was a unit which could combine minimum manpower demands with maximum possibilities of surprise.

Great advantage could be derived from the element of surprise and the protection of the night.

The desert made his plans feasible. The fighting between the two armies was concentrated along the coast road, and the Germans had a very vulnerable flank in the form of a vast expanse of unguarded desert. A handful of men dropped by parachute deep behind enemy lines could hide by day, attack German airfields by night, then slip away under cover of darkness.

It was an ingenious plan. Now all he needed was permission. But there was no time for bureaucratic red tape. He had to bring it to the immediate attention of the hierarchy.

After failing to bluff his way past the sentry at the Headquarters Middle East Command in Cairo, he scaled the fence and hobbled off as fast as his injuries would allow.

He eventually found the Deputy Chief-of-Staff, Middle East Forces, General Ritchie, explained he had come on vital business and handed him a pencilled memorandum.

Soon afterwards, Stirling was given permission to recruit 66 men from what was left of Layforce and told the unit was to be called L Detachment of the Special Air Service Brigade.

Stirling immediately recruited Jock Lewis, an Oxford graduate and rowing blue. Later, when the SAS got its own cap badge and insignia, the colours of light and dark blue were chosen because in the original unit there was a representative of each of the Oxford and Cambridge boat race crews – Lewis of Oxford, and T.B. Langton of Cambridge.

The Winged Dagger design symbolised the legendary King Arthur's Excalibur, a sword to win freedom from the invader. The Egyptian-looking wings were inspired by a fresco in a well-known Cairo hotel. The motto chosen was "Who Dares Wins". It was to prove an apt choice.

Training the hand-picked volunteers began at Kabrit, a small village 160 kilometres (100 miles) from Cairo. Unfortunately, the SAS's first operation ended in disaster when, due to severe sand storms, landmarks were obliterated and the airborne parties were dropped in the wrong area. Aircraft were lost and men swept away.

The force that took them back to safety was the vehicle-borne Long Range Desert Group, a reconnaissance and intelligence unit. Stirling could see the advantage of using the LRDG and initially they were used to transport the SAS to their targets.

The SAS, collaborating with the LRDG, destroyed 100 German planes within a few weeks. A Rhodesian, Mike Sadler, acknowledged as the best navigator in the Western Desert, was to transfer from the LRDG to the SAS.

By the end of the desert war, 400 enemy aircraft had been destroyed by SAS raiding parties. It was the type of classic operation latter-day SAS men longed to do and it would not be until the Falklands War of 1982 against the Argentinians that they would get their chance to once again destroy enemy aircraft on the ground.

The SAS pioneers also destroyed workshops and hangars full of spares ... hijacked lorries ... mined roads ... set petrol dumps alight and demolished enemy railway lines. Thousands of Germans had to be diverted from other military tasks to try and guard the scattered airfields and vulnerable lines of communication from daring SAS attacks.

Adolf Hitler recognised the Special Air Service men's qualities only too well. In a back-handed compliment he ruled: "These men are dangerous. They must be hunted down and destroyed at all costs."

Such was David Stirling's fame that German radio was soon referring to him as *The Phantom Major*. He featured in Erwin Rommel's diaries and tales of his exploits spread throughout the Eighth Army.

As the war in Africa drew to a close, the SAS featured in daring exploits in Sicily, Italy, Belgium, Holland, Germany and France where they also trained the French Resistance Movement.

In September, 1944, the ADC to General F.A.M. Browning, KB, DSO, broadcast to SAS men still behind German lines: "The operations you have carried out have had more effect in hastening the disintegration of the German Seventh and Fifth Armies than any other single effort in the Army."

When the fighting was over and there was no longer a need for the SAS, 1 Regiment SAS (the original L Detachment), 2 Regiment SAS and HQ SAS were disbanded. The Belgian and French Regiments were handed over to their respective armies and retained.

For the British, it seemed the SAS days were over, but after a War Office analysis of the role the specialised force played during the war, it was realised that it would be ridiculous to let all that invaluable knowledge and experience go to waste. The SAS was reborn as a *territorial* unit and merged with the resurrected Artists Rifles to become 21 SAS (Artists).

* * *

Malaya, 1951 – 1953

Distance for Rhodesians, wrote one military historian, has always made the heart grow patriotic. Rhodesians were certainly keen to do their bit for the "motherland" and their proud military tradition was second to none in the Empire.

No less than 64 percent of the country's available manpower served in the First World War and when the world was plunged into war for the second time, the Rhodesians once again rushed to Britain's aid.

The whole of Rhodesia volunteered almost to a man and restraints had to be brought in *not* to call people up ... but to *stop* them going, for it was the only way to preserve the country's essential services.

As it was, Rhodesia supplied more troops per head of its population to the British war effort than did any other country in the Empire. Some 6 650 white and 1 730 black Rhodesians served outside Rhodesia and more than a quarter of them served in the Royal Air Force, including the man destined to become the country's most famous Prime Minister, Ian Smith.

He was a fighter pilot and after a long run of successes, one of which put him into hospital, he rejoined his Squadron to lead a strafing trip to the Po Valley picking on the most attractive targets of locomotives and fuel tanks. There was no sign of opposition and he made the mistake of going back for a second run.

As he pulled out of his dive, a resounding thud shook his Spitfire and he was forced to bale out. Later, while attempting to return to the Allied lines, he worked with the partisans, becoming a member of a company high command and inner war council, planning and taking part in raids and ambushes.

Then 11 years after the war, Rhodesia's proud military tradition was maintained when the Communists began giving trouble in the Far East and a Commonwealth Force was needed to help the United Nations in Korea. Rhodesia was still part of the Empire and only too willing to send a token force to Korea.

Only 100 men were wanted for the Far East Volunteer Unit. Twelve times that number, including South Africans living in Rhodesia, volunteered. Men and boys, old campaigners and civilians ... the scheme caught their imagination and it was all the able-bodied could talk about. It was an opportunity to put all that wartime experience into practice again; and for those too young for the last lot, here at last was their chance ...

The young Sandhurst-trained lieutenant who was to raise and train the force to fight Communist Terrorists on the other side of the world was Peter Walls. He could hardly have guessed that a couple of decades later, as Rhodesia's Military Supremo, he would again be leading Rhodesians in the fight against terrorism. Or that many of the successes of the Rhodesian war would largely be attributed to the experiences and lessons learned long before in Malaya.

There was another soldier destined to play a major part in Rhodesia's military history. But in those days of the Far East Volunteer Unit, Ron Reid-Daly was very much a raw, inexperienced new boy.

In fact, going off to the other side of the world was the last thing the 22-year-old post office technician wanted, and he told the rugby friend who had "volunteered" his name for the scheme as much in no uncertain terms.

Then his mate dropped the magic word "parachuting" into the conversation and Reid-Daly began to think that perhaps it *wasn't* really such a bad idea. After all, there had to be more to life than playing around with telephone wires for eight hours a day.

He decided to toss a coin to determine his future. If it was heads, he'd damn well chuck up his job and try his chances in the Far East. If not, well, he still had his rugby and baseball, didn't he?

It was heads – and the start of a soldiering career that would one day take Reid-Daly into the pages of military history as the extraordinary leader of Rhodesia's famed unit, the Selous Scouts.

Ninety civilians and ten regulars, some of them with wartime service, were selected for the Far East Volunteer Unit and the average age was 24. Then they learned they were not going to Korea after all, but were destined for the bitter, unrewarding war in the foetid swamps and green hell of the Malayan jungle, where the fanatical Chinese Communists were waging a bloody revolution to seize control of the country in a campaign which had become known with some understatement as The Emergency.

In less than two years, the communists had killed more than 1 300 civilians, police officers and soldiers for the loss of more than 1 130 of their own men. One thousand terrorists had been captured yet still the war raged on.

By 1951, 5 000 terrorists were firmly embedded in the remote heart of Malaya, hoping by frequent and savage attacks on the white population and the sabotage of key installations to force Britain to relinquish the valuable colony. Malaya's rubber industry, the biggest in the world, had been brought almost to a standstill. British planters were being murdered at the rate of one a week and morale in Malaya was generally low.

With the terrorists' detailed knowledge of the terrain, and the hit-and-run tactics which they had down to a fine art, they clearly had the upper hand.

The dense jungles, tall grass and endless swamps of inland Malaya where the water was full of tree roots and snakes, was certainly a terrorists' paradise. Gangs would live in the jungle, emerging only to destroy stocks or machinery, slashing rubber trees, bringing production to a halt, ambushing convoys and trains, and extorting food from the vulnerable local population.

The conventional troops kept to the fringes of the jungle, seldom making contact with the bandits.

An acknowledged expert on guerilla warfare, Major J.M. "Mad Mike" Calvert, holder of 13 decorations and a legendary character, was tasked to produce a detailed analysis of the rapidly escalating jungle war together with recommendations for its solutions. Calvert's study later formed the basis of a controversial strategy named the Briggs Plan after the British Director of Operations, General Sir Harold Briggs, who put it into effect.

It was clear to Briggs that terrorists had to be denied access to the local population. This would not only cut off the terrorists' intelligence and source of food supply but would protect the villagers ... and some 410 villages in the affected areas were uprooted, and entire rural Chinese populations were moved to new, fortified villages.

Briggs's other recommendation was that if the enemy was to be defeated, their base areas, training camps, courier lines, had to be attacked and destroyed.

It would involve deep-penetration operations, taking on the enemy on their own ground, seeking, flushing out and destroying them, something conventional troops were not trained to do.

What was urgently needed was a special forces reconnaissance unit to live in the jungle, denying the enemy sanctuary and rest. Calvert's argument was that British troops should be able to survive in the jungle far longer than the maximum for an orthodox infantry patrol.

Calvert was instructed to form such a unit, known as the Malayan Scouts. They were to link up with 21 SAS, the territorial unit formed after the Second World War, to form a *regular* unit to be known as 22 SAS (Malayan) Scouts. The Malayan Scouts part of the name would eventually fall away.

The aim of the unit was not so much to kill the enemy in great numbers but to harass them and drive them on to the roads and more civilised areas where other British Army units would do the killing.

With manpower being the first priority, Calvert began an intensive recruiting campaign travelling some 35 000 kilometres (22 000 miles) in three weeks in his drive for men. His whirlwind tour included a trip to Rhodesia, where, he briefed the 100 Rhodesians on the situation in Malaya.

The Rhodesians were to be known as C Squadron SAS (Malayan Scouts) and would wear identifying Rhodesian shoulder flashes. There was also an A and B Squadron, British Army formations, and later, a D Squadron and full headquarters, to complete the regiment.

The idea was for Peter Walls and his second-in-command, Lieutenant Ron Campbell-Morrison, to train the Rhodesian contingent, after which, an older soldier with wartime experience would take over command and take the Rhodesians to Malaya. A British-trained Major would then be appointed as their squadron commander, should they stay together and not be split up.

In the event, the Rhodesian Army could find no one to take the token force to Malaya. And Peter Walls, who described himself as no more than a "buckshee lieutenant", was called in, told he would lead the force to Malaya ... and that he was now a temporary captain.

The newspapers were full of stories of the lucky 100 men, and their spirit of adventure and loyalty to the Commonwealth was greatly admired by all.

When they marched off on the first leg of their journey to Malaya, the scene resembled that of a wartime victory parade. It looked like the whole of Salisbury had turned out to line the streets as the volunteers decked out in jungle kit and bush hats, proudly marched from the city centre to the railway station. There, to give them a typical wartime send-off, were 3 000 cheering friends and relatives.

To the strains of *Auld Lang Syne* and deafening applause, the train pulled out of the station en route to South Africa – and adventures unknown.

Four days later they arrived in Durban where they boarded a Dutch liner, and set sail on a journey that would take them to the other side of the world for almost two years. Ahead lay the jungle, hot, humid, hostile – very much unknown. And it was an excited and apprehensive group of young Rhodesians indeed who disembarked into the stifling Singapore heat of a March day in 1951.

A couple of days later they got their first really good look at Malaya on the train journey to Kuala Lumpur en route to their regimental base camp at Dusun Tua where they met up with the men of B Squadron.

"A" Sqn, they would soon learn, was made up of some "fairly interesting characters", some whose discipline left much to be desired, and some of whom were unwanted by their own regiments. "A" Squadron comprised men from units in the Far East and no particular criteria had been set down for selection. Such was the urgent need for men that to have been too discriminating would probably have meant the unit would never have been resurrected.

Despite their shortcomings, they did have some very good jungle soldiers and fine officers, and the Rhodesians would be impressed with the way some men could use themselves around the jungle. They had some excellent navigators and navigating was no easy task where it was often impossible even to see the sky.

"A" Squadron too spent the longest single spell in the jungle and returned from their record-breaking four month jungle stint shortly after the Rhodesians arrived at the camp.

When their convoy pulled up, it was a desperate-looking bunch of men indeed who piled out. The new boys from Rhodesia had never seen men looking so rugged and tough in all their lives.

They sported ferocious beards, their toes were sticking out of their canvas jungle boots and they all had pieces of ragged old yellow parachute silk carelessly tied around their necks.

"Is that the old debonair fighter pilot type thing?" curious young Rhodesian, Corporal Reid-Daly ventured of one man.

"My backside!" the veteran replied with feeling. "This is to stop us shooting at each other; everyone does it. You either put it on your hat or neck or somewhere. Then, if you see something move, you look for the colour. See?"

The Rhodesians clearly had much to learn about the ways of the jungle and the techniques of operating in the tight close undergrowth, just as men in the other Squadrons had. Many of the problems were unique to Malaya and the best way those pioneers had of finding out was to stagger into the jungle themselves and learn the hard way.

C Sqn got its first introduction to the jungle during a six-weeks training operation where they learned the ropes of jungle navigation and patrolling. The Rhodesians also learned to use their eyes and ears more than they usually did, sharpening their senses in the process.

The training, devised by Calvert, was directed at realism and live ammunition was used. Shooting fast from the hip at point-blank range was another skill that had to be mastered. The jungle was so dark in some places they would only be able to see a few paces in front of them and the undergrowth would have to be hacked away step by careful step ... and all providing wonderful cover for the quick-off-the-mark ambushing enemy.

By the end of the Rhodesians' training operation, the British had decided against splitting the Rhodesians up and against putting a British officer in charge of

C Squadron. Again Peter Walls was called in and told he had been appointed Squadron Commander and promoted to Acting Major.

Walls was only 24 and admits to being overawed at the challenge, particularly as a lot of older men with similar rank had rows of ribbons and years of experience behind them. However, he did have supreme confidence in his men. Rhodesians were used to being leaders at an early age and counter-insurgency depended greatly upon leadership, right down to the quality of a two-man patrol.

At first, the Rhodesians were confused when it came to tracking. It was completely different from tracking back home where the sun was a vital factor and where the dust, sand, rock, dry leaves, wild animals and their habits all helped.

In the jungle, the packed foliage blotted out the all-important sun and sky, reducing daylight to twilight and the only time they saw it was on the welcome occasions when they crossed a river or cut a helicopter landing zone. Only occasionally did the speckles of sunlight filter through the leaves of the sixty metre (200ft) high trees, intertwined at the top to form a canopy.

Seeking and flushing out the elusive bandits from the dense cover of their jungle sanctuary was uncomfortably hot work, too. Coming from Africa, the Rhodesians were well used to high temperatures, but the high humidity of the jungle took some getting used to, combined as it was with the heavy tropical rainfall which nourished the dense vegetation.

Major Calvert was invalided home suffering from an assortment of tropical diseases, and the SAS was withdrawn from the jungle for a period of reorganisation and retraining, during which some of the unruly types were sent packing and discipline was restored.

When the SAS returned to the jungle, it was for a historic operation that marked the first large-scale airborne operation of The Emergency.

Parachutists were to drop into a remote almost inaccessible jungle valley near the Malaya/Thailand border to take it from the terrorists. The locals in the Malay settlements there had been forced to supply the 100 terrorists with food, and the operation aimed to exterminate the bandits, evacuate the locals to safety, and destroy all the food supplies and habitation the bandits were likely to use.

Fifty-odd parachutists from B Sqn, plus one experienced Rhodesian paratrooper – Lieutenant Charles Pavlich – dropped into the Belum Valley, while ground units trekked through the jungle to link up with them.

There were strong air currents that day and only four of the paratroopers, including the Rhodesian, landed on the dropping zone. The others ended in trees but had been given thirty-metre long ropes to aid their descent. The mission was successful and the regiment went on to clear the bandits from the valley.

Most of the Rhodesians were parachute trained by the time their tour of duty ended, and when the second airborne operation was mounted in Malaya, it was the Rhodesians who made up most of the numbers.

Off-duty, the Rhodesians became the best of friends with the black Fijians, making nonsense of some claims that the Rhodesians in Malaya were a shade too colour-conscious. The truth was the Rhodesians with their background were better orientated towards mixing with blacks and coloureds than the average British troopie who seldom associated with them.

For the most part, the Rhodesians had been a bunch of inexperienced soldiers when they had left on their Far East adventure. They were young, new soldiers in a totally foreign environment. But they developed as they went along, and had acquitted themselves well.

11

Peter Walls was awarded an MBE for his work in Malaya but says it was definitely in recognition of the entire squadron's efforts.

The Rhodesians' commitment lasted almost two years but the SAS Regiment went on to spend a total of nine years in Malaya, perfecting their jungle fighting. The Emergency was declared over in July, 1960. Their commitment over, the Rhodesians returned home, most of them reverting to civilian life.

For the few who did continue to make soldiering their career, the Malayan experience had provided a tremendous grounding. Malaya had been a valuable experience and they had learned the elementary principles of counter-insurgency warfare.

They learned the technique of tracking; had learned what it was like to be ambushed; what the principles were in establishing their own ambushes; the sort of things that could give them away.

These and others, were the sort of pertinent lessons that were taken home and adapted to local conditions and developed way beyond the original.

Peter Walls and Major (later General) R.R.J. Putterill, who had been to Kenya to study the Mau Mau campaign, were to pass on their knowledge at rural training camps.

The Combined Operations concept introduced in Rhodesia in 1977, where the military and civil forces all worked together with the common purpose of prosecuting the war and defeating the enemy 24 hours a day, seven days a week, under one supreme commander, stemmed from those Malayan days.

"The terrorists don't play golf on Sundays, we won't play golf on Sundays," the dynamic Governor and Supremo of Malaya, General (later Field Marshall) Gerald Templar had ruled.

Templar's comment made a lasting impression on young Peter Walls, who would one day be appointed to a post similar to Templar's. That remark became a catchphrase of his over the years.

Major-General Putterill, OBE, who as Army Commander, presided over Rhodesia's own COIN operations from 1966-1968, believed that Walls ranked alongside Templar as one of the finest modern operational practioners of counter-insurgency warfare. (interview with Michael Evans).

The protected village idea where the vulnerable, unarmed local population were moved and resettled into villages to deprive the enemy of his target and means of support, while providing better community facilities and a more sophisticated infrastructure, was also introduced in Rhodesia.

Even so, Peter Walls says, had some of the experiences and lessons been implemented earlier, the Rhodesian troubles might well have been stamped out in their infancy. Whereas the Rhodesian Army and Air Force had learned from the overseas experiences, the Police who had never been overseas didn't have such a fund of experience to draw upon.

When it was pointed out that the same pattern was happening in Rhodesia as had happened in Malaya and Kenya, the Police refused to accept this. Their view was that they did not need to heed the lessons and learn from the experiences of people in other countries. Rhodesia, the police argued, was not the same as Malaya or Borneo; they had their own methods.

Their minds were not attuned to trying new methods, the author was told. And the country's top-level Security Council supported the view that the Police knew best.

C Sqn was disbanded on its return to Rhodesia, but the value of the SAS concept could be clearly seen. And when thoughts of establishing a parachute unit were first mooted in the days of the Federation of Rhodesia and Nyasaland several years later, someone suggested: "Well, if we're going to go for parachuting, let's go the whole hog and have the best. Let's have the Special Air Service."

and that's precisely what happened . . .

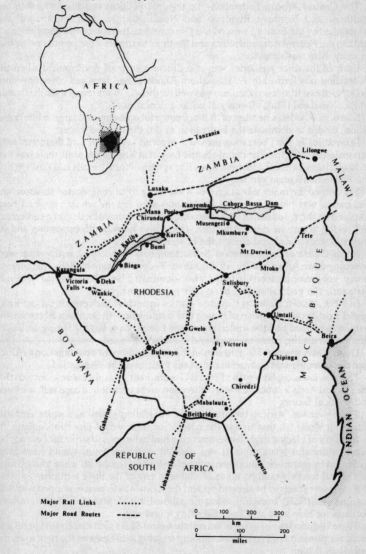

Rhodesia, her neighbours and her position in Africa

13

C Squadron SAS Arrives In Africa, 1961-1963

Until the sixties, Rhodesia had never had a regular white Army, just a black regular Army with a staff corps of white instructors. But all that was about to change.

The Central African Federation, the regional political structure, which linked Southern and Northern Rhodesia and Nyasaland had been encouraged and established by the British Conservative Government. It involved five governments – Britain, the Federal Administration and the three territories – the premise being that in unity there was strength.

Each of the three territories was at a different stage of development when the Federation was formed in 1953. Southern Rhodesia had been self-governing since 1923, Northern Rhodesia (Zambia) was well on the way to achieving a similiar status, while Nyasaland (Malawi) was still under colonial rule.

Southern Rhodesia, because of its more powerful economy and larger white population, tended to dominate the Federation as did their armed forces.

Economically, the Federation proved a tremendous success and there was great expansion in all fields. The hydro-electric project at Kariba was built, there was vast industrial development and there was a fine system of trunks roads laid down to link the Federation's main centres.

Yet despite the many advantages of what was a most complicated structure, the Federation was bitterly opposed by Africans who felt the whole plan had been imposed on them. Indeed, black nationalist, Joshua Nkomo stood up at a conference in London to state he rejected the idea. The British knew of this opposition and yet they still went ahead and created the Federation.

It was the era of decolonisation. Self-determination and black nationalism were sweeping down Africa and the Africans in the Federation wanted their own independence, not junior partnership in the white-dominated land. They wanted Britain to dismantle the Federation and hand over power to the people.

In 1959, African National Congress parties in each of the component territories began a deliberate campaign of rioting and intimidation. In Southern Rhodesia, the party was banned and the leadership placed behind bars, but the rioting, intimidation, crop-burning, cattle-maiming and assaults continued.

Under heavy pressure from the nationalists, the British sent a commission to Africa and the outcome was a suggestion that the Federation be dismantled.

This was not acceptable to the Federal Government . . . and it became obvious that the Federal Army's structure needed alteration and expansion to cope with the internal political factors.

There were four African battalions in the Federation as well as a white territorial force, but it was felt that should the need arise, these would prove inadequate.

In an era of black nationalism, something had to be done to strike the balance between white and black units. It was decided that force levels would have to be increased by recruiting Europeans into newly-formed regular all-white units, which, as Federal forces, would be made available to any of the three territories.

Rearmament was to be stepped up and the Army was to be re-equipped with self-loading rifles (SLR). Ironically, to test the political attitude of the British Government, requests for help were sent from Salisbury – and met.

These included the delivery of several thousand SLRs with associated spares and tools, the provision of Ferret scout cars and training facilities, and the right to recruit openly in Britain.

During the negotiations, several force level options were studied. They included raising one infantry battalion (The Rhodesian Light Infantry) and one armoured car squadron (The Selous Scouts). Another suggestion was that a parachute squadron be formed to be called C Squadron, Special Air Service, after the Rhodesian unit which had served in Malaya.

But first, it had to be discovered if regular parachuting, including basic training, was in fact possible in Central Africa, for the landing height would be well above sea level and landings could be expected to be harder.

A Parachute Evaluation Detachment was formed to find this out and to examine the practicalities involved in forming and training the SAS Squadron. The officer commanding was Squadron Leader Errol Minter, of the Royal Air Force, who had arrived from Britain in 1960.

The Parachute Evaluation Detachment comprised black and white volunteers from the Army and Air Force, and Lieutenant Ian Barclay-Loggie, who came directly to Rhodesia from the British Parachute Regiment.

Initially the instructors concentrated on physical training to ensure that the volunteers were brought up to a reasonable standard of fitness. The chief instructor for this phase was "arch fiend", Colour Sergeant Bob Bouch, an Irish giant of a man, also known as "Troat", as whenever he instructed in unarmed combat he constantly urged his pupils to seize the enemy by the "troat" and squeeze the life from him.

After that came the parachute training. The first military parachute descents in Rhodesia were in the form of a demonstration for members of the PED at New Sarum air base, Salisbury, and carried out by Chief Technician Bill Maitland, Lieutenant Barclay-Loggie and Sergeant George Sizeland. Less than a week later the course members made their first descents outside Salisbury to be followed by further jumps in Lusaka (Northern Rhodesia) and Lilongwe (Nyasaland).

After Squadron Leader Minter's submissions, it was decided to go ahead with the formation of an SAS Squadron.

Volunteers were called for from the Royal Rhodesian Air Force, to undertake training to qualify them as parachute jumping instructors and from Army personnel to be instructed in SAS selection and training methods. The Air Force volunteers were to train at Abingdon, near Oxford, England, where the SAS men were also to undergo a basic parachute training course.

The inclusion of the SAS met considerable opposition – largely based on ignorance – from many serving, senior and middle-grade officers with limited or no combat experience.

Nor did they care for the creation of an elite band who would, inevitably, attract to themselves and accept for service only those officers and men of the highest quality.

This thinking was easy to understand and deserved sympathy. The country was huge and the Army tiny in proportion. Even so, the quality of all ranks within it, prior to the expansion, was extraordinarily high. Cadets going to Sandhurst were expected to, and often did, figure in the top graduating ten places. Several Swords of Honour and Merit Prizes were won over the years, a distinction indeed, in such a highly competitive field.

By early 1961, the financial arrangements were concluded for the new units and staff plans made. Concurrent recruiting for the new units began in Britain, in Rhodesia and in South Africa with a trickle from elsewhere.

A small team, the nucleus of the resurrected C Squadron, was selected and plans made to attach it to 22 SAS in Britain for several weeks, after which, they were to return home to form the squadron.

Those chosen were the OC designate, Major Courtenay Welch (ex-Rhodesian African Rifles); Captain Jack Crutchley the 2IC, (ex-Sword of Honour winner – King's African Rifles); Lieutenant Dick Tilley, a signals officer who was to be OC of the signals troop; WO2 Stan Standish, an Arnhem veteran and ex-2nd Parachute Battalion member who was to be the Squadron Sergeant Major; Bob Bouch, who was to be the physical training instructor and Acting Corporal van der Merwe, a volunteer from the RLI.

With no precise idea of how best to prepare themselves, they aimed to become physically fit and as professionally proficient as they could in the limited time available.

The programme they set themselves, they were to find out later, was a good deal tougher than the selection course at Hereford.

Welch recalls one gruelling forty-mile trek across the Matabeleland bush, one of the most rugged parts of the Federation, full of scree, scrub and dense undergrowth, ravines and valleys. He rubbed up an enormous blister on his heel, which eventually burst.

Later that night, the footsore, wet and bedraggled group arrived at a remote American mission station where it was at first assumed they were a band of robbers. After having been well fed, they were required to attend a prayer gathering at which the Almighty was asked to give strength to "these boys fallen from the sky and to lessen their hardship". There was a twinge of approval from Welch's heel, and muttered insubordination from his inferiors.

After some weeks, they were more than ready to go to Britain, but inter-government delays held up their departure until April, 1961.

Eventually, the Rhodesians arrived in Bradbury Lines, the home of 22 SAS in Hereford, England. Everyone was very accommodating but there appeared to have been no plans made for their training.

At this time, 22 SAS were still regretting the passing of the Malayan Emergency and were striving to create for themselves a major role in Borneo, which they eventually did, with high distinction.

The UK, for them, was a place to recruit, train and rest in. Operations were, so far as they could see, always likely to be overseas, and to them the Rhodesians were a mild curiosity and a big nuisance, distracting them from their main aim.

But the visitors were persistent. They wanted to do everything, try everything and learn everything. To this end, they completed their basic parachute course at Abingdon, went on a regimental exercise to Denmark, took the selection course, sampled canoeing, rock climbing, navigation and the art of demolition, and plunged into the myriad intricacies of organisation and equipment.

During this time, Van der Merwe broke a leg and returned home. He did not serve with the squadron again.

The officers mess in Bradbury Lines was of old-fashioned design, being a well-founded, wooden building of impressive age. It ran on an unfamiliar, almost self-help basis and only one type of dish was provided for each of the three main meals of the day. This was curry. It brewed constantly in a huge iron pot in the kitchen and was a cult-symbol from the jungle days.

The officers of 22 made no complaint, so neither did the Rhodesians. At least not in their company. Luckily, they were not there much, being more often than not chased over the Welsh mountains on their selection course. Let no one imagine these mountains to be of no significance, particularly at night with a 40lb load!

At Abingdon, they met Flight Lieutenant Smudger Smith, who had helped train the C Squadron parachutists in Malaya. He was later to go to Rhodesia on second-ment to open the Parachute Training School at New Sarum. The Rhodesian Air Force volunteers were also there at the same time before returning home to run the PTS. And so were the South Africans who started 1 Parachute Battalion in Bloemfon-tein (the Parabats).

During their three-month attachment to 22 SAS, the Rhodesians went with them to Denmark for exercises with the Danish Home Guard. Since it does not get dark in early summer in those latitudes, it proved an exhausting experience.

The whole population joined in the game, including children and pet dogs. If caught, the captive was subjected to a rigorous interrogation, the likes of which, these days, would call for an investigation by the Human Rights Organisation.

Later, when it was all over, there were wild celebrations in the Tivoli Gardens, local breweries, and neighbouring establishments, during the course of which the OC designate had a chamber-pot dropped on him from a height of ten floors. Twas a glancing blow, and, in a spectacular way, marked the end of the visit.

Before they left the UK, they visited Rhodesia House, where they interviewed scores of applicants for the Army, the product of a very active recruiting campaign.

Returning to Salisbury, Court Welch became immersed in the setting up of the squadron. They decided on six Sabre (combat) troops of 17 men, the total strength of the Squadron being 184. This number was necessary as they were to be an indepen-dent unit in all respects and had to provide their own support back-up.

The argument raged back and forth as to where they should be located. It seemed obvious they should be at New Sarum where the Parachute Training School was due to become operational in late October.

But in the end, Ndola in Northern Rhodesia was chosen for political reasons. It had to be shown that the money was being spread across the constituent parts of the Federation. The Selous Scouts were also to be based in Ndola. For the SAS, it was a bad decision and the unit was to suffer for it.

Ndola was no place to lock up 184 young men, most unmarried and in the prime of life. They would have to be worked hard and constantly to keep them out of mischief as there was little for them to do in their spare time, and what entertainment there was, was expensive for them. The problem was to manifest itself in the state of the gate post across the entrance at the guard room. It was in constant need of repair.

Perhaps though, the greatest disadvantage was the need to fly the squadron to Salisbury in rotation for parachute training and continuation training. Needless to say, there were accommodation and transport problems once there, and the whole business was a constant headache calling for complicated planning, which was itself dependent on the co-operation of others, hundreds of miles away.

The cost involved in this "bussing" was just one indication of a bad choice, made for bad reasons.

Captain Jack Crutchley, the 2IC, set up the first selection courses in the Matopos mountain range which was selected because of its remoteness, lack of human habita-tion and for ease of control by the directing staff.

They modelled the course on the lines of the British SAS selection course and endeavoured to make their selection as stringent and all-encompassing, if not better than that of Hereford's, within the framework of the Central African situation. Everything was done to break the men mentally and physically.

The hot weather in the Matopos had to be taken into consideration, particularly in the endurance speed march. Bob Bouch was a merciless overseer of this, the most dif-ficult of all tests, and he was largely responsible for setting such a high standard on the course.

ing team was thus able to select the very best material, particularly in where a man was physically lagging but showed exactly the mental determination which personified the ideal SAS soldier.

The success rate of those early selection courses was very low and the training team aimed to set an extremely high standard. Careful selection was of course the first all-important step on the road to making an SAS soldier into an elite specialist operator.

The selection board never lost sight of the fact that in wartime, the SAS soldier would be called upon to operate behind enemy lines, on reconnaissance and sabotage; tasks that called for cunning and initiative as well as great endurance.

Those early volunteers were frankly staggered by the high standards expected of them and one man could only describe selection as "bloody iniquitious". He was one of the lucky ones, too. It is not known what the failures felt.

It was found that slightly more mature men faired better than the teenagers. The young had strength on their side, the others had stamina.

Those lucky enough to be selected set themselves high standards and helped to set a pattern for the future.

After selection, which included physical agility tests, initiative tests, speed marches and the dreaded endurance march, they underwent a basic course receiving a grounding in such subjects as signals, first aid, navigation, unarmed combat, demolitions and gunnery.

They then went on to their parachute course at the Parachute Training School – the first descent being in November, 1961 – and then the "sickener" phase, Exercise All-In, which was the culmination of an intensive programme. It was only after having done all this that they qualified to don their coveted SAS wings, sand-coloured beret and blue stable belt.

As for those early troop commanders, they were among the very best officers in the Federal Army.

From time to time, the squadron planners gave recruiting talks to drum up trade at Brady Barracks in Bulawayo . . . and were not too well received by the instructors. It was fairly obvious to them that they were after their best men.

It was an uncomfortable period. This of course was common in all so-called elite units as small as C Squadron, for they simply did not have the capacity to train from enlistment and, in any case, they needed the experience that the trained men brought with them.

In 22 SAS, they looked only at men aged 23-plus with at least three years' service. Of necessity, the Rhodesians were taking 17 and 18-year-olds, quite often with only two months' service. The promise that they would, in time, come back as better trained men seemed hollow to the donor units since the aim of a full career in the Army was not generally held.

Men in other units too were jealous that so much was spent on the SAS, that they were travelling in their own expensive Sabre Land-Rovers, had so much access to helicopters and had their own special selection course and own specialised equipment.

Gradually, order came out of chaos and a steady stream of successful qualifiers began their basic training, were formed into the first of the Sabre troops and then went off to do their parachute training. Meanwhile, the barracks at Ndola were under construction and the vehicles and equipment issued.

The whole business was a remarkable achievement and a huge tribute to everyone involved . . . the old, the new, the planners and the trainers.

That it all came to pass in so short a time, reached such a high pitch of readiness, served so well in later years and then was cut down, is not something that the first OC, who saw it all take shape, would wish to comment upon.

The novelty of the Army expansion and in particular tales of the supermen of the SAS, prompted much newspaper coverage. Many of the articles, seeking notoriety, exaggerated and romanticised the cold facts given by the officers.

Eventually, they became so irritated by one sneering, persistent and uninformed sniper in the readers' letter columns, that they asked him – a Mr Pete Morris – if he would care to give up one afternoon to take part in one of the exercises involved in the selection course.

Mr Morris and a group of his ex-RAF mates had claimed that Army life was not what it used to be and that the SAS's 15-mile march through some of the roughest country in the Matopos was "a bit of a dawdle". If he could not do it, he would offer drinks all round, he said.

Mr Morris foolishly accepted the SAS challenge and on the appointed afternoon, in a blaze of publicity, he set off with Bob Bouch and others, duly weighed down with the standard load.

He lasted only five of the 15 miles before collapsing in a heap in the full glare of all the cameras and under the vindictively satisfied eyes of those he had been tormenting. Mr Morris took back all he had said – then set up the beers. It was altogether a most satisfactory afternoon.

Early in 1962, the SAS left for Ndola, driving their vehicles up in long columns. They were to share the barracks with the Selous Scouts, but being the larger unit by far, they were to administer the establishment.

Despite the SAS's growing skills at canoeing, freefalling, demolitions and battle medicine, it became clear that the odd brigade exercise, although interesting and testing, was not enough to maintain the necessary training edge.

Something more was needed if they were not to become just a parachute squadron of infantry.

Exercises against other troops generally cast them in conventional roles and any tendency toward their natural mode of operation called forth heated and uninformed criticism from the controlling HQ and opposing units. This was partly due to the small size of the Army, the few units that were available on account of distance, and cost and a preference for the "book" by the more senior officers who had not been exposed to post-war "revolutionary" experience.

Whenever the chance arose, Court Welch pressed any distinguished visitor, serviceman or politician, to further their need for overseas training, preferably in an operational theatre. The political problems involved were considerable and so were those of a purely military nature.

No one was certain whether they and the UK were friends or not and force levels were never anything but dangerously inadequate and to have a Squadron away for several months was a serious matter.

But eventually, insistence paid off and it was agreed that the SAS should have a joint exercise in Arabia, in the East Aden Protectorate with 22 SAS in 1962. As it turned out, Welch's plot did not go quite as planned as elements of 22 were committed to operations elsewhere in the world and only a skeleton Rear Headquarters and two Squadrons were able to take part.

Not only would it give them the opportunity to get to know the UK SAS and get them thinking along SAS lines but it would be the first time the Squadron had operated as a unit. They had a lot to learn about the simple things of soldiering.

The British SAS comprised troopers with several years' service both in the SAS and in other regiments and corps before that. Some had been NCOs and had given up their rank to serve in the regiment, initially as troopers. They were therefore a self-confident outfit, maybe over-confident, operational service under their belts, a wealth of experience to draw upon, and led by equally experienced officers.

The Rhodesians, on the other hand, were equally good material but largely inexperienced. Most had never served abroad and they had barely time to shake down as a Squadron. Some of the troopers had been on selection course only four weeks before and this general lack of experience had to be watched carefully. The exercise for them was as much personal tutoring as squadron training. This was particularly important in the wild type of terrain they were to enter. Court Welch was not sure that 22 SAS realised the situation the Rhodesians were in and felt they probably expected too much of them.

The terrain was extraordinary and impressions were legion. Woad-covered tribesmen without a stitch of clothing ... ancient walled cities some of which contained Lancashire mill girls who married their "sheik" while he was working temporarily in the UK ... the bitter, lethal, inter-village feuds ... old men with powder horns and muzzle loaders (their sons would have AKs and sophisticated machineguns).

"Beau Geste" forts manned by 14-year-old National Guardsmen, whose signallers, without a single word of English, could send Morse with an accuracy and speed the SAS's best could not match ... the stories of the breaching of the great dam at Marib which set in train the occupation of Dhofar and the decline of the ancient Yemini civilisation ... sandstorms ... overturned Land-Rovers, the frustration of not knowing the language ... the Queen of Sheba and King Solomon ...

A lot of this was lost on the sons of the Oud Transvaal and those from Stepney, but all were awed by the antiquity and wild glory of the forbidding land.

It was a wonderful opportunity to encourage leadership, initiative and all those skills the Rhodesians had learned at home, especially navigation!

It was the first tempering of the Squadron, never to be repeated abroad again, despite frantic effort. The plan had been to send them to Malaya for experience in jungle warfare, but politics once again wove webs in which to trap the simple soldier, and they did not go.

Back home from their Arabian adventure, they returned to their familiar training cycle with large numbers of the Squadron scattered all over the country pursuing their various specialist skills of bush survival, long range navigation, canoeing, parachuting, weapon handling, demolitions and matters medical.

Truth to tell, the threat was hard to define in those days, except for the ever present "internal security" scene.

The Portuguese were still in Angola and Mozambique and seemed likely to stay there forever, despite growing security problems. General Antonio de Spinola visited Ndola from Mozambique with a monocle in his eye and a cowpat-cap on his head. He seemed a spry and rather unworldly figure. And so, later, he proved to be.

On the political front, a new Constitution had been negotiated in 1961 between Southern Rhodesian and British Governments which was to widen the franchise to bring Africans on to the voters roll. It meant that for the first time in Rhodesia's history, Africans would have been allocated seats in the 65-member white-controlled parliament and that they would have a say in the day-to-day running of the country.

At first, Joshua Nkomo approved the constitutional proposals, then changed his mind.

The call for nothing less than one-man-one-vote had grown and the Africans turned to violence.

Later that year, there were again rumblings from the African nationalists and the internal situation became bad. There was much industrial unrest and some small scale burning of wattle plantations in the country's eastern highlands. Eventually, after much badgering, Major Court Welch managed to persuade Army HQ to move the SAS south.

This period coincided with the first troubles in the Congo and Katanga. An endless stream of Belgian refugees were fleeing south. It was clear things were changing in Africa and that they were living in troubled times.

Having arrived in Salisbury, it was agreed to parachute troops in the Melsetter area to help quell the wave of arson in the region. It was September 1962 and it marked the unit's first operational jump. They did not achieve much from the operational point of view, but at least it gave the Army and Air Force planners the opportunity to practise the airborne deployment of the squadron and its resupply in the field. Everyone learned a good deal and it was yet another vital step on the road to moulding a viable unit.

It was an early introduction to the area that was to become all too familiar to the security forces in later years as a major war zone. The terrain was quite different from any the SAS had operated in before, both in its immensity and the scale of the hills and valleys.

There, too, they saw the mysterious irrigation system cut into the hillside, some said in pre-historic times. Even in those days the area seemed somehow sinister. The Honde Valley struck at once as being a prime approach route into Rhodesia from the east. The valley straddled Rhodesia and Mozambique, was densely populated and obviously vulnerable.

Halfway around the world, the war in Viet Nam raged and, knowing they could never get there, the Rhodesians read all they could of American special operations, and tried out those that were possible with the facilities and equipment available.

Before the troubles ran out of steam in the south, they had the opportunity to work extensively with the recently-formed Alouette Helicopter Squadron. The Air Force, like the Army, had undergone changes and had taken delivery of more sophisticated aircraft.

The time spent with the Alouette squadrons proved to be most valuable to both squadrons, and techniques were evolved which were later to be honed by operational experience.

Meanwhile, the Congo situation had begun to brew in earnest and massacres followed, creating yet another flood of refugees. At the end of 1962, the SAS was deployed to control the main border crossing from the Congo into the Copperbelt to keep the Congolese soldiers from raiding across the border into Zambia. It called on them to dig in, an unusual occupation for SAS troops, although a programme of active patrolling deep into the Congo was also to give them a good insight into the situation within. It was bad.

At home, the politicians were highly vocal in their endeavours to save – or dismantle – the Federation, depending on who they were. South Africa seemed the only stable part of southern Africa.

This period of uncertainty coincided with the unit's formative years. Being so young and diverse of origin, it is not surprising that many young men began to wonder if they had made a good choice in seeking a new life in the Federation.

Eventually, it became clear that Britain's great African experiment was crumbling and that the Federation was destined to break up.

It had been created by Winston Churchill's Government by men who believed in the concept of the Empire. Their successors did not and the time came when the British, realising the Empire was breaking up, decided to pull out of Africa. Their future lay not in the colonial past, but in an economic alliance with Europe.

Back in Africa, the uncertainty of the situation had its effect on morale in the SAS. The unit had just got into full swing, the training had been completed, they had been to Aden with 22 – then politics had called a halt.

Some of the troops felt the unit ought to move south before the Federation broke up, as there might not be an SAS afterwards. But others felt that such a suggestion was a hot potato. To pull the SAS back to the south might be interpreted as a deliberate manoeuvre to give strength to the whites.

The SAS men would just have to wait and see.

When the crunch came, the three territories in the ten-year-old Federation were to become separate countries. Northern Rhodesia was to become an independent Zambia, and Nyasaland an independent Malawi.

But what was to be granted to the others, was to be denied to Rhodesia. She was to enter a new era of trying to negotiate independence with the British. It was to be a long haul.

The Federal Army, like the country, was to be carved up. Fortunately for Southern Rhodesia, the British allowed her to inherit the entire fighting force of the Royal Rhodesian Air Force, a move that enabled Rhodesia to retain air supremacy throughout the war that was to follow.

The northern territories had no need for the wholly white units of the SAS and Selous Scouts, and it was merely a question of finding out the wishes of each person as to what he wanted to do.

There were a number of options open to them. They could return to the south to the Southern Rhodesian Army. If they were officers, NCOs or specialists, they could stay put north of the border with the Northern Rhodesian Administration's Northern Rhodesia Regiment. There was also a British Army option. Or they could leave army life altogether and take the generous golden handshake.

They had to think the future out for themselves.

As most of the troops were from Southern Rhodesia and South Africa, there was naturally a big draw to the south.

The Rhodesian Army however was not offering much – an option to apply for a job. They stressed they could not take everybody. There were no guarantees a man would get a job; no guarantees there would even be an SAS. It was an expensive unit to run and Rhodesia had a small military budget. In short, there was little incentive for men to head south.

The Northern Rhodesian Administration, on the other hand, could see the Army and the men with soldiering skills disappearing across the border and was making some pretty attractive offers – increased salaries and a step-up in rank, with a bonus at the end of it.

For the young troopers, it was a chance to get their hands on a bit of money, and most chose to take the handshake and call it a day. All the officers, including the OC, elected to stay in Northern Rhodesia and in the end only 31 "other ranks" volunteered for service in Southern Rhodesia.

In the event, there was to be an SAS in the south and the new Officer Commanding was to be Major Dudley Coventry with Captain Peter Rich as his second-in-command ... and they arrived in Ndola in November, 1963, to take the volunteers and the unit's equipment south.

It was the parting of the ways, the beginning of a new period in Central African politics. It remained to be seen if the south could hold out against the pressures that might come.

In the black nationalists camp, they were fighting among themselves. The Reverend Ndabaningi Sithole and his supporters – including Robert Mugabe – dissatisfied with Nkomo's indecisive leadership, split with Nkomo and formed ZANU (the Zimbabwe African National Union).

Nkomo, meanwhile, had formed the People's Caretaker Council (PCC) to continue the activities of the banned ZAPU.

Nkomo's supporters came from the Ndebele-orientated tribes in Matabeleland in the west, while ZANU's power base lay among the Mashona tribes in Mashonaland in east and central Rhodesia.

Some of the most bitter incidents in nationalist politics followed as former colleagues turned on each other. Black nationalist politics were much in keeping with traditional African politics, beset by tribal and ideological differences, a situation that would not improve with the passing of time.

It was in white Rhodesia's interests that the nationalists continued to fight with each other, and not present a united front. In later years, Rhodesian security forces would deliberately stir things up among the different factions, for while they were fighting each other, they were not waging war on Rhodesians.

As for the SAS, it too, was going through a difficult phase. And when those 31 volunteers pulled out of Ndola barracks to begin a new chapter in their history, it was in the knowledge that the Squadron's strength had never been lower ...

A New Era

Rhodesia Defies the World

With the "winds of change" rapidly blowing down Africa and independence assured for her northern neighbours, Rhodesia's destiny now seemed very uncertain.

Rhodesia had been "occupied" in 1890 by the Pioneer Column in the name of Queen Victoria, and the capital, Salisbury, named after the British Prime Minister of the day. The man behind it all had been Cape Colony politician, financier and mining magnate Cecil John Rhodes, who had sought to extend British influence – not to mention his own – in Africa.

In 1888, the territory's Matabele king, Lobengula had signed a concession giving Rhodes the sole right to the mineral exploitation of Mashonaland. Legend had it that the territory north of the Limpopo River was the location of King Solomon's famous mines, and that promise of glittering wealth was ultimately to be fulfilled.

Rhodes then got Queen Victoria's blessing together with a Royal Charter to administer Mashonaland in her name, and the British South Africa Company was formed to administer the territory.

As Rhodesian author John Lovatt says in his book, *Contact*, both African and Briton were less than honest with each other. The wording of the concession document seemed to camouflage Rhodes's intention of colonising Lobengula's Mashonaland fiefdom . . . while Lobengula no doubt hoped that by signing the concession, he would keep other hunters at bay.

Two years later, 500 mounted infantry – the British South Africa Company's police – and 180 Pioneers trekked northwards and arrived in what was to be called Cecil Square. The British flag was run up, there were three cheers for Her Imperial Majesty – and yet another new territory was added to Queen Victoria's long list of far-flung colonies.

The lean years that followed were difficult, precarious, fraught with disease and danger, the latter coming from the warrior tribe, the Matabeles, offshoots of Shaka's dreaded Zulu race, who had realised too late what was happening and had then forbidden the settlers' entry.

But those tough adventurers survived, civilisation gradually spread and the country began to prosper. Farms were cut out of the virgin bush and businesses grew and flourished.

From the very beginning, there was a constant influx of new settlers. The early ones trekked northwards across the rugged bush terrain in creaking ox-drawn wagons, seeking adventure, gold and a new life in the young, uncharted country. It was the stuff of which great adventure tales were made.

Rhodes fulfilled promises made to the Matabele chiefs and set land aside for them.

The African chiefs were given greater powers and the authority of the British South Africa Company was reduced. The settlers were given four representatives in a Legislative Assembly and Rhodes promised them eventual self-government.

When the early settlers made the long trek to Cecil Square in those difficult pioneering days, they had done so with a spirit of adventure, a search for a new life and the hope of finding mineral wealth, not with any burning desire to colonise new territory for Queen Victoria.

Britain had taken no part in founding the country and had not rallied when times were hard. As Rhodesians saw it, the fact that the charter giving them the right to administer the country bore the word "Royal" did not give the British the right to meddle in their affairs.

In 1923, Rhodesia voted for Home Rule and became a self-governing colony. The British paid three and three-quarter million pounds to the British South Africa Company as compensation for 33 years' administration (two million would have to be repaid to Britain by the Rhodesian Government) and the company was allowed to keep its commercial and mineral rights.

Britain gave Rhodesians the right to legislate, maintain an Army and run the Civil Service . . . all of which they had been doing anyway. And the British Government retained supervisory powers.

Forty-one years later, in 1964, Ian Smith, farmer, World War-II Royal Air Force hero, became Prime Minister. He was the first Rhodesian-born premier and he was determined to get independence from Britain and remove her reserve powers. The country was self-governing after all, which was more than could be said for her more backward ex-Federal partners.

But Britain argued that it was not going to grant independence to Rhodesia as its franchise was more restrictive than any other British territory to which independence had been granted. Later, British Premier Sir Alec Douglas-Home told Smith that if he wanted independence under the 1961 Constitution – which widened the franchise to allow Africans in Parliament for the first time – he must show it was acceptable to the people as a whole.

A referendum duly tested the white electorate, who voted ten to one in favour of independence and an *indaba* – a meeting – of 622 African chiefs and headmen supported the move.

But by then, Britain had a new Prime Minister. Harold Wilson and his Labour Party were determined to complete the decolonisation process of Central Africa through majority rule in Rhodesia and refused to accept the meeting with the chiefs as a valid indication of African opinion.

Britain was not going to grant independence until majority rule was guaranteed – and that meant African majority rule.

Ian Smith, however, had stated that there would be no African nationalist government in his lifetime. Such a government would mean the end of the European and the civilisation that he had brought to the country. People were getting tired of hearing that Africa was going to be preserved for people of every race and colour with the exception of the European. He seemed to be the only one who did not come into the picture.

If far-away socialist Britain would not grant Rhodesia independence, then Rhodesia would just have to take it unilaterally.

Around the world, speculation was rife. Would Rhodesia dare to declare UDI, and would Britain send troops to Rhodesia to crush the rebellion? While the Tories had been opposed to an armed intervention against their Rhodesian "kith and kin", no one knew for certain what the Socialists would do.

Only the use of force would have delayed the rebels taking their independence. But then Harold Wilson declared there would be no invasion to settle Rhodesia's constitutional problems, and that option was ruled out.

The way was now clear . . . and on Armistice Day, November 11, 1965, the 11th hour of the 11th day of the 11th month – a reminder to Rhodesia's own kith and kin across the other side of the world of Rhodesia's past and proud war record – Rhodesia defied Britain, convention and the world by declaring UDI, the Unilateral Declaration of Independence. It was the first rebellion against the Crown since the American Revolution of 1776.

Addressing Rhodesians and the world, Ian Smith explained: "There can be no happiness in this country while the absurd situation continues to exist where people such as ourselves, who have ruled themselves with an impeccable record for over forty years, are denied what is freely granted to other countries who have ruled themselves, in some cases, for no longer than a year.

"The decision which we have taken today is a refusal by Rhodesians to sell their birth-right, and even if we were to surrender, does anyone believe that Rhodesia would be the last target of the communists and the Afro-Asian bloc?"

Harold Wilson, acting on intelligence from his MI6 men in Rhodesia – responsible for intelligence, espionage and counter-espionage operations overseas – said famously that the rebellion would be over in weeks not months.

Britain's solution to bringing the rebels to heel was to use economic measures, not military means. But Wilson had grossly overestimated the effect of trade sanctions against Rhodesia and underestimated the country's ability to get help from neighbouring South Africa, Portugal and elsewhere, in overcoming them. Smith too, had talked of the three-day wonder. He thought that by declaring UDI on a Friday, after the stock exchange had closed, all the excitement would have died down by Monday. Both men were wrong.

Britain first imposed sanctions, then an oil embargo. Eighteen months later the UN ordered a total ban on trade with Rhodesia. Such measures were designed to bring Rhodesia to her knees, yet from 1969–1974 – before the world recession and the fall of white rule in Mozambique – Rhodesia's economic growth was more impressive than Britain's. While many luxuries were in short supply, Rhodesians soon learned to do without them.

If they couldn't get British goods, they could get Japanese, French and West German substitutes, which were better anyway.

Nor had Harold Wilson and successive British Prime Ministers reckoned on Rhodesian ingenuity. What essentials they could not acquire by devious means, they made and grew themselves, becoming amazingly self-sufficient, an attribute that came in useful when the war got into top gear and Rhodesians were able to manufacture their own weapons to overcome procurement difficulties.

Rhodesian businessmen became masters at overcoming UN sanctions and trade with her northern neighbours – as well as the West – flourished. Many African States ignored sanctions completely and most members of the OAU traded with Rhodesia. As President Bongo of Gabon once said: "If I do not give a list, it is out of courtesy."

The black States might well have condemned the white racists in the south, but behind the scenes it was all very different. It was Rhodesian beef and South African wine which graced the tables of African presidential palaces. The maize train spoke louder than a hundred speeches at the UN and it was Rhodesian maize which fed countless thousands of Africans in black Africa, including those determined to bring down the fall of white Rhodesia.

Immediately after UDI, Wilson (*"I Hate Wilson"* stickers sold like hot cakes) dispatched RAF Javelin jet fighters to Zambia (air traffic controllers in Salisbury kindly guided them in) but they were not to be used against white Rhodesians.

Officially, they had been sent to defend Zambia's airspace, but according to authoritative journalist Chapman Pincher, their purpose was simply to occupy the airfields to prevent the Russians from doing so. Such was the value of the "kith and kin" factor, that the RAF officers toasted Smith's health during their New Year's Eve celebrations in their Lusaka mess.

As for the SAS, the unit became a "lost legion", cut off by politics from its parent unit in Hereford. Personal friendships did, however, continue.

UDI was a factor that would affect Rhodesia for the rest of her days. It set in motion a sequence of events that would gather momentum and change the map of Africa once more. British and American politicians would come and go in search for the all-elusive settlement, and it would be 14 long years before the rebellion was over and majority rule attained. And when it was, the incoming government would be far worse than anything the white Rhodesians or the British could have imagined. Tragically, 30 000 Rhodesians would die and thousands injured or maimed before an uneasy peace and recognition came.

Back in the defiant mid-60s, however, the drums of African nationalism had largely been silenced and the prospects of war seemed very remote. Joshua Nkomo, Ndabaningi Sithole, Robert Mugabe and hundreds of others had been cast in prison where they would remain for ten years.

Nkomo's party, ZAPU, and Sithole's ZANU, had been banned and their young lieutenants had fled into exile.

In the post-UDI era, the black nationalists, now totally committed to the forceful overthrow of white political domination, looked to Britain to act for them. But that was a mistake in their strategy. Britain would not take up arms for them: they would have to do the job themselves ...

The SAS Go External

Within a few months of UDI, twenty-one ZANU had infiltrated Rhodesia from Zambia, then split into three sections. One group headed for Umtali in an abortive bid to blow up the Beira-Umtali oil pipeline and kill white farmers, and a second group headed for Fort Victoria. Both were rounded up.

The third group was chased by 120 police and reservists in the biggest counter terrorist operation the country had seen. They infiltrated 250 kilometres (155 miles) into Rhodesia and reached Sinoia some 120 kilometres (74 miles) from Salisbury.

An informer working for the Rhodesian Special Branch had infiltrated the gang and managed to slip away from his comrades to tip off the police ... and on April 29, the net tightened, a fierce battle ensued – and seven insurgents, some trained at the Nanking Military College near Peking, were killed.

The battle had been nothing more than a fiasco for the terrorists, but it had been the deepest penetration into Rhodesia to date and ZANU would mark it as the first day of their war of liberation, their *Chimurenga* Day.

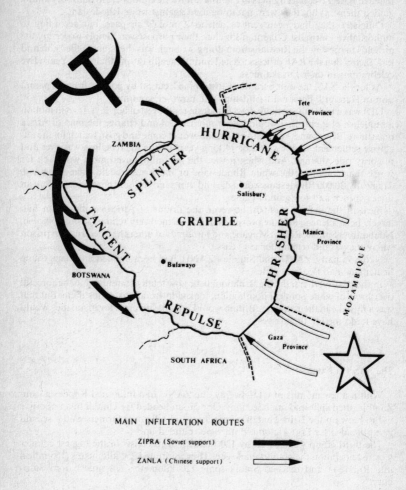

MAIN INFILTRATION ROUTES

ZIPRA (Soviet support)

ZANLA (Chinese support)

The operational areas of Rhodesia and the terrorist infiltration routes

28

But for many people, however, the real war began three weeks later when a white farmer and his wife, Johannes and Barbara Viljoen, answered a knock at the door of their remote farmhouse 25 kilometres (15 miles) from Hartley and armed men began shouting at them.

"Then Mummy and Daddy lay down and went to sleep on the floor," their young son told police. The Viljoens were the first Rhodesians to die at the hands of Communist-trained and armed terrorists.

As for the SAS, they planned to put things right and their first external operations into Zambia began.

Top secrecy was clamped on the missions and so sensitive were they that only the Army Commander, General R.R.J. Putterill, the Director of the Central Intelligence Organisation – an umbrella agency handling internal and external intelligence – Ken Flower and the SAS Commander, were briefed about them.

As the unit was run by the senior NCOs, it was obvious they chose to carry out the operations themselves.

Yet this policy of using the same people each time for clandestine operations, while excellent for security, was very bad for morale. It wasn't long before the operators were being dubbed *The Secret Seven* or the *Sinful Seven,* by members who were naturally upset at not having the opportunity of having their crack at special operations.

Not only did it cause a great deal of unhappiness throughout the unit, but as it involved the most experienced operators, it was also putting all their eggs in one basket.

Then in October 1966, the SAS commander, together with W.O. II Bob Bouch, Colour Sergeant Mick Cahill and Colour Sergeant Geordie Wright and a policeman seconded to the unit for the operation, Chief Superintendant John Wickenden, formed the team chosen to travel to Lusaka, the Zambian capital, where they were to destroy the ZANU headquarters.

Sergeant Jannie Boltman was to have been included in the party. He had been in on all the rehearsals, but the op had been cancelled a number of times and eventually Jannie decided he had to take his annual holiday. His place was taken by Geordie Wright.

The plan was to cross the Zambezi just below the Chirundu Bridge by canoe. The explosive device, which had been made up in Salisbury, was transported to Chirundu by vehicle. Then the collapsible canoes and the explosive device were portered to the crossing point.

The five men began assembling the canoes and making the final preparations. The SAS commander, moved away from the others for a moment and began to tie his bootlace.

Just as the commander bent down, a terrific explosion tore through the air. The explosive device had accidentally detonated, and the SAS commander was knocked unconscious.

He came to with his hair alight and both ear drums perforated . . . and the scene that greeted him was not a pretty one. Bob Bouch, Mick Cahill and John Wickenden were dead. Geordie Wright was still alive but it was obvious there was no hope for him and he died in his commander's arms.

The cream of the unit had been brutally wiped out, and, but for the protection of a fold in the ground, the SAS commander would have also died that day.

Nearly two kilometres away at Chirundu police camp, Sergeant Major Al Tourle of the RLI, with his commando on border patrol duty, heard the explosion. He had no forewarning about the operation and was more than a little surprised when the explosion rumbled across the countryside.

As he rushed down to the river's edge to find out what had happened, he bumped into the survivor on his way up from the Zambezi in search of help.

"Hullo, Sergeant Major, how are you?" the SAS commander asked in his normal, calm, cultured tone, not sounding at all like a man who had just escaped death by a miracle. Nothing, it seemed, could rattle the SAS man.

The remains of the bodies were collected next day and soon after first light, a Rhodesian Air Force chopper arrived to transport the OC and the bodies back to Salisbury.

The chopper reached the height of 100 feet and then just to round off the whole thing, the engine cut out. The pilot executed a very professional auto rotation crash-landing which saved the SAS commander and a precious helicopter.

The commander stepped out of the aircraft, brushed his handle-bar moustache and contemplated what was to happen to him next!

The cause of the explosion was never discovered. The device was prepared with a built-in time mechanism and it can only be assumed that the vehicle trip must have damaged or unseated this mechanism. It was a very expensive way of finding out that initiating devices should only be placed in a charge when at the target. But in those early days of the war all Rhodesians were inexperienced in this type of operation and they did not know any better.

The day after the tragedy, the SAS were lined up and told of the deaths. The men were stunned. Jannie Boltman, who by rights should have been on the mission, was especially shocked.

The four men were awarded posthumous Meritorious Conduct Medals. It was Geordie Wright's second tribute to his bravery.

Six months earlier, he had been on duty at Kariba Power Station when the peace of the afternoon was shattered by an explosion. An African civilian had climbed over the bilingual warning notice and the double fence surrounding a minefield near the power station and had stood on a mine. Now the man lay bleeding and groaning in the middle of the field.

Geordie immediately volunteered to go in and get the injured man, but was advised to wait until they could get hold of the plans showing exactly where the mines were planted.

Geordie could see the sense of that and waited – and waited. Thirty minutes ticked by and the sound of moaning drifted across to the SAS men on the other side of the fence, yet still the plans had not materialised.

Geordie decided he could wait no longer and scaled the minefield fence, unaware of exactly where the mines were planted. Using his bayonet, he probed a path through the minefield, inching his way forward until he reached the injured man.

Then, after retracing his path to the protective fence, he re-entered the minefield with a stretcher and together with Lieutenant Harry Harvey, returned to the casualty and carried him to safety.

The prompt action of Geordie and Harry Harvey, undoubtedly saved the life of the man, and both SAS men were awarded a Commendation for Brave Conduct.

* * *

A couple of months after the tragic deaths of the four men, a further clandestine operation was planned, once again in conjunction with CIO. The mission – codenamed *Sculpture* – was to destroy terrorist documents and records held in the ZANU headquarters in Lusaka. They had to get into the building surreptiously and place on various filing cabinets a number of incendiary devices, which were designed to raze the building to the ground.

The plan called for the infiltration of three SAS operators – Lieutenant Brian Robinson, Sergeant Jannie Boltman and Sergeant Dan Hartley – into Zambia by light aircraft. The aircraft, bearing false registration numbers, was to land on a deserted airstrip some distance from Lusaka under the cloak of darkness and without lights on. Having landed by moonlight, the three men were to meet a Zambian-based agent who would transport them to the target area.

Two weeks before the operation, rehearsals took place in the Bulawayo area. Landing a light aircraft at night without lights and with only the moon to guide them calls for considerable skill, and this part of the operation was rehearsed several times over the same distance the plane would fly on Operation *Sculpture*.

Someone spotted the plane one night but no one seemed to be able to account for it ... and in the next day's paper there were reports that an unidentified flying object had been sighted near Brady Barracks. The SAS were not about to put the record straight.

The three operators encountered numerous operational problems which appear so easy in the adventure movies. Breaking a window silently proved a major difficulty as Brian Robinson remembers.

"We tried bricks wrapped up in newspaper covered in syrup, so the glass wouldn't fall on the ground. We also tried a glass cutter. Neither of these methods was successful and we ended up using a pellet gun pistol, which allowed us to make a hole big enough to insert a wire, which in turn enabled us to open a window ... a most unprofessional method of breaking and entering."

They were to wear civilian clothing with all the *Made in Rhodesia* labels removed and in the event of things turning nasty and they were stopped at a roadblock, they would have terrorist weapons to "talk" their way out.

Late one night behind the drawn curtains of one operator's city home, the team worked on the ringmain; the device linking up the various charges that they planned to spread around the target and which would enable all the charges to go off together. They planned a thirty-minute time delay, to give them enough time to get out and away.

The intelligence for the op was sketchy. It had apparently been gleaned from the pages of a South African magazine which had carried a story on the ZANU headquarters. Not an ideal method of getting information, but in those early days of the war, it was the best they had.

Nevertheless, it was a very sophisticated operation and the risks to the three operators were great. They were to be far from home with no help at hand. They didn't even have radio communications with the south.

Finally, all the rehearsals and trials were over and it was time for the real thing. At last light, the three men flew out of Rhodesia; their destination a private flying club 64 kilometres (40 miles) from Lusaka.

The pilot, Peter Kale, flew low under radar cover. Finding an airstrip without a flare path at night, with only a moon to assist, is not easy, but the navigation was spot on and the trip uneventful.

The pilot carried out a glide approach to keep engine noise to a minimum and brought the Cessna 206 down, taxiing to a halt at the far end of the runway, well away from the clubhouse. As luck would have it a rowdy party was in progress that night and the arrival of the plane went unnoticed.

As the aircraft came to a halt, the three men prepared to deplane, eager to get clear of the Cessna as soon as possible. But the pilot had forgotten to raise the electric flaps, which prevented them opening the back door, and the tension inside the plane mounted.

After what appeared to be an eternity, the flaps were raised and they were able to pile out.

Then the Rhodesians were off, running to the safety of the bush fringing the airstrip. The pilot opened the throttle and took off into the night.

But from the start, things went wrong.

The three SAS men immediately set about locating the agent. But nobody had specified which end of the runway the rendezvous was to take place and Brian Robinson was furious with himself for neglecting such an important detail. The three men subsequently trudged up and down the edge of the 900 metre runway hugging the cover of the bush, trying to make a rendezvous.

When the meeting eventually took place it was something straight out of a Peter Sellers' comedy about the bungling French moustacheoed Inspector Clousseau.

In keeping with the spy role demanded of him, the agent was wearing a full-length leather jacket and a hat pulled down well over his eyes. And Brian Robinson was so relieved to see him that he stuck out his hand and pumped the agent's arm vigorously for about twenty seconds before giving the password.

Now it was time to go and destroy the terrorist headquarters. The SAS men picked up their Castle Lager cooler bags containing the incendiary bombs and piled into the agent's car.

The agent clipped a new number plate on to the old one and they headed off into the night for the Zambian capital.

"Oh, by the way," he said matter-of-factly, "the police have been mounting road blocks lately." But apart from the odd policeman on night patrol which almost caused them an instant coronary, the journey to Lusaka was uneventful.

There were no road blocks into town, no one to stop their progress. Everything was going well. Soon the yellow street lights of Lusaka loomed before them. Then came the shock.

The agent decided to drive slowly past ZANU headquarters to give the team an on-the-spot run down of the target. As they passed the target, they were amazed to see the streets full of youths in the middle of an interfaction riot. The lights of the headquarters were going on and off every two minutes and the area was teeming with people.

It was chaos – and incredibly bad luck for the SAS.

Undaunted by the unexpected turn of events, the agent dropped the team off and they made their way to a piece of open ground to the south of the target where they watched the proceedings with wide-eyed amazement.

Leaving Jannie Boltman behind with the charges, the other two men eased forward to reconnoitre the building and from their place in the shadows, they watched the battle.

Lieutenant Robinson tried to get into the building from every possible angle, but it was just no use. The area was so well lit that a surreptitious entry was impossible.

They had been dropped off at 23h00 and the fighting raged for a full ninety minutes. The pick-up time was 02h00 and it was obvious that even if the battle did subside, there would not be time to complete the operation.

There was no option but to abort the op and rendezvous with the agent. The agent arrived spot on the appointed hour, then drove them to the perimeter fence of Lusaka's main international airport. Quickly the three men scaled the fence. Then with their deadly packages still in tow, they made their way to the apron on the runway which was still in use.

Now they had to wait for their lift. But the pilot was late and as they waited in the darkness, their disappointment at having failed to pull the job off, gave way to worry.

What if something had gone wrong and the pilot didn't come? What would they do? How would they get home?

Thirty minutes after the apppinted pick-up time, the sound of a plane flying low penetrated their thoughts. At last! The airfield was still very active, but the Rhodesian pilot simply joined the circuit and landed immediately after a Zambian Airways aircraft.

He came to a halt and the three anxious men out on the apron were so relieved that he had arrived at last, that they flashed their pencil torches at him – the pre-arranged signal – for what must have been a thousand times.

The door of the aircraft was flung open and the three operators leapt in dragging their unused incendiary devices behind them.

The pilot opened his throttle and they were airborne within 300 metres. Lusaka control tower hadn't even bothered to call them up as they cleared the circuit and disappeared into the night.

They gave the pilot and navigator their sad news, then the sorry team slept for the remainder of their journey as the plane headed for Kariba where the three men were debriefed by the SAS commander and a CIO man.

They were bitterly disappointed at the failure of the mission. But as Brian Robinson recalls, a number of very valuable lessons had been learned which would stand them in good stead for the clandestine missions yet to come.

They had discovered the absolute necessity for accurate intelligence, complete detail and the need for alternative plans if things went wrong.

Had the pick-up not been planned for the same night, they might have been able to remain in the area until the following day when things had quietened down. They had not specified which end of the runway to meet the agent and didn't have a plan if the agent failed to meet them ... and there had been no recovery plan if he failed to meet them at the ZANU headquarters.

Operation *Sculpture* was to be the first and last secret operation without High Frequency communications.

Another early operation involved the attempted sabotage of 12 500 tons of Rhodesian-bought coal being stockpiled in Zambia, allegedly accumulated for the time Zambia closed the border. If the coal could be destroyed, perhaps Zambia would continue buying Rhodesian coal ... ?

An SAS team planned to help the coal ignite with their specially-made firebricks, but the half dozen mountains of coal that awaited them, would have taken far more than a piecemeal attack. In the event, the coal was moved, the border was not closed and Zambia continued to trade with Rhodesia for several years.

These and other early undercover operations were to remain a closely-guarded secret. So delicate were they in fact, that the SAS men were told if they were captured or killed, the Rhodesian Government would disclaim any knowledge of them.

Lighthouse Incident

There was a certain lieutenant in the 1st Battalion, Rhodesian African Rifles who had distinguished himself on Operation *Nickel* in 1968 . . . an operation mounted in the wake of the first major terrorist incursions into Rhodesia.

He had carried out a follow-up operation of some 85 kilometres (54 miles) in just 48 hours, and such was his determination that he had to take a boot resupply.

He always led from the front and during a brief pause, he heard the click of a safety catch or a similar sound made by the withdrawal of a grenade pin, indicating that he was in the centre of a well-concealed enemy position, and the middle of an ambush.

Acting on reflexes, he immediately fired towards the sound, killing two terrorists and causing four others to surrender. On learning that other terrorists were concealed nearby, the lieutenant, with complete disregard for his own safety, immediately positioned himself where he could subject the area to fire, and in the ensuing battle, a further six enemy were killed and two appeared with their hands held high above their heads.

The lieutenant radioed for helicopter support, eased springs and returned to base camp, wondering what the fuss concerning terrorism was all about.

The success of the action was entirely due to his quick, fearless reactions and remarkable qualities of leadership, and he was later awarded the Bronze Cross of Rhodesia for his gallantry.

Having seen action with the RAR he decided to try his hand with the SAS and duly passed selection in 1969. There was a shortage of officer accommodation at the time and a number of men were given permission to live out of the camp. The lieutenant decided to choose a fellow subaltern as a flatmate.

During a slack period, the two friends were "on the town" as usual and after removing a "Men at Work" sign and putting it outside the Nurses' Home, they decided to check the "talent" at *The Lighthouse* nightclub in Avondale . . . a popular gathering spot for the youth of Salisbury, and where most of the RLI and SAS members met when off duty.

On entering the circular nightclub, they decided that things definitely needed livening up. Everyone appeared subdued. It was the weekend, after all, and a bit of merriment was clearly needed.

Our lieutenant returned to his vintage Jaguar which served both as a car and armoury. Selecting the missile of his choice – a teargas grenade – he returned to the club.

Popping his head around the door, he nonchalantly tossed the grenade into the subdued smoke-filled nightclub atmosphere. Then, closing the door behind him, he strolled into the night air, looking like innocence personified, took up a comfortable position outside the club, and waited for the fun to start.

He did not have long to wait– about 4,5 seconds in fact!

It became apparent very quickly to the occupants that something was amiss.

The gas attacked their skin, eyes and nasal senses causing immediate respiratory stress . . . and not being able to breathe equals panic! Within a matter of seconds the scene in the club changed from tranquility to pandemonium.

Chivalry fell by the wayside as everyone fought for the door, leaving a trail of destruction. Furniture was crushed like matchsticks and the breakages were fantastic.

The management disregarded orders to allow customers out first and decided they too must abandon the *Lighthouse*. The fight for fresh air took priority.

Yet, despite the commotion, one enterprising RLI trooper managed to keep his wits about him. Not one to let an opportunity pass him by, he quickly made off with the *Lighthouse* till – only to be brought down in a rugby tackle by one of the management a few centimetres from the door as he attempted to make good his escape.

The hitherto peaceful scene outside had now taken on a new appearance. People were crying, gasping and vomiting in every direction. Some were bent double leaning over the outer club walls ... others were lying prostrate, trying to regain their composure.

It was like a First World War battle scene and the culprit responsible was in hysteria watching it all.

But during the mass confusion, the vigilance of the law remained unimpeded.

It was not long before a policeman spotted our man and asked if he wouldn't mind assisting them in the investigations.

He was politely asked to open the boot of his car ... and the eyes of the BSAP officer came out on organ stops as the lieutenant's private arms cache was revealed. Armaments varied from 7,62 millimetre ammunition to thunderflashes to – *teargas grenades* ... Teargas grenades!

The game was up and our hero was in deep trouble.

By now, his flatmate had decided to retire to his flat and continue his little party with his friends.

The police officer was convinced that a bigger and better arms cache existed somewhere else, and, escorted by the policeman, the lieutenant was asked to proceed to his home for further investigations.

On reaching the flat in one of the city avenues, it was very apparent another party was in progress. Blaring music and hoots of joviality could be heard from the street.

As they opened the door, the expression on the policeman's face was a picture. For the centrepiece of the party appeared to be a teddy-bear which was in the process of being roasted on the rotisserie.

A search of the flat unearthed more materials of war, whereupon the two flatmates were invited to accompany the officer to the station.

The Lighthouse culprit was obviously in big trouble. Telephone calls were made to Major Peter Rich, the OC, revealing the sad sorry tale. Hurried visits were made to and from Army HQ and hushed conversations took place at all levels behind closed doors.

Our hero was to be formally charged and would go on trial for a number of offences, varying from disturbing the peace to malicious damage to property.

During the court case, suppressed giggles could be heard through the courtroom as the facts unfolded.

Even the magistrate could be seen biting on his lower lip. An African interpreter – who sat in on every case – was becoming progressively gigglier and finding it very difficult to contain himself, much to the annoyance of the magistrate who had by now taken a grip of his own emotions.

He had almost subdued his desire to burst out laughing when the guilty party was asked why he placed the "Men At Work" sign outside the nurses' home. When he replied, "I thought it would be a bit of a giggle", it was all too much for the interpreter and he broke down and howled with mirth.

The lieutenant's superior officer at the time of Operation *Nickel* was called to give evidence in mitigation and, because his plea concerned current operations, his evidence was heard in camera.

He must have put up a command performance as he related the brave exploits of the lieutenant. He must have played on the stress factor and the fact that the young operational officer had to have some form of emotional release; that his behaviour was really only high spirits.

The court accepted this and the young lieutenant was spared a prison sentence in favour of a heavy fine.

He eventually left the Rhodesian Army and went off to fight in the Middle East, where by all accounts, he was held in high esteem.

Out of the bush he was a bit of a nuisance. He was, however, a typical example of a superb operational soldier and a fearless and natural leader.

His men would have followed him anywhere ... even, as one young soldier quipped, if it was just out of curiosity ...

Into Mozambique, 1969-1972

Up until the late sixties and early seventies, guerilla incursions into Rhodesia were not militarily successful for a variety of reasons.

A very real factor was the vigilance by security forces and other government departments in the Zambezi Valley. The farmers too, who in the main were members of the Police Reserve and had the benefit of training programmes, were a force to be reckoned with.

The few large-scale incursions there had been had left the terrorists severely mauled by the security forces. The Zambezi had indeed become a valley of death.

Then in 1967 ZIPRA made a political blunder when they infiltrated with the South African ANC (African National Congress). Pretoria immediately dispatched a number of policemen to strengthen Rhodesia's security. They became more involved from the following year and were to stay patrolling the Valley until 1975.

A massive incursion took place in 1968 and the six-week operation, codenamed *Cauldron,* lasted six weeks and involved the army, air force and police. During the operation, the SAS picked up a thoroughly emaciated insurgent who hadn't had a drop to drink or anything to eat for ten days. They gave him a packet of Army "dog biscuits" which he ate – and to their utter amazement, dropped stone dead at their feet. Next day, Captain Brian Robinson sent a signal to the Quartermasters' Stores congratulating them on their first kill!

Smaller urban groups had penetrated Rhodesia intent on striking at the heart of the country's administration, but in the main, although a few explosive devices were detonated, the impact was negligible and the police were able to deal with the matter.

The enormous hardships encountered by groups in the Zambezi Valley was another very real deterrent and gave the defender an advantage.

The Zambezi River and Lake Kariba were natural barriers that had to be crossed. The valley was extremely hot; there was disease and little water. And there was no one to give them food, shelter and intelligence.

Insurgents would cross the Zambezi loaded down with ammunition and those who did not drop dead through lack of water, had the stuffing knocked out of them by the security forces, while others failed the river crossing attempting to escape. South of the river were high bare hills, ravines and a vast expanse of open bush. It was a good thirty days' journey from Zambia before a man could get into action against a reasonable target; another thirty days back to get an ammunition resupply.

Infiltrators also made the basic errors which in insurgency led to certain death. They moved in columns, wore green fatigues and a standardised boot with a distinctive pattern which made tracking easy.

The Rhodesians' intelligence network was excellent and continually had the nationalists guessing.

Political strife within the two opposing factions of ZANU and ZAPU did not help their plans to take Rhodesia through the barrel of the gun, either. Neither did their initial lack of recruits.

In the early days of the war, only one country could really be used as a springboard for incursions and that was Zambia. Although Botswana was used in a limited way, Zambia was the only liberated country to share a frontier with Rhodesia where large concentrations of men could be assembled.

To the east was Portuguese-ruled Mozambique, which meant a hostile passage for the terrorists. But time and history were destined to change all that.

* * *

There was an airline advertisement which regularly told Rhodesian television audiences of the delights of a Mozambican coastal holiday. "The Portuguese have been there a long time," it said, as it showed fleeting visions of sand, sea and platters piled high with seafood.

Whether by air or by the long tortuous road leading eastwards, landlocked Rhodesians would flock to Beira or Lourenco Marques (later known as Maputo) and were particularly lemming-like at long weekends in their quest for prawns and cheap vino.

Yet there was another face to Mozambique and it was not tourism that concerned others in the country . . . they were interested in severing Metropolitan Portugal's 400-year-old rule on its far-flung African Province.

They were members of the black nationalist movement FRELIMO (The Front for the Liberation of Mozambique); they wanted black majority rule and were determined to get it by armed struggle. The war, which had begun in the early sixties, had become increasingly bitter and FRELIMO were having a fair amount of success.

Prior to FRELIMO beginning its campaign to oust the Portuguese, the Mozambique Province had been the perfect overseas posting for Portuguese Army officers who generally hailed from high-class families. The main concentration of inhabitants stretched along almost one-third of the East African coast and the officers joined them for a fine life under the African sun.

But then things began to go sour. FRELIMO started making their presence felt about the countryside and Mozambique very rapidly lost its appeal – many high-ranking officers packed their bags and returned to the safety of Portugal.

To counter the growing problems in Mozambique, the Portuguese shipped out the *povo* – the peasants – men who had not been made welcome there before, and, as it was generally a conscript army, morale was not good.

In March 1968, FRELIMO opened up the Tete front in the east, adjoining Zambia, Malawi and Rhodesia, and in 1969 an SAS tracker team was asked to go into Mozambique to hunt down FRELIMO for the Portuguese.

They were the first white Rhodesian soldiers to go into Mozambique and their presence there was top secret. FRELIMO had not yet forced their way south across the Zambezi River, and the SAS teams operated right to the extreme north of the country near the Malawi/Zambia/Mozambican borders.

But the Portuguese were extremely loath to come out of their garrison camps. Their hearts were simply not in the war, and with a few notable exceptions, they generally only wanted to get back to Portugal in one piece.

Junior officers and NCOs objected to being pulled out of university for three years and sent to Africa to fight for people who were important in Mozambique but would be of no consequence back home.

On the rare occasions they did venture out of their garrisons, they did so in strength, and were not prepared to break into smaller groups where they stood the chance of greater success.

Their discipline left much to be desired, and their standard drill when getting lost in the bush was to fire shots in the air!

Often to the horror of the SAS trackers closing in on fresh spoor for them, the Portuguese would break open beer cans and start drinking . . . or bang tins or planks to deliberately frighten the enemy away. Most of the contacts the SAS trackers had, turned into running punch-ups.

When the Rhodesians located an enemy camp for them, the Portuguese would often do a dry run with their jets. Then they would do the real thing the next day. By then, of course, FRELIMO had fled.

But apart from giving the Portuguese a hand, the SAS men did gain a knowledge of the terrain. And the exercise gave them battle experience that proved useful in later years when their own war got into full swing.

Then, in 1970, FRELIMO conducted a large offensive and managed to cross the Zambezi River near Chicoa. It was a decisive phase in Mozambique's war and it opened up Mozambique from the Zambezi River down to Rhodesia's north-eastern border.

But Portuguese forces were stretched. This predicament ensured the unimpeded progress of FRELIMO and ultimately their complete dominance of that part of Mozambique.

The Rhodesians – the SAS, RLI and Air Force – were naturally eager to keep FRELIMO away from their own border and prevent the war spilling into their own country, so they carried out a classic combined operation with the Portuguese. Even at this early stage, the security forces were concerned that Rhodesian terrorists might piggy-back on FRELIMO routes.

They aimed to show the Portuguese both the tracking concept and the joint-operations concept of counter-insurgency warfare where air and land operations were integrated. Yet when it came to tracking, it was the Rhodesians who were to learn the biggest lessons.

Up until then, they had viewed tracking as the magic ingredient for success. Their own victories had been in the remote, unpopulated regions of the Zambezi Valley where, if there was no interference from the rain, tracks would remain for anything up to a week.

They soon found that tracking was an entirely different proposition in a heavily-populated area where it was pouring with rain the whole time. It was the first indication to the Rhodesians that should things go wrong and the war be taken to the population, they too would have similar problems.

They were not to know it then, but by the time their own war got into full swing, the need for tracking would virtually fall away. There would be so many enemy running around Rhodesia that there would be no need to track them down; and there would not be enough trackers to do the job anyway.

* * *

38

The Beginning of the End

Over the years, Zambia-based ZANU/ZANLA had been having a serious re-think about the question of access into Rhodesia. It had long ago become obvious that the confrontation tactics of 1966-71 had to be discarded and an alternative infiltration route found to the suicidal Zambezi Valley.

The solution had to be hitherto hostile Mozambique. But now that FRELIMO were out and about, why couldn't they infiltrate into Rhodesia in the wake of the safe corridor FRELIMO were creating in their own push southwards? Access would be quicker and easier and the Mozambique/Rhodesia border with its forests and mountains providing good cover from the air, made it excellent guerilla country.

Apart from the need for that vital infiltration route and strong rear base, the Chinese-trained ZANLA leaders also felt that the key to successful incursions was to exploit black discontent and motivate the local population by politically indoctrinating them, so as to be prepared for the coming confrontation. It was the tried and tested Maoist theory of peasant mobilization.

An approach was made to FRELIMO to use the Tete region of Mozambique as a vital rear base. But FRELIMO considered ZANLA no more than a splinter group, and of no real consequence, so apart from allowing a small team to join them in Tete in 1970, that all-important permission was not granted.

Besides, FRELIMO had offered the Tete facility to ZIPRA, their old friends. FRELIMO themselves were operating right to the Rhodesian frontier and were keen to help ZIPRA gain access to Rhodesia that way and were prepared to guarantee their supplies. The fact that ZIPRA did not seem in any hurry to take up their offer, did not unduly worry FRELIMO at that stage.

Yet two years later, it was a very different story. FRELIMO had still been unable to persuade ZIPRA to take up the offer and despaired of ever selling the idea to them.

FRELIMO had been under the mistaken impression that ZIPRA enjoyed the support of all black Rhodesians. But the truth was that Rhodesian Africans bordering Mozambique were Shona-speaking and, as such, supported ZANLA, *not* the Sindebele-speaking ZIPRA. ZIPRA realised only too well that they would have had a very difficult passage through a hostile area where the locals didn't even speak their own language and were historically antagonistic towards their Matabeleland-based tribe.

Had ZIPRA taken up FRELIMO's persistent offer, the final outcome might well have been very different for Rhodesia.

Eventually, after two years of negotiations with FRELIMO, ZANLA was given permission to establish close links with FRELIMO outposts and "liberated areas" in Mozambique.

For ZANLA it was a major breakthrough in their bid to bring majority rule to an independent Zimbabwe; for white-ruled Rhodesia, it was to mark the beginning of the end.

It meant that ZANLA could operate close to the border, recruit, gather intelligence and move in ammunition to north-east Rhodesia. The politicization of the local population meant that incoming groups could be offered assistance and intelligence and not reveal their presence to the security forces. Invariably, political motivation would win the day and recruits would join the "struggle".

The Sindebele-speaking ZIPRA would continue to infiltrate across the rugged, sparsely populated Zambezi Valley.

Thus it was that the Rhodesian security forces were to face two enemy armies each using different tactics – one, ZANLA, which moved often in large groups working with the local population as a political force ... and the other, ZIPRA, which operated in small groups and worked solely in a military way.

Then in March 1972, police intelligence confirmed the presence of a ZANLA reconnaissance group which had travelled from Magazine in Zambia to ZANLA's base in Chifombo near Mwamjawanthu in Mozambique, ostensibly to select a route from Zambia through Mozambique to the Rhodesian border. The areas selected for infiltration covered a wide front.

Detective Section Officer Pete Stanton, of the Special Branch Terrorist Desk, Salisbury, was assured by local informers, sources in Zambia, and Mozambican refugees crossing into Rhodesia fleeing from FRELIMO, that there were ZANLA *comrades* from the Sipolilo area of Rhodesia at FRELIMO's Matimbe base. When he studied his map, he knew it had to make sense.

The camp was right next to the border. What would FRELIMO need with a base there? ZANLA, on the other hand, needed to be close to their recruiting sources. It was obvious ZANLA were carrying out a reconnaissance of the border area and assessing the attitude of the Rhodesian locals.

The Portuguese had always denied that ZANLA were in Mozambique or involved with FRELIMO. There was just no evidence. Rhodesians had the added worry that by the time the Portuguese troops reacted to a terrorist threat, the birds had flown.

Pete Stanton knew that if they were to get their evidence, it was necessary to outsmart the Portuguese. So at the next Portuguese Joint Operational Command meeting, Pete said he had information about a terrorist presence at Musengezi, which was in fact in the opposite direction from where the real threat lay.

As he had hoped, the Portuguese agreed to mount an operation there. Then Pete casually asked if the SAS – at that time already deployed in Mozambique – could patrol near Gungwa Mountains. The Portuguese agreed and the SAS mounted a strike on Matimbe camp. They killed several enemy, although it was difficult to establish at that stage if they were FRELIMO or ZANLA, as they were all dressed alike.

But huge sacks of documents were recovered ... and in a little black notebook, Pete Stanton found all the documentary evidence he needed. "Go and tell Evensi that the Zimbabwe boys have arrived. This is secret. Don't tell anyone", the message said in Shona. Pete knew of Evensi and that he came from Sipolilo in the northern part of Rhodesia.

Further intelligence revealed that the locals had been politically indoctrinated and numerous recruits collected to undergo external terror training.

ZANLA were making no secret of the fact that they were planning a new strategy.

Following the resounding "No" vote given by Africans to the 1972 British Test of Acceptability of new settlement proposals to the Rhodesian issue, ZANLA leaders in Lusaka announced that after the upheaval caused by the Test, there were now enough Africans in Rhodesia willing to pick up guns and use them.

Several trusted cells had been set up in the rural areas and an all-out effort was being made to smuggle arms and ammunition into Rhodesia, ZANLA declared.
* Their aim was to break the "resistance threshold" of white Rhodesians. Explained the man behind it all, brilliant lawyer and ZANLA Operations Chief, Herbert Chitepo: ZANLA's revolutionary warfare strategy was: " ... to attenuate the enemy forces by causing their deployment over the whole country. The subsequent mobilization of a large number of civilians from industry, business and agriculture would cause serious economic problems. This would have a psychologically devastating effect on the morale of the Whites ... "

*Michael Evans 40

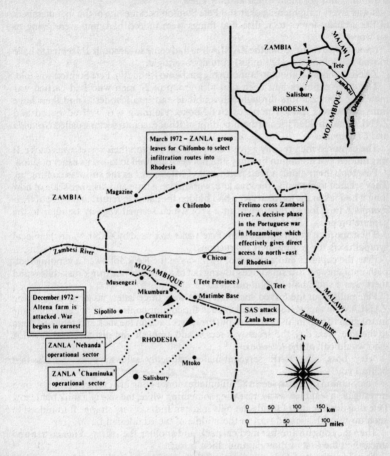

The ZANLA offensive begins

Map labels:
- ZAMBIA / Tete / MALAWI / Salisbury / RHODESIA / MOZAMBIQUE / Indian Ocean / Zambezi
- March 1972 – ZANLA group leaves for Chifombo to select infiltration routes into Rhodesia
- ZAMBIA
- Magazine
- Chifombo
- Frelimo cross Zambesi river. A decisive phase in the Portuguese war in Mozambique which effectively gives direct access to north-east of Rhodesia
- Zambesi River
- Chicoa
- MOZAMBIQUE (Tete Province)
- Musengezi
- Mkumbura
- Matimbe Base
- Tete
- MALAWI
- December 1972 – Altena farm is attacked. War begins in earnest
- Sipolilo
- Centenary
- SAS attack Zanla base
- Zambesi River
- ZANLA 'Nehanda' operational sector
- RHODESIA
- ZANLA 'Chaminuka' operational sector
- Mtoko
- Salisbury
- N
- 0   50   100   150 km
- 0   50   100 miles

* As far back as March 1969, a Mr Davis M'Gabe had predicted: "Chimurenga is a Shona word which means 'war of liberation'. Shona is the language of the native peoples of Zimbabwe, the land which the recent settlers call Rhodesia. If I were to tell you that a war of liberation is unfolding in Rhodesia you would probably call it wishful thinking. You could be wrong."

During October and November, 1972, intelligence came to light that insurgents had infiltrated through Mozambique into north-east Rhodesia ... and an internal operation, codenamed *Tempest*, was launched, involving the RAR.

Three ZANLA men were picked up by SB ground coverage during the operation and Pete Stanton sat them down in a little trench for a bit of privacy, shooed away the scorpions, and got them to tell all they knew.

It was a very enlightening chat and Pete Stanton became one of the first members of the security forces to realise that things were indeed bad, and were going to get worse.

It was hard to believe that the ZANLA line had come so far south. It seemed to have moved 200 kilometres (120 miles) virtually overnight.

ZANLA was now about to launch a big push into Rhodesia, Pete Stanton was told.

The three captures had been part of a group of 27 men who had carried war materials from Zambia through Mozambique and into Rhodesia, and their huge arms cache was hidden north-east of Mtoko. Planning was well advanced and ZANLA had divided the northern portion of Rhodesia into sectors, called *Nehanda* and *Chaminuka.*

The captured men readily agreed to show Pete Stanton their secret arms cache. It was hidden at a mountain but they had not been allowed to know its exact position.

Pete took them along a road north-east of Mtoko just as the sun was coming up. They seemed to recognise the area and, working on a time and distance scale of how long it had taken the terrorists who had hidden the cache to return to the rest of their *comrades,* they found themselves in a spot which seemed vaguely familiar to the captured men.

Then one man said he would show Pete a *letter-box,* used by ZANLA and their local sympathisers for getting their instructions.

Pete, the captures and a couple of members of the RAR, followed a winding foot-path until they got to a small tree growing out of a hill. The tree trunk was hollow and there was a stick, half-in, half-out of it.

Pete pulled out the forked stick and there were three letters attached to it, telling ZANLA what they were supposed to do in the coming confrontation. Pete copied the instructions down in his notebook, put the letters back on the stick and returned them to the tree. Next day, the security forces would ambush and dispatch two ZANLA who would call at the *letter-box.*

"Hey boss," the RAR sergeant-major suddenly said to Pete, "what's that behind you?"

Pete Stanton turned to see an 82 millimetre mortar lying in a crevice. As he got up to investigate, a leaf blew away, revealing something white, the size of a milk bottle top. Pete dug out a bottle of headache pills made in India, a very strange find indeed in such an unsophisticated spot in the middle of the Rhodesian bush.

Then they dug up another medical pack, and another, then scraped near a tree and unearthed the first of many ammunition boxes.

They literally unearthed a mountain full of weapons, landmines and ammunition. There were 9 000 smallarms rounds alone. It was a vast haul and nothing like it had been seen in Rhodesia before. Soon the choppers were arriving to take it all away, and three loads were recovered from the mountainside cache.

In early December 1972, ZANLA together with large groups of porters carrying weaponry, and under the command of Rex Nhongo – later one of the ZANLA hierarchy – wound their way through Mozambique and entered Rhodesia between Mkumbura and Musengezi.

The scene was now set for ZANLA's new offensive, the start of the new war of Chimurenga (the old being the rebellion against the whites in the 1890s).

As a result of the ZANLA men being picked up in the Mtoko region, the plan to infiltrate from that sector was abruptly called off.

It was now left to the group which had infiltrated in the *Nehanda* sector to make the first move. ZANLA had planned their new offensive for Christmas or the New Year when the country was celebrating and many soldiers would be on leave, but in view of the Mtoko party's arrest, they decided to launch their attack earlier.

Their target was fairly random although they had heard allegations that the farmer at Altena Farm in the Centenary district, fifty kilometres (31 miles) from the border and 200 kilometres (124 miles) from Salisbury, had poor relations with his staff.

On the evening of December 21, the ten ZANLA closed in on the humble farmstead. Inside, the owner and his family slept soundly on that peaceful Wednesday before Christmas. Outside in the darkness, peace and goodwill were the last thoughts on the minds of the ZANLA men with their sophisticated RPG-7 rocket launcher and AK-47 assault rifles.

Suddenly, they stepped from the shadows . . . and then their communist-supplied weapons sent a frightening clatter of rounds ripping through the homestead, peppering the walls with a deadly hail of lead and injuring a young girl inside.

Then ZANLA's thirty-second burst of bravado, designed mainly to impress the local African population was over and they fled into the nearby bush. But they were better trained than previous insurgents and took the precaution of planting a landmine, and cutting the telephone wires to hamper follow-up operations.

It was not a particularly spectacular incident and had little strategic value. But it did mark the first shots in the decisive phase of the war. From then onwards, terrorist attacks and incidents would be continuous, not sporadic as in the past.

Initially, there were many sceptics who, lulled into complacency by the insurgents' inactivity through the previous few years, were making such comments as: "We'll sort this little lot out and be home by Christmas." But it was to take another seven Christmasses before peace came to war-ravaged Rhodesia.

For, from that first half-minute act of aggression, the country was to be plunged into years of bloody warfare, which would only end with the signing of the Lancaster House ceasefire agreement.

Fortunately, from the outset of *Hurricane*, as the new anti-terrorist operation was to be known, the Special Air Service was fully prepared.

Even before the attack, the unit had already been called out to Centenary where a terrorist-indoctrinated witchdoctor had been captured and disclosed the whereabouts of an arms cache.

Within hours of the alarm being raised at Altena Farm, a group of young SAS trackers were rudely awakened at Cranborne Barracks in Salisbury.

They looked at their watches. It was 04h30. Someone was standing over them telling them that a farmhouse had been attacked at Centenary and they were to get their kit together. A chopper would be arriving to pick them up in half-an-hour.

By the time they got to Altena Farm, the landmine had been found in the road near the homestead. But the terrorists had learned their anti-tracking lessons well, and despite intense effort by the SAS men, the spoor petered out. The elusive ZANLA were just nowhere to be found.

The SAS set up their headquarters at a nearby farm. By now a Joint Operations Command (JOC) had been established at Centenary where the uniformed Police, the Army, the Air Force and Special Branch co-operated and worked in harmony to pool their intelligence.

Then another farmhouse, *Whistlefield*, was attacked and once again the SAS trackers were shaken awake. But they were picked up in the darkness and there was nothing much they could do until it got light.

43

The trackers teamed up with an RLI support group and together they boarded a truck and set off for spoor.

As they approached a bend in the road, the SAS trackers got off and cut across the corner section to continue the search. Almost immediately, they picked up spoor and called the RLI over on their radio.

As the truck swung around the corner, disaster struck.

There was a tremendous thunderclap and the truck was catapulted into the air as the back wheel detonated a landmine that had been well-camouflaged in the sandy soil.

Corporal Norman Moore, who had been standing on the tailboard, was flung through the air, receiving serious injuries, which were to prove fatal. Several other RLI men were injured.

Quickly an SAS corporal raced to the wreck and pulled an injured soldier off. An RLI corporal had already leapt from the truck to aid his injured colleagues.

The SAS, the 15 RLI men and an old African Police tracker, immediately set off on the spoor. Their blood was up and they were determined to get the men responsible.

They tracked the entire day and slept that night on the spoor. As soon as it was light enough they set off again and got so close to them that when they came upon the hidden ZANLA camp, the fire was still burning.

Meanwhile, back at Centenary, the new SAS OC Major Brian Robinson decided to put stop-groups along the Musengezi River to cut the enemy off.

Corporal Danny Smith and his four men were hurriedly choppered in to a commanding position on some high ground near the river and had no sooner taken up their positions when they saw some ten enemy advancing in single file towards them, armed with automatic weapons, a machinegun and an RPG-7 rocket launcher.

Smith had deployed his men into favourable positions. As he saw it, the enemy had three routes available to them. Unluckily for them they chose the wrong one – and ran straight into Smith's callsign.

At the end of the contact three terrorists had been killed and another surrendered. Next day, another wounded man surrendered. It was the first engagement since the war began in earnest and Smith was to get a Military Forces Commendation for his action that day.

By now, security force officers were no longer talking about sorting out the affair by Christmas. Now they were making it plain that it was going to be a long operation. A huge security net had been thrown around the Centenary area and it was declared a restricted area with no unauthorised visitors allowed in.

Territorial soldiers helped guard Centenary farms over the Christmas holidays and farmers joined their police reservist units in the massive seek-and-destroy sweeps through the rugged countryside.

The Rhodesians would soon realise that they were up against a better calibre of enemy than they had faced in the past. Soon the killings would begin and the farming community, some initially irritated by the troops trampling over their crops, would begin to realise their vulnerability.

"It is no fun living behind a three-metre fence, no fun spending nights at a time lying in ambush outside one's own tobacco barns," wrote visiting British journalist, Max Hastings. "Least fun of all when they know that they can reach no end; and that this is only the end of the beginning."

Most of the SAS stayed in the Centenary area until early in the New Year on follow-up operations. But SAS OC Major Brian Robinson wanted his unit out of the area.

He had been totally against the SAS being involved in what was an infantry role, wandering around the countryside tracking down terrorists. The function of the SAS was external, not internal like other units.

They knew where the insurgents were coming from and it was obvious that if they were to be stopped, the war had to be taken to them while they were still in Mozambique. The sudden upsurge in incursions had to be stemmed. Their camps inside Mozambique had to be reconnoitred and their infiltration routes ambushed.

While several SAS trackers were to remain in the Centenary area for three months assisting other units to react to the increasing number of attacks, the rest of the squadron was pulled back to Salisbury to await the time when they could go external again.

They would not have long to wait ...

First Operational Freefall Jump, January 19, 1973

It was now blatantly apparent that Rhodesian insurgents were openly collaborating with FRELIMO and had established infiltration routes and bases on a wide front on the Rhodesian north-eastern border. The routes were in constant use serving *Nehanda* and *Chaminuka* sectors with logistical and manpower requirements.

The Rhodesians knew there were two very important crossing points used by the insurgents to get into the country. They were travelling from the Chifombo region of Mozambique down to Umpapi, north of the Zambezi, and from there, they crossed the river at two points.

Complaining to the Portuguese didn't do much good. Troops were sent to investigate, but the message coming back to Salisbury was always the same – "No, there's no one there."

Undeterred, the Rhodesians continued to look for an excuse to get back into Mozambique and sort the insurgents out.

Then, on January 8, 1973, 18 days after the Altena farm attack, at Centenary, there was a new development.

Three white Rhodesian Government land inspectors, Gerald Hawksworth, Dennis Sanderson and Bob Bland, and their two black messengers, were ambushed as they drove along a lonely road in Mount Darwin in the north-east of the country.

As the vehicle rounded a bend in the road, there was a sudden burst of machine-gun fire and Bob Bland and Dennis Sanderson were cut down, making them the first white civilians to be killed in Rhodesia since May 1966, when Johannes Hendrick Viljoen and his wife were murdered at their remote farmhouse.

Hawksworth and his African staff were to be spared, but not freed ... and the ZANLA terrorists headed back to Mozambique with their prisoners. The two Africans managed to escape, but Hawksworth was destined to continue marching to Mozambique at the insistence of his captors.

Here at last was a golden opportunity for the SAS to get back into Mozambique, and permission was sought from the Portuguese. After a great deal of diplomatic wrangling and negotiation, the Rhodesians gained permission for the SAS to operate in depth between the Zambezi River and the Rhodesian/Mozambique border in the Tete Province.

It was essential that the SAS be deployed secretly in order to gain complete surprise, and to achieve this it was decided to deploy two groups by freefall and static-line parachute.

(Freefall parachuting had been introduced a year before after the persistent badgering of Brian Robinson and Frank Hales of the Parachute Training School. Frank, an experienced freefaller, who had emigrated to Rhodesia from England, had realised that in terms of the African environment, freefall parachuting – high-altitude, low-opening – had many advantages. The opposition didn't have much in the way of sophisticated radar or anti-aircraft devices to detect or reach a plane flying at something like 18 000 feet above the ground. It was extremely difficult to hear a plane that far away – and even if the enemy did, they would not be expecting to find paratroopers floating down some time later.)

One SAS group was to deploy to the west of the Musengezi River some 36 kilometres (22 miles) inside Mozambique where there was one of the known crossing points; the other to the east, near the second crossing point, both about 15 kilometres (nine miles) south of the Zambezi River. Then, having broken down into smaller groups, they were to cut off the infiltration routes and prevent insurgents getting into Rhodesia.

Before the main body of men arrived, it was imperative that the SAS deploy two four-man freefall pathfinder teams – one for each of the two parachute groups – to ensure the area selected for the main drop was uninhabited.

Having selected a suitable drop zone and determined the wind speed, the main drop of static-line paratroopers was to be controlled completely by the pathfinder leader. He was to select the run-in direction for the plane, and tell the pilot to go left or right and make corrections if necessary in order to drop the paratroops precisely where he wanted. Then he was to give the "Red light on" instruction, the signal to the dispatchers to shout the "Stand in the door" command to the static-line paratroops.

Finally, the pathfinder leader would give the "Green light on" command . . . while above, the dispatchers bellowed the "GO" sending the troops tumbling out of the Dakota on their way down to Mozambique.

Lieutenant Chris Schollenberg was to be the leader of the four-man pathfinder team on the western side of the Musengezi . . . the SAS 2IC, Captain Garth Barrett, was to command the other four-man group on the east of the river.

Finding suitable dropping zones for the main body of static-line paratroopers following them into Mozambique at midnight was not going to be easy, as the two pathfinder teams soon realised when they looked at the maps and aerial photographs of their area. There was just nothing that met the regulation requirements.

If Army regulations were to be followed, the two DZs had to consist of even, cleared ground 1 000 metres long and 750 metres wide. The teams could not find anything that even vaguely looked suitable on their photographs. Hopefully, they would be able to find somewhere once on the ground.

On January 19, 1973, in the operations room of Two Brigade, Brigadier John Hickman gave a briefing to the SAS troops. It was the first time a brigadier had briefed Rhodesian SAS troops for an operation.

He told them of ZANLA's route and the two crossing points and where they were to drop to cut off the gang and, with luck, secure Hawksworth's release. He said the chances of getting Hawksworth were slim, but they had to kill as many enemy as they could while in there.

This would prove to the Portuguese that the terrorists were in Mozambique, that there was a route, and that the Portuguese were not doing their job and stopping them getting to the Rhodesian border. The more they got, the stronger was their case for staying inside Mozambique. The SAS had to get in there and "turn off the tap."

Rehearsals were held at the Parachute Training School and on that warm January evening, OC Major Brian Robinson gave the orders for the first Rhodesian airborne military operation outside the country since the counter-insurgency days of Malaya in the 50s.

It was going to be the first operational freefall for the pathfinders; the first time freefalling had been used in anger; the first operational static-line descent for most of the Squadron members. And it was to be the first real night descent for many of the young soldiers.

Excitement and apprehension were in the air. No one knew what to expect, what the terrain was like, how many ZANLA or their FRELIMO comrades roamed the countryside, and if they would land in the middle of a terrorist camp.

SAS commanders, airmen, Special Branch members and Brigadier Hickman were all gathered to hear Brian Robinson give his orders.

"In order to remain clandestine," the SAS commander said, "casualty evacuation will only be carried out if death in the field is imminent."

The audible gulp of medic Sergeant Richard Thorne, echoed through the stunned, silent orders group.

The Dakota with the two pathfinder teams on board was airborne at precisely 17h30 and the plan was to drop the pathfinders just on last light. The timings for the drop were absolutely critical. One minute too early and the freefallers could be seen during daylight. One minute too late and they would not be able to read their altimeters.

Thirty minutes from drop time Squadron Leader Derek de Kok, of the Parachute Training School, ordered the men to "saddle up" – to get their kit on.

The military freefaller is a most cumbersome sight dressed up in full equipment. The Bergen rucksack weighing 25 kilograms was secured by hooks and straps behind the knees, with a rifle inverted and strapped to the left shoulder and side.

The Dak was flying at 11 000 feet to avoid detection from the ground and in heavy equipment at that altitude, with oxygen on, the men were soon perspiring despite the low temperature.

As the drop time approached, the atmosphere became electric. There was some cautious talk, but they didn't want to say too much in case their fear showed in their voices.

Some were laughing, trying to be casual. Others were silent, wondering exactly what emotion Brian Robinson was hoping to see in their faces.

"Others pretended to nod off to sleep and I was trying to give an air of complete confidence whilst sitting with my stomach in a knot . . . and I didn't have a parachute on my back," Brian Robinson recalled.

The new SAS commander was very proud of his lads in the Dak at that moment, he stressed. This was history in the making. Normally a solemn man, that night he was in a cheerful mood.

The leader of the first pathfinder team, Lieutenant Chris Schollenburg remembers being worried about the jump, but more concerned for the lads who would be parachuting in at midnight by static line. The pathfinders only had a couple of hours to find a suitable dropping zone for them, and it was a great responsibility.

Conditions were extremely hazy and both the pilot and dispatchers were having great difficulty finding the correct dropping zone.

But eventually they located the spot south of the Zambezi where they had to drop off the two small teams.

Five minutes out from the dropping zone, the dispatcher gave the order to number off for the equipment check. Each man laboured to his feet, hardly able to support himself under the weight of all his equipment.

47

"Eight men okay . . . seven men okay," he said as he checked out their equipment from head to toe. Helmets . . . reserves . . . handles . . . altimeters . . . every piece of equipment was checked first by the SAS operators, then by the dispatcher. Then he counted down to "One man okay . . . stick okay."

Thumbs up, thumbs up. Everyone gave the signal that meant all was well.

Most of the men attempted to give the impression of joviality as they finished their equipment checks and wished one another good luck.

Then came the "action stations" command. The team took up their positions in the aisle.

Their kit was now weighing very heavy on their backs. They did not have the oxygen now. Everything went quiet. They were particularly anxious at that moment, wondering if they would faint; hoping they would not.

The dispatcher was now in a lying position with his head sticking out of the gaping hole which once contained a door. He was studying the terrain below and wore a mask over his mouth to speak to the pilot, to tell him to go left or right, to make the last-minute corrections. The slipstream was distorting his face so much that he looked like something out of a horror movie.

Chris Schollenberg now stood with both hands on either side of the lights above the door, his right foot forward, minutes away from launching himself into space.

Now Brian Robinson could sense that the butterflies had disappeared and knew each man was privately going through the well-rehearsed routine . . . maintain aircraft heading, arch the body, bring in the hands and legs, check the altimeter, look for other parachutists, track away from them, watch the altimeter, then when the time was right, with one last look at the altimeter, hands in and pull the handle.

"Stand in the door!" shouted the dispatcher at last above the roar of the aircraft's engines and the rush of the slipstream.

Schulie removed his hands from the top of the door and placed them at waist level on either side of the door.

The green light came on.

"GO!" screamed the dispatcher, at 18h50 above the noise from the engine, slapping Schulie on the back of the calf.

In less than three seconds, Schulie was gone, falling through the evening to a spot south of the Zambezi River. He was followed by Corporal Danny Smith, Lance Corporal Dave Cale and Sergeant Frank Wilmot.

Five minutes later the second team led by Captain Garth Barrett and his team of Lieutenant Ron Marillier, Pete Marshall and *Horse* Green left the aircraft just as darkness descended.

The first stick fell to earth and were heading for more or less where they wanted to land. There was the flat countryside, the little bit of a ravine they had seen on the aerial photographs.

At 10 000 feet, Dave Cale, the third man out of the plane, watched in horror as Frank Wilmot, the number four man who should have been stacked up high above him, came spinning past him. His parachute was not open.

Frank was in a right-hand spin and getting faster and faster . . . and Dave Cale and Danny Smith were utterly helpless to do anything to assist him as they floated down. There was no way they could see him getting out of the spin.

At 2 000 feet, Schulie pulled the ripcord of his parachute. It opened and he looked up to see a couple of parachutes crack open as his team obeyed orders and pulled at the regulation height of 2 500 feet.

48

It was then that he saw Frank Wilmot hurtling down. He was still in a right-hand spin. Neither his main parachute nor his reserve was out.

"PULL!" the pathfinder leader bellowed at the top of his voice as Frank spun past him. But there was no reaction.

"Oh my God!" thought Schulie immediately, giving himself a fright at having shouted. If there were any terrorists skulking around below them, he would have blown their entry for sure.

Schulie, Dave Cale and Danny Smith were still up high in the sunlight. Below, the dusk had fallen on that Friday evening as Frank continued spinning earthwards.

The lack of light below prevented Schulie getting a clear picture, but he distinctly saw Frank land in an open patch, then saw a puff of dust as he hit the side of a little gully.

There had been no flowering of a parachute. Neither Frank's main nor his reserve chute had opened. The pathfinder leader knew there was no hope for him. He had spun into the ground.

Meanwhile, Major Brian Robinson as yet unaware of the tragedy and flying somewhere over Mozambique sat anxiously waiting for the reports from below. The news when it came, shocked him to the core and as Schulie's gutteral Afrikaans voice came over the aircraft's VHF radio, his first words were to remain with him for the rest of his life.

"This is Pappa-One," Schulie said. "One of my men has gone straight into the ground ... "

"We were all initially stunned and then a spate of thoughts as to what should be done next shot through my mind," the SAS commander recalled.

"How was I going to find the body? If I did, how was I going to recover it without giving the game away? Should I cancel the whole operation?

"Forcing myself to think clearly, I decided to continue with the operation, but decided against telling the rest of the squadron of the death. Having sworn the aircrews to secrecy and hearing the all's well from Captain Garth Barrett over in the second pathfinder group, they set course for New Sarum arriving at the Parachute Training hangar where the rest of the Squadron waited at 20h00."

As he hurried into the hangar, he was appalled to see the Army padre handing out Bibles to a group of bewildered SAS soldiers.

"Jesus!" quipped Sergeant Pete Cole. "I remember being frightened at Aden, but this really takes the cake!"

Convinced that the padre had been told of the parachuting death, Brian Robinson threatened the well-meaning padre with violence if he put the wind up his men.

He found out later that the padre knew nothing of the death of Frank Wilmot, but had merely gone out to the Parachute School to wish the boys well. But it was a most ill-timed visit as far as Robinson was concerned.

By 23h00, the static-line paratroops had boarded the two waiting Daks and the aircraft had set course for Mozambique.

Meanwhile on the western side of the Musengezi River, Schulie had already landed and watched the rest of his pathfinder team touch down safely.

They regrouped, bundled up their parachutes and cached them. "Right let's see if we can find Frank," Schulie said to his team.

They had a quick look but without success. It was already dark and they were under a lot of pressure to find a suitable dropping zone for the static-line paratroopers coming in a couple of hours time. They would have to abandon the search for Frank for now, get cracking and find a DZ before what visibility there was disappeared altogether.

They moved off counting their paces and their times, with Schulie using a compass, so that they could return to the spot later and resume the search.

They trudged on through the bush, and with each step they took they worried that they would never find an open space within the limited time frame. The other lads due to jump that night would not thank them for the broken bones they would undoubtedly sustain if they got the all-clear to jump in such wooded terrain.

But the trees did not thin out and Schulie decided there was nothing for it but to keep on walking through the night until they heard the drone of the Dakota above them.

When they did hear the plane, the terrain had not improved and they were still surrounded by trees.

"Right, we are ready to jump," came a voice from above towards midnight. "Have you got a DZ for us?"

"Negative," Schulie radioed back. "There's no DZ and that's that. The guys can jump, but it's all trees down here."

It was the second serious problem that night. For the entire operational deployment had revolved around two separate DZs.

Captain Garth Barrett, leader of the other pathfinder team, had by now come up on his radio to report finding a DZ on the eastern side of the Musengezi. The first one they had found was strewn with large rocks and they had pressed on looking for another. By 23h00, they had found one with fewer rocks and less danger to the paratroopers as it consisted mainly of trees . . . and Brian Robinson now decided to deploy both callsigns into Barrett's area.

It meant that the group which should have been working in Schulie's area under the command of Captain Howard Inman would face a fifty kilometre (32 miles) trek through the bush to join up with him.

At midnight, Garth Barrett's radio crackled into life as the pilot told him of the arrival of the main body of paratroopers. Soon the drone of the aircraft's engines could be heard and the pathfinder team guided the Dakotas on to their position and directed the drop.

Then all the paratroopers leapt out at Barrett's DZ. Except that was not really a DZ either!

They had to take their chances among trees, small rocks and uneven, unsuitable terrain, for there was hardly a clear space at all. The DZ was purely a figment of the pathfinder's imagination, they discovered.

The deployment had also become the first operational night drop without a proper DZ!

Amazingly, save for the broken ankle sustained by New Zealander, Lieutenant Martin Knight-Willis when he landed on a small rock, the drop went without a hitch.

Perhaps the regulations did state that a DZ ought to consist of a cleared piece of ground 1 000 metres long and 750 metres wide! The SAS certainly had news for whoever wrote the regulations.

Despite Brian Robinson's earlier instructions that there would be no casevac unless death was imminent, he sent a chopper to recover Martin Knight-Willis. Another was already on its way to collect Frank Wilmot's body. Brian realised that it was an *Alice in Wonderland* idea to expect so many men to operate behind enemy lines without air support.

Schulie and his team were already making their way back to their original DZ, counting their steps as they travelled over the flat, featureless countryside. They were to await the arrival of the chopper on its way to collect Frank Wilmot's body. But first, they had to find him.

At about 02h00, they realised they were back in the area of their original DZ. It was an amazing stroke of luck. For even meticulously counting their paces was not guaranteed to produce accurate results, specially at night over countryside with no features to make the job easier.

They found the cache of parachutes, then, aided by the light from the moon, started searching for Frank's body.

Three hundred metres from their cache, Danny Smith suspected they were in the right area. Then he saw a glint in the moonlight. Closer examination revealed that it was an army ration tin, which had burst from Frank's pack on impact with the ground.

They found Frank at the bottom of a sandstone gully next to a tiny tree. They were working at such a rate, that the horror of their find did not sink in at the time.

The canopy of Frank's main parachute trailed behind him up the gully. The rigging lines were neatly folded and it was clear they had only come out of their sleeve on impact. The reserve was open beneath him and puffing up around him. It was obvious that the main and reserve canopies had burst open only when Frank smashed into the ground and skidded down the gully.

Schulie and Danny turned Frank over on to his back and folded the reserve parachute over him, careful not to disturb anything. They carried him to a safe spot, then once more searched around for a landing place for the chopper.

Again they could not locate one – and at 04h00, chopper pilot, Flight-Lieutenant Peter Woolcock, radioed he was near them.

"My friend," said Schulie "We are sorry, but there's no LZ. Can *you* find one?"

"No problem!" replied the Flight-Lieutenant, "I know where you are."

As the pilot and his technician, Bob Mackie, flew along the Musengezi River, the moon virtually disappeared . . . and as they got closer to the pathfinder team, they switched off their landing lights and flew in almost total darkness. They had no idea if there were any enemy in the area, and had no desire to attract attention to the pathfinders.

Suddenly, the pilot picked up Schulie's torch flashing out its urgent signal through the darkness.

He came down cutting his way through a tree to land in the gully, the blast from the rotor blades sending the grass dancing like waves on the ocean. Only in those last few crucial moments before touch-down did the pilot switch on his landing lights. Then, as soon as he landed he cut his engines to reduce the risk of compromise.

It was remarkable flying and something the security forces were to become accustomed to over the years.

Frank Wilmot's body was loaded on board. Schulie knew there would be an investigation and told the pilot that was exactly how they found Frank and that they had not disturbed any of the equipment.

The chopper lifted, the pilot and technician gave a wave and then they were off again, skimming the tree tops and heading for home.

Theories about Frank's death varied from the spin causing him to black-out . . . to a parachute malfunction . . . or its wrapping around his body. As both the reserve and the main canopy deployed on impact, the true story will never be known.

A member of the Parachute Training School recalled that Frank had an automatic opening device on his reserve parachute but it was impossible to determine whether or not it had worked, and, if it had, whether his body attitude had prevented the correct deployment.

When body and equipment were taken to the mortuary, someone removed the parachute and equipment. Investigators conducting the subsequent Board of Inquiry were presented with everything in a huge bundle and were thus unable to determine what, if anything, had gone wrong with the parachutes.

Captain Howard Inman who had to jump out at Garth Barrett's DZ instead of at Schollenberg's, led his men on the long arduous trek westwards to rendezvous with the first pathfinder team. They walked all day in the sweltering January heat, and eventually the tired team, drenched in perspiration, reached the banks of the Musengezi River, only to find it in full flood.

Howard stared in disbelief at the 100 metre torrent that separated them from Schulie's team, aware that the longer they lingered, the greater the danger of their being seen. But soon they found a dug-out canoe carelessly left on the banks of the river by a local fisherman. They stripped off and swam the raging river, ferrying the dug-out back and forth until all their kit and equipment was safely on the other side.

All reached the safety of the opposite bank uneventfully, donned their uniforms and started out on the final leg of the journey to link up with Schulie and his team.

Three days after the first pathfinder group had dropped into Mozambique, the two groups met up. Half expecting them to have a morale problem after having wrapped up Frank Wilmot, Howard Inman greeted Schulie and said he bet they were glad to see them.

"No, no, no!" replied Schulie who had already been busy conducting one-man missions. "I like being by myself."

It was the first intimation his friends had that Schulie enjoyed operating by himself or in very small groups, unlike others who preferred the group feeling. It was a *modus operandi* that was ultimately to make him a legend in Rhodesian military history.

The SAS then broke down into callsigns in their search for the enemy, and Captain Garth Barrett in charge of one group soon found an ideal ambush position. The Captain and his partner, Stan Hornby, were dug in on either side of a huge anthill and a massive tree hid them from view from the path below.

They were at their post as usual one morning and Stan was beginning to think the terrorists would never come when suddenly Garth whispered a warning that two men were approaching.

Stan looked from behind his anthill to see men walking next to each other coming down the track. Both were totally offguard, carrying SKS rifles with bayonets fixed slung over their shoulders.

They passed in front of the ambushers. Garth Barrett sent a round towards the man at the back and he slumped to earth, mortally wounded. His companion fled, dropping his rifle in his panic.

Luckily the dead FRELIMO was carrying a letter and although it was in Portuguese, the SAS picked out the name *Hawksworth.*

It asked the FRELIMO commander of that particular sector to allow Hawksworth and his captors to pass through on their way to his ultimate destination. It was the nearest they were to come to Gerald Hawksworth, and it was certainly better than the Army and hierarchy had hoped for anyway.

Hawksworth was force-marched at gunpoint more than 1 600 kilometres (1 000 miles) through Rhodesia and Mozambique before finishing up in a flea-ridden Tanzanian jail. A British subject, he was used as a ZANU propaganda prize in a bid to get recognition for the party in exile, and was released a year later after representation by the British Government.

While Hawksworth was stumbling through Mozambique, the SAS were familiaris-
ing themselves with the terrain and procedures that would become second nature to
them over the years.

In previous operations, they had normally been involved in border control where
people did not bother too much about snoring or banging their mess tins.

But all that had changed overnight. Men were beginning to get upset about how
much noise a neighbour made when he shook out his bivvy or rattled his mess tin
with his spoon. Noise could compromise them, alert terrorists to their presence. It
could have fatal consequences.

Schulie had always been aware of these problems and when he first joined the
squadron from his native South Africa, he was eyed with a certain amount of
suspicion.

He camouflaged all his kit – his spoons ... mess tins ... notebooks ... Even his
locker at camp was sprayed camouflage colours. It would not be long however before
the others realised the advantages of camouflage.

Nothing annoyed Schulie more in the bush than a man coughing. To Schulie it was
inexcusable.

His particular callsign happened to have two members afflicted with this irritating
habit and the worst offender, a certain Fred, quickly earned the apt nickname
The Cougher.

"If you can't control your cough – and it's all psychological anyway," the lieutenant
threatened, "I'm going to leave you behind."

Fred obviously thought it was an idle threat and continued to cough, and, as a
result, when they based up at night, Fred and his mate were dropped off 500 metres
and sometimes as much as a kilometre away from the rest of the callsign.

Schulies' idea was that if Fred coughed at night the terrorists would find him and
not the others!

They really didn't expect too much from Fred as his coughing tended to override
everything else. Then one day Fred was left on guard while the various callsigns
awaited the arrival of a re-supply plane. Suddenly, two shots rang out from
Fred's direction.

Everyone raced to find *The Cougher* proudly standing over two terrorists, one dead,
the other wounded in the head. Even Schulie was impressed – not that he let Fred
back into base at night!

The operation lasted almost a month and as the rainy season was in full swing, the
SAS were soaked day and night. They accounted for many totally unprepared enemy
who didn't have a clue that the Rhodesians were abroad in what was assumed to be
friendly terrain.

Cameras were dropped in and dead terrorists were photographed to prove to the
Portuguese that ZANLA were indeed operating in Mozambique, and to build up the
squadron's case that the SAS should stay in Mozambique.

The squadron captured many arms, picked up when running ZANLA dropped
everything in an effort to get away. Their haul included the first RPG-7 rocket
launcher captured in the war.

The SAS were in Mozambique chasing terrorists in their home bases, hitting them
before they could infiltrate into Rhodesia. And they were in officially. For having got
in there, they began picking up definite signs of enemy camps, some jointly shared by
FRELIMO and ZANLA and which the Portuguese knew nothing about.

The situation gave the SAS a valid reason to stay in Mozambique and the Portuguese gave approval. Big real estate was about to become the SAS's business.

Externals – An Everyday Occurrence

Macombe Days, 1973-1974

Shortly before Rhodesia staged her rebellion and declared UDI, Brian Robinson, one of the unit's new young lieutenants, went to Britain on attachment to 22 SAS, absorbing all he could about the role of the SAS and soaking up atmosphere from the masters.

He was only the second Rhodesian SAS officer to have been attached to 22 and it was an invaluable experience; one which was ultimately to have a direct effect on the way the Rhodesian Special Air Service was to develop.

For all Brian's initial ideas were based on what 22 were doing on their operations behind enemy lines. By living with them, talking to them, thinking SAS 24 hours a day, the young Rhodesian gained a unique insight into what the SAS was all about – what they should do, and perhaps just as importantly, what they should not do.

It was 1965 and 22 SAS were working right into Borneo, and the closer Brian Robinson got to know the operators, the more he heard about the sort of operations they were doing there . . . seeking out enemy camps, leading in the infantry to attack them, melting into the night and going on to their next task. It was the typical everyday work, the deep penetration behind-the-scenes clandestine work that made the SAS what it was.

Suddenly, all the SAS's well-known clichés – *long range deep penetration, seek and destroy, shoot-'n'-scoot* – became part of Brian's life.

Then, having got himself on the flight manifest to go to Borneo with 22 SAS, UDI happened, and the adjutant called Brian in to spell out exactly what it meant to the Rhodesian soldier.

"Look, I'm awfully sorry about this," he told Brian "but you are no longer welcome here."

And that was that. Brian Robinson was on the next plane to Rhodesia.

It was a big blow and Brian was bitterly disappointed. He knew he could have gained a wealth of experience in Borneo that could have been used back home in Rhodesia.

Now that it was 1973 and the Rhodesian SAS was working externally in Mozambique, he saw it as an ideal opportunity to employ his men in their proper role, just as 22 SAS had done in Borneo.

The squadron could act as the eyes and ears of the Rhodesian Army, providing the infantry with information for their attacks on terrorist bases and routes. The SAS's role was not necessarily to do the killing, as most people in Rhodesia thought. Since the desert days, the SAS's role was not to engage the enemy, but to outwit them.

But getting that message across was not such a straight-forward task.

54

For the first few months after the Frank Wilmot incident, the SAS were working south of the Zambezi River, watching and monitoring ZANLA and FRELIMO movements.

It became very apparent that the so-called Ho Chi Minh trail was far more than one simple route, which would have been easy to ambush. It was a whole series of routes running through villages and kraals, in a vast area that was something like seventy kilometres (45 miles) wide.

But sitting and watching paths, and acting as the eyes and ears, took time, and the average soldier sometimes could not understand why the SAS were doing it.

Rhodesian SAS soldiers were young, magnificient – and like all soldiers, they wanted action. And they could not help feeling that by making them sit and watch paths for weeks on end, their commander was messing them around.

Nothing could have been further from the truth. Brian Robinson realised that it took time, often months, to build up a picture, to establish where the many infiltration routes were, which could ultimately lead to big ambushes being mounted and to large-scale camp attacks.

Yet while the SAS continued to follow their traditional role and act as eyes and ears for the infantry, the plan was not followed to its logical conclusion because – according to Brian Robinson – the SAS did not have the benefit of adequate support troops.

All SAS information was passed back to Two Brigade ops room where the staff spent their time putting lines and stickers all over the maps where they intended positioning cut-off troops. It all looked extremely impressive on the maps. On the ground however, it was not so good.

It became extremely frustrating for the SAS, having risked their lives and located groups of 150 or so ZANLA moving southwards each day, to call in a group of infantry which was unable to react effectively and eliminate the insurgents . . . thereby leaving ZANLA to continue on their way unopposed and infiltrate into Rhodesia.

Ideally, what was needed, Brian felt, was a superior infantry unit like the British Parachute Brigade. But that was just not available in Rhodesia and Brian eventually conceded that if their information was not followed-up effectively, the SAS were just wasting their time.

Having at long last managed to convince everyone that the SAS's role was *not* to kill the enemy but to act as eyes and ears, Brian then began to fight for the right to do the infantry's job for them – to kill the enemy!

He was basically fighting against himself, but he had no choice. If the enemy were to be stopped, the SAS would just have to do the job themselves . . . and what started as reconnaissance turned into a hit-and-run, hunter-killer role, which was acceptable to Brian Robinson as it was the *shoot-'n'-scoot* of the Borneo days – a volley, inflicting casualties then disappearing into the night as soon as possible.

The SAS troops themselves certainly welcomed the opportunity to be unleashed and do something positive to put a stop to the enemy.

As they were working so far from Salisbury, a tactical headquarters was established at an old mission station at Musengezi in Rhodesia from where the helicopters and aircraft were on standby to speed across the border for casevacs, airstrikes, resupply, trooping and extraction.

It didn't take too long for the Rhodesians to realise that if they were to turn the terrorist tide effectively, they needed to get right to the source – and that meant operating *north* of the Zambezi, taking the war right to the Zambian border where ZANLA were crossing over in their journey down Mozambique and into Rhodesia.

It meant doing deep-penetration operations; it also meant they needed a permanent forward base *inside* Mozambique ... and in September, 1973, the SAS established a permanent tactical headquarters at Macombe, a Portuguese aldeamento (a strategic protected village) with an all-important airstrip on the south bank of the Zambezi.

Aircraft remained on standby at Macombe forward tactical headquarters during the day and were pulled back to Musengezi rear admin base at night, for they would have been sitting ducks to any enemy hidden in the thick surrounding bush and armed with mortars or rocket launchers.

Macombe aldeamento – housing civilians to protect them from the rampages of FRELIMO – was at one end of the grass and dirt airstrip and the SAS tactical headquarters was in a tented camp part way down the runway. The troops based up in bivvies under the trees around the camp.

A number of armed black militia guarded Macombe and although they came under the control of the Portuguese Army in Tete, they had been left very much to their own devices.

There were few roads and these were so heavily mined the militia ventured out from the safety of the aldeamento only every few months to make the long and hazardous trek to their nearest control station at Zumbo, sixty kilometres (37 miles) away, to collect their pay.

The arrival of the SAS at Macombe was one of the most classically successful counter-insurgency operations of the entire war. The RAR were to join them later and they kept the area south of the river clear of enemy while the SAS worked north.

Although their boundaries were set to some extent by the Portuguese, the SAS's area of operation became more and more flexible and the greater successes they had, the more terrorist camps they destroyed, the more they forced the enemy northwards and away from the Rhodesian border.

The SAS began at the Zambezi and just kept walking towards Zambia, dominating the area and keeping the enemy on the run.

So successful were the SAS's hunter-killer tactics, and so deep inside Mozambique were they, that for a while, the enemy were taken totally by surprise and didn't know where they had come from.

When ZANLA and FRELIMO finally worked out that the SAS were in the area, they actively went in search of them, increasing their groups from twenty to sixty to give them more confidence. They even brought in dogs to hunt down the SAS men.

The SAS would parachute into a single DZ previously selected and reccied by a freefall pathfinder group, and cache their parachutes in plastic bags. They would then split up into their various patrols and fan out towards their prescribed areas to carry out their tasks of ambushing, patrolling, observing and locating camps and the main infiltration routes into Rhodesia.

Unless there was a need for them to regroup for a camp attack, the patrols would not meet up again until the end of their six-week stint.

If they were not pulled back to Macombe forward tactical headquarters, a parachute resupply would be dropped in to them every 14 days with food, radio batteries, medical supplies and ammunition.

This period became known as the *Macombe Days* – and it served to sort the men from the boys.

Many soldiers fell by the wayside when Brian Robinson began insisting that every SAS man hiding away in a little corner of SAS HQ, who was fit and able and drawing para-pay had to go on ops into Mozambique. Those who did not were posted to other units.

The length of the operations took their toll on some of the married men too. The normal operation was six weeks in the bush and ten days back in Salisbury, which in those early days of the war was unheard of.

The Macombe saga lasted more than a year, but long before it came to an end, many married men, placed under a lot of marital pressure, had moved on to join units which were not so demanding.

Waging war north of the Zambezi was tough and those SAS men who managed to overcome the rigours of the *Macombe Days,* went on to become the mainstay of the SAS in later years.

The *Macombe Days* era was an entirely new ball game. They were a very long way from home and left very much to their own devices.

It was new even to the most experienced combat soldiers who had seen service in Viet Nam or Aden. In those particular theatres there was always air support somewhere near at hand, and no matter how deep into the interior they were, they could be confident that within a matter of minutes of calling for support, the planes would be overhead dropping off their deadly payloads.

That was not the case in the *Macombe Days.* Generally, an ageing Provost plane had to struggle up from Musengezi rear administrative base in Rhodesia to do an airstrike, and the SAS were basically relying on it to frighten the enemy away rather than for any damage it could inflict.

To add to the SAS's troubles, there were also the deadly anti-personnel landmines liberally sown around the countryside, which opened up an entirely new dimension in the war for them.

The bush was extremely thick and often there was no option but to use the few overgrown tracks that there were. Every soldier knew that with each step he took he ran the risk of having a leg blown off.

It was not conducive to good nerves and enemy AP mines claimed two SAS lives before the *Macombe Days* were over. Thereafter the SAS had very good cause to have a healthy respect for AP mines. The SAS occasionally laid AP mines themselves, but some men were totally against using them at all unless they could be absolutely certain the enemy would walk on them straight away.

For the AP mine was a double-edged sword that could claim Rhodesian lives, especially if planted in a remote area on the offchance of scoring a hit. Often they were planted in the dead of night and the operator might not know exactly where he was, making it difficult to keep an accurate log.

The SAS were often tasked to go back into the same area weeks, months or even years later, running the risk of blowing themselves up on their own mines.

The extremely rugged mountainous terrain north of the river made patrolling over long distances carrying extremely heavy packs, particularly tortuous. The merciless blistering heat, bathing every operator in sweat during the long summer months and the torrential tropical downpours during the rainy season, only added to their discomfort.

Virtually every soldier experienced enormous weight losses on each bush trip. Some lost more than nine kilograms (24lb), a situation made worse by their meagre diet.

Being run-down made them particularly susceptible to veld sores. The exceptionally cruel African bush, with most trees, bushes and creepers harbouring vicious thorns, took its toll.

Even the grass was an enemy and cut into them. In normal circumstances, minor cuts and scratches could be ignored, but the SAS had to meticulously paint theirs with antiseptic as they could very quickly become septic and develop into runny bush sores which were impossible to heal. Many SAS men still carry the scars from those as a reminder of the rugged *Macombe Days*.

There were perpetual problems with malaria-carrying mosquitoes, which were the most concentrated they were ever to experience. Despite religiously taking anti-malarial tablets, men still went down with malaria.

Water had to be constantly purified with tablets to prevent the particularly unpleasant intestinal disease, bilharzia. Other diseases, long since forgotten by the civilised world – cholera, typhoid, blackwater fever – were still common in those areas. Often troops returning from long bush trips would go down with diseases the doctors were unable to classify.

Once they were in the bush, they were in, and would only get casevacked if seriously injured.

The terrain was wild, with thick bush and reeds, and often nil visibility. It was just bush, bush and more bush, with few signs of life; less of civilisation. Mist hung along the riverlines, and low clouds clung to the mountains and huge rock kopjes, often making resupply difficult.

It was like being transported back in time to an Africa of hundreds of years before, except now there were few wild animals, as many had been killed by FRELIMO and ZANLA.

There were no telegraph poles or roads leading anywhere and the few tracks they came across were overgrown, and the hardly distinguishable foot paths were often criss-crossed with hundreds of felled trees, chopped down by FRELIMO to stop the Portuguese convoys travelling the countryside.

South of the river, there were the occasional cut lines gouged out of the bush years before by the Portuguese in their anti-tsetse campaign.

The enemy were not only ZANLA, but the locals too, and the SAS soon learned to steer well clear of civilians, who invariably reported their presence to FRELIMO.

For even though the SAS donned camouflage cream and appeared as black as the enemy, they could not pass close examination. And even if they did, the locals generally knew everyone in the area and reported them anyway.

The SAS's bushwork quickly developed and became superb.

Every man was alert to the possibility of a hostile civilian, FRELIMO or ZANLA watching through the thick bush, and the little things that could give the enemy away – the crackle of twigs . . . scuffling noises which sounded like baboons but without the familiar chatter . . . the sudden noise as a flock of birds flew off and turned into the sun . . . even an eerie feeling that told them something was not quite right . . . the seeping of water into fresh spoor, and the feeling that hit them in the pits of their stomachs that they were about to walk into an ambush . . .

Or the times when, in their search for terrorists, they investigated track patterns picked up in the thick bush by aerial reconnaissance . . . when the tracks led them through dark narrow tunnels of undergrowth and the hairs stood up on the backs of their necks. Times when they couldn't go left or right, they could only go one way . . . and with every step they took they could lose a leg on an anti-personnel mine, or every corner they turned they could be met by a hail of machinegun rounds and have their heads blown away.

They learned not to linger too long in one place; not to base up for the night in the same spot where they had eaten their last meal of the day; not to take the presence of even a solitary herdboy for granted . . .

Tactics which they had learned back in Rhodesia suddenly took on new meaning; for now the war games were for real and from the moment they leapt out of the Dakotas they were in enemy territory, in unknown country, and there could be no relaxing until they got back over the border again.

They always spoke in a whisper and only when necessary. They might well have been on a long bush trip in the company of a lot of other soldiers, but they would only exchange a few words with them the entire stint.

When they took a smoke break, there could be no sitting in little groups chatting about this and that. One man would always go forward to watch the front and the last one would face the opposite direction to cover their spoor. The others would face outwards, so the patrol was facing the four points of the compass.

It was during the *Macombe Days* that Brian Robinson introduced what was for Rhodesia the fairly revolutionary idea of reducing callsigns from six-man to four-man groups to enable them to cover more ground, and to make them more acceptable as an Alouette load.

Initially, there was a considerable amount of determined resistance from the troop commanders, tough courageous men, who thought that it was a ridiculous idea, and that their commander was sending them to certain death. With the smallest FRELIMO group being thirty-strong, there was certainly good reason for the troops to feel apprehensive.

But Brian was merely getting them thinking along traditional SAS lines, and eventually, his men saw the sense of the four-man callsign and realised it was ideal for the *shoot-'n'-scoot* hunter/killer tactic. It was a concept that was to be used with lethal effect from the *Macombe Days* right until the last days of the war.

The Portuguese were still allowing the Rhodesians only a limited time in Mozambique, but the SAS always managed to find an excuse for staying in – they had found new tracks or had killed a few terrorists – and each time the Portuguese extended their visit.

The attitude of the Portuguese troops to the war had not improved and the SAS were amazed to find that there were Portuguese garrisons and heavily populated aldeamentos not ten kilometres (six miles) from FRELIMO camps. It was not so much as if the Portuguese security forces were condoning the presence of FRELIMO; just that they were not interested in them.

The SAS soon realised that if they told the Portuguese they were going to attack a terrorist camp, there would be a wink and a nod from the Portuguese and ZANLA and FRELIMO would be gone by the time the SAS hit it. In the end, the SAS, having learned their lesson, didn't bother to tell the Portuguese. That way, they got results.

After one particularly successful ambush, the SAS made their way into an aldeamento at Mucamgodzi, which had an exact duplicate of a French Foreign Legion tower with a crenelated top. After the endless bush and the rugged largely unpopulated terrain, it felt as if they had arrived in London, so great was the contrast.

The white Mayor of Mucamgodzi, half a dozen Portuguese troops and thirty-odd black militia saw them coming and turned out to greet them, treating them like the heroes they were.

They gave the SAS soap and towels to rid themselves of the grime of their weeks of patrolling and laid on a huge feast of fish, rice, vegetables and cold beer. The SAS were to find on frequent return trips, that the mayor and his friends would invariably break open their last bottle of beer for them.

The Mayor was the first to appreciate that while he and his militia stayed within the safety of their aldeamento, the SAS were out and about in the heavily-mined roads and enemy-infested bush doing their job for them.

During the SAS's occupation of Macombe aldeamento, it weathered many a storm including floods, occupation by millions of mosquitoes and two terrorist attacks. After the SAS pulled out, it was engulfed by the waters of the giant Cabora Bassa man-made lake.

Then, an event took place in far-away Lisbon which was destined to change the face of Africa and have a very dramatic effect on the Rhodesian war.

It began with a book written by General Antonia de Spinola, who maintained that Portugal could not win its African wars by military means and that only a political solution could end the troubles in Mozambique, Angola and Guinea-Bissau.

The Portuguese had grown war-weary and the long fight had cost them more than 7 600 lives, many of them national serviceman, who had no link whatsoever with the overseas provinces. The cost of the war was staggering and had affected the economy of Portugal, one of the poorest countries in Europe.

The book triggered a left-wing revolution in Portugal and on April 25, 1974, Dr Marcella Caetano's Government was overthrown in a military *coup d'état* . . . the only time a European army revolted against the retention of colonial rule.

Spinola's idea of a political solution fell short of total independence. Instead, he advocated some form of federation. But within three months, he changed his tune and began talking of transferring power to the people of Angola, Mozambique and Guinea-Bissau.

Four hundred years of Portuguese rule was all but over. Ironically, it happened at a stage when the Portuguese Army was containing the terrorist problem in Angola, and starting to gain the upper hand in Mozambique.

Even before there was talk of transferring power to the nationalists, the Portuguese Army collapsed in the three provinces.

The black nationalist group FRELIMO came to power in Mozambique, while in Angola, the pro-Soviet People's Movement for the Liberation of Angola (MPLA) would emerge the victor in the civil war that followed the Portuguese collapse.

Power was transferred to FRELIMO in June, 1975, something which even in their wildest dreams they had not anticipated happening for another ten years. Even before then, however, they were seen around the towns and formed a transitional government in October, 1974. The Portuguese streamed out of the country in droves . . . and a new era began.

For beleaguered Rhodesia, the fall of the Portuguese administration represented a strategic nightmare. Overnight, it meant that the whole of the exposed eastern border adjoining Mozambique – some 1 100 kilometres (680 miles) of it – suddenly became very vulnerable.

Apart from a 200 kilometres (125 mile) stretch bordering friendly South Africa at the Limpopo River, Rhodesians, always short of manpower, now had an enormous 3 000 kilometres (1 800 miles) of hostile border to guard, and over which the enemy would eventually pour from every angle.

The country's import and export lifeline which carried most of Rhodesia's sanctions breaking oil supplies from the east coast ports of Beira and Lourenco Marques (Maputo) now ran through a country which was dedicated to the overthrow of white-ruled Rhodesia.

It would be two years before FRELIMO leader Samora Machel closed the border with Rhodesia thereby severing her links with Mozambique ports, but by then, having anticipated such an event, Rhodesia would have a new rail link, a single economic artery, from Rutenga in south-east Rhodesia to Beitbridge and on to Johannesburg. The 145 kilometres (90 miles) of rail line took just 93 days to lay and was finished 21 months ahead of schedule.

White-ruled Rhodesia, virtually surrounded by black Botswana, Zambia, Malawi and Mozambique, and already isolated by international sanctions, was now even more dependent on "Big Brother" down south.

The SAS withdrew from Mozambique immediately news of the Lisbon coup became known, but went right back in again the next day. They would never need permission again.

Now more than ever before, they needed to monitor and kill as many terrorists as they could. With FRELIMO in power, it would not be long before ZANLA took advantage of the situation and opened up new sectors enabling them to infiltrate into Rhodesia on a wide front.

Ultimately, ZANLA would abandon their bases in Zambia and move their entire operation into Mozambique to direct their infiltrations from the east. (This followed the assassination of ZANLA Operations Chief, Herbert Chitepo by a car bomb, said to have been the work of fellow ZANLA, but probably planted at the instigation of Rhodesian security forces. Several ZANLA were rounded up and imprisoned, including a member of the high command, Josiah Tongogara. As a result, the war was brought to a virtual standstill.)

Logistical supplies would be more readily available because of air and sea routes, and as road transport was available, greater quantities of material could be moved more readily.

Newly trained personnel would not have to walk vast distances and could be transported directly to crossing points. There was not such a desperate need to rely on porters, and medical treatment would not be far away, which would do wonders for morale. The psychological impact of the Portuguese *coup d'état* would also turn the trickle of recruits into a flood.

In November, 1974, there was talk of detente and in keeping with the spirit of the exercise, the SAS were pulled out of Mozambique.

While the unit had already stopped using Macombe base, it was the end of the *Macombe Days* era. A lot of invaluable soldiering lessons had been learned, which would stand the men in good stead for the many hazardous operations that were to follow.

A Change of Scenery

By April, 1974, there had been many changes in the unit, and according to notes written at the time by one officer, Lieutenant Chris Schollenberg: "In little over a year, Brian Robinson had done much to make the unit one of the best in the Rhodesian scene. From a peacetime army, the SAS became one of the most professional units in Southern Africa, if not the world."

But now Brian Robinson was out of action with hepatitis and Captain Garth Barrett, the 2IC, was acting OC.

Since the start of Operation *Hurricane,* the SAS had been involved in operations against terrorist and logistics bases in Mozambique. However, fresh intelligence coming in was about to bring a change of scenery.

When the existence of three Zambian-based ZIPRA camps became known to the intelligence agencies, it was decided to send in an SAS reconnaissance team to pinpoint one of them known as Pondoland East "B" and believed to accommodate some fifty ZIPRA.

On the evening of April 9, 26 members of the SAS arrived at the district commissioner's camp at Sibankwazi police station on the Rhodesian bank of the Zambezi River, with CIO officer *Sneaky Jack,* two SB representatives, a former SAS adjutant Ken Phillips, now the 1 Brigade intelligence officer, boosting their numbers.

As usual with cross-border missions, the operation was shrouded in secrecy and most activity took place at night, so as not to arouse undue suspicion from the northern bank.

The command group and the reconnaissance team moved into their allotted houses by the river. The windows were covered with blankets and movement was restricted to the rear, well away from the prying eyes of the Zambian fishermen, who wisely hedged their bets and fed the Zambian-based insurgents and the Rhodesians alike with intelligence.

The main body of men, meanwhile, set up their camp in a gully near the river.

Then, while the officers and some of the men threw themselves into the preparation phase, others got on with the more devious business of reconnaissance.

In the early days of the war, it was not unusual for white fishermen to be seen at the DC's camp . . . and Ken Phillips, the SB representatives and CIO man *Sneaky Jack* turned this to their advantage.

Dressed in suitable clothing, they boarded a boat and under the guise of being fishermen, silently reccied the river banks for suitable crossing points and logged the whereabouts of the ever-changing positions of the black fishermen on the northern banks.

To any interested onlooker on the Zambian bank they would have passed for the real thing. And, as a bonus, the fish they caught made a welcome change to their normal army *ratpacks.*

They were hopeful too that their little trips would ultimately lead to the netting of much bigger fish . . .

Other SAS troops took up observation points on the rugged terrain through which the Zambezi wound its way, where, from their high positions, they silently watched the Zambian banks for any signs of enemy activity.

During the day, the pseudo fishermen withdrew so as to leave the peaceful atmosphere undisturbed and the real fishermen and the enemy unsuspecting.

The reconnaissance team meanwhile studied their maps and aerial photographs and worked out how they could find ZIPRA's Pondoland East "B" base.

Chris Schollenberg was to command the reconnaissance team and Schulie had chosen Bob McKenna, Brian Jackson and Jop Oosthuizen to go along with him. The estimate of fifty terrorists said to be in the camp did nothing to soothe their nerves.

They knew that the area under investigation was about 15 kilometres (nine miles) from the Zambezi; was sparsely populated and generally only used by fishermen travelling from the interior down to the Zambezi.

Occasionally, fishermen travelling on the only old track down to the river were stopped by ZIPRA and quizzed about security forces activity on the southern shore. Often, the fishermen saw two and three-man ZIPRA hunting parties searching for game.

In view of the vast numbers of game trails criss-crossing the countryside, the

Rhodesians had been unable to pick up the exact location of the ZIPRA camp. From the air it was impossible to differentiate between the track patterns of small and hidden bases and that of game trails near a water-hole, vital for both game and guerillas.

Pinpointing the enemy came down to a simple process of deduction and elimination. They had to be somewhere close to the old track which snaked on its way down to the river; they had to be near water – and there were not many rivers carrying water at that time of the year.

It was impossible for fifty men to hide for long in an uninhabited area with sparse vegetation. There were only few dense patches of trees too where the enemy could be hiding.

The ZIPRA men had to hunt to replenish their rations and enemy shots could be heard over long distances.

The SAS knew that if there were ZIPRA troops in the area, they would have no difficulty finding them ... and by studying the maps and the aerial photographs, two areas were selected as likely hiding places that needed investigation.

On secret cross-border operations such as these, it was crucial that every contingency be catered for ... from what to do if there was a contact ... what action they had to follow on an ambush ... what to do if they got separated and lost ... Even on the most mundane missions, nothing could be left to chance.

They would wear *Black Is Beautiful* camouflage cream to give them the edge ... and to add to the deception, they would use bare feet on paths just as the local civilians did.

Small binoculars and nightsights would prove vitally important items. A more mundane but essential item, was the torch each operator would carry to aid his pick-up from the river bank. And, as a last-resort measure, they would carry cyanide phials.

Timings for the operation were going to be crucial. For the mission to succeed, they had to cross the Zambezi unseen and unheard. Too much light, and they would be seen; too little, and they would be unable to find the terror base.

It was felt that the most suitable time for the river crossing was a day or two after the full moon. Between dusk and the rising of the moon, there would be a state of total darkness over the Zambezi ... while the moonlight afterwards would serve to speed the recce patrol along once inside enemy territory.

For several days there was much frenzied activity as preparations neared completion. Launching positions were found and a route was chosen on which to man-handle the equipment needed for the river crossing.

A Zodiac was to be used as a rescue craft in case the recce party got into difficulties. The inside of the engine cowlings were lined with polystyrene and the whole engine was covered by a blanket to muffle the sounds.

The night of the full moon came and went. Finally on April 15, it was time to go.

The four-man reconnaissance team was to be taken across into Zambia by the ferry party which would return later for the pick-up ... while a mortar team was to remain south of the river to provide protection if need be.

The timings turned out to be perfect. Under cover of that pitch black night, their kit was transferred to the water's edge and the canoes were assembled and placed in the river.

The reconnaissance group and the ferry party climbed into the canoes, which were designed to take two men, but it was a tight squeeze that night – there were two operators, a ferryman and a mountain of equipment to each canoe.

Commander Garth Barrett wished them a good trip and they silently set sail for terrorist country.

63

But then, within twenty metres, came a problem.

A fast-moving whirlpool suddenly sucked the front canoe into the murky, swirling waters of the Zambezi, tossing Brian Jackson and ferryman Ben Botha into the river . . . and sending all the untied equipment to the bottom of the river.

Brian Jackson and Ben Botha remained on the surface, then began to float downstream on the current – leaving Bob McKenna, the third passenger, hanging upside down in the overturned canoe, trapped by his webbing which had caught on the struts and hooks.

With almost superhuman strength, Bob McKenna managed to twist himself up into a contortionist's position, then he began trying to free himself with one hand and grip on to the boat with the other. But no amount of struggling was helping to set him free.

He had a mere five centimetres of air trapped in the canoe and as he drifted downstream in the swiftly-moving current, all he could think about was what little air he did have, would eventually disappear altogether – and that the canoe would sink with him still trapped in it.

Brian Jackson, by now striking out for the shore, suddenly realised that Bob McKenna was missing and turned back to rescue his friend.

When he caught up with the canoe, he half climbed on to it . . . and Bob's precious few centimetres of air suddenly began to diminish.

Bob gurgled a "Get off" and Brian Jackson obliged.

Then a much-relieved Bob squeezed his rescuer's leg to indicate he was all right. The two men whispered to each other through the skin of the canoe as they continued to be washed downstream, ever-conscious that a raised voice could alert anyone watching or listening on the Zambian bank.

Brian eventually set Bob free at about the same time the rescue boat started up its engines and began purring softly towards the drenched, drifting men.

Then to round the whole thing off, the steering mechanism on the second canoe came undone, allowing only port steer. But with a bit of luck, and skilful paddling, the canoeists managed to return to the launching spot after a huge circle battling the fierce current.

The crossing had been a catastrophe. Equipment needed for the mission was missing and although their rifles had been tied to the boat, they were drenched. Two members of the reconnaissance party were soaked to the skin and one had barely escaped with his life.

The recce commander asked for a postponement to get a re-issue of equipment, but the 2IC Garth Barrett said they had to continue. They could not delay any longer, for the chance of compromise could only increase as time progressed.

In the east, a glow appeared in the dark sky which preceded the rising moon.

If they were to cross unseen that night, they would have to get going.

With Bob McKenna and Brian Jackson now out of the operation, volunteers were quickly called for from the main reserve. Tim Hallow and Willie *Mac* McIntosh volunteered to go along.

Mac was just a young soldier but he had become an old hand at volunteering. Whenever Schulie asked for volunteers, Mac was always the first to join him, and it was to become the accepted thing for him to go along with Schulie. Mac could not have asked for a better tutor. He learnt his lessons well and close-in reconnaissance was to become his own particular speciality.

Schulie had only 15 minutes to put them in the picture about the task ahead, and while they shoved borrowed rations and maps into make-do packs, he quickly ran through the situation from his brief notes. Once the new boys were satisfied with the plan, the team once again shoved off for Zambia.

This time there were no mishaps and the canoes beached successfully on the northern bank. The moon started to rise with only minutes to spare.

Hopefully, the fisherman next to his fire a few hundred metres downstream was unaware of the crossing. Crossings normally took place near rapids where any sounds made by the infiltrators were smothered by the rushing waters; but that had been impossible this time. The actual beach was rocky so there would be no give-away footprints to tell the tale next day.

They slung their packs down at the first high ground they reached, and hastily rearranged their kit.

The initial panic was over. Schulie was always relieved to reach the stage where everyone else was off their backs and the pressure off. From now onwards the team alone dictated the conduct of the operation with only minimum interference from control at the other end of the TR-48 radio, the *Big Means*.

By midnight, they had reached the first area under suspicion. But there were no signs of the enemy and no spoor from terrorist boots on the dry, sandy road.

Suddenly, using their nightsight, they picked up the soft glow of the dying embers of a fire.

Carefully, they approached the centre of the dark vegetation stopping many times to listen for breathing ... snoring ... talking ... ever-alert to the possibility of stumbling into unseen enemy or their bushy hideout.

As soon as darkness came down, they checked a gully using the shaded light of their torches and found a man-made footpath crossing over it. Now they were on to something.

Quickly, Schulie and Jop Oosthuizen left their packs with Mac McIntosh and Tim Hallow just off the newly discovered footpath and quietly discussed rendezvous procedures. Then Schulie and Jop moved towards the denser area near the river which had all the makings of an ideal enemy hide-up position.

Schulie briefed his companion to wait off the path to warn of anyone coming from the rear. Then he slowly moved in to carry out a one-man close-in reconnaissance.

He lay low in the darkness and waited.

From behind the thicket to the right of the path came the sound of a tin being banged against another metal object. It was the first indication of an enemy presence.

Then, he heard the sound of a radio with the volume turned low; then the low voices of three men talking.

Schulie moved around the camp to establish its size. It was a time consuming but productive exercise, revealing two occupied positions.

He heard snoring coming from at least five terrorists; but in view of the size of the camp, he felt it could well be occupied by dozens of enemy.

He rejoined the others, and they agreed they had pinpointed the enemy camp and could definitely pick it up on aerial photography the next day.

Their mission over, they melted back into the night and headed south. Back at the river's edge, the pin-prick glow from their shielded torches told the boat party waiting on the southern shores that they were ready to return ... and they were soon on their way home.

As anticipated, they were able to locate the terror base from the aerial photographs and a track showing a vehicle turnaround point was clearly visible on the pictures.

Within a few weeks, a much larger group of blackened-up SAS men tramped through the night arriving on the outskirts of the ZIPRA camp several hours before their planned first-light attack.

They were hot and sweaty from their long walk, but it was a bitterly cold winter's night and their perspiration seemed to turn to ice. Most had not expected to arrive so soon and were totally unprepared for what seemed to the Rhodesians to be Arctic conditions. Even the chaps from Britain, traditionally made of sterner stuff when it came to wintry weather, were feeling the cold.

Many tried to snuggle into the ground to get warm and some climbed into the bags in which they had carried their RPG-7 rockets.

Eventually, dawn broke over the sleeping camp and the SAS silently got into an assault formation and eased forward, eager to get going at last.

They got so close to the motley collection of grubby white and green tents that they expected to be seen any second by the sentries. But there was no reaction; no movement. All was silent.

Then they let rip, firing low into the tents, hoping to catch the enemy as they lay asleep in their beds. Again there was no reaction from the fifty or so enemy they hoped to catch inside. They slashed an entry through the sides of the tents and discovered the reason – ZIPRA had vacated the camp.

The attackers did, however, manage to account for the camp logistics officer, but missed another man, who with impeccable timing had slipped out of his tent to answer the call of nature.

The early-morning visitors salvaged many weapons, including brand new RPG-7 rockets which would go to augmenting their own meagre supplies, then blew up what was left.

A couple of landmines were laid in the access road, then, confident no one would see them, the SAS returned home.

Next day, an aerial reconnaissance was carried out and a gaping hole found where once the landmines had been – as well as an upturned Land-Rover straddled across the treetops. A few more ZIPRA had died.

The SAS continued to plant mines on all access roads to all camps they attacked throughout the war ... and almost invariably the enemy continued to hit them.

The kills, captured arms and a few valuable documents which were to lead to even bigger stuff, had made the mission worthwhile.

Operation Big Bang, August – October 1974

ZIPRA had learnt the folly of large-scale incursions the hard way and had now adopted a much more devious method of waging war.

The early tactic of infiltrating 100 men at a time had proved a fateful lesson. The security forces had hunted them down and wiped them out virtually to a man.

Now, instead of sending large groups across to get massacred, ZIPRA had decided to build up an internal network of arms caches and subversive cells.

Operating clandestinely from Francistown in northern Botswana, Russian-trained agents were planning to set up a long chain of arms caches throughout the Matabeleland Tribal Trust Lands with the help of an internal network of ZIPRA sympathisers. The scheme was called the 3-2-3 network and the idea was that, when the time was right, the locals were to ferry ammunition to the arms caches for the terrorists. The network was also responsible for recruiting men for terror training.

ZIPRA had planned it all very carefully. They had devised a series of secret signals to enable one person to recognise the next in the chain. It was a cut-out network so that if one man was picked by the security forces he could not pinpoint the others.

But Rhodesian Special Branch officers were clever too and acting on some exceptionally good intelligence, they were able to capture a Russian-trained agent in Bulawayo, pick-up all the key people and smash the network. They also located all the holes dug in the TTLs to receive the ammunition.

The SAS, meanwhile, had been called in to pinpoint ZIPRA camps in south-west Zambia, after incursions effected from one end of Lake Kariba to the other.

Documents captured on the Pondoland East "B" camp attack told of another camp a day's walk to the west. That would have placed the new camp in the area of the Ngwemanzi River some 11 kilometres (seven miles) inland . . . and due north of the subversive and recruiting cells set up in Wankie TTL. Aerial reconnaissance was able to pick up the camp, and photographic interpreters felt there could be as many as twenty people in it. Special Branch sources considered that the camp could well be the headquarters of a number of ZIPRA satellite camps.

Lieutenant Chris Schollenberg, who had pinpointed Pondoland "B" camp, was tasked to lead in another reconnaissance team to establish if the Ngwemanzi River camp was still occupied. If it was, then the SAS planned to attack it.

At 20h00 on August 9, Schulie and his team of Corporal John Ross, Lance Corporal Mac McIntosh and Trooper Jo Bresler, dressed in terrorist kit and with AK rifles, crossed unseen over the invisible border to the Zambian bank at a point downstream of Victoria Falls.

Within minutes the ferry party, having deposited the team, pushed off again for the southern shore.

The moon was not yet up as the reconnaissance team crept passed the fires of unsuspecting Zambian fishermen. Then they left the fishermen far behind and headed north into the night . . . and for some eight kilometres (five miles), they cautiously moved through the rugged, broken countryside, inhabited only by game.

Slowly, conscientiously, they eased their way into the Zambian hinterland . . . lying up . . . listening for gun shots, the sounds of wood being chopped . . . looking for smoke . . . checking for spoor . . .

After a couple of nights, five shots rang out across the bush. It was the first indication of a terrorist presence. The locals would not be using high-powered rifles. The terrorists were obviously making use of their rifles to bag something for their cooking pots.

The four SAS men moved in closer to the area of the suspected camp.

As they lay up that day they heard the strangely out-of-place rumble of a vehicle in the distance. Then they saw a green truck travelling westwards. It was similar to a Rhodesian Army Land-Rover but had a longer bonnet.

Now they were on to something . . .

What was a vehicle doing in this rugged primitive countryside in the middle of nowhere? It was not between two towns or villages . . . there were no places of interest marked on the maps . . . and the local Africans did not use vehicles.

Certainly the sight of any vehicle would have been immediately suspicious, but the fact that this was a *military*-styled one confirmed their theories that this was no civilian vehicle.

It could only be a terrorist vehicle – and it had to be going to the same place they were heading.

Briefing John Ross and Jo Bresler to wait behind for them, Schulie and Mac McIntosh moved forwards to try and pinpoint the camp.

They had gone only one kilometre when three shots from a terrorist weapon rang out across the countryside. John and Jo, thinking the others had been shot or compromised, followed their orders for such an event and returned to their pre-arranged rendezvous point. The shots had come nowhere near them in fact, but due to a communications problem, Schulie was unable to let the others know . . . and John and Jo continued to follow SAS emergency procedures and crossed back into Rhodesia next day.

The other half of the reconnaissance team meanwhile had located the camp and were keeping it under surveillance.

Shortly after midnight, Schulie and Mac slunk into the camp which straddled the river. There was not a single person to be seen. The stark framework of a hut which stood silhouetted against the moonlight was proof that the terrorists had abandoned the base several nights before.

A few Russian matchbox wrappers lying around what had once been the main fireplace, bits of scrap paper with Russian writing on them, and the seldom-seen early-warning device of tins threaded on string, was the only evidence they found that ZIPRA had been there.

There was no sign of the green truck. They could find no tracks. They had not seen it move. So where the hell had it gone?

They skirted the camp searching for the tracks then struck out for high ground to check the road where they had seen the truck. It was then they saw a new road leading off the old one and going eastwards. It ran alongside an old rutted bicycle path and had been made by simply by-passing the bigger trees and demolishing the smaller bushes in the drive to get access to the east.

On investigation, they found tracks which could only have come from that elusive truck.

It was obviously a route which needed further investigation. They felt that the truck had to be going to a ZIPRA camp, probably the one that replaced the abandoned base. Having obtained the blessing of Garth Barrett back in the SAS base, they decided to follow it to its logical conclusion.

Slowly, cautiously, they picked their way eastwards over the flattened grass of the new track. Thinking that they might bump into the re-sited terrorist camp at any moment, they removed their boots to aid their stealthy approach.

They lay up next day and that night were back on their travels. As they headed eastwards they suddenly heard the sound of men's voices and went to ground.

They took out the nightscope for a quick look; saw the glow of a fire and four African men sitting around it talking. To get a closer look they put down their packs and moved forward.

Then, the nightsight slipped from Mac's hands with a thud. For a moment the two soldiers hardly dared breathe as they lay low in the shadows.

An African got up and wandered out to investigate. He shone his torch towards them but they hugged the ground and were far enough away not to be seen.

The man lingered only a minute, anxious to return to the warmth of the fire and the companionship of his mates. Convincing himself that there was no one out there, he snapped off his torch and hurried back to his friends.

Quickly, Schulie and Mac left, skirting the area looking for tracks or some indication that this was a terrorist camp. But there was no sign; it was merely a temporary resting place.

But where was the base? Where had that truck gone? Obviously it had to be further east.

They moved off once more and set up an observation post on a hill overlooking the track. Next day they saw several ZIPRA cycling towards the area where they suspected the base to be and heard shots coming from the same direction.

Again they moved on, confident of finding the camp at the end of the track.

They had now been in Zambia far longer that was normal at that stage in the war. By remaining to exploit the possibilities for a couple of days longer, they had overstayed their visit. While Garth Barrett had given his blessing, CIO had not, and on their next radio communication with Barrett, they were told to return to base as soon as possible.

It would mean pulling out without having found the camp. But orders were orders and they had no choice.

Within three weeks, Schulie was back in the same area. This time, Captain Mick Graham and Sergeant Bob McKenna were with him.

Their mission this time was to check if the spot where the four men had been chatting around the camp fire was still occupied. They also had to find a camp east of the Mazanga River – the one the first reconnaissance team might have discovered had they been allowed to continue eastwards along the road. They further had to check out a suspicious looking hole picked up by aerial photography.

Again they spent several days quietly easing into the area, lying up, listening, searching, and all the time working their way towards the place where Schulie and Mac had seen the four men around the camp fire.

They found no signs that anyone had been there lately; they then retraced their steps, followed a footpath leading off the main track that ran down to a river. The terrorists would need water; maybe they would find the camp somewhere nearby?

They crossed the river but still found nothing of interest. Time was going. It was already becoming daylight. They had only limited rations for their visit and would have to return to Rhodesia soon.

Schulie realised it had been a mistake to take this route. The elusive camp had to be way in the distance somewhere. And he hadn't a clue how to get there either.

He told his two companions of his dilemma, then, leaving them in a little gully looking after his pack, he wandered off alone with his rifle.

He moved cautiously around the area, searching the countryside for a clue, no matter how small, that might point him towards the enemy base.

Then he heard sounds of village activity and saw large herds of goats and cattle grazing along the Mazanga River. Occasionally, the excited shouts of the herdboys rang across the countryside as they scolded their charges.

At night, Schulie moved in closer. It was Saturday and just after last light, a beer drink got underway. A gramophone, drums and a whistle, ably assisted by the barking of dogs, provided music throughout the long night.

It was clearly a civilian complex; yet what of those suspicious-looking boot tracks Schulie had seen on and off the paths at each end of the village?

During the early morning, he heard the distinctive sound of a vehicle to the north, and, remembering the truck from the first reconnaissance, he moved to investigate, and halted on high ground.

Below, about a kilometre away, a green truck was moving. It was bigger than the first he had seen three weeks earlier, being about a four-tonner.

He saw a couple of men offloading kit; then the truck was driven under the trees and screened from view.

All the activity was taking place near a large hole . . . obviously the one picked up on the aerial photographic run, and the one they had been tasked to investigate.

It had to be a civilian road construction gang at work. Still, he would check it out and confirm it just the same.

It was broad daylight now and Schulie eased right down to where the activity was taking place. He crawled among the long grass, carefully creeping towards the noises.

The grass was long but not long enough to afford him cover if he stood up, and he lay low in a hole underneath a clump of small palms, right on the edge of the river junction.

He was 150 metres from three unarmed Africans and from all the talking, he reckoned that there had to be six to eight men at work in the hole.

For three hours, a continuous hammering sound like that of nails being driven into wood, could be heard. Occasionally, he heard the sounds of wood being sawn.

It sounded suspiciously as if they were making a roof for the huge hole. The wood was obviously going to keep the structure up.

Metallic noises similar to that of a metal drum being hit by a baton came from the hole throughout the morning. Eventually, he worked out that in the absence of a ladder, the men were using the drum to get out of the hole and, as they jumped up, they made that tinny noise.

The sun was flashing on some shiny objects under a canopy not 100 metres from Schulie. He suspected they were weapons, but couldn't risk standing up for a closer examination.

It was becoming more and more apparent that this was no ordinary construction gang going about its business. These were ZIPRA, and it suddenly flashed across his mind that had he known they were not civilians, he would have stayed well clear of the area.

But what could they be working on so diligently? Perhaps he had stumbled on to an underground cache in the making . . . ?

Then he fell asleep. For it was boring waiting for someone to move in closer to him and he was weary from his previous night's activities.

The hot September sun beat down on the sleeping soldier.

Suddenly, he forced himself awake.

"No, no . . . I mustn't fall asleep, 'cos just now I'll snore and someone will come and investigate," he silently reminded himself.

At noon, the work party downed tools and wandered off for lunch.

Schulie's eyelids began to grow heavy again and he felt himself about to nod off once more. It was definitely time to pull out.

There was plenty of fresh spoor from terrorist boots leading south to the village, which was obviously handy for food and women; and it was clear the ZIPRA men had attended Saturday night's beer drink.

Back in their little gully, Mick Graham and Bob McKenna sat chatting and wondering what Schollenberg was up to, wondering what they would do if he did not come back. They dined on their high-protein *Tarzan Bars*, which virtually represented the sum total of their rations that trip.

Eventually, in the late afternoon, Schulie returned to report he had pinpointed the target . . . and they all crossed back to Rhodesia.

Schulie had obviously stumbled on a new camp complex still very much in the preparation phase, and it was felt that the hole could only be an underground arms bunker.

When the Brigadier heard the SAS had no immediate plans to mount an attack, he flew down to their base camp on the banks of the Zambezi. For a moment it looked as if commander Garth Barrett was in hot water for pulling his troops out before attacking the camp.

But as Barrett pointed out, the camp was definitely not in a position to be attacked. Were they to hit it too soon, they would achieve virtually nothing.

He got his point across and thereafter the activities at the hole were monitored by aerial reconnaissance. When the photographic interpreters reported that the roof was going on and the hole was probably filled with stores, the SAS decided that the time had come to pounce. It was essential to strike before ZIPRA had the chance of disposing of their arms supply inside Rhodesia.

Some forty-odd SAS troops moved down to the forward tactical headquarters south of the Zambezi, the same one used for the earlier reconnaissances. It was close to Sidinde Island, a District Commissioner's camp, and used many times by the security forces.   A former SAS OC, now with CIO was to be the base commander and the strike force going external would work back to him, keeping him and his stay-behind party in the picture about developments on their operation.

They set up a small communications station . . . the radios rested on old batteries . . . blankets were spread on the tables in the tents. At night they had the dullest of lights, powered by a car battery. For with Zambia just a couple of metres away and with steep mountains possibly affording terrorists an ideal observation post, they could take no chances.

During the day, the Zodiac boats for the river crossing were hidden under camouflage nets at a small stream running into the Zambezi. At night, the troops rehearsed their beaching drills for the crossing.

Finally the plan was ready and the rehearsals were at an end.

Schulie was to go into the camp to confirm occupation before the main body of men arrived.

He had just come out of hospital after a recurrence of jaundice and was not feeling his fittest. Bob McKenna and Mick Graham, who had been with him on the second reconnaissance, were not available for the mission, and the task of checking the place out, then positioning stop groups, fell to him.

He took in the three stop group commanders and showed them where they would have to attack.

The following night – October 3 – the main group climbed into their boats and shoved off to the northern shores. The engines were muffled, but there was still a bit of noise.

Once across the river they reorganised and with Garth Barrett, the 2IC leading, they set off in single file on the long approach, to link up with Schulie who had already plotted the way for them on a time-and-distance basis using compass bearings.

All told, there were 43 SAS chaps, the biggest number of Rhodesian security forces to go external on a single operation into Zambia since the start of the war.

As they got close to the last ridge on their way inland from the Zambezi, Garth Barrett heard movement in front of him. He was convinced it was human movement. If so, it could mean they had been seen as they crossed the river. He got out his nightsight, but could see no one.

They continued to travel northwards through the night.

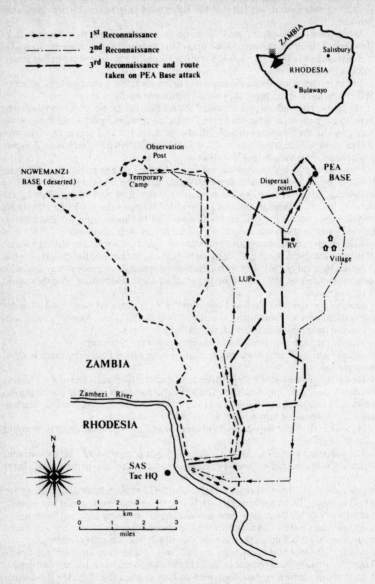

Operation *Big Bang:* Routes taken by reconnaissance teams and assault force prior to attack on ZIPRA camp

72

Ali Barrett and his forty thieves, as they called themselves later, were quite pleased when they came across a huge bush fire. Now they could have that much-needed smoke without having to worry about terrorists or locals seeing the light from their cigarettes.

Back at the forward base on the other side of the Zambezi, all was still. The full moon shone on the peaceful camp.

It was 02h00. Corporal Phil Cripps had just woken. There was another ten minutes before he went on guard. It was just long enough to snatch another kip. He tried to get back to sleep.

The next he knew, the sound of an AK was ripping through the camp. Phil thought that he was dreaming. Then he heard the attackers changing magazines and realised this was no dream; this was for real.

Two ZIPRA had slipped unseen right up to the camp and emptied their magazines on the eight members of the rear party. Corporal Willie Erasmus sleeping not ten paces from the terrorists was seriously injured. After the first couple of shots he rolled off his stretcher and the terrorists continued firing over him.

The SAS could not return fire as it meant shooting over the heads of their own men. Then as quickly as they came, the attackers faded into the night ...

Phil Cripps, who proceeded to have his first smoke for 18 months, had been slightly wounded, as had the former SAS OC.

Perhaps the movement Garth Barrett had seen as they wound their way northwards had come from the attackers watching the main body of men crossing the river? Perhaps the young African boys they had seen herding cattle on the northern banks had told ZIPRA of a security force presence? Maybe it was the usual fishermen who had talked? Subsequent intelligence revealed that the attackers had been en route to the camp the SAS was about to attack, when they decided to take on the sleeping base camp.

In any event, the SAS learnt the hard way that they should never use the same spot time after time for their forward base. Possibly the security forces were complacent in those days thinking that because it was Rhodesia it had to be safe. But as the place was so close to Zambia and as it had been used so many times before, the spot was a natural target for the enemy.

The base staff decided against telling Garth Barrett of the attack, feeling he might abort the mission and return to his wounded men.

The strike force walked all night and set up their firm base next morning, lying up in the stifling heat of the day.

The mopani trees had no leaves, there was no other natural shade, and they were unable to put any up for fear of being seen. They tried to sleep that day, but it was far too hot, so they were glad to see the sun set, even though it meant they would soon be on the move again.

In the early hours of October 5, they met up with Schulie at the pre-arranged rendezvous point. It had been a hard night's slog and there were many who thought they would never make it. But somehow they managed to make good time.

Schulie led the way to the dispersal point. He told the three stop group commanders to select their routes. The two assault teams, one led by Schulie, headed north of the camp.

Garth Barrett had the command stop group on the south-west of the camp and there was a support and other stop groups.

Soon, all the 43 SAS troops were lying low around a still-sleeping camp. Only their eyes moved, but as yet there was nothing to see.

All was quiet, except for the usual night noises – the birds, the animals, the noise from the nearby stream . . . Now all they had to do was to wait for the dawn. They were cold, tired and a little nervous – and it seemed as if the morning would never come.

At last it was just light enough to see.

The assault group positioned themselves in a little gully right on the northern edge of the camp. They could just see a guard moving from one bivvy to another.

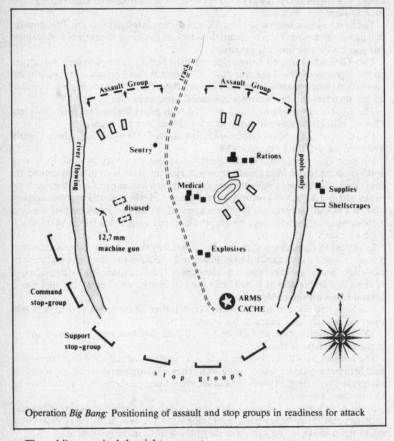

Operation *Big Bang:* Positioning of assault and stop groups in readiness for attack

The soldiers awaited the right moment . . .

As the guard came back, he stopped and looked in their direction. At that, Schulie pulled the first shot, then all hell broke loose.

The sudden roar of automatic fire proceeded to rip the camp apart as the SAS men fired non-stop, their rifles spewing spent cartridges like popcorn machines. They were well organised and were working in pairs, so that when one man stopped to change magazines, his partner took over the firing.

As soon as the attack went in, the SAS saw movement in front of them.

God! The bloody terrs were sleeping in shellscrapes not ten metres from them. They would not have gone that close had they known.

But the terrorists were more intent on getting away than taking on the early-morning callers.

Within five minutes, some 2 500 rounds had been directed at the fleeing ZIPRA.

They headed straight for the stop groups positioned around the camp. Some of the enemy had AKs with bayonets fixed on them. One man, shot twice in the chest at point blank range, cartwheeled forward throwing his AK into the air, stopping literally dead two paces in front of his attacker. His bayonet stuck into the ground nearby, with the AK swaying to and fro above it.

"I'm dead, I'm dead," claimed one injured terrorist hiding in a clump of trees. His prediction was to prove correct.

All told, nine ZIPRA, the only ones there that morning, had died in the attack.

But the big prize was still to come. After the camp was cleared, the demolition group quickly moved towards the centre of the camp to inspect the bunker.

A metre of soil and grass hid the entrance from view. Quickly it was removed to reveal a small trap door.

The demolition group lowered themselves through the trap door, dropping on to the drum which Schulie had heard on his reconnaissance. From there they dropped to floor level. They stared in wide-eyed amazement at their incredible find. It was a complete underground reinforced concrete bunker so big an army truck could have quite comfortably turned around in it.

ZIPRA had always hidden their caches underground, but spread over a wide area; never on such a grand scale as this.

The cache, which had breathers built into the roof, contained a veritable Aladdin's Cave of arms and ammunition. The Rhodesians had never seen anything like it. It was stacked from top to bottom with hundreds of boxes of ammunition and explosives. There were rifles, rockets, mines, pistols, magazines, holsters, safety fuses and ancillary equipment.

There were boxes and boxes of limpet mines, something the Rhodesians had never seen before. There were even two-metre-long 122 millimetre rockets – they had not seen them before either.

There were millions of rounds, something like 5 000 detonators, Tokarev pistols, 200 Garand rifles from America, never again seen during the war, light machineguns, 12,7 millimetre heavy machineguns, 100 boxes of anti-tank mines, dozens of boxes of anti-personnel mines, AK-47s, SKSs, RPG-7 rockets, 75 millimetre recoilless rifles, bayonets, shells ...

Most of the weapons were in specially constructed racks with chains securing them in place. Much of the ammunition was still in its original packing, with weapons still in grease.

Demolitions expert Rob Warraker reckoned there had to be three tons of explosives. There were also large quantities of webbing and clothing.

Just about everyone involved in other tasks around the camp found time to pop their heads into the hole to give the amazing arsenal the once over.

Sergeant Pete Cole, tasked to compile the inventory, did not have the time to check out all the equipment. For the demolitions team, working to a limited time frame, had soon finished laying their charges and wanted him out of the bunker.

Some of the contents – the limpet mines, AKs, bayonets and Tokarevs – were saved for their own use and in the hole went a 12,7 millimetre heavy machinegun, a 75 millimetre gun, huge boxes of electric detonators, rolls of detonating cord and safety fuse found above in the camp.

There was enough food in the camp to feed an army. A Rhodesian Army map of Gwelo was found which showed the route ZIPRA planned to take to attack the School of Infantry there.

Landmines were laid on the road, the bodies were searched and documents gathered. Then the majority of the groups began to move out, leaving Rob Warraker to set up the charges and with 2IC Garth Barrett and signaller Dave Cale bringing up the rear.

With an estimated three tons of explosives going up they needed to be at least a kilometre away from the blast.

Rob Warraker caught up with them when they were 500 metres from the cache. They had only gone another fifty metres when the biggest explosion they were ever to experience throughout the long bitter war rumbled across the Zambian country-side.

The shock waves came through the trees like a fierce wind, lifting some men off their feet and throwing them forward.

Ammunition was going off in all directions and enormous chunks of concrete screamed through the air sounding exactly like jet aircraft. For a moment they thought the Zambian Air Force was reacting to their camp attack, and couldn't quite understand how they had got there so soon.

Then the whistling blocks of concrete obeyed the forces of gravity and hurtled groundwards, burying themselves into the shaking soil. It was all rather frightening.

The mushroom cloud from the explosion could be seen ninety kilometres (56 miles) away in Rhodesia.

Back at their base camp over the Zambezi, the ground shook, the water rippled, and the leaves fell from the trees. And over the air came signaller Dave Cale's message in Morse: "Mission successful".

Then, as the clouds of dust and smoke billowed around the wrecked camp, the SAS began their long hot walk back to the Zambezi, weighed down with captured ammunition, limpet mines, Tokarovs and AK bayonets, stunned by their experience and their ears still ringing from the explosions. But there were big smiles all around.

At a waterfall they stopped to rest. Schulie, still recovering from his bout of jaundice, was now feeling very sick.

He was finished; he could not go on, he told the 2IC. Could they not just leave him there to find his own way out, he asked? He certainly knew the damn route by now.

But the boss was against the idea of leaving him on his own. Dave Cale was tasked to cook a meal for him . . . and a portion of rice mixed with mashed pilchards helped perk him up.

As they neared the Zambezi, they radioed base for pick-up and, as they crossed over, they learned of the ZIPRA attack on the SAS base camp.   The operation – forever nicknamed *Big Bang* by the SAS – was a major victory for the Rhodesians, a catastrophe for ZIPRA.

The camp – Pondoland East "A" base – had been the central logistical base for the whole of ZIPRA's operations into Matabeleland.

The cache was being built up to feed the small local caches dug in the Matabele-land TTLs. The internal network had been smashed; now all the ammunition for the internal caches had been blown to smithereens.

The attack set ZIPRA's programme back considerably. It took them about six months to resuscitate themselves into a formidable force again.

At that time, *Big Bang* was the biggest external operation of the war, and Garth Barrett who led the attack was awarded the Order of the Legion of Merit.

Schulie, who had carried out the close-in reconnaissance for *Big Bang* and the previous camp attack on Pondoland "B" base was awarded the Silver Cross of Rhodesia, the country's second highest gallantry medal for "conspicuous courage and gallantry over and above the call of duty" and undertaking "personal reconnaissance of enemy positions with considerable danger and with the risk of discovery".

He became the first member of the Special Air Service to be awarded the Silver Cross.

His only wish was that Mac McIntosh, who had been with him on the first reconnaissance, could have shared the award with him, he said in a letter to Mac.

Schulie was to become the first holder of the country's highest award for gallantry, the Grand Cross of Valour, equivalent to the Victoria Cross and the American Congressional Medal of Honour. It was awarded while he was serving in the Selous Scouts. Only one other soldier – an SAS officer – was to receive the honour.

Schulie, accepted as the foremost exponent of reconnaissance in the Rhodesian Army, if not the world, was described by his SAS colleagues as "a man who emerges only once in a generation".

His courage, such as displayed on the *Big Bang* reconnaissances, became legendary in the Rhodesian Army.

Ceasefire, 1974-1975

Then, there was a ceasefire! At least, there was supposed to be. Detente had become the fashionable word in Africa and under pressure from South Africa, Rhodesia had become involved in the detente exercise.

South Africa was keen to make friends with the new order in Mozambique and maintain its detente policy with black Africa. Despite its own domestic policies, South Africa felt it essential that Rhodesian whites reach an agreement with the black nationalists.

South Africa's ally in the detente exercise, Kenneth Kaunda of Zambia, was anxious for the bickering black nationalists to unite and talk to the Rhodesian premier. He had much to gain from a settlement. Abiding by sanctions and reducing trade with Rhodesia had cost Zambia dearly. According to the UN Economic and Social Council, the cost to Zambia from January 1973 to mid-1974 alone was £112 million.

Ian Smith was persuaded to resume talks with the nationalists ... and the nationalists agreed to come under one umbrella organisation of the reconstituted ANC, with Bishop Abel Muzorewa as the compromise chairman.

In December, 1974, a ceasefire was announced. Detainees, including nationalist leaders, were to be released and negotiations without preconditions would be held.

But it soon became obvious that the nationalists had no intention of abiding by any ceasefire, and less than two weeks after the ceasefire announcement, four South African policemen were cut down.

Ironically, it was the ceasefire which had cost them their lives. They were stopped on a road in north-eastern Rhodesia by apparently peaceful ZANLA pretending to be observing the truce. But it was all a hoax and the four policemen were disarmed and then murdered in cold blood.

By dropping their guard and allowing the nationalists time to comply with the ceasefire, Rhodesia had effectively spared the lives of countless enemy inside the country and lost ground in the process. The nationalists were able to move out of Rhodesia with impunity.

Releasing the nationalist leaders back into the terrorist fold, at a time when the metropolitan government in Portugal was handing over to FRELIMO, would ultimately lead to an escalation in the war. Nkomo, leader of ZIPRA, demanded and got every family in his support area of Matabeleland to send one man out to Zambia for training, and his recruits were streaming out of the country at the rate of 3 000 a month.

In January, 1975, as part of the detente scenario, South Africa ordered the withdrawal of the South African Police from positions along the Zambezi Valley. The SAP had been technically supporting Rhodesian forces since the late 1960s to prevent South African-born terrorists infiltrating through Rhodesia to South Africa.

They were to be withdrawn totally on August 1, 1975, as an inducement to the nationalists to attend another constitutional conference. However, the conference, held at Victoria Falls, failed to produce an agreement.

(Elements of the South African Defence Force – members of the crack reconnaissance units – would however, secretly return to work with the SAS on external missions, operating towards the end of the war as D Squadron, SAS.)

The detente period was a particularly difficult time for the security forces. All external operations were stopped and security forces were ordered not to shoot or take offensive action against insurgents heading away from Rhodesia – and therefore back to their bases. They could only be eliminated as they made their way towards Rhodesia.

The SAS, having been stopped from their cross-border role, embarked on a period of internal operations and retraining ... but when it became obvious that the ceasefire was not working, the SAS were tasked to get back into Tete.

A flamboyant brigadier at Army Headquarters put the SAS commander Brian Robinson and his intelligence officer, Scotty McCormack, in the picture.

"Okay chaps!" he said. "Blue Sector (Tete Province) is on. You can go back in – but you've got to go in quietly."

Scotty immediately turned to the SAS commander to ask: "Have you got any silent landmines sir?"

It was obvious that landmines were out ... and they were told quite categorically that they were not to tangle with FRELIMO.

What followed was a very low-key exercise – reconnaissance and intelligence-gathering, checking the roads, establishing the routes; typical SAS work.

It was to be a terrible phase. The conditions were bad ... the bush was incredibly thick and the operators had to carry copious quantities of water. Yet despite the hardships, the SAS's intelligence dossier was growing.

Part of the unit's job was to try and increase the effectiveness of the new border fence which had gone up over an extensive part of the north-eastern border and to sweep it for enemy spoor, acting as advanced eyes and ears for the rest of the army.

In September, 1975, the various patrols were choppered from their camp at the airstrip at Marymount Mission in the north-east.

Within a few days, tragedy had struck. A twenty-strong group of FRELIMO had closed in on an SAS patrol, using the cover of dead ground. Then, with the FRELIMO leader shouting his orders, they swept through the bush with weapons blazing.

Corporal Kelvin Storie was killed immediately and another man wounded. Then with the FRELIMO leader standing over the dead man's body, patrol commander Sergeant *Flash* Smythe and national serviceman Gary Stack mounted a counter-attack, killing the enemy commander, chasing the numerically-superior FRELIMO away and recovering their radio, which FRELIMO were about to capture.

Flash had done a first-class job as he was to do throughout the war and national serviceman Gary Stack had also acquitted himself extremely well on his first bush trip. He had done everthing he was supposed to . . . obeying *Flash's* commands and helping to contribute to the successful counter-attack.

But one man had been killed and it had been a sad incident.

The Missionaries, The Military and The Minister

Marymount Mission – where the unit was based – was administered by a German missionary . . . and at this time of the war, missionaries and the soldiers were not always on the same side.

Missionaries tended to hold anti-Government, pro-nationalist views, and the German missionary, who was suspected of actively assisting the enemy, was certainly not keen to have the SAS based at the end of his airstrip.

But, as he pointed out to Lieutenant Bob McKenna, he really didn't have any say in the matter – they had the guns and he didn't.

Nevertheless, the two men established a workable relationship and the missionary finally offered the soldiers the use of his swimming pool and showers. Bob negotiated the timings for his men to use the pool as they had to fit in with the missionaries timetable and that of his black staff.

Unbeknown to the missionaries, the flamboyant Minister of Defence P. K. van der Byl had arrived for a visit to his troops in the bush.

"PK" as he was affectionately known to Rhodesians, was frightfully British and old school tie. He was a master of the Churchillian phrase and generally considered eccentric. The troops thought he was magnificient.

There was no one quite like PK in their eyes; and indeed no other Defence Minister had such a rapport with the troopies.

"Good bugger, old PK," remarked one SAS soldier after the minister had arrived. "And more to the point, he's brought a bottle of whisky with him. Imported of course."

PK arrived at Marymount wearing khaki shorts and displaying a large expanse of pale spindly legs. He was wearing a British stable belt and had a captured AK over his shoulder.

He told Brian Robinson that he couldn't make up his mind what uniform he was going to wear. Perhaps, just to keep everyone happy, he said, he would wear an RLI stable belt and SAS wings.

"Well, I don't know about the stable belt, Minister," replied Brian Robinson witheringly. "But you certainly won't be wearing SAS wings!"

During his stay at Marymount, some of the SAS troops returned from the bush and went for a shower out of the prescribed times . . . and the German missionary was most unimpressed with them.

At 10h00, still dressed in his baggy pyjamas, he stormed down to the SAS camp in a highly agitated state to demand an interview with the military.

Bob McKenna tried to be as diplomatic as he could but the conversation was beginning to get slightly heated.

"What can I do?" the missionary wailed yet again. "You've got all the guns."

"Yes," the SAS officer agreed, "*we've* got all the guns."

Listening to the unholy row from the inside of his tent was the Minister of Defence. Suddenly, the lanky figure of PK emerged from behind the flaps of his tent. Introducing himself as the Minister of Defence, he drew himself up and continued:

"Listen, my dear fellow," he pointed out, "if you don't like these chaps using your swimming pool, I will take away your swimming pool. And if you don't like that, I will take away your whole mission – all the buildings, all the tractors and everything in it – and close it down.

"And not only will I take away your swimming pool and close down the mission, but I will also deport you . . . and you'll never see this place again.

"Now – what have you got to say to that?"

Needless to say, there wasn't much the poor trembling missionary could say. He turned tail and, with his pyjamas flapping around him, stormed off mumbling to himself in German. The timetable was thrown away and the troops were showering and swimming in the pool that afternoon.

Uninvited Guests

For some time, a ZIPRA reconnaissance platoon had been basing up on the northern shores of Lake Kariba, crossing over into Rhodesia to gather intelligence, then returning to their sanctuary in Zambia.

Special Branch knew they used a house close to the lake shore as their headquarters and staging point, but for some time they could not pin it down. Then they eventually got lucky and the house was located at an isolated spot on the lake shore at a place called Chipepo. Originally a civilian fishing cottage, it went by the name of the Chipepo Guest House.

There were the usual scatterings of locals' huts in the area, but the guest house itself was several hundred metres from the nearest habitation.

The missing piece of the jigsaw slotted in while the SAS's "A" Troop were operating from Weather Island, eighty kilometres (fifty miles) west of Kariba village. Lieutenant Bob McKenna and his men had already spent three exhausting days along the Zambian shoreline searching for ZIPRA crossing points. They were able to locate one and, as an added bonus, unearthed a two metre-deep supply bunker. ZIPRA had failed to booby-trap their bunker, so the SAS climbed down and did it for them!

Their mission over, the weary men climbed back in their boats, set sail for Rhodesian waters and began looking forward to a well-earned sleep. But there was to be no sleep for them that night. Waiting to greet them back on Weather Island was the SAS 2IC, Mick Graham, with the news that they would be out on the lake again that night.

Chipepo Guest House was about to get some uninvited visitors, and an attack was to be mounted immediately, before the ZIPRA men could be alerted and make good their escape.

The plan called for the raiding party to spring their attack on the house early in the evening, when the terrorists were off guard . . . capture everyone inside . . . and return to Rhodesia before first light.

Up-to-date intelligence given by any captures could only prove useful to the Rhodesians – and might very well lead to other operations being mounted – so the aim of the mission was to bring back prisoners, Mick Graham told Bob McKenna, who would be commanding the actual attack.

Taking prisoners would be a severe tactical handicap and Bob set about working out a plan of action. Perhaps they could surround the house and get in without firing any shots? Then again, maybe they would be able to capture the enemy while they were asleep?

Just after dark, 16 blackened-up SAS men climbed aboard a security force command boat and two inflatable rubber motor boats, and set sail for Zambia. On the command boat were six canoes to use on the last stretch of the journey.

They sped across the vast expanse of water separating the two countries, but a navigational error was made and by the time the boats neared the Zambian shoreline it was close on midnight.

The command boat and the two rubber boats cut their engines and the 12-man raiding party disembarked, climbed into the six canoes and paddled into the night. Their four friends were to wait for them out on the lake . . . to pick them up when their mission was over or to speed to their rescue if there was a problem.

There was a very bright moon that night and the canoeists could only hope there would be no locals, fishermen or enemy up and about by the water's edge to see their silent approach.

The only noise that could be heard was from the water as it gently lapped against their paddles.

Cautiously, the 12 men approached the shoreline. It was now getting on for 01h00. Surely everyone would have long ago gone to bed?

As they put in to shore, they saw no sign of life. The terrain was as they had imagined it . . . typically open, with just a few trees dotted here and there.

Immediately in front of them, well-illuminated in the eerie stillness of the moonlit night for all the uninvited visitors to see, was their target – the Chipepo Guest House. It was of brick construction with a corrugated iron roof, and just 150 metres from the water's edge.

Leaving the canoes on the beach, the dozen shadowy figures silently moved up to the house.

Bob whispered to his men to take up their positions around the building. Soon, the ZIPRA headquarters was completely encircled with well-armed SAS men. Bob went up to the front door. It was time to try out his first plan.

He intended walking straight in to see what was going on, then take things from there. He turned the handle, but, contrary to the locals' practice, the ZIPRA platoon had taken the precaution of locking it.

It was time for Plan B.

The sound of knocking thundered through the guest house. It was certainly an unearthly hour to go visiting. It was followed immediately by the unmistakable sound of a white man, and an American one at that, as he bellowed:

"COME OUT AND GIVE YOURSELVES UP. WE'VE GOT YOU SURROUN-DED . . . THROW YOUR WEAPONS OUT OF THE WINDOWS . . . COME OUT WITH YOUR HANDS UP AND WE WON'T HARM YOU."

With that, there was a great clattering from inside, as the startled ZIPRA began cocking their AKs. Bob decided to give it one more go.

81

"COME OUT WITH YOUR HANDS UP ... WE WON'T HARM YOU ... "

But the men inside plainly did not believe the last part of the instruction and began firing rounds out of the windows all around the house and through the locked door.

Then Bob did the movie trick of shooting at the lock. He fired about 15 rounds into it, but still the lock did not budge.

By now the terrorists had begun heaving grenades out of the windows and it was time for Plan C.

Around about this time, Bob was resolving that the capture of prisoners would simply have to be a lucky by-product of the mission, not the aim.

However, they still would not use maximum force just yet. He was hopeful it might still be possible to get something in the way of a capture.

"GRENADES!" he shouted to his team ... and high explosive and white phosphorus grenades were thrown through the windows, and a volley of rifle fire was put down.

Occasionally, ZIPRA would lob a grenade out of the windows, sending the SAS men lurking below, dashing away. They would wait for it to go off ... then, when it did, they would return to take up their positions beneath the windows.

Flames begun by the white phosphorus and tracers started to lick the building. Inside, choking white smoke filled the house.

The terrorists were putting up a determined resistance ... and the SAS on the outside were relentlessly keeping up their attack.

Then the burning began to get out of hand. The blaze had quickly spread from one room to the next. As flames leapt ever-nearer to the enemy they were forced to flee to safety, seeking sanctuary in one room at the corner of the house.

With the flames getting closer and the house surrounded, the terrorists were finally cornered.

The room they were confined to had two windows, one on one corner, one on the other. Shots continued to smack both in and out of both windows as the enemies fought it out.

The SAS commander still had it in mind to get his prisoners, yet he didn't want them to burn in the process.

"GET SOME WATER AND PUT THAT FIRE OUT," he yelled to some of his troops above the noise of shooting, crackling flames and crashing masonry.

Grabbing pots, ammunition tins and whatever containers they could find, the water party hurried down to the lake. They were soon back and set about attempting to douse the blaze.

"GRENADES!" the lieutenant ordered again to the troops positioned at the two windows.

And while some of his men followed that order, the others continued to subdue the flames.

Eventually after many trips to the water's edge, the fire was extinguished ... but a pall of heavy black smoke filled the house and hung in the air.

And still the enemy were nowhere near surrendering. Inside the smouldering house they were scheming new moves.

Suddenly, there was a long burst of bullets from one of the windows; then a grenade was thrown out.

It almost landed on Bob's foot, but he and his men had seen it coming and again they ran around the side of the house to take cover.

As the grenade exploded, three ZIPRA leapt from the windows and made a break for it, trying to get away under the cover of the pall of smoke from the house fire and from that kicked up by the exploding grenade.

They ran for their lives through the dense choking smoke, chased by a merciless hail of bullets.

So thick was the smoke that the soldiers could not tell if they had shot any of the ZIPRA men or not. But judging from the appalling odour wafting through the cordite-filled air that morning, they knew that at least one man had taken a hit in the guts.

Bob McKenna mentally gave the fleeing men full marks. They had obviously sorted out their escape quite well and executed it without it being a complete failure.

But he was rapidly losing patience with the order about having to capture the enemy, and was now thinking of other measures.

They *still* had not got that front door open and once more they turned their attention to it.

Again Bob tried the other Hollywood trick of trying to kick the door in with his boot. Again it failed to work. Eventually, a strongly-built trooper pushed him out of the way. "Allow me, sir . . . ," he mumbled.

The trooper moved back slightly and paused for a moment. Then he hurtled forward and took a flying rugby tackle at the door, whereupon it fell straight in with the trooper still lying on top of it, and Bob standing over him.

They were confronted with the spectre of a man on his hands and knees and glowing in the darkness. He shone like a human torch from all the white phosphorus that covered his entire body.

As the door crashed down, the wounded man threw out a grenade and it rolled between the SAS lieutenant and the trooper. As it did so, a burst of rifle fire from Bob McKenna's FN thumped into the glowing enemy and he fell dead before them. But the grenade continued rolling on its way coming to a sickening halt right at the two soldiers' feet.

There was no time to take cover. The worried pair could only wait for it to go off. But nothing happened.

Then they realised that although the injured enemy had the presence of mind to heave a grenade at his attackers, he was so badly wounded that he had not had the strength to pull out the pin. Someone was definitely looking after them that night, and the two men offered up a silent prayer.

They stepped over the bleeding, still-glowing terrorist and cautiously moved into the smouldering headquarters.

Swiftly, silently, they checked out the blackened rooms, establishing that the glowing ZIPRA had been the last one alive in the house. One man lay dead under a bed; the others had cleverly escaped through the window and run off into the night.

Having missed their men, they grabbed every document and it made quite a reasonable haul and would no doubt prove very useful to SB.

By now the unchecked flames had spread and the house was again starting to burn furiously.

Bob glanced at his watch. Time was going. They checked out the area around the guest house in the hope of finding any wounded, but there was no sign.

Bob got on the radio to Mick Graham waiting out on the lake to put him in the picture; together with the request to come and collect them. The boats sped in for the pick-up.

The captured kit and their six canoes were loaded on to the boats. One hour before daylight, the raiding party climbed aboard and left Chipepo.

Behind them flames shot high against the greying early-morning sky as the guest house continued to blaze. When the fire spread to the armoury it took on new dimensions as landmines, rockets and rounds began exploding, and brilliant flashes fuelled the flames.

As for the men responsible, they had no sooner got clear of the bay than their problems began. A storm had blown up while they were dealing with the guest house, and soon one of the engines of the main boat began to give trouble as they ploughed into the howling wind and wild waves making almost no headway. However, the motors in the two smaller boats were running reliably and they were faring a bit better.

An urgent signal was sent out over the savage waters of the lake, telling of their problems and requesting immediate help.

When daylight dawned, they were still inside Zambian waters and feeling slightly uneasy.

They continued battling into the storm. Then the command boat ran out of fuel and the passengers were left adrift.

Soon afterwards, the distinctive, welcoming whirr of a Rhodesian helicopter could be heard approaching in answer to their earlier call for help.

The chopper lowered fuel to the main boat and the two motor boats alongside. But the problem with the bigger boat's engine still remained.

"YOU'D BETTER GO ON AS BEST YOU CAN," 2IC Mick Graham yelled to make himself heard above the din of the storm to the men in the two smaller craft.

Left behind on the main boat were Mick Graham, Bob McKenna, mechanic Tex Wills and a few of the troops. Tex got the motor going, while the chopper pilot lowered a rope to take the boat in tow.

But as the boat bobbed up on a monstrous wave it almost smashed into the bottom of the chopper . . . and when it dipped into another trough, it dragged the chopper down with it. The chopper came within centimetres of crashing into them and plummeting into the angry black waters of the lake.

Everyone agreed the helicopter trick was not a good idea and cut the chopper loose.

With a friendly wave from the relieved pilot, the chopper flew home, leaving the soldiers to continue their battle with the storm with one engine working and the other struggling.

Then, just as they reckoned they had arrived in friendly waters, they saw a large Rhodesian boat in the distance, and immediately began firing rockets to attract the driver's attention.

Across the spray and the turbulent waters, the driver, a Police Reservist, saw coloured flashes dart across the sky.

To the SAS's relief he roared in for the rescue. He did not seem in the least bit surprised to find a team of heavily armed, blackened-up soldiers returning from the Zambian side of the lake, and without so much as an explanation from them, he promptly towed them back to their base on Weather Island.

Bob McKenna was pleased with their haul of documents but he silently vowed that this would be the last time he would ever accept an order where the capture of prisoners was the *sole* aim of the mission.

A ZIPRA, sporting scars from white phosphorus burns would one day tell SB how he and another wounded and burnt colleague had managed to escape from Chipepo House and lived to tell the tale. The third man had been killed, and they had carried him away under cover of the pall of choking smoke.

In northern Rhodesia, another Fireforce action was underway.

Fireforce was the unique and lethal blend of air and ground units used with maximum skill, inflicting enormous casualties on terrorist groups. Such was the cutting edge of the concept that the kill ratio was to reach a remarkable sixty to one.

Once terrorists had been located by observation groups, a fireforce reaction group – manned by the RLI, RAR or both – was called in from a strategic area and the enemy were then subjected to a vertical envelopment by helicopter-borne combat troops. Later in the war, paratroops were also used.

The reaction troops were dropped off on likely escape routes, and while the troop-carrying Alouette helicopters – fitted with twin MAGs of Belgian design – withdrew to safety, the Rhodesians would fight it out with the terrorists on the ground. Overall control was from the Alouette command ship, the K-Car (Kill Car), which had a twenty millimetre cannon mounted.

The security force sweep lines would then drive the enemy into the path of pre-positioned stop groups. Faced with the fireforce, the enemy had three options – to stand and fight and be annihilated . . . scatter to a pre-determined rendezvous point . . . or bombshell – to break in all directions.

The ground commandos relied on bush skills to locate and kill, and murderous engagements occurred at close range in the form of personal duels.

Positioning the ground troops was once described as a lethal chess game . . . and to outsmart the enemy, fake insertions were made, with a helicopter hovering at treetop height to give the impression that troops were de-planing. The insurgents would then take another escape route – the one that the airborne commander had planned they would take. And they would run straight into the path of cut-off troops waiting in readiness for the kill.

Yet the Rhodesians didn't always get things their own way. The wild countryside dotted with huge kopjes, the thick bush, long elephant grass and endless msasa trees were an enemy, too, providing ideal cover and at times giving the terrorists the edge in the hide-and-seek game of life and death. It all went to make the task of ground troops trying to hunt and flush them out, fraught with unseen dangers.

The fireforce action on July 19, 1975, was one such occasion.

Part of the action took place in a dry riverbed which wound through a thickly bushed and very rocky area. There were huge boulders dotted all over the riverbed, interspersed with clusters of small rocks. Erosion had taken place, and here and there were washout underhangings along the banks.

It was from one of these washouts that a gang of ZANLA watched as two Rhodesians silently made their way down the riverbed looking for signs of the enemy.

The ZANLA men could not have got themselves into a better position. The washout formed a cave-like hideaway, and a curtain of enormous tree roots draped the entrance, concealing them from view. Their little cave was just one metre up from the riverbed and they had the advantage of not only remaining undetected, but of having a grandstand view of the two unsuspecting trackers moving down the riverbed beneath them.

Then, when the two soldiers were just ten metres away, ZANLA opened fire and the Rhodesians fell.

For their RLI colleagues looking down on the scene from a three-metre high embankment, it was extremely difficult to see where the two men were. And, because of the boulders all over the riverbed, it was hard to tell if the men were injured . . . or dead . . . or merely taking cover behind the boulders.

It was also hard to work out precisely where the terrorists had fired from – or, where they had moved to – if they had moved at all. A K-Car tried to winkle them out of the area, but because of the difficult terrain, it proved a futile exercise.

After failing to draw ZANLA's fire, the general feeling was that ZANLA had moved from wherever they had been hiding, to a spot further down the riverbed.

Then the sounds of moaning floated up from the riverbed. Former SAS soldier Corporal John Coey, an American and the callsign's medic, leapt from the embankment to help his wounded colleagues – and as he did so, more shots cracked out and he fell into the riverbed. For the ZANLA gang had not been down the riverbed as imagined, but directly beneath him.

By now, RLI officer Joey du Plooy had arrived on the scene and began organising RLI and RAR stop groups around the area. Then he attempted to sort ZANLA out himself by shooting and throwing grenades into the riverbed.

But because the enemy's little cave was off the riverbed, the grenades were having virtually no effect. They were merely bursting into the riverbed, with the fragments spreading in every direction – while ZANLA, holed up in their cave, remained unharmed.

And because the RLI officer was not too sure if the three soldiers down in the riverbed were dead or alive, he was unable to do precisely what he wanted to do anyway.

Joey du Plooy and his men then began to skirmish forward to get into a better position. But once again, ZANLA opened up ... and one Rhodesian soldier was shot and killed.

Joey du Plooy received a graze in the head in the incident and another man was wounded in the leg. The casualties were mounting – and still the men responsible had not been located and accounted for.

Much to his dismay, the RLI officer was ordered to get into a chopper and return to base. It was with great reluctance that he obeyed the command, for he was eager to get to grips with the men responsible for their troubles that day.

As a casevac chopper climbed out of the LZ and turned for base, Joey du Plooy left behind a number of stop groups positioned around the area ... and three colleagues down at the bottom of the riverbed, whose fate was still very much unknown.

The RLI continued firing into the area of the enemy position. Occasionally, they got return fire and sometimes they were greeted only with silence, until eventually no one was quite sure if the ZANLA gang was still there or not.

One long hour followed another and the problem remained unresolved. Eventually the SAS, based at Mount Darwin at the time, were told of the situation and warned that they might be called in to help.

But as the day wore on and no further word was received, it seemed as if the panic was all over.

But as dusk descended at the dry riverbed in northern Rhodesia, the problem had still not been sorted out. The three men lay somewhere in the riverbed – and no one had been able to work out if they were dead or alive.

It was time to call in the SAS.

Lieutenant Bob McKenna, rounded up volunteers and told them what sketchy information he had. Within minutes, Bob and his team of *Horse* Green, *Torti* King, Sergeant *Flash* Smythe, Alan Hider and medic Wolfgang Hucke, were airborne.

It was dark when the two chopper pilots flew out from Mount Darwin and set course for the troublespot north-east of Rushinga. Unusual as it was for helicopters to fly so late at night, the pilots were undeterred by the hazards involved ... without night-flying equipment and the ability to see the horizon, they might end upside down with fatal consequences.

But Rhodesia's plucky pilots were prepared to take their life in their hands when circumstances called for it; and this was definitely one such time.

Luckily for them and their passengers, there was virtually a full moon that night, and while the conditions were not ideal, it was not quite so dangerous.

It was a cold, crystal-clear night and Bob McKenna was wearing a much-prized British Army smock, designed for climates similar to the one the Rhodesians were experiencing that crisp winter's night.

The brilliant glare from the moon shone on the helicopters as they flew through the still, silent night probing the darkness. The choppers' red and green navigational lights flashed through the black of the night, while inside the Alouettes a faint light came from the pilots' shielded instrument panel.

An hour after take off, the pilots turned off their navigational lights as they began their approach to the embankment above the dry riverbed. For they had no wish to attract attention to themselves, their passengers or the other troops in the area.

As the choppers came in to land 100 metres from the embankment, a young RLI corporal, Butch Alexander, who had taken over control and had been running things since Joey du Plooy had been casevacked out, sprinted across to greet them.

He reported that the situation was much as it had been for some time. No one could tell if the enemy were still in the riverbed, although the general feeling was that they had gone. No one had been able to pinpoint the position of the bodies – or had been able to establish if they were bodies and not wounded men.

Positioning two of the SAS team – both with night sights on their rifles – to give covering fire, Bob McKenna and the RLI corporal crawled to the edge of the embankment overlooking the riverbed to carry out a reconnaissance. They stopped only to chat to a couple of RLI men who had been left on guard and were told that there had been no movement or moaning coming from below for several hours.

The SAS officer inched forward and peered over the edge. The figures of the three injured men were sprawled beneath him in the riverbed, well illuminated in the moonlight. Bob McKenna watched for a few moments, but saw no movement. It seemed obvious to him that the three men were dead.

But where were the enemy?

To pinpoint their position, he got the RLI guards to throw grenades, including phosphorus, into the riverbed. Although there was no reaction, Bob realised the enemy might not have left. Perhaps they were just lying low? Perhaps they were trying to conserve their ammunition until the time the rest of the Rhodesians ventured into the riverbed?

For fifteen minutes, the SAS team fired rounds into likely hiding positions. But they were unable to provoke any return fire at all.

Although ZANLA's hideout had still not been pinpointed, Bob eventually decided there was nothing for it but to go down into the riverbed and find out exactly what the situation was. He certainly had no intention of jumping over the edge to get riddled with bullets as fellow American John Coey had. And if something wasn't done soon, they would be there all night.

Bob repositioned some of the SAS team to cover any likely escape routes and provide cover, then asked *Horse* Green to go along with him into the riverbed.

87

When the RLI corporal Butch Alexander heard what they were planning, he insisted on going with them. The corporal pointed out that the three men down in the riverbed were his buddies and it was only right he should go along.

Bob McKenna agreed, then prepared himself for a fight. Shedding his webbing and leaving his rifle behind, he armed himself with his pistol and stuffed the large pockets of his British Army smock with hand grenades.

Then Bob, *Horse* Green and Butch Alexander went 150 metres downriver to where they felt they could safely enter the riverbed.

The bright moon was creating a mass of eerie shadows in the dry riverbed that night, as Bob, pistol in one hand, grenade in the other, started to slink up the riverbed snake-fashion leading the way through the mounds of boulders.

Crawling twenty metres behind him came Butch Alexander – and bringing up the rear was *Horse* Green who had been given the MAG machinegun together with instructions to blast away the moment he heard or saw anything untoward.

All was silent as they slithered around the rocks, snaking ever-closer to the suspected ZANLA position.

Suddenly, *Horse* Green heard something and without so much as a word of warning, fired off several long bursts from his machinegun. Every fifth round was a red tracer and they were ripping in sheets over the heads of his two companions. *Horse* let loose 100 or so rounds ... and his two companions, although startled, continued crawling through the night, without a word spoken.

Then, just as unexpectedly as it had started, so it ended and all fell silent again. There was just the moon, the boulders, the long shadows and the eeriness ...

Eventually, Bob McKenna arrived at a spot where he could see the three soldiers. They were lying within arm's length of one another and now, there could be no doubt as to their fate. They were all dead.

As the SAS officer and his two companions crawled closer, they could see white phosphorus glowing through the thick curtain of tree roots as it clung to the walls of ZANLA's little cave-like hideaway. At long last, the enemy's position had been pinpointed.

The three soldiers lay in the riverbed just ten metres from the cave, listening for the sound of breathing or coughing that would tell if ZANLA were still holed up inside. But there wasn't a murmur and Bob McKenna reasoned that after all this time the enemy must have fled.

He lobbed a couple of grenades into the still-glowing cave and as the last one went off, he summoned up all his courage and, with his pistol in his hand, he leapt up into the hideout – while below, *Horse* Green and Butch Alexander prepared to give covering fire.

But there was no reaction. Behind the screen of tree roots there was only an empty cave. The enemy had gone, escaping through a gap in the stop lines, pausing only long enough to take their victims' machinegun and ammunition.

An SAS tracker team followed up next morning, but the enemy had made their escape across a maize field, which was criss-crossed with the tracks of the local population, thereby making identification of the ZANLA spoor impossible. The search was abandoned and the only thing they found was the captured machinegun ZANLA had dropped when it became too heavy for them.

The SAS had been very impressed with the young RLI corporal who had taken charge and run things before their arrival. Butch Alexander had done an excellent job in very confusing, difficult, and at times, extremely demoralising circumstances.

They tried to get him to join the SAS, but although keen, the corporal was always busy with fireforce actions and never found the time to apply.

With four good men cut down and two others wounded, July 19 was to go down as a dark day in the history of the RLI.

As for the SAS rescuers and the RLI corporal who had volunteered to crawl up the riverbed and face the unknown with them, it had been one of the most harrowing jobs of their soldiering careers.

Selous Scouts

The concept of pseudo counter-insurgency, which was to play a large part in the Rhodesian war, was studied from two separate angles in the early days.

On one hand, hunter and consultant ecologist Allan Savory who had run bush-craft survival courses and advocated the use of tracker-trained troops and anti-terrorist units had worked on his concept in which he believed the best way to hunt down, fight and understand the enemy was to think and train as a terrorist. And if ever overrun, men could penetrate and operate as terrorists behind the lines.

On the other, Brigadier John Hickman, ultimately to become Commander of the Rhodesian Army, was also staunchly advocating the pseudo idea.

Hickman had been in Malaya and had gained a wealth of knowledge about pseudo-operations, gangs and counter-gangs. As well as having researched the topic, he had written papers on the benefits to be gained from "turning" captured terrorists. Then, to take that one step further, he advocated that a unit be formed to incorporate the "turned" terrorists so that they could be used in counter-insurgency; using them, in effect, against their former comrades.

To take an enemy, put a rifle in his hand and stick him in the Rhodesian Army, was a totally revolutionary idea and Hickman got nowhere with the concept.

Rhodesia's answer to any terrorist who was caught was clear. After he had his day in court, and no matter how much he had helped the police track down his former comrades, he invariably had a date with the hangman.

Brigadier Hickman had aired his views when he was a major. The next time he raised the matter was as Brigade Commander at JOC *Hurricane* following the Centenary farm attacks.

Special Branch officers involved in the war from the outset, and even before, were particularly keen on the pseudo plan.

Their role was to piece together the many snippets of intelligence from wherever they could get them ... and through well-placed informers, they knew what the terrorists had planned over the years and knew where their training camps were throughout Africa and abroad.

But now that the war had been taken into the local population and the masses were being politicized, that job might not be so easy. It could mark the beginning of the end. To stay current, to stay ahead before events got out of hand, would call for a wealth of intelligence.

What was needed were people who could pose as terrorists, passing themselves off among the local population and to be convincing enough to fool the enemy themselves. Their role would be to gather intelligence, locate insurgent groups and when the time was right, eliminate the terrorists; or stir things up and set one group of nationalists against another.

Brigadier Hickman approached SAS Sergeants Andre Rabie and *Stretch* (Alan) Franklin and RLI Sergeant Pete Clementshaw in the *White Rhino* pub at Kariba and put the pseudo idea to them. They all liked the idea and Andre and *Stretch,* who were instructors at the Tracking Wing at Kariba, were detached to John Hickman for special duties.

It was a top secret assignment and none of their friends knew where they were and whether in fact they were still in the SAS. Being SAS-trained, they knew better than to ask.

Andre, *Stretch* and Pete were joined by three African soldiers from the RAR. They also had a captured terrorist, one of those responsible for the Centenary farm attacks, who had been caught by Portuguese troops and handed over.

The little team was called *The 4949s* after the number on the file kept at Special Branch headquarters.

At first the three white soldiers put the black troops through their paces and then SB officer Pete Stanton came in to teach them terrorist methods – what to eat, what not to eat, is an art in itself – for if a local did not trust them and offered them certain foods, which they accepted, he would immediately realise they were pseudos, and not real terrorists.

The enemy were constantly changing these foods and it was SB's task to keep abreast of the changes, as out-of-date information could have fatal consequences.

Once Pete Stanton had trained the soldiers, he handed them over to the captured terrorist and *The 4949s* learned all they could from him.

Special Branch provided *The 4949s* with their money and kit and found them a *safe-house* to use between their deployments.

It was still a highly sensitive operation and as the north-east remained a hot area, fairly elaborate arrangements had to be made to get them to their *safe-house,* for had they been seen – blackened-up and armed to the teeth as they were – they would have been shot out of hand.

They only travelled in their covered van in the dead of night when there were no road blocks to stop them, and it was only when the African house servant had been sent out of the way did they dare risk nipping into the safety of the house.

The houseboy never got to see them in their blackened-up state. All he really knew of the mystery was that he was going through bath cleaner like it was going out of fashion.

Sadly, Andre Rabie was accidentally killed while working on the pseudo idea. He made a tragic map-reading error and was killed by another member of the security forces. His death was a tremendous blow to the SAS and the Army. He had been one of the personalities of the squadron. Andre received a posthumous award, making him a Member of the Order of Legion of Merit (Military Division) for distinguished service over and above the call of duty on operations.

Eventually, Prime Minister Ian Smith ordered that an army regiment be formed to carry out pseudo work, and the Selous Scouts unit was formed with an ex-Malayan SAS soldier, Major (later Lieutenant-Colonel) Ron Reid-Daly, a former RLI Regimental Sergeant Major, as the founder commander.

*The unit was named after the famous nineteenth-century scout and hunter, Frederick Courteney Selous, upon whom Sir Henry Rider Haggard based his equally-famous character, Alan Quartermain in *King Solomon's Mines.*

Overnight, the army had got itself a glamour unit.

To the SAS hierarchy, this particular aspect was perfect. The SAS deliberately played down their role . . . they certainly did not want the glory, the publicity and the focus that was suddenly being given to the Scouts.

The new regiment attracted men from other units and former SAS members were there to play a very important part in founding the Selous Scouts. SAS strength was reduced to 25 men as a result, which was fewer than when the unit moved down from Ndola.

It was a difficult time for the SAS, but the commander was adamant that there was going to be no lowering of standards just to boost numbers. Far rather have 25 good men than 100 mediocre ones.

The SAS was a special forces unit with a unique professionalism – and that's the way it was going to stay.

Frosty Reception

Since C Squadron's resurrection in the '60s, manpower had always been one of its major problems. First they had to find men, then train them, and this created the unit's own identity, which differed slightly from the original SAS mould.

But that identity may have been altered again had the SAS hierarchy got their own way and been permitted to accept non-Europeans into their ranks.

Until the late '60s, the unit was organised, trained and equipped to some extent, along European theatre of war lines.

And, up to that time, that was adequate, in that the unit functioned satisfactorily, although according to commander Brian Robinson, they should have seen the light much earlier. Only one example is needed to make the point.

The SAS used to run escape and evasion exercises where the fleeing troops were bound to a *pipeline*. In that broad belt of land they could make contact with various agents or receive help from "safe houses".

The exercises were good – but very European.

For on subsequent operations inside Mozambique, they soon learned there were no safe houses or friendly agents. If a four-man patrol was compromised, that part of Africa became the hunting ground, the entire population became the hunters, and the SAS were open season!

And the people of their hunting grounds were almost exclusively African and therefore movement through an area, and understanding what was going on in it, was that much easier if the intruder was also an African.

SAS men may well have dressed up and disguised themselves as Africans wearing *Black-Is-Beautiful* camouflage cream and may even have disguised their footprints. But in reality, whites cannot pass close examination, as their features are different – and to the discerning eye even their spoor is different.

Then there was the problem of language. Very few SAS soldiers were fluent in Chishonas (prevalent in the north and east of the country) or Sindebele (in the south and west) or both. And it was often very frustrating for a patrol to close brilliantly on a terrorist base camp, listen to the occupants having a serious discussion, but be unable to report back because they did not really understand what was being said.

The SAS tried private tuition, language laboratories, and had African soldiers teaching them, all of which were fairly successful. But within weeks of developing a talent, it would be gone through lack of conversational practice.

There were more than six million Africans in Rhodesia, so that was hardly a justifiable excuse. Commander Brian Robinson concluded that they were idle and lazy in this respect, but that was the common failing of the white man in most of central and southern Africa.

91

Their next policy in seeking a solution for the inadequacies on operations was to have seconded to the SAS a number of specially selected and experienced African soldiers from the 1st Battalion, Rhodesian African Rifles.

One African soldier was attached to each four-man patrol and the operational results were greatly improved.

SAS troops were generally full of praise for the professionalism of these attached African soldiers and what interested Brian was the great mutual affection exhibited between them all when off duty. They all celebrated the coming of 1975 with the roasting of a buffalo they had shot and slightly more than a few beers. Throughout the long celebrations, the Africans remained part of their patrol and did not segregate; and on the other side of the coin, the white members were obviously enjoying their company and were natural with them.

Perhaps it was because they were with exceptional 1 RAR soldiers and that they were all soldiers together. Either way, it convinced the SAS hierarchy sufficiently to approach the Army Commander, Lieutenant-General Peter Walls, and formally request they be allowed to embody African troops into the unit who had successfully passed the selection course and the parachute and SAS skilled-training courses.

They were turned down flat.

They would, they were told, allegedly be duplicating the role of the Selous Scouts, and that was not necessary.

But it was hardly likely at that time . . . the Selous Scouts role was that of tracking down terror gangs *within* Rhodesia.

The SAS meanwhile were talking of purely *external* operations, of close reconnaissance and destruction of camps and communication lines, and perhaps organising counter-groups from the locals within Mozambique – typical SAS work in other words.

The result in fact was that the Selous Scouts ended up encroaching on the SAS's role to some extent.

The Scouts did *not* have the benefit of any previous experience of "special" operations and the army commander was obliged to give both units specific areas in which they could operate.

Considering the all-encompassing nature of SAS work in a guerilla war, this was absolutely ludicrous and did little to promote good relations between the two units, Robinson felt.

At about this time – early 1975 – there were two other incidents that convinced the SAS that official policy on integration in army units was not what it should be.

The first involved a Lance Corporal Frost, a very light-skinned coloured and a member of a neighbouring army transport company.

For as long as he could remember, Lance Corporal Frost had admired soldiers, and the SAS, whom he used to watch training near his company, epitomised everything he dreamt of in the military.

He noticed that the day started early for the SAS training troop with PT and a seven kilometre (four mile) run at 05h45.

Armed with the knowledge that the SAS was a volunteer unit demanding high standards of physical fitness, he approached the instructors one morning and asked to join the physical training squad.

"Well, it's your funeral," the somewhat nonplussed instructor said, shrugging his shoulders.

So Frost joined the squad and from that moment didn't miss a single morning PT session . . . in fact, so keen was he that he was very soon a regular member of the afternoon PT class as well.

Time passed and Frost applied to attend SAS selection and this was granted as a matter of course.

The only problem was that the SAS did not know he was a coloured as the transport company also had white NCOs.

Having eventually mustered all candidates for the selection course, the training troop departed for the rigours of the Eastern Highlands.

Lance Corporal Frost had successfully completed one leg of the course when the SAS received the news from Army HQ – who had been told the names of the SAS volunteers on selection – that Frost was a coloured.

He was ordered to rejoin his unit.

It is easy to imagine the tremendous disappointment experienced by Frost, who without doubt would have passed the course through sheer determination to realise his dreams and elevate himself from a rather second-grade citizen to a prestigious SAS soldier.

It was not easy telling Frost either; he was well liked by the training troop.

To his credit he held no umbrage against the SAS . . . and such was his determination that he tried to join the "Supers" for a second time about a year later.

Although his application was submitted, it was refused again – and there ends the tale. Perhaps it was being sentimental, but Brian Robinson felt Frost deserved better than that.

At the same time, the SAS also had in its ranks a Lieutenant Martin Knight-Willis, a well-decorated soldier who had come from the New Zealand SAS.

Through correspondence and visits home on leave, he obviously described the conditions and experiences to be enjoyed in Rhodesia . . . and this resulted in queries from New Zealanders who were interested in joining the Rhodesian unit.

Among them was a sergeant, well known to Martin, who spoke very highly of the applicant. The sergeant was a Maori.

The SAS made enquiries to Army Headquarters and the reaction in a nutshell was "Bloody good those Maoris – but what about his family? Would they fit in socially?"

Brian Robinson was livid.

His whole point was that the unit was always short of manpower. The SAS was a volunteer unit with very stringent selection. If there was any doubt surrounding an individual, the SAS got the benefit and on his way he went.

Standards started high and if anything had got higher over the years, so to have mixed races in the unit would not be allowed to affect their proficiency, he felt.

The consensus at the time was wholeheartedly behind the OC, although there were some who believed otherwise . . . that the unit's professionalism would have dropped had other races been accepted into their ranks.

The SAS commander, however, was a fierce taskmaster as men who did not fit their commander's high standards found to their cost. The unit, *not* the personality, came first in Brian's book and he stood no nonsense from anyone, be he black, white or coloured; trooper or officer.

But it was not to be . . . and the SAS remained exclusively white.

SAS Training

The average British SAS man is a unique specimen in his late twenties with years of military experience in other units before volunteering for the Special Air Service. Except on formal occasions, 22 SAS do not wear badges of rank, and communications among the ranks is normally done on a first name basis.

But it was all very different in the Rhodesian SAS – and it was basically because they had no choice.

When Brian Robinson returned from England after his attachment with 22 SAS, he argued that the average SAS trooper had to be 25 with at least three years' service. But because of the chronic manpower shortage throughout the Rhodesian Army, he realised, even as he advocated such a policy, it was an impossible dream.

The average age of the Rhodesian soldier, therefore, was under 21, and towards the end of the war, most SAS members had no previous military experience before joining.

They wore their rank badges except on operations, and officers were addressed as "Sir" – although Brian Robinson readily concedes to having heard some bold souls mutter on a couple of occasions: "Spelt with a C!"

This was not the SAS's own ostentation, however, merely a Rhodesian Army system they were obliged to abide by. From the top downwards, the system was that NCOs were addressed by their rank, and other ranks by their surnames.

Generally, the SAS abided by this rule, but much use was also made of Christian names and nicknames, for it was very difficult to remain aloof when part of a four-man patrol on a six-week operation.

The Rhodesians certainly envied 22 SAS their access to trained manpower. Nevertheless, Brian Robinson felt that the SAS founder, David Stirling would have been proud of the Rhodesians wearing the coveted sand-coloured beret.

Initially, the 1st Battalion, The Rhodesian Light Infantry, was a good source of volunteers to the SAS, and numbers were also boosted by men from foreign armies or those from the signals, engineers and occasionally the air force or police. Although already trained, they still had to undergo the rigours of the SAS's special training and selection course. Not all made the grade either.

Eventually, the RLI complained that just as they were getting men trained, so the SAS were poaching them, and in the end, the SAS more or less agreed not to look to the RLI for recruits.

Then the Selous Scouts was formed and the SAS's strength dropped to 25 men. There was simply no other source of manpower available to the SAS and it was then that Brian Robinson embarked on two different ventures, which, despite tremendous opposition from qualified SAS men, was to work exceptionally well.

He decided that the only solution was to train their own men from scratch – to take raw recruits straight out of school and into the army to do their compulsory national service . . . rather than wait until they had finished their basic training in some other unit as in the past.

The beauty of the plan was that they did not have to sort out a man's bad military habits. They could take him straight off the street and teach him SAS discipline and methods, and orientate him to the SAS's way of thinking right from day one.

It was a unique idea and totally contrary to the SAS doctrine according to the 22nd chapter. But, as the Rhodesians were to learn, it was amazing what they were able to develop through rigorous training and practical work with more experienced colleagues.

Whereas 22 SAS selected their men first then trained them, the Rhodesians were to do it the other way around – train them, then select them.

The "All-In", the culmination of a recruit's training, a testing exercise to see if he had assimilated all the SAS skills before being awarded his SAS beret and belt, was now to be scrapped.

Brian felt that to put a recruit on "All-In" when they desperately needed the manpower was wasting time.

The answer was to give a soldier the real thing, the best test of all. He would have to prove himself under battle conditions in the bush. He would carry a rifle and be expected to fight.

It meant that the SAS would have to be extremely careful. Putting a new man in a four-man patrol was 25 percent of the patrol and lives other than his own were at stake. Brian Robinson acknowledged that it was a bit much to ask a seasoned soldier to take a new man along, but there was no choice. They needed the men and it had to be done.

However, although a recruit would go on patrol, he would not receive his SAS belt and beret until he had proved himself operationally. It might take several bush trips before he was badged – and even then he was not "safe", as his beret could be taken away at any time, just as it could with other more experienced operators.

Despite the urgent need for manpower, the standard of training and selection remained high right to the end of the war. There was still a 75 percent failure rate during selection and on one course not a single recruit was considered good enough for the SAS.

The second revolutionary idea to bolster numbers was to take in TA men, civilians (often former SAS men) on call-up with other security force units who had already received some form of military training. However, as they were trained men, it was not necessary for them to do the entire recruit course. They joined the recruits during the final phase of selection with the officers having to do additional tasks.

There was the inherent security problem in taking in TA men, and the SAS hierarchy were worried that in view of the sensitive nature of SAS operations, there might be a security leak.

But Brian Robinson was realistic enough to concede that despite the most stringent precautions, leaks occur in the best of circles.

(It is unheard of in other armies for regular and TA troops to work together on active operations. Generally too, the regulars in those forces consider TA troops inferior. But in the Rhodesian SAS, this unique relationship was a success. As the TA troops were called up so often – and because they were mostly former SAS men anyway – they were accepted by the regular SAS troops as a working force and as equals.)

While the methods of SAS training varied to some extent over the years, the basic idea remained the same – to see if a man had the mental and physical stamina to do the job and to see if he was compatible.

To determine that meant reducing a recruit to the lowest form of life . . . to exhaust him, then see if he could think under stress.

While an SAS soldier had to be able to act as an individual on his own initiative, he also had to spend long periods in very small groups across the border, and compatability was absolutely essential.

To live cheek-by-jowl on the wrong side of the fence for six weeks with someone who ate noisily, had a permanent sniff, or picked his ear, could have disastrous results for the offender.

Idiosyncracies which were not irritating in normal circumstances could become so magnified that by the end of a six-week bush trip, one soldier could end up wanting to kill another in the same callsign.

If a man's character was such that this type of reaction was likely after ten days instead of six weeks, then he was not the sort of man the SAS wanted.

Positive, quick-thinking, self-disciplined people were the men the SAS needed. Stamina, fitness, endurance, initiative, courage, compatibility, individuality and logic were the criteria.

It was not necessarily the supermen, the six-footers with the bulging muscles, who made the grade either. As Brian Robinson once pointed out, any reasonably fit Rhodesian could pass selection and a candidate didn't have to be able to swim across Lake Kariba with a knife between his teeth.

Experience proved that it was often the large fit rugby players who were the first to give up and fall by the wayside, whereas others who had the right mental attitude would switch off and doggedly stagger on, regardless of how many times the instructors goaded them and did their best to encourage them to give up.

The SAS wanted people who, even if they fell down exhausted, would not give up.

From the outset, the Who Dares Wins motto took on a very real meaning.

Over the years, a variety of people ran the selection courses, each with his own idea of what selection should be and resulting in a variety of standards being set.

Brian Robinson conceded that occasionally some training officers went a bit too far in trying to get their standards high, and were just being cruel for the sake of it. It was something the hierarchy had to watch.

According to some critics – themselves involved in training – the selection courses, run at Inyangombe Mountain, Inyanga, the highest mountain in the country, became predictable.

While Inyangombe Mountain was rugged terrain and had to be taken seriously, the same rendezvous spots were used time and again for the speed marches and some enterprising recruits arranged for friends to give them lifts. In some respects this was accepted and as long as a recruit was not caught, he did not necessarily fail selection because of it.

Then, at about the time Brian Robinson decided to train youngsters fresh from school and take in TA, a couple of other changes were made that were to make a marked difference to the SAS's training methods.

Captain Rob Johnstone was appointed permanent training officer, thus providing the continuity that was so necessary to ensure that the standard remained the same from one selection course to another.

His team of instructors also remained fairly constant over the years too, and while they were masters at dreaming up new endurance and initiative exercises, by the same token they knew just how far they could push recruits.

Rob Johnstone, who was the training officer for five years, was instrumental in getting the venue of the arduous selection course changed from Inyangombe in the east to the Matopos in the west.

By the mid-70s, the war had begun to hot up and Inyanga had become part of the operational area. As recruits had to use dirt roads on selection, there was the very real problem of mine warfare to consider.

The Matopos was ideally suited to SAS needs and tested not only recruits' endurance but their map-reading abilities, too. Unlike Inyanga, it was impossible to see any of the rendezvous points either.

Even if the training staff had used the same RVs over and over again – which they did not – the Matopos was so rugged and remote that it was largely impassable to vehicle traffic, and certainly out of the question for recruits to arrange lifts with their friends.

Initially, training and selection courses took place over six months, but because of the desperate need for men in the bush, the training staff had the task of transforming raw schoolboys into hardened men in just four months.

They started each course with about 150 recruits chosen from the thousands of 18-year-old school leavers who reported to Llewellin Barracks, Bulawayo, for their compulsory national service. The national servicemen had numerous options open to them as to their choice of unit or corps they wanted to join.

Rob Johnstone and his training team had to sell the SAS idea to them but the problem was how to tell a bunch of schoolboys what the SAS was about – and, at the same time, because of the sensitive nature of SAS operations and the need for security, *not* tell them what the unit's role was on ops.

To capture their imagination, they displayed the various SAS specialist equipment – the diving gear, the canoes, and the enemy heavy weapons . . .

Having selected their nucleus of schoolboys, it was back to Salisbury where training began in earnest. It was stressed from the outset – just as it had been down the years – that a recruit could withdraw from the course at any time he wished, and that if he did, it would not be a disgrace. By the same token, he could be kicked off at any time.

Rob Johnstone's main criterion for selecting a Rhodesian SAS soldier was simple: "Would I take this bloke with me on a punch-up with the terrs?"

The recruits began their soldiering careers with a six-week period of basic training during which they were taught map-reading, signals and medics, and familiarised themselves with their own weapons and those of the enemy.

Rhodesian SAS men were renowned for their exceptionally high standard of shooting and, apart from one entire day spent dry shooting, recruits used live rounds on training, unlike the rest of the security force recruits, who used blanks.

The use of blanks led to wild shooting, a loss of control and a waste of ammunition – and that was not wanted in the SAS.

Blanks tended to give recruits a false sense of security and it was found that as soon as they began using live rounds, they were so busy concentrating on the bangs going off around them, that they forgot to listen to their orders.

By getting recruits used to a heavy-noise situation from the outset, they had confidence and did not hold back when it came to the real thing.

Using realism from the start was to pay handsome dividends for the SAS, and it was a rare occasion indeed when an ammunition resupply had to be called for during an operation.

To improve recruits' shooting, the worst shottist of the week had the dubious honour of being presented with the SAS's special *Shit Shot Bell.*

On receiving the large cow bell, the hapless winner had to do a victory lap of honour accompanied by the clanging of the bell – and worse still, the humiliating sound of applause from the rest of his course.

Then, he had to give a quick talk on how he had managed to qualify for the award – and wear the bell around his neck for seven days until he could hand it over to the next holder. Needless to say, shooting accuracy picked up remarkably.

As fitness was one of the requisites for a Special Air Service soldier, the recruits ran everywhere for the entire twenty weeks of their training and selection.

SAS operators always knew that there were recruits somewhere in camp by the unmistakable clanging of the *Shit Shot Bell*, as the new boys, their young bronzed bodies bathed in sweat, sprinted somewhere on another leg of their training.

By the time their basic training was over, the instructors were left with a hundred recruits.

They now moved down to the Gwaai River Mine – a former copper mine – north of Wankie National Park where all their field work, tactical training, patrols, map-reading, canoeing and demolitions were done, the main emphasis being on their quick shooting and ability to practise the basic principles of war.

The whole idea of the six-weeks Gwaai phase was to be as authentic as possible . . . to enable recruits to see what the real war would be like, set in rugged bushy terrain under realistic conditions.

The tactical training included splitting recruits into two teams: one to build a proper COIN warfare terror camp from where they would do their patrolling and organise their guard systems – the other to patrol and locate the camp. Then having found the base, they would set up their observation posts and keep watch on the camp.

The groups would then change over, with the "terrorist" camp growing bigger the second time around as the new group continued building.

It was a very intensive phase and everything from classical warfare to an attack on their newly-built camp was included. By the time this phase came to an end, the re-cruits had become fairly conversant with the whole war situation and were able to lead their own patrols.

Sweating it out behind a school desk was child's play compared to their new life-style. They got up at 04h30 for a PT session, ran everywhere, worked all day and invariably attended lectures until 21h00.

During the last ten days at Gwaai, officers and NCOs from other units, and TA men wanting to get into the SAS, would join the course. They would be given revision work, a series of separate exercises and a group of recruits to work with, enabling the instructors to assess their knowledge. The officers would also be expected to give military appreciations on the unconventional SAS type of operations.

This phase culminated in an attack on their terror camp, when they were tested on their lessons learned. The officers and NCOs had to give complete orders and organise the recruits for the attack.

Then followed the really hard part – the final selection to see if a recruit had what it takes to become an SAS soldier.

By this stage, more recruits had dropped out – and the course was left with between 50-70 percent of its original members.

Gone, too, were all the schoolboys. They were now a superbly fit bunch of tough men who had reached such a pitch that to have put them through a selection course straight away would have been pointless.

The idea now was to physically wear them down and soften them up before selec-tion . . . to repeatedly take them up to a certain stage and then let them relax; to bring everyone down to the same level and to give each man an equal advantage.

They now moved to Llewellin Barracks, Bulawayo, for the dreaded and intensive pre-selection *Rev* phase which included a series of arduous tasks thought up by the instructors. The *Rev* was split into hour-long stints during which the recruits boxed, ran, played baseball, wrestled in a mud bath, had a tug-of-war competition, PT sessions, swam and among other equally exhausting activities, competed in a *chariot race* in which they pulled the instructors around in vehicle trailers.

The instructors worked them up to such a state that they could barely move and after each physically exhausting stint, they would let the recruits relax. It was the sitting down part which failed most recruits . . . they would simply not get up again. Most stints were done carrying a rifle and a heavy steel ball.

Meal times were just something they thought about ... and as they were not allowed to speak to each other either, the only things which past their lips were water, glucose, salt tablets – and hushed curses.

One incentive to give up was a fresh meal. It was certainly a tempting inducement.

And all the time, the training team kept telling them what a waste of rations they were, urging them to give up, trying to wear them down.

Eventually, this phase was over and the instructors were down to about thirty determined recruits. Those lucky enough to get through the rigours of pre-selection were rewarded with the greasiest of eggs, the weakest of coffees.

Finally, the still-hungry recruits were taken to the rugged Matopos mountains for the last leg of their SAS training, the all-important selection course.

They were dropped off at last light and told that their next RV would be at 18h00 the next day. Then Rob Johnstone put on a command performance and cursed his team for forgetting to bring the correct map and instructor Nick Breytenbach would join in the little act, mumble his apologies and throw a huge bundle of maps at the recruits' feet.

By then Rob Johnstone would be reeling off a six-figure grid reference of where they were and another of where the recruits were to go to.

As the recruits tried to get their torches to work and began scrambling for their notebooks, Rob Johnstone and team would let out their clutches and roar off, leaving them to get to their rendezvous by themselves. Just for company, they had to take along a tin trunk full of iron, or a log.

It would be the first time in four months they had been left completely to themselves.

Having been dumped at the foot of the mountains, the first thing the recruits would do was to collapse in a heap and eat all their rations.

Then the squabbling would begin as to who should carry the log or trunk, and which way they should go.

Various men would begin to assert their authority, and having finally decided that a massive hill was the best route to take, they would eventually stagger off carrying their log and their 4,5 kilogram (10 lb) loaded rifles, while weighed down with their tortuous 36 kilogram (80 lb) Bergens, and the steel balls still in their hands.

They had long ago got used to the weight of SAS packs. Regular soldiers in other units often found it hard to believe how much kit SAS operators had to hump around the bush. Many found difficulty in even lifting an SAS Bergen off the ground and SAS packs became legendary.

The training team could not have chosen a more rugged, punishing spot in the whole of the country for the selection phase. Uphill was very definitely uphill and downhill was decidedly downhill.

The bush was thick, there was quite a lot of game, and wherever they went in the Matopos they were bound to hit a rough patch.

The hills were strewn with giant boulders and there were a number of false crests. Just as they got to the top of one, so they were confronted with another.

Even if they climbed to the top of the nearest hill, which could only be done in a circuitous route, there were very few hills where they could see the whole area. And generally when they got to the bottom again, they were disorientated.

Their 15 kilometre (nine mile) trek would take them all that night, and often they would fall asleep on their way after the hardships of their *Rev* phase.

There would still be a lot of haggling and name-calling, particularly over the tin trunk, which would not go around corners, and kept getting stuck in trees and bushes.

They were under a lot of pressure, too, as they had been told there was a deadline to meet. Unknown to them, the time-frame didn't really matter that much to the instructors. They were more interested in knowing how the recruits operated as a team.

Eventually, they would stagger into the RV, and if the instructors were not there to meet them, they would have left a map and a message to meet them further along the route, just to get the recruits in a worse frame of mind.

If they had not shaved or cleaned their weapons or kit by the time they met up with the instructors, they would get another steel ball to carry for the next phase.

The instructors would then quizz them on their buddy rating – who in order of preference they would want to work with again, and who they thought was no good.

It was a very revealing exercise, and if there was a borderline case as to whether a recruit passed or failed, the instructors would refer back to the buddy rating and make their final decision based on that finding.

Then followed the individual effort – a one-day hike. Recruits were dropped off at different points along the road, told where they were, given a map, told their RV point and the time they were to get there.

Just to make things interesting, the roneoed maps had all the roads and paths removed and each recruit had to map-read his way through the hills, not an easy task in the Matopos where many of the hills were only ten metres high and not depicted on maps anyway.

Finally, there was a speed march in which they had to cover 25 kilometres (15 miles) in five hours. So determined were recruits by this stage that the average time was three-and-a-half hours.

After four extremely hard months, with the constant worry hanging over them of not knowing whether they would shape up or not, the sheer delight of being told they were good enough for one of the world's most formidable units can only be imagined, and reduced many to tears.

After passing selection, they did their parachute course; then joined the troops and went to the bush to prove themselves operationally, each soldier on his way to becoming an elite, specially-chosen operator – a man among men.

Mick Reeves

Tales of courage and adventure abound in the annals of the world-wide Special Air Service, some are public knowledge, and others must for security reasons remain forever untold.

One of the most famous stories involves the daring mid-air rescue by Sergeant Mick Reeves of 22 SAS, who is mentioned in this history as he subsequently emigrated to Rhodesia and joined the ranks of the Rhodesian SAS.

In September, 1967, Mick, then 36, was spending the weekend at a civilian sport parachute centre in the English Midlands and was acting as jump master for a group of novices – a task that involved leaning out of the plane on the final approach to the drop zone and shouting corrections to the pilot.

Once over the correct spot, Mick instructed the pilot to cut the engine to reduce the slipstream, then told one of the novices to jump out of the plane.

The man obeyed the order, but instead of floating down under his canopy, he found himself spinning precariously at the end of his static line, the thin webbing strap attached to the aircraft at one end and a parachutist's pack at the other. The parachutist is suspended on this line until it pulls his chute out of his pack.

This time the static line had malfunctioned and the parachute was not going to mushroom.

It was impossible to pull the man back into the plane, and had he pulled his reserve parachute, it would have entangled in the plane's tail. And if the plane had landed with the man still attached to the static line, he would have been dragged to his death.

Mick got the pilot to pull away from the built-up urban area and return to the drop zone then instructed him to keep circling until the problem was sorted out.

He then left the aircraft and coolly climbed down the static line. The friction burned through his gloves but his grip never faltered.

Having reached the man, he wrapped his legs and an arm around him and signalled the plane that all was well. By now the plane had climbed, giving them more height and time. Then, having checked they were back over the drop zone, Mick cut through the static line with his knife.

As they fell, he grabbed the handle on the man's reserve parachute, and yanked it, then held on to the novice again. The reserve canopy opened, and Mick released his grip on the man, and hurtled away into a freefall.

The novice landed safely and Mick's own freefall rig opened just a few seconds before he hit the ground. He rounded off his remarkable performance with a classic textbook landing roll.

He was duly awarded the George Medal for his actions, and it was no wonder that by the time Mick reached Rhodesia, he was already something of a legend.

Reconnaissance Mission, South-east Mozambique, August, 1976.

Mac McIntosh had been tasked to command a reconnaissance patrol to establish the presence of a suspected terrorist camp near the Zamchiya business centre, twenty kilometres (12 miles) into south-east Mozambique.

The region itself was a frozen "no go" area to security forces other than the Selous Scouts who were operating there in their normal pseudo role, and apart from this SAS reconnaissance mission, no other troops were allowed into the area for fear of mistaking the Scouts for the enemy and eliminating them.

The Selous Scouts had twice attempted the same reconnaissance in their pseudo role and had been compromised on both occasions, and Mac McIntosh didn't really think that he and his small team could do any better, particularly in view of the vast numbers of locals in the area, who were very pro-ZANLA.

A glance at the map alone, showing the many African kraals throughout the region, was a good indication of the problems they might encounter.

To have a white four-man callsign, albeit blackened-up and wearing terrorist gear, skulking around that neck of the woods, would certainly not be without its risks.

Mac was a fitness fanatic and he chose three other superbly fit soldiers to go on the mission. There was Guy Peel, the toughest Dutchman in the unit and as tall as he was broad, Melvin Bellman, as fit and as tough a soldier as anyone could find, and Rog Hartman, who boasted the longest legs in the squadron.

The four men deployed into south-east Mozambique by chopper and were put down some distance away from the target area to avoid any suspicion and to give them a sporting chance of pulling off the mission.

It was obvious from the outset that the mission was going to be no walkover. There were so many African kraals in the area that in some places they were only 500 metres apart. And, even though it was quite late, there were groups of Africans milling around.

Carefully, the four SAS men eased their way into the area, skirting around the many clusters of huts, lying low at the sound of voices, the yapping of dogs, until they had eventually negotiated their way through dozens of kraals and were on the outskirts of the last little village.

It had taken them all night and by now the sun was coming up. They would have to find some cover soon before the villagers were up and about.

There was a distinct lack of cover but a slight drop on the other side of a footpath offered some hope. They based up there for the day but it was so open that they couldn't sit up for fear of being seen . . . and the four soldiers spent a very uncomfortable day virtually lying on their backs, hoping that no one would walk into them.

Miraculously, they managed to escape detection that first day . . . and that night, they continued their approach towards the area of the suspected terror base.

The following morning found them with not too much time to spare and at the base of a slight hill. There were scatterings of bush and a few trees on the hill, and so much foliage that they felt it might prove an ideal spot to hide them from the prying eyes of interested passers-by.

They could sit the day out there and venture out that night to do a close-in reconnaissance of the surrounding area to establish the presence of ZANLA.

They headed for the cover of a huge baobab tree about one-third of the way down the hill on the far slope . . . and were particularly careful no one saw them as they cautiously snaked their way through the dense undergrowth.

They based up near the baobab tree, and the commander positioned Guy Peel up the massive tree to keep a look-out for intruders. The broad baobab was so tall and so well branched that it was highly unlikely he would be seen in such a hiding place.

Mac McIntosh ventured out from their base to take some bearings and determine their exact location . . . then he, Melvin Bellman and Rog Hartman settled down to catch up on their sleep while the going was good, leaving Guy Peel – celebrating his 21st birthday that day – up his tree keeping watch.

All was quiet. There was just the faint rustle of grass. The sun beat down on the three SAS men dozing in the shade of the giant tree.

Suddenly, sentry Guy Peel glanced down from the tree to see three ZANLA men. They had silently made their way through the thick undergrowth and were now standing directly beneath his tree.

The incredulous soldier eased off his branch and stood pressing his body flat against the tree trunk, trying his best to keep a very low profile, hoping against hope that the three men would not look up and see him; would not walk around the other side of the giant tree where his three colleagues were sprawled out, off-guard and maybe even asleep.

The three ZANLA lingered at the base of the tree for a while, then turned and retraced their steps, leaving a relieved but nevertheless agitated soldier still safely hidden up his tree.

As soon as it was safe, he clambered down and shook Mac McIntosh awake.

Mac was just as amazed as the trooper that ZANLA were out looking for them. Had they been seen moving through the night? Had someone seen the commander when he went off on his own that morning? What had put the terrorists on to their spoor? A hundred possibilities flashed through his mind.

Off in the distance, the four SAS men could hear women shouting in the fields. Then men joined in. Mac didn't like their predicament one little bit. They would have to leave the hill and get going.

He had no sooner ordered his men to gather their kit together and get ready to move out, than an incredible volume of fire, the likes of which they had never experienced before, was directed towards their hill.

Thousands of smallarms rounds were being fired at them, and occasionally an RPG-7 rocket would hurtle through the air.

It didn't take many minutes for the four SAS men to realise that the forty-odd attackers out there didn't know their exact location . . . and they lay low holding their fire so as not to give away their position.

Signaller, Rog Hartman got out a message to the base in Chipinga and called the choppers to extricate them. But although the choppers had been earmarked specially for the mission, they had gone out on a fireforce call, and there was thus no immediate air support available for Mac and his men.

The enemy fire lasted twenty minutes then began to subside, although every so often there would be sporadic bursts from different areas.

Finally the firing ceased and the Rhodesians lay low.

Now the four SAS men could hear ZANLA shouting at each other as they worked their way towards them from the opposite side of the hill.

At midday, the radio crackled into new life and an SAS man back in base assured them he had personally been to sort out *The Blues*, and that if the pilots didn't recover the SAS immediately they had returned from their fireforce action, he would go and knock their blocks off.

Meanwhile, back on the hill, everything had become deathly quiet. There was no shooting and no shouting. Perhaps everyone had gone home? But the firing soon started up again and it was more intense that the first barrage.

This time, 100 enemy had encircled the hill and were running around saturating the area with smallarms fire, rockets and mortar bombs. They were still trying to draw the Rhodesians' fire, but the SAS very wisely lay low.

Shouts of "Stop your fire – we're sweeping through", were followed by the sound of running, then another bout of saturating fire.

Quickly, the SAS signaller got back on the radio with an urgent request for emergency air support. The choppers were still unavailable but the good news was that a Lynx was on its way.

The SAS had their haversacks and rifles ready, but the time was not quite right to make a break for it. There were far too many people out there searching for them at this stage; better lie low as long as they could.

The four men could hear enemy voices getting closer. Suddenly, two ZANLA men appeared on the scene, one from either side of the baobab tree . . . and one opened up on Mac McIntosh and Rog Hartman lying nearby.

Immediately, Melvin Bellman swung into action and peppered both enemy with a hail of rifle rounds. Simultaneously, Mac and Rog Hartman opened fire on the other ZANLA . . . and both wounded enemy took off into the thicket.

The SAS grabbed their kit and sprinted up the hill, back the same way they had come.

Sometimes the commander was in the lead, occasionally Rog Hartman with his long legs overtook him. The order was all very changeable as they ran for their lives.

Before long, they had left their hill behind and were heading for open ground – the only route available to get them back to white man's land and home.

As they ran across the path leading to the open patch, they were fairly bunched up, the total distance between the front man and the one at the back was a mere 15 metres.

The first two SAS men darted across the path. Then, incredibly, before the other two could do the same, a lone ZANLA ran straight between them, then continued on his way unsuspecting, not noticing the blackened-up Rhodesians for what they were. It was just like a scene from the movies.

The SAS were now beginning to get slightly more confident. Having successfully got clear of their hill, no one seemed to be chasing them. Maybe, ZANLA and their FRELIMO and militia friends thought they were still hiding up on the hill?

They felt really done in, and for the first time since beginning their cross-country run, they afforded themselves the luxury of a stop, resting in a dip near some loose rocks, to catch their breath, have a drink and make a plan.

They were bloody lucky to have got away safely from the hill, the SAS told each other; not, they conceded, that they didn't have problems ahead.

They looked around and studied the countryside, realising that if something went wrong and they were forced to lie low, they would still be totally exposed. For there was no cover anywhere ... just acres of old cut and burned out maizelands.

There were four African huts to their south. An old man and a young boy were standing nearby staring at the four soldiers. Then the old man raised his gnarled hand and gave them a friendly wave.

All too soon, it was time to get going again. They slung their packs on their backs, picked up the rest of the kit and set off, walking this time, sensing the pressure had eased.

But they had barely gone ten metres when all hell broke out around them again and machinegun rounds pounded the rocks.

It was a classic ambush – and it was top marks to ZANLA. They had lined up six RPD machineguns behind the little huts in the kraal not fifty metres from the SAS ... and as the four soldiers scrambled hell-for-leather up the ledge of loose rocks, ZANLA began to put down more than 1 000 rounds.

Rog Hartman was moving so fast and so low that he walked all over his hands, tearing his fingers apart and crushing his nails. But it was his hide, not his hands, that was concerning him right then.

Then Melvin Bellman fell. The rounds were bursting all around him and the rocks and soil were spraying in every direction. But he soon righted himself without so much as a scratch.

Then it was Mac McIntosh's turn. He stumbled and fell, and the dust from the ZANLA bullets covered his face.

Bellman shouted across and started to run towards him. But Mac waved him away and the soldier knew his commander was all right.

Incredibly, they all got over the ridge without so much as a nick or a hit through any of their packs or equipment.

But this was no time to congratulate themselves and they were off and running again, this time heading across the open undulating countryside in the direction of a river.

The four Rhodesians had soon reached the river, and, while running through a herd of grazing cattle, they came in for another burst of machinegun fire.

The enemy were getting clever, but not that clever. ZANLA were making sure not to get too close to the fleeing soldiers. Every now and then, the SAS would catch a glimpse of the forty-odd follow-up group chasing them with their mortars and rockets.

The Rhodesians would stop, turn around, send a few rounds towards ZANLA who would drop to earth – and the SAS would travel on a bit further.

Up and down the undulating countryside they ran . . . over open areas . . . through little kraals . . . around kraals.

There were civilians everywhere, and as soon as the soldiers raced by, they all shrieked: *"Vari-pano, Vari-pano* (They're here, they're here)".

A little picannin with his jacket pulled over his head was walking along in front of them just like a helpless little old man. But as the soldiers flew by him, he too screeched *"Vari-pano, vari-pano"* to the follow-up group.

Through the kraals and maizelands the four men raced and it was their sheer speed, adrenalin and a love of life that was keeping them ahead of the mortar bombs and machinegun fire.

As they ran, strange thoughts flitted across their minds.

What if one man stopped a round? Would they – could they – finish him off? It was certain that there was no chance of one man surviving on his own. On second thoughts, perhaps they would all decide to stand and fight alongside the injured man? But then, being up against such heavy odds, they knew damn well that even as a group, they would not escape with their lives.

Everything was on the opposition's side; nothing on theirs. When on earth would the Lynx arrive?

Somehow the enemy follow-up party had managed to put little groups along the route to cut them off. As Mac McIntosh and his men sped along, they couldn't quite understand how that had happened. They had been running practically non-stop, so it couldn't be people from the same group who had overtaken them and were trying to stop them. The main group must have some sort of communication with the cut-off groups waiting further ahead, they finally reasoned.

Now they had their old enemies chasing behind, mortaring them as they ran . . . groups running with them . . . civilians aiding and abetting – and there was much shouting and excitement.

Then ahead, a fate almost as dreaded as enemy bullets – a thicket entwined with painful buffalo beans. As they ploughed their way through them, sending fine, almost invisible, clouds of tiny hairs billowing into the air to settle on their skin and clothes with irritating, tearful consequences, they gritted their teeth and thought of the alternatives.

Then they managed to stop and catch their breath. Quickly Rog Hartman got out another signal requesting immediate hot extraction and air cover.

This time it was good news. The Hunters would be with them in one hour; the choppers 25 minutes later. If only they could hang on until then.

By now, the SAS reconnaissance team had had all they could take. The general feeling was that they should stop and fight it out. But the commander insisted they keep going. They could make it, Mac McIntosh urged them, and he knew he was right. There wasn't one weak member in the callsign to slow them down.

All too soon, the battle began again . . . and, as Rog Hartman's long legs carried him away, the antenna of his radio dragged in the dirt behind him.

There were a couple more incidents and then they reached the end of the maize-lands. Now they had arrived at a fairly wooded area. It was the first bit of decent cover they had seen since they set off twenty kilometres (12 miles) and almost three hours ago.

Here at last was the chance of getting into a good position, enabling them to draw the enemy into the killing ground. On the other hand, it was on a riverline. They could get themselves trapped.

They glanced at their watches. It was 14h50; still twenty minutes until the Lynx appeared overhead. They must only be about two kilometres from the border, not, they knew, that it would deter the enemy from pursuing them.

They decided to go into the bush after all; but Rog Hartman and Guy Peel stopped in their tracks before they could join the other two in the undergrowth. They saw a very well-armed group looking for spoor, watching to see if they had gone through the riverline into the bush ... and the two SAS men sank to earth.

They watched the enemy trackers link up with another group of 120 men running along the ridgeline only 100 metres away from them. There was a cut-off group on their right, another on the left and the back-up group closing in behind – and they were blocked in.

They were surrounded, outnumbered and the situation didn't look like improving just yet. ZANLA had already fired 5 000 rounds in exchange for their twenty. There were 180 heavily-armed men against four.

Every now and then they saw the box slowly closing in on them. ZANLA had got the SAS in a no-win position and it was clear the enemy were enjoying the cat-and-mouse game. It was a ploy adopted by both sides at one time or another when they felt in a position of confidence. This time, it was the Rhodesians who were the mice.

During the lull that followed, Mac decided against trying to get out of the spot they were in. Instead, they would try to hold the position as long as they could. But if ever there was a time for a hot extraction, this was it. The little group called for immediate air support. Now they just had to wait and hope for the best.

If ZANLA were to rush them, they would probably be able to account for several before being completely overrun by such superior numbers.

The ZANLA men closed in again ... teasing ... holding their fire ... prolonging the cat-and-mouse game.

Away to the north, well out of vision, a Lynx was already airborne with a request to Mac and his team to state their exact position.

The four men were unsure. They had entered the area at night and they had been running non-stop for hours. All they knew was they had been heading in the general direction of good ol' Rhodesia and home.

To add to their problems the radio was faulty and was only working intermittently. Eventually though, they gave a few general directions and very soon afterwards the familiar sight of a friendly Rhodesian war plane could be seen ten kilometres (six miles) to the north.

It was one hell of a comfort to see it, but there was still a long time to go until the choppers could swoop in for the rescue.

ZANLA's decision not to take on the vulnerable, cornered men the moment they had them boxed in was a big mistake. For now it meant that the callsign were in with a chance of escaping with their lives.

As the Lynx, armed with an MAG machinegun, came overhead, the enemy was forced to turn their collective attentions away from the SAS and on to the circling plane, which although keeping fairly high, was close enough to be in real danger if a

106

lucky shot hit it. The ZANLA men were certainly doing their best to shoot it from the sky and were even firing mortars at it.

The minutes ticked by. The SAS consulted their watches again. Would the choppers never come?

Then, at long last, they heard them.

Below, some of the ZANLA men began to get a bit bolder and were creeping forward, shooting into likely cover, still unable to see Mac and his party, but hoping to draw their fire nonetheless. The four Rhodesians had no intention of giving the game away now and continued to maintain their low profile.

As the two choppers came over the treeline from the west, the soldiers threw phosphorus grenades to indicate their positions. The choppers swooped in and hovered. The four men threw their kit in, then jumped aboard. Then up they climbed, plucked from the middle of a hornets' nest and snatched to safety.

Within a minute, the pilot had told them that they were back over the border.

"So guys," he said turning to them, "what's all the excitement about then?"

The four sweating men exchanged a look and said nothing. They were too tired and too relieved to tell of their close call.

It was only after they had been dropped off at Chipinga and they had time to reflect on the events of those past few days, that they had to agree that someone had very definitely been looking after them.

Three of them privately paid tribute to Mac McIntosh for what he had done for them. His reading of the situation, his drive and his ability to keep them going when they had had enough, had largely contributed to their successful escape and survival.

For when they totted up all the odds – ZANLA's great numbers, the very good ambushes they had set up, the help of the locals – the SAS knew that they hadn't really deserved to get out of their predicament.

It had demonstrated again just how difficult it was for blackened-up white soldiers to operate clandestinely in such a heavily-populated and hostile area.

They had more than conclusively achieved their aim. They could report a very strong enemy presence indeed in the area. The suspicion was now a certainty, vividly etched on four men's memories.

And it was certainly one hell of a way to celebrate your 21st birthday ...

Malawi Adventure, September 1976

By 1976, tensions were running high in the sub-continent. It was the era of the Angolan war, of revolution and of white mercenaries ... and the SAS men preparing to visit neighbouring black-ruled Malawi would have to be very careful.

Although Rhodesia and Malawi had no fight with each other, the Malawi Youth Wing was very active and could be expected to be alert to the possibility of trouble. The discovery of six "mercenaries" in their midst would be a prize indeed.

Malawi did not harbour anti-Rhodesian insurgents and it was one place that the SAS didn't normally go visiting. It was, however, geographically well situated to play a part in an operation against ZANLA lines of communication, and as such, offered the SAS a back-door route into Mozambique.

It had been learnt that ZANLA were moving weaponry to the Rhodesian border over a bridge in northern Mozambique, but because the bridge was out of helicopter reach, a much more elaborate manoeuvre was necessary to get the SAS saboteurs and their explosives to the target. Thus it was that six SAS men landed one of the most interesting missions that year.

Passing themselves off as tourists, they were to fly to the Malawian capital of Blantyre ... then travel down to the border with Mozambique in hired transport, where, after taking delivery of a consignment of explosives at a bush airstrip, they would nip across the unmarked boundary into northern Mozambique and march to the bridge.

The homework had been done and Major Brian Robinson and Captain *Big John* Murphy, the mission commander, had already spied out the land, examined the airstrip and walked the distance to the target. An aerial photographic reconnaissance of the bridge had been carried out and the explosives prepared from the interpretation.

The six operators had been selected both for their demolitions experience and for their foreign passports. *Big John* was American, the others, South African and British.

Even though businessmen and tourists travelled to and fro between the two countries, it was imperative that these particular tourists did not appear connected in any way with Rhodesia. It was essential, too, that their passports did not reveal they were involved with the military.

Any reference to having been in South Africa in the preceding months was carefully removed by the backroom boys of the Central Intelligence Organisation, who also issued them with doctored vaccination certificates and had stamped their passports with the latest immigration stamps.

Arriving uneventfully in Malawi, the SAS made their way to the rendezvous point near the Malawi-Mozambique border to await the arrival of their explosives.

As dusk approached at the little bush airstrip, three operators lay low in the bushes, ready to offload the special cargo the moment the plane touched down ... while at the opposite end of the airstrip, their hired Land-Rover stood parked with its bonnet up. Every so often, *Big John* Murphy gave it a kick to convince the locals it had broken down, hoping to distract them while the plane landed.

Brian Robinson was to bring in the explosives in the Rhodesian Prime Minister's official aircraft which had been freshly painted for the mission and was sporting a Malawian registration number.

The airstrip dipped sharply at one end, which luckily, was the end furthest away from a cluster of houses.

The plan was that the aircraft would land, turn around at the bottom, and as soon as it was out of sight, the explosives would be offloaded. The plane would taxi up the runway to give the impression it had landed in the wrong place.

In the event of anything going wrong, two of the operators were to run up the centre of the airfield, whereupon the plane would circle and fly home again without landing.

Precisely at the appointed time, the three SAS men waiting in the bushes heard the hum of a plane coming from the south.

As they glanced down the airstrip to check all was well, they saw to their horror two Africans sprinting down the runway. It was their signal that something was amiss; that the mission was off ... and it couldn't have happened at a worse time.

But fortunately good luck was with them. It wasn't yet dark and Brian Robinson was able to see that the men running along the airstrip were Africans and got the pilot to land just as planned.

In the dip at the bottom of the airstrip, the door of the plane swung open and Major Robinson enquired: "How's it going?" Then he stretched out his hand in true Rhodesian fashion to indicate he wanted to shake hands and wish them well. But there was no time for idle banter, even if he was the boss.

"I haven't got time for that now," said Iain Bowen, as the three operators snatched up the five heavy Bergens containing the explosives and staggered off to the safety of the bushes.

The door slammed shut, the plane turned and headed off down the runway. It rose into the evening and then was gone ... Soon, all fell silent again.

The sudden appearance of the plane had not aroused the slightest suspicion. It was merely some pilot who had landed in the wrong place, then, realising his mistake, had taken off again.

Besides, the locals were far too interested in the "broken down" Land-Rover. By now a large crowd had gathered and everyone was offering advice on how best to fix the troublesome vehicle.

Eventually, they were persuaded to leave and the three operators darted from the bushes, lugging their explosives with them. They piled into the vehicle and headed off for the drop-off point near the unmarked Malawi-Mozambique border.

Leaving Iain Bowen to drive back to Blantyre, the five-man bridge-blowing team crossed unseen into Mozambique and tramped off to the target. But unfortunately for the Rhodesians, that was where their luck ran out. The aerial photographic interpretation had been wrong and the SAS had insufficient explosives with them to demolish the bridge properly. They did, however, manage to crack the foundations, putting it out of commission for many months, slowing down ZANLA's arms supplies to Rhodesia and causing the enemy considerable inconvenience.

Iain Bowen was waiting for them back at the pick-up point with shaving gear and clean clothes, then the SAS split into two parties and went their separate ways, only meeting up again at Jan Smuts Airport, Johannesburg.

The SAS rounded off their mission with a few drinks in the airport bar; then it was back home to Rhodesia. It had been an interesting trip and something different. Stranger still, it had been the only time they were ever to use their passports to operate in a neighbouring country.

Peace Talks – The War Hots Up: October - December 1976

On the political front, the bitter war of words had begun again.

At a summit meeting in Pretoria, the American Secretary of State, Dr Henry Kissinger, made it abundantly clear to Ian Smith that he was in a no-win war; that Russia would increase its commitment to Smith's enemies and that the pressures on Rhodesia from the free world would continue to mount. And America would simply write off Rhodesia.

But there was, it seemed, a way out. Kissinger handed Smith a piece of paper which set out a five-point package deal suggesting Rhodesia agree to majority rule within two years ... agree to meet the black nationalists ... and that an interim government should consist of the Council of State, half black, half white, with the job of drawing up a majority rule constitution.

The Rhodesian premier, who had vowed there would be no majority rule in a thousand years, was unimpressed. They wanted him to sign his own suicide note, he commented flatly.

The heat of international pressure was on and the Rhodesian Cabinet had no option but to go along with the Kissinger proposals. South Africa would make sure the Rhodesians signed.

Kissinger, who hoped to pull off a settlement just before the American presidential election in November, realised that the key to breaking Ian Smith was South African premier John Vorster.

As far as Pretoria was concerned, the Smith regime, recognised by not a single country in the world and the cause of raised tensions in the region, had outlived its usefulness. Rhodesia had become an embarrassment to Pretoria's "outward policy" and an obstacle in the way of better relations with Black Africa and the West.

South Africa wanted a gradual, peaceful transition to a moderate pro-Western black ruled country north of the Limpopo. Kissinger's plan was that America would help Vorster set up a Kenyan-style government in an independent Rhodesia/Zimbabwe.

That South Africa – under seige herself and with an uprising in the black township of Soweto – was in turn under pressure from the international community, was obvious.

South Africa paid half of Rhodesia's defence budget, and to get the point across, the money, weapons and ammunition had suddenly dried up. The Rhodesians had been waiting months to hear if South Africa would support them for another year. Rhodesians were brave, but even they couldn't fight without ammunition.

Then South Africa turned her attention towards Rhodesia's main export and import artery which ran through South Africa. Soon, some Rh$125m (R72m, US$82m, £50m) worth of Rhodesian goods had piled up in South Africa. The border was closed during the Kissinger Summit and Rhodesia's precious oil supplies were down to an all-time low of 19,6 days. The situation was critical and leaders of business and industry urged Smith to act rapidly.

But Big Brother "down south" was going for the jugular and there were no options left.

Kissinger told Smith that the proposals were essentially British ones, with American backing. (The British, however, felt a settlement was impossible as long as Smith remained in office.) Kissinger would support the proposals as long as he (Kissinger) remained in power, but that if Jimmy Carter won the elections, there would be no settlement anyway.

In return for accepting the proposals, the British and American Governments assured Smith there would be an end to terrorism, lifting of sanctions and an injection of development capital. The Rhodesian premier had grave reservations that the enemy would oblige and end the war, and correctly predicted an increase in terrorist activity.

He insisted that the head of the Council of State and the Ministers of Defence and Law and Order be whites and Kissinger agreed to consult the front-line presidents on such points of detail.

The nationalists didn't like the Kissinger package either, but they too, under pressure from the frontline states, would go to the summit to be held in Geneva. They even formed an "alliance" called the Patriotic Front, but it was no more than a fragile coalition. It did, however, bring them together as a joint negotiating team, reducing the possibility of Smith, the British and Americans playing on divisions.

Whatever the outcome of the conference, the Kissinger shuttle had forced white Rhodesia to change course. The suicide note had marked the death knell of white-ruled Rhodesia, setting in motion a chain of events that would end almost 1 000 days later with the first one-man-one-vote elections.

The war, meanwhile, continued unabated ...

110

SAS Second-In-Command Mick Graham declared in the squadron diary that no one in the unit got over-excited about the Kissinger proposals, firstly because they were too busy; secondly because people changed their minds too often, and for most people, it was too mind-boggling anyway!

The white politicians and the black nationalists were to meet in Geneva and the Geneva Conference era marked an intensive phase for both security forces and enemy.

An unprecedented number of insurgents poured across the border during the last three months of the year ... and for their part, the security forces struck at external bases, disrupted infiltration routes and destroyed and captured tonnes of arms and ammunition.

Operation *Mardon* was the first major external during that phase and was planned to counter an imminent ZANLA infiltration threat in the north and eastern areas. It constituted a 72-hour pincer air-ground thrust, one from *Hurricane* in the Tete Province, the other from *Repulse* into Gaza, covering in all a 241 kilometre (150 mile) arc.

In Tete, the engineers cut the *cordon sanitaire* (landmine) fence and cleared a path into the province, and the SAS and RLI marched on to their first targets. Then some 83 vehicles crossed the border to carry troops to their next targets.

Horses belonging to the Grey Scouts carried the heavy 81 millimetre mortars across a river and through the breach, and it was only through the determination and skill of an SAS sergeant, who swam across the river with the horses, and made them leap off huge rocks into the swirling waters below, then guided them through the very small breach, that the animals made it at all.

Several camps were attacked, many enemy killed and the troops discovered so many arms caches that by the end of the first day, it had lost its novelty. Much of the weaponry was recovered and the remainder destroyed. The Rhodesians also captured FRELIMO's Portuguese paymaster and his one million escudoes, and "liberated" a precious tractor. Two Rhodesians – SAS Trooper Ed Lotringer and RLI Trooper Grahame Fanner – were fatally wounded and a Grey Scout lost a leg when he walked on an anti-personnel mine washed out of the mine cordon.

As the column pushed deeper into Tete Province, it became apparent that ZANLA had fled to Tete town, and the column commanders eventually decided to call it a day.

"The other point is, that having by now travelled nearly 100 kilometres (62 miles) inside Mozambique, the 'hot pursuit' ruse was starting to wear a little thin," commented the SAS Second-In-Command.

* * *

Within days, the SAS and RLI were back inside Mozambique attacking the Mavue terror base and killing 31 enemy. From now until the end of the year the security forces continued to hit ZANLA with good results ... and in December a combined SAS/RLI force attacked a camp at Rambanayi a few kilometres from the Rhodesian border which housed a platoon of Tanzanians, the first the Rhodesians had encountered.

The Tanzanians were holed up in a complex of underground bunkers, and while most of the twenty-strong platoon fled for their lives, the others chose to fight it out.

Winkling them out proved a time-consuming business. There were many sharp corners which were difficult to reach and many bunkers were covered by large logs and earth. Various methods were tried which were all unsuccessful and the attackers finally solved the problem by using the Viet Nam trick of pouring petrol through the weapon slits, then throwing in a match.

Ultimately, as a result of the lessons learned at Rambananyi, the army, with much SAS assistance, developed a bunker bomb which was designed to lift the lids straight off trenches.

By the end of the day, many Tanzanians, FRELIMO and ZANLA were killed and the Rhodesians lost RLI Corporal Butch Alexander in the attack. SAS Lieutenant Bruce Burrell and Trooper Enslin Van Staden were killed when they detonated a landmine on the walk out. The operation had been a success and the SAS had acquitted themselves well, but as two troopers, Steve Seymour and Boet Nel had been killed a few days earlier, the unit was somewhat stunned at losing four good men in such a short space of time.

By December, the Honde Valley on the eastern border had become a very hot area. There were continual infiltrations and ZANLA had carried out large-scale attacks against Ruda police station. Then just before Christmas, 27 African tea estate workers were rounded up, forced to lie on the ground and massacred in one of the bloodiest single incidents of the war.

Captured ZANLA revealed that insurgents were staging from Mavonde, a small base just ten kilometres (six miles) from Abervoyle Tea Estates. The operation that was mounted marked the beginning of the SAS's interest in house-fighting and was excellent training for the major operations that were to follow.

The buildings in Mavonde were in three rows and the assault team split into groups and moved into town, firing their RPG-7s, scuttling in through doors and windows, advancing efficiently and systematically from building to building, keeping pace with each other, and only advancing on a new target when the other teams were abreast of them.

Iain Bowen successfully blew up the nearby bridge and the various booby traps he left behind later scored hits, bringing the total of enemy killed on the mission to 44.

* * *

By now it was obvious that a negotiated settlement was as elusive as ever. The seven-week Geneva Conference, doomed even before it had begun, had ended inconclusively, never to be resumed.

Kissinger had conceded details to Smith, which according to the Frontline Presidents, who had the job of bringing the nationalists to heel, should have been points for negotiation. In any event, the nationalists – who would never lay down their arms while the whites were still in control of the security forces – hadn't even been consulted, and Kissinger had met only Joshua Nkomo.

The American had spent some seven minutes with Nkomo and he "spoke in short sentences in a dull, flat voice, like a businessman doing a quick deal," said Nkomo in his autobiography. "His ideas were of no interest to us."

Smith stuck to Kissinger's five points, arguing they were not negotiable . . . while the black nationalists considered them irrelevant. One described the conference as "a load of crap", and there were many in the opposition camp who would not have argued.

In a letter to *The Rhodesia Herald,* a reader suggested that as the enemy had sent a delegation to Geneva and as the conference had already passed the point of the ridiculous, it would surely not be remiss of the army to send a delegation from the SAS in hot pursuit.

SAS scribe Major Mick Graham commented that the unit would have loved to oblige; but it was a shame that nobody had come forward to sponsor such an operation.

"A few of your mates from Rhodesia to see you."

By now, South Africa had taken the heat off and promised more guns and oil. Kissinger had lost his job after the American elections brought Jimmy Carter to power. Mugabe and Nkomo had gone their separate ways – and the war continued much as everyone back in Rhodesia suspected it would anyway ...

The War Escalates

Harassing Programme

By 1977, the SAS were fully committed to the strangulation of Mozambique's Tete Province, and for the first few months they were constantly in and out of the region stirring up trouble and causing havoc.

The latter half of 1976 had been characterised by the unit being deployed on a very ad hoc basis, and according to Major Mick Graham, no one at Army Headquarters seemed to have any idea how to use special forces.

"They had no overall stategy or plan for external operations and hence the ad hoc deployments, and us bouncing from crisis to crisis."

As for the SAS, he reported, they undertook to put matters right "which in terms of military procedures is mind-boggling, but unless *we* did something, the unsatisfactory state of affairs would persist."

Attacking enemy base camps was clearly out. The nationalists had learned from experience how devastating they could be and now either deployed by vehicle from major towns, or remained in camps normally attached to FRELIMO complexes for short periods – where they knew they would not be touched.

Attacking major enemy camps was politically unacceptable to the Rhodesian hierarchy at that stage too.

It was therefore decided that the enemy's major vulnerability was on the routes from the main centres to the Rhodesian border.

If the SAS destroyed their vehicles, the enemy would have to walk, which would be a hindrance to them since only limited equipment could be portered.

Terrorists on vehicles made excellent targets as well. By ambushing and mining vehicles carrying enemy, the SAS could expect to get a high kill rate. Indeed, it might even be possible to get more kills than large-scale attacks as the target was concentrated. A four-man group, armed with landmines, claymores and automatic weapons could successfully take on such a target. By dividing into such groups, the SAS could cover a vast area and several of the routes concurrently.

Having decided that this was the correct strategy and tactics for the SAS, the next problem was to discover what routes the enemy were using.

Using various forms of entry, the SAS were able to map all known and likely terrorist routes leading in and out of the *Hurricane* and *Thrasher* areas.

In strict terms of the SAS role, they should do the locating and then advise army or brigade headquarters of their findings and leave them to place troops to do the offensive work. But the Rhodesian Army force levels were such that this could not happen ... and it fell on SAS's shoulders to take the offensive action.

"Not that that was such bad news," commented the Squadron 2IC. "In fact, I firmly believe we are the only unit that can go offensive externally in small groups, make hay *and* get away with it."

It was a very aggressive phase . . . anything that moved – ZANLA, FRELIMO or donkey – was eliminated.

The SAS was to strike and strike again at the main infiltration routes from the Tete Province into Rhodesia.

Tete town itself was the hub with a major ZANLA base being sited there. From Tete, ZANLA travelled in a variety of routes to get to the border. The routes were ZANLA's lifeline and the SAS were determined to do all they could to destroy any ZANLA wanting to make use of them.

Small SAS teams were deployed by freefall and others by static line and on one occasion, a small group even infiltrated by horseback.

The year got off to an excellent start with a very successful ambush led by Andy Chait, who did sterling work and accounted for most of the dead himself.

Meanwhile, Sergeant Bruce Fraser and his small team were also having their fair share of success on a stretch of the road north of Mkumbura.

Within 24 hours of dropping in, Bruce's task was complete and he came up on the radio asking for uplift back home. Their hidden landmine had already destroyed a Unimog vehicle heavily laden with ZANLA supplies, nine ZANLA and two FRELIMO. All the survivors of the initial mine blast were blown off the vehicle on to the side of the road where the SAS were waiting for them. The startled enemy ran straight into the claymores and were promptly killed.

Not to be outdone, American Corporal Dick Biederman and his callsign were walking into the bush to take up their ambush positions when a convoy could be heard bumping along towards them.

It was an opportunity too good to miss and they successfully accounted for several vehicles and many enemy. Amazingly, after the first vehicle was attacked, the drivers of the remaining vehicles insisted on driving straight through the ambush.

As the SAS were setting light to one vehicle, one "body" sat up and said: "I am ZANLA, do not kill me." As the SAS scribe recorded at the time: "We saw no reason to give him any preferential treatment."

The "B" Troop boys, meanwhile, were sitting it out on a main road to establish if it was being used as an infiltration route . . . and to take on any likely target.

After a couple of days, the commander felt the vehicles were moving a bit too fast for an effective ambush . . . and when a truck with a broken-down Land-Rover on the back came along, he and a couple of his men sauntered out on to the road and commandeered it.

The Land-Rover was dumped on the side of the road and a suitcase left behind in the front seat was booby-trapped. Aerial reconnaissance later revealed the broken-down Land-Rover had become a blown-apart Land-Rover . . . and that the unfortunate soul who had lifted the booby-trapped suitcase had not lived to tell the tale.

The SAS also demolished a store and a grinding mill, putting paid to ZANLA's last-minute resupply facility on their infiltration route.

The strain of SAS's harassing tactics were beginning to tell and FRELIMO were forced to push more armed military into the region to counter the increasing threat from the trouble-makers across the border.

Meanwhile, "A" Troop Commander, Captain Bob McKenna, had been looking at different ways of getting into Tete undetected – and remaining so.

Whenever a Dakota took men into Mozambique, there was always a chance of their being seen by the enemy despite diversionary tactics adopted by the pilots. Walking around the bush playing cat-and-mouse games with ZANLA and FRELIMO also had severe limitations.

What they wanted was a foolproof way of outfoxing the enemy. They needed to infiltrate undetected, strike and melt into the night... then pop up again elsewhere to mount another attack, with the enemy not knowing where they came from or went to – or where they were likely to hit next.

Ideally, what they needed was somewhere safe to operate from. And some sort of transport to get them from one target to the next.

Vehicles were obviously out. They could not run around Mozambique in them for long and still remain undetected.

Then Bob turned his attentions to the giant Lake Cabora Bassa, one of the biggest man-made lakes in the world, straddling north-west Tete Province and formed a few years earlier by damming the Zambezi at the Cabora Bassa Gorge.

When Bob studied his map, he knew the lake offered endless possibilities. To the south of the lake and a few nights' march inland were Daque, Mague and Chinhanda Crossroads – the very infiltration routes the SAS wanted to hit and there were FRELIMO targets to the north, too.

The lake was about 250 kilometres (155 miles) long and as much as fifty kilometres (31 miles) wide in places depending on the rains. It was a vast area and there could be enormous problems. But surely it made sense to include the lake in the overall strategy, use it as a firm base and put an SAS team on it?

They could base up on shore or on one of the rocky islands during the day, attack the enemy on their own territory at night, using ZANLA's own hit-and-run tactics of landmining and ambushing. Then, they could return to the sanctuary of the giant lake and canoe on to their next hiding place.

The enemy would never dream of looking for them on the lake, not when the Rhodesians could get to the target areas by other, far simpler means.

The lake offered them both mobility and refuge and it was agreed at SAS head-quarters that Bob McKenna should lead an operation on the lake.

The idea was that Bob and his team of *Cockleshell Heroes* were to disrupt road traffic on the Tete-Mague-Mkumbura road and harass ZANLA and their FRELIMO supporters whenever they could find them.

All told, 12 "A" Troop men were selected to experience the novelty of the very first lake op on Cabora Bassa. Every man was thrilled at having been chosen; delighted at the prospect of operating from the lake and of pioneering a new concept. There was a bit of apprehension, too, as there always was about the unknown.

But perhaps the most excited man of all was territorial trooper Dave Arkwright. For years, Dave had dreamed of gaining a first-hand knowledge of the massive lake. As a university student, he had intended doing a thesis on Cabora Bassa for his town planning degree. It would have meant walking right around the lake, a mammoth undertaking indeed.

But the war had interfered with his plans. A white man – and a Rhodesian at that – strolling around Cabora Bassa in the heart of enemy country would have been most unwelcome, not to mention a wonderful target or a propaganda prize. Dave was forced to forget his dream of seeing the lake and had to choose another project.

But now, when he had given up all thoughts of ever seeing the lake, he had suddenly been given the chance to see much more of it than he had ever thought possible. He would not have to walk either. It remained to be seen if six weeks of paddling would cure his fascination!

Rehearsals as always, were the time-tested secret of success, and the canoes from which they were to live and operate for six weeks were taken out to Lake McIllwaine, near Salisbury, to iron out possible problems.

The 12 men soon found that their personal kit would have to be minimal. With two people to a canoe, there was little room left once they squeezed themselves in with their weapons and equipment, much of which had to be made waterproof to prevent it becoming useless.

Resupplies – food, ammunition, canoe spares, equipment – were to be parachuted in to them by Dakota. They also planned to boost their ammunition supplies by capturing enemy equipment.

The clandestine canoeists were to be in daily contact with the SAS HQ back at Salisbury and special codes had to be worked out for every single canoe part to avoid lengthy messages when ordering spares.

Eventually, Captain McKenna and his team were ready and on January 17 they set off for the long drive to the north-eastern border. They were going to infiltrate to the lake by way of the Musengezi River near the Musengezi Mission in Rhodesia. It was the most devious, the most surreptitious access they could have chosen. It would take them a full day to reach their starting point, but far better that than being choppered in, risking being seen before they could start operations.

They broke their journey with a stop-over at the Centenary forces canteen, then it was on to the Musengezi, a long laborious journey, much of it spent on a dirt road, always a hazardous business with its attendant risks of landmines.

A final six kilometre cross-country ride through the bush brought them to a lonely spot at the river's edge and to the start of their operation.

As they climbed from their truck they were hot, dusty and more than a little tired and stiff. Then they assembled their canoes and packed in their equipment. For they were to be on their way immediately and planned to paddle down the Musengezi River and be on Cabora Bassa by the early hours of the following day.

They donned their regalia of war – their green terrorist-type uniforms – some pulling on leather gloves to protect their hands from the rigours ahead.

They then checked out their weapons, the usual assortment of AKs, FNs, RPDs and an RPG-7 rocket launcher. Every man carried a pistol in a shoulder holster, so that should his canoe capsize and he become separated from the main weapons, he would still be armed.

It was 18h00 and still light when they stepped into their heavily-laden canoes.

The red half-ball of the sinking sun filtered through the bush at the rivers' edge and danced on the water as they pushed off for terrorist country. The peaceful beauty of a Rhodesian sunset was unmatched anywhere . . . and the war seemed a very long way from such a tranquil scene.

Along the muddy banks of the narrow river were the unmistakable shapes of crocodiles sleeping in the dying heat of the day. The canoeists sitting very low in the water were taking no chances and kept a very cautious eye on the crocs as they drifted and gently paddled by in single file.

The crocs did not seem to hear the silent approach. Softly, the paddles brushed the water as the flotilla continued on its way. Suddenly, first one, then another croc woke up, caught sight of the intruders and dashed headlong into the river.

But they harboured no evil intentions. They had merely been startled by the canoeists' sudden appearance and only wanted to get into the comparative safety of the muddy waters to hide from the strange new creatures in their territory.

There were encounters too with leaping fish which hit them on the head and landed on their laps. Then, disaster.

As they rounded a bend, they were whipped away, spinning and crashing into a set of rapids, hitting trees, then sinking. Canoe structures were broken, kit and equipment were soaked. There was to be no going on that night, if indeed at all.

They settled down for the night, and next morning set to in earnest patching and repairing canoe frames and drying out clothes and equipment.

Fortunately nothing important had been lost and the radios were all working with Salisbury-strength five, the maximum strength.

The weather was hot enough to dry out every item and at 18h00 on the second night of the op they set off again, but their journey was impeded by a lone hippo, snorting and snuffling to himself as he stood guard over his domain, determined not to let them through a particularly narrow stretch of the river.

The paddlers had only one option if they wanted to get on to the lake. They had to land and start the laborious time-consuming task of portering their canoes and equipment around the resolute beast – it was an enormous task, and all for a hippo.

Later, they witnessed a fascinating phenomenon when thousands of silver fish came advancing towards them, leaping and battling their way upstream, passing them in the night like a huge silver wave. Then they were gone and all was silent again
. . .

At last, they paddled through the mouth of the Musengezi to the very edge of Lake Cabora Bassa.

Immediately there were problems with large patches of reeds, and canoes getting lost and it became necessary to follow the main course of the river until 22h00 when they were able to turn and travel in the direction they wanted to go.

The wind was now against them and the going was hard. A lion was making a terrible racket but it was far enough away not to worry them. They bumped along, negotiating the clumps of dead reeds, careful not to make any unnecessary noise.

The last hour of their journey was spent paddling through a couple of kilometres of partially submerged mopani forest as they looked for land. By now everyone was tired and stiff.

At 03h00 they reached land at last. Or at least mud. But it had been a long night and they were glad to be even on that muddy, smelly piece of land, surrounded by its evil-looking water.

* * *

Next day, they put up bivvies for shade from the blistering sun as there was no natural shade anywhere near their base. All around was mud and desolation. Hundreds of trees reached forlornly out of the water near the shores, a legacy from the pre-lake days. There was no way of describing the atrocious smell of the once magnificent mopani forest now drowned and putrifying.

The sunset over the peaceful lake was incredible. And the stark surroundings and mountains looking as if they had been chiselled from a giant slab of marble, gave the canoeists the uncanny feeling of having been suddenly transported back to the Stone Age where time stood still.

Captain McKenna established radio communication with SAS Intelligence Officer Scotty McCormack flying somewhere over Tete Province. It was reassuring to think that someone was thinking of them, Bob mused. They were very conscious of being a long way from home and help, very much on their own, and if anything untoward were to happen, there would be no immediate back-up, no prompt casualty evacuation.

Their first resupply was due a few nights later . . . and they called the Dakota pilot up ten minutes before his drop time. Five minutes later they spoke to him again.

He was flying with his navigational lights off and they talked him on to them by the sound of his engines. Above, the pilot looked for the twinkle of their strobe lights flashing down below in the darkness. Then the SAS saw the silhouette of the resupply plane against the backdrop of stars.

"Left . . . left . . . green light on . . . NOW," Bob McKenna instructed . . . and the parachute with its box of supplies fell into the black night from 800 feet.

The Dakota turned and set course for home, leaving the dozen men to their own devices on the dark, desolate lake below.

It had been a good drop and their resupply had landed just twenty metres away from them, although it took them all of 45 minutes to scramble over the rocks and obstacles to retrieve it.

The kitchen staff at SAS HQ had done them proud. There were freshly cooked chickens still warm in tin foil, oranges, bread rolls and milk. It made a pleasant change from their usual tins of sausages, baked beans, nuts and boiled sweets. They felt very privileged. Sometimes it paid being in special forces . . .

The main purpose of the drop however, had been to enable them to establish an ammunition dump with additional landmines and rockets from Salisbury. But someone forgot to send the ammunition and Bob had to make a slight change of plan. They forgot the cigarettes, too, so the smokers would have to go easy there.

Their feast over, they buried the parachute and its harness together with some batteries, biscuits and a bottle of rum. They would return and recover them later.

* * *

The operation had been underway a week and a four-man patrol led by Colour Sergeant Karl Lutz now prepared to venture out to get on with the business of fighting the war.

The four operators exchanged their sandals for walking boots and were dropped on the mainland at 17h15. They were to trek inland to the Mague-Caponda road to leave a surprise on the ZANLA infiltration route snaking its way through the bush to Rhodesia.

Back on the lake their friends waited for their return. It was as hot as hell on their little island – 37°C (100°F), an unbearable situation made worse by the lack of natural shade.

Pete Cole's log read: "We have allowed the guys to sit in the lake to keep cool. But the lake water is also hot; so hot in fact that the captain cooked his instant rice by leaving it in the water. He said it was okay. It must have been his day, as for the first time since we started out, the tube of milk he used for his tea was not off."

Morale was good although the smokes were running low. There was still enough food for another week but as someone had forgotten to send the gas cylinders in the resupply, there was not enough fuel to cook it with and the use of wood fires was ruled out because of the giveaway smoke.

Towards dark the following day, the men on the lake saw a green flare shoot into the night over on the mainland. It was Karl Lutz and company, back from their landmining foray, unable to attract the attention of the rest of the paddlers with their out-of-order radio.

Their colleagues hastened to recover them and learned that they had been forced to return barefoot to avoid leaving boot spoor on the dirt roads. The commander decided to give them a few hours to rest their sore and blistered feet and catch up on their sleep, but at 03h00 it was back in their canoes to spend a very long time crashing and manoeuvring around the mopani forest.

They were still able to cover ten kilometres before sunrise, stopping in the midst of a swamp on another muddy smelly island just two feet above the waterline. The trees were draped with moss and weed and it was all rather eerie. It could easily have doubled for the Florida Everglades, they agreed.

At 09h15, a loud explosion rolled across the Mozambican countryside. It could only be Karl Lutz's landmine. "First blood to us," the commander logged. It was nice to know the op had started in earnest. Intercepts later reported that the 2IC of Mkumbura FRELIMO garrison had been killed in the blast.

"We are trying to read books but it's much too hot even for that," Pete Cole logged. "I went and sat in the water for a while, but it's so warm and dirty, it's not much help. I was glad when it started to get dark and we could be moving. I also buried the remains of my gloves today. They were completely worn out but I think my hands are hard enough not to need them any more."

Within a few days, ten of the *Cockleshell Heroes* had left the lake on another mission. Leaving sentries to guard the camouflage canoes, they set off to the road half way between Mague and Daque, which even by Mozambican standards was in poor condition. There was very little vehicle and no pedestrian spoor.

Bob McKenna, Pete Cole and Karl Lutz who carried out a reconnaissance of the road agreed to move further east to find a good ambush site. Having found one, they showed each man where he was to be positioned during the ambush.

Then, when everyone was satisfied where he had to go, they moved back into the bush where there was more cover and more natural shade and where they could hide until a target appeared.

With weapons ready and two men on stag at a time, they remained in their position among the bushes for nine hours. Finally, their wait was over. The sound of a vehicle could be heard approaching.

Immediately they leapt to their feet, eager to do battle at last, snatching up their weapons and racing to their pre-arranged positions 14 metres from the road.

A new Land-Rover was approaching. It seemed loaded down and because of the state of the road was not travelling fast.

In the bushes the ten blackened-up men waited expectantly, every index finger curled around a trigger.

The Land-Rover bumped along.

Bob McKenna and Pete Cole were to give the signal by opening fire. Their FN rifles were fitted with Trilux scopes, making their targets look that much closer. They could not miss at that range and as the truck drew level, Bob picked off the driver and Pete shot the first passenger.

The others joined in immediately. There was a roar from the SAS weapons . . . and the Land-Rover hurtled off the road and crashed headlong into the bushes with bodies being flung off the back as the rounds slammed into them.

The ambushers moved forward, cautiously covering each other and checked out the occupants of the vehicle. All were dead or dying.

There had been ten altogether – three in the cab, seven in the back. Two were completely rigged out in FRELIMO uniform; two sported FRELIMO trousers and boots with civilian shirts and the remainder were dressed in an assortment of clothing.

There was very little in the way of documents although later examination of the paperwork revealed one man was ZANLA.

The small quantity of smallarms ammunition, FRELIMO clothing, cigarettes and stores all pointed to it having been a supply vehicle. At last the SAS were able to replenish their own meagre supplies.

They searched the bodies, reloaded their RPD belts from the ammunition in the Land-Rover, while a couple of men watched the road for any reaction.

The commander and his assistant meanwhile prepared to burn the vehicle. But destroying a vehicle is not the easy job it is always made out to be in the movies. And it is much harder with diesel fuel.

They had tried a variety of methods before, so knew the shortcuts. Soon the vehicle was prepared for destruction.

"EVERYONE READY?" the commander yelled at last.

"Okay ... Light up!" he ordered.

The Land-Rover was soon blazing away. The bodies had been left either in the vehicle or where they fell.

The ambush party was moving fast, leaving a trail of footprints in the dirt track. Pete Cole was tasked to booby-trap the spoor.

While the others took a breather, he took two camouflaged tins and pegged them down, one on either side of their spoor. There was a grenade in each tin and a tripwire attached to both grenades stretching across the path of their spoor.

The pins were removed from the grenades, with the levers being held down by the tins. The idea was that when someone walked into the tripwire it pulled the grenades out of the tins, releasing the levers – and bang!

It was not the most sophisticated method, but it was a simple and effective means of discouraging the enemy from following up. As Bob was to comment in his log: "It's easy being a terrorist."

They walked until just after dark, then they lay up until first light, keeping a guard as always. Then it was back to the canoes to join the two who had had to stay awake throughout the ambush party's absence to keep radio contact with them and Salisbury.

They spent the rest of the day cleaning their weapons and kit, reloading magazines and resting. They put a sentry in position to watch their spoor, in case someone came along, but it remained quiet. No one came to investigate – no one suspected them of operating from the lake.

Again they set off, first paddling three or so kilometres through the treetops that afternoon, then as it got dark out on to the open lake and into a slight head wind.

They had spent almost two weeks on the lake and were to cross to the northern side to stir up things there for a change and draw attention from their spot of action on the southern shore.

After the desolation, shallow stretches and foul water of the southern side, they were delighted to find the northern bank grassy, the water clear and altogether much more pleasant.

The area had been hilly before the lake was formed and they were able to make their base 100 metres above the waterline with good natural shade and cover.

Now they planned to attack a small FRELIMO base next to Nhende aldeamento village, and, as they were due to be resupplied with ammunition, landmines and rockets the following night, they could afford to expend a fair amount of ammunition on the attack.

Bob gave his orders and all twelve men set off at 17h30. They moved through the thick thorny bush towards a dirt road and Karl Lutz had the unenviable task of walking in front, getting his hands, arms and clothes torn as he led the way. Once they got on to the dirt road that ran from the lake to the barracks town, the going was easy.

Trooper Dale O'Mulligan had a landmine and Pete Cole an entrenching tool and on the commander's order, laid the mine in a puddle in the road. They were soon on their way again and arrived at the bottom of an airstrip on the outskirts of the FRELIMO camp. It was now 21h00.

There was a line of buildings that looked very much like an army barracks running down the side of the airstrip and they could see a radio mast near the largest brick building. There were plenty of lights on and they could hear the unmistakable throb of a generator.

Bob McKenna, Pete Cole and Karl Lutz moved forward on to the airstrip for a closer inspection of the buildings, and just then, the generator stopped and most of the lights went out.

They got to within 100 metres of the barracks and studied the area with their nightscopes and binoculars. Fifteen minutes later they had made their appreciation and returned to the others.

They were to split into three groups of four and it was 22h00 when the little groups advanced towards their various firing positions eighty metres from the barracks.

Inside a radio was playing.

Fifteen minutes later, Bob initiated the attack. Sniper-trained Dale O'Mulligan was, as always, quicker off the mark than everyone else and his rocket smashed into the building. Then everyone joined in, putting down a fierce weight of fire.

Rockets slammed into the buildings, smallarms fire was aimed into the windows and vehicles, and rifle grenades were fired over the buildings into the courtyards and parade square beyond.

But there was no return fire. The radio had stopped playing. But no one ventured out from the nearby Aldeamento village. Not even a dog barked.

When all the rifle grenades had been expended, the three group commanders heaved white phosphorus grenades at the main barracks. Then, having caused enough commotion for one night, they withdrew behind the smokescreen.

They had to be on their way before FRELIMO rounded up their men and gave chase, and they still had an eight kilometre (5 mile) walk to where they had hidden their canoes.

Their journey was to take them along the shoreline and it meant clambering over rocks and fallen trees, which proved extremely hard going.

As they struggled over the boulders, shots rang out from the direction of the barracks . . . the only apparent reaction from the enemy. It was pitch black and the terrain was becoming more and more appalling. In the end Bob, not wanting to risk a broken leg or ankle, was forced to call a halt.

They waited until it got light enough to continue their struggle, and at 04h40 they reached their canoes to find they had only been a couple of kilometres away from them after all.

It had been one of the worst walks they had experienced and they would not be trying the shoreline trick again.

Daybreak found them basing up on yet another little island. It rained practically all day, but nothing could dampen their spirits once they heard the landmine that they had buried in the puddle go off. As they watched the smoke and dust billow into the air, they wondered what and who had hit it.

The weather had cleared long before the resupply arrived that night. They never got to meet the pilots who flew these particular sorties, but they were grateful for their skills.

The Dak dropped four boxes that night and one landed just ten paces from Bob's bivvy. The food, ammunition, mines, rockets, canoe spares and batteries would keep them in business for a while longer.

They awoke to a sunny morning and spent the day drying kit, sorting out the resupply, distributing rations, equipment and ammunition, and patching canoes. As usual, they were out on the lake again that night . . . and the following night they experienced one of the worst storms of the trip.

They tried rafting-up in a small group of trees but the waves were far too big and began throwing them dangerously close to the trees. The storm showed no sign of abating.

"Let's make a dash along the shoreline," Bob yelled above the roar of the elements, as he tried to make himself heard.

It was still very hard going and they were taking in water from some of the larger waves. They had travelled about one kilometre when they found a sheltered spot to beach and to wait out the storm.

The guard was briefed to watch for a change in the weather as they intended moving on again when the weather calmed. But 03h00 came and went and still the lake was far too rough to venture on. Would it never calm, they wondered? But the lake gave back no answer. The weather was certainly controlling this op.

Next day, Pete Cole was briefed he was to lead a six-man mining party to the ZANLA infiltration route at Chinhanda Crossroads south of the lake. They spent most of the day preparing their equipment and landmines . . . and late that afternoon, changed into their walking boots, blackened-up, and were ferried back to the southern shore.

They walked for six hours and at times had to struggle through extremely thick thorn bush. This time Corporal Dave Berry was leading the way and did a great job. His hands were torn and bleeding. He had cuts and scratches everywhere and his clothing was ripped.

They allowed themselves the luxury of a break, then they were soon on their way again . . . and nine hours after beginning their journey, they eased their packs from their aching backs and settled down in the bush. It began to rain almost immediately and as water was now short, they stretched bivvies between the trees to catch some rainwater and soon had enough to brew some tea.

They stayed there for the 12 hours of daylight then continued after dark, moving through the thick bush using elephant trails which ran roughly in the direction they wanted to go. Three-and-a-half hours later they reached a road near Chinhanda Crossroads . . . the ZANLA infiltration route.

It was a dirt road with plenty of vehicle spoor. The fresh boot patterns told that a FRELIMO patrol had recently walked towards the crossroads, then returned. But the coast was clear, and they set to work immediately.

The six men had their mine-laying drill off pat. They selected a place to lay the mine . . . put a bivvy on the road to avoid leaving spoor. With early-warning sentries posted on both sides of the roads, the others prepared the mine . . . began digging . . .

collected topsoil putting the remainder into a bag ... the anti-lift device went into the hole followed by the landmine. All except one man moved away ... he armed the mine, filled in the hole with soil, packing it down well, hiding surplus soil well clear of the road.

Then they camouflaged the spot to look like the surrounding area by taking a mugful of water from a waterbottle and flicking the water hard on the topsoil to give the impression that large raindrops had fallen recently, which had in fact happened. Thus the area easily blended in with its surroundings.

The road was wet and sandy and it took only thirty minutes to complete the job. The commander was satisfied the mine was well-camouflaged, confident that patrols would not find their mine; equally confident that a ZANLA or FRELIMO vehicle would, as those were the only vehicles in the area.

They checked the area, called in the early-warnings; then it was back to the road crossed earlier to plant another mine.

Then they returned to the lake, bypassing a native kraal where the dogs barked as always. But the SAS saw no one and were soon on their way back to the island base and relaxing with tea and a well-deserved rest after debriefing ...

* * *

It was now three weeks since they left Rhodesia. They were almost at the eastern end of the lake and Bob told his team they would be starting west.

The next task was to be a vehicle ambush some 15 kilometres (nine miles) east of Daque, another FRELIMO garrison town on the southern shore. Leaving two sentries behind to guard the canoes, the others started another long difficult approach march.

Even at night the weather was as hot as hell and they had to add salt to their water to prevent heat fatigue. The availability of water, would in fact determine how long the ambush position could be manned.

The group reached the target area, found a suitable ambush site and moved back from the road slightly to hide up in the bush.

A small group went forward and laid a landmine to assist the ambush and that job was completed just before sunrise.

Cautiously, Pete Cole and a sentry checked out the camouflaging of the landmine. A little pat here ... pick up a bit of dark soil from the lighter there ... flick up a bit of grass that had been trodden on ... it all looked perfectly natural, so good in fact that he had to place a stick on the opposite side of the road to indicate exactly where the mine was.

The mine-layers moved back to join the others and settled down to wait. It was not a pleasant wait. It was extremely hot, there was little water and swarms of mopani flies gathered, tiny black flies the size of a matchhead; they drove men crazy in the bush in their search for moisture.

And this day, the mopanis came in droves ... settling and walking in the men's hair, ears, eyes and mouths and up their noses. And the more that were killed, the more arrived, attracted no doubt by the strange smell the flies gave off when swatted.

The flies were indeed a scourge of the bush and many men wore headnets for protection. But these could only be worn while waiting for a target, as they tended to restrict vision. Soldiers certainly couldn't risk wearing them while walking through the bush.

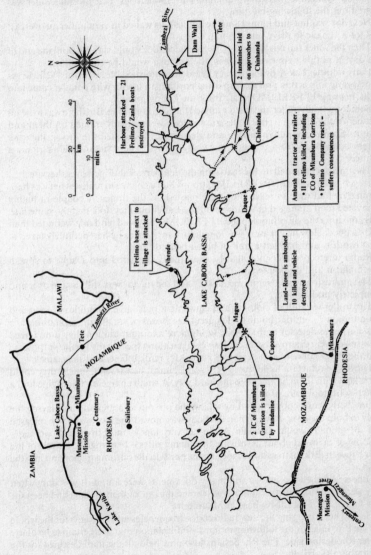

Harbour attacked — 21 Frelimo/Zanla boats destroyed

Dam Wall

Zambezi River

Tete

2 landmines laid on approaches to Chinhanda

Chinhanda

Ambush on tractor and trailer.
• 11 Frelimo killed, including CO of Mkumbura Garrison
• Frelimo Company reacts = suffers consequences

Daque

Frelimo base next to village is attacked

Nhende

LAKE CABORA BASSA

Land-Rover is ambushed. 10 killed and vehicle destroyed

Mague

Caponda

Mkumbura

RHODESIA

MOZAMBIQUE

2 IC of Mkumbura Garrison is killed by landmine

MALAWI

Zambezi River

Tete

MOZAMBIQUE

Mkumbura

Centenary

Salisbury

RHODESIA

Musengezi Mission

Lake Cabora Bassa

ZAMBIA

Lake Kariba

Centenary

Musengezi Mission

Musengezi River

Operation *Cockleshell Heroes*: The mighty Cabora Bassa, home of the SAS's *Cockleshell Heroes*

125

The only traffic on the road all day was an African on a bicycle. That night, the commander sent out a water party, who found a puddle but they were only able to scoop out enough to fill two two-quart (4,5 litre) waterbags. This precious water was shared out the following morning.

Next day was hot and humid and the ambushers waited in vain under an overcast sky for a vehicle to drive into the trap.

Then the water ran out altogether. Bob decided they would stay put until the end of the day; if nothing appeared by then, the ambush would be called off.

Forty minutes before deadline, they heard the unmistakable sound of a vehicle. As they sprang into action and took up firing positions, a tractor with a trailer came into sight, bearing 12 FRELIMO straight for the killing ground.

Somehow, both trailer and tractor missed the SAS landmine. But there was to be no escape for the enemy. Ten Rhodesian weapons were already trained on them and within seconds, rounds from Bob and Pete's rifles had killed the driver; then the others opened up from a range of twenty metres. Their victims didn't stand a chance.

The tractor continued up the road with the dead driver slumped over the wheel ... and even before most of the FRELIMO troops had a chance to realise what was happening, or had time to react, they were blasted off the trailer. A couple of highly motivated men managed to scramble off the trailer but they, too, met the same fate.

By the time the shooting stopped, 11 FRELIMO lay dead, and one wounded man had escaped. How he got away was to remain a mystery as he had definitely taken at least two hits and had left a trail of blood behind him.

Radio intercepts later indicated he had finally staggered into Daque to spread much alarm and despondency.

The ambush was all over in seconds .... and the tractor was still ticking over and completely undamaged.

The trailer was full of clothing and equipment plus large quantities of food and ammunition ... mortar bombs, stick grenades, boxes of smallarms ammunition, a Russian mine detector and 11 AKs. Equipment and ammunition they didn't need themselves were destroyed with explosives taken along specifically for the purpose ... and the RPD gunners and personnel with AKs refilled belts and magazines.

They were reluctant to destroy a very good, almost new tractor, but, as they could not take it with them, it had to go the hard way. A small charge on the engine and a match soon took care of it.

One body was booby-trapped by taking the pin out of a grenade and laying the body to hold the lever down. When the body was moved, the lever would be released and the grenade would detonate. Again not very fancy, but it invariably worked.

Some of them set about destroying the enemy rifles – bending the barrels of the AKs between forks of trees and scattering the parts on the burning tractor and into the bush.

Others searched the bodies and many documents were found. It was only when they were examined further that it was learned the one of their victims had been the new CO of the FRELIMO base at Mkumbura.

He had been carrying the new radio codes, frequencies and callsigns for the whole of Tete Province for the following months – information that was certain to be of use to the Rhodesian side. The Rhodesians also now held all the mail destined for the Mkumbura Garrison.

Then it was back to the lake. On the way they found water in a riverbed and made a well-deserved brew. Morale was now extremely high.

The next day, the dull thud of an explosion in the distance indicated the success of the landmine but it was several weeks before the canoeists heard the details. According to radio intercepts, the wounded survivor had staggered in to the nearby FRELIMO base to tell of the ambush and a patrol was sent to investigate. When they saw the effects of the ambush, reinforcements were called to help recover the bodies and vehicles.

A whole company of FRELIMO arrived to sweep through the ambush area in search of the attackers. Then they sent for another tractor and trailer to collect the bodies.

In the meantime, the booby-trapped body was picked up – and three FRELIMO were wounded as the hidden grenade exploded.

When the new tractor and trailer arrived, the driver travelled down the side of the road to avoid all the bodies spread out in front of him. He reversed and loaded up all the dead and wounded, then set off back to base. As there were no longer any obstacles littered around, he drove straight down the centre of the road.

The tractor passed over the SAS landmine uneventfully. Not so the trailer. The ensuing blast tore into the trailer, causing even more casualties and flinging the pile of dead bodies and booby-trap casualties in all directions.

At that, FRELIMO lost all interest in the affair. The wounded were helped back to base but the bodies were abandoned.

The flotilla meanwhile was continuing on its way ...

* * *

Within days, the SAS arrived back on an island where some boxes of captured FRELIMO rations had been cached, not substantial enough to live on but making a pleasant change, containing tins of fish from Norway, chocolate milk and cheese from Holland, corned beef from Tanzania and fruit juice from Portugal.

Despite the slight variation to their diet, some men were starting to feel run down and a weight loss was becoming very apparent. Two corporals had become noticeably thin and Dave Arkwright was looking particularly skeletal.

They were very low on supplies and some men had already eaten their last food; everyone had used his last tea bag. There were only six dehydrated meals left among the whole group.

There was no sugar left at all and when the resupply failed to arrive the second night, Pete Cole wrote in his log: "The operation has now turned into a survival exercise. We spent all morning catching fish in the net and grenading the shallow shoreline, finally ending up with 14 large fish. We boiled them in an old ammo box, which satisfied everyone.

"The lack of sugar is a problem, so we chopped out a mopani nest for honey, but there was not enough to make much difference. It took Dave Berry and I three hours to chop it out of a tree and it was hardly worth the effort.

"We have located two beehives in trees and will try and smoke one to get some honey during the night if the resupply doesn't arrive.

" ... Despite the lack of food, morale is still high and it certainly took a boost when the resupply finally arrived at 19h15. The drop was accurate and by 19h30 we were eating the customary chickens."

Weapons had already been cleaned and oiled, and knives rubbed with vaseline to keep them rustfree, and when the canoe repairs were carried out the fleet was fully operational again.

* * *

They were now on their way back home. It was almost beyond belief that in almost six weeks, they had not paddled for a single night where the wind had been favourable. For the three weeks they went eastwards the wind blew from the east . . . and now they were going westwards it was blowing from the west.

Eventually after six long and eventful weeks the operation drew to a close. That last night on the lake they had coffee laced with rum to celebrate the successful conclusion of the mission.

Fortunately, they did not have to take their leave of the lake via the Musengezi River. The choppers would be coming to take them home the following morning.

In a way, they would be sorry to leave the lake but after the total isolation of their surroundings they were certainly looking forward to getting back to civilisation with the chance to talk to someone else other than the same group of men they had lived and eaten with for six weeks.

That they all got on with each other for six long weeks of living in such close proximity to each other was a measure of their special selection and training. Only mature, self-reliant troops were capable of such missions.

The following morning they cleared a landing zone for the choppers by blowing down two large trees, then cleared the rest of the trees with matchets and entrenching tools. Soon, five Alouette choppers arrived to recover them and their equipment. They must certainly have looked a dirty dozen. They sported beards, their hair curled on to their shoulders and their clothes were tattered and torn.

They flung their kit into the choppers and clambered in after it. The sun was shimmering on the vast, smelly, beautiful lake as the choppers climbed out of the LZ taking the troublesome intruders back home.

And so ended the first extremely successful lake op on Cabora Bassa. They had paddled 540 kilometres (335 miles), 140 kilometres (87 miles) more than they had planned . . . had left a toll of dead and wounded including the CO, 2IC and Political Commissar of the Mkumbura FRELIMO garrison and had disrupted the traffic on the only access road from Tete to Mkumbura. So effective was their mining and ambushing that attempts were made to build a parallel road on some stretches.

They had amply proved that operating from the lake was a viable proposition . . . and it would not be many weeks before *Cockleshell Heroes* Part II got under way . . .

Colour Sergeant Karl Lutz and his crew mate, Corporal Dave Berry, were to become old hands at the paddling game. They were to take part in phase two and three and were to spend 13 out of the first 17 weeks of the year canoeing around Cabora Bassa.

On the third trip, the SAS reduced every boat at the lake's largest harbour to matchsticks. As the black of the night turned to a vivid red and boats burned and crackled and drums of petrol helped fuel the flames of destruction, two of the saboteurs, Karl Lutz and Mick Graham were caught in the glare as if on a stage.

They paddled a bit faster and reached the safety of darkness uneventfully. The blaze was a spectacular sight and the mission was the most successful operation on the lake.

The first lake op was undoubtedly the hardest, however. In subsequent ones, the operators were choppered to the lake shore, avoiding the long hazardous trip down the Musengezi River.

The many valuable lessons learned from the mistakes and experiences of those first *Cockleshell Heroes* were to make subsequent lake ops by the SAS and Selous

Scouts far easier, for the commander returned with a lengthy list of recommendations to improve conditions next time around.

All the lake ops had achieved their aim of disrupting movement on the infiltration routes from Tete to north-eastern Rhodesia. And, as anticipated, ZANLA and their FRELIMO friends didn't have a clue where the SAS had come from.

Chioco Garrison Attack, March 24, 1977

ZANLA had established a fairly strong presence at Chioco garrison, one kilometre south of Chioco town in Tete Province from where they deployed straight into Rhodesia over a very wide area.

The Rhodesians were determined to do something about the 100 or so enemy based there ... and a decision was made to destroy the place.

ZANLA had the luxury of a properly-built camp with all the comforts of barrack blocks, electricity and a water tower.

The garrison had been built by the Tanzanians but they pulled back to Tete and FRELIMO had taken it over. Then their ZANLA comrades had moved in.

ZANLA were well fortified with an excellent trench and bunker system and could be expected to put up a fight.

The SAS was to get the task of sorting out the garrison and its occupants, and the mission commander, Captain Dave Dodson, realised that decisive firepower would be crucial to the mission ... and every one of the 22 operators from "A" to "B" Troops was told to draw unusually large amounts of ammunition for the job.

The odds were five to one against the attackers, but they were planning that their extra ammunition and the element of surprise would tip the scales in their favour, enough to rout the enemy, force them to abandon the camp and push them further back to Tete ... and away from the Rhodesian border.

Having moved out to Mtoko forward air base in preparation for the operation, Corporal Imre Baka, the storeman in charge of the ammunition truck, was kept busy most of the day with ammunition requests.

As always, security was tight and although Imre Baka was in the SAS, he was not told what the mission was about. However, in view of all the ammunition he was issuing, it took little imagination to work out that it had to be a large ambush or a camp attack.

Much frenzied activity went on around the base and the preparations went on until well after sundown.

Then Sergeant Andy Chait wandered across to see Corporal Baka in the ammunition store to tell him he had been selected for the mortar team. Baka was to get his kit together and be at the briefing at 09h00 next day. For Baka, normally a base soldier, it was a chance in a million.

Later, Sergeant Iain Bowen visited the ammo truck for some claymores. The commander had just returned from a quick aerial reconnaissance of Chioco garrison and brought back photographs showing that there were several buildings made of corrugated iron ... and claymores would be the perfect thing to blow them away.

The sergeant said he wanted to set up a bank of ten claymores against the walls of the two barrack rooms ... and in less than a minute Bowen and Baka had worked out how a wiring harness could be used to blow the two groups of claymores simultaneously. After an hour of scrounging, they had a harness made up that could be put in place and ready for action in a very short time.

The harness was wound on to a cardboard reel . . . and they made a few dry runs to see how long it would take to set up.

At the briefing next morning, a small model of Chioco terror base was on display. Ration boxes substituted for buildings and were labelled with what type of construction they were made of. Prominent terrain features – hills, bunkers and trenches – were also depicted.

Then the commander gave a thorough briefing, designating which callsigns would go in first and their positions in the assault . . . how many enemy they could expect . . . the types of weapons at the camp and where they were positioned. There was a 75 millimetre recoilless rifle near Chioco police station and they would be taking in a 60 millimetre mortar to counter it.

Then they moved off to a remote part of the airfield for a few dry runs of the camp attack, just to ensure everyone knew his job.

After lunch, they left for the long overland trek to Marymount, a former mission, close to the border where the police had a base camp. They helped each other cover up with Black-Is-Beautiful, and within minutes were transformed into Africans.

The first lift boarded the choppers . . . the rotor blades bit into the air . . . and they were off for Mozambique once more. The Alouettes shook in protest as they struggled towards the top of the escarpment.

The three choppers were flying in V-formation and, as they cleared the crest immediately dropped out of sight to keep them off the skyline – and out of enemy sights – as much as possible.

The whole panorama of the Zambezi Valley lay below them in the distance, the dark green ribbon of the Ruya River rushing up to join the Mazoe, then on to join the Zambezi.

Eventually, the choppers banked sharply to the left and dropped down to the bush, the rotor blades making the waist-high grass dance like giant waves at sea.

There was not a single place to put them down and the choppers hovered while the soldiers made a jump for it. Then having dropped the troops some 17 kilometres (11 miles) west of their target, the choppers returned to Marymount to bring in the remainder of the team.

As the second lift came in, the new arrivals could just make out the shapes of the other SAS men in the treeline where they were in all-round defence.

The newcomers joined the others in the defensive circle with their weapons at the ready. Soon the noise from the choppers faded into the distance and the bush became quiet again.

Everyone was straining his eyes and ears to detect some movement, sound, or smell.

The call of a hornbill broke the silence and a slight breeze started to move through the bush.

The commander motioned the callsign commanders to gather around him. They were to march a kilometre or so until they found some good cover where they could hide until the moon came up.

The going was difficult and their equipment heavy, but they soon reached the cover of thick bushes. After posting sentries, the others propped themselves up against their packs and were asleep almost immediately. Yet such was the nature of their work, that the slightest sound or movement, or even a thought, would have them awake in an instant if the need arose.

All too soon, Sergeant Andy Chait was coming around and whispering to them that it was time to get going. The word was passed back along the line and, by the light of the full moon, the SAS moved off again through the bush ... snaking their way up and down around hills, through dry river beds and in and out of the dense bush.

They all carried mortar bombs and their equipment seemed to treble in weight, the straps of their packs cutting into their shoulders. They walked for fifty minutes then rested for ten ... then were on the march again.

They walked all that night by the light of the moon and, at the first signs of morning, moved into the cover of the thick bush. Everyone cleared a space for himself, removing crackling twigs and noisy leaves before promptly passing out from exhaustion, all that is, except the usual sentry who would get his turn later.

That afternoon, Captain Dodson called the other callsign commanders together – Andy Chait, Iain Bowen and Nick Breytenbach – to give them their final briefing ... and, that night they were back on their travels again.

At about 23h00, they came out of the bush and on to a footpath and walked down each side of it en route to Chioco, a stone's throw from their target, Chioco garrison.

Twenty minutes later, the unmistakable sound of African music and singing floated across the still night from the direction of the town ... and the whole line ground to a halt.

It was coming from a radio or record player in Chioco. There were voices raised in song and it clearly told them that one hell of a party was in progress.

They moved off through the night again ... and very soon an airfield with fuel drums scattered over it, the outline of buildings and a water tower loomed into view. Next to the buildings, they saw the glow of a couple of campfires. There could be no mistaking this for anything but the target.

They stopped once more and the commander told the mortar team to follow him. A sergeant, and a corporal obeyed the command and Corporal Imre Baka fell in behind them ... they turned off the path into a maize field that was between the camp and the path.

Dodson had selected this as an ideal spot for the 60 millimetre mortar: it would not be seen from the camp and the mortar team would have a clear field of fire with no big trees impairing the upward flight of bombs. Their role was to mortar Chioco town one kilometre from the garrison and more particularly, the police station, just to keep their heads down and out of the fracas, while the rest of the SAS attacked the camp itself.

Everyone dropped off his Bergen and mortar bombs at the mortar position and walked off through the bush ... then Dave Dodson, Andy Chait, Iain Bowen and Nick Breytenbach, the four callsign commanders, moved 500 metres south of the fenced camp to do their final reconnaissance.

Turning to Nick Breytenbach, the commander whispered that he wanted him to take his callsign to the northern corner of the camp. The idea was that once the attack went in, the other three callsigns would drive the terrorists towards him.

"Sir, is there going to be another callsign next to me?" Nick enquired, remembering his briefing that there were 100 enemy in the garrison.

"No," came the reply, "only the four of you ... "

H-hour was to be at first light on March 24. The plan called for Nick to set off his eight claymores on the northern corner at the same time Sergeant Iain Bowen detonated the claymores against the two barrack room walls on the west of the camp. Nick and Iain synchronised their watches to ensure the plan went smoothly.

Immediately the claymores went off, Frank Booth, Nick's second-in-command, was to throw two high explosive hand grenades into an enemy-occupied bunker inside the camp.

The exploding claymores would be the signal for the three assault teams to move through the sleeping camp – Iain Bowen was to take the left side; Dave Dodson, commanding the main assault team would move through the centre ... and Andy Chait and his team would be on the right. And any interference from the town was to be dealt with by the mortar team.

A couple of hours before the attack was due to go in, Nick and his team headed around to the left of the camp and up through open bush, crossed over the main road to Chioco town, and eased in to their position on the northern corner of the garrison.

Nick and his 2IC did their final recce. They could hear two terrorists snoring and pointed some of the claymores towards them; then positioned the remainder right up against the corrugated iron buildings.

Nick showed Frank Booth where he had to throw his grenades; then they settled down to await first light.

The other three callsigns meanwhile were slowly easing forward across the dirt track and crouched on the outside of the fence.

Corporal Baka was busying himself with the mortar when Sergeant Chait came over and asked him if he would like to be in his assault group. One of his troopers had a slight cough and had to be replaced, Andy explained. Baka again jumped at the chance. The man he was to replace could do all the coughing he wanted while dropping bombs into the mortar. Leaving the coughing trooper to nursemaid the mortar, he followed Andy.

Andy's callsign was already in position behind the wire fence, and Andy and Baka slithered under the three-strand fence and crawled up a slight rise. The sergeant told him who was on his left and right, wished him good luck and moved off to take up his own position.

Below them, the camp was quiet. There were no lights on and the music and singing in the town had stopped some time before.

All that separated the SAS assault team and 100 enemy were a few blades of grass. It was a fairly cool morning and they lay low in the wet dew trying not to think what could go wrong, hoping no one saw them.

Just before first light, Dave Dodson's and Iain Bowen's teams forming the main assault group, crawled under the fence through a gap between two trenches and placed their claymores along the walls of the two barrack rooms.

Then they discovered that instead of both buildings being made of tin, one of them – the one allocated to the commander and his callsign – was of brick.

Swiftly, they set about positioning the claymores, placing one down, unravelling the wire from the cardboard reel, placing another, then running out another ... soon, there were five in position along the back of each barrack block.

The eastern sky began to get lighter.

There was a flicker of light in one of the barrack block windows, then a faint glow of a cigarette as a man took a long pull on it. The glow disappeared, then appeared at the next window, then the next, moving closer to the door at the end of the building.

Outside, Iain Bowen had just put the last claymore down and was unravelling the wire to take it back to the detonation position.

Suddenly, the door opened and a naked black man with a cigarette dangling from his lips sauntered out of the building and proceeded to urinate just one metre from the SAS man.

Iain gripped his rifle and hardly dared breathe. The urine splashed on to the concrete steps of the barrack block ... but the dozy terrorist did not see the Rhodesian soldier lurking in the gloom of the coming morning.

When he finished, he shook the last few drops, cleared his throat and spat with feeling into the dust, then turned and sauntered back into the building. Iain watched the glow of his cigarette and followed the man's progress as he made his way back to the window where he had first lit up his cigarette.

Iain hurried back to the overgrown trench system, crawled under the fence, checked that the circuit lights on the Shrike exploder connecting the claymores were working. For if there was a short, the claymores would not work. He was relieved to find that everything was in order.

It was 04h30 – another thirty minutes before the fireworks. They all settled down now to await first light.

The adrenalin was racing as it always did before an attack, each man thinking of his role in the forthcoming action.

Despite the trenches and bunkers the enemy obviously felt very safe in their garrison camp ... the unmanned weapons positions and the totally unprotected high ground would soon be evidence of that.

In the north, Frank Booth began to sneak up to the bunker with his two high explosive grenades. He pulled out the pins, held down the levers and with a grenade in each hand, waited patiently for the claymores to go off.

As one long minute followed another, he knew he could not possibly relax his grip on the grenades. To do so would send the levers flying, and if he wanted to live, he would have to throw them. And he did not want to do that, until the time was right ... until the claymores went off.

Fifteen minutes later, exactly at the pre-arranged time, the commander gave the order for the attack to go in.

Immediately, an ear-shattering explosion broke the silence as Nick Breytenbach set off his claymores on the north ... followed a couple of seconds later by those against Iain Bowen's and the commander's barrack blocks. Bowen and Dodson had waited just long enough for the terrorists to sit and stand up in the barrack blocks, thus making them better targets.

The claymores did little damage to the commander's masonry barrack block, but they certainly knocked the stuffing out of Iain Bowen's.

A split second later, Frank Booth had tossed his gift of two grenades into the bunker ... then ran back to take up his position in Nick Breytenbach's callsign in the north. Two muffled explosions added to the commotion as the grenades did their job.

Immediately everyone in the main assault group got to his feet and started moving forward. The SAS advanced at a walk and the green tracers of their AKs and RPDs were interlacing with the red tracers of their FNs.

Andy Chait's callsign was moving parallel with the main assault line but firing across their line of sight, thus catching the terrorists in an L-shaped assault and forcing them either to fight or die or take off towards Chioco.

The din of the smallarms fire was punctuated by the explosions of RPGs and grenades.

Iain Bowen put a rocket into his building to blow a hole in it, then fired low through the outer wall, spraying the floor with rounds, trying to catch any enemy lying low in the building.

They fired a magazine each, then firing slackened off as they did a quick reload and went in.

Sergeant Bowen paused for a second at his barrack room door to check that all the men had reloaded. They had, and he ran in to see a terrorist trying to escape through a window.

Two shots in quick succession rang out and the man fell dead, shot in the rear with a double tap from Iain Bowen's FN. By now the rest of his callsign had joined him and were sweeping through the building, firing under the beds, behind chairs, anywhere the enemy was likely to be hiding.

The room turned out to be somewhat deserted, as many of the ZANLA men had already made good their escape and others had gone to the party in the town that night.

Everywhere there was devastation. The claymores, the rocket and the blistering deafening weight of fire as the troops swept through had left the walls holed and pockmarked and the few personal effects ZANLA had were in complete disarray.

Near the main entrance to the camp and twenty metres from Sergeant Bowen's barrack room was a sentry position, and by now the two duty guards were returning fire.

Iain Bowen and team, having finished with the barrack block, opened up on them and the two guards suddenly lost all enthusiasm for the fight as they went clean through the side of their guard house in their haste to be gone. The whole side of the guard house was torn out in the process ... and the two Africans dashed off up the road practically carrying it with them ... and followed by a stream of angry tracers.

The remains of the building clattered down into the dust.

To the north, Nick Breytenbach was reeling in the wires of his claymores and putting them in his pack. Suddenly, he looked up to see the terrorists right on top of him and tripping over the wire he had laid out for the claymores. Some were jumping past and over him. Some had nothing on; others wore just underpants; others sported only chest webbing, some had no weapons at all ...

Immediately, the northern stop group sprang into action and began to have a field day picking off the fleeing ZANLA. One fell fatally wounded on top of one of the troopies.

The trench system was such that the terrorists could hop into the trenches inside the camp and move to the outside of the fence without being seen. The trenches ended a couple of paces away from Nick's left-hand side and he could clearly hear a couple of them talking against the background of firing.

Nick, who spoke fluent Shona, heard them say that this surely was the day they were going to die.

"These maningis (bad whites) here are going to slaughter us," one said to his companion.

By now the commander and his team had cleared their barrack block and were turning their attentions to the trench system and tossing in bunker bombs.

The advancing assault groups were getting return fire from the bunker on the other side of the camp. They could actually see the grey streaks of the bullets coming at them as they moved forward shooting.

As one thought after another tumbled through their minds, they couldn't hear their own weapons firing as they advanced, and it only registered that they themselves were firing when they saw their empty cartridge cases spewing out ... and now and then saw their tracers burning.

The crescendo of return fire was so intense that the men in the mortar position were convinced the SAS had run into a battalion of enemy and been overwhelmed. They could see huge quantities of red and green tracer rising into the air all around the garrison. It was a spectacular sight.

Andy Chait's group on the right-hand side of the camp were now dealing with the trenches. Several enemy tried to jump out and make a run for it. Those who did were no match for one corporal and his RPD. The earth erupted around them and they collapsed like rag dolls.

The steady crump of the SAS mortar could be heard above the rifle fire and exploding bunker bombs and it was followed almost immediately by the corresponding explosions as the bombs landed in Chioco town.

Sergeant Chait yelled for his team to sweep towards the water tower. A corporal opened up with his RPD and the others followed suit. In less than a couple of seconds the water tank resembled a sieve and the water poured out like a giant shower.

The commander's team meanwhile were sorting out a troublesome RPD gunner in the garrison's command building on the corner of the parade square ... while Iain Bowen's team moved down to a bunker.

The armoury went up with a fairly big whoosh as the thatched roof caught fire.

In the north, despite one man's weapon having a gas stoppage and another a malfunction, the bodies were piling up around the SAS as their colleagues elsewhere in the camp drove the enemy towards them.

* * *

Andy Chait's advance was blocked by a deep gully, but there was a makeshift bridge made from a few planks of wood, and Andy told his men to cross over one at a time.

At the other side of the bridge, a lone terrorist came running out of a partially-concealed two-storeyed house – a strangely-out-of-place building with red bricks and white window shutters.

The man had no intention of dying without a fight and dropped to one knee and brought his AK to his shoulder. He was killed immediately.

The din tapered off and Andy Chait indicated to his men that he wanted them to wheel to the left. They moved away from the house, crossed a narrow field, scrambled up a three-metre-high dirt mound and came out on to a maize field.

From the top of the mound they raked the field, their tracers ricocheting and arching into the sky.

Cautiously, they moved out between the maize stalks. Five metres from the edge of the field someone fired at them. They hit the dirt. But luckily the terrorists were aiming high and the rounds cracked over their heads.

To their front was a trench and they saw the muzzle flashes of terrorists intent on killing them. Everyone sent a blistering rate of rounds towards the trench and some threw grenades.

Andy shouted to Imre Baka to throw a white phosphorus grenade. Baka pulled the pin and threw it, shouting "white phos" as he did so. As the cannister arched towards the trench, he knew it would be on target.

It exploded in the trench like a firework display. The white smoke billowed out, obscuring their vision. There were several more explosions and more white smoke.

The firing from the trench stopped. The agonising screams of the injured enemy filled the air as the white phosphorus burnt into their bodies. Those lucky enough not to be hit, fled – straight into the path of the commander's callsign. Their luck finally ran out and they too died.

By now the maize field was on fire, set alight by the terrorists' tracers or some of the white phosphorus ... and Andy Chait and his team were forced to move away.

The trench still had to be cleared and they poured automatic rifle fire along the whole length of it. They heard no more from the enemy.

Andy Chait and his team were to remain in their position until the main assault group finished the sweep.

Firing broke out to their front, about fifty metres away. A steady stream of tracers were climbing into the sky from the bottom of a large anthill which formed part of the trench system. It looked as if someone down in the trench was firing an RPD through the opening. Everyone opened up at where he thought the trouble was coming from.

Andy shouted across to Imre Baka to give him a hand grenade. Imre tossed him one. Andy put his AK down and was just about to pull the pin and sort out the gunner, when the earth erupted around them.

Bullets were hitting the ground. Someone saw a terrorist stick his rifle out of the trench and take pot shots.

Baka looked at Andy for direction; then heard a loud slap and saw Andy's denims tear open on the outside of his right thigh.

Andy yelled that he was hit, grabbed his thigh above the wound and rolled into the trench. The grenade rolled in with him. The terrorist responsible was also in the trench and had to be killed before anyone could get to Andy.

Andy, still holding his thigh, called the commander over and said his injury was a bad one; they had got the artery.

He was lifted out to the edge of the trench, but because his colleagues had to kill the terrorist first, they lost a precious thirty seconds before the medic could put on a tourniquet.

Baka recovered the grenade, pulled the pin and threw it at the anthill. The firing coming from there ceased.

Quickly, the operators picked up Andy and moved him to a safer position in cover behind one of the buildings. Someone ran to fetch a bed to try to make him comfortable.

When Iain Bowen, busy finishing off clearing the bunker, realised what had happened to Andy, he immediately sent his medic to help . . . and he sprinted across the parade ground with bullets bouncing all around him.

The whoosing sounds of enemy 75 millimetre recoilless rifle rounds were passing over their heads as they helped care for Andy . . . then 60 millimetre mortar bombs sped from the opposite direction as the SAS mortar replied.

By now four men had carried Andy towards the landing zone next to the mortar position. The casevac chopper had been sent for . . . and it was time to make tracks. The commander had already called for the Hunters to put in an airstrike on Chioco if there was any trouble during uplift.

Nick Breytenbach counted 25 bodies piled around his position. Another 13 lay dead around the trenches and the camp. Later intelligence told that many more were wounded. The shindig in the town that night had undoubtedly saved many ZANLA who had been partying instead of defending their barracks.

FRELIMO were still firing at them from the town but their firing was becoming more erratic.

By now the whole garrison was ablaze. There was not much left to fire at in the camp at all. The debris of the battle could be seen in open areas . . . buildings were burning and demolished, dead enemy lay strewn in the open and at the bottom of trenches. The SAS knew the smoke of the battle would be visible for miles around.

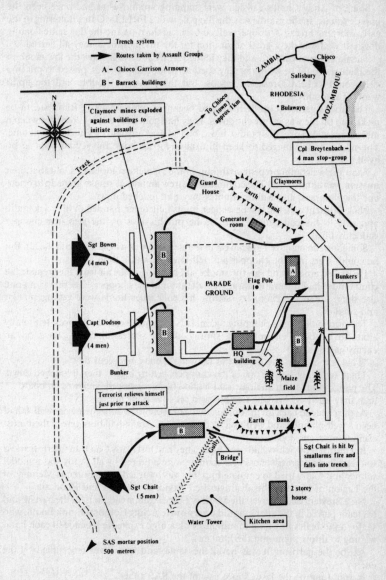

Legend:
- Trench system
- Routes taken by Assault Groups
- A – Chioco Garrison Armoury
- B – Barrack buildings

ZAMBIA
Chioco
Salisbury
RHODESIA
Bulawayo
MOZAMBIQUE

'Claymore' mines exploded against buildings to initiate assault

To Chioco (town) approx 1km

Cpl Breytenbach – 4 man stop-group

N

Track

Guard House

Earth Bank

Claymores

Generator room

Sgt Bowen (4 men)

B

PARADE GROUND

Flag Pole

A

Bunkers

Capt Dodson (4 men)

B

Bunker

B

HQ building

Maize field

Terrorist relieves himself just prior to attack

Earth Bank

B

Gully

'Bridge'

Sgt Chait is hit by smallarms fire and falls into trench

Sgt Chait (5 men)

2 storey house

Water Tower

Kitchen area

SAS mortar position 500 metres

The Chioco garrison attack

137

It was a helluva sight and they wished they had brought their cameras.

Some of Andy Chait's callsign were standing around what had once been the parade square. In the middle was the flagpole with a FRELIMO flag fluttering in the early-morning breeze. A trooper walked over, cut the rope and the flag came floating down. It would make a great decoration for the troopies mess, they all agreed.

Then a chopper came in and they loaded Andy aboard. By now the low moan of the Hunters could be heard as they sped across the upper skies, poised to put in a strike on FRELIMO reaction troops. But there was no trouble and the uplift went off smoothly.

The troops gathered up their kit and began marching back to Rhodesia, to be picked up on the way by the choppers. They had gone only a few kilometres when a message crackled over their radio. It was bad news; Andy had died on the way home. The medic had managed to keep him alive for an hour, but it had been to no avail.

Soon the welcoming repetitive thump of the Alouette rotor blades told that their mission was almost over. The commander threw an orange smoke grenade to orientate the choppers, and within minutes they had touched down.

Nick Breytenbach, the last passenger in his helicopter, handed in his pack, radio and rifle to his colleagues. Then, as he put his foot on the step, the chopper suddenly lifted.

Somehow, he managed to grab on to the step and was whisked up into the air. But he couldn't get into the chopper and fell to earth with a thud.

He looked around and saw the smoke still hanging in the air from the grenade the commander had thrown to attract the attention of the choppers. There was no one else there – and the choppers bearing his colleagues home were getting smaller and smaller.

The adrenalin began pumping again as Nick considered his chances, left totally alone in a hostile environment, shortly after a successful camp attack on an enemy garrison!

"This is it *Nickers*," he thought to himself. "You've had your day."

Then, suddenly, he saw one of the choppers getting bigger; then it touched down. The pilot mumbled an apology; said he had been convinced Nick was on board ... then they lifted off over the treetops and set course for home.

As they headed back for the border, they knew they had done their work well. It had been a well-planned and well-executed operation. And it had been one of their most exciting missions, too.

But the price of victory had been high. They had lost Andy Chait, an utterly fearless soldier, whose aggressiveness and courage were admired by all. Andy was a model soldier and many tried to emulate him. He was awarded a posthumous Member of the Legion of Merit for his distinguished service to the SAS and Rhodesia.

Nick Breytenbach received the Military Forces Commendation for the part he and his team played in the attack, as did a very brave Acting Corporal Frank Booth, who sat for an unbelievably long 15 minutes with a high explosive grenade in each hand waiting to throw them into the bunker.

As for the garrison, it was never the same, and was never reoccupied by the enemy.

It would not be the last Chioco saw of the SAS either ...

Chioco Revisited, May 1977

ZANLA had no sooner gathered their belongings and their thoughts and moved from the ruins of Chioco garrison into the nearby town, than the SAS were back in the area again.

Having made the garrison untenable, they now planned to do the same with the entire town, which ZANLA shared with FRELIMO.

They were to harass the area and give the occupants the jitters ... take it over for themselves, then raze it to the ground so it was no longer viable as a staging area.

Initially four callsigns, led by Captain Dave Dodson, were deployed into the area after a very long approach march ... and within a day, three explosions had rocked the neighbourhood as the enemy kept blowing themselves up on SAS landmines.

The trouble-makers continued skulking around the neighbourhood on a glorified anti-tracking exercise, laying landmines and periodically making mischief.

They were on the move the whole time and walked endless kilometres. But that really was what SAS work was all about. To outsmart the enemy, they had to keep ahead ... keep a low profile ... be devious ...

Having caused a fair amount of alarm and despondency, the commander decided that the time had come to get into town. They were expecting to find some thirty ZANLA and FRELIMO in residence and a much stronger assault force was needed ... and they moved away from Chioco to await the arrival of a dozen reinforcements, who were to parachute in that night.

The Dakota came in nice and low. Its landing lights flashed once and the ground troops picked up the signal, immediately hurrying to mark out the dropping zone with their hand-held strobe lights.

The 12 reinforcements, led by Mac McIntosh, launched themselves into the night, and the main force followed their progress as the chutes cracked open and they floated gently to the earth. They cached the parachutes, gathered up their weapons of war, and set off immediately, snaking their way through the bush to Chioco, walking for most of the night and stopping only for a few hours to wait for the moon to come up.

As the 28 men silently approached the town, they passed the site of one of their anti-tank mines. But the mine was no longer there and in its place was just a gaping crater and bits and pieces of vehicle strewn around.

But by now, the locals' earlier SAS-initiated troubles seemed to be over and everything had quietened down. The street lights were on and the generator was ticking over smoothly. It all looked very peaceful.

The mortar team and protection party crossed a small wooden bridge at the bottom of the town and went off into the maize field to set up their two 60 millimetre mortars. Everyone else followed, dropping off packs and mortar bombs.

Then the assault force moved in closer to the town and lined up in a large rainwater drain, in readiness for the attack.

The stench in the drain was atrocious, yet they had no option but to put up with it until daybreak. Only then would they realise they had spent part of the night in the community latrine. Never had their Who Dares Wins motto been tested more fully.

SAS trooper Manny Carvalho, who had grown up in Mozambique, was rather looking forward to getting into Chioco. He had been there in the old days when it had boasted a thriving Portuguese community. It was ironic that his return visit was to blow the place off the face of the earth.

Within a couple of hours, the eastern sky began to grey and it was time for the attack.

The commander waved the advance and the SAS came out of the twilight.

Now the smell from the drain was forgotten as they advanced on Chioco in two separate extended lines. Behind them in the maize field, the mortar teams took up their positions to deal with any interference and give the attackers' support as they swept through the enemy town.

Ben Robins and his team were to destroy the buildings and neutralise any opposition on the right-hand side of the town, while Mac McIntosh and his men took care of those on the left. Once all resistance had been overcome and the town secured, Dave Dodson was to set up his command post in the town.

Chioco sprawled before them, calm and still. It was a typical olde-worlde town with a tree-line boulevard, which stretched roughly the length of two rugby fields. It boasted a dozen buildings on both sides of the main road, which led north to Tete and south to Rhodesia.

There were a couple of two and three-bedroomed houses, a post office, a hall, a meteorological station with radio masts, a water tower, an administrative building where the mayor lived, and a large civilian complex . . . and all served by a cantina and a brand new shop.

There was an old disused airstrip at the far end of the town, too, but as the SAS had found on their previous visit, FRELIMO had taken the precaution of scattering old fuel drums along it to prevent Rhodesian war planes landing there.

As the SAS closed on the silent town, Trooper Manny Carvalho could see that Chioco was no longer the quaint little town of his childhood haunts. Gone were the manicured lawns and trim flowerbeds of the good old Portuguese days.

Now, Chioco was neglected, overgrown, pathetic . . . Still, there was no time for nostalgia and it didn't really matter anyway. They were about to reduce it to even more of a shambles than it already was.

On the signal, the attack went in.

Mac McIntosh tossed a bunker bomb into the first building on his side . . . and everyone in his team doubled around behind it to take cover. Bunker bombing never did much good to a building and the explosion tore into the house, shattering the silence of the morning; heralding the SAS's arrival.

On the opposite side of the road, two men lobbed bunker bombs into a three-bedroomed building and ducked behind the wall. There was an almighty thunderclap and the house collapsed like a pack of cards.

The walls crashed down on the two men, and the corrugated roof lifted and flew through the air, winging its way back to earth at speed. Luckily, no one was in its path to be neatly sliced in half and it clattered into the dust uneventfully.

Groggily, the two operators climbed from the rubble and brushed themselves down. They were a bit bruised and battered by the experience but much relieved at their lucky escape.

Then, with chilling precision, the SAS advanced down the high street, throwing their bunker bombs and lobbing their grenades. They worked in tandem, in a fluid motion, each team destroying a building at the same time as the other . . . while the mortar crew in the maize fields behind them, increased the range of their two mortars and blasted ahead at a safe distance, giving covering fire.

Masonry was falling, tin was clattering and belching clouds of smoke filled the streets. And behind from the maize field came the crump of mortars. Everywhere there was chaos and commotion.

Yet amazingly, there was no return fire and no resistance. Chioco appeared deserted, which made their takeover of the town a bit disappointing. It was always more interesting when someone shot back.

Undaunted, they continued sweeping through the buildings, meticulously clearing each one, shooting in every possible hiding place, before ducking out and progressing to the next building, just in case FRELIMO and ZANLA were keeping a low profile. But there was no sign of anyone.

In less than half an hour, the SAS had swept right through the town and by the time they had finished, all that remained standing were pock-marked shells.

On the commander's orders, they put a rocket into the cantina and within seconds, the place was ablaze, exploding *Coca Cola* bottles adding to the confusion of the morning.

Next to nothing was salvaged from the cantina, but luckily the store next door escaped unscathed and they were able to rescue a few tins of food and milk and a few bottles of *Manica* beer – at least enough for a celebration.

There was only one victim of their takeover that day and that was a chicken which had made the fatal mistake of hanging around town; it became the star attraction at the party.

With the SAS out and about the countryside, the other occupants had left town and were now sleeping in the thick bush, not twenty metres from the SAS mortar position. The SAS's harassing programme had given them the jitters and they had taken the precaution of not being caught in their buildings at first light, a popular time for the SAS to strike.

By the time they awoke and got organised, the commotion had died down and Chioco was under the complete control of the SAS.

As the enemy opened up on the SAS mortar team, something exploded into the tree next to the startled crew. A sergeant leapt over one man to get to the mortar, swung it around, popped a few bombs into the barrel and without knowing exactly where the problem lay, blasted away at where he thought the enemy were.

All fell silent and there was no more trouble from that quarter.

The sergeant had scored a direct hit. Later, they would find one man with his foot blown off and in a dazed state. Webbing thick with congealed blood told that another victim had taken a chest wound before being carted away.

In the town, the salvaged food was being ferried from the store in preparation for the victory celebrations. The commander tasked Ben Robins and Mac McIntosh to finish demolishing Chioco, and for them, it was back to work with a promise of a share of the goodies later.

The others, meanwhile, had found some old easy chairs and a table in the mayor's house, and, with the commander's permission, dragged them outside.

Next came a teapot, cups and saucers and fine white linen. They set the table under the shade of a tree, spread out the tablecloth and laid the cutlery.

Someone with a sense of ceremony picked a few flowers and weeds and arranged them in an old tin can. It made the perfect table decoration.

Then, still blackened-up and filthy from their morning's labours, they relaxed in the armchairs and got on with the festivities.

The Chioco tea party was not without its security, but it was a leisurely, enjoyable affair, the culmination of the SAS's domination of the Tete Province.

As the sun filtered through the overhanging tree, the grimy soldiers cocked their little fingers delicately in the air and slowly sipped *Manica* beer out of their china tea cups.

Soon, the smell of fried chicken mingled with that of the burning, smouldering buildings.

One of the troops found a pet monkey among the rubble and sat it on the table, breaking open a couple of tins of mangoes for the little chap.

Then, with the SAS in complete mastery of the town, their victorious commander stood on the front porch of the mayor's parlour and officially pronounced himself the new Lord Mayor of Chioco. To a man, they agreed it was an honour well deserved.

Special Branch were choppered in to glean whatever intelligence they could from the mountain of captured documents, and as most of it was in Portuguese, SAS trooper Manny Carvalho got the job of sifting through it.

A huge masonry tower, a monument to the Portuguese era, was found to conceal a massive ammunition cache, much of it ancient weaponry, including Second World War Mausers with German crests. What the SAS couldn't make use of themselves, they piled into a giant heap, and come the end of the day, the square-shaped tower was blown up.

Following hard on the heels of the garrison attack, the assault on the town was to serve as the final nail in the coffin for the enemy. The comforts afforded to ZANLA and FRELIMO at Chioco were never to be offered to them again . . . for the town and garrison were never rebuilt.

Their celebrations over, the SAS split into two parties to continue harassing and ambushing the enemy. Mac McIntosh and twenty men remained in Chioco and sat on the road day and night to stop ZANLA and their resupplies getting through to Rhodesia . . . while the commander and his team went north to Chinhanda Crossroads to stage a few surprises there.

Mac's stay-behind party remained on the outskirts of the devastated town for several days, but it proved a difficult area to ambush, and they moved back into the ruins, rigged up the mortar, and waited for a FRELIMO reaction party, which they knew wouldn't be too long in coming.

Although FRELIMO came in strength, only three men had the courage to risk going into the town . . . and the SAS watched and waited as they warily moved down the main road, expecting a trap, an ambush . . .

There was a sudden crump of mortar fire and one man dropped, the green of his uniform stained blood red. Fortunately for the other two, they were hidden from view by all the rubble, and managed to escape. Not so lucky was the Tanzanian lieutenant who came face to face with an SAS early-warning group that afternoon.

But FRELIMO and their Tanzanian friends were not prepared to allow the SAS to reign supreme in Chioco . . . and before long, a combined force of 100 men, supported by mortars, arrived on the outskirts, and for every bomb the SAS fired, they got ten back in reply.

Then a lucky mortar bomb, the only one fired with any accuracy, landed next to the SAS command post, slightly wounding Mac McIntosh and Corporal Dave Arkwright.

The SAS were big enough to admit that chaos reigned for a short while, but talk of abandoning the town was met with sharp words from the SAS commander in Salisbury.

After the two injured men were casevacked, Captain Bob McKenna came in to take command of the Chioco siege. But there was no more fight left in FRELIMO and their Tanzanian friends . . . and a few days later, the SAS finally took their leave of the smouldering ruin that once was Chioco.

142

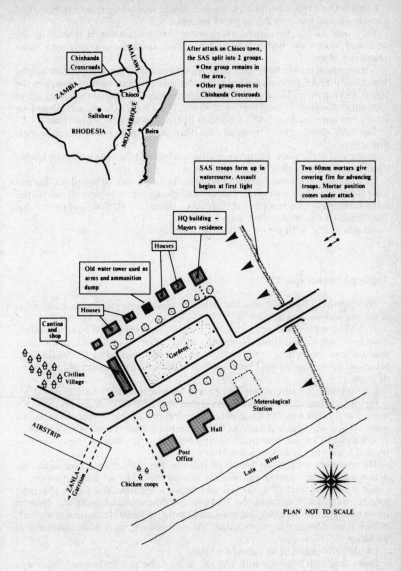

After attack on Chioco town, the SAS split into 2 groups.
• One group remains in the area.
• Other group moves to Chinhanda Crossroads

SAS troops form up in watercourse. Assault begins at first light

Two 60mm mortars give covering fire for advancing troops. Mortar position comes under attack

HQ building – Mayors residence

Houses

Old water tower used as arms and ammunition dump

Houses

Cantina and shop

Civilian Village

'Gardens'

Meterological Station

Hall

AIRSTRIP

ZANLA Garrison

Post Office

Chicken coops

Luia River

N

PLAN NOT TO SCALE

Chinhanda Crossroads

MALAWI

ZAMBIA

Chioco

Salisbury

RHODESIA

MOZAMBIQUE

Beira

Chioco revisited

143

Captain Dave Dodson and his team, meanwhile, were sitting it out at Chinhanda Crossroads and having a fair share of success.

They were having one contact after another, and had no sooner cleaned up the road and hidden the bodies behind a hill, than another group of enemy came sauntering along.

A letter found on one body indicated they were part of a larger group from nearby Jeque, and the SAS, RLI and Air Force mounted an immediate airborne attack on the ZANLA camp there. Those fortunate enough to escape ran straight into the path of Dodson and his team sitting waiting for them at Chinhanda Crossroads. Their luck finally ran out – and the SAS's mound of bodies took on new proportions.

The SAS tidied up the road as best they could and waited for their next victims . . .

By the end of the week, 24 enemy had been accounted for, the ambushers having been forced to move their position only once.

Having reached the two dozen mark, the commander decided to call it a day and leave the enemy alone for a while. The SAS had spooked them sufficiently, and if they harboured any doubts beforehand, there was a mortuary full of bodies to prove that the Rhodesians most definitely meant business . . .

All told, it had been a very productive deployment.

Training Exercise, July, 1977

For Captain Colin Willis, attached to the School of Infantry in Gwelo, it seemed as if the war was passing him by.

He had done his initial recruit training in the SAS way back in 1970 and was within a week of doing his parachute course and joining a troop, when he decided his career might take off better if he were an officer. He was duly selected for the officer cadet selection course, passing out 13 months later at the School of Infantry, third in order of merit.

But that did not mean he could go back to his parent unit, the SAS, as an officer.

For the unit insisted that SAS officers – other than a few experienced senior NCOs already in the unit who had undergone officer-training – serve at least two years in a conventional unit before joining the SAS . . . and as a result of that ruling, Colin was posted to the RLI where he stayed for four years, earning the Bronze Cross for gallantry and leadership in action in the process.

Then he went back to the School of Infantry, this time as an officer instructor, which was an ideal posting and another step up the ladder for a career officer.

But it was now mid-1977, the war had begun to escalate, and Colin, like most soldiers, wanted a bit of the action. He knew that if he stayed where he was, his next move would be the inevitable, but mundane, posting to Army Headquarters as a staff officer. It would mean more responsibility, more money, more office routine –but no action.

On the other hand, if he joined the SAS . . .

Colin sought an interview with SAS OC Brian Robinson. Fortunately, Brian was equally keen for Colin to "return" to the unit, but told him that he would have to do another selection course. It was not going to deter Colin, but he was surprised that having already done *one* selection course with the SAS the unit wanted him to do *another*.

144

The SAS, however, had definite ideas about "outside" officers wanting to join its ranks. No matter what their background, experience or previous training, they had to undergo the stringent selection phase to assess their leadership potential and their ability to command SAS troops in the more unconventional SAS operations.

And if the normal selection course for ordinary SAS soldiers was tough, the officer's course was designed to be even more arduous.

The customary gruelling long-distance march with heavy loads was the great leveller, bringing everyone – officer, raw recruit and men from other units – down to the same physical state of fitness. But then Colin and the other two officers along on the same selection phase, soon found that in addition, they, as officers, were expected to write military appreciations and make plans and decisions whilst totally worn out from the most strenuous of conditions.

SAS training officer Captain Rob Johnstone and his team were particularly interested in making the training phase as realistic as possible. To this end the three officers were assembled and tasked to carry out a reconnaissance, as an undercover group, on the central ammunition depot at Llewellin Barracks in Bulawayo, which housed supplies for the whole of Matabeleland and the Midlands.

A couple of days later, the three officers, blackened-up, dressed as African labourers, and carrying grass-slashers sauntered casually up to the perimeter fence of the central ammunition depot.

In Rhodesia, Africans working on the side of a road seldom warranted a second glance and no one, least of all the white security guards on duty, paid the slightest attention to these particular chaps as they kept to the bushes and scythed through the long grass with their slashers.

They were back again the next day, studying the depot from all angles and assessing the security situation. Then, their reconnaissance over, they returned to Salisbury, where they worked out their written military appreciations on how they would get in and out of the depot . . . and then, working from a model, they had to give orders on how they proposed to destroy the target.

Colin was very impressed with the way things were going.

In all his years in the army, this was the first time that full operational verbal orders were given with models and all the other paraphernalia that the School of Infantry taught officers they would get to use in their units, and which Colin knew seldom happened. He would soon find that this was the norm in planning SAS operations.

After a further 24-hour gruelling phase to test fitness, training officer Rob Johnstone addressed the students:

"Right, you've done the recce. Now – go and attack the place ... "

One of the three officers was tasked to command the mission but the man felt he could not handle the job – and by his admission, ruled out all chances of a career in the SAS. It was then that Colin found himself in charge. Now, all the theory and the time spent in the classroom was to be put to the test.

It was the height of the war and the central ammunition depot, which would make an ideal target for terrorists, was surrounded by a wire fence and patrolled by twenty European guards who kept watch from a series of towers. The substantial floodlighting all around the depot would not make the SAS candidates' job any easier.

Colin and his team knew they would have to be good. If they were not, they knew they would not pass selection. It was as simple as that.

The SAS training officer took the precaution of tipping off the commandant of Llewellin Barracks as well as the officer who would be on duty on the night of the attack. The base armourer was also asked to remove the firing pins from the guards' weapons.

In the interests of realism, however, the guards were not informed of the plan.

A few days later, for the second time, blackened-up men approached the arms depot. This time they came by night, came in strength and were dressed in an assortment of khaki uniforms. They took cover in a blind spot between two arc lights, then crept up to the security fence. They were now right beneath two of the watch towers.

They waited for a few seconds, then, certain that no one had seen them, cut an entrance through the wire. The two officers, Colin Willis and Mac McIntosh, slowly inched their way into the depot.

The two men silently made their way to the main guard building, ready to take on the duty guard outside. But there was no one in sight. The mission was getting easier by the minute.

Meanwhile, the unsuspecting guard commander, his 2IC and the relief guards were gathered in the building waiting to take their turn in the watch towers later than night.

Suddenly, the door burst open and two "black" men dressed in khaki terrorist gear stormed in, their silenced weapons bristling and pointing straight at the twenty assembled men.

The element of surprise was total and the look on the guards' faces was a picture. The startled guards had no time to react and only one of the twenty men lounging around tried to reach for his rifle.

The duty NCO sat with his feet up on his desk. His cap was pulled over his eyes and he was fast asleep. One of the unexpected visitors gave him a good hard kick in just the right place. He flew up and the befuddled look on his face disclosed he had not the least idea what was going on around him.

The trembling guards, firmly convinced that the late-night intruders were ZIPRA, were bundled into a small armoury and locked up. The main gate was opened and the remainder of the SAS selection course poured through to assume their respective roles in the attack on the depot.

Meanwhile, Colin Willis and Mac McIntosh had persuaded the watch commander to accompany them to each of the watch towers, the barrel of an Uzi that was firmly stuck in his ear playing no small part in his willingness to help.

Without too much prompting, the watch commander called seven of his eight guards down from their towers, and the eighth one, asleep in the grass nearby, was duly rounded up.

The commander and all his guards were tied to one of the towers, then they watched helplessly as Colin and his team quickly moved through the night securing the depot. But there were no deafening explosions and no killings and the petrified guards soon realised that the visitors were not ZIPRA after all.

But it had been amply demonstrated that had they been the enemy, they would have no problem destroying everyone and everything in the depot. The exercise had not only tested the ability of the raiders but shown up the sorry state of security at the vital installation.

The depot commandant was not amused by the 400 Rhodesian dollars worth of damage inflicted on the fence but was impressed enough to order a major tightening of security at the installation.

The guards were not enchanted with the SAS either and some were to spend a few uncomfortable days in the stocks for neglecting their duties that night.

Colin Willis and the other students passed selection ... and thereafter, whenever the word got around that the SAS was visiting Llewellin Barracks, even the Regimental Police at the gate who normally carried only sidearms or no weapons at all, were armed – and very much on the alert.

* * *

Combined Operations Headquarters housed in Milton Buildings in the heart of Salisbury was the nerve centre of the Rhodesian war machine and as such was the most important building in the land.

And no one could get past or outfox the security people there, the Prime Minister's personal security officer boasted to SAS 2IC Major Mick Graham.

Despite Mick's assurances that the SAS was perhaps the one unit that could do it, the man remained adamant. Security was so good, he claimed, that not *even* the SAS could pull it off.

Ever one to rise to a challenge, Mick knew what had to be done. The unit with the Who Dares Wins tradition was not about to be written off by a bunch of security guards. At least, not without a fight.

Shortly afterwards, Captain Colin Willis, recently back in town from a bush trip, found himself tasked with getting into ComOps.

Colin knew that this particular exercise was not only going to be a fair test on ComOps security, but, as he would be working alone, it would also be a fairly stringent test of his own abilities and initiative.

He had never been to ComOps before and knew only that General Peter Walls and the Prime Minister worked in the building.

A few days later, Colin sprinted up the steps that lead to the hallowed corridors of Milton Buildings. He was dressed in civilian clothing and carried a briefcase packed with plastic explosives. It was with some trepidation that he approached the security guards' post.

"Morning," he said to the two guards on duty, in a crisp, businesslike tone that served to hide his nervousness.

"I've come to see Mr Mitchell in the PM's Department. He's expecting me," he continued, omitting to give his own name or say where he had come from.

"Fine, sir," said the guard, in an equally businesslike manner. "Just fill this in first."

The guard pushed a roneoed questionnaire across the desk to Colin and the SAS officer was deliberately vague about the details he gave and simply signed in as "Mr Williams".

Satisfied with the visitor's particulars, or rather the lack of them, the guard accompanied him up the stairs to the first floor. Colin somehow managed to walk in front, and then with an authoritative nod of his head, he dismissed the guard telling him that he knew the way.

The security man took his word and disappeared down the steps to take up his post by the entrance once more, while Colin, still with his explosives by his side, took off along the corridors of the Prime Minister's Department as if he owned the place.

Then he wandered around the first floor until a civil servant approached. Colin got him to point the way to the ComOps Department and when the man headed off for his office, Colin darted in to the nearest gents' toilet and sat himself down in the first cubicle.

So far, so good. Quite frankly, he told himself, he couldn't believe his good luck. As far as he knew, there was no one working in the Prime Minister's Department by the name of Mitchell. That, as they say in army circles, had been sheer bulldust on his part.

The guards had not bothered to ask for his ID or check out his suitcase. So much for the tight security, he thought. Still, he knew that he wasn't out of the woods yet.

Although it was his first visit to ComOps, he was known by some of the hierarchy as an SAS officer and he knew if they saw him wandering around, they would get suspicious.

He initially decided to stay in the toilet all day until most people had gone home, then, once the coast was clear, he would come out and get into ComOps. But then he remembered he had signed in. If security was what it really ought to be, they would notice he had not signed out and might even mount a search for him. He decided to return that night when things had quietened down a bit.

When the corridor was clear, Colin retraced his steps and with a brisk, "Cheerio" and a friendly wave to the guards at the door, he left Milton Buildings –for the time being.

Back home, he set about preparing his suitcase for his return visit. Inside went 10 kilograms of plastic explosive, *Cordtex* detonators, a timing device, a saw and other bits and pieces of sabotage equipment.

Then, at 19h00, when all the civil servants had left for the day and there was only a skeleton staff on duty, Colin once again approached Milton Buildings.

This time, there were new faces on the security desk but Colin had come prepared with a better cover story, and felt more confident than on his first visit. Still in civilian clothes and packing a pistol in a concealed holster, he flashed a card with a picture of a helicopter on it.

It was a Viet Nam War Veteran's identity card borrowed for the occasion from SAS captain, American Bob McKenna. It bore Bob's name too, but the guards did not seem to notice, as nothing was said when the visitor signed himself in as Capt M.U. Gabe, a name not dissimilar to that of the ZANLA leader!

Colin informed the guards that he was going up to ComOps, and before they had time to strike up a conversation, he was on his way up the stairs, plus suitcase.

There was no one to be seen in the corridors and he was soon outside the ComOps door. There were security bars on the windows but he decided not to try sawing them immediately.

Experience often proved that the simplest solutions were best. And so it turned out to be on this occasion. He turned the handle and the door opened. The amazed captain stepped into a small waiting area, and luckier still, there was no one around to bar his entry.

There was another door in the waiting room, which Colin assumed could only lead into the ComOps inner sanctum. But it had no handle, which meant it probably operated on some form of timing device from the inside.

Now he had a problem. He had not anticipated this sort of hurdle. He was just contemplating what to do next, when he heard footsteps approaching down the corridor.

Quickly, the SAS captain clambered under the only desk in the waiting room. His heart was making a terrible racket, and it flashed through his mind that it might give him away.

An Army officer entered the room and walked straight over to the desk. The SAS captain crouched lower and thought that his little game was up before it had got started.

The ComOps man put his hand over the desk and reached underneath. His hand was dangerously close to Colin's head. Then, he pressed a little button concealed under the desk top, and with a *bzzz,* the inner door magically swung open.

Colin was delighted. His dilemma had been solved for him ... and he watched the man go through the door and saw it close shut behind him.

As soon as he thought it safe, Colin pressed the same button and as the door opened once again, he scrambled out from under the desk, hurriedly brushed his clothes down and walked cautiously through the door.

There was not a soul to be seen ... and for the next ninety minutes, Colin pussy-footed around ComOps laying dummy-charges using real plastic explosives but without the detonators.

He got into General Walls's outer office without anyone disturbing him and did the same in the police representative's office, which was littered with maps showing ZANLA's main deployment routes into Rhodesia. Just to prove how abysmal the security was, Colin collected them up and bundled them into his briefcase.

A beautiful silver letter opener gracing the police officer's desk caught his eye and that, too, was stashed into his briefcase together with bits and pieces of other booty from the desk.

He also spread his charges around the office of the Head of Psychological Operations. That ought to give him something to think about.

He located the duty officer's room and found the man's beret and briefcase lying on the bed where he was going to sleep that night. Colin stole the man's pistol and put plastic explosive under his beret.

He pseudo booby-trapped the ComOps ammunition store – and no one came near him or into the office the whole time. It couldn't have been simpler.

His mission complete, Colin left Milton Buildings, and with a rather confident "Night, then" to the smiling guards on duty at the main entrance, he waved goodbye.

Next day, there was much consternation at ComOps when the staff realised that their bastion had been penetrated and there were a couple of things missing.

They were not to get their chattels back ... for the victorious SAS captain had presented his trophies to the SAS Corporals' Mess long before the hue and cry had erupted.

The maps were returned and the pistol was handed back to a very annoyed and embarrassed duty officer.

Colin subsequently spent a couple of sessions with the Prime Minister's security chief, explaining just how easy it had all been.

Colin's exercise had certainly exposed the vulnerability of the most important building in the land and it was readily conceded that security left much to be desired.

As Colin pointed out, there was every reason to believe that had he been a terrorist he could have got into the Prime Minister's office and eliminated him.

For the ComOps staff who had taken time off to attend a farewell party in another office that night, it had been a lesson well learned.

Needless to say, a couple of security guards got their marching orders and the security arrangements were speedily re-organised and improved.

And SAS officers would soon find that whenever they reported to the ComOps security desk in future, they were *always* escorted everywhere they went!

Rifle Ambush, October, 1977

Security force missions owed much to the men in a certain red-bricked building in Salisbury's civil service belt. These were the signallers who monitored enemy messages around the clock, and who were aided by experts who pieced together the snippets of information until a picture emerged that would be of use to the war effort.

It was from this intelligence that they were able to glean not only Zambian Army, Police and FRELIMO movements and reactions, but also the activity of their ZIPRA and ZANLA comrades.

Towards the end of September, one of the Salisbury eavesdroppers switched in to a rather interesting signal that gave the intelligence boffins something very definite to work on.

The gist of it was that sometime during the following ten days, 24 *Comrades* would be returning to Tete from Rhodesia for resupply, refit and debrief.

The FRELIMO signals operator had made the mistake of giving the exact route the ZANLA squad would take. For the Rhodesians, it was a stroke of luck. Operations had certainly been initiated on a lot less positive intelligence.

News of the possible opportunity target was quickly radioed to "A" Troop, based at Mtoko on the north-eastern border with Mozambique ... and Troop commander Bob McKenna gave the job to Captain Colin Willis and a team of eleven men.

It looked like being a fairly straight-forward ambush job, Bob told them. The two dozen ZANLA men were on their way from Mkumbura to Chioco – their major transit jump-off base – and from there they would be travelling to Biriri then on to Tete.

The SAS were to lie in wait for them on the main access road between Tete and Chioco.

They were to parachute in, then walk to the target area. The local civilians and FRELIMO had by now become very wise and wary to security force infiltration tactics and all normal activity usually stopped in any area overflown by a Dakota.

Thus in order to try and confuse the enemy and, at the same time, provide the ambush party with a fair chance of success, the callsign would be infiltrated by parachute some fifty kilometres (31 miles) from the target area. The tactic of a long approach march would make it very difficult for the enemy to learn of the callsign's real mission.

They would need to carry a large supply of water. For apart from their fifty kilometre trek, they didn't know how long they would have to sit it out in their ambush positions, and at that time of the year in Southern Africa and particularly in Mozambique, water was indeed a very vital and scarce commodity.

Sergeant Bruce Fraser was to lead a four-man pathfinder team to find and secure the dropping zone, and the rest of the party would drop in the following day.

That night, the pathfinder team boarded a Dakota and were soon over hostile territory. They were flying at 16 000 feet, and at a point some sixty kilometres (38 miles) from the border, they leapt out into the darkness.

Down through the night they fell, deploying their canopies at 2 000 feet and landing on Mozambican soil uneventfully within seconds of each other.

Having checked that the area was uninhabited, they set about clearing the mopani scrub for the eight paratroopers who would be joining them from Rhodesia the following night.

* * *

After midnight on September 22, the remaining eight men stood up in the lurching Dakota and checked their kit and equipment. They were five minutes out from the drop zone, and below them in the mopani scrub the pathfinder force sat patiently waiting for them.

Pathfinder leader Bruce Fraser looked at his watch. It was 00h59. One minute to go. He strained his ears for the familiar drone of a Dakota high above in the hot hazy atmosphere.

It was a perfect night for a drop. There was a gentle breeze and the moon was full, only occasionally being obliterated by the odd stray cloud skittering across the sky.

Then Bruce Fraser heard the unmistakable sound of a Dakota coming from the south, and tasked Captain Frank Hales, formerly with the Air Force and who had just joined the SAS, to call up the pilot.

"Cyclone 3 – this is 11. Do you read? Over."

"11 Juliet 3, read you loud and clear. We should be with you in four minutes. We have your Sunray with us who should be joining you shortly. Do you require me to circle or do you want a straight run in?"

"Juliet 3, this is 11, Roger," came the reply from below. "Do not circle. I have you visual. Keep coming as you are. Steady, steady ... left a bit; roll out, Roger ... keep her there. Red light on, Roger. Dead right ... steady, steady ... green light on."

"GO, GO, GO," shouted the PJIs in the Dak ... and eight heavily-laden men shuffled through the open door, to be whisked away in the slipstream. Quickly, the drills which were so instinctive to them were completed and then they were gently floating earthwards, their Bergens and vital operational kit dangling below them.

Another mission had begun.

Suddenly, a bright flare lit the night. Then came the pop-pop-popping of smallarms rounds.

God! thought commander Colin Willis as he floated down. His men were having a contact even before they were out of their harnesses.

Someone had been waiting in ambush for them. The area was supposed to be clear of people. Where was Bruce Fraser and his pathfinders? Had they been captured? What was going on? A dozen possibilities flashed through his mind as he touched down and struggled to free himself from his harness.

But there was no cause for alarm. There were no enemy and all his men were safe.

It had only been an accident caused by a man's Bergen bursting into flames as he touched down. An anti-personnel landmine had been set off and the flash from that had set off plastic explosives and ammunition. Within minutes his pack was destroyed and the hapless trooper had to quickly manufacture a makeshift one from his parachute harness. His food too had gone up in smoke, but he knew his mates would help contribute towards his diet from their rations.

Quickly they regrouped, cached their chutes and surplus water. There was no time to be lost and they set off immediately for the ambush area.

Ahead of them was a very long approach march and each man carried forty kilograms of ammunition, batteries, kit and enough water and rations for a two-week bush trip.

It was hot. Very hot.

The merciless September sun had left the night-time temperatures just below 43 degrees Celcius (110 degrees F) and the approach march was going to be far more difficult than they had expected.

It all became too much for one trooper and during the first night's walk he collapsed from a severe case of heat fatigue.

While his friends put up a drip and tried to get fluid into him, Colin Willis decided they would have to wait until the man was stable, for he was in no condition to march.

They were now losing time but the commander had no intention of leaving an escort with the sick man thus depleting his callsign. He didn't want to call for a casualty evacuation either, as it might well compromise the mission. There was nothing for it but to wait until the man was fit enough to continue.

They had to put a second drip in the sick trooper and it took 12 precious hours before the unfortunate man responded and Colin was sufficiently satisfied with his condition to enable the group to proceed.

His kit was shared out among the rest of the team and they set off once more towards the ambush area. With each step he took, the commander was becoming more and more concerned that the delay might have cost them the mission.

Despite the extreme heat and heavy loads, the ambush group made good time. The sweat was pouring off them, running into their *Black Is Beautiful* and huge salt marks stained their uniforms.

Eventually, 48 hours after drop time, the tired but alert men, arrived in the target area – the main road between Tete and Chioco – and it didn't take them many minutes to realise that it was not going to be such a straight-forward ambush after all.

There was very little foliage at that time of the year anyway, but what grass and undergrowth there was, had been deliberately burned out by FRELIMO to prevent Rhodesians springing the sort of surprises they were planning right now.

How on earth was Colin going to conceal his killer group and their assortment of deadly weapons?

His original plan had been to hide the ambush party and their landmines and heavy weapons just 100 metres from the road. But that idea was obviously out. Any enemy worth his salt would easily pick up the wires and claymores.

Eventually, after a detailed appreciation and lengthy discussion with the other NCOs, he decided to cut the killer group down to six men. They would put two three-man early-warning groups in good vantage points overlooking the road two kilometres either side of the main killer/ambush group.

They would simply have to forego using any ambushing aids. It would have to be a straight-forward rifle ambush.

It meant that the six men in the killer group would have to make their first shots count. But that would only be six of the 24 ZANLA down. What of the other 18?

The initial rifle fire would give them a second or two to react before the SAS would be able to switch targets. The survivors would obviously be fast-moving, highly-motivated and unlikely to hang around.

Colin felt that if they could eliminate half the group, they would be doing well under the circumstances.

Using bits of burnt branches, the ambush party camouflaged a suitable position near the road from where they could spring their ambush. Then they moved back 200 metres from the road so that they would not be seen by anyone going about their day-to-day business along the road. The early-warning groups took up their positions on either side of the main party.

Then they settled down to wait. It turned out to be a long process.

The incredible heat beat down on the ambush party, who were fighting for what little shade they could claim from the dry, withered stalks of the mopani trees. The heat was sapping their strength and their water supplies were dwindling fast. It was taking a fierce discipline and determination to stop water being guzzled down their parched throats.

The trooper who had collapsed that first night had still not fully recovered and he sat patiently waiting in an early-warning group for the ambush to be sprung so that he could be casevacked.

Colin had split the main killer/ambush group into three two-man buddy groups and they were fairly well spread out. It meant that one man could be reading or sleeping while the others stayed on guard. It also meant that each group could be constantly vigilant and all directions were monitored.

The captain had teamed up with Sergeant Bruce Fraser and they spent their days manoeuvring around and around a tree as they chased the shadows in search of a cool place.

They were kept constantly amused by the smallest, most ridiculous things. A group of ants kept them occupied for two whole days and the two soldiers watched with intense interest as they built a firm base next to a pile of spilled sugar. They proved fascinating friends and, if nothing else, at least helped pass the time.

Around the eighth day, they were beginning to feel the strain of waiting. It had long ago become natural to talk in a whisper.

A constant stream of locals and even the odd FRELIMO patrol wandered along the road ... but still there was no sign of the 24 ZANLA men.

During the nights they practised getting in and out of their ambush positions so that when the time came they could move in a slick, well-drilled movement.

Colin was constantly enacting the little scenario he hoped to be played out, wondering what the enemy's reactions would be when six men jumped up and started firing at them. It was a constant worry to him that their success would depend on rifle fire alone.

After nine days of laying in wait under almost unbearable conditions, nerves taut, Colin convinced himself that the ZANLA party had surely slipped by on a different route or had gone past on that first day when they were attending the sick trooper.

They were now in a very unpleasant situation. Daytime temperatures were still very high and they were now down to two water bottles to each man. Much against his wishes, Colin decided that he would have to send out a water-party soon to try and locate a water hole. It would mean thinning out the killer party to three men to allow the other three to search for water. But it was a risk that had to be taken.

The morning of the tenth day dawned and looked like being no different from the others. The heat was still shattering and the water had now almost finished. The water party would definitely have to go out that night, Colin decided.

Then at 12h15, the radio which had been silent for a couple of hours, suddenly cracked into life.

It was Franz Vickers, commanding one of the two early-warning teams. "Confirmed 22 ZANLA moving along the road from west-to-east towards ambush position," he warned. "They are moving in single file. They are well strung-out and cover at least 300 metres."

The commander quickly signalled to the other buddy groups and the adrenalin was already flowing as they rushed to their pre-planned positions.

153

Colin had planned the ambush in an L-shape with two soldiers, Bruce Fraser and Dave Bole, the RPD gunner, on one side of the road ... and the remaining four members of the killer group twenty metres away on high ground but on the other side of the road.

His idea was to let the enemy pass right in front of their high ground team waiting on their high ground overlooking a dip in the road. Then, as soon as the first ZANLA drew level with Bruce Fraser and Dave Bole, they would open up and initiate the ambush. Thus the ZANLA men would be covered by rifle fire from both sides of the road, and if all went well, the SAS would get the maximum number of enemy.

The six soldiers were totally exposed as, hardly daring to breathe, they cradled their rifles and pressed their bodies into the hot earth to avoid being seen.

It seemed to take hours before Colin saw the lead man walking towards them ... and to his great disappointment he saw they were indeed well spread out, just as they had been warned.

Quickly, he counted to see how many would be in the actual killing ground before Bruce Fraser down the road squeezed the trigger to initiate the ambush. There would only be eight.

The ZANLA party seemed to be moving painfully slowly. Then, within ten paces of Bruce Fraser's position, the ZANLA leader stopped and turned around.

Bruce's rifle was already trained on the man but the SAS commander's immediate thought was that they had been seen; that he would have to initiate the ambush himself before it was too late. But something told him to hold his fire for a moment.

Then, the most incredible thing happened.

It looked as if the ZANLA leader had suddenly tired of walking and had decided to call a halt. With a wave to his men to get a move on, he stood in the middle of the road resting his weary feet and waiting until the other twenty-odd armed ZANLA caught up with him.

Having finally assembled his men in one big bunch, the leader turned around ready to move off once more. He did not get very far.

As he glanced towards the side of the road, he suddenly found himself staring down the muzzle of Bruce Fraser's 7,62 millimetre folding-butt FN. The surprise was vividly etched on his face, yet he did not have time to take in the situation properly or to move his men to safety.

A shot rang out and the round stopped squarely in his chest. He was dead before he hit the ground.

Within a fraction of a second, everyone else in the SAS killer group had opened up. And just as Colin had anticipated, their first shots struck and six ZANLA slumped to earth without knowing what had hit them.

Then the ambush group ran forward on their high ground overlooking the road and either stood or knelt as they picked off the rest of the targets below, pouring a deadly hail of lead and copper into a completely stunned enemy.

Then, silence. Bruce Fraser down the road, jumped up to investigate what the problem was. The survivors had run right up to the bank on the side of the road and because the ambushers were above them on their hill, the SAS could not see them.

Being able to see right down the road, Bruce Fraser was in the ideal position to take them on, however, and he walked into the middle of the road and began to sort them out. But he could not deal with them fast enough and quickly shouted across to his partner, Dave Bole, to join him.

Together the two men walked down the road, raking the sides and centre of the killing ground. The surprise was absolute. The ambushed men didn't really stand a chance. They were so shocked at being ambushed so deep inside their safe host country that at first they thought a terrible mistake had happened and cried out "Comrade! Comrade!" to their attackers, thinking them to be FRELIMO.

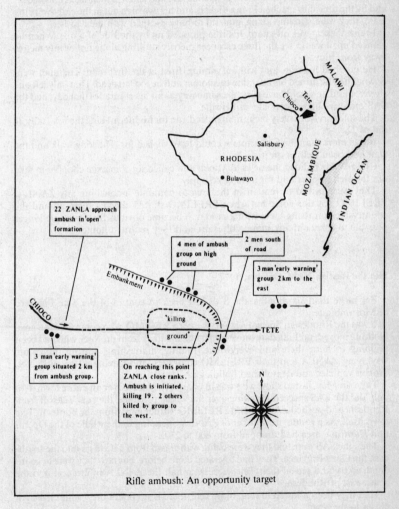

22 ZANLA approach ambush in 'open' formation

4 men of ambush group on high ground

2 men south of road

3 man 'early warning' group 2 km to the east

Embankment

CHIOCO

'killing ground'

TETE

3 man 'early warning' group situated 2 km from ambush group.

On reaching this point ZANLA close ranks. Ambush is initiated, killing 19. 2 others killed by group to the west.

MALAWI

Chioco   Tete

Salisbury

RHODESIA

Bulawayo

MOZAMBIQUE

INDIAN OCEAN

N

Rifle ambush: An opportunity target

But their pleas were answered only by the roar of Rhodesian weapons and Colin gave the ceasefire exactly 45 seconds after the first rifle shot had downed the ZANLA commander.

The silence was deafening as the SAS surveyed the scene before them.

Nineteen ZANLA fresh from their latest forays into Rhodesia, who a minute ago had been happy and content and looking forward to a spell of R and R, lay dead in the middle of the road, their lifes' blood oozing into the parched soil of what they believed had been friendly terrain.

Three of the ZANLA party at the end of the line had taken to their heels and fled . . . and by the time they reached Franz Vickers and his two men out in the early-warning team, they were strolling along, grateful to have escaped with their lives.

Franz Vickers was off-guard, his rifle propped up by the side of a tree. When he glanced up, it was to see the three escapees merrily strolling along not twenty metres away from him.

He grabbed his rifle, and without aiming, fired at the first man. The man went down. Then he turned his attention to another and he too fell dead. That only left one survivor and he would have gone the same way as all his comrades that day, had the SAS man not had a stoppage in his rifle.

The sole survivor, a very lucky man indeed, ran for his life, making the final tally 21 out of 22.

It was more than the SAS captain could have wished for. The long walk and the wait had been well worth it.

Colin Willis radioed the news to Mtoko and called for a casevac chopper to take out the sick trooper and for a water resupply.

They were tasked to remain in the area to continue ambushing any ZANLA/ FRELIMO reaction force but when FRELIMO started chasing them around the countryside, harassing them with a mortar, it became obvious that it was no longer possible to carry out any more ambushes, and they returned home.

Into the Russian Front, October, 1977

For more than six months, the SAS had been in control of the Tete Province of Mozambique.

It was the Rhodesian Special Air Service, *not* FRELIMO, who controlled the area. Nothing moved; nothing dare move for fear of an attack from the SAS, who had been popping in here, there and everywhere, mining, ambushing, stirring things up, waylaying ZANLA and their FRELIMO comrades, and leaving a trail of bodies, broken vehicles and demolished buildings.

Then, in May, just to show who was in charge, they took over an entire town. Not only did the SAS succeed in taking over the whole province, they cut Tete off from Rhodesia and pushed ZANLA and FRELIMO further away from the border to Tete town itself. As a result, the number of ZANLA operating in the whole of the Operation *Hurricane* area had dropped from 800 to 210.

Then the SAS were told they were being withdrawn from Tete to go into the south-east, the Gaza Province. They had operated there before, but now they were to go in-depth to try and repeat their Tete success, to halt the ZANLA infiltration into the south-east of Rhodesia.

Had they been allowed to remain in Tete, there is no doubt they would have got closer to the town.

As it was, the security force unit which replaced them did not have the expertise or the staying power to maintain the SAS's good work. It may well have been boring for them, as there was nothing much going on because of previous SAS activity.

In the event, the province eventually reverted to what it had been before the SAS started their campaign of intensive harassment. The replacement unit took a hammering and FRELIMO got bolder. The Tanzanians began clearing the roads of landmines for them and as a result, terrorist incursions into Rhodesia stepped up.

There were simply never enough SAS men to be everywhere they were needed. Unlike other units, which boasted 600 and 1 000 men, the SAS only ever had 200 operators at any time, and then only on specific large scale operations when the commanders had to call up TA and extra regimentally employed members.

The SAS was to take over from the Selous Scouts, who had been having a terrible time in the south-east and were telling the SAS all sorts of horror stories. There were some Scouts who said the SAS would be run out of the area by FRELIMO. The SAS said that remained to be seen.

The Scouts had previously attacked the terrorist camp at Mapai, blowing buildings and taking over the airfield. As a result, ZANLA and FRELIMO could be expected to be more alert in their endeavours to locate Rhodesians entering their territory.

Apart from the Mapai attack, the Scouts had generally concentrated their attacks on the rail line, and had done a good job, too.

But the SAS now planned a new tactic, one that the enemy would not be expecting ... they were to operate south of Mapai and harass the parallel road system and convoy route from Barragem to Mapai.

Not only had the SAS to get into the south-east undetected, but they had to remain so, at least until their first task was completed.

Then commander, Major Brian Robinson hit on an idea. Surely they could carry out a HALO entry (high altitude low opening)? After all, the higher they were the less suspicion they would arouse from people on the look-out below.

It was the only logical answer. But unlike previous missions, Brian wanted 24 men to freefall in, not just a couple of four-man pathfinder teams in separate areas.

If successful, it would be the largest number of freefallers to jump on a single operation during the Rhodesian war. It was a daring idea. But it was not without its problems.

The mission called for two dozen men to leap out of a plane at dead of night *without* a moon, in the heart of very hostile territory and with almost double the amount of kit they would normally carry.

As they would need enough equipment to carry out their first ambush, they would be jumping with rifles, 60 millimetre mortars and RPD machineguns, and each RPD gunner would have 500 rounds of ammunition on him.

They would have to land on a single DZ and regroup before first light. To do that, they would have to exit the plane virtually touching each other; then keep as tight a formation in the air as possible, but without getting entangled with each other.

They were to infiltrate from 12 000 feet above ground level, which was *just* on the oxygen level. To add to the risks, there would be only *one* emergency oxygen bottle in the plane to revive anyone who passed out.

In addition, they were to take along three boxes of additional kit to resupply themselves after their first ambushing task – and that, too, had to end up in the same place.

The boxes with their parachutes were to be pushed to earth first and would carry a flashing strobe light to enable the freefallers following to know where they landed. Fixed to each box would be an automatic opening device designed to release the parachute at a pre-determined height.

The strobes would flash all the way to the ground and continue flashing once the boxes had touched down, thus enabling the parachutists to zero in on them, and providing them with a single rallying point.

The freefallers, led by the mission commander, would have red or green lights on their helmets. As they jumped out of the plane, they would either turn right or left depending on their number and colour.

Thus, if everyone managed to stay close together on exit, there would be one stream of red lights descending through the darkness and another of green – and hopefully, they would not get entangled with each other.

Although they were to use civilian pilot Jack Malloch's DC-7 for the actual drop, their practise jumps with kit were from a Dakota. And although they were able to work out their exits from the plane, correct their body angles and try out their red and green light system to avoid mid-air collisions, they would find the Dakota just did not give the same effect as the DC-7.

The rehearsals, too, were carried out with packs of only average weight. Come the day of reckoning – October 11 – they were to find they bore no resemblance to the proper thing.

As their packs were strapped underneath their buttocks to rest against the backs of their upper thighs, and as the amount of kit each man carried began to mount up, the parachute training staff responsible for checking their equipment at New Sarum began to get worried.

Yet despite their exceptionally heavy loads, there was some debate among the more experienced freefallers about the necessity of having to wear the automatic opening device. Some felt they did not need them. But Brian Robinson and the parachute training staff wanted no unnecessary heroics, and insisted.

Their checks over, the 24-man freefall team lumbered into the DC-7, taking up their places on the makeshift benches. Then it was off across the border into the Gaza Province.

As the DC-7 sped through the night, the atmosphere in the plane was tense.

Would their additional weight affect their exit speeds? Would they be able to keep a tight formation? Would the lack of moon make if difficult for them to assess the wind drift, of prime consideration to the freefall paratrooper? And would they pass out?

The pilot and navigator had their own problems too. Not for Rhodesian pilots the fancy navigational aids of more sophisticated air forces. The aircraft had no navigational equipment other than a compass and the drop was to take place in enemy territory without a moon.

Pilot Jack Malloch and his navigator were to drop the troops on a time and distance basis in the dead of night. They had worked out their timings and distances precisely ... but without a moon and sophisticated equipment, would it work?

Then as they approached the border, a brilliant white glare lit up the night as an SAS operator based at Mabalouta forward headquarters, threw a flare to help the pilot pinpoint his position.

Towards 03h00 and 12 000 feet above ground level, a trooper collapsed through lack of oxygen. A dispatcher hurried across, revived him with the emergency oxygen set, then helped the visibly pale man back on to the bench.

But the operation they were about to undertake was a complicated one and time was short. The red light was already on. They would have to get going.

The woozy operator would have to be left behind. Quickly, they took the man's mortar equipment from him, the commander, Dave Dodson delegating someone else to carry it.

The rest had already lumbered to their feet and staggered to the open door. The three boxes containing their additional kit were lined up on rollers on the opposite side of the open door, now seconds from falling through the darkness into Gaza.

Then off the boxes went, crashing over the rollers, their flashing lights already working.

Immediately, Dave Dodson launched himself out into the night, following the flashing lights of the boxes down through the darkness. The second man stepped into the air after him.

One by one, the heavily-laden freefallers shuffled towards the door. But the angle of the rollers became a major hurdle as they squeezed through the doorway and attempted to get into a good exit position.

Normally, kitted-up freefallers would swivel around on a ninety degree angle from the door to face the engine, presenting themselves square on to the slipstream and getting into a good face-to-earth freefall position.

But because they were being particularly careful not to step on the rollers, they were unable to get into a good exit position . . . and, as the DC-7 was much bigger and faster than the Dakota, having two engines instead of just one outside the door, the slipstream they encountered was far greater than they had been expecting.

And those freefallers who presented only half their bodies to the slipstream ended up tumbling and spinning head-over-heels through the air.

Then one man, weighed down with kit, tripped one metre from the door, slowing down the flow of exiting troops. The dispatchers picked him up bodily and threw him out of the plane.

Far below, Captain Dave Dodson was on his way down through the night. He pulled his ripcord at 2 500 feet. The other chutes were to crack open higher up, a precaution to avoid mid-air entanglements, thus creating a staggered effect.

The heavily-laden troops were finding their ability to manoeuvre around the sky impaired by all their kit, and instead of the nice red and green line of lights, it was beginning to look like a checkerboard as they skated across the night sky.

The last man out of the plane, Jan Greyling, staggered to the door under the weight of all his kit. Then just as he leapt into space, he blacked out . . .

By now the three boxes had landed and the commander followed the flashing strobe lights down. He landed nearby, climbed out of his harness and waited for the rest of his party to join him.

They were scattered all over the bush and when he totted up, he found that four of his men were missing. Most of them wandered in at first light, and Iain Bowen, who had landed on the side of an anthill, was carried in piggy-back style.

Of the 23 men who had jumped in to Gaza that night, Iain Bowen had a broken leg, two had twisted ankles and one had a stick in his buttocks, all the result of wearing heavy equipment and being unable to see exactly where they were landing. And one was missing.

It was quite an entrance into the south-east.

But the pilot – without a moon or sophisticated navigational equipment to help him –had dropped the troops on time and within five kilometres (three miles) of their planned DZ. It was an amazing achievement.

Missing was Sergeant Jan Greyling, who had lost consciousness as he leapt from the plane. Jan had come to floating down under his canopy. An experienced freefaller, he had been one of the men against using an automatic opening device. Now he owed his life to Brian Robinson for insisting he wear one.

Yet despite his relief at having an automatic device firmly in place and working, Jan was a worried man. He couldn't see any of the red and green lights twinkling in the darkness beneath him, and even before he landed, he knew he was completely alone.

It was the first time he had been in the area and he did not know his exact location. And tonight of all nights, he did not have a radio with him.

But now, despite his initial misgivings, his SAS training and survival instincts were beginning to take over. He knew he could not sit where he was and wait until someone came and found him. He would have to go and find them.

Drawing a map in the sand with a stick, he worked out that from the aircraft speed and the average gap between each man out of the door, that he must be seven kilometres (four miles) from the rest of the crew.

To the west was the Limpopo River and beyond that South Africa and the Kruger National Park. He decided that if he couldn't find his companions, he would strike out for the South African border.

He reviewed in his mind what he would need with him – what was essential, what could be safely left behind. He buried his main and reserve chute and all the unnecessary kit; and at first light set off with his water and troop medical kit, which he might well need should he ever meet up with the others.

Then he heard the familiar sound of parachutes being torn down from trees.

Cautiously optimistic, yet sure it was friends, Jan eased through the bush and closed nearer to the sound – only to find himself in the midst of a herd of elephant ripping the branches off trees. He nimbly skirted away and took off through the bush.

Hour after hour he trudged through the scrub searching for the 22 other freefallers, getting more concerned all the time, cautious about what lay ahead and who might be following behind.

Once he heard a shot ring out. But was it FRELIMO? Could it be friends?

Jan kept setting himself objectives. After midday, he would go west, then the next stop would be the Limpopo.

That afternoon, he began to pick up spoor of boots and equipment. It looked like a typical sweepline searching for someone. Obviously FRELIMO, he told himself. Now he was even more cautious than before.

Then came the distant sound of someone chopping at a tree. Was it the freefallers trying to communicate, indicating their emergency RV? Perhaps it was FRELIMO signalling their men to regroup? On the other hand, it might just be a local chopping firewood.

Perhaps the spoor he was still following belonged to his SAS friends after all?

He fired a shot and almost immediately the sound of a double tap, two shots in close succession, came back. That, Jan told himself, was definitely a signal and he cheered up.

The mission commander, who had dispatched search parties at first light, now sent out another patrol to locate Jan. And 15 hours after jumping into oblivion, a much-relieved Jan was delighted to see the familiar faces of SAS men approaching through the bush.

The final tally was four men injured and 19 men fit and ready for action.

Jan Greyling patched up the casualties, and although Iain Bowen with his broken leg qualified for immediate casevac, they were all to remain in the bush until the first ambush had been sprung. To send for a casevac chopper beforehand would have alerted FRELIMO and ZANLA to their presence in the area, and they would have lost the element of surprise.

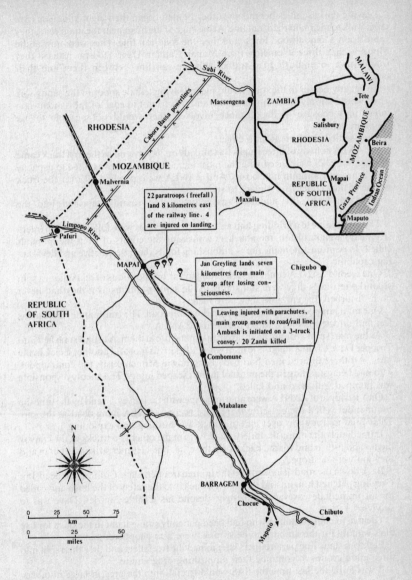

Into the Russian Front

Leaving the casualties behind, the other 19 men began their eight kilometre (five mile) walk to the main road/rail line. At the edge of the bush near the main road, they came upon a sandalwood forest and then the road/rail line. They were now at the Mpuzi siding, three kilometres from Mapai. Captain Dave Dodson realised they would have to ambush road traffic with the rail line between them and their target.

To get any nearer to the road would mean leaving telltale spoor in the sandy soil. They would simply have to mount the ambush from the edge of the sandalwood forest, and because of the distance involved, they would not be able to use claymore mines.

They settled down to await a target.

A ZANLA convoy of three trucks was already on its way and as the first truck came in sight, the SAS were faced with the most incredible sight. It was filled to capacity with arms and ammunition boxes. And ZANLA were perched all over the truck wherever they could find a place to sit.

Then suddenly, the ambush was initiated and rounds smashed into the driver's cab.

The truck came to a grinding halt and the opening shots were followed by an intensive heavy weight of fire, the attackers witnessing the effects of what the manuals called "maximum automatic fire" – ambushing for its sheer destructive and devastating capability.

One second ZANLA could be seen sitting in various positions of relaxation; a split second afterwards they were still sitting in the same positions as if they had never been disturbed. Except now, they were lifeless.

One man jumped off the truck and ran down the road. The commander leapt to his feet and directed his men to get the fleeing ZANLA.

As the man spun around, he sprayed automatic fire at them. A round smashed into Trooper Dave Collins' head, one man got a bullet in his foot and another a nick in the head. All three injured men had been lying down. Miraculously, the commander, who had been standing in the midst of them, escaped injury. The enemy responsible was pumped with lead and killed.

Only a couple of ZANLA were able to escape with their lives . . . and by the time the commander yelled the ceasefire there were twenty ZANLA lying dead in the sun. Their final journey was over and the truck was burning and exploding.

Immediately the ambush started, the drivers of the other two trucks in the convoy did an about-turn and roared back down the road. But a Hunter strike was put in and they too were destroyed.

Back down the road, it looked as if the injured trooper, Dave Collins, was dead. Jan Greyling patched him up and they moved back into the safety of the bush and called for an immediate casevac. Amazingly, despite his terrible injuries, Dave was to survive.

The five freefall casualties who had been patiently sitting it out in the bush for five days waiting for the ambush to be sprung, were also choppered out.

Eighteen static line paratroopers later joined the freefallers and they then split into three main groups to continue their ambushing programme.

It was to be the last time the SAS would freefall into the area in large numbers. Thereafter any plane which went over was immediately suspect.

As expected, ZANLA had been caught unawares by the attack on their convoy and they and their FRELIMO friends would now be more alert to the possibility of road ambushes.

As far as the SAS could determine, the south-east was nearly as hard as the Selous Scouts had warned them, and it was going to get harder. From now until the last days of the war, the SAS would be operating in the south-east, and they were big enough to admit it was a particularly difficult area to master.

There were no high points in the region. They would find that water was desperately short at some times of the year, and the few pans of water there, were very difficult to find. The SAS would listen for frogs at night for an indication of where to find the odd oasis. And when they did locate water, they would often discover it was undrinkable.

The soft, sandy soil made anti-tracking exceptionally difficult. And the security forces were almost always reported to FRELIMO by the local civilians, who were extremely hostile and would even help FRELIMO track down the SAS.

The Rhodesians would never have enough heavy equipment with them and what little they did have was up against FRELIMO tanks and armoured personnel carriers.

The south-east was also a long way from any air support. A chopper flight from Mabalouta to Mpuzi, for instance, was two hours, and as a result, close air support was seldom used by the SAS.

FRELIMO in the south-east were far more aggressive and numerous than those the SAS had encountered in Tete and would actively go in search of a fight.

The main route where the security forces located ZANLA and FRELIMO was on the parallel road and rail line, and there were constant patrols along the route.

The longer the SAS operated in the area, the more FRELIMO and their advisers developed better methods of locating them. Eventually, FRELIMO groups were based at all the various sidings down the rail line. Then, whenever an aircraft was heard in the area, the various groups would begin patrolling, covering their portion of ground and looking for spoor, which because of the sandy soil, was easy to find.

If the SAS were looking for action, they knew they would find it in the south-east.

"A" Troop (later Squadron) was to have a particularly active time in the south-east and much SAS blood was spilled there. There is no doubt that had the Selous Scouts returned to the region when "A" Troop were there, they would have found it considerably harder than before.

Operating in the region would ultimately become more a battle of wits between the SAS, FRELIMO and their Russian and East German advisers. So bad did it become, the SAS dubbed the region "The Russian Front".

Operation Melon, November, 1977

By October, a new tactical picture was developing in south-east Mozambique.

FRELIMO who were already very aggressive, now intended getting even tougher with the Rhodesian security forces. They were more than a little upset at the Rhodesians' continued presence in Gaza Province and had instructed all units to engage actively and rout the border-hopping Rhodesians.

They also intended supplying as much war material and spiritual assistance as possible to their ZANLA comrades.

163

For Rhodesia's security forces operating against ZANLA's entry and resupply routes in the province, it had become increasingly difficult to distinguish between FRELIMO and ZANLA. The more ZANLA was attacked, the closer they moved into the FRELIMO confines – and the more the *Freds* protected them.

And ZANLA, realising the obvious benefits to be obtained by travelling the roads with their FRELIMO friends, were in the process of switching from using civilian buses and other forms of transport, to the relative security of travelling in FRELIMO convoys.

It was a dilemma which was becoming more and more frustrating to SAS commanders and their troops as they vainly tried to stick to the Rhodesian Government policy of leaving FRELIMO alone ... whilst at the same time, always hitting positively identified ZANLA targets.

Then at the end of October, the radio interceptors tipped the SAS off about a six-vehicle ZANLA convoy which was on its way from Maputo docks to Mapai, the major military FRELIMO garrison in Gaza. Thereafter, it would travel onwards to the border carrying ZANLA commanders and reinforcements straight to the south-eastern operational area of Rhodesia.

It was a ZANLA only convoy, and as an added bonus, the vehicles were brand new. It was certainly an opportunity not to be missed ... and Captain Colin Willis and 15 other men were immediately deployed to the forward operational base at Mabalouta in the south-east to prepare for the mission.

At 18h00 on November 1, they boarded a Dakota and crossed the border, flying low, and pursuing a zig-zag course, a routine procedure carried out in the south-east to confuse any observers as to their true destination, and to infiltrate under FRELIMO radar cover which was capable of picking up aircraft movement within a 160 kilometre radius of Mapai. Their DZ was 120 kilometres (75 miles) into Mozambique and they were well within that radius.

At 19h00, the 16 men leapt into space from 500 feet above ground level ... while above them, "A" Troop commander Captain Bob McKenna strained his eyes to watch as his men floated gently through the twilight, before landing safely in an open pan in the middle of a sandalwood forest.

The Dakota, still flying low, droned on its way through the darkness, and every so often, the aerial resupply dispatchers threw out alpha bombs – small 1 kilogram steel balls which bounced before exploding in the air – a ploy to convince the enemy that the Dakota was on a bombing mission, *not* a parachute run.

The Dakota turned, then headed for home.

Some fifteen minutes later, the pilot saw a fire glowing through the darkness. The night had come down suddenly and the fire was the only thing visible through the gloom of the evening.

Ahead lay FRELIMO's Mapai garrison, but all was quiet and there was not so much as a chink of light to be seen.

The aerial resupply dispatchers disgorged another cluster of alpha bombs to give the chaps sitting around the little camp fire a rude awakening, then the Dak continued on its way.

Suddenly, all hell was let loose inside the plane.

The pilots had unintentionally overflown Mapai, and the enemy gunners, having been alerted to the Rhodesians' presence by the last drop of exploding alpha bombs, were ready and waiting for them.

A barrage of bullets, green tracer and flak poured through the cockpit, zinging down the fuselage, narrowly missing the aerial dispatchers and gouging holes in the plane.

Alloy was pinging in every direction from the effects of FRELIMO's 23 millimetre anti-aircraft shells, 12,7 millimetre heavy machinegun rounds and smallarms fire.

The co-pilot was blasted out of his seat in some sort of instinctive muscular spasm, and crashed on to the controls. The next barrage of rounds went through the plane's direction finder and aluminium sliced through Bob McKenna's face.

The plane meanwhile had dived from 500 feet and was heading straight to earth. Bob McKenna, and SAS officer Percy Johnson, who were both standing in the cockpit, were thrown off balance and now lay on the floor staring in horror at each other.

The commotion about them prevented their sharing their fears aloud, but each was convinced that both pilots had been killed – and that they were heading for a crash.

Suddenly, just 200 feet above the ground came a miracle. The plane began pulling out of its dive and when the two SAS men looked up it was to see that the pilot was still very much alive and in control of his plane.

The dive had merely been a brilliant evasive action to get them clear of the anti-aircraft fire. And by the time the FRELIMO A/A gunners had adjusted to the Dakota's new range and altitude, the Rhodesians had made good their escape.

By the time the Dakota pulled away, the co-pilot had pulled himself up from the control panel and had clambered back into his seat and both pilots were busily checking the plane was still flying and would get them safely across the border.

Fortunately, there were no fires on board and their main worry was the damaged direction finder. They started to map-read their way home and although the going was a bit rough and it took some considerable time, the plane managed to limp back to Buffalo Range airstrip.

On landing, the shaken pilots and passengers immediately jumped out and rushed to the mess for a quick drink to regain their composure and celebrate their good fortune.

Next morning, they found 23 holes, some as big as a man's fist, had been punched into the plane. A bullet had also cracked the cylinder head of an engine. They had been extremely lucky and they would remember not to go near Mapai again in a hurry.

* * *

Meanwhile, Captain Colin Willis and his team of 15 paratroopers, having cached their chutes, were on their way to the main Mapai-Maputo road, a trek of 15 kilometres (nine miles), which had to be completed by first light.

The ZANLA convoy was expected two nights after the drop, giving the SAS ambushers one night's buffer time to establish their trap.

By 10h00 on November 2, they had found a reasonable place to site their ambush . . . and as the mine-laying party set to, the men in one of the early-warning positions saw two FRELIMO and one ZANLA strolling along the road. The SAS opened fire, but the thick bush prevented them downing the enemy with their first shots and a small fight developed between the enemies. However, the exchange was swiftly over and three ZANLA lay dead on the road.

Colin realised that since the contact may well have been heard by FRELIMO troops on duty at the various sidings along the main road, there was a very real possibility that the enemy, who were particularly active after any air activity, would now have positive evidence they were in the vicinity and would come looking for them.

165

There was nothing for it. The SAS would just have to pull out and look for another site. Luckily, they still had some buffer time, enough to allow them to move a healthy distance away and set up the ambush all over again and still be within the time frame to catch the convoy.

The bodies were left on the road and booby-trapped; and some mines were left. The troops gathered their belongings and pulled out, eager to put at least 15 kilometres (nine miles) between their original ambush site and their new one.

But they had travelled only four kilometres when the sounds of heavy vehicles could be heard adding weight to Colin's worst suspicions. All along he had been worried that the convoy would come on the first night, not the second, and they would miss the chance to ambush it.

And now it was too late to set up another ambush. The convoy would be on top of them before they could complete their preparations. There was little they could do but wait and hope.

Still, their landmine was in place at the old ambush site and they were in with a chance of hitting at least one vehicle and halting the convoy long enough for them to dash back and get to grips with the remainder.

As the vehicles rolled closer through the early evening, it was becoming apparent that it was no ordinary convoy. The noise told there had to be far more than the six ZANLA trucks they were expecting. It was becoming obvious it was a well-disciplined military convoy of some considerable size and importance.

The 16 SAS men could only assume that the extra numbers meant it was a joint ZANLA/FRELIMO convoy travelling together for protection. They were not to know it then, but it would prove a much bigger prize altogether.

An enormous, but not unexpected, thunderclap reached them across the bush as their landmine and claymores exploded. At least, they consoled themselves, they had scored one hit.

But moments later, the initial blast was followed by an even bigger secondary explosion. For FRELIMO and ZANLA had made the foolish mistake of putting an ammunition truck at the head of their convoy – and were to suffer dearly for it.

The truck and its contents continued to blaze away fiercely for the next few hours, preventing other vehicles getting past the burning, exploding obstacle.

Over and above the sounds of the explosions, other noises told their story. Vehicles were revving, moving to and fro and lights were going on and off. The enemy, having decided against returning back down the road in the direction they had come, were basing up for the night and were moving into some sort of defensive or protective formation. The enemy commanders no doubt hoped that the fire still raging in the ammunition truck would burn itself out, and they would be able to continue their journey the following morning.

For the SAS watching and listening to the fireworks from down the road, it was another opportunity not to be missed.

If they could be allowed to direct strike aircraft on to the extremely vulnerable convoy, it would indeed be a prize target for the Air Force.

By the watery light of the moon, Colin Willis instructed the signaller to send a detailed report using the Morse code giving their location and the estimated strength of the convoy to the tactical HQ at Mabalouta. Then he asked for the men of No 1 Squadron, the Rhodesian Air Force to come and join the punch-up.

The information was passed back to the SAS headquarters and ComOps, and within thirty minutes he had received a reply. It was "affirmative".

The SAS moved in closer to the road to give a better target indication to the aircraft and to get themselves in an ambush position to stop any vehicles fleeing past them.

Then, with the ammunition truck continuing to explode into the night, they settled down to await first light.

* * *

As dawn approached, sounds of activity could be heard coming from the direction of the convoy. Vehicles were manoeuvring into the cover of the bush, as the enemy commanders, realising their vulnerability, began to prepare for a visit from the Rhodesian war planes. For the ammunition truck was still burning, and it was still impossible for them to get past.

At first light, although they could not see it, the SAS could hear the drone of a Rhodesian Lynx high overhead. All vehicle movement down below ceased immediately.

As soon as the Lynx got within radio range, Colin established communications with "A" Troop commander Bob McKenna on board the plane and began giving him a sitrep. Using the burning ammunition truck as a reference point, the ground commander indicated the area where the convoy vehicles were hiding.

"We haven't got them visual yet. There are too many trees," pilot Flight-Lieutenant Giles Porter radioed Colin. "We're coming around again for a closer look . . . We need to get a bit lower," he added.

But Bob McKenna, who had read the danger in his ground commander's voice, wasn't so sure that was a good idea. "Well, I'm staying up here on a cloud," he was heard to mumble in the background.

Giles Porter descended to treetop level and flew up the road, passing the SAS position and heading straight towards the blazing ammunition truck.

As the Lynx closed on the target, the clear, still morning was rent by the deafening roar of some 400 automatic rifles, several 23 millimetre anti-aircraft guns, machineguns and assorted missiles including Strela.

One moment the SAS party down the road saw the Lynx, the next it had disappeared into a billowing black cloud of flak, as the full wrath of the enemy was brought to bear on the pilot, his passenger and plane in what had to rate as the heaviest concentration of firepower Colin had witnessed during the long bitter war.

As for pilot Giles Porter and SAS commander Bob McKenna, they thought their last hour had come. For Bob, it was the second such feeling in two days. But there is no substitute for luck and the pilot deftly managed to pull his plane safely away. Amazingly, neither it nor the men on board had taken a single hit.

Down the road, Colin gulped and turned to tell his 15 men to dig in. But they needed no telling. With hundreds of heavily armed enemy just a few kilometres away from them, the odds suddenly didn't seem so good any more and they were already furiously digging.

Then the Hunters swept in, locating their targets from the muzzle flashes of the weapons firing at the Lynx, and from the windscreens reflecting in the early-morning sunlight, a point the enemy had overlooked when attempting to hide their vehicles.

By the time the Hunters had done their first few strikes, the scene below them resembled something out of a Viet Nam movie. Ammunition trucks were burning and exploding, terrorist rockets were zig-zagging all over the show, the wrecks of vehicles were cartwheeling in every direction and there were massive fireballs everywhere.

The smoke from the Hunters' 30 millimetre guns added to the spectacle and often, as one Hunter swooped in to attack and a truck blew up behind it, the second supporting Hunter would be flying through the debris exploding from the first strike.

For the next five hours an intense and spectacular land/air battle raged.

The Hunters kept up the momentum, making strike after strike, hitting the vehicles, with one pair of planes replacing the next as their weaponry was exhausted and their time overhead ran out, and they had to return to base to rearm and refuel in readiness for their next strike ... and the defenders grimly hitting back with everything they had.

After the fourth strike, the SAS raiders decided discretion was the better part of valour and leaving *The Blues* to sort out the convoy, they vacated their holes and quickly moved away from the road.

A very strong follow-up group, making use of a 12,7 millimetre anti-aircraft gun mounted on wheels, was soon hot on their spoor, highly upset that the small SAS team had managed to cause such havoc.

Colin Willis and crew were determined to shake off the enemy and find a lying-up point where they could lay low for a couple of days and let the heat die down before returning to ambushing road traffic.

They were careful not to leave spoor but, as always in the south-east, the ground was such that anti-tracking was impossible in some places ... and in those areas, they booby-trapped their spoor and left a few other surprises scattered around to discourage the enemy.

A couple of times they heard their booby traps go off. They hoped it was to the detriment of the enemy, but as it also served as a reminder that the hunt was still on, they got moving again.

They set up a small base in the escarpment of the Limpopo River and on the fourth day when everything had gone quiet, they were ordered to return to their DZ forty kilometres away to await uplift. In view of the success of the operation, the powers-that-be decided to pull them out and let things die down for a while.

But as they made their way back to the DZ, their radio told that ComOps now wanted them to get back to the scene of the holocaust to make an accurate assessment of the damage inflicted on the convoy ... how many vehicles and who exactly was involved ...

It was not the most popular request with the ground troops and Colin was annoyed that they were being asked to carry out a reconnaissance, particularly as an aerial photograph could well have sufficed with no risk to life.

Having seen the large number of troops involved and the intensity of their firepower, no one was particularly keen to go skulking around in the target area and bumping into large groups of determined enemy who were clearly better organised and trained than the ones they normally encountered.

But orders were orders and Colin sent 12 men back to the DZ to unearth the parachutes, while he and three others returned to the target area. He felt that a smaller group would be much easier to control, easier to avoid trouble and less likely to stumble into the enemy.

They were extremely apprehensive about encountering a still very active and highly upset enemy and it took them a further day of very slow, cautious movement to ease into the target area.

That night, it was a very careful group of SAS men indeed who closed in on the black hulks of wrecked vehicles. They were half expecting to find an aggressive reception party lying in wait for them.

But there was no one and nothing had been left buried in the scorched soil to take them unawares. They were greeted only be an eerie silence and a scene of utter devastation. After the apprehension of returning to the scene the four SAS men experienced a feeling of almost comic relief to find the place totally devoid of enemy.

Around them lay the remains of what had been a convoy of brand new vehicles. All told, there were 21 damaged vehicles. Only one had managed to flee from the carnage.

They found a mobile operations centre, and the more they looked around, the more obvious it became that they and their Air Force friends had taken on the whole FRELIMO 4th Brigade HQ (Mobile), which had been moving up to Mapai in compliance with their orders to supply closer support to ZANLA and to set up a forward base to conduct the war against Rhodesian security forces.

They found enough evidence to convince them the convoy was led, managed and organised by Russian advisers. It was the first time that the Rhodesians had seen definite proof that the Russians were operating in Mapai.

The SAS collected much incriminating evidence from the debris of the Russians' presence, including Russian uniforms and numerous documents. The Russian/Spanish dictionaries they found, also indicated there had been a Cuban presence.

The damage inflicted by the air strikes was virtually complete and the four soldiers were gratified to see the amount of brand new Russian trucks, trailers, fuel and water bowsers, operations and command centres, support weapons and spares which had been rendered useless on their first trip from the docks.

There were also bogies, track and ammunition for T34 tanks, making it the first indication of tanks in Gaza Province – and the first time tanks had been found so close to any Rhodesian border.

Colin assessed that a few of the vehicles could be repaired and just to prevent that happening, the Hunters screamed in a few days later to put them out of action for good.

The SAS also found evidence of a ZANLA presence in the form of two trucks, the remains of which carried ZANLA literature, uniforms and documents.

There was only one body, but the evidence of used medical equipment, bloodied uniforms and helmets with skin attached to them, indicated that many had been wounded or killed ... and subsequent intelligence revealed there had been fifty casualties.

Colin and his small team radioed their findings to ComOps, then, after dodging a couple of FRELIMO patrols, rejoined the rest of their group. They were uplifted and recovered to Rhodesia without incident, the enemy and their Soviet advisers in the *Russian Front* having been dealt a very severe blow indeed.

Operation Dingo

> *"We are fighting for the existence of law and order here*
> *and you cannot just sit back and let bases like that exist.*
> *Yes, we will continue to operate behind enemy lines."*
> *– LIEUTENANT-GENERAL PETER WALLS*

Nineteen seventy-seven was drawing to a close and it was almost twelve months since SAS commander Brian Robinson had called in his intelligence officer, Scotty McCormack and given him a special task.

The SAS commander had been tipped off about the presence of a huge ZANLA complex ninety kilometres (56 miles) inside Mozambique, and Scotty was given the job of finding out every scrap of information he could about the place.

Unlike the Selous Scouts, the SAS did not have their own SB officers to provide them with up-to-the-minute intelligence, and, as the information about the ZANLA camp was not coming in to them, they would just have to go and find it for themselves.

Scotty began his investigations immediately and learned that an increasing number of ZANLA being caught in the *Thrasher* operational area had been telling SB that they had been at the camp which was roughly opposite Umtali. Some called it New Farm; others Vanduzi or Chimoio, as it was only 17 kilometres (10 miles) north of Chimoio town.

All this information had been forwarded to the Central Intelligence Organisation in Salisbury. And there it sat. Nothing was going to be done about the camp.

Scotty was able to glean more information about the Chimoio camp from Pete Stanton, of SB, and from the Selous Scouts intelligence officer, Alan Lindner. His dossier was getting fatter; but he wanted more.

"Okay then," Scotty said at last to the people in the aerial photographic department, "let's fly it."

When the film from the photographic run was processed, it was obvious he had not been wasting the pilot's time.

The camp was enormous, with 13 separate areas, and was far bigger than anything he had imagined. The photographic interpreters carried out a head count and totted up 700 ZANLA on the rifle range alone.

Scotty got the photograph enlarged as big as it would go, then sent for Captain Jacques Dubois, of the Intelligence Corps. In civilian life, Jacques worked in the Surveyor General's office – the government mapping department – and Scotty asked him if it was possible to make a model of the camp.

Jacques assured him it would be no problem, then, armed with the photograph and maps giving all the contours, he set to work.

Top secrecy was clamped on the project and as Jacques couldn't be seen working on the model at the Intelligence Corps headquarters, he had to build it in the SAS presentation room. He was helped by a sergeant from the Intelligence Corps and a woman from the photographic interpretation department, whose husband was a professional model maker.

Jacques and his team worked diligently for six solid weeks getting the detail absolutely correct and the model perfectly to scale.

Initially, to give them the detail they were after, coloured foil was placed over separate negatives of the aerial photograph. These were then placed on two overhead projectors, thrown on to a screen and viewed through coloured glasses. Thus a 3-D effect was obtained and all the camp's features and characteristics were highlighted. The aerial photograph was then fitted over the papier-mâché model and according to those who saw it, "surpassed all expectations in its splendour".

Then, just as the finishing touches had been put on the model, came a stroke of luck. Umtali SB came up with a capture who had left ZANLA's Chimoio camp two weeks earlier.

He was sent immediately to Salisbury where Scotty sat him down before Jacques Dubois' model.

"Right," said Scotty, "there's the camp. Remember, you are looking at it from above. Now – tell me what you know."

And the man went through the whole layout from beginning to end, placing the jigsaw together until a picture emerged that was both revealing and worrying.

The camp was the biggest, the most important ZANLA base in Mozambique ... the headquarters and nerve centre of Robert Mugabe's war machine.

FRELIMO had allocated the entire Chimoio/Vanduzu/Pungwe area to ZANLA and since fleeing Rhodesia after the abortive detente exercise, Mugabe had begun to reconstruct the war effort from Chimoio. The ZANLA leader and his two top commanders, Rex Nhongo and Josiah Tongogara, directed operations from their high command headquarters, in an old farmhouse.

It was from Chimoio that the thousands of ZANLA brought back from Tanzania, China and Ethiopia after training, deployed straight into Rhodesia to wage their war.

The main part of Chimoio covered five kilometres (three miles) and there were many satellite camps, specialising in a variety of tasks, as well as a centre for women combatants.

The enemy were extremely well dug-in in trenches and bunkers. There were a multitude of anti-aircraft positions in pits. And there were look-out towers for anti-air early-warning, which were positioned throughout the camp and manned by ZANLA with whistles.

Civilian farm buildings, houses and grass huts were scattered throughout the complex. ZANLA had learned their lesson and eventually realised that if they positioned their base camps in confined areas, they could be boxed off and everyone in them annihilated.

They hoped, too, that by spreading themselves among the local population, the civilians would provide them with early-warning of a Rhodesian attack.

Chimoio camp was also close to a large FRELIMO base, and ZANLA had rightly guessed that the Rhodesians would be very reluctant to kill civilians and would not want to involve FRELIMO in their fight with ZANLA.

Then, parallel with his study of Chimoio, Scotty turned his attention to another major ZANLA camp, called Tembue, responsible for incursions into the *Hurricane* operational area. It was north-east of Cabora Bassa, 225 kilometres (140 miles) from Rhodesia. Tembue was easily located on aerial photography and another papier-mâché model was made and the camp brought to life.

FRELIMO had moved in close to the Tembue camp to monitor ZANLA movement, desertion and theft.

Scotty now had the low-down on the two most important terror bases in Mozambique, responsible for all ZANLA infiltrations into Rhodesia.

Recruiting had been high and there were thousands of enemy amassed in the two camps. But there were not enough weapons for everyone and approaches had been made to FRELIMO to supply them with weaponry and ammunition.

With all their anti-aircraft precautions, ZANLA felt extremely secure in their two camps. Not only had they sited them near civilians and FRELIMO as double insurance, but as Chimoio was ninety kilometres from the border, they were confident that the Rhodesians wouldn't *dare* attack it. It was just too far.

As for Tembue, that was twice as far from the border; the Rhodesians wouldn't even *dream* of striking 200 kilometres into Mozambique. It was a ridiculous notion.

They had not, however, reckoned with the determination of the SAS commander, Brian Robinson, his second-in-command, Mick Graham, Scotty McCormack, SAS troop commanders, and Air Force Group Captain Norman Walsh. For massive pre-emptive strikes against the two camps were precisely what they had in mind.

171

Unlike other armies where the initiative came from the top, this time it came from a small nucleus of officers who were morally supported by Special Branch.

They realised only too well that the insurgents had to be stopped at source. It was no use waiting until they were inside the country. Despite the lethality of fireforce, that concept could not stop the momentum of insurgent infiltration. Only pre-emptive strikes against external enemy bases could do that.

The most daring operation of the war to date, the Selous Scouts raid into Nyadzonya/Pungwe base – commanded by ex-SAS officer Rob Warraker in August, 1976 – had taken the operators forty kilometres (25 miles) from the border as the crow flies, although it had involved a long devious journey to get there.

But Chimoio was twice as far and Tembue five times that distance from the border and planning pre-emptive strikes against them posed a number of interesting problems.

How could they get to the camps undetected? And how could they account for the maximum number of enemy? And, even if these problems were solved, would Com-Ops give their blessing to such an audaciously *overt* operation so far from home anyway?

In view of the distance involved, it was out of the question for a strike force to drive to the targets as the Scouts had done. Tembue in the north was too far to go. And it was impossible to drive to Chimoio and remain undetected. It was a heavily populated tribal area and word would have reached the camp long before they got there . . . and they didn't want to run the risk of finding the camp vacated.

That left only air effort – and that was something that had been forbidden by the hierarchy, except for casualty evacuation, and then only in the case of serious injury.

Undaunted by the difficulties, Brian Robinson, Norman Walsh and team pressed on with their planning, knowing that if *they* didn't push for attacks on the camps, nothing would be done at all . . . the camps would remain in being . . . the insurgents would pour into the country in their thousands.

* * *

Years of watching camps during attacks had proved to the Rhodesians that no matter how often the enemy had been shown where the escape routes were, they never stuck to them. Experience had shown that when the Rhodesians arrived, the enemy had run in whichever direction they happened to be facing at the time.

Thus, it was no good positioning stop groups on *likely* escape routes. If a camp was to be hit effectively, it was obvious the whole camp had to be surrounded.

Brian Robinson and Flight-Lieutenant Frank Hales had developed a method to do just that. Called *the box*, it involved sending Dakotas or helicopters to all four sides of a camp . . . disgorging troops to act as stop groups all the way around the target . . . enabling every possible escape route to be blocked.

The element of surprise was total. They literally got the drop on the enemy – and they achieved the best possible results in terms of kills.   But having decided *the box* was the best method of attacking Chimoio and Tembue camps, Brian Robinson and his team were then faced with the major problem of how they were going to get all the helicopters to the target.

The ParaDaks – Dakotas bearing paratroopers – could get to the targets in one trip, so there was no need to worry about them.

But the Alouette IIIs, the only helicopters Rhodesia possessed, had a very limited range and it was impossible to get them to even the nearest target in a single flight.

It would call for a refuelling stop on the way in to the target – and another on the way out.

In the case of Chimoio, the choppers could refuel at an administrative base inside Rhodesia to get to the target, but they would need somewhere close at hand where they could go to refuel and rearm to enable them to carry out strikes on the camp... and to top up for the journey home. Getting helicopters to Tembue, which was twice the distance from the border, called for an even more complicated manoeuvre.

There was only one possible solution. They would have to take over a piece of Mozambican territory and establish a forward administrative base *inside* enemy countryside for however long the operation lasted.

They would only need one such base for the Chimoio raid, but because of the vast distance involved, they would have to set up *two* when they attacked Tembue.

It was a daring idea and nothing like it had ever been done before. But again, would ComOps go for it?

Brian Robinson and his team naturally wanted to get the best results from both camps, too. Ideally, they needed to hit them simultaneously, but the hard facts of life were that Rhodesia simply did not have sufficient aircraft to do that.

It meant the Rhodesians ran the risk of arriving at the second target to find the enemy forewarned and the camp vacated. The team was then faced with another problem – which camp to hit first to get the maximum kills.

* * *

Eventually, they were satisfied with their plan and invited the hierarchy to visit SAS HQ to listen to a presentation of their proposed mission.

With the magnificent models spread out before them, Scotty McCormack gave an intelligence briefing on the two biggest terror bases in Mozambique. Then Brian Robinson and Mick Graham presented the army case and Norman Walsh, the air force's.

They had to sell the entire concept to the ComOps team – the attack itself, the necessity for it, the advantages to be gained, what would happen if they did not attack it, and the admin base idea.

The hierarchy listened in fascinated silence as the proposed plan unfolded and clearance was sought for the raid. And they didn't like it one little bit.

They didn't believe the security forces could get the huge numbers of kills Brian Robinson and his team were saying they could with the limited amount of air weaponry available. As for the amazing suggestion that they establish admin bases *inside* enemy territory ... well, they were not sold on that at all.

The Tembue plan calling for *two* bases to be set up in Mozambique, was totally out of the question. The camp was simply too far away to even be considered as a target.

What worried ComOps was that the external admin bases would have to be set up almost as far from the border as the targets themselves. In the event of the helicopters being discovered as they rearmed and refuelled, they would be sitting ducks. While the Rhodesians would protect the vulnerable aircraft, all the enemy needed to do would be to put a few mortar bombs in among the choppers and there would be chaos.

If the planes were destroyed, it would be impossible to get the troops out of the target and they would face a very long trek home with all the attendant problems. Brian Robinson, Norman Walsh and their team were not keen on this aspect either, but considered it a calculated risk that had to be taken.

As in all major missions, too, the aggressor nation had to apply a percentage aircraft loss. While nations like America could suffer a loss without being seriously affected, Rhodesia with her limited air force, sanctions, and shortage of foreign currency to replace the aircraft, could not.

Rhodesia simply could not afford to lose a single aircraft. And to lose as many as ten, would be catastrophic. They would never be able to replace them and the Rhodesian Air Force would become virtually non-operational.

As it was, considering the enormous scale of the proposed operation, the Rhodesians would be working with minimal numbers of aircraft. It was a ludicrous situation and everyone knew it.

But what terrified the hierarchy most of all was world opinion. For if an aircraft was shot down in enemy territory, it would be *blatantly* obvious to the world who the aggressors were – not, that the world would not know anyway. World reaction would be far from favourable. Rhodesia, already under intense pressure from all sides, would be well and truly roasted.

No doubt, too, the rest of the world would claim refugee camps were attacked, just as they had done on the Nyanzonia camp attacked by Selous Scouts a year beforehand. The ammunition belts on many of the bodies had been conveniently ignored by those who screamed "refugees".

When the idea was first mooted, it was the era of Kissinger and the Geneva Conference. Could Rhodesia be seen to be acting so *overtly* when they had agreed to peace talks?

Finally, the ComOps hierarchy said that the Chimoio target was a possibility, but turned the Tembue plan down flat. Brian Robinson and his team would have to go back to the drawing board and have a rethink about that phase.

The first presentation had been given in November, 1976. A year had passed – and still the operation had not been given the go-ahead.

After the first presentation the whole idea had gone dead for a while. In the meantime, the camps were being photographed once a week and mushrooming at an alarming rate. Every single ZANLA captured inside Rhodesia was telling SB that he had either been at Chimoio or Tembue. Ships were docking along the east coast and trained ZANLA were being offloaded en route to the camp ... planeloads of men were arriving in Beira from Dar-es-Salaam ... and trainloads of ZANLA were passing through Chimoio on their way into Rhodesia.

Eventually, almost a year after the camps had first been picked up by aerial photography, the figures at Chimoio stood at between 9 000 and 11 000, making it the largest concentration of enemy ever to be in one camp at that stage of the war.

By comparison, the figures at Tembue training camp in north-east Mozambique were small. But the 4 000 enemy there could do an awful lot of damage if they crossed into Rhodesia.

It had become extremely frustrating to SB officers and security forces in the know to see the problem growing – and knowing that nothing was going to be done about it.

Eventually, the possibility of attacking the camps was resurrected and Brian Robinson, his troop commanders and Air Force Group Captain Norman Walsh began an intensive phase of trying to convince ComOps that the time had come to attack the two camps. As before, they emphasised the same old argument . . . that the only way to stem the flow was to turn off the tap.

As for the enemy, they had become even more confident that they were never going to be attacked by the Rhodesians.

Finally, SAS intelligence officer Scotty McCormack was called upon to give another presentation to the ComOps team. It was his 12th presentation – the 12th time he had tried to sell the idea.

By now Scotty knew the two camps like the back of his hand, and without a single note before him, he stood up and gave a detailed briefing, stressing the precise points he knew the hierarchy wanted to hear. Cataloguing the military facts of life, Scotty emphasised how the camps had grown, and how, if left unchecked, they would continue to grow.

He explained the advantages to be gained in striking offensively; told how ZANLA would want to push as many people into Rhodesia as possible before the seasonal heavy rains began and before the infiltration routes got too bad.

The hierarchy needed no reminding that at that time of the year the bush became an enemy, too. For the rains provided ZANLA with plentiful water and lush vegetation cover, and seriously hampered security force operations.

They needed no telling of the terror that could be caused by vast numbers of infiltrating ZANLA. The enemy were learning more than their Chimurenga songs of liberation at the two camps. The number of people on the rifle ranges alone proved that.

Incursions were on the increase and attacks had been mainly directed towards black civilians in the rural area. Two hundred civilians had been murdered in the previous two months.

Then the two chief architects of the plan, Brian Robinson and Norman Walsh, presented their case for the Army and Air Force. The hierarchy went away to consider all they had heard and weigh up all the pros, cons and ramifications of such a raid.

They would have had to consider the same aspects as the year before – the possible aircraft loss; what the world would say about such an overt mission . . . the biggest cross-border offensive of the war to date. On the other hand, the situation in the country was critical. Could they sit back and allow such bases to exist, particularly the two biggest camps in Mozambique, responsible for all ZANLA incursions and drastically affecting the conduct of the internal war?

The people at the top had never stopped believing either that the Rhodesian problem could be solved politically. But the Geneva Conference had failed to bring a ceasefire and the war was more intense now than it had been when the idea of striking the two camps was first put to the national planners.

To the astonishment of Brian Robinson and Norman Walsh, their endless bulldozing had paid off. The green light was given and the operation was to be called *Dingo*, with Chimoio given the codename Zulu-1, and Tembue, Zulu-2. The time had come to stem the tide, to deliver a telling blow to the ZANLA war machine – to eliminate the enemy, gather intelligence and disrupt the enemy's logistics.

The detailed and very complex planning for the two-pronged thrust into Mozambique began immediately. Busiest of all at that stage were the people in aerial photographic who sat for days scanning photographs of Mozambique to find suitable sites for the three external admin areas.

The admin areas – one for the Chimoio raid, two for the Tembue phase – had to be 10-15 minutes flying time from the target; in the most isolated areas possible; somewhere that could take all the helicopters; and in places where those security forces defending the aircraft during the camp attacks could parachute into.

There had to be high ground nearby where they could position sentries . . . and well away from access tracks. Nor had the admin areas to be anywhere near a position the enemy could take advantage of to mortar the planes.

It was a tall order, but eventually three suitable sites were found.

The admin base for the Chimoio raid was to be eighty kilometres (fifty miles) inside hostile territory and only ten kilometres (six miles) from the target. The admin bases for Tembue, 225 kilometres (140 miles) from the border, were to be set up on a huge flat-topped mountain south of Cabora Bassa, nicknamed *The Train;* with the second base sited ten kilometres from the target.

Both Chimoio and Tembue were formidable targets, and with a minimum of 9 000 ZANLA at Chimoio and 4 000 at Tembue, the 185 Rhodesian ground troops who were to attack the two camps would be sorely outnumbered.

Of the 9 000 to 11 000 at Chimoio, 4 000 were known to be fully trained, operational and armed. It is standard military doctrine that during the attack phase, the attacking force must have a three to one superiority. Rhodesians, short on manpower as they were, were not going to pay any attention to that.

Only surprise, the well-used principle of war, could help. Repeated visits by *The Blues* would help to even up the odds, however. Nevertheless, the planners were working on a thirty percent casualty rate.

Using every aircraft Rhodesia possessed, they could get no more than 200 troops to the targets at any one time.

And as the whole aim was to achieve maximum surprise, it could not be done in more than one wave. It was futile to take in one wave of troops, then go and collect another wave. For by the time the second wave got there, the enemy who had survived the initial attack would have already fled.

Both raids were to be basically similar and were to prove classic examples of vertical envelopments.

Chimoio – the bigger of the two camps – was to be attacked first and the 97 SAS and 48 RLI parachutists were to land on two sides of Chimoio . . . while forty helicopter-borne RLI troops were put down on the third. It was envisaged that the fourth side would be theoretically boxed in by the fire from the K-cars.

Timings would be critical, with the paratroopers arriving in Chimoio exactly two minutes behind the initial air strike.

The idea was that the anti-aircraft defences would be too busy shooting at the strike aircraft to pay any attention to the Dakotas bearing the SAS and RLI paras. The helicopter-borne troops would be put down near the camp shortly afterwards . . . and exactly eight minutes later the K-cars would swoop in to close off the cordon.

The ground troops would kill any enemy fleeing the strafing of the aircraft, sweep forward flushing out others hiding in the bush, then advance on the main complex itself. Aircraft meanwhile would continue to pound the camp for as long as necessary.

To the troops involved, it seemed a straight-forward enough plan. But for the SAS Officer Commanding Major Brian Robinson and Air Force Group Captain Norman Walsh, *Operation Dingo* was a planner's nightmare.

For the plan to succeed, it was absolutely critical they achieve total surprise. Having at long last got the go-ahead to mount the strikes, the two planners were haunted by the possibility of arriving at the targets to find the enemy were on to them and the camps vacated.

Yet, how could an armada of noisy aircraft arrive over the target without giving the game away?

If the wind was blowing in the wrong direction, it would send the sounds of the advancing helicopter gunships straight towards the camps. It would give the enemy, whom they hoped to catch unawares, a good ten minutes early warning ... long enough to scatter or take cover, and sufficient time to man their anti-aircraft guns in readiness to take on the vulnerable Dakotas flying over the camp at 500 feet.

So what could be done to maintain their security? How could they outsmart ZANLA, whom they planned to attack at their regular 08h00 muster parade when they were at their most vulnerable and concentrated?

Then Norman Walsh hit on an idea. He felt that if the assembled enemy were to hear a jet scream over the camp ten or 15 minutes *before* the first strike went in, they would break ranks and dive for the safety of their trenches, thinking the Rhodesians were about to attack them.

When nothing happened, they would take up their positions on the parade square again. Planes were seldom heard in the area and they would probably think it was a stray airliner. It would give them a false sense of security for the time the noise from the *real* enemy aircraft was heard overhead.

The Rhodesian planners were banking on the enemy reasoning that as nothing had befallen them the first time around, they would not bother to run for cover a second time. And that would seal their fate.

The scheme had the virtue of never having been tried before. But would it work? Civilian pilot Captain Jack Malloch, owner of a sanctions-busting airline who was always ready to help out with any security force plan, readily agreed to lend his DC-8 jet and a pilot for the task, which had to be worked out with split-second timing so that ZANLA were back on parade at precisely the time the Rhodesian jets appeared overhead.

Then another worry. The two planners could not dismiss the awesome prospect that the weather might be against them and they would get to the point of no return to find Chimoio in cloud. The strikes were timed for late November and there was a very real possibility of rains and cloud.

If – after the noise from the aircraft had alerted the camp to their presence – they then had to turn around and go all the way home without the attack going in, they knew that would be that; they would never get the go-ahead to mount the operation again.

In addition to their other worries, Brian Robinson – who was to command the ground troops – and Norman Walsh – to command the air effort – would carry a further psychological load.

The hierarchy had imposed a strict limit on their time across the border, and as they were still concerned about world reaction, they wanted the entire operation over and every man and machine back in Rhodesia in three or four days.

The two planners would then have the extremely difficult job of organising the extraction phase. Everybody who had parachuted in or had been choppered to the target and all those held in reserve in the forward admin area had to be brought out again.

They had to bear in mind that they were swinging from an easterly target to a northerly one within 48 hours, which from a logistical, manpower and airpower point of view was an enormous problem.

The mission which was to set a number of operational precedents, would be the first time a senior army and air force officer were to command a major external battle from a helicopter. As far as the planners could see, it would be stupid *not* to use a helicopter to command the battle. A commander needed to read and feel the battle, and it was difficult to do that if he was not near the target. Previous experience had shown that unless air and ground forces could get a quick response to requests, the battle tended to get bogged down.

A helicopter would provide the two commanders with the most mobile platform possible. They could fly wherever they wanted, follow the battle around from their elevated position, be more involved in the proceedings and in radio contact with everyone. And as Norman Walsh was a pilot, what could be better than having him fly the chopper and direct the air force side of the operation with Brian Robinson sitting next to him, commanding the ground troops?

An Alouette III was modified to suit their needs and proper radio plugs installed so that they could transmit at the same time but on different networks. Both seats were next to each other and faced forward.

As well as the command chopper, there was also going to be an Admin Dakota with a command element, although it would have nothing to do with the battle itself. General Walls was to fly in the Admin Dakota, twenty-thirty kilometres (12-18 miles) north of the battle zone and his role was to be very much politically-orientated. He would have a direct link via a teleprinter back to the Prime Minister in Salisbury, and his function was to decide such things as what action to take in the event of FRELIMO scrambling their MiGs.

Eventually, all the rehearsals and attention to detail were over and it was time for the real thing. The strike planes were bombed up, and the SAS and RLI troops began arriving at New Sarum Air Base, Salisbury. The magnificent model of Chimoio was moved into a hanger and stands arranged around it for everyone who was going to be involved in the operation. Other intelligence information – aerial photographs, maps, charts – were arrayed on boards.

Then the general, the air marshal, the rest of the brass, and all the soldiers and airmen filed into the hangar and took up their seats to hear Brian Robinson and Norman Walsh give their orders.

It was certainly a strange way to give orders. Brian Robinson was a major; and yet there he was giving orders to the top brass when it ought to have been the other way around.

And the orders were thorough and in-depth, catering for most eventualities.

Although Chimoio housed 13 separate camps, it was out of the question for the Rhodesians to attack them all because of the limited numbers of aircraft available, and SB had been tasked to select the five most important camps to hit.

The ground troops would be wearing normal Rhodesian camouflage to make them easily identifiable to each other during the battle, and their caps were to be turned inside out to reveal bright orange "dayglo" patches, making them recognisable to the pilots and airborne commanders.

It was stressed they were not to engage FRELIMO. The raid was against ZANLA only, not their host country's troops.

Each para-stick commander had been given written orders and after the two planners gave their overall briefing, the commanders then gave their own detailed orders, telling each member of his stick where he was to be positioned ... his fire and movement drills ... who the sub-commanders were ... who was to be the medic ...

Then, to ensure the written orders were followed to the letter, they carried out their battle preparations until everyone knew where to go and what his role in the action was to be.

The Dakotas carrying the 97 SAS and 48 RLI paratroopers were to fly straight to the target . . . while the forty helicopter-borne RLI would fly from Lake Alexander, a forward air base a few kilometres from the Mozambican border.

After the mission, the helicopters and all the troops would exfiltrate through the external admin base, then return home via Lake Alexander and Grand Reef air base.

Eventually, final equipment requirements were drawn and the forty RLI troops who were to be choppered into the ZANLA camp began the long drive to Lake Alexander to await the arrival of the helicopters.

Ahead of them went SB officers Pete Stanton and Pete Dewe who were to interrogate prisoners and sift through captured documents. The two men were dressed in police reservists uniforms and the local water bailiff stopped by for a friendly chat.

"Hello chaps," he said, "what are you doing here?"

"We're waiting for some mates," they replied, explaining they were going to camp by the lake for the night.

Next morning, the water bailiff passed by again to see the air force knocking white tabs in the ground for the choppers. Later, he saw every helicopter Rhodesia possessed lined up along the lake shore.

"You *have* got a lot of friends," he remarked with a shake of his head when he saw the two SB officers in a restaurant later.

* * *

D-Day Minus One was extremely tense for Brian Robinson and Norman Walsh. They had a couple of drinks in the mess to help them doze off, but it didn't really work and they spent a very restless night.

They knew only too well that they had planned the enormous in-depth cross-border raid down to the last detail, but as they tossed and turned throughout the long night, they continually quizzed themselves if they had forgotten anything . . . if it would work . . . if the enemy would still be there by the time the jets arrived overhead . . . And, indeed, if the mission was still on.

For they could not help sensing even at that late hour, that the hierarchy were still apprehensive about the operation, still uncertain they would be able to get the vast number of kills they claimed.

Certainly, no one, hierarchy or planners, knew what to expect.

Sleep eventually overtook Brian and Norman . . . and when they awoke, it was to find that it had rained during the night. It was their first of many worries that long, eventful day; for they had no idea if the target would be in cloud.

As the two planners stepped out on to the tarmac that crisp early morning, they were confronted by the magnificent sight of row upon row of camouflaged helicopters lined up on the wet tarmac, all ready for the order to lift off. There were the ten troop carriers, all the K-cars to be used in the attack, and the command chopper.

They now knew that, except for atrocious weather, there would be no cancellation. They were committed.

As the incoming flights of aircraft had been arriving at New Sarum from other centres in readiness for the mission, Salisbury folk up early that morning were quick to guess something big was afoot. Those old enough to remember World War II were to liken it to D-Day all over again.

The pilots climbed into their aircraft, eager to be gone. Then the commander of the Air Force, Air Marshal Frank Mussell came on to the runway to see them off, and at

05h00 on Wednesday, November 23, the pilots started their engines and headed eastwards in waves of five.

The country's most audacious pre-emptive mission to date had begun and it was a year to the day since the idea had begun to take shape.

Elsewhere in New Sarum, the 48 RLI paratroopers from 3 Commando (under the command of Major Gerry Strong, BCR) and the 97 SAS operators were fitting on their parachutes, strapping their rifles in place and would soon take up their positions inside the six Dakotas. In Thornhill air base, Gwelo, the bombed-up jets were taxiing on to the tarmac. Soon Jack Malloch's DC-8 jet would be streaking across the border towards Chimoio.

Altogether the massive air effort seen over Rhodesian skies that morning totalled 42 helicopters, eight Hunters, six Vampires, three Canberras, six Dakotas and a dozen Lynx's.

* * *

At Lake Alexander, close to the Mozambique border, there was a sudden flurry of activity. The helicopters had landed uneventfully and soon, the refuelling was complete and they were ready for the last leg of the journey to Chimoio.

The task of leading the armada of helicopters to the target rested squarely on the shoulders of one man, Squadron Leader Harold Griffiths.

He had made his flight plan and had marked out all his reference points and knew exactly what was going to happen every minute of the journey.

The forty RLI helicopter-borne troops climbed into ten choppers and the squadron leader's chopper lifted. Then, one after the other, the rest followed, flying low to get into Mozambique under radar cover.

As the squadron leader map read and led the way to Mozambique, Brian Robinson and Norman Walsh in their command chopper were questioning each other on codewords and the position of stop groups during the forthcoming battle. After endless weeks of dry runs, it was their first live rehearsal. Next time, it would be for real.

Just before the armada reached the border, their journey took them through a valley. Suddenly, as the squadron leader led the way down the valley, he was confronted with a blanket of solid cloud. There could be no going on.

He did a quick U-turn and headed back down the valley . . . followed by the entire armada. His carefully-laid plans and timings had now been thrown out, and, having been forced to change plans mid-air, he had to virtually map read by the seat of his pants.

Luckily, the squadron leader found another valley that was clear of cloud, but the detour had cost them precious minutes and the planners immediately began to worry about the fuel situation.

The DC-8 jet meanwhile, had screamed over Chimoio with taps full open, making as much noise as possible – and the enemy fled for cover, just as the planners had hoped.

The Dakotas bearing the paratroopers were flying direct from Salisbury and the tension inside the planes was thick.

SAS captain Colin Willis was thinking that he must have been crazy to leave the safety and security of a job at the School of Infantry to get involved in something like this. This was no small task, and the odds – almost 200 Rhodesians against 9 000 to 11 000 – seemed ridicuious even with surprise and air back-up. As he looked around at the grim, determined faces in the Dakota, he wondered as he often did, who would be coming back.

As it got nearer to H-hour, the paratroopers were relieved to see they were no longer alone. There was now a multitude of aircraft accompanying them to Chimoio. Jets were passing them, other Dakotas were flying with them, and they in turn were overtaking helicopters.

The jet pilots were anxious to know what the weather was like into the target. Norman Walsh, flying ahead in the command chopper radioed it was all right, although he personally didn't consider it particularly good.

The peace and tranquility existing in the biggest war base in Mozambique could now be measured in minutes.

Brian Robinson and Norman Walsh glanced at their watches once more that morning. It was now almost H-hour.

In Chimoio, ZANLA were gingerly coming out of their tranches. They thought the jet that had just flown over had heralded the start of a Rhodesian air strike. But nothing happened and they considered themselves safe. By 08h00 they had all taken up their places for their daily muster parade.

Suddenly, they became aware of an aircraft very high in the air, coming from the south. At first, they thought it might be Samora Machel, the Mozambican President about to pay one of his periodic visits.

But the base commander was not so sure and he gave the order to dismiss. But by then the bomb doors of the Rhodesian jets had opened and their cargoes were already on their way. The bomb aimers in the Canberras saw a sea of faces looking up at them from the parade square. Then came the "bombs gone".

Huge columns of black smoke and dust were enveloping the camp . . . people were running in every direction . . . fires were starting all over the complex. The unexpected had happened . . . and they had no hope.

The two men who had planned the mission, sat in the command chopper a few minutes flying time from the camp, anxiously awaiting a quick sitrep to learn if the jets had been on target or not. They glanced at their watches again. It was way past H-hour. Things had still not quietened down sufficiently for the Hunter squadron leader to give his report yet. Finally, Norman Walsh could stand it no longer.

"Red One," he said to Richard Brand over the air force net, "were you on target?"

The voice of the squadron leader crackled over the air immediately. "What a question," the pilot replied reassuringly in a very casual air force drawl.

After that, the tension went out of the whole thing and the planners knew they were in business. The weather had been okay after all and the DC-8 ploy had enabled them to maintain their security. The swiftness of the assault and the rapidity with which it was pressed home came as a total surprise.

By now, the SAS and RLI stick commanders in the Dakotas were listening in on their headsets for a blow-by-blow account of what was going on ahead of them. Two minutes from jump time, having removed their headsets and put their helmets on, they heard the deafening crunch of the airstrikes over and above the noise of the Dakotas.

Now they could see the multi-coloured tracers of anti-aircraft and smallarms fire streaking across the sky towards them.

The red lights came on and everyone waddled along the fuselages towards the open doorways with characteristic gait, the mood not quite so apprehensive now. As the commanders stood in the doorways, they could see the many satellite complexes sprawled beneath them exactly as in their scale model. The crackle of smallarms fire passing the Dakotas punctuated their thoughts as they prepared to leap out.

The Dakotas were flying at between 450 and 500 feet, the normal height for operational jumps. Any higher and the descending troops became easy targets; any lower and it would be too hazardous to jump, resulting in heavy casualties.

They came to the run-in and the green lights went on – and precisely as planned, two minutes after the first air strikes went in, they jumped into Chimoio. And the game was very much on.

As the command choppers came within range, Brian Robinson and Norman Walsh were confronted with the unbelievable sight of Hunter strikes, Vampire strikes and everything that flew going into the target. Then came the armada of Dakotas – and the air was filled with the puffs of countless parachutes.

Next, the helicopter-borne RLI troops were put down on their side of the camp . . . and eight minutes later the gunships arrived to close off the cordon. The camp was surrounded and everything was going according to plan.

(Meanwhile, other troops were being dropped into the forward admin base ten kilometres (six miles) away by the DC-7, to secure the area and await the parachute drop of helicopter fuel.)

As soon as the paratroopers left the Dakotas, they could see the airstrikes going in and by concentrating on them, were able to orientate themselves in relation to their own specific targets.

After the noise of the Dakota, the static of the headsets and the noise of the air-strikes, the silence was almost deafening as they floated down under their canopies.

Suddenly, the anti-aircraft gunners were trying to shoot them from the skies. As the ground rushed up to meet them, they could see scores of ZANLA running beneath them.

"Christ, but these guys can only move," thought one paratrooper, remembering they had been positioned far enough away from the camp for the enemy to get there *after* they had landed.

From the moment they got out of their harnesses, they began engaging the fleeing enemy. They could not shoot and exchange magazines fast enough and within a few minutes of landing, one four-man group had accounted for eighty ZANLA.

Few ZANLA entertained any serious thoughts of retaliating. They only wanted to get away as fast as possible.

Several paratroopers landed in trees and were now trying to struggle free of their parachutes and take on the men running beneath them, before they could turn their attention to the soldiers dangling in mid-air above them.

Captain Colin Willis's parachute was entangled in two trees and no matter how hard he tried, he couldn't get out of his predicament. His rifle was still firmly held in place by the body band of his parachute and by the time he had grabbed his pistol, the ten armed enemy running straight towards him were only thirty paces away.

He blasted away at the men, who by now were running directly beneath him. One man fell mortally wounded at his feet. Realising his commander was going to have a problem, Sergeant Les Clark raced to the rescue and downed six of the nine enemy.

The pressure now off, Colin swung himself across to one of the trees, released his harness and dropped to the ground, feeling much safer and happier being on the soldier's normal environment with plenty of good cover around him.

Now the stop group commanders consolidated their stop lines, took cover and watched and shot, just as their orders had instructed.

The volume of fire from both attacker and camp defender was intense. The Hunters and K-cars continued to pound the complex with everything they had and the enemy anti-aircraft gunners grimly fought back.

Within the first five minutes, every aircraft over the target had taken a hit, including the command chopper, and Brian Robinson and Norman Walsh were forced to retire from the battle and return to the forward admin area.

It was a serious setback. The alternative army commander was on the ground and could not be uplifted because of the thick trees. As he was unable to see the overall picture from his position, he was virtually ineffective and could not control the battle.

It would be the security forces first lesson of the day. Next time, they knew that the alternative commander needed to be airborne as well. There was now no one to control troop movement other than *The Blues*, and it was an extremely frustrating time for the ground troops who were eager to get to grips with the A/A gunners still firing at the aircraft.

Back in the admin base, the two planners managed to scrounge a lift in other aircraft and they would use them until the command chopper was repaired and they could get together again.

The whole episode had cost them a precious thirty minutes when they desperately needed to be over the battle to control it.

As soon as Brian Robinson appeared over the camp again and started redirecting the battle, the stop lines began pushing through the bush to the main camp. ZANLA were flushed out and only token resistance was offered, their enthusiasm for the armed struggle suddenly wearing very thin. By the time the troops reached the camp, they had several prisoners who were more than happy to co-operate and point out the best routes and hiding places.

For the rest of the day, the SAS and RLI continued to have battles all over the camp. The enemy were hidden in a variety of places and the soldiers had a job to winkle them out. The A/A gunners only abandoned their positions once the troops closed in.

There were areas where the two planners had to bring in airstrike after airstrike to try and clear the enemy. The Canberras were to return to the camp several times to deliver their deadly payloads . . . the Hunters were going back to Thornhill air base, Gwelo, to refuel and return to strike their targets time after time . . . and the helicopter gunships bustled back and forth to the nearby admin area to refuel and rearm before going back to Chimoio.

As one SAS group advanced on the ZANLA garage, the enemy opened fire. Corporal Trevor Kershaw looked to see if the sweepline was straight, and as he did so, a single shot struck the man next to him between the eyes.

The stick commander bellowed to his men to get down and take off their dayglo caps, for that was what the enemy were shooting at. The SAS sank to earth. But there was no cover and the enemy were still shooting at them. While Sergeant Phil Cripps sent out an urgent request for the casevac chopper and a K-car to flush out the enemy, another man crawled towards the injured soldier, who had now stopped breathing.

With the enemy still firing at them, he gave mouth-to-mouth resuscitation and breathed life back into Frans Nel while the medic sorted out the drips. But thirty minutes later, Frans was dead. A K-car arrived to strafe the area, and when all fell silent, Frans and a couple of other injured men were lifted out.

Inside the command helicopter – repaired and back over the battle within a few hours – the amount of radio traffic filtering through the chopper was phenomenal.

183

There were 64 individual army radio stations alone and scores of air force ones, and the two commanders had to handle all requests for casevac, ammunition re-supply and air strikes. These in turn were channelled through the Admin Dakota which acted as the airborne link to the external admin and main bases in Lake Alex-ander, Grand Reef, Salisbury and Thornhill, from where support would be forthcoming.

Although the commanders were transmitting on different channels, they could not separate them and it meant they were listening to everything at once.

During the day, a FRELIMO reaction force positioned at Vanduzi Crossroads fired at a Vampire piloted by Flight-Lieutenant Philip Haigh. He got the plane back to Rhodesia but was killed in a crash landing.

* * *

The din of the battle had died down now and towards last light on that first day in Chimoio, an SAS corporal shinned up a tree and held aloft the green and white flag of Rhodesia, just to show who was in charge.

As darkness descended, the troops were put into defensive positions and settled down for the night. There were several contacts with ZANLA who stumbled in on them and several were killed when they wandered into the buildings, thinking the Rhodesians had gone home.

But there had been no sign of the leadership element and if the top commanders were there, they certainly did not stay to rally their men.

The wife of Edgar Tekere, destined to become an outspoken and controversial figure in Zimbabwe politics, managed to escape detection by standing in the communal latrine for three days.

By now, the wounded were staggering towards Chimoio town and the press would soon be on to the raid. Back home, security was tight. The operation was not yet over and the Rhodesians would have to wait for details.

* * *

Next morning, the stop groups began re-sweeping their previous days' targets and destroying whatever was still standing.

Captain Bob McKenna and his team moved down to the main transport area to find twenty vehicles in various states of repair. One belonged to Robert Mugabe and the sticker on another told it had been serviced at a Salisbury garage a few days before.

They destroyed the ZANLA workshop, petrol tank, then used the sole remaining vehicle, a Peugeot pick-up truck, to collect the anti-aircraft guns, which were to be taken back to Rhodesia.

The distances between the various anti-aircraft positions were vast and Bob and his team reckoned they got to see more of the battlefield than anyone else. They collected seven 12,7 millimetre guns, and destroyed a Chinese 37 millimetre twin-barrelled anti-aircraft gun which was too heavy to take back home.

Finally, it was all over and the Rhodesians began to leave Chimoio. Men, kit, the captured weapons and a mountain of documents, were, bit by bit, pulled back to the forward admin base ... then to Lake Alexander ... and on to Grand Reef Air Base, Umtali.

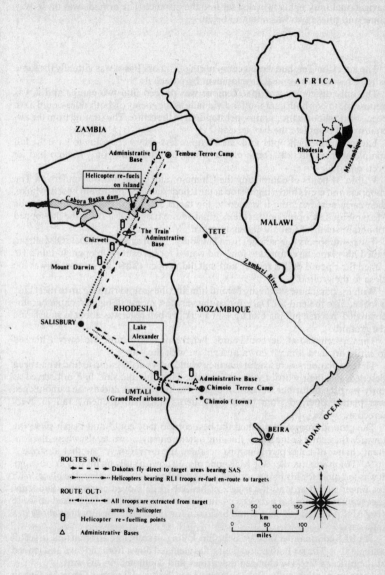

AFRICA

ZAMBIA

Administrative Base

Tembue Terror Camp

Helicopter re-fuels on island

Cabora Bassa dam

MALAWI

TETE

'The Train' Administrative Base

Chizweti

Zambezi River

Mount Darwin

RHODESIA

MOZAMBIQUE

SALISBURY

Lake Alexander

Administrative Base

Chimoio Terror Camp

UMTALI (Grand Reef airbase)

Chimoio (town)

BEIRA

INDIAN OCEAN

ROUTES IN:

- - - → Dakotas fly direct to target areas bearing SAS
.... Helicopters bearing RLI troops re-fuel en-route to targets

ROUTE OUT:
••••◄•••• All troops are extracted from target areas by helicopter

🛢 Helicopter re-fuelling points

△ Administrative Bases

N

0   50   100   150
km
0   50   100
miles

Operation *Dingo:* The helicopter and Dakota routing for the attacks on ZANLA's Chimoio and Tembue bases

185

It was almost dark when they began their approach to Grand Reef. A long line of navigational fairy lights twinkled far into the distance. The armada was on its way home and phase two was about to begin.

* * *

The attack on Tembue recruit camp north of Cabora Bassa was virtually the same as for Chimoio – a vertical envelopment by parachute.

The only difference was that Tembue was divided into two camps and it was impossible to box both camps off individually as the enemy on both sides would have been able to shoot at the paratrooper stoplines in the centre. The strafing from the aircraft would complete the box instead.

Except for one helicopter and one Vampire less, they were going to have the full complement of aircraft. Those planes which had taken hits on Chimoio had all been repaired.

Within 24 hours of completing the Chimoio raid, phase two was underway. The choppers and crews had a night-stop at the Rhodesian forward admin base at Mtoko, then early next morning it was on to the target 225 kilometres (140 miles) inside Mozambique, stopping only at the external admin base on *The Train,* the flat-topped mountain south of Cabora Bassa, to refuel.

The paratroopers flew straight from Salisbury . . . and as Sergeant Dale O'Mulligan exited his plane, he counted to four and waited for his canopy to open. It didn't. He pulled the ripcord on his reserve and that didn't open either, for by now he was too close to the ground.

With his parachute streaming behind him and the ground rushing up to meet him, it looked like the end for Dale. But at the very last moment, his parachute became entangled in a tree pulling him up with a jerk just before he was about to smash into the ground.

The very relieved soldier could hardly believe his good fortune. He lowered himself to earth, brushed himself down and got on with the war.

The two planners were fearful that they would arrive at the camp to find it had been deserted, but their worries were unfounded. The Chimoio raid had not served as early-warning of further Rhodesian aggressive intentions – and as the camouflaged war planes emerged from behind the trees, the terrified enemy ran in every direction.

The ground troops established the best cordon they could and began sweeping towards the centre of the camp, flushing out the enemy . . . while, elsewhere, the constant chatter of helicopter gunships heralded the arrival of yet another airstrike.

"A" Troop commander Bob McKenna moved down a gully on his way to the camp. It was too quiet for his liking and there was a feeling of danger about the place. With his finger curled around the trigger of his AR-15 he moved cautiously. Suddenly, there came the sound of a rock as it bounced down the cliff face. He looked up to see six ZANLA armed with ten-round SKSs waiting in ambush for him high above in a little cave.

The SAS commander fired from the hip, killing all six before any had time to get off a single shot. The six bodies and their rifles clattered down from the cave and landed at the officer's feet. He changed magazines and continued on his way.

Later, in another gully, Bob, Sergeant Les Clark and Trooper Gerry McGahan came face to face with a large group of enemy.

Standing back-to-back, the three soldiers blazed away while the enemy fled into the bush and dived for cover. Fortunately for the Rhodesians, Bob and Les carried automatic rifles, and Gerry an RPD light-machinegun. In the whole of the war, the three men had never fired so rapidly or changed magazines so quickly.

The contact lasted three minutes and by the time they had finished and other troops had arrived to help, 86 enemy lay dead. There were three SAS men who could be forgiven for thinking they had won the war single-handed.

There was a FRELIMO presence three kilometres to the north in Tembue town, but helping their ZANLA comrades was the last thing on their minds. The Rhodesians could see them through their binoculars as they stood on their roofs watching the proceedings – and cheering.

Ten kilometres away in the Rhodesian-owned admin base, technicians were examining a chopper which had taken a hit. Their verdict: if it was to fly again, it would need a new engine. Unusual though it was to change an engine in the field, it had to be done. A new engine was flown in, and then, standing on a fuel drum, the technicians took the rotor blades off, changed the engine and made it serviceable again – and did it all in six hours.

By late afternoon, SB came up with a capture who reported another camp thirty kilometres (18 miles) to the north where 500 trained ZANLA were holed up. The information came too late in the day for a full-scale camp attack, but at 17h00 the Canberras made a single run and the pilots reported the strike had been successful.

By evening, the RLI, SAS and the Air Force had the camp fairly well buttoned up although the odd ZANLA could be seen darting furtively from cover to cover. Most of the troops got back into the choppers, leaving Bob McKenna and his small group to be uplifted last.

As the choppers flew home in waves, one began to run short of fuel as it approached Cabora Bassa. Norman Walsh, flying behind in the command chopper, got the pilot to put down on a tiny island in the middle of the lake, then asked Jack Malloch in the DC-7 to come around and drop four drums of fuel off for them. The drop went without a hitch and several of the choppers hovered around the island while the pilot topped up his plane. Then he gave the thumbs up sign, and off they went heading south again.

There was a refuelling stop on *The Train* admin base, then they set course for home. But there was a massive line of storms, and many choppers began to run low on fuel. Everyone tried to make it back to Mount Darwin, instead of the small emergency forward admin base right on the border, but the weather that pitch black night was filthy and a dozen choppers went missing.

The first wave managed to get over the escarpment and were landing in various clubs around Centenary ... and when club members suddenly saw the red navigational lights coming through the blackness from the direction of Mozambique, they believed it to be a Mugabe invasion force.

The second wave which included the command chopper could only make it as far as Chizweti. Brian Robinson and Norman Walsh clambered out of the chopper into the pelting rain, then hurried straight to the pub where they proceeded to get screaming drunk. Five days of constant worry and tension were over. The mission had been a success and a few days' R and R lay ahead.

Meanwhile, Bob McKenna and his men were still far away in Tembue and after a night when the silence was repeatedly broken by the sound of FRELIMO vehicles and heavy machineguns firing north of Tembue town, they were uplifted and flown home without incident.

As the waves of helicopters returned to Salisbury carrying home the fatigued yet triumphant soldiers, Rhodesians greeted their safe return and heralded their success by flashing their car lights and throwing their hats in the air.

The ComOps' switchboard was jammed by calls from Rhodesians eager to congratulate the commanders of the two raids. Major Brian Robinson, MCM, and Group Captain Norman Walsh, BCR, were to be made Officers of the Legion of Merit – for distinguished service to Rhodesia – for their planning of the raid.

Operation *Dingo* had been a spectacular success. It had been a classic example of a meticulously planned and brilliantly executed joint security force operation. It was the biggest kill rate of any camp attack of the war; more than 2 000 enemy had been killed and several thousand others wounded.

Both camps had been decimated, vast quantities of weapons destroyed and captured, and the mountain of captured documents was to keep SB busy for nine months sifting through it. There was so much they had to empty prisoners out of three of Umtali's police cells to store it in. The documents gave a tremendous amount of information on ZANLA's internal operations and routes and the security forces were kept busy for months waylaying and killing gangs.

The Rhodesians had lost one soldier and one airman and eight men had been wounded. Considering the odds, they had been extremely lucky. Despite their success, ComOps were still worried about world opinion and sat for days waiting to see what would happen.

Dr David Owen, the British Foreign Secretary, while condemning the raid as a "savage and pretty brutal attack," said "it might show the PF that the Rhodesian defence force is simply not on its back."

As expected, ZANLA went running to the United Nations, and claimed that innocent women and children had been killed. Although unable to take a seat at the UN, the Rhodesians were able to answer the allegations with documentary and photographic evidence.

There had certainly been teenagers at the camp, but from the blackboards the soldiers found, it was clear they had not been studying the three Rs. It was Marxism and the theory of smallarms fire that had been on their timetable.

Eight captured photographs showed a platoon of women practising rifle drills with fixed bayonets. There were pictures of women in camouflaged steel helmets grouped around a 12,7 millimetre anti-aircraft machinegun and another showed Josiah Tongogara and two women wielding AK rifles. There was one document which listed the Chimurenga names of eighty women.

On the subject of civilians inside the camps, a memorandum by ZANLA commander, Bataimoyo Munhukwayie read: "There is a problem of Mozambican masses staying within the camp, where they indulge in magical affairs, but getting them to leave is difficult."

The Rhodesians concede that there were many unarmed people at Chimoio, but that the soldiers were not there to take chances. In some contacts, it was found that the enemy were armed with folding butt FN rifles, and when cornered put up heavy resistance.

The raid was labelled a massacre by many critics. But the security forces point out, it must not be forgotten that Chimoio was a terror base and the people there, if not already trained, were destined to become the next crop of ZANLA infiltrators, whose role was to sally forth and terrorise Rhodesians.

Indeed, as General Walls explained: "We are fighting for law and order here and you cannot just sit back and let bases like that exist. Yes, we will continue to operate behind enemy lines." He added that if there were women in the camps, "then we just have to accept that we might kill some women."

As for the survivors, their morale was completely broken. They now knew that it was no longer safe to hide deep inside Mozambique and the fear of being involved in anything similar was very real indeed and would haunt them for years to come.

As a bonus for the Rhodesians, the raid served to sow the seeds of discontent within the ZANLA central committee and high command.

Trouble had been brewing for some time and the leader of a dissident group, Cleotus Chigowe, and his supporters were not satisfied with the way the high command was running the war. Chigowe blamed the losses at Chimoio on Mugabe's complacency, accusing him of failing to arm some of the occupants for fear of being overthrown by the dissidents.

Then, with morale at rock bottom, the rebels plotted a coup to topple Mugabe. However, Edgar Tekere persuaded FRELIMO to arrest two dissidents and when word reached Chigowe, he captured Tekere and Dr Herbert Ushewokonze, tied them to trees and beat them. Mugabe supporters in turn rescued their comrades, ambushed the rebel leader and several supporters ... and FRELIMO finally stepped in and rounded up forty rebels.

The coup was foiled, but what with one thing and another, all was not well in the Mugabe camp ...

The Command Dakota

After the successful raids on Chimoio and Tembue, the airborne method of command was developed further.

While the army and air force commanders favoured the helicopter method of command as it allowed them to be more involved in the battle, helicopters were particularly vulnerable ... it was necessary to leave the battle from time-to-time to refuel ... and it was also tying up a valuable helicopter that could be used on another task.

It was finally decided that the total command of a battle should take place from a command Dakota, but that as a back-up, there should also be an alternative or subordinate command element. Sometimes a chopper was used, occasionally, a Lynx.

A high frequency command radio and radio plugs and teleprinter were installed in the command Dakota, special mapboards with photo-overlay facilities were built in and the seats turned around so that the army and air force commanders could face each other.

New Times, New Tasks

Hot Pursuit, Botswana, February 1978

To the west meanwhile, there were other enemies. Throughout January and February, 1978, a Special Branch informer had been monitoring a ZIPRA presence near his kraal close to the Botswana/Rhodesia border – and it had become very apparent that ZIPRA had set up another transit camp inside Botswana.

The Botswana Government's policy had always been to give sanctuary to Rhodesian "refugees" as well as ZIPRA deploying from Rhodesia for rearmament and rest and recreation.

The so-called "refugees" were largely ZIPRA recruits – volunteers or abducted teenagers – who, after undergoing training in Zambia or elsewhere, returned home as fully-fledged terrorists. It was estimated that eighty percent of ZIPRA were taken at gunpoint through Botswana.

In August, 1976, the Lusaka-based ZIPRA high command had dispatched the influential Dumiso Dabengwa to Francistown to persuade the Botswanan Government to allow an intensification of the terrorist war effort. Dabengwa wanted Botswana's authority to infiltrate large numbers of armed men into Rhodesia via the common Botswana/Rhodesia border. Although the request was reportedly denied by Botswana, which had always claimed it maintained a neutral stance, ZIPRA's activities began to increase almost immediately.

Botswana-based ZIPRA hierarchy were responsible for masterminding an upsurge in recruiting and abduction campaigns within Rhodesia ... as well as an increase in acts of terrorism along the Bulawayo/Plumtree railway line; robberies, landmine incidents, disciplinary killings and attacks on isolated farmers ...

The latest intelligence coming in to Victoria Falls-based SB Officer Mike Howie put the new ZIPRA transit camp about 15 kilometres (nine miles) south of Kazangula and some six kilometres (four miles) across the border inside Botswana. It was an ideal site, affording ZIPRA a quick and uninterrupted supply and deployment route into Matabeleland.

When the SB officer's informer made yet another report about the suspected camp, Mike Howie decided the time had come for a further investigation. The SAS's "B" Troop, were based up at the game rangers' houses on the banks of the Zambezi, a few kilometres from Victoria Falls, and he had a quiet word to the Troop's new commander, Captain Colin Willis, about the latest ZIPRA threat.

The SAS were only too willing to help, Colin said ... and a four-man reconnaissance team was tasked to pinpoint the camp. (The SAS were now operating in three external countries at once.)

At sunset that night, the recce team crossed unseen into Botswana and it didn't take them long to travel the few kilometres to the area under suspicion. Having sought the safety of a small escarpment, they settled down to watch for any signs of ZIPRA.

They overlooked a large open area – there was a small quarry with water in it, a couple of villages . . . and, on the other side of the clearing, there was a wooded area.

Two uneventful days and nights passed without any sign of ZIPRA. Then, on the third night, 18 healthy young men stepped out of the trees into the clearing. Some wore drab green uniforms, others were in khaki and the rest were in East German flek pattern. They were in a very regimented sort of group, although they carried no weapons.

The SAS watched intently as the 18 youths prepared to hold a meeting. It was very apparent that this was no ordinary group of youths milling around. One man very soon emerged as their leader and whenever he spoke, the others showed obedience to him.

Then, their business over, they dispersed. Five youths strolled off to bathe in the quarry where they removed and replaced three sets of clothing, a very significant move, as terrorists operating inside Rhodesia often wore more than one set of civilian clothing or uniforms, or both, to enable them to merge with the population and to outsmart the security forces.

There was no doubt in the minds of the reconnaissance team that the group was ZIPRA. They were convinced, too, that their camp had to be behind the far treeline.

Ideally, the SAS needed to carry out a close-in reconnaissance to confirm their suspicions. But the reconnaissance commander was suffering from ticklish night-time coughing attacks, the result of a chest infection, and that idea was abandoned. A simple cough could give the game away and the commander was not prepared to take that chance.

They radioed base to report the presence of ZIPRA to Colin Willis . . . and it was agreed that they return to Rhodesia the following morning, when Colin planned to retask another commander to do the close-in reconnaissance.

* * *

Next day, SB officer Mike Howie was due for another intelligence gathering meeting with his informer friend on the Rhodesian side of the border on the main Victoria Falls/Kazangula Road.

SAS Territorial Captain Jeff Telfer was to go along for the ride, and when the new SAS doctor, Jon Thomson, heard about the trip, he tried to cadge a lift too.

The doctor had just passed selection and his parachute course but still had another two weeks to go before his orientation course – to check and complete the training of attached personnel – after which he would qualify for SAS colours.

But Jon was getting fed up with hanging about. He hadn't joined the SAS to sit around the camp, he complained. He wanted a bit of action . . . and the commander finally agreed to let him go along on the trip . . . then asked the three men to try raising the SAS reconnaissance party on their radio as his own communications with them were not good.

The SB officer met up with his hunter informer and a couple of other agents, and they produced a hand grenade found in Botswana . . . yet more evidence of a ZIPRA presence.

Then the three men set off on the return journey, and, instead of going back the way they had come, they travelled down the narrow, seldom-used dirt road close to the four-strand barbed wire cattle fence that separated Rhodesia from her western neighbour.

It was a particularly bad road, fraught with danger for unsuspecting travellers . . . an ideal spot for terrorists who might care to leave a few lethal surprises planted along the lonely, dusty track.

Only a couple of weeks before, Mike Howie had chanced upon a landmine. A nosey elephant had sniffed at it, disturbing the red soil sufficiently for Mike to see it. The SB officer had lifted it, then continued on his way . . . only to find more evidence of another landmine a few kilometres further along the road. Next to a huge crater gouged out by an exploding landmine, lay one very dead elephant.

Mike Howie decided that they would go a little further down the road before trying to make radio communications with the SAS reconnaissance party now making their way back to Rhodesia.

Suddenly, an almighty bang reverberated around the Land-Rover, and all three men thought that was it – they had hit a landmine. Then they heard the rattle of smallarms fire and saw tracer screaming past the windscreen, and realised that men were firing at them from just twenty metres away.

The explosion had not come from a landmine after all, but from an RPG-7 rocket which had missed the Land-Rover, but exploded nearby, sending shrapnel showering in all directions.

Standing in the waist-high grass of the marshland were ten very aggressive ZIPRA . . . and directing an incredible volume of fire at them.

The enterprising enemy, in Rhodesia on a reconnaissance mission, had quickly sprung into their ambush positions the moment they heard the Land-Rover crunching towards them, and, thinking it had to be the routine Kazangula police patrol vehicle, they were agreed it was too good an opportunity to pass up.

For the three Rhodesians, there was no time to be lost.

Mike Howie put his foot down flat . . . and with Jeff Telfer and Jon Thomson giving covering fire out of the door, they emptied their magazines as the Land-Rover sped through the ambush. A hail of lead followed their every move.

In the split seconds it was taking to change magazines, Jeff told his companions that he had been shot. He had taken a hit in the foot, not that it deterred him from keeping the ZIPRA attackers at bay.

"I've been hit too." Mike suddenly said, as the police Land-Rover lurched along kicking up a cloud of dust all around them. The doctor noted that Mike was already turning a sickly shade of white. Mike's left leg had been shattered. His right leg was also injured, but, fortunately, he was still able to operate the accelerator. But he was so badly shot up, that he couldn't change gear.

ZIPRA were still firing at them, and it was imperative the three men get clear of the ambush. Quickly, they made a plan.

With the SB man accelerating with his good foot and steering, and the doctor in the centre operating the clutch and changing gears, they roared off, while Jeff Telfer continued to give covering fire as before. But Mike was on the verge of collapsing at the wheel, and warned his friends he was about to pass out.

"No! No! Carry on!" he heard a voice urge. And although extremely weak, the SB officer managed to obey the command and remain conscious.

The vehicle lurched faster and faster down the rough track. Then its tyres burst. On and on they sped, desperately trying to put as much space as possible between them and their attackers.

Only when the ambushers were a good three kilometres behind them and the sounds of firing had died down, did Mike Howie feel they were relatively safe at last. He brought the Land-Rover to a grinding halt . . . and his two companions carefully lifted him from the driver's seat and laid him next to the vehicle.

It was only now that the doctor realised just how bad the SB officer's injuries were. Both main bones in his leg were severed . . . and his leg was literally hanging on by the skin. Everything pointed to him losing the limb.

The doctor found a medical kit behind the driver's seat, got a drip going, and administered a pain killer. Then, he turned to deal with Jeff Telfer's injury, finding that a round had passed through his foot. Jeff was wearing a beautiful pair of imported running shoes – his pride and joy – and one very blood-stained shoe was eased off and his injury patched up.

Jeff set about trying to make communications with someone to report the ambush. But he was unable to raise Colin Willis back in Victoria Falls on the army radio and tried the police radio in the Land-Rover.

The Kazangula police patrol was due along the road, and it was imperative they be warned not to come, for there was a very real possibility that the ambushers had also planted a landmine in the road.

Only then did the SAS doctor realise that he too had been shot in the foot. It was not as bad as the others', but sore nonetheless. Leaving Mike groaning and Jeff trying to raise someone on the radio, Jon Thomson hobbled off to lay an ambush in case ZIPRA decided to follow-up.

As he lay in his ambush site, trying to ignore his injury and concentrate on the broken ground ahead and watch all sides at once, he worried that ZIPRA would try and outflank them. He rather hoped they didn't come along at all. Both of his companions were injured and he was alone in his little ambush position. He hadn't been properly trained yet. He had never seen a shot fired in anger. Hell, he thought to himself, he hadn't even got his SAS beret yet!

The minutes ticked by slowly as he kept up his lonely vigil.

Back down the road, Jeff Telfer had finally managed to get word to the police station about the ambush . . . and the news was quickly passed back to Colin Willis who immediately dispatched a casevac chopper to the scene with a medic on board.

Meanwhile, the SAS reconnaissance party, had crossed back into Rhodesia, and heard the sounds of firing . . . and when the news of the ambush was flashed to them, they raced to the rescue.

By now, the ZIPRA responsible for the troubles that morning had hotfooted it back across the border to the safety of Botswana, leaving a legacy of three injured Rhodesians . . . a reconnaissance team hurrying through the bush to their colleagues' aid . . . a casevac chopper on its way to the scene – and, one very upset SAS commander.

Colin immediately radioed ComOps for permission to conduct a hot pursuit follow-up from the ambush area into Botswana to track down the men responsible. Then he had to wait for an answer.

* * *

Forty-five long, worrying minutes after the ambush was mounted, Mike Howie, Jeff Telfer and Jon Thomson saw the friendly faces of the SAS reconnaissance team emerge through the bush. Within minutes, the casevac chopper had touched down and they were loaded aboard.

The chopper was soon at Victoria Falls airstrip, where Sergeant Major Peter Cole was already waiting for the casualties with an ambulance. Then he and Doc Thomson put a fresh drip in Mike Howie while they awaited the arrival of an aircraft to fly all three casualties to Wankie Hospital.

Just before the plane arrived, an agitated Jeff Telfer shouted across to the sergeant major. Presenting him with his blood-stained track shoe, Jeff instructed him: "Look after that for me. It's imported. It was *very* expensive. And can you get it scrubbed clean? Put it in the sun to dry and make sure it's returned to me *personally*."

Back at base, meanwhile, Colin Willis had gathered together 27 men in readiness for a hot pursuit operation. But official word hadn't yet come and time was running out.

They boarded their troop carrier and shot off along the narrow, dusty road that ran along the Zambezi. Colin intended joining forces with the reconnaissance party, still out in the bush, and once ComOps had given permission, they would all get to grips with the ZIPRA ambushers.

On their way, they passed the sergeant major stopping long enough for Colin to tell him to "hold the fort" while they were away. Then, with a roar and a cloud of dust they were on their way, leaving a disgruntled SSM in a dust-covered ambulance, nursing a bloodied trackshoe and rather hoping they wouldn't find any terrorists, as he would be missing out on the action.

He sat staring at the trackshoe, silently cursing the officer who shouldn't have been wearing them in the first place. He suddenly let out the clutch and the ambulance leapt forward as he returned to camp and follow his orders to hold the fort.

* * *

As Colin and his men roared along the dusty track, he silently debated what would be the best course of action. He knew that before he could do anything, he needed ComOps authority. He radioed back to base to be told that ComOps had now approved a hot pursuit operation into Botswana.

But, when he weighed up the evidence, the SAS commander decided against following the spoor. He would go straight to the suspected terrorist camp instead. After all, their reconnaissance had just confirmed a definite ZIPRA presence in the area. Not only that, but the suspected camp was very close to the ambush site.

Time was of the essence and the commander reasoned that if they were to get their men, they ought to go straight to the camp, assess the situation, then decide what to do. If there were no ZIPRA to be seen, they would return to the ambush site inside Rhodesia and start tracking the enemy down from there.

They met up with the reconnaissance team and the whole force of 33 men crossed the border. It had now been five hours since the ambush.

The reconnaissance commander led them to a hill in more or less the same position where his team had spent the previous few days. Leaving the others behind, the recce commander, Colin and Lieutenant Dale Scott moved down to a good spot overlooking the area where they suspected the camp to be. The recce commander gave a short orientation briefing and pointed out where ZIPRA had been the day before.

They didn't have too long to wait to see their first ZIPRA emerge from the trees. Colin was quite convinced the man was ZIPRA. He was wearing the same sort of uniform that ZIPRA operating in that area usually had, and he carried an SKS rifle.

There were a number of similarly dressed men moving in and out of the treeline. Colin was studying the area very carefully and doing a mental appreciation on how they would attack the camp should he decide that was the best plan.

Off in the distance, the sound of vehicles could be heard. Shortly afterwards three

Botswana Defence Force Land-Rovers came roaring along the dusty track. To the amazement of the SAS men, the Land-Rovers screeched to a halt and parked right in front of the suspected camp. One of the 18 men on the BDF vehicles was dressed in East German flek camouflage, the sort worn by ZIPRA.

Colin and crew, hidden 400 metres from the little track, were now taking a very keen interest in the goings on below them.

The SAS commander now faced a dilemma. Was this a genuine ZIPRA camp? Or was it a Botswana Defence Force patrol base? If it were a terrorist camp – and everything pointed to it being one – all well and good. If, on the other hand, it was a Botswana defence base, then it was not such a clear-cut situation.

If they attacked it and it turned out to be the latter, unpleasant things would start hitting the fan. And Colin would be up to his neck in it.

Then, as the Rhodesians watched, a lone ZIPRA man came from the camp and spoke to the 18 men on the BDF Land-Rovers. The entire group moved into the camp. Colin and his team could not see what was going on in the treeline, but twenty minutes later, they saw them all come out again.

As they emerged from the trees, it was very apparent the BDF were escorting a group of terrorists, and it seemed to the SAS commander that they were the best of friends.

There was a marked difference in their uniforms, walk and tidiness. The BDF were well turned out in their normal kit; ZIPRA were in the usual assortment of camouflage and civilian clothing. The BDF carried pistols, sub-machineguns and FN rifles; the terrorists had communist weapons.

The BDF escorts were carrying the same heavy packs that were being carried by the terrorists. Together, they were heaving kit and equipment, landmines and ammunition-type boxes – and it was all being loaded into the BDF Land-Rovers. The evidence all pointed to this little scenario being a pick-up.

The SAS had never come across or heard of open collaboration between the BDF and ZIPRA before, but it seemed clear to Colin that somehow the BDF had heard – obviously on their radios – that the Rhodesian security forces were abroad on a follow-up and were worried that the ZIPRA camp would be located. And that would prove embarrassing to the Botswana Government which firmly maintained it hosted "refugees" only, and *not* ZIPRA.

It was obvious that ZIPRA were being moved away to start their troubles afresh somewhere else.

For Colin, time was running out. He had to make an on-the-spot decision whether to let them get away – or, put a stop to them then and there.

All the evidence and the events earlier that day were too overwhelming. As far as he could see, there was only one course of action that he could take.

To hell with it! He wasn't going to let them get away. If the BDF wanted to get involved with ZIPRA, then they must suffer the consequences.

"We're going for it," he said in a whisper to the two men at his side.

Quickly, quietly, they left their hideout and scrambled 100 metres uphill to the rest of the party. Colin hastily briefed them about what he had seen and what the plan was to be. They moved off briskly in extended line. Time was not on their side and they needed to get into an ambush position down by the road before the BDF vehicles came along.

They were half way to the road when they heard the sound of vehicle engines suddenly rumble into life. Immediately, the SAS were off and running.

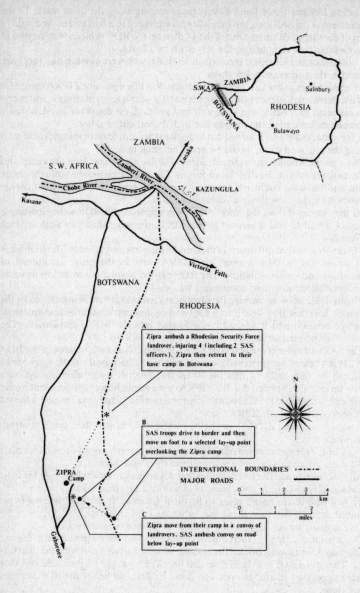

Zambia / S.W.A / Botswana / Salisbury / RHODESIA / Bulawayo

ZAMBIA
Lusaka
S. W. AFRICA
Zambezi River
Chobe River
Kasane
KAZUNGULA
Victoria Falls
BOTSWANA
RHODESIA

A
Zipra ambush a Rhodesian Security Force
landrover, injuring 4 (including 2 SAS
officers). Zipra then retreat to their
base camp in Botswana

B
SAS troops drive to border and then
move on foot to a selected lay-up point
overlooking the Zipra camp

ZIPRA
Camp

INTERNATIONAL BOUNDARIES ·—·—·—
MAJOR ROADS

0 1 2 3 4
km

0 1 2
miles

Gaborone

C
Zipra move from their camp in a convoy of
landrovers. SAS ambush convoy on road
below lay-up point

Map showing the SAS's hot pursuit operation into Botswana

196

As the Land-Rovers roared nearer, the Rhodesians maintained their extended line and arrived in some semblance of ambush overlooking the road at about the same time the first BDF Land-Rover swung around the corner.

Some of the SAS went straight into a kneeling position readying themselves for the contact. A few chose to stand. There was no time to decide who should go where. In any event, there was very little cover and they knew they would be visible from the road.

They could see six ZIPRA among the 18 BDF men in the three Land-Rovers. Then, when the front Land-Rover came into the killing ground, Colin, still standing, lined his first victim in his sights.

The unsuspecting man was sitting on the bonnet of the Land-Rover acting as a scout or landmine sentry. The SAS commander took aim and opened fire.

As the round thumped into the man's chest, it catapulted him off the vehicle and into the dust. That was the signal for the commander's men to follow suit with rifles and machineguns . . . and the volume of fire was intense and devastating. In less than a minute, all three Land-Rovers had ground to a halt and were raging infernos.

So intense and fierce was the attack and so taken unaware were the victims, that the BDF and ZIPRA got off only a few shots in return. They were far more interested in getting out of the Land-Rovers than fighting it out.

Some of the passengers managed to clamber out of the blazing vehicles, only to be picked off as they attempted to scale a three-metre high embankment in their bid to escape. Burning and wounded, they slithered to the bottom of the hill to form a mound of bodies.

Five somehow managed to clear the summit and escape with their lives by a miracle, getting away under cover of the dust kicked up from the gun fire and the pall of smoke that hung in the air.

Within minutes it was all over and the commander had waved the ceasefire.

Once the firing died down, Colin decided to wait where they were until the flames were snuffed out. They should really be pulling out before the escapees raised the alarm. But Colin wanted to collect the weapons, even those that had been partly burned as well as cartridge cases that lay around. Ballistic tests would prove conclusively that there had been ZIPRA on the BDF vehicles.

He didn't need a crystal ball to realise that any incident directly involving the Botswanans would cause shock waves throughout the sub-continent and heighten tensions even more in the region. Without definite ballistic evidence he doubted if the world would believe the Rhodesians' story.

Judging by the amount of weapons they collected, none of the ZIPRA men had escaped the ambush. Four of the bodies were positively identified as being ZIPRA from the rice-flek uniforms and the usual terrorist boot patterns. Some of the BDF men too had paid the ultimate price for supporting ZIPRA.

Heavily-laden with their evidence, the SAS ambushers returned to their base in Rhodesia where the sergeant major was anxiously awaiting them.

Things were already buzzing, he reported. ComOps had been on, Army HQ had been on, everyone wanted to know where the ambush party was – and, more particularly, what had happened.

For, even as Colin and his men were still leaving Botswana, the news had already broken via diplomatic circles. The Rhodesian Ministry of Foreign Affairs had already learned a BDF convoy had been ambushed and destroyed. Foreign Affairs Minister P.K. van der Byl was in the hot seat and had to know what had taken place.

The Botswana Government was claiming the attacked men were all from a para-military unit, that they had been carrying out a normal border control duty, and that the Rhodesians had acted without provocation, murdering their men in cold blood. To suggest that the BDF was collaborating with ZIPRA was a "blatant lie".

It was a grossly-exaggerated story to save face. But, be that as it may, ComOps was not amused, and it looked like Colin was in hot water.

The SAS hierarchy immediately flew down to listen to Colin's version of the story. Then they all had to await the findings of the ballistics reports on the weapons and ammunition found at the first ambush site inside Rhodesia as well as those collected from the second ambush attack in Botswana.

The immediate reaction from the Botswana Government was to close the Kazangula border with Rhodesia, which was a considerable blow for trade in the region.

The border position was one of the most strategic points between black and white Africa being where four countries met on the Zambezi – Rhodesia, Zambia, Botswana and South West Africa (Namibia). It was the only remaining link between white and black Africa since the Zambia-Rhodesia border closure in the early 1970s.

The matter was raised at the United Nations and a ballistics expert was dispatched to Rhodesia to make his findings. Eventually, the Rhodesians were able to prove their case and prove the Botswana Government wrong.

Cartridge cases collected from the first ambush were identified by ballistics experts as having been fired by the same weapons captured at the second ambush involving the BDF. They were also tied into documents relating to ZIPRA weapons held by SB in Bulawayo.

Despite being found with egg on their faces, the Botswanans, taught a very severe lesson, would not back down and the border remained closed.

As for the three men injured in the initial ambush, Mike Howie luckily did not lose his leg... Jon Thomson went on to earn his coveted SAS beret... and Jeff Telfer was reunited with his expensive blood-free trackshoes, and vowed *never* to take them to the bush again.

ZANLA Barracks Attack, May, 1978

Until now, strategic targets in urban enemy areas had been out of bounds to SAS ground troops, or any other special forces for that matter.

But it was now May, 1978, and the war had been raging in earnest for some five and a half years, and when a high-ranking ZANLA capture pinpointed a prize of a target close to a major Mozambican town, ComOps began to give it serious attention.

The talkative capture, in on many ZANLA secrets, had provided the Rhodesian war effort with detailed information on a number of major targets, helping to piece together vital bits in the intelligence jigsaw. One item of particular interest was an entire ZANLA barracks, occupied by 100 enemy at a time – and all destined for Rhodesia.

The building – known as Battariao Barracks – also housed the provincial head-quarters of ZANU, the political wing, and in addition to the 100 transitory terrorists, there were resident ZANU general staff, mechanics, drivers and assistants. There were four long barrack blocks interlinked by an ablution complex, a filling station, a separate logistics stores and a spares room.

While it was an ideal target for security force attack, there were certain difficulties.

Battariao Barracks was on the edge of a major heavily populated town of Tete, the main centre and hub of Tete Province, where there were more than one thousand FRELIMO soldiers in residence.

Just to make life interesting for any would-be attacker, the main FRELIMO barracks was near ZANLA's Battariao Barracks, there was another FRELIMO building right next door, and a guard outpost on the other side of the river.

The captured terrorist had forewarned the Rhodesians too that there were three unarmed sentries on duty on the main gate of Battariao Barracks, who if challenged, would ask for a simple password. It was nice to know of course... but the Rhodesians had no intention of walking in through the front gate.

Tete town was 100 kilometres (62 miles) as the crow flies from the border and to infiltrate right up to the doorstep of the major FRELIMO stronghold would be an ambitious, high-risk operation. Entry was going to be a major problem.

How could they get to the target undetected? And how could they get safely away again before FRELIMO and ZANLA or both had time to react?

It was impossible to walk operators in to the target. It was just too far. Parachuting anywhere near to the barracks would be a risky business, too.

They could be choppered in, but would have to be taken so far away from the target that they would need vehicles to get in close. And with all those methods of entry, they ran the very real risk of bumping into FRELIMO or ZANLA before reaching the target.

What they needed was a totally clandestine method of entry and exit. The mission was offered to the SAS and it was obvious to Captain Dave Dodson that the solution lay in the actual position of the barracks themselves.

The building was on the north-western tip of Tete, right on the banks of The Zambezi River – a sitting duck for a water-borne assault.

By canoeing downriver, the saboteurs could get access to the barracks, lay their explosive charges around the building under cover of darkness and be back on the river and away again before the big bang went up and the alarm was raised.

Like the operations on Cabora Bassa pioneered by the SAS the previous year, it meant that they could loom out of the darkness, attack their target and melt into the night before the enemy knew what had hit them.

The beauty of the plan, too, was that the element of surprise would be total.

ZANLA were extremely confident that they were safe from Rhodesian security force attack. They felt that as they were so close to such a major heavily populated town with a very strong FRELIMO presence, the Rhodesians would never dare attack them.

In the unlikely event of them thinking seriously about it after that, they would naturally expect them to infiltrate overland after being airlifted into Mozambique. They would never expect them to infiltrate down the river – an ardous, time-consuming and circuitous route.

So confident were they, the barracks was only fenced on three of its four sides – and the unprotected side was the one facing on to the river.

After laying their charges around the barracks, the raiders would have to travel past Tete town ... under the giant Tete bridge spanning the Zambezi – and past FRELIMO's main barracks. There were armed militia guarding the bridge too but they were there to protect it from attack from both sides. They were hardly likely to expect trouble from the river itself.

It would be a daring, difficult operation. And it would be something completely different from anything the security forces had done before. Yet SAS officer Dave Dodson was confident that, given the chance, it was well within SAS capabilities.

Fortunately, ComOps shared his view and the plan was finally given the green light. Dodson, who was to lead the mission, chose seven other operators to go with him, and preparations and rehearsals got underway immediately.

It was going to take 250 kilograms of explosives to destroy the barracks, and it took a team of outside demolition experts, specially called in for the mission, three full days of intense activity to prepare the 12 Rhodesian-manufactured *Wrecker* charges.

They were planning on using a minimum time delay of ninety minutes to give them sufficient time to get clear of the barracks before the explosives ripped the buildings apart, and the trials proved more or less accurate within five minutes.

They were to use a number of different types of timing devices so that if one device failed to go off, there were several back-up mechanisms. Having gone so far and taken so many risks, they were not intending to take any chances of equipment failure.

At last, all the preparations and rehearsals were over and everyone was ready to go. The eight operators deployed to the Selous Scouts fort at Mtoko, in north-east Rhodesia to prepare for the mission, and on May 30, they boarded the choppers for the first and easiest part of the operation. They were soon in enemy territory, flying over the endless mopani forests and scrub to a spot some 75 kilometres (46 miles) upriver of Tete.

It was still daylight as the choppers began their descent to the treetops and the eight SAS men could see that the Zambezi was in full flood – and knew immediately that they were in for a very interesting journey.

Quickly, they jumped from the choppers and yanked out their explosives, weapons and canoe bags. The choppers lifted, then were gone ...

All fell silent again. There was not a soul around to see them as they busied themselves assembling the four canoes. There were the usual scatterings of kraals dotted around the riverbank, but the sudden chatter of helicopters had sent the locals scurrying for cover, just as it always did.

Meanwhile, Sergeant Major Pete Allan and his mortar team were also on their way to Tete Province with their mortar bombs slung in special bags under the helicopters. Their role was to create a diversion near the ZANLA terrorist staging post at Chinhanda Crossroads and take the attention away from Dodson and his helicopters. They hoped that by harassing Chinhanda Crossroads, the enemy would think they were being attacked and react by concentrating their troops there, thus taking them away from Tete where the real threat lay.

Back at the river, the eight SAS operators, blackened-up and clad in FRELIMO uniforms, were getting on with their preparations.

There were to be two men – and big ones at that – to each of the four canoes and it was obvious that with their heavy charges and accessories, an RPD light machinegun to each canoe, together with their personal weapons, it was going to be a very tight squeeze.

It was clear too that the weight of the charges combined with the current would make it impossible for them to travel independently without getting into serious difficulty.

As soon as night began to fall, they pushed the canoes into the water and lined up side-by-side, holding on to the canoe next to them for a raft effect, thereby providing greater stability.

Once everyone got the feel of the fast-flowing current, Dodson gave the word and they set sail for Tete, using the rudders, and with the men on each side of the "raft" paddling. But the current was so fast and they were hastened along so quickly that there was very little paddling done that night . . . and they swiftly bumped and crashed on their way to Tete under the cover of darkness. So weighed down by explosives were they, that they were riding just above the waterline.

Then they heard the unmistakable rush of rapids and waterfalls across the night. But apart from one hair-raising moment when the current snatched at their raft and swung them around in a circle, they managed to manoeuvre around the rapids without difficulty.

Around 03h00, the distinctive muffled grunts of hippos could be heard through the darkness as they grazed along the riverbanks and splashed in the shallows.

As the new day began to dawn and the chance of compromise became greater, they looked for somewhere to base up for the rest of the day before continuing their travels again that night. They had done well and had covered about 45 kilometres (28 miles). Only thirty kilometres (19 miles) to go.

They beached at a little tributary and began laboriously humping their extremely heavy, tightly-packed canoes as far away from the river as possible. It was a thickly-bushed area and they had specially chosen it to screen them from view. Unfortunately, they found that a well-used footpath crossed the tributary and although they based up well away from the path, they were seen at midday by a group of young Africans.

A quick burst on a silenced Czechoslovakian-manufactured Skorpian sub-machinegun sent them on their way, but the SAS were concerned that the youngsters would report them to FRELIMO . . . and immediately began to take precautions in case a strong heavily armed group came to hunt them down.

They planned to leave the canoes and explosives behind; walk out of the area and be recovered later by chopper. But they had no intention of letting FRELIMO get their hands on their explosives or twenty thousand Rhodesian dollars worth of precious canoes, and rigged them up for demolition.

Then, with the early-warning groups on the look-out for trouble, they laid low in the thick bush and waited for the FRELIMO troops, who must surely come. But amazingly, none did.

The operation was still on and they dismantled their demolition kit on the canoes, and that night were back on the river again. The current was much the same as the previous night and they were buffeted further along into enemy waters without much paddling.

Everything was going according to plan and they were well within their timeframe. There was going to be plenty of time to get to Tete, do the job and get away under cover of darkness.

As they crashed on their way through the black of the night, each man was apprehensive, yet quietly confident that the job was all but in the bag.

Then, way off in the distance they saw the faint glow of lights and knew they were getting close to their target. It looked just like normal lighting and would not be a problem.

But then it happened. As they swung around the corner, the black security of the night and their confidence suddenly disappeared as they found themselves under the merciless glare of high-powered searchlights beaming out across the river from a nearby power station.

The Salisbury saboteurs and their deadly cargo of explosives were centre stage, a few hundered metres from the ZANLA barracks and from the nearby FRELIMO barracks – and beautifully illuminated for all to see. Never had they felt so vulnerable.

Quickly, the canoeists on either side of the raft paddled furiously away eagerly seeking the safety of the shadows once more, while every other finger was on the trigger.

They were fully expecting to be challenged or shot at any second, but miraculously, nothing came of it and they continued on their way unseen and unopposed, hardly daring to believe their good fortune.

Four hundred metres further on they pulled into the bank and rafted-up in a clump of partially submerged trees. It was already 22h00 and they had an hour to kill before moving down to the ZANLA barracks.

They were now on the outskirts of Tete and only 500 metres from the target. The barracks, a mere 100 metres from the riverbank, was completely lit up and a bit further downstream, the twinkle of lights could be seen in Tete town, which lay calm and quiet – and unsuspecting.

Eventually, it was time to get going and they unloaded their explosives. Leaving two men behind to watch over their canoes, the others carefully moved towards the target, ZANLA's Battariao Barracks.

A close-in reconnaissance was carried out to see exactly where the sentries were positioned and where the charges were to be placed to the best effect.

The explosives meanwhile had been dropped off at a central point and were to be carried to the outer walls as they were needed. As the demolition team set about laying the charges, commander Dave Dodson and the others kept a look-out for intruders.

Suddenly, the commander bumped the button on his high-powered strobe light in his webbing pouch – carried to attract aircraft and for emergency rescue signals – and although dulled by the webbing, it flashed on and off . . . on and off, across the night.

Everyone held his breath again waiting for some sort of reaction. The strobe continued to flash out its urgent signal for forty worrying seconds before it could be stopped.

But once again, nothing happened and no one came to investigate. They offered up a silent prayer, grateful that good fortune was with them that night.

Quickly, quietly, the demolition teams got on with their task, returning every so often to the central point to get more explosives. As Dave Berry hugged the shadows and helped lay the charges, he could hear the unmistakable sound of someone snoring inside the ZANLA barracks.

Then a man wandered out of the barrack block to relieve himself close to the building, too lazy to walk across to the ablution block.

The soldiers froze and kept to the shadows as he went about his business. But the man didn't see them and when his toiletry was complete, he sauntered back into the barracks, oblivious to the activities out in the darkness.

Soon everything had been done and it was time to go. The *Wreckers* were all propped up around the building, the ringmain linking them had been run out, and the various time delays attached.

As stealthily as they had arrived, so they retraced their steps and left the barracks.

They climbed into their canoes and pushed off, riding much higher in the water now that they no longer had their cargo of explosives.

There was no need to raft-up any more and the eight canoeists moved out into

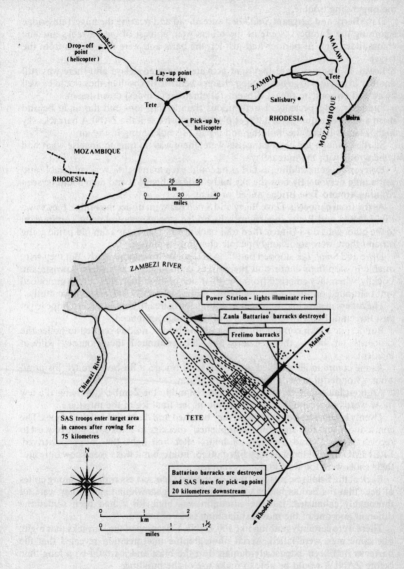

Drop-off
point
(helicopter)

Zambezi

Lay-up point
for one day

Tete

Pick-up by
helicopter

MOZAMBIQUE

RHODESIA

0   25   50
km
0   20   40
miles

ZAMBIA

Salisbury •

RHODESIA

MOZAMBIQUE

MALAWI

Tete

Beira

ZAMBEZI RIVER

Chimari River

Power Station - lights illuminate river

Zanla 'Battariao' barracks destroyed

Frelimo barracks

Malawi

SAS troops enter target area
in canoes after rowing for
75 kilometres

TETE

N

Battariao barracks are destroyed
and SAS leave for pick-up point
20 kilometres downstream

Rhodesia

0   1   2
km
0   1   1½
miles

The clandestine route taken by eight operators on the SAS's first infiltration and attack into an
urban enemy area

203

midstream and headed off into the night, the current carrying them swiftly away from the impending trouble.

Dave Berry and Sergeant *Small Bez* were ahead and nearing the huge Tete bridge spanning the Zambezi; some of the others were abreast of the barracks and the commander and his partner had just left the bank and were fifty metres from the target.

It was 15 minutes since they had activated the time delays and there was still another 75 minutes to go before their charges went off. But by then, they would be well away and en route to their LZ twenty kilometres (12 miles) downstream.

Suddenly, unexpectedly, a tremendous thunderclap tore into the night behind them as almost a quarter of a ton of plastic explosive sent the ZANLA barracks sky high. Flames licked the building and a pall of smoke hung in the air.

Startled though the eight canoeists were, there was no time to analyse what had gone wrong with the time delays.

Everyone began paddling as fast as he could, each man feeling very vulnerable and just a little nervous. By now the sky had a reddish hue to it and men could be seen running around Tete Bridge ahead of them.

As the front canoeists, Dave Berry and *Small Bez* went under the bridge, they saw a FRELIMO Land-Rover shoot across the bridge, stop at a control point, continue on to the other side; do a U-turn, then roar back again. There was a fair old panic going on and there were some angry people charging around.

Dave and *Small Bez* stopped paddling and got their weapons ready. But they were unable to stop their canoe and the current continued to carry them downstream. Luckily, when they emerged from the other side of the bridge, they did so unnoticed and continued on their way passing the main FRELIMO barracks uneventfully.

The others meanwhile, were still paddling downstream, hoping against hope to get past the main FRELIMO barracks and the bridge unnoticed.

But despite much coming and going on the bridge, no one seemed to notice the canoeists far below them – and they too continued their journey without incident.

As the commander paddled under the giant bridge, it flashed through his mind what a wonderful target it would make one day.

An hour later, they all met up on a little island in the Zambezi, exchanged a few hasty words of greeting and then set out on the final leg of the mission.

Twenty kilometres from the target they beached and disassembled the canoes. The commander sent the "mission accomplished" message to Mtoko with the request to recover them ... and a couple of hours after first light, the choppers arrived. FRELIMO fired at them as they lifted off for home, but it was token show only and their shots were too wild to do any damage.

Back at the Selous Scouts fort, they celebrated their success with welcoming crates of beer that the Scouts had waiting. After two nights without sleep, they were all thoroughly exhausted. But the adrenalin was high, for it had been something different and one of the most exhilarating tasks of the war.

There were certainly nothing like 100 ZANLA sleeping in the barracks that night, but some men were killed. Aerial photographic interpretation revealed that the barracks had been extensively damaged in the blast and it would be a long time before ZANLA would be able to make use of the building.

Sergeant Major Pete Allan's diversionary mortar tactics were successful, too, and the radio interceptors confirmed that the enemy had been convinced that Chinhanda Crossroads was under attack.

The operation had marked a turning point in Rhodesian SAS history, clearing the way for more daring operations against strategic targets in urban enemy areas. And it had been a walk-over, just as the commander had suspected it would be.

As for ZANLA, they were never able to work out how the SAS got to the target – and from then until the last days of the war, they could never be certain when or where the SAS would strike again.

Operation Elbow, January - June, 1978

By March, 1978, the political situation in Rhodesia had changed considerably. Following the ill-fated Geneva Conference and an unsuccessful bid to divide the PF leaders by embracing Nkomo, the need to bring about a political settlement had become critical.

The Anglo-American proposals were unacceptable to the Rhodesians – and the only option left was an internal settlement.

On March 3, history was made. An internal political settlement was finally signed between Ian Smith and the three internal moderate blacks, Bishop Abel Muzorewa, Rev Ndabaningi Sithole and Senator Chief Jeremiah Chirau.

The thorny question of the number of white parliamentary seats was resolved, and it was agreed the whites would get 28 seats in the 100-seat government.

The white politicians had hoped for 34 seats, but even so, there were many Rhodesians who found it hard to believe that the internal blacks had agreed to so much (the Anglo-American proposals had only given the whites ten seats), and the agreement was hailed as a triumph of moderation.

There was to be a new constitution, which still had to be worked out ... a transitional government comprising an executive council of the four signatories to the March 3 Agreement ... and a ministerial council of black and white co-ministers, who were to share equal responsibility. Together they would work towards steering the country to black rule and, hopefully, peace. The first one-man-one-vote elections were to be held at Christmas and would produce the country's first black Premier.

After eighty years of white rule, Rhodesia was about to enter a new era. Ian Smith, who had vowed there would be no majority rule in his lifetime, had successfully negotiated the white tribe into a position of a political minority. Even more amazing, the whites had given their blessing in a referendum.

The war had cost thousands of lives. Perhaps a political compromise could stop the killing. Even Britain's Foreign Secretary, Dr David Owen heralded the agreement as a step in the right direction.

Yet the internal agreement was bitterly condemned by Joshua Nkomo and Robert Mugabe, and the black-white alliance only served to add a new dimension to the long war. Indeed, instead of the war being scaled down as had been hoped, it was to escalate.

By now, Nkomo had begun to build up his army and had thousands of trained men in Zambia ... and Special Branch desperately wanted something done to stem the increasing numbers of ZIPRA infiltrating from the north.

ZIPRA had established a new forward base, known as DK camp which was only a few kilometres inland from the Devil's Gorge region of the Zambezi and an ideal crossing point. The river at that particular point was sluggish, easy to cross and only

100 metres from one unpopulated spot on the Zambian side to another unpopulated point on the Rhodesian bank. With two days' hard march, the ZIPRA men could be in the heart of their support area in the Lupane region of Matabeleland.

The SAS attacked the camp, killed 27 enemy . . . and the landmines they planted on the access roads caused several casualties including Zambian army and police.

Within a month, ZIPRA had reorganised and established another base four kilometres further inland and again the SAS struck, killing several ZIPRA, recovering 92 sophisticated Russian anti-tank mines – and pushing ZIPRA even further away from the Rhodesian border . . . until by June, ZIPRA were 32 kilometres (20 miles) from the Zambian shore.

Now the SAS and RLI planned to cause them more setbacks by continually harassing them . . . killing or capturing them . . . and locating their resting places and arms caches.

An SAS reconnaissance party had established that ZIPRA were now staging from the Kabanga Mission area (where there was a Zambian Army brigade HQ) . . . moving through the night . . . stopping at the Simani semi-precious stone mine for equipment . . . then heading southwards into Rhodesia.

From his hidden vantage point on a large hill overlooking Simani Mine, Mac McIntosh had reported numerous sightings and had seen ZIPRA milling around the staff compound before heading south towards Kariba.

Russian-made and supplied *Gaz* and *Zil* lorries had been seen transporting ZIPRA between Kabanga and Simani during the day.

However, despite the overwhelming evidence that the new DK set-up was somewhere in the Simani Mine area, the Rhodesians decided against going in and sorting them out immediately. Instead, they planned to ambush ZIPRA where they were most vulnerable – on the road between Kabanga and Simani. That way, they would not only account for dozens of ZIPRA, but would also destroy one or possibly more of their precious troop-carrying Russian lorries.

They were also hoping that, as a result of the ambush, there would be a build-up of ZIPRA at the suspected camp in the Simani Mine area. Then, having assembled all the various scatterings of ZIPRA in one place, they would swoop in for the kill with a RLI fireforce action.

But first, the ambush . . .

The task was to go to "B" Squadron, at that time based with their tactical headquarters at Deka forward camp, a few kilometres from the northern border. They planned to plant a mine in the road between Kabanga Mission and Simani Mine, and to follow-up the resulting devastation with rifle, rocket and machinegun fire.

Their plan all hinged on their hidden landmine. It had to be powerful enough to destroy an enemy lorry, evening up the odds in the subsequent fire-fight.

Sergeant Major Pete Cole had the task of constructing a special landmine which had to be even more potent than normal. Using an existing landmine, he boosted its killing potential by removing all the unnecessary parts and filling every available space with additional plastic explosive. Then he converted it from a normal pressure mine which was detonated solely by the weight of a vehicle, to one he could control and set off at the touch of a button from his hiding place.

The landmine and detonators were to be buried in the middle of the road and connected to an electric cable running under the road surface and back to an exploder mechanism at his side. He chose a British-manufactured mechanism, which gave him the ability to test the wires, detonator and connectors from his ambush position without actually firing the mine. This was a crucial check, for, if the landmine failed to go off at the very moment they wanted it to, they stood the risk of compromising themselves and being overrun by the many enemy they were likely to encounter.

Just to make sure everything would go according to plan, he made a duplicate landmine, pressed the command button and the mine blew exactly as he hoped it would come the real thing.

The party was to consist of 12 men, commanded by Captain Pete Fritz. Eight men would form the main ambush/killer party ... and the others, led by Sergeant Phil Cripps, would be in an early-warning group passing on intelligence and covering their flank.

Just before last light on June 13, the operators got out the *Black-Is-Beautiful,* and the usual green uniforms to make them look and pass for ZIPRA terrorists or Zambian soldiers ... enabling them to pass for another terrorist or army group ... giving them the initiative to get the first shot in if need be ... or to move back into the bush and continue their task unsuspected.

Within minutes the transformation was complete and they packed their camouflage cream in their packs, for they would need it with them if they were to continue looking as black as the enemy.

They boarded three Alouettes and within thirty minutes the pilots were depositing them on the other side of the border. They were in Zambia once more and another mission had begun.

As the choppers and their crews flew back to base, the dozen SAS men quickly moved away from the landing zone. They lay-up in the thick bush near the road they were to use later that night, and remained hidden there for three-and-a-half hours without anyone making a sound.

They watched and listened, making sure that the old dirt road, overgrown and washed away in places, was not being used by anyone.

At last the commander, Pete Fritz, gave the order to move out. There was very little moon that night, which made walking on the old, rough road difficult, specially as they were weighed down with heavy packs, containing radios, medical equipment, ammunition, and enough food and water to last them for a ten-day stint in their ambush position.

For the next five-and-a-half hours, they trudged through the darkness. They did their best to forget the heat of the night and attempted to ignore the sweat that was mixing with the *Black-Is-Beautiful,* making their eyes sting and running into their mouths.

The journey was a slow, tedious business with many listening stops to check for locals, ZIPRA or Zambian soldiers, and they allowed themselves only a couple of rest breaks.

They were heading for a junction where the old road linked up with the Kabanga Mission-Simani Mine road. Once over the junction, they were to skirt around the bush, returning to the main road nearer Simani Mine.

As they neared the junction, progress became even slower, for the area they were entering was well populated with a number of kraals along the road. But apart from the occasional dogs barking as they passed the scatterings of huts, there was no other sign of life.

They were particularly careful not to leave spoor at the junction, and the two empty sandbags taken along for just that purpose made ideal stepping stones.

By 04h00, the ideal spot to lay up for the day had been found and the tired troops settled down to sleep in a thicket, leaving two men on guard. As dawn approached and the light gradually improved, they spread out in pairs and crawled deeper into the thick bush, which would give them protection from the heat of the day as well as from passing locals.

With one man able to sleep and the other awake and watching out, they had a fifty percent alert should anyone stumble into their position . . . which is precisely what happened later when a group of herdboys drove cattle right through their hideout.

The sleeping men were hurriedly shaken awake and everyone carefully eased himself further into the clumps of bushes to avoid detection.

The unsuspecting herdboys were within metres of a dozen camouflaged Rhodesians, who were busy dodging the occasional stone thrown to chivvy the cattle out of the bushes. The herdboys shrieked and belted their charges with sticks and the cattle crashed on their way through the bushes.

Pulses raced as the SAS feared detection, but fortunately, they remained unseen. All they had to really worry about after that were a number of very smelly deposits left nearby.

Later that afternoon the patrol continued on its way, making slow progress through the thick bush. By 23h00, they were tired enough to need a break. At 03h00, when there was a little more moon, they were off again, heading east and soon locating a stream which would lead them to the ambush area.

Leaving the others behind, a reconnaissance party struck out for high ground where, by the grey of first light, they selected the ambush positions.

The spot chosen for the killing ground was in a valley with the stream running through the centre and crossing the road. There was a suitable rocky area right next to the road where the ambush/killer group could hide before springing their attack . . . and fifty metres back from the road was a hill liberally scattered with boulders which were big enough to conceal them during the major part of their wait.

They selected another spot 800 metres to the west of the ambush group on a piece of high ground where the early-warning group would be able to see the road on either side of the ambush area.

The early-warning group moved off to begin their vigil while the eight men in the killer group took up their places among the rocks above the road.

At last, they all removed their packs, easing their sore shoulders and backs, already feeling the sweat starting to dry cold on their backs.

Everyone in the ambush group was told exactly where he had to go once the target appeared, and what he was expected to do. They established communications with the early-warning group and the signaller called up Deka base to report the ambush was now is position.

* * *

Sergeant Major Pete Cole and three men later moved down to the road to lay the landmine. With one man positioned on the road in either direction to warn of approaching traffic, the sergeant major and Corporal *Lucy* set about chipping out the hardened soil with entrenching tools.

The road was made up of sand, stone, and rock . . . and it took them two-and-a-half hours to dig a hole deep enough to take the landmine. Then, just for good measure, 13 kilograms (29 lbs) of plastic explosive was added, making a total of more than 20 kilograms (44 lbs).

Once the landmine was laid and its wires buried as far as the nearby stream, they had to find a way to get the wires over the stream without getting them wet, and keeping them concealed. Pete decided to lay a log across the stream and run the wires along the side of it. Then he continued running the wires through the bush, camouflaging them as he went, back to a boulder in the ambush position from where the landmine would be detonated.

He connected the exploder to the wires and tested the circuit. A green light came on. Everything was working. The landmine would go off when he pressed the button. Now all they needed was a target.

At first light, he checked the camouflaging of the landmine, then the killer group rehearsed what they would do in the ambush. Captain Fritz and the sergeant major sited each man giving them their arcs of fire, and the sergeant major took note of a tree he could use as his aiming mark. When the first enemy vehicle reached the tree, it would be squarely over the landmine and pressing the button at that precise moment would achieve the best effect.

They returned to the LUP among the boulders on the hill to await a target. It was to be a long wait, calling for extreme dedication.

ZIPRA lorries normally travelled the roads by day, but they had to be prepared to spring their ambush at any time. Someone had to sit by the radio around the clock to await the word from the early-warning group. Weapons and rockets had to be kept at the ready and ammunition pouches, grenades and other equipment essential for the ambush had to be worn constantly by day, and at their side by night.

As in all SAS ambushes, no one could ever speak above a whisper and often hand signals were the only means of communication. Equipment taken out of packs had to be replaced immediately it was used. Their small gas cookers had to be turned down low to avoid noise and there could be no cooking of strong-smelling food.

Smoking was strictly limited to certain times during the day. There could be little or no movement in the position and there was strict discipline regarding movement at night.

Water parties and men wishing to relieve themselves ventured out only at night and everyone made sure he told his colleagues exactly where he was going – a life-and-death procedure, essential if he was to avoid being mistaken for an enemy blundering into the position and being shot.

Only wooden spoons were used to avoid making a noise. All tins of food, mess tins and cookers were camouflaged with green paint. And before they set out they had checked that no one was carrying white handkerchiefs or shiny plastic bags – anything that could give the game away. All rubbish went in sandbags which they kept in their packs at all times.

There could be no washing at all. It was essential that their hands and faces remained blackened-up and they constantly had to renew their camouflage, checking each other for glimpses of pink flesh.

During their vigil there was a fair amount of local traffic ... and the cyclists and pedestrians and the people in cars, lorries and Land-Rovers passed unaware of the 12 heavily armed ambushers lying in wait.

A meticulous log was kept of all movement, and from the type of clothing worn by some of the passengers, they assessed the Land-Rovers were ferrying ZIPRA.

Time passed slowly and with a fifty percent alert, the rest killed time by reading. Every book was camouflaged and passed from man-to-man in the main group. There were all types – spy books, westerns, thrillers ... There were even war books, as if the real thing was not enough.

Another pastime with Pete Cole, Lieutenant Laurie Walters and Corporal *Lucy* was watching and feeding rock rats, welcome visitors seen only at first and last light.

The soldiers fed them on rice and bits of army biscuits and Laurie Walters discovered they were specially partial to sugared peanuts.

The rats became quite tame, providing shows by chasing one another around the rocks and playing hide-and-seek with the soldiers and each other. Eventually, the men began to look forward to the break in routine provided by their new-found friends. Laurie Walters talked of making a trap to catch them, but his superiors did not approve of his scheme.

Remaining under such conditions inside hostile country, surrounded by locals and under constant threat of discovery or worse, placed a great strain on everyone. As in all long-term ambushes, it called for a great deal of self-discipline, team work, give-and-take, patience, stamina, and above all, the ability to wait.

By the fifth day, there was still no intelligence from the radio interceptors as to when a target might arrive, and they realised that they would either have to pull out in another four days or take a resupply of rations.

The commander opted for a resupply, and six men were chosen to rendezvous with the resupply chopper.

Two days passed and some time after last light, the six men carrying light weapons with enough rations and water for one day, and the tins and rubbish from all the ambush party, but otherwise empty packs, moved from the hill and down to the road.

Pete Cole, who would be leading the team, decided to use the road. It would be a risky business but there was no alternative.

Time was extremely limited and they had only one night to travel the 15 kilometres (nine miles) to the resupply point and find a safe position where they could hide up for the day to await the arrival of the chopper. Their return journey would also have to be completed in one night as it was essential to have the ambush group back to full strength as soon as possible.

They had just begun walking up the side of the hill when a vehicle suddenly shot over the crest of the other hill behind them. Quickly, they dived off the road, cradling their rifles to their chests, and lay still. Their hearts were pounding and they hoped that they had not been seen.

The lights of the vehicle were very dim. The soldiers lay perfectly still, listening and watching the lights without actually looking up.

They were about half way up the hill, which was fairly steep, and as the vehicle slowly struggled up the incline, the soldiers tightened their grips on their rifles, then faced the road and slipped the safety catches to fire.

The vehicle came to a stop about four metres downhill from them and the lights were snuffed out. Pete Cole decided to chance it and see what was happening.

It was dark and the moon was not yet up. But the night glittered with a million stars and he could see three of his group were crawling into better cover.

The vehicle, a Land-Rover, contained about three or four men. One had a torch. It was the same Land-Rover they had logged going up and down the road and it obviously contained ZIPRA.

The light came on very dimly and the engine ticked over. The Land-Rover skidded, struggled, moved a few metres and stopped almost opposite the sergeant major. Then the lights went off.

The chap with the torch came from behind the Land-Rover. This is it, the Rhodesians thought. Pete Cole sited through his nightscope, his finger was around the trigger.

But now he could see what the man was doing. Every time the Land-Rover stalled, he and his friends were placing large rocks under the rear wheels to prevent it rolling back down the hill.

They all appeared to be in civilian clothing and unarmed . . . and were far too busy trying to get their ailing vehicle up the hill to pay any attention to the sides of the road.

Off they went, a few metres at a time, and had soon passed the men hidden in the bushes. They continued in this way up the hill, and on reaching the top, got in and drove off.

It had been a close shave all round. The late-night drivers would never know how close they had come to trouble.

The six SAS men returned to the road and continued towards the junction with the old road, the same one they had crossed over that first night a week ago.

Once again, they were careful not to leave spoor. It was not really a problem where the road was hard and dry and had been used by numerous pedestrians. But, even though they wore similar patterned boots to the locals, six sets of tracks through a muddy area might arouse suspicion and on a couple of occasions, they were forced to leave the road and by-pass muddy patches.

Eight hours after setting out, the weary men reached the resupply area, and sought the sanctuary of a nearby hill . . . and later talked the pilot on to them, unloading the resupply and throwing their sandbags full of rubbish into the chopper at the same time.

Almost eight hours later, they arrived back in the target area, once more. The weary men were glad to get their packs off and grab an hour's sleep before first light. The group was now back to full strength and ready for business.

* * *

Over in the early-warning position, Sergeant Phil Cripps and a lance corporal had been taking it in three-hour stints to keep watch on the road while two other men behind them provided protection. Their position was the best possible, but had limited views of the road.

At precisely 11h15 on June 24, eleven days after the mission had got underway, Sergeant Cripps was watching the road intently as usual, when, to his great astonishment, around the corner swung a huge brand-new dark green Russian manufactured Zil truck.

Not only that, but it was laden down with what looked very much like brand-new ZIPRA in crisp new khaki-coloured uniforms and floppy hats, carrying brand-new AK-47s.

Quickly, the excited sergeant got on the radio to the main ambush group.

"Here it comes," he reported.

"How many trucks?" came the voice at the other end of the radio.

"Not sure," the sergeant replied, "I only saw one."

Down in the ambush group, books were hastily discarded, equipment fastened, weapons and rockets grabbed. Instinctively, they carried out their well-rehearsed drill of checking that everyone was ready, then they were up and running to take up their places in the ambush position.

The sergeant major tested the circuit. The green light came on. Everything was as it should be. They took off their safety catches and waited.

Meanwhile Sergeant Phil Cripps had returned from the radio to his earlier position and could see a truck on the stretch of the road that was visible through the bush. But now he couldn't tell if it was the same truck he had already seen – or another one.

211

When another truck swung around the corner, the sergeant and his companion worked out that there had to be three trucks in all . . . and all carrying terrorists. Quickly, Phil relayed the information to the men in the ambush position.

"Well, where are they?" the ambush party demanded to know.

"I don't know," the equally-puzzled sergeant replied. "The engines keep stopping then starting up again. But they should have reached you by now." Perhaps, he thought to himself, they had stopped for a smoke break.

To the group lying in wait, it seemed like an eternity. What should have taken only a couple of minutes took an agonising ten before the first Russian truck came into sight.

The convoy was moving cautiously and the ambush party could see why. There was a sweepline of ZIPRA troops walking ahead of the first truck and it was divided into two teams of four men on either side of the road.

They were checking the road for landmines and examining the sides of the road for the likes of the very people who were already primed and watching. The ambushers could clearly see machineguns on the first truck. All three lorries were crowded with enemy. Some were standing; some appeared to be sitting on what looked like equipment.

The sweepline advanced moving ever and dangerously nearer to the eight SAS soldiers lying in ambush behind the pile of rocks on the side of the road.

There were, in fact, not one but two dips in the road and, having meticulously swept through one looking for trouble, ZIPRA were obviously taken aback to find yet another ahead of them.

They decided that they had done enough checks for one day. They couldn't be bothered with any more.

The sweepline halted just ten metres from the Rhodesian landmine. Then ZIPRA climbed on to the first truck and it moved off again. The other two trucks were now about 200 metres apart.

Corporal *Lucy* with the RPG-7 rocket launcher and two companions had been tasked to take on the trucks in the event of the command-detonated landmine failing to do the job. *Lucy* could not conceal himself satisfactorily and knelt by the road waiting to put a rocket into the truck.

The sergeant major meanwhile was watching his tree – his aiming mark – and the first vehicle. Stand by . . . prime . . . wait . . . wait . . . wait. Then the back of the truck passed over the hidden landmine.

A split second earlier, *Lucy's* companion shouted a warning to him that the enemy had seen him and were shooting at him. *Lucy* sent a rocket into the vehicle.

But by then Captain Fritz had already given the word to initiate the ambush. The sergeant major pressed the button and that was it. The enemy didn't have a hope.

There was a sudden wind-sucking *whoosh* and the first truck vanished in a gigantic mushroom-shaped fireball of smoke and flames 15 metres in diameter. Amazingly, the ambush group never heard the explosion.

Lucy's rocket had merely added to the commotion of the moment. When he looked for the enemy who had been shooting at him a fraction of a second before, he had disappeared.

The size of the fireball came as a complete surprise to the ambush party. It was certainly nothing like the trial run back at Deka.

And no wonder. For there was more than ammunition exploding that day. The lorry had been carry a highly-inflammable cargo and as the landmine exploded it ignited the ammunition – and a 200-litre drum of petrol.

Lieutenant Ken Harvey *(back right)*, who at 19 was awarded the DSO for his courage and gallantry behind the German lines. He later became the Rhodesian SAS's Honorary Colonel

SOUTHERN RHO
FAR EAST VOLUN
UNIT

Where it all began. . . one of the lucky volunteers chosen for service with the Malayan
Scouts (SAS)

For the entire duration of the Rhodesian bush war, the operational control was in the hands of one man, Lieutenant-General Peter Walls *(Left),* the commander of the original C Sqn. SAS

Lieutenant-Colonel Ron Reid-Daly, SAS, legendary founding commander of the Selous Scouts *(Right)* who served in Malaya with C Sqn SAS *(second from the left)*

SAS Comanders: Major Dudley Coventry *(above left)*, Major Peter Rich *(above right)*, Major Court Welch *(right)*, and Major Brian Robinson *(pictured below with Prime Minister Ian Smith)*, who, as the longest serving OC, commanded the SAS through the major part of the war

Karl Lutz *(above)* and Dave Berry, who spent 13 out of the first 17 weeks of 1977 canoeing on operations on Cabora Bassa

Above: Lieutenant Chris Scollenberg, the SAS's first Siver Cross Soldier

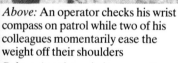

Above: An operator checks his wrist compass on patrol while two of his colleagues momentarily ease the weight off their shoulders

Below: Another mission over, the SAS arrive back in the relative safety of their base camp

Right: Chioco revisited – and Mac McIntosh with some of the spoils of war

The *Cockleshell Heroes*

Above: A photograph taken from a camera captured at Chimoio, which some western voices claimed was a ''refugee'' camp. The rifles tell the true story

Below: Unable to carry home this heavy anti-aircraft gun, the SAS later destroyed it – ensuring the enemy would not use it

Above: "A" Troop commandeer a ZANLA truck to collect vast quantities of enemy heavy weapons at Chimoio

Below: As the SAS pushed deeper into Mozambique during a major vehicle operation, a landmine had to be detonated to allow the convoy to continue

Above: The Dakotas carry the SAS deep into Zambia to ZIPRA's Mkushi camp

Centre: Mkushi is razed to the ground

Below: The Russian emblem daubed on the wall illustrates the Soviet influence at the ZIPRA terror training camp

Operation *Bastille:* The long road north

The ammunition store at ZIPRA's Mkushi camp deep inside Zambia blazes
fiercely as the SAS destroy the base

The Chambeshi rail bridge, in northern Zambia, destroyed by the SAS in a dramatic operation

Below: Part of the vast arms cache which fell into the hands of the Rhodesians during the Mkushi raid

Going . . . going . . . gone . . . One of the bridges destroyed in Mozambique

RAID INTO LUSAKA

Military targets shattered, says Walls

RHODESIAN WARPLANES struck at a terrorist base in Zambia yesterday . . . as the Commander of Combined Operations, Lieut-General Peter Walls, was explaining that the daring raid into Lusaka was not a political assassination bid on the life of Joshua Nkomo.

The general told a crowded Press conference in Salisbury: "Our record shows if we wanted to kill him we would have done so."

Sunday Mail Reporter

THE Commander of Combined Operations, Lieut-General Peter Walls, briefs local and world newsmen in Salisbury yesterday.

Nkomo claims he was home when attack was launched

LUSAKA.

LUSAKA residents were woken by a big explosion at about 3 a.m. on Friday.

A fistul of escudoes: Lieutenant Charlie Buchan and the charismatic leader of the Mozambique National Resistance, Andre Matangaidze, after Andre and his men had sacked a FRELIMO town. The money was handed out to the locals.

Left: And afterwards, after lucky escape, one for the album

Above: A dredger sinks into the muddy waters of Beira harbour, Mozambique's second largest port

Left: The flag of the Mozambique National Resistance movement. The red depicts the blood of the revolution, the arrows, five centuries of resistance and the blue, the pursuit of freedom

Right: Colin Willis *(left)* chats to Pete Cole *(centre)* and Les Clarke about their bomb to be left in Beira

Operation *Chicory:* The SAS and Air Force prepare their surprise attack on Joshua Nkomo's hidden arms cache near Lusaka – a vi: destined to have a significant effect on Nkomo's invasion plar

Above: Was this convoy just a show of strength during the hysterical days before the 1980 election results were announced? Or was this SAS Squadron occupied on a more devious task?

Below: Squadron commander, Captain Bob McKenna, who was responsible for planning one of the most important phases in the top secret mission, *The Op That Never Was*

Left: Lieutenant Rich Stannard, Bronze Cross of Rhodesia, Wings On Chest

Below: Former Prime Minister Ian Smith shares joke with SAS officers during their last official dinner

Captain Bob McKenna, SCR, BCR, WOC, admires the unique array of miniature medals awarded to Rhodesia's *Phantom Major,* holder of the Grand Cross of Valour *(left),* Silver Cross of Rhodesia *(centre),* Bronze Cross of Rhodesia *(right)* as well as Wings on Chest

Above: Operation *Uric:* Using an elaborate system of ropes and pulleys, the SAS were able to get under the spans of the double Barragem Bridge to lay their charges

Below: The bridges blow. *(Inset)* The SAS captured a 23 millimetre anti-aircraft gun, then turned it on the enemy and used it to protect the demolition teams

The Chongwe River Bridge, forty kilometres from Lusaka, demolished during Operation *Dice*. The unfortunate driver of the vehicle at the bottom of the gorge was transporting maize to the capital – and unaware that the bridge was no longer there

ROUTINE 191005Z DEC 80 (006)
FM HEREFORD
TO KABRIT
BT
TO CO AND ALL RANKS 1 SAS REGIMENT FROM CO AND ALL RANKS 22
SAS REGIMENT PD FAREWELL TO A MUCH ADMIRED SISTER UNIT
PD YOUR PROFESSIONALISM AND FIGHTING EXPERTISE
ON 31 DEC 80 HAS ALWAYS BEEN SECOND TO NONE THROUGHOUT THE HISTROY
OF THE RHODESIAN SAS PD BEST OF LUCK TO YOU IN THE FUTURE PD
C SQN STILL REMAINS VACANT IN 22 SAS ORBAT
BT

Above: The Rhodesian SAS flag comes down for the last time . . .
and the memorial plinth is smuggled out of the country to the
safety of a South African resting place

The fireball was so enormous that for one horrifying moment the Rhodesians held their breath as they feared for the lives of *Lucy* and party positioned a mere 15 metres from the detonation point.

But they were safe . . . and the moment the landmine detonated, *Lucy* and his team jumped to their feet and put rockets into the two remaining trucks as fast as they could, while the remainder of the party raked the trucks with machinegun and rifle fire.

The second lorry was also carrying a 200-litre drum of petrol and that too went up in flames as it ran into the wreck of the first truck, which was still burning, the exploding ammunition feeding the fire.

The driver of the third vehicle fled. The door was wide open as his truck careered down the hill and crashed into the other two, where it too immediately burst into flames.

The scene was an absolute holocaust. Trucks were blazing and exploding; there was the constant roar of gunfire and the air was filled with the screams of burning and wounded enemy.

All the ZIPRA on the first truck had been killed in the initial explosion. The ZIPRA men on the second and third vehicles attempted to flee in all directions. But they were either killed by the exploding ammunition or cut down by smallarms fire.

Several wounded managed to get clear and eventually staggered in to the Zambian Army base at Kabanga to report the ambush.

The ambushers had no concept of time but the event they had been waiting for so long to be played out must have only taken minutes.

The ambush group stopped firing and remained watching the area. The radio operator and a trooper moved back to the hill to report the ambush to Deka.

As the early-warning group moved in to join the main party, a burning figure stumbled towards them his flesh hanging in shreds. They shot him and he went down.

They rejoined the ambushers and swept the area, avoiding the immediate vicinity of the trucks which were burning and the ammunition still exploding.

Wounded enemy lying among rocks and thick clumps of bush opened fire, but the ZIPRA men were quickly outflanked and a further four were killed.

A body-count and search was carried out, documents and weapons were retrieved and photographs were taken of possible commanders and of the ambush site.

Their count, arrived at from the number of whole bodies plus parts of others, revealed that 69 ZIPRA had been killed. It was the highest kill-rate from any ambush in the entire war.

Pieces of bodies, arms, legs, chunks of flesh and intestines, even a rib cage, were hanging in the surrounding trees.

Charred bodies lay scattered in the surrounding undergrowth close to the trucks.

A line of dead was sprawled for 100 metres along the edge of the road, killed as they attempted to jump and run from the last two trucks as they careered out of control and into the ambush area.

A trail of new hats lay in a single line along the road, blown off by the force of the wind as the survivors ran away. They had kicked off their shoes as they fled . . . their hard bare feet better suited for running.

Every man had been in freshly-issued kit. They had even had new toothbrushes still in wrappers in their pockets.

As the explosions died down, all enemy weapons were recovered or thrown into the still-blazing trucks.

The SAS moved back to their former position on the hill to collect their packs. Suddenly, they saw the same burned terrorist who had been shot by the early-warning team get up and with super-human strength, stumble away from them. He was shot again. This time he did not get up.

A party was sent to lay landmines either side of the trucks in the hope of getting even more enemy when they came to investigate. Then, they regrouped and moved along the road to await extraction.

A group of Zambian civilians and their donkeys sauntered towards them, and, fearing the weight of the heavily-laden donkey cart might set off their new landmines, the soldiers detained them while they awaited the arrival of the choppers.

Soon the faint beat of rotors could be heard. The SAS released the locals with a warning not to go down the road. Then they slung their kit into the choppers and were gone.

Two choppers containing the main ambush group flew back to Deka ... but for Sergeant Phil Cripps and his team in the remaining chopper, there was still one more job to do.

They headed down the road towards Kabanga Mission and the pilot landed them far enough away from the ambush site not to arouse suspicion. They were near a kraal, so quickly moved into the bush and pulled back to the hills.

The Rhodesians were now planning to bait the big fish. They knew that the terrorist hierarchy made a practice of visiting the scenes of major incidents ... but only after a few days' grace during which the local army contingent checked the area for anything the Rhodesians might have left lying around.

That night, Phil Cripps's mine-laying party moved back down the escarpment towards the road. It was a beer-drinking night in the local kraals and as the SAS men lurked in the bushes by the side of the road, they could hear a drunk stumbling along the road whistling and singing to himself.

The man blundered down the road and soon all fell silent again. The mine-party cautiously moved out into the road.

Aided by what little light there was from the poor moon that night, Corporal *Lucy* set about digging a hole for the landmine, while two men kept watch either side of him.

Sergeant Phil Cripps was on hand to remove the excess soil and spread it among the bushes, but it was to be some time before he had any. The road was rock hard and Corporal *Lucy* had to chip it out bit-by-bit with his bayonet. In normal conditions where the soil was in granular form, the job would only have taken an hour. This time it took him four, and by then his hands were cut and bleeding from his labours.

The hole he eventually carved was just large enough to take the mine and he wasn't happy with it.

There was no space to put anything fancy like anti-prod devices or boosters. It would have to be just a straight-forward landmine.

The mine really needed to be deeper in the road and camouflaging it was not going to be easy. Vehicle tracks had been engraved into the dry hard road and it would be impossible to reproduce that sort of look.

Then *Lucy* heard the sound of cows and had an idea. He knew that a huge pile of dung would provide the perfect solution. Better still, he managed to find a suitably brittle piece that had been well and truly flattened by a passing vehicle. Carefully, he eased it on to his bivvy then carried it over to his mine. It fitted perfectly.

The sun was just coming up as he patted the cow dung in place. Soon, the locals would be up and about and maybe even the Zambian Army would be along to sweep the road for landmines.

They gathered up their kit and anti-tracked away . . .

Three days after the ambush, ZIPRA hierarchy and their bodyguards travelling in two Land-Rovers rolled along the road to carry out an on-site inspection of the devastation. Included in the VIP party was ZIPRA army commander Alfred Nkita Mangena . . . a big fish indeed.

Hidden under a piece of cow dung was the very thing, which, if activated, could strike right at the heart of the enemy's command structure.

But the two vehicles passed over the landmine uneventfully and the passengers continued on their way unharmed.

Their inspection over, the VIPs reversed and roared off in the direction they had come. Nothing untoward had happened on their way in. The Zambians had already swept up and down the road, checking the area out for landmines after all. There was every reason to feel confident on the way out.

But the ZIPRA men could not have been more mistaken. The rear wheel of the last Land-Rover bearing Alfred Mangena detonated the SAS landmine . . . and the ZIPRA army commander and three of his colleagues went up in the blast . . . When the dust settled, it was found that in addition to the three dead men, six others, three of them senior commanders, had been injured.

Back at Deka, the SAS had been monitoring Zambian Army messages in the days after the ambush and when Captain Colin Willis heard the Zambian Army commander at Kabanga telling his HQ that the "comrades" had hit a second landmine, he scrambled the choppers, organised a small SAS stick and crossed the border once more in the hope of getting hold of Mangena's body and claiming it as a propaganda prize. But by the time they got there, it had already been taken away.

It had certainly been a bad week for ZIPRA. Both the ambush and the landmine incident were major blows, and the death of Mangena was to hit the ZIPRA high command hard and have a demoralising effect on the men in the field.

Had Mangena survived, he would have gone on to be the most powerful man in ZIPRA next to Joshua Nkomo. According to SB thinking, his death was equivalent to having accounted for 1 000 run-of-the-mill enemy.

Mangena's death was to cause considerable friction between ZIPRA and the Zambian Army. ZIPRA blamed the Zambians for it. They were supposed to have checked out the road after all. They even accused the army of calling in the Rhodesians.

The Zambian Army very reluctantly cleared up the ZIPRA corpses and eventually convinced the local Africans to help them bury the bodies and remains. The burnt-out shells of the trucks were never removed and right until the last days of the war they were still there, serving as a reminder to ZIPRA of what might befall them if they strayed too close to the border.

* * *

In the days following Mangena's death, SAS reconnaissance groups reported numerous sightings of ZIPRA in the Simani Mine area . . . and Captain Colin Willis and Captain Fred Watt, of 1 Commando, RLI, decided that the time had come to go into the mine complex itself.

They planned a vertical fireforce envelopment in the hope of flushing out ZIPRA . . . and while Fred Watt remained airborne in a K-car directing movements in the sweep operations, Colin and a small SAS party were put down to pay the mine manager a visit. They were not the most welcome callers.

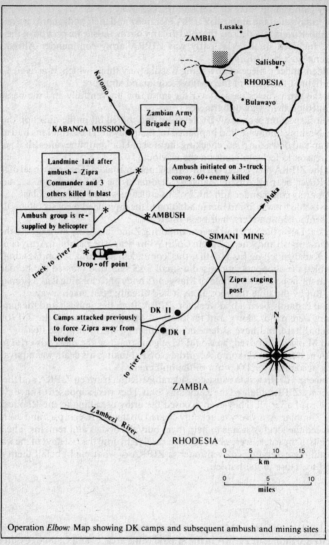

Operation *Elbow:* Map showing DK camps and subsequent ambush and mining sites

Not only was the elderly miner petrified about his fate at the hands of the Rhodesians, he was equally concerned about what would happen to him in the event he survived his ordeal. He was quite convinced that if ZIPRA came to interrogate him, they would kill him for assisting the Rhodesians.

He confirmed ZIPRA were moving around the area although they were not actually using any of the mine buildings.

216

Then between them they concocted a plan to protect the miner from reprisals. The SAS stressed they didn't want to harm him in any way, but if he wanted to avoid trouble with ZIPRA, they would have to make out they were assaulting him to force information from him. After that, they would tie him up but would do it in such a fashion that he would be able to free his bonds within half an hour of their leaving.

The miner agreed and gave a command performance for the benefit of his staff outside. His blood-curdling screams sounded realistic as the SAS proceeded to thump the table and kick the sides of his desk to get some genuine beating sounds. Occasionally, the SAS men yelled back at him then wacked the table a bit harder.

But time was getting short and they still had to search the mine and Colin decided to speed things up by borrowing the manager's private Landcruiser.

Assuring the miner that they had no intention of stealing his vehicle, they promised to repatriate his keys by dropping them on his lawn from the chopper.

Their search failed to turn up any ZIPRA however and as they flew over the manager's house, saw he had failed to keep his part of the bargain to remain fettered until they left.

Obviously not believing a word they said about not returning his vehicle, he had already freed himself and was running around outside in a state of panic. Colin tossed the keys out of the chopper and after satisfying themselves the miner had seen them, the Rhodesians disappeared back over the border.

This particular phase of the operation was unproductive and, as a direct result of the ambush and the Mangena episode, the area went quiet, as ZIPRA had once again been pushed further away from the border.

Captain Chris Schollenberg, Grand Cross of Valour, June, 1978

Captain Chris Schollenberg – Schulie to his friends – the first SAS man to be awarded the Silver Cross of Rhodesia, earned a place in the world's military history books by becoming the first holder of the Grand Cross of Valour, the country's highest bravery award.

The GCV, the equivalent of the Victoria Cross, or the Congressional Medal of Honour, was awarded to Schulie, then with the Selous Scouts' Reconnaissance Troop, for "deeds of the most conspicuous gallantry and daring ... in which he exhibited extreme devotion to duty and courage of the highest order".

Schulie earned the honour for his very detailed reconnaissances of targets far behind enemy lines.

Lieutenant-Colonel Ron Reid-Daly, the founding commander of the Scouts, had recommended Schulie for a bar to his Silver Cross, but the medals' committee clearly felt that was insufficient tribute to the world's foremost exponent of close-in reconnaissance.

He was awarded the GCV, and after receiving his medal from the President of Rhodesia, some one and a half thousand men, the largest contingent of Selous Scouts ever assembled, broke into the Scouts' specially-composed funeral song to pay their own tribute to Schulie. The African members of the unit regarded Schulie as a hero and said that no man who had done what he had done, ought still to be alive.

Viscount Disaster, September, 1978

It was Sunday, September 3. A day Rhodesia would never forget.

It was the day the many faces of terrorism suddenly took on a new ghastliness. Joshua Nkomo, accused by rival Robert Mugabe of not being aggressive enough, was, in a single day, about to correct that impression.

A firing mechanism found at Victoria Falls Airport some time before was the first indication the security forces had that a new dimension was about to be added to the long, bitter war.

It belonged to a SAM-7 missile launcher (commonly known as a Strela), a Russian hand-held weapon which fired a surface-to-air heat-seeking missile that could zero in on an aircraft's engine with devastating effect. Later, part of a second SAM-7 was found.

Both Strelas had been fired at South African Airways flights but something had gone wrong with them and they had missed . . . and two plane loads of tourists continued their journey unaware of just how lucky they had been.

They were the first attempts of aggression against civilian aircraft and the incidents were hushed up. Only a handful of security force people knew about them.

ZIPRA was not amused that the holiday makers had escaped with their lives. They accused their Russian backers, who had supplied the missiles, of tampering with them and making them ineffective. A Russian technician was immediately sent to Lusaka to examine the Strelas still held there and he came to the conclusion that there was nothing wrong with them. If they were not functioning properly, it was ZIPRA's own fault, he said.

They were obviously transporting them too roughly to the war zone: if they wanted results, they would just have to be more careful.

* * *

Shortly afterwards, a planeload of suntanned holiday makers who had been spending a relaxing weekend break at Kariba boarded an unarmed Air Rhodesia Flight RH 825, the Viscount *Hunyani,* for the return journey to Salisbury.

Despite the war, the lakeside holiday resort had continued to flourish and Kariba remained a tourists' paradise of game-viewing, water sports, fishing, evenings in the casino, and unmatched sunsets.

It was a retreat to fly to. Air travel was the best way to go: everyone knew that. It was far safer than travelling by road, which carried all the risks of hitting a landmine or being ambushed.

Within minutes, the 58 passengers and crew had left Kariba and the great manmade lake dividing Rhodesia from Zambia was behind them. They were still climbing, flying over the endless scrub and remote, sparsely populated bush that made up the vast Urungwe Tribal Trust Land.

In an hour, they would be back in the capital. But first there was a sundowner to look forward to on the plane to round off their break in routine. Children were laughing and hostesses Brenda Ann Pearson and Dulcie Esterhuizen were handing around the drinks.

Then, just minutes out of the airport, disaster struck.

Something smashed into two of the plane's four engines with a thud, violently shaking the Viscount. Flames streamed past the windows; pieces of metal pinged off the skin of the aircraft.

218

One of Nkomo's Russian-supplied deadly heat-seeking missiles had finally found its mark, its infra-red guidance control automatically homing in on the heat given off by the still-climbing Viscount.

It struck the trailing edge of the jet pipe of the number three engine, spraying shrapnel into the wing and shattering the fuel pipe. Its incendiary device started a fierce fire in the wheel well, which was filled with spilled fuel.

"I can't . . . " First Officer Garth Beaumont said in part of a message picked up by a National Parks plane at 17h11. The rest of the message was never heard.

A minute later, Kariba Airport picked up his desperate May Day signal.

"I've lost both starboard motors, we are going in . . ."

Inside the cabin, one man jumped up and dashed along the aisle shouting for a fire extinguisher; another tried to get through a window as the plane nosedived. One wing was already in flames.

Calmly, gallantly, a hostess instructed the frightened passengers to fasten their seatbelts and put their heads between their knees. Captain John Hood spoke over the intercom, telling them to brace themselves for a forced landing.

They were heading for a clearing in the thickly-treed terrain. It looked like a cotton field. Miraculously, the captain crash-landed his stricken Viscount, putting it down almost like a feather. But before he could stop it, the Viscount ploughed into a deep concealed ditch dividing the field. The right wing hit two trees, tearing portions off the wing tip, and the plane disintegrated.

An intense fire broke out, consuming everything that was burnable.

Air Rhodesia Flight 825 was over.

* * *

In Salisbury, relatives who had gone to meet the flight were told to go home. The plane had left Kariba on time but there was no news of it. The airport would let them know the moment they heard anything.

Not far away, the telephone jangled discordantly at SAS Major Garth Barrett's home in the suburbs.

It was ComOps. Could the SAS Commanding Officer put some "paramedics" as the caller described them, on standby and ready for an immediate operation? When pressed for a reason, the voice at the other end of the telephone told him that a Viscount was missing.

After an exchange in which the ComOps man refused to say what the cause of the plane's disappearance was, and did not accept Barrett's theory that it had been shot down or that the incident was a terrorist action, the SAS CO agreed to provide a small tracker and medical team.

An hour after the distress message had gone out from the stricken plane, a series of telephone calls were made to the SAS to "get into camp as soon as possible."

All told, twenty men were rounded up, including two doctors, an operational medic, an officer skilled at tracking, and RSM Pete Allan.

Garth Barrett quickly put them in the picture. The doctors helped supervise the packing of five panniers of kit – slatted wooden boxes designed to break open on impact with the ground. Everything that could possibly be needed for a casualty station was packed.

About 22h00, the CO told them to fall out. There was nothing more they could do. They had better go home and report to New Sarum at 05h00 next day, he said.

There was to be no sleep for the relatives and friends of the missing passengers and crew. As one long hour followed another, there was still no news of the Viscount or its 58 passengers and crew.

Air traffic controllers at Kariba were convinced it had been hit by a Strela and that there would be a fire on board. An aerial grid pattern search was conducted throughout the night but there were so many fires from locals in the TTLs that it was impossible to identify any as a plane burning.

The morning paper and radio carried reports of the missing plane. It seemed the whole country either knew someone on the plane, or knew someone who did. In a country with a small European population equivalent to that of an average British town, it was hardly surprising.

A special edition of the paper would be put out as soon as further details were known, readers were told. Journalists began ferreting for stories and pictures of the missing crew and passengers. The rest of Rhodesia hoped and waited.

Meanwhile, somewhere low over the Urungwe TTL, a Dakota containing the SAS medical/tracker team was circling, searching the rugged, densely-treed terrain for anything that might give them a lead.

It was extremely hot and the Dak was flying at just 1 000 feet. Most of the men were violently sick from the turbulence.

Then, as they reached the end of their grid search, Garth Barrett and the pilot spotted the wreck of the missing plane. It was still smouldering, and even from the air it was obvious that there had been a vast amount of devastation. The plane was broken up and most of it had been completely burned out.

The CO passed the news to the SAS paratroopers in the back. Another message was flashed to ComOps.

They did several low-level circuits and Garth Barrett saw a group of bodies lying under some trees.

Inside the plane the grim-faced SAS waited for the cue that would come any minute now. They stood up, checked their equipment and shuffled systematically towards the open door.

First came the red light. Then the green. As the first stick jumped out, the sudden rush of wind tore at their faces and uniforms making a pleasant change from the hot stifling atmosphere inside the Dakota.

As they floated down, they could see the wreckage strewn around the cotton field and the scorched earth near the fuselage.

The CO, Garth Barrett, medic Bruce Langley, RSM Pete Allan and a fourth man climbed out of their harnesses, grouped together and moved forward. Then they stopped in their tracks, confronted by an appalling sight they knew they would never forget.

There was a bundle of bodies, ten in all, the same ones seen from the air. A little boy ... a middle-aged woman, an old man with twenty dollars sticking out of his pocket ... the air hostesses, one of them, the sister of an SAS soldier, the girlfriend of another ...

Their injuries told a gruesome story. Somehow, these ten had survived the horror of the crash. Then they had been mowed down by automatic rifle fire from close range at the hands of a separate gang of ZIPRA.

The hardened SAS men who had witnessed death in many a battle, could only gape in horror at the scene ... while the Dakota circled overhead dropping the other parachute stick.

While some of the SAS quickly encircled the crash site, the first stick moved off to search for other victims.

Then they saw a white hand wave at them . . . and three people popped out of the bush at the bottom of the field.

For a moment, the soldiers could hardly believe it. After what they had just witnessed, they were not expecting to find any survivors.

They sprinted forward to help them, and as he ran, medic Bruce Langley shouted across asking if anyone was injured. Amazingly, there were no broken bones.

The three survivors were a honeymoon couple . . . and Anthony Hill, a close friend of RSM Pete Allan. It must have indeed been a comforting sight to Mr Hill to see a familiar face coming down the track . . . and the SAS man had soon brewed up a cup of tea for his friend.

Bruce Langley set up his stove and made the bride coffee. She gulped it down in one go. Some of her clothes had been torn away in the shock of the blast and someone organised a blanket for her.

Bit by bit, the survivors told what had happened . . . of how they had escaped from the broken wreck, helping some of the injured to safety. They returned to look for warm clothing and blankets and were searching the luggage when a group of terrorists arrived carrying AKs.

"Don't worry," the ZIPRA men had shouted. "We won't harm you," . . . and they laughed as they ran towards the wreckage.

At first, some of the survivors thought they had come to help them. Some were even thanking them. But then ZIPRA suddenly turned on them and mowed them down.

The three survivors ran towards a ridge. As the bridegroom ducked to retrieve his wife's dropped wedding ring, the attackers fired over his head.

Five other survivors, including a four-year-old girl, had also crawled to safety from the wreckage but were searching for water when ZIPRA arrived. They heard the shots and fled into the bush.

Of the 58 passengers and crew, 18 had escaped from the wreckage and ten of them were massacred.

Another grisly scene confronted the soldiers at the wreck. The charred bodies of children lay outside the plane. A doll was lying forlornly under the baking African sun and would never be played with again.

As for the passengers in the plane, they had never stood a chance. The horror of it all cannot be imagined. The heat from the smouldering plane was intense. The stench of burned fuselage, molten rubber, synthetic fabric and death, hung in the air.

Realising there was nothing much that they could do to help the survivors, some of the soldiers went off and sat in the riverbed. A couple chose to sit quietly on their own and make themselves a cup of coffee.

By now other security forces began arriving from Karoi to search for the five other survivors still wandering the bush and they were soon picked up.

Scores of angry farmers joined the hunt for the men responsible.

A nursing sister arrived by helicopter and went hysterical at the incredible scene. Two minutes later she was on her way out again.

The SAS men had played their part and flew home. The ghost of flight RH 825 would haunt them and Rhodesians for always.

221

In a BBC interview, Joshua Nkomo proudly took credit for the Viscount disaster. *The Fat Man* cackled as he boasted that it had been ZIPRA who had shot down the plane. He denied they had killed the survivors, but Dr Callistus Ndlhovo the ZAPU man at the UN, admitted ZIPRA had killed the survivors ... but not the children.

In his autobiography, Nkomo said that while his men helped the survivors to safety and took them water, "I have no idea how the ten died. I do not believe they were killed by our people. I hope not."

A few weeks earlier Ian Smith had offered Nkomo the hand of friendship and some power-sharing in the transitional government at a secret meeting in Lusaka. Nkomo was always viewed as the lesser of the two evils, but there was no way Nkomo – after the incident Ian Smith called him a "monster" – could be welcomed back.

Rhodesians were beside themselves with anger at the ruthless and cowardly outrage. The country mourned and morale plummeted to new depths. The mood was not helped by inaccurate reports in South Africa that the white victims had been raped before being shot.

Outspoken MP Mr Bill Irvine said the slaughter of the injured and dazed survivors was an action more barbaric than anything in the annals of Ghengis Khan.

"The people of this country will not let these innocents go unavenged ... I can promise the leaders of the PF skulking in Lusaka and elsewhere that those who seek to ride the wind, will reap the whirlwind."

In South Africa, the Friends of Rhodesia Society offered a reward of one hundred thousand rand to anyone who could bring the murderous Nkomo back to Salisbury for trial. No one collected the reward.

The trip to Lusaka to capture Nkomo was not necessary either. For amazing as it may seem, Nkomo was having dinner with white friends in the exclusive Salisbury suburb of Highlands two days after the tragedy.

A memorial service was held in Salisbury's Anglican Cathedral five days after the atrocity and was attended by some of the survivors. The church had never been fuller and the 2 500 mourners had to queue to get inside. There was not enough room for all of them and 500 had to stand outside.

Passers-by wept as they walked past the grim silent crowd. The SAS men who had found the broken, burnt and butchered bodies were there, too, to pay their last respects to the victims.

Within a few years, the Russians would shoot down a South Korean plane carrying 269 innocent passengers. The western world would be united in its condemnation of such a barbaric act. But there was no such reaction to the Rhodesian atrocity.

Only, as the Dean of Salisbury's Anglican Cathedral, John de Costa, pointed out, a "deafening silence".

" ... Nobody who holds sacred the dignity of human life can be anything but sickened at the events attending the crash of the Viscount *Hunyani* ... this *bestiality,* worse than anything in recent history, *stinks* in the nostrils of Heaven. But, are we deafened with the voice of protest from nations who call themselves civilised? We are not. Like men in the story of the good Samaritan, they pass by on the other side."

There had been no loud condemnation by Britain's Dr David Owen, nor from the President of the United States, or the Pope, the Chief Rabbi, or the Archbishop of Canterbury, he said in his sermon.

Blame lay not only with those who fired the guns, but also with the United Nations and their church equivalent, the World Council of Churches " ... from the safety and comfort of New York and Geneva, high moral attitudes can safely be struck. For us in the sweat, the blood, the suffering, it is somewhat different.

" ... The ghastliness of this ill-fated flight from Kariba will be burned upon our memories for years to come."

* * *

Within a couple of months, the tracker who had been in the team which had found the wreck of the Viscount, returned to Urungwe ostensibly to run an SAS officer selection course. However, while there, he used their skills to ambush known paths in the hope of getting some of the men responsible for the Viscount episode. After a tip-off, the SAS accounted for three of the men responsible for killing the survivors.

Five months later, a second Viscount was downed. Again, the SAS were called in to help. Then they were told the panic was over. Their services were not needed. This time everyone on board had perished ...

Operation Snoopy, September, 1978

By September, there were 2 000 ZANLA at what had become known to the security forces as the Chimoio Circle, the area north of the old Chimoio camp site, attacked by the Rhodesians the previous November.

Gaining clearance to mount another camp attack proved a lot easier the second time around. It had been done before and had proved successful. There had been no great international outcry – a few rumblings at the UN; then the world got on with its business. Besides, this time, the intelligence people were able to prove that four white Rhodesians, abducted from their homes a few months earlier, were being held at the new Chimoio.

ComOps gave their blessing – and on September 20, another major external, involving the SAS, RLI and air force was mounted on Chimoio.

The plan had been to attack the new base and then to destroy large amounts of periphery camps that had existed in the area for a number of years.

Initially there were only a few enemy to be seen in the new camp and it appeared it had been abandoned. But as the troops prepared to pull out, a Lynx carrying out a reconnaissance on the periphery area was shot at 35 kilometres (22 miles) to the south. Troops were sent to investigate and came under fire from a different place.

Reinforcements choppered in from the abandoned camps also met the same determined resistance ... while, practically every aircraft over the new target was spotting trenches ... tracks ... and small camps – and drawing heavy anti-aircraft fire.

The new target was ten times bigger than the Rhodesians had originally thought being thirty kilometres (19 miles) by forty kilometres (25 miles), comprising dozens of small camps, many gun positions, an extensive trench system and wide scatterings of very angry and determined ZANLA. Soon, virtually every callsign was having contact after contact, and because the targets and security forces were so spread out, it was very difficult to use air support effectively.

The pilots were having an extremely difficult time pinpointing their targets, and to add to their problems, the haze that hung over the target worsened once the camps began burning.

Day two was no better – and the Canberras were running in one direction ... Hunters were doing high altitude pinpoint diving strikes in another ... Lynxes were milling around ... helicopters were dodging in and out ... and it was happening in various stages of daylight and twilight and was so confusing, it was difficult for the airborne commanders to keep a grip on the situation on the ground.

During the confusion a tragic mistake was made when a pilot bombed a hill occupied by the SAS and Trooper Steve Donnelly was mortally wounded by a sliver of bomb casing. It had been a genuine mistake and a direct result of the appalling haze which enveloped the camp that day. The SAS, fully appreciating the difficult circumstances that had existed, never held a grudge, nor did they allow the incident to mar the excellent working relationship they had with *The Blues*.

Nine FRELIMO tanks arrived to harass the Rhodesians during the night, but apart from blundering around through the darkness and keeping everyone awake, no serious damage was done.

Next morning when the tanks had left, a search was made for the four white prisoners, but there was no trace. Only an old ledger containing their names and the campaign medals belonging to a 61-year-old retired British Army major, Tom Wigglesworth.

Three Russian armoured personnel carriers which arrived in the camp were destroyed by Hunters, and later that night, an RLI contingent attacked and destroyed another and killed ten FRELIMO.

On day three, the Rhodesians pulled out, leaving behind dozens of dead enemy as well as the main HQ and numerous bases razed to the ground.

The security forces had encountered much tougher resistance than normal and had experienced the heaviest anti-aircraft fire to date with a large number of aircraft hit by smallarms and missile fire. The Rhodesians simply didn't have the resources to keep the action going or the manpower to take on a camp spread over such a vast area.

For the four white abductees subsequently moved to Tembue camp in the north however, the operation had been a success. SB were able to produce the captured documents to the International Red Cross, and it was exactly the lever needed to ensure their release.

Five months later, they were handed over to Amnesty International and flown home ... and Tom Wigglesworth was finally reunited with his medals. Commenting about the return of the medals in his own book about his captivity and hardships, he said: "Truth is certainly stranger than fiction, and I would have had difficulty in believing that if I had read it in a book."

Operation Gatling, October 19, 1978

> *"If we worried about what the west says,*
> *we would have had our necks wrung a long*
> *time ago"* ... LIEUTENANT-GENERAL PETER WALLS

Rhodesia now began to turn her undivided attention to Zambia. The SAS had of course, been in and out of Zambia since the beginning of the year, destroying ZIPRA camps ... springing ambushes, and laying landmines. And in an operation led by Mac McIntosh, 17 enemy boats were destroyed on the Zambian shore of Lake Kariba.

But as was the way of SAS operations, it had all been low-key work – making their hits, then fading into the night again. Now, the security forces were planning to go into Zambia in depth, in force and very much more overtly.

The ominous lull that followed the downing of the Viscount was about to end with the first major combined air and ground pre-emptive strike into Zambia.

The offensive was aimed at delivering a telling blow to the thousands of ZIPRA amassing across the northern border – and it promised to be the largest and the most ambitious mission of its kind to date.

By now, Joshua Nkomo had thousands of trained ZIPRA at various camps in Zambia and their presence and numbers were causing ComOps considerable concern.

By siting his camps deep inside Zambia, Nkomo was confident they were well out of the reach of the Rhodesians. His main camp was FC (Freedom Camp) at Westlands Farm, 15 kilometres (nine miles) north of Lusaka, and much too close to the capital for the Rhodesians to ever contemplate attacking. Or so he thought.

There were 4 000 ZIPRA undergoing training at FC which also doubled as ZIPRA's main military high command – equivalent to army headquarters – where ZIPRA operations were planned and launched . . . and, as the most important terror camp in Zambia, it would be the first the Rhodesians would attack.

The plan was . . . after the fighter-bombers had pulverised the camp and delivered ZIPRA their first body blow, they would return to Rhodesia to rearm before heading out to Zambia again to bomb Mkushi camp, 125 kilometres (93 miles) to the northeast of Lusaka, where there were believed to be 1 000 enemy.

Although the detailed intelligence on Mkushi camp was very sketchy, the aerial photography was good and the Rhodesian eyes in the sky had picked up 500 uniformed ZIPRA on parade, and others were seen undergoing weapon training in the centre of the camp. The main base was surrounded by eight satellite camps.

After the initial air strikes on Mkushi, 120 SAS paratroopers and 45 SAS helicopter-borne troops including an 81 millimetre mortar team would carry out a vertical envelopment of the camp, then destroy it.

To round off the day's massive pre-emptive activities, a Vampire, Lynx and four helicopter K-cars would attack ZIPRA's CGT-2 (Communist Guerilla Training) camp, south-east of central Zambia and 100 kilometres (62 miles) east of Lusaka, and thought to house more than 4 000 enemy. After the strikes, RLI paratroopers and helicopter-borne troops would arrive to envelop the camp and complete the damage.

In view of the distances and logistics involved, an assembly area had to be set up at Kariba airfield . . . another at Mana Pools . . . and a third inside Zambia, five minutes helicopter flying time from Mkushi camp, where the helicopters could rearm and refuel.

The 120 SAS paratroopers were to fly direct from New Sarum to Mkushi, while the 45 helicopter-borne SAS men would take off from Mana Pools. For the attack on the CGT camp complex – the RLI paratroopers would jump off from Kariba, and the helicopter-borne RLI would leave from Mana Pools.

The personnel manning the Rhodesian-held assembly area inside enemy territory would parachute into Zambia at the same time the Air Force was making its initial strikes on Mkushi terror camp.

The force for the admin area was to be provided by the RLI under the command of their RSM. The party had just completed their basic parachute course and carried out six jumps. After their final jump at New Sarum, they had climbed aboard trucks expecting to return to their barracks. Instead, they turned left into the SAS barracks and were placed under quarantine.

The next morning, they would carry out their seventh jump, not as expected on to New Sarum, however . . . but a very long way outside their home country.

Every single SAS soldier in the regiment was called up and recalled to Salisbury for the mission. There were 270 including TA men, the most ever involved in a single operation. Those not directly involved in the raids, were to man the various admin areas.

Security was tight and the men were confined to camp. ComOps staff then travelled the 14 kilometres (nine miles) to the SAS's new barracks near the airport called Kabrit – after the SAS pioneers' first camp in the Western Desert – and presented their briefings to the squadron commanders, who, in turn, briefed their troops until every man was fully conversant with his role.

As the first chinks of dawn appeared in the greying sky on October 19, the SAS climbed into their trucks for the short drive to nearby New Sarum.

Before climbing into the command Dakota at the start of that day's raid, General Walls suddenly spotted one rather elderly paratrooper with grey hair saddling up. He was Arnhem veteran, Sergeant Major Stan Standish, who had gone to England in the days of the Federation to find out about the SAS. Stan, now a TA soldier, had smelled something in the air, and, not wanting to miss out on the action, he had got himself attached for the week.

General Walls chatted to some of the SAS lads, then wandered over to Stan.

"Hell, I don't know Stan," the General said. "Is there anybody else here who could have been at Arnhem as well as you?"

"Only the bloody aircraft sir," came the reply.

Later, the SAS squadron commanders climbed into the air force control tower to listen to the results of the air strikes on FC camp, on the outskirts of Lusaka.

The Rhodesians had no fight with the Zambians themselves, but they had no wish for the Zambian Air Force to interfere with the raid. The intelligence was that there were MiG 17 and 19 aircraft based at Mumbwa, Zambia's main air force base 100 kilometres (62 miles) north of Lusaka. There was also the possibility of the Rapier missile system and Strelas being used against Rhodesian aircraft.

The Rhodesians had an extraordinary plan to neutralise such threats – one that was to earn a place in the history books.

Heading north and entering Zambian airspace at that time, were two Hunters, four Canberras and four K-car helicopter gunships. Other Hunters orbited Lusaka airport and two more were en route for Mumbwa air base, to keep watch and retaliate in the event of Zambian Air Force reaction to the strike on FC camp.

At 08h30, high above the assembled target, the Hunters attacked, spewing death on the assembled ZIPRA below with their thousand pound bombs. Then came the Canberras and their cargoes of alpha bombs to compound the utter devastation on the parade square beneath.

The K-cars came next with their 20 millimetre cannons spitting high explosive shells into the scattering, totally stunned enemy.

The pilots reported that the ZIPRA anti-aircraft pits were unoccupied. Smallarms fire only had been directed at the planes but from two positions only. The element of surprise was complete.

Then came the extraordinary and now famous Rhodesian take-over of Zambian airspace. It was, as *The Rhodesia Herald* declared, a bizarre conversation.

Squadron Leader Chris Dixon, the Canberra commander, with the callsign *Green*

Leader, called up Lusaka international airport, whose radar covered the whole of Zambia and was in direct contact with the Zambian Air Force at Mumbwa.

"Lusaka Tower, this is *Green Leader*," he began.

Then *Green Leader* politely but firmly asked the air traffic controller to pass a message to the Zambian Air Force station commander at Mumbwa.

"We are attacking the terrorist base at Westlands Farm at this time. This attack is against Rhodesian dissidents and not against Zambia. Rhodesia has no quarrel – repeat no quarrel – with Zambia or her security forces. We therefore ask you not to oppose or intervene in our attack.

"However, we are orbitting your airfield at this time and are under orders to shoot down any Zambian Air Force aircraft which does not comply with this request, and attempts to take off."

Asked if he had copied the message, the controller replied in brisk, businesslike manner: "Copied."

Soon afterwards, the controller came through asking if the Rhodesians had any objection to two civilian aircraft taking off.

Green Leader replied: "We have no objection there, but we advise you for the moment to stand by on that. We request that you hold on for a short while, half an hour or so."

And for the next thirty minutes, the Rhodesian Air Force maintained control of Zambian airspace, while the Rhodesians continued to pound the ZIPRA camp to the north of the capital.

A huge pall of black smoke, clearly visible in Lusaka, hung over the destroyed FC camp. Men, wounded and dying, many carrying AK rifles, staggered out of the camp into the bush. Inside the camp, the number of dead ran into hundreds.

Dolphin 1 – the Rhodesian command Dakota bearing Air Force Group Captain Norman Walsh and General Walls – then took over the transmission from *Green Leader*, who peeled off out of range.

As *The Blues* were winding up their raid at FC, Dolphin 1 allowed a Kenyan aircraft from Nairobi to land at Lusaka airport. When the Kenyan pilot, who had been asked to make an orbit of the airfield, thereby delaying his landing, asked who had priority, the air traffic controller replied:

"Well I think the Rhodesians do at this time."

Then General Walls introduced himself as the Rhodesian Sunray (commander) and told the controller to tell the Zambian Government to "wind its neck in."

General Walls asked to speak to someone in the Government and even though the controller obligingly made a telephone call, the Zambian at the other end of the line declined to speak to him.

"Okay, you can carry on now," Norman Walsh instructed the controller, signing off the transmission.

* * *

In Salisbury, the SAS squadron commanders, listening to *Green Leader* and the strikes on FC climbed down from the New Sarum control tower and quickly passed the news of the successful air attacks on to their troops. Then they filed into the six Dakotas and took up their seats in readiness for the attack on Mkushi camp.

Once over the lake dividing the two countries, the pilots flew low level at treetop height and under radar cover. Soon the bumpy ride began to take its toll and many paratroopers swiftly filled their air sickness bags.

The attack on Mkushi had started badly with only one pair of Canberras dropping their weapons on the target. But the Hunter strikes were good, and at 11h45 the Dakotas bearing the SAS turned into Mkushi on their approach run.

The paratroopers could see the Hunter strikes ... the craters ... the columns of smoke and dust and the fires as the bombs did their damage.

For the occupants below, all hell was breaking loose.

By now, the first men due to go out of the Dakotas were standing by the door, one hand on their containers, the other on the static lines, moments from dropping into the ZIPRA camp.

In another Dakota, Sergeant Major Stan Standish stood ready and waiting to drop into the forward admin base, a few minutes flying time from the main camp. Stan was in SAS colours and on his chest was an impressive row of 11 campaign medal ribbons. As the oldest paratrooper in the Rhodesian Army jumped out, the young men following behind, couldn't help but feel a sense of occasion.

Within moments of landing, the admin base party had climbed out of their harnesses and were getting down to business. The first airdrop of helicopter fuel was expected any minute to allow refuelling and there was no one so nervous as a chopper pilot out of fuel deep inside hostile territory. If the admin party did not have the fuel ready for them, the conversation tended to be unprintable.

Stan Standish was to be seen everywhere on the DZ that day, rolling drums, collecting chutes and exhorting the RLI troops to greater efforts. When the RLI RSM learned how old Stan was, he shook his head and promptly lashed into his men with words of: "If a 60-year-old SAS man can roll drums, you can roll 'em a damn sight faster."

The SAS paratroopers meanwhile had been dropped off around Mkushi. Three of the six sticks had been dropped 1 500 metres from their target while other paratroopers were put down a bit too close for their liking.

They were having contacts with fleeing enemy before they could get into a semblance of a sweepline. Then a heavy grassfire, started from all the shooting and the wind, began blowing it straight towards the SAS. The stop group commanders cleared their men away from the blaze, and the fire swept on destroying many parachutes.

Next came the 45 helicopter-borne SAS, including an 81 millimetre mortar team. But commander, Captain Bob McKenna and his team in one of the helicopter stop groups was put down eight kilometres (five miles) from their target and faced a frustrating time waiting for the helicopters to return from refuelling to reposition them.

Then SAS lance corporal Jeff Collett in another group was fatally wounded. The khaki-clad ZIPRA responsible was swiftly made to account for those fatal shots, and, as the soldiers glanced at the form of the dead enemy, they realised it was a woman.

As their briefings had not mentioned anything about women ZIPRA, the troops were slightly taken aback. Indeed, as the planning had been based mostly on aerial photography, no one could tell them that.

It took a bit longer for the other stop groups to realise that they were attacking a predominantly women's camp. For they were all in camouflage shirts, trousers, black boots and webbing and many carried rifles just as their male comrades did.

Bob McKenna and his group, having finally been put in the right place, were sweeping towards the main camp.

Suddenly, a male, obviously an instructor to all the women running around, opened up on them, – and Bruce Langley went down, part of his face blown away and a wound in his shoulder.

SAS doctor, Jon Thomson hurried across and began putting a drip in his semi-conscious patient. Then a grass fire swept towards the little party bustling around Bruce and they lifted him on to a pole stretcher. But Bruce, no lightweight at 99 kilograms (220 lbs), broke the stretcher. He was picked up bodily and rushed through the fire to safety.

The instructor responsible for Bruce's injury realised that his cover was disappearing rapidly and began shooting at them again. As the SAS shot back and silenced him once and for all, the doctor, oblivious to all but his patient, finished putting up the drip.

Hardly a minute was passing without an action of some sort happening in the camp. There were hundreds of individual foxholes all over the camp and the K-cars with their 20 millimetre cannons were clearing them before the ground troops followed up.

Most of the enemy, although armed, seemed more intent on surviving than putting up a fight. They were hiding in the foxholes . . . behind rocks . . . in crevices . . . behind trees . . . in bushes . . . in the river . . . in buildings . . .

Those who did fight back were very aggressive, far more so than the women at Chimoio. There was no question in anyone's mind that they knew how to use their rifles.

Mac McIntosh and his little party commandeered a Russian built and supplied Zil truck, and used it to lay four landmines in the access road to delay any enemy reaction group. Afterwards, they drove around the camp collecting all the arms and ammunition they could from inside the foxholes and depositing them in the centre of the camp.

In the heart of Mkushi, the SAS found huge parade grounds and a library daubed with a Russian hammer and sickle. There was an enormous kitchen with a massive cauldron, a training ground, an underground armoury and a bunker which the women were forced to dig when on punishment and used by camp Chief-of-Staff Moses Pinda as his headquarters.

The camp was beautifully laid out and was far more military orientated and had more amenities than any of the ZANLA camps the SAS had seen in all their years in Mozambique. Valuable documents, including signals equipment and ciphers, were recovered by the SB boys, and Scotty McCormack captured a Russian general's uniform complete with medal.

Then a Zambian Air Force MiG flew over the admin base and Mkushi main camp, sending the Rhodesians below scattering for cover. But it harboured no aggressive intentions and tended to hide away behind puffs of cloud and smoke. Just to make sure it didn't get involved, the Rhodesian Hunters were prowling about keeping an eye on it.

Behind the scenes, the Zambian authorities were in a state of intense panic. Intercepts told that the Zambian Air Force was far too scared to retaliate.

The Rhodesians' cross-border activities that day so unnerved six Zambian police officers at one nearby station that they ran away and were never seen again.

Meanwhile, a signal from the army base at nearby Kabwe was describing the situation as "very critical". Another said: "The person who was in charge of the radar at the time of the bombing (on FC camp) and the commander of ZNDF, Lt.-Gen. Pete Zuze must be sacked because they are useless. If they are not sacked, Zambia will experience more bombings."

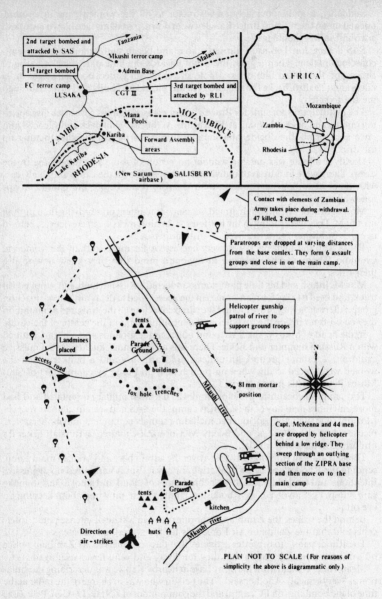

Operation *Gatling:* Map showing attack on ZIPRA's Mkushi terror camps with inset showing other phases of operation

230

By now, the air force and the RLI had attacked CGT-2 terror base, but word of the earlier attacks had spread and the birds had flown. There was therefore only token resistance, but at the end of the raid, 51 enemy lay dead at CGT-2.

By 16h00, Mkushi was more or less secured and, on the SAS's suggestion, a decision was made to bring in the *Vultures* – the security forces name for the press, as they turned up when everybody was dead. Despite reports to the contrary, the Rhodesians were not about to deny that there were women at the camp, or conceal the hundreds of communist weapons, Chinese literature, military training manuals and instructional notes that proved it had indeed been a ZIPRA training centre and not, as Joshua Nkomo would allege, a place of shelter for students and sick people.

At ten that night, the wounded were still being ferried from FC camp to the University Teaching Hospital in Lusaka. Private vehicles belonging to the South African ANC and SWAPO, the Red Cross and police had been used throughout the day, and ZIPRA had asked the OAU Liberation Committee for 15 lorries to ferry the wounded.

Many of the wounded had fled into the bush and could not be picked up. Others, beyond hope, were left where they were to die in the bombed-out camp. One commander, realising it was all over, turned his gun on himself.

Meanwhile, the Zambian Government had gone into an emergency session to discuss the devastating raids.

And in Mkushi, the SAS settled down for the night, ambushing known paths and tracks and shooting a couple of enemy vehicles that tried to get close under cover of darkness.

* * *

Next day, the *Vultures* arrived on the dusty parade square of Mkushi. It was 24 hours after the attack had gone in; the SAS were still mopping up and the air was full of kites wheeling high over the bodies.

A women prisoner, Phinah Malaba, dressed in khaki slacks and jacket, was brought forward to speak to the journalists. Phinah was one of seven prisoners taken back to Rhodesia. Phinah had been a training instructor and all the 13 male instructors at Mkushi had been trained in Angola.

There had been two separate groups in the camp – one for 1 000 trained enemy and the other for 1 000 new arrivals, who were still undergoing their training. The overall strength of Mkushi totalled 2 036.

The 1 000 trained women had spent six months learning bayonet charging, combat tactics, logistics, foot and rifle drill, camouflage and concealment in the bush, weapon handling and firing a variety of rifles and rocket launchers, ambushing and skirmishing, guerilla warfare administration and urban warfare.

Joshua Nkomo had gathered so many women to his cause over the years that the time had come to do something with them. Sadly for them, and acting very much against the Russians advice, Nkomo opted to give them military training. They were thus trained military personnel and as far as the Rhodesians were concerned, another enemy.

Even though their role was eventually to be staffing forward bases, it was felt that had they ever found their way into Rhodesia, they would have had a serious impact on the country. And not having had any prior knowledge of them, the security forces would have had no counter to them.

While the Press took their pictures, the troops set about burning everything they thought ZIPRA could use again. More than 1 000 weapons went up in smoke, and the Russian Zil truck was destroyed.

* * *

Next morning, the SAS prepared to pull out of the still-smouldering camp and moved to the north-east to await the choppers. After half the party was choppered out, the very excited voice of one of the sentries suddenly came up on the ground commander's radio to warn of a large party of men approaching the camp in sweeping formation.

The group included 64 Zambian Army, 17 policemen and several ZIPRA, dressed in an assortment of uniforms and carrying a variety of weapons.

The Rhodesians allowed them to get close – then opened up with devastating results. Clive Cripps initiated the ambush and the ensuing contact lasted twenty minutes. By the end of it, 47 enemy lay dead and two men were taken prisoner.

One capture was a Zambian Army corporal and the other the ZIPRA logistics officer at Mkushi, Mountain Gutu, who turned out to be one of the most important prisoners the intelligence people had had to date.

He had been to Russia on a commander's course, knew all the ZIPRA hierarchy and was able to give SB a valuable insight into the top ZIPRA men, which, until then, they didn't have. As the logistics officer, he had travelled around Zambia delivering supplies and was able to pinpoint the many ZIPRA camps beginning to spring up throughout Zambia and the routes used to get there.

Within days of Gutu's capture, the bombers were on their way to Zambia to destroy a logistics base near Lusaka. He also told how ZIPRA were holding dissidents and captured black members of the security forces in an underground prison 140 kilometres (87 miles) into Zambia. The Selous Scouts subsequently rescued 32 Africans, including security force members and civilians abducted for terror training.

The captured Zambian corporal was ultimately returned to Zambia and Mountain Gutu became the chief firearms instructor for the Muzorewa youth wing, undergoing training at a secret farm in Bulawayo.

Operation *Gatling* had been the most devastating operation yet mounted in Zambia. The death toll was high: between 800 and 1 000 were killed at FC camp, and another 600 wounded. The Mkushi figure was put at about 600 dead, and at CTG-2, fifty.

The offensive sent Zambians into a state of panic and for weeks afterwards, ZIPRA shot at every low-flying aircraft approaching Lusaka airport. Several domestic flights were struck by smallarms fire as they came in to land and several months later they succeeded in shooting down two Zambian army jets.

The Zambians began harassing whites and saw spies behind every tree. ZIPRA were convinced that the success of the raids had been due to intelligence received from white Zambians. Some people were beaten, others murdered. And everyone wondered when the Rhodesians would strike again.

The Zambian offensive had coincided with other self-defence attacks against ZANLA bases in the Chimoio circle, both described by General Walls as "enormously successful." He said he "did not give a damn what the rest of the world said about Rhodesia's raids into neighbouring territories.

"If we worried about what the West says we should do, we would have had our necks wrung a long time ago. It seems to me that we are constantly being advised to lie down and take it. But nobody else in the rest of the world has to do it – only us."

Operation Shovel, December 15, 1978

Just before Christmas, SB got themselves the best present of all – the secretary of the ZANLA high command for Tete Province, whose immediate superior was top operational commander Josiah Tongogara.

Not only did he know Tete like the back of his hand, he was also familiar with terror camps elsewhere in Mozambique and Tanzania and was able to give SB a wealth of intelligence.

Then he told them about a massive arms dump being hoarded in a hangar at Tete airfield. A Hunter was immediately dispatched to the airfield and with a single rocket blasted the ammunition dump . . . and the hangar . . . and the surrounding buildings off the face of the earth. So intense was the force of the explosion that the pilot almost knocked himself out of the sky, but as he turned for home, he took comfort in the sight of the utter devastation below him.

It was obvious that ZANLA would lose no time re-establishing and resupplying their ammunition stockpile. Soon a trainload of ammunition would rumble northwards from Beira to Moatize, the station nearest to Tete, and ZANLA would be back in business once more.

If the security forces could follow the devastating air strike by destroying the rail line . . . a bridge . . . and, as a bonus, hitting a train as well, so much the better.

Not only would it prevent the ammunition dump being replenished, but with the line blown, nothing and no one – particularly ZANLA – would be able to use the track for some time. ZANLA were using the line to travel from Chimoio to Tete and nearby Chingodzi . . . and from there, they were deploying straight into Rhodesia.

The demolition task was offered to Lieutenant Mac McIntosh, who had just come back from a stint in the bush and about to head off for a well-deserved holiday.

It was a hot target and Mac jumped at the opportunity. It was a chance in a million and he immediately postponed his holiday.

The name of the op was to be *Shovel*. If all went well, the enemy could soon be shovelling the remains of a bridge and train out of a riverbed.

The aerial photographic interpretation had already been done and, based on the information gleaned from it, the explosive charges – 1 000 kilograms of TNT – had been made up specifically for the task.

Thereafter, everyone involved in the sabotage task moved quickly. Equipment was loaded on to trucks and they set off for Mtoko where they established a tactical head-quarters. That night they boarded a Dakota and parachuted into Mozambique.

Their plan was to establish themselves on the ground, find the bridge and carry out their reconnaissance. Once Mac MacIntosh had evaluated the situation, he would call in the Dakota and the 1 000 kilograms of charges would be dropped right next to the bridge. For there were only twenty men in their party; not enough to carry such a heavy load of explosives over long distances.

They found the bridge without difficulty and established themselves in a lay-up position near the bridge . . . and the next night, Mac called in the Dakota.

Soon the dull throb of an aircraft engine could be heard. The Dakota was bang on time. Mac began to talk it in to their position. Above, the dispatchers stood by the open door of the plane and waited for the order to send the explosives through the night.

But the inexperienced dispatchers on duty that night jumped the gun and pushed the mound of explosives out the door a few vital seconds before the final order . . . and

233

those all-important seconds made all the difference between the charges landing next to the target as planned and dropping eight kilometres away.

The ground troops watched in dismay as the parachutes flopped open in the distance. They knew they were in for a hard night's slog and a few choice words over the radio reached the ears of the very embarrassed dispatchers.

There was a mumbled apology from above, then the Dak turned and headed homewards carrying the men responsible for their troubles that night to the comfort of a warm bed.

Back at the Mecito bridge in Mozambique, there was no time for recriminations and no time to be lost. They had to locate every box of explosives and bring them all back to a safe position by the side of the rail line before first light. For there were villages and sidings down both sides of the line and they couldn't afford to be seen by the locals.

For hours they laboured – locating the explosives ... sweeping ... struggling through the bush until eventually all the charges and the parachutes were recovered.

The hot, tired team hid the explosives in a ravine and camouflaged them from prying eyes. As if to round off their troubles that night they had just finished doing that when there was the most torrential downpour. The weary, now wet, men settled down for what was left of the night.

Next day, the recce party ventured out for a closer inspection of the bridge and found fresh problems.

To their dismay, it transpired that the photographic interpretation had been totally incorrect. From the air, the bridge must have looked closer to the ground. In reality, it turned out to be twice the size the photographic interpreters had thought.

As the explosives had been made up from the photographic interpretation, it meant that they were far from custom-made for the bridge. It also meant that the all-important accessories for getting the saboteurs under the bridge and the charges in position – the metal ladder and lengths of rope – were useless.

The ladder would not even reach half way up the bridge. Instead of being an aid, it was nothing more than a nuisance, for now they had to waste time burying it as its discovery could lead to detection.

Now faced with an enormous drop, the demolition team would have to be extremely careful. A careless moment, a slip of the foot, and they would plunge to certain death.

It was a severe set-back but the mission would still go ahead. They would just have to improvise with what they had.

Back in the safety of their lay-up position, the SAS schemed how to place their charges to the best advantage, and with some initiative and some fairly bright lads – particularly Nick Wilson, who had just come off a demolition course – they managed to sort out a system that would get Mac McIntosh and a corporal under the bridge and the explosives safely in position.

That night, Mac and the corporal returned to test the plan.

Following their normal procedure, they placed two early-warning groups out, one on either side of the bridge. New SAS officer Lieutenant Mike Rich had the task of sitting on the railway line with the radio, co-ordinating the early-warnings and giving Mac and crew the shout if anyone or anything came along.

They fastened their length of rope – which had been extended by paracord – on to one of the rail lines and tied a rock on the other end of the rope. They then slung it underneath the bridge ... up the other side ... took the rock off and tied the rope on to the opposite rail track.

Mac and the corporal climbed under the bridge and shuffled along it, using the rope to go hand-over-hand along the pier. When they got to a gap, they pulled themselves up on to the ledge. Their legs dangled precariously over the edge of the 13 metre-high bridge and it was such a tight squeeze that they were sitting shoulder-to-shoulder. They were, however, ready for business ...

Using a chain formation, the incredibly heavy charges were passed down from one man to the next, each steadying them with one hand, then pushing them against the side of the bridge and down to the next man.

One of the two men under the bridge would lean out, clutch the charges to him with both hands and pull them in under the bridge. Then, as there was no room to manoeuvre, one man would lean out of the way while the other slapped special *Wonder Glue* on little wooden blocks and stuck them firmly in place under the bridge.

The blocks had hooks attached to them; and the paracord tied around the charges was threaded through the hooks, then drawn up tight.

It was a slow, tricky business and they could tell from the beginning that it would take several nights to get all the charges in position.

As one long hour followed another and the night came down, they made use of their torches.

Eventually Mac called a halt. They had not finished yet and would have to spend another night perched under the bridge.

Mac debated if they should wire up the explosives then and there. If they were compromised, it meant they would be able to blow the bridge before withdrawing. On the other hand, if a local went into the riverbed and looked up, he might catch a glimpse of the wiring system. Mac decided not to take the chance.

Mac and the corporal took their leave of the bridge, glad of the chance to stretch their legs and rest their aching arms. They met up with the others again then settled down to wait the day out before returning to the bridge again that night.

During the day, they got a message from Rhodesia warning them to be careful ... FRELIMO were very suspicious that their bridges might be demolished.

Within half an hour, that signal had taken on new meaning. Trundling down their stretch of track came a member of the militia driving a small railway trolley. The trolley passed over the bridge, then slowed right down, cutting its engine just as it got out of sight. Then silence!

Back in the bushes, the atmosphere was electric. Would the driver come and investigate and discover their explosives? Mac cursed himself for not wiring them up after all.

Five long minutes ticked by, but the militiaman never came to investigate. The trolley rattled on its way without the Mozambican so much as stretching his legs. It had been nothing more than an incredible coincidence.

As evening approached and the temperature dropped, the railway lines began the now-familiar nightly clatter as they contracted. Darkness falls quickly in Africa and it was not long before the demolition team had slipped back under the bridge to complete their task.

By the time they had finished, there were layer upon layer of charges hanging in place. There could be no doubt as to the fate of the bridge or whatever was on it when the bang went off. The charges together with the weight of the train equalled overkill.

The demolition was ready. All that was needed was to hook up the exploder, turn a handle and press a button. They also needed a train.

Both steam and diesel trains travelled up and down the line and Mac had to consider which was the most important. Maybe their luck would hold and they would get a troop train. Then while he was trying to make up his mind, the decision was taken out of his hands.

The enemy ammunition resupply had not yet left for Moatize and it was vital that the bridge be dropped before it got through.

Back in Salisbury, Lieutenant-Colonel Brian Robinson, now with the ComOps planning team, was more interested in the urgency of the demolition and felt that the sooner a train – any train – was dropped on the bridge, the better it would be. His idea was passed on to the operators and that night – December 15 – Mac and his men took up their positions.

The commander and his partner moved to their initiation point. By their side was the exploder device. The rest of the men under Lieutenant Mike Rich lay low by the side of the track ready to attack from the rear of the train. Then they settled down and waited.

At 21h00, a steam train came heaving up the line from the Mozambican coast. Soon Mike and his men saw the twinkle of carriage lights through the darkness. Then as the train passed within ten paces of them, they saw the fireman shovelling coal into the fire.

As the engine got on to the bridge, Mac McIntosh did his stuff with precision timing. He pressed the button; the bridge erupted and the train blew with it.

The bulk of the charges hidden under the side of the bridge nearest to the train blew first, followed a micro-second later by the others on the far side. There was a mighty roar, a hiss of steam and all sorts of peculiar noises and crunches. The remains of the engine plunged into the gaping chasm where the bridge had once been – and ended its journey in the riverbed with a deafening crash.

As it fell, it dragged several open wagons in its wake . . . and they were left dangling forlornly over the edge. There was so much wreckage it almost filled the gap where once the bridge had been.

Metal grated upon metal and a big steam cloud hung in the air.

The lights of the four carriages and small guards van were snuffed out, their power source having come from the wrecked engine.

By a stroke of luck, the terrified passengers had escaped with their lives. The rail tracks had been blown off the embankment and the passenger carriages had ploughed into the shaking soil instead of continuing on and plunging into the riverbed.

Mike Rich's group advanced down the track firing their RPDs and RPG-7s into the back of the train.

A group of FRELIMO got off the train in a panic. There was a token exchange with the SAS and the Mozambicans made off into the night.

Scores of nervous Africans tumbled off the train along with their goats and chickens and some passengers had the presence of mind to dive straight for the bush.

The saboteurs swept through the carriages coach-by-coach in search of others. They moved down the corridors systematically, forcing open the doors and beckoning the passengers outside. They assured the passengers no harm would befall them, but not everyone believed it. Two were so nervous that the urine stains could be seen seeping through their trousers. Others, relieved that they were to be spared, were over-friendly and readily did as they were bid.

They were all herded outside and quizzed about FRELIMO activity in the area and willingly supplied the answers. At last, the SAS commander had all the information he wanted and told them to clear off. The passengers, grateful to have escaped death twice that night, took to the hills without a second bidding, muttering among themselves as they fled.

The SAS used up their left-over explosives to blow the wheels off the coaches and prevent FRELIMO salvaging them.

After burying a landmine under the big granite chips in the rail track, Mac and his team left the still-protesting engine and struck out for a mountain three kilometres to the south, from where they could monitor any recovery train FRELIMO sent to collect the remains of the one now languishing in the riverbed. Then they would climb down from their mountain and destroy that as well.

As the sun came up, they could see right down from their mountain perch into the valley and could see another bridge not one kilometre from the destroyed one. It had not been marked on their maps and the intelligence people had known nothing of it.

Had they known, Mac and his men could have destroyed both of them and the coaches would have been nicely marooned between the two demolished bridges, thereby doubling the time it would take FRELIMO to salvage them.

When FRELIMO did come, they came in strength and were clever enough to send a train from both ends of the rail track, then deploy troops on either side of the line in a very wide extended line formation to look for the saboteurs. Luckily for them, no doubt acting on a tip-off from one of the passengers, they unearthed the SAS's landmine.

The prize was a diesel train, but there were FRELIMO troops milling around it all the time ... and Mac decided against hitting it. It was impossible to get out of the escarpment, effectively hit the train and get back into the escarpment safely again without encountering intense opposition from an extremely upset enemy. There were only twenty SAS operators and they would be sorely outnumbered by a heavily armed enemy.

* * *

Meanwhile, other plans were afoot to thwart ZANLA moving ammunition northwards by alternative means.

As part of a three-pronged exercise to stop enemy ammunition getting into Rhodesia, a 12-man SAS group was in position along the road to Tete and awaiting the arrival of a ZANLA munitions truck.

The intelligence coming in was that now the track had been sabotaged, resupplies were to be ferried up by road from Maputo . . . and that the convoy carrying them was due to reach Guru within a couple of days of the Mecito bridge being demolished.

The SAS ambush party were waiting in the pouring rain for them ten kilometres north of Guru. It was a busy road and the ambushers lying low some fifty metres from the tar, remained undetected in the cover of the thick bush.

At 05h00, five days after the rail bridge was demolished, Sergeant *Small Bez* was sitting on guard in his bivvy when he heard a rumble in the distance. Unsure if it was a vehicle, he called for another opinion from the chaps on the hill above him.

"Yes," came the reply, "I can definitely hear vehicles; in fact I can see lights coming," he was warned.

It didn't take long to get the action going ... and soon an assortment of guns and rocket launchers were lined up along the edge of the road. A command-detonated landmine had already been buried in the tar road.

At 05h30, the first vehicle came into sight. It was still dark but the men in the bushes could see that it was a pantechnicon with huge green lights shining through the early-morning downpour. But it looked more like a civilian vehicle than a ZANLA one and they allowed it to get clear of the killing ground.

Next came an open-backed truck bearing a group of men with tarpaulins pulled over their heads. They were huddled together for protection from the rain and cold and there could be no mistaking this for anything other than what it was – a ZANLA troop carrier.

Corporal Rob Slingsby looked down the sights of his RPG-7 rocket launcher, and as the troop carrier crunched nearer, there was a bright flash and a tremendous bang as his rocket left the launcher and sped on its way.

He hit it smack centre, sending it careering out of control ... and straight towards him. He leapt out of the way in the nick of time, seconds before it hurtled passed him. It ploughed over one of his rockets, then crashed through the bush taking its petrified passengers on the final journey.

The mission commander meanwhile had pressed the button to activate his hidden landmine and the third vehicle – a Land-Rover – went up in a huge bang and disintegrated into nothing.

The explosions were enough to bring the twenty assorted trucks following behind to a grinding halt. They did a quick U-turn and beat a hasty retreat, but they were spotted hiding in an orchard by a Lynx pilot ... and at 08h30 when the clouds began to clear, the Hunters screamed in with all guns blazing and accounted for every vehicle that could be seen. Then a ZANLA petrol bowser which had gone unnoticed in the initial attack, caught one pilot's eye and just before he peeled off home, he destroyed that as well.

The huge mushroom that billowed into the sky as the explosion went off and the petrol ignited, was clearly visible to the SAS ambush group on their hill ten kilometres (six miles) away.

It was the end of that particular consignment of enemy ammunition ... and, their mission complete, the ambush group returned to Rhodesia.

* * *

Back on the mountain overlooking the demolished Mecito bridge, the SAS were still monitoring the activity of FRELIMO and their associated helpers. The enemy had eventually worked out how to overcome their problems until repair work could start and with the help of the not-so-willing locals, were operating a shuttle system – offloading goods from a train on the south of the track and carrying them to one on the north, from where the goods were railed to Moatize.

It was something that the Rhodesians were to remember. Next time, FRELIMO wouldn't get the chance to be so clever ...

238

It was a somewhat apprehensive Lieutenant Rich Stannard who drove through the gate of the SAS barracks one Monday morning.

The last time he had been there he had been an SAS corporal; since then he had been overseas, done a spell in the Selous Scouts, and completed an officer's course at the School of Infantry in Gwelo.

Now, he was returning to his parent unit as an officer and he knew those first days were going to be nerve-racking.

He had done fairly well during his time as a corporal, but being an SAS officer was going to be a different experience entirely. It was not enough to have done well at the School of Infantry . . . he was going to have to prove himself to his fellow officers. The "other ranks" would be watching his performance too.

Rich didn't have too long to wait to lead a team into action.

He was sent to Mabalouta where Captain Bob McKenna called the new subby to the ops room and tasked him to take a team into south-east Mozambique to ambush ZANLA/FRELIMO vehicles travelling up to Malvernia. They were to hide up midway between two railway sidings south of the Malvernia forward staging post.

A few days later, Rich and the 19 men who now fell under his command were floating down under their canopies. When they got their bearings, they found they had been dropped in completely the wrong place and it would take a good two nights' walk to get to their ambush site.

There was no time to lose so they set off immediately, and as always in the south-east, the conditions and the terrain were against them. On the morning of the third day, it was an extremely tired and parched bunch of men who pushed their way through the last bit of bush. Their long trek had brought them out to the north of the railway siding that was to be their target area.

They were now desperately short of water. They had been unable to find any on their long march, and what little remained in their water bottles was very precious indeed. They knew that they would have a real problem if they didn't find water soon.

Rich Stannard, his 2IC, Sergeant Billy Gardner, and the main body of men were to form the killer/ambush group, with Sergeant Dale O'Mulligan and his partner in one early-warning group . . . and Sergeant Willum Butler and his partner in the other.

The early-warnings took up their positions either side of the main ambush group, and Sergeant O'Mulligan had no sooner dropped his pack and settled down to await ZANLA vehicles than his partner whispered that there were civilians approaching.

As he looked up, he could see a group of kitted-up ZANLA men sauntering into sight along the rail line. He quickly passed the news to the mission commander, then counted forty terrorists strung out along the rail track. The SAS callsign, caught completely unawares by the *walking* ZANLA men, watched in the bushes in amazement – and let them walk by.

The new SAS lieutenant knew he had blown it. Rich Stannard cursed himself but knew it would be no use explaining he simply had not been expecting ZANLA *pedestrians.* He knew his mistake would neither be forgiven nor forgotten. How *could* he have let such an opportunity pass?

"After this Stannard," his men ribbed, "you'll be off to the Guard Force."

Forcing such negative thoughts to the back of his mind, the commander began to concentrate on other more pressing matters.

The lack of water was still very much on everyone's mind and as they lay in wait for vehicles that day, Rich began to plot how they could take over the buildings at the railway siding, kill the occupants and capture their water. After that, they could take up their places in the bushes again and continue their task.

In the grey dim light of the following morning, Rich sent out the early-warnings to take up their positions again.

At 05h30, Sergeant Dale O'Mulligan and his partner heard the sounds of talking again – then saw yet another group of ZANLA walking along the rail line.

Snatching up his radio handset, he gave the alert once more. But Rich's radio was giving him trouble and Dale's voice was barely scratching through its important message. Dale tried again and this time, the message got through loud and clear and the commander knew what he had to do.

Rich really couldn't believe what was happening. They were supposed to be waiting for vehicles, yet all they were encountering were ZANLA pedestrians. Well, Rich thought, there was no way he was going to let such an opportunity pass a second time. Walking or riding, ZANLA were ZANLA after all.

When he thought about it, they were in the most fantastic killing ground he had ever seen. The enemy would be silhouetted in the early-morning light as they strolled along the embankment and the SAS would have no difficulty picking them off.

Rich told Dale to carry on counting the ZANLA men and let them go past, and told his 2IC by his side to wait for his signal to initiate the ambush.

Rich reasoned that if this lot were strung out like the first group of enemy, the SAS could get them all nicely trapped between the two early-warning groups.

Soon, eighty ZANLA had strolled past the early-warning position and the SAS had grown tired of counting. An unbelievable number of ZANLA were already in the killing ground and it was time for action.

On the signal, the 2IC opened up and four ZANLA men went down in the initial volley. Even before they hit the ground, the rest of the killer group were up and getting stuck in.

"GRENADES!" 2IC Sergeant Gardner yelled above the roar of rifle fire – and grenades it was.

One group of enemy crumpled and fell in a heap in the killing ground. Others, many of them injured, tried unsuccessfully to crawl away to avoid being burnt by the exploding phosphorus grenades.

Some of the enemy managed to return fire and as they did so, SAS Corporal Mo Taylor fell mortally wounded.

Other ZANLA ran straight into the path of Dale O'Mulligan, a trained sniper. The kill rate was soaring.

By the time Rich had called the ceasefire, 17 terrorists lay dead. The others had escaped but intercepts would reveal that another 28 died in the bush.

Then, even before the dust of battle had settled, the main ambush group sprinted forward into the killing ground, ripped the water bottles from the mound of dead terrorists and drank their fill.

As they wiped the water from their blackened faces, and stood over the pile of bodies, some still glowing from phosphorus grenades, two characters, totally unaware of the events at the railway siding that morning, came sauntering along the road towards them without a care in the world.

Kitted out in spotlessly-laundered FRELIMO uniforms, one man was tall and lanky, the other was short and fat with an RPG-7 rocket launcher casually slung over his arm.

"Look!" Rich muttered to his companions as the two men strolled along, "Mutt and Geoff!" Then he asked: "Don't you think we should move off?"

"No, No," his 2IC replied, "just act naturally and let them carry on."

The SAS commander and his 2IC, still surrounded by the heap of bodies, beckoned the two strangers over with a friendly wave. The tall thin recruit and his short, fat friend kept walking towards them.

Then their pace slowed as it eventually dawned on them that there was something not quite right about the mound of mangled bodies ahead of them. Slowly, the short, fat one unslung his RPG-7 and put a rocket in.

As he did so, the SAS sergeant laying low in the grass in an early-warning position, offloaded some rounds in their direction. He missed; but his rounds hit their rocket, it went off – and the two men dropped.

"And that," said Rich, matter-of-factly to his companions "is the end of Mutt and Geoff."

The SAS collected the enemy's ammunition, weapons and mortar bombs and a bonfire was soon raging. Their unexpected opportunity target had turned out to be one of the highest killrates from a single SAS ambush. The 45 enemy they had accounted for that morning would never cross the border to terrorise Rhodesians.

But the loss of Corporal Mo Taylor took the edge off their victory. The mission 2IC was particularly upset. Mo had shared half his last water bottle with him, and that was something a man simply did not do in conditions where every drop of precious water was needed for a soldier's own survival.

The success of the Malvernia ambush had involved the most incredible luck. Had they not been dropped too far out and spent time travelling to the ambush site, they might well have withdrawn before the enemy came along.

Rich was thankful that he had Sergeant Billy Gardner, a very experienced soldier by his side to suggest throwing in grenades at the precise moment the circumstances called for them. From now on, the two men ran a very diplomatic callsign and would sit down and thrash out tactics. It was a partnership that was to work well to the detriment of the enemy.

For Rich, the ambush had been an even better start to his officer's career in the SAS than he could have hoped for.

After that, he didn't have to worry about being accepted by his fellow officers, men who had all had their fair share of big successes. The new boy would not be hived off to the Guard Force after all. For having proved himself, he was welcomed into the officers mess as an equal.

Behind Rebel Lines

*"It was war, and in war
all things are allowed."*
– KEN FLOWER, HEAD OF THE RHODESIAN
CENTRAL INTELLIGENCE ORGANISATION

There are many ways of fighting fire with fire and in dark days of 1976 when the storm clouds began to gather over the country and the situation didn't look like improving, it became obvious to the Rhodesians that a new approach was necessary.

After the lull following the assassination of ZANLA operations chief, Herbert Chitepo – the man behind the 1972 offensive – ZANLA had moved their head-quarters from Zambia to Mozambique where they were being provided with a safe haven and crucial rear base facilities. They had resumed the war with a vengeance and were flooding across the entire length of the rugged largely-exposed Mozambican border at an alarming rate.

Robert Mugabe and his two military commanders, Josiah Tongogara and Rex Nhongo, had based their strategy on continuous infiltration through the thick bush border of eastern Rhodesia. The mountainous Honde Valley became an infiltration corridor while the tribal trust lands became tunnels for the insurgents in which they could merge with the local population, according to military historian M. Evans.

* They began their series of rolling infiltrations into the eastern highlands and south eastern lowveld in February, 1976, with the threefold objective of infiltration saturation to stretch the Rhodesian military membrane to breaking point . . . disruption of Rhodesia's vital road and rail links with South Africa to damage tourist and export traffic . . . and the harassment of the agricultural economy by attacking the prosperous timber, tea, fruit and cereal producing estates in eastern Rhodesia.

* Farmers were ambushed, roads mined and black labour dispersed, the intention being to wreck the country's commerce. The TTLs were used as launch pads for attacks against the government infrastructure, and African council offices, stores and cattle dips became soft targets.

* In Mozambique, Robert Mugabe followed the Chitepo strategy and began to expand ZANLA by creating a network of transit and staging bases, while shuttling recruits to Tanzania under Chinese instructors.

Then, Samora Machel announced he was putting his country on a war footing and closed the border with Rhodesia. Overnight, Rhodesia lost her links to east coast ports and an outlet for a high percentage of her exports. (Rhodesia had however, anticipated the problem and had been diverting traffic by rail via South Africa and Botswana.)

But the pressure was mounting, the war was escalating and resources and man-power were limited. The threat on the military level was serious.

The problem facing the Rhodesians was whether they could sit back and quietly allow Mozambique to support and export violence and terrorism? It was obvious that if they were to prevent the country being overrun, they could not. The time had come to hit back.

Mozambique and not just ZANLA was an enemy and something drastic had to be done to counter the increasing threat from the east.

How Rhodesia proposed to defend her borders and pre-empt that threat was to remain one of the best-kept secrets of the war. Rhodesia, already masters of the innovative, tactically flexible approach, now planned an even more unconventional counter-insurgency campaign in her war against ZANLA.

As head of the Central Intelligence Organisation Ken Flower explained later: "It was war and in war all things are allowed."

* * *

The plan for the highly sensitive operation was unfolded in a letter that appeared on the desk of a senior CIO officer one morning in 1976. His brief was simple:

Making use of the strong anti-FRELIMO feeling that already existed in Mozam-bique, he and his department were to establish a black resistance movement . . . con-duct a psychological and clandestine campaign against the Marxist Mozambican government – and create a sufficiently strong opposition to challenge the existing authority.

Thus Rhodesia, committed to stopping guerillas taking Rhodesia by force, was to actively encourage an organisation with a similar motive in neighbouring Mozambique.

Should the plan succeed, Machels' Marxist administration would be replaced by a democratic western-orientated government, one sympathetic towards Rhodesia . . . and one inclined to boot ZANLA out of Mozambique.

That, of course, was the long-term plan. Until such time as that happened, the Mozambique National Resistance Movement (also known as Renamo) would indirectly assist Rhodesia achieve her prime role to destroy, hinder and disrupt ZANLA forces operating out of firm bases in Mozambique.

For in addition to eliminating FRELIMO in their bid to take the country, a Rhodesian-supported resistance movement could be well placed to provide an intelligence network on ZANLA rear bases and movements inside Mozambique . . . information that could be passed back and followed up by Rhodesian security forces.

But whilst top priority was placed on the secret operation, the mission was beset with problems, the least of which was that because of the strains on the country's limited resources, no money had been made available to the CIO. To make matters worse, they were given no weapons – and no time-scale.

Undaunted by the difficulties, the CIO officers pressed on with what they could. They spent most of 1976 studying the mood among Mozambicans in the border area, confirming original assessments that there was indeed an intense hatred against FRELIMO.

When FRELIMO had taken over the reins of office, they had promised the earth. But things hadn't quite gone as planned and life for the average Mozambican was much worse than it had been in colonial times. There was much to feel bitter about.

No one had been more taken aback than FRELIMO when, in the wake of the Lisbon coup, the terror group had suddenly been handed Mozambique on a platter. It was what they had been fighting for all along, but when it happened, they were totally unprepared. They had no idea how to run the country and no structure to cope with it.

A very hard attitude was taken against the Portuguese and they streamed out of the country in droves taking their finance and expertise with them, leaving the country's twelve million blacks to pick up the pieces. Thousands lost their jobs and the white braindrain left a huge vacuum in the administration and general running of the country.

Soon, Mozambique had become one of the world's poorest nations with the UN officially listing it as an undeveloping country.

Within a month of independence, Machel had made sweeping changes, nationalising land, schools, hospitals and funeral parlours. Next came rented buildings and the gradual takeover of companies. Freedom was eroded. The enforced communal system of agriculture caused production to fall drastically, and nationalised factories operated at reduced speed. All was not well.

Yet, despite the intense natural hatred for FRELIMO, few Mozambicans were willing to take up arms at that stage. Certainly not enough to form an army. And even if there were, there were no weapons for them.

Then came a new development in the raising of the rebel army. The CIO began their bitter war of words, using as ammunition, the power of the pen and FRELIMO's poor track record.

To crystallise the hatred and discontent against FRELIMO and to push the Mozambique National Resistance creed out to the common man, they started an undercover radio station *The Voice of Free Africa* using a huge old-fashioned 400 kilowatt transmitter nicknamed *Big Bertha,* said to be based "somewhere in Southern Africa", but actually situated in Gwelo.

The staff of *The Voice* monitored Mozambique's news commentaries, immediately rewrote them to support the Mozambique National Resistance and then pushed their own communiques back into Mozambique.

The results were immediate and encouraging.

Soon people were switching off *Radio Maputo* in favour of *The Voice* and it wasn't long before *Radio Maputo* became too frightened to say anything for fear of the treatment their communiques would get. Eventually, Machel became so worried about the harmful effects of the radio station that he called in the East Germans to silence it. But the transmitter was just too powerful to jam, even with the most sophisticated equipment.

Such was the response to *The Voice* that the CIO planners were then faced with the embarrassing situation of having countless FRELIMO deserting to join the resistance – but being unable to find it because it existed in name only.

Apart from confirming there were now people willing to do something positive about overthrowing Machel, it was obvious that unless the CIO got their military programme off the ground, they would lose that support. For while grievances existed, the guns still did not.

Then, after months of not really getting anywhere, things started to happen.

Several countries around the world began to see the swing to the east in Marxist Mozambique, and having been sold on the concept of the pro-western resistance movement, saw it as a suitable alternative. They came up with the necessary finance, and although the CIO would have liked more, there was enough to buy arms for the handful of recruits who had been rounded up.

Training recruits for the top secret operation began at an isolated farm, at Odzi near Umtali, and initially the CIO made the mistake of using Portuguese men to train and boost the MNR's numbers. The Mozambican blacks under training resented them, thinking they were trying to recapture Mozambique for themselves . . . and they were replaced by several former SAS men, working with the CIO.

But there was one vital ingredient still missing. The rebel force had no dominant leader, no inspiring figurehead, so necessary in a guerilla movement.

Then, one day, a former FRELIMO platoon commander, Andre Matangaidze, escaped from a FRELIMO re-education camp and made his way across the border to Umtali. He had heard all about the resistance recruiting campaign and the idea fascinated him. Having been locked up by FRELIMO, he had a definite axe to grind and sought out the resistance recruiters.

He had the remarkable charisma of a born leader and he had no fear . . . and what's more, he assured CIO that attracting FRELIMO to the ranks of the infant resistance movement would be easy. CIO recognised Andre's potential immediately and struck up a deal with him – if he could get the men, they would groom him for the MNR leadership.

To prove he could come up with the goods, Andre's first task was to go back to Mozambique with a nucleus of resistance men, attack his old re-education camp at Gorongoza, and release all the prisoners, most of whom were former FRELIMO soldiers.

It was a tall order, but Andre Matangaidze was as good as his word. When he and his small band of rebels closed in on the camp, they did not hesitate.

Led by the incredibly aggressive and inspiring Andre, they stepped from the shadows, mounted a successful attack – and released 500 prisoners. And that was that. The Mozambique National Resistance movement had a leader.

Three hundred released men opted to take to the bush and throw in their lot with the rebels. Together they set off for Rhodesia, stealing tractors and low loaders and shooting at any FRELIMO they came across on the long trek back to the border.

The pattern had been set for the future. Andre had proved it was possible to mount such daring attacks and get away with them. He had put new life into the movement and it was obvious from the start that his men would have followed him anywhere.

It was mid-1978 and Mozambique's second war of liberation was about to begin. From then onwards, the resistance would go from strength to strength, with the response to recruiting so overwhelming that it would become difficult to keep pace with, and potential recruits would often have to be turned away.

Soon the rebels were notching up an amazing string of successes about the country-side and FRELIMO were faced with similar running bush warfare tactics they had used when fighting to wrest independence from the Portuguese.

The rebels came up with a wealth of intelligence on the whereabouts of ZANLA bases and this was followed up by the Rhodesians.

When ComOps suggested the MNR attack ZANLA, the CIO pointed out that as the resistance's main objective was to overthrow Machel, the very last thing they wanted at that stage was to become involved with ZANLA.

The CIO won the day that time, but ComOps had their own way later when FRELIMO started using ZANLA against the increasingly troublesome rebels. That so irritated the resistance that they carried out spontaneous attacks on ZANLA – and it was an added bonus for the Rhodesians.

Politically, a number of splinter organisations and moderate factions were looked at by the CIO, including several which had returned to Portugal. But in the end, it was decided to concentrate on the military who were indoctrinated politically anyway. Africans are born politicians and it was felt that when the time was right, a natural political leader would emerge as an alternative to Machel.

In January, 1979, the SAS began operating with the resistance and later, small ad hoc groups were attached to them in a training and advisory role.

* * *

Their operational relationship got off to a spectacular start with a successful attack on the Mavuze hydro-electric power station on Chicamba Real Dam.

Having knocked out the turbines – the dam's sole generator – and a transformer station with 75 millimetre recoilless rifle projectiles, Corporal *Lucy* was down to his last target ... and his last projectile. The target, the valve house, was a good two kilometres away on top of a hill ... a mere speck on the horizon with just the faintest glow of the coming day piping the edges.

It was a long shot and he told the commander as much. But there was no need to worry. *Lucy* was on the ball and hit the jackpot with chilling precision. Then to round off the night's work, the SAS and MNR blew down an electricity pylon.

Suddenly, over and above the crunching of the ailing turbines, came the unmistakable sound of tank guns firing at them. It was no time to be caught in the middle of FRELIMO manoeuvres and they hurried away, crossing rivers and anti-tracking as they went. The heat was on and they had far to go.

They walked all that day and most of the night and managed to shake the enemy off. It was one of the longest walks the operators ever had. By the time they reached their LUP, their round trek totalled 120 kilometres (74,5 miles) and some of the men had lost so much weight that they were having to keep their trousers up with string.

Despite the long walk and the untimely arrival of FRELIMO, the SAS and MNR had severed the electricity supply to a vast part of Mozambique and it would be some time before the damage was repaired and service restored.

The MNR's local knowledge had played a significant part in the success of the mission. They had guided the SAS to the target and had been used as "faces" among the local population – gathering intelligence and spreading the MNR gospel – while the SAS remained under cover ... and it was to become their *modus operandi* for joint missions from then onwards.

* * *

The rebels designed their own flag and badges and eventually reached the stage when they felt they were making headway. The time had come to establish semi-permanent bases inside Mozambique where new recruits could come for training and rally to the flag. Such bases would also enable them to extend their activities more rapidly.

One operational base was established in the hilly, heavily-wooded countryside at Gogoi 35 kilometres (22 miles) from the Rhodesian border, while the headquarters and nerve centre of the rebel organisation was deep inside Mozambique in the thick bush of the remote Serra Da Gorongoza mountains of Sofala Province.

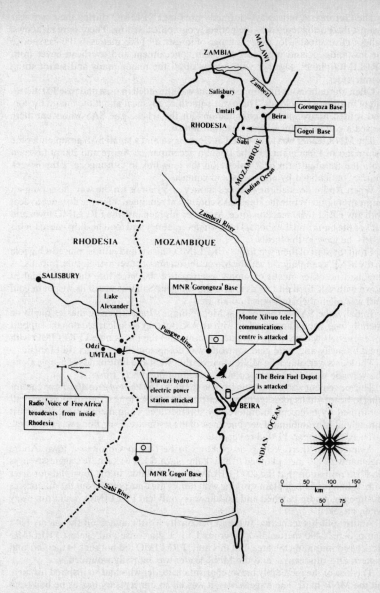

Rebel country: Home of the SAS-trained Mozambique National Resistance movement. The map shows the Resistance's main bases and depicts a few of the joint SAS/MNR operations

247

The Gorongoza hideaway – formerly used by FRELIMO during their own war against the Portuguese – was the perfect geographical setting. There were meadows, valleys, clear streams for water, a fringe of forests, all 1 863 metres (6 100 feet) above the lowlands ... and providing excellent concealment and overhead cover from FRELIMO planes, together with a view of all the major roads and surrounding countryside.

Often, the enormous flat-topped plateau was shrouded in mist and rose 300 metres out of the top of the clouds. There was something mystical about the mountain, too, and it held many spiritual connotations for the rebels. The SAS who went there sensed a certain eeriness about the rain forests.

The MNR leader was to be based at Gorongoza and a small SAS group under the command of Lieutenant Charlie Buchan accompanied Andre and 200 of his men from the training farm in Rhodesia on the long trek to Gorongoza, a three-week journey punctuated by ambushes and contacts.

When Andre decided they needed money and rations on the way, he sprang an impromptu raid. While the small SAS contingent remained off in the distance to deal with any FRELIMO reaction force, Andre led his men into the FRELIMO town and sacked the bank and the shops. Then, whatever money and food he didn't need for his rebels, he gave to the locals.

From the start of their war to oust FRELIMO, "hearts and minds" played a big role in the MNR's campaign to win the Mozambican masses over to their side. Initially, as they had no other means of supply, every patrol staggered into the bush weighed down with salt, food and seeds to give the villagers. Salt was worth its weight in gold and was often their passport into an area.

Initially, the SAS suspected that Mozambique's long-suffering masses might be friendly to anyone who turned up with an AK. But they soon learned that the support for the rebels was spontaneous and genuine, and the locals hated FRELIMO with great intensity and were glad someone was doing something to get rid of them.

The locals welcomed the MNR wherever they went and little bands of people along the wayside would join their columns, swelling the rebels' ranks.

The movement was going from from to strength. *The Voice of Free Africa* was continuing to beam out its message to good effect. The MNR's long string of successes – all confirmed by intercepts monitored by sophisticated equipment – were broadcast throughout Mozambique. Everyone knew of the resistance. Everything was going well.

Then, in October, 1979, disaster struck.

Assured that there were good pickings to be had in Gorongoza town, Andre together with 110 men planned to attack the place. Such was Andre's aggressiveness and determination that the 400 FRELIMO and six tanks in the town did not deter him. When the SAS captain working with him at the time pointed out the differences in strength, Andre laughed and said he was confident FRELIMO would run away when attacked.

Andre split his team into two and personally led the attack on the enemy base camp, across 400 metres of open ground, up a sharp rise and against FRELIMO trenches dominating the area. But this time, FRELIMO did not stick to their normal pattern and run away – and the MNR leader was mortally wounded.

The loss of the incredibly brave, charismatic leader who had so inspired his men, hit the MNR hard. The tragedy was, it was all so unnecessary too, as he had been warned of the risks he ran by his personal involvement in attacks and advised to direct operations from his headquarters. But Andre had insisted on leading his men from the front and had paid the ultimate price.

After a brief power struggle, Andre's deputy Alfonso Dhlakama, emerged the new leader. It was something he had not envisaged in his wildest dreams but when the opportunity presented itself, he grabbed it with both hands and with sheer dogged determination, overcame tremendous odds and measured up as a more than capable leader.

In stature, he was a short bespectacled man, whereas the other main contender was a big burly individual, whose physique alone contributed to his leadership of men. The well-educated Alfonso Dhlakama, on the other hand, was much more of the intelligensia, and eventually that was where his strength lay and how he won his troops over.

Yet, despite the brief internal upheaval, the resistance continued operations, proving themselves a viable proposition. ComOps was impressed with their results and suggested that the SAS now get more positively involved with the rebels, attaching larger groups in their classic role of supporting and guiding the resistance.

The few SAS who had been involved with the MNR to date considered the resistance highly motivated and well worth supporting – and, knowing the contribution the SAS could make, the CIO were fully behind the suggestion.

As for the SAS, the MNR operation – codenamed *Bumper* – marked a new and interesting facet in their counter-insurgency war and much thought and preparation went into their resistance programme, just as it did with all their many and varied operations.

The SAS could, of course, draw on their many years of unique experience. When they operated on the Rhodesian side of the border, they did so as counter-insurgency experts. When they worked externally, they operated as guerillas and their own impressive string of successes bears testimony that they were good at that role, too.

But there were always lessons to be learned from other campaigns, and Captain Bob McKenna, whose "C" Squadron was to go into the MNR camps first, and Lieutenant Pete Cole, of "B" Squadron, who was to take over from them, got together to study the whole spectrum of counter-insurgency warfare and how it applied to the rebels and their own particular role. They read everything they could lay their hands on, both from the western viewpoint to the thoughts of Mao.

They had many British Army pamphlets to refer to and American-born Viet Nam veteran Bob McKenna had the benefit of experience with American special forces, whose particular role was to train indigenous guerilla movements.

His collection of US special forces pamphlets and field manuals became their blueprint for everything they needed to know – from how to get to the guerilla camps . . . politicizing the locals . . . to growing crops and becoming self-sufficient. Very little modification was needed as the American special forces envisage that the guerillas the operators would be working with would be peasants, as was the case in Mozambique.

The main difference between the American forces and that of the Rhodesians was that Uncle Sam provided US troops with all the support in the world . . . whereas the Rhodesians were unable to give their men as much help as they would have liked.

The SAS set up their tactical headquarters in a deserted farm at Odzi, close to the MNR's secret training base inside Rhodesia, and groups were sent to Gorongoza headquarters and the smaller secret operational base at Gogoi.

Alfonso Dhlakama had not long taken over as leader of the resistance and moved to Gorongoza and the SAS's first job was to help him build permanent structures on his mountain hideaway. The first team, under the command of Lieutenant Rich Stannard, slept in bivvies in the forests with the MNR while the camp was being built. They helped the rebels site their defences, build a rifle range and select access tracks. Later groups would build hospitals and underground caches for bulk ammunition, and reorganise the stores, teach hygiene and signals.

They improved the rebels' shooting with the AK – the true weapon of the revolution – and the much-favoured RPG-7 rocket launcher. They taught the rebels how to be as devious as the SAS . . . how to derail trains . . . where the best places were to lay ambushes and landmines . . . and how to do it quickly.

The Rhodesians, masters at improvisation, taught them how to salvage whatever could be useful to their cause . . . how to fashion corrugated iron into buildings . . . how the bits and pieces of old weapons lying around their bases could be cannibalised into workable weapons . . .

Self-sufficiency was essential and seed was flown in to them to start their own maize and vegetable gardens. Generally, guerillas in other conflicts were too mobile to grow their own crops and were forced to get their supplies from the locals. The MNR, however, had no need to force Mozambicans to feed them – they readily gave what little they had – but local production was subsistence and couldn't hope to feed the growing number of rebels.

Each platoon was encouraged to have a commissar to politicize the masses . . . to convince them that one day they would be victorious and overthrow Machel . . . and ZANLA's system of holding all-night political meetings in villages was adopted by the rebels.

There were some colourful characters, with a style all of their own. Some had spiky hair, others multi-coloured beads and many had sweat bands, or maybe a monkey tail around their waists.

When they moved off from Gorongoza and snaked their way through the thick bush on yet another operation, the commander's entourage would often carry a sunshade, a battery-operated transister or a tape recorder in a bag made from curtains stolen on another mission. Some carried folding tables and chairs for the senior personnel.

Here and there a coloured helmet could be seen, legacy of a spell spent working on a South African mine. But the wearers knew that a vividly coloured hat could get a man killed when he closed for a contact, and he would exchange it for green headwear.

Often the battalion tailor and his captured pedal sewing machine went along to do running repairs. For a mission could last months and it could take its toll on their uniforms and webbing.

The weekly flag-raising ceremonies helped maintain discipline and morale. As the flag broke and fluttered in the breeze, the hundreds of rebels assembled around the parade square would begin singing and clapping.

Within seconds, the clapping would grow in intensity and volume as the war cry of the rebel army rang out across the valleys and streams and floated down below the blanket of mist covering the Gorongoza hideaway to the thick bush of the lowlands.

Soon, the familiar chant of *Basha FRELIMO* would echo across the country. Then came FRELIMO's own and best-known slogan – *A Luta Continua* (the struggle continues).

There were other songs too – stirring, highly-motivating ones, telling how they were going to live in the bush . . . sleep in the rain . . . suffer every type of deprivation, taking on FRELIMO with their AKs and RPG-7s.

Individuals would be singled out and praised for their efforts and groups congratulated. A chain of runners kept the resistance leader informed of a company's progress while on operations.

With Rich Stannard's arrival at Gorongoza, a much more aggressive approach was taken than with previous attached groups. A combined SAS/MNR team attacked a FRELIMO farm at the bottom of the mountain range with cannon and mortar fire and when they swept down the mountain, FRELIMO had fled, leaving behind 75 000 rounds of AK ammunition, 200 x 82 millimetre mortar bombs, 200 x RPG-7 rockets and a dozen rocket launchers to be captured and used by the rebels in the classical guerilla war tradition.

There were vast quantities of grenades and heavy weapon ammunition, blankets, tents – one which became the MNR leader's operations room – marquees, a kitchen unit, food and 170 cattle.

It had been a good day's work and there was much singing and partying up on Gorongoza that night with the SAS firmly acknowledged as thoroughly good chaps to have around. To honour their advisers, the rebels made the SAS gifts of goats and piglets, and later presented them with bottles filled with wild honey gathered from trees in the endless valleys.

Soon, the SAS had moulded the resistance into an organised workable system. MNR morale went up immediately the SAS became involved with them, and operational results improved considerably.

"The presence of the SAS with their expertise has advanced the MNR in both training and operational fields, and accelerated their progress beyond measure," the CIO commented.

As each month went by, the MNR gained new ground, and became accepted by a vast proportion of the population as a viable opposition to the Machel government. Every successful ambush produced more captured weapons, food and great experience.

The movement continued to grow in popularity with civilians, and disillusioned government troops were attracted to their ranks. They didn't have much before they joined the rebels' ranks, so the excitement and comradeship they had with the resistance was certainly a big improvement compared to the dull, poor life in the countryside.

They were convinced their cause was just; that there had to be a better way of life; that they could secure a better future for themselves. No one thought it would be the following day. But perhaps one day . . .

When the MNR first began its campaign to topple Machel, *Radio Maputo* referred to the rebels as "bandits". By 1979, they had changed their tune and were calling them "the enemy". So seriously did he take the MNR, and so alarmed was he at the widespread nature of their activity, that Machel was forced to withdraw 200 FRELIMO operating inside Rhodesia in support of ZANLA.

* * *

By 1980, events were moving quickly in Rhodesia. There was a fragile ceasefire and the country was gearing itself up for its first all-party British-supervised elections. The British monitoring forces were on the tail of the SAS and although they suspected they had been working externally with the MNR, they couldn't catch them at it.

Machel had saved the Lancaster House talks by persuading Mugabe to stay talking at the conference table and to repay the favour, the British put a stop to the rebels' Rhodesia-based radio station.

While the CIO denied any connection with the station, the British – then in control of the country – knew better, and *The Voice of Free Africa* went off the air in February, 1980.

The rebels' training camp inside Rhodesia was closed down and the CIO and SAS connection with the rebel army ceased.

It was not, however, the end of the Mozambique National Resistance. Things had come a long way since those early days of 1976 and the resistance was now some 5 000 men strong. Left to determine their own future, they were sent rejoicing into the bush to begin a new and successful chapter in their campaign to topple Machel.

While the MNR had provided an excellent intelligence network, the plan to overthrow Machel and install a government sympathetic to Rhodesia had been overtaken by time and events. And yet, say CIO officers, it might well have been different.

Had the necessary arms, money and other resources been available when the idea was first mooted and a definite time-scale been set, they feel they would have been able to accomplish the aim. By the enforced delay in getting established, they had created their own problems as the resistance within FRELIMO had built up accordingly.

Whilst they would have had to convince the purist conventional military man that the use of guerilla troops was a viable alternative, the CIO felt that the MNR could have brought about a change of government in Mozambique . . . ZANLA could have been kicked out of Mozambique . . . and the Rhodesian war could have been all over bar the shouting by 1978/1979.

As for the SAS, they had played their part and felt that helping to get the MNR going was one of the most lasting, significant missions of their careers. They had been faced with the potential of moulding one of the most formidable guerilla armies in Africa – and if the MNR's impressive string of successes is anything to go by, they didn't do too badly at it either.

* * *

Postscript: At the time of writing, the Mozambique National Resistance movement is still a major force to be reckoned with in Mozambique, and FRELIMO have been unable to quell the rebels who are tightening their grip around the capital.

With the historic signing of the Nkomati Peace Accord with South Africa, Mozambique, having embraced the east for so long, now seems set on turning to the west.

Machel has pledged to bring stability to his country and peace to the region. But perhaps only dialogue with the leader of the MNR can bring genuine peace?

In the meantime, the struggle for Mozambique continues . . .

Towards the End

Wings on Chest

For ten years the SAS had been battling for the right to present its own special award to outstanding operational soldiers.

It was an award which meant more to an SAS operator than any other, and it had its traditions back in the Desert days of the Second World War.

SAS founder, David Stirling had ruled that if a soldier had distinguished himself on operations, he was eligible to wear his coveted operational parachute wings on his left breast, instead of on his right arm.

It was this prestigious award that the Rhodesians wanted for their own outstanding operators, those who had done a series of good jobs or a single task. Yet the army hierarchy would not hear of it. And the Air Force objected to the *Brown Jobs* wearing wings in a traditional *Blue Job* position.

Undeterred, the SAS continued to push for it, but it was not until late 1978 that the unique Wings on Chest award was finally given official blessing.

A special committee, comprising the CO, the past COs, the RSM and squadron commanders sat to decide who warranted the honour. Even the trooper had his say, making his recommendations to his NCO who would pass it up through the chain of command.

The standard that was set was high and there were many who felt that had a recipient been in any other unit, he would have been recommended for a Bronze Cross of Rhodesia. Certainly, some who had the BCR valued their Wings on Chest more. It was, after all, a measure of how their fellow soldiers rated them – the greatest test of all.

On January 5, 1979, history was made when 55 past and present Rhodesian SAS operators received their Wings on Chest award at a special open day held at their new barracks at Kabrit. Several others received them later in the year.

The occasion also marked the dedication of a SAS marble memorial plinth, an impressive and everlasting tribute to the war dead killed on operations since January 1, 1964.

But the war was far from over and within a week one more name was eligible to be added to the plinth. It was that of Sergeant Clive *Chipo* Cripps, killed when the SAS was ambushed while deploying to the operational area. There would be other names too and one of them would be Trooper Richard Hickman, son of the Army Commander, General John Hickman.

Operation Neutron, February-March, 1979

Within six months of the security forces raid on ZANLA's Chimoio Circle, the area had once again become a problem. ZANLA had now moved into what was known as the Vanduzi Circle, 15 kilometres (nine miles) from Chimoio town, and had resited their camps between two mountains, Monte Bossa and Monte Urueri.

ZANLA were now very alert to the possibility of security force attacks and their new site was in a thickly-treed area, providing good cover from Rhodesian war planes.

The camp was very dispersed and far too spread out for a conventional attack ... and the Rhodesian planners decided to put someone in the area to assess where the critical areas lay, then at the right time, carry out an air strike. They also hoped to bait the inevitable hierarchy who usually came to inspect the bombed camp ... whereupon, the Rhodesians would mount another attack.

Former SAS Captain Scotty McCormack, now with the national intelligence team, had learned from a capture that ZANLA even had the services of a unique early-warning system – a couple of tame baboons which went by the name of John and Janet.

So shell-shocked were they from their previous airstrikes that the faintest hint of a plane approaching would send them into a frenzy. The berserk baboons would rip up grass, leap into trees and frantically tear off leaves. Blessed with an incredible sense of hearing, their sudden peculiar behaviour was all ZANLA needed to send them running for cover.

A four-man SAS team, under the command of Lieutenant Rich Stannard, was choppered into the area one night to recce the camp and monitor the occupants' movements and habits.

They had been told that the camp housed 5 000 ZANLA and judging by the amount of spoor they were finding, the SAS could well believe it. The tracks were so worn that the occupants had gouged a twenty centimetre furrow in the dirt.

ZANLA were carrying out clearance patrols, checking for unexpected visitors and landmines up to ten kilometres (six miles) from the camp ... and in the end, Rich considered the security so good that they could not safely carry out a close-in recon-naissance ... and they returned to Salisbury.

"C" Squadron commander Martin Pearse called Rich to his office and told him they would give it a break for now and would try going back into Vanduzi a few weeks later.

Rich had very definite ideas of how he wanted to handle the op the next time around and put his theory to Martin.

He pointed out that the four-man team did not really work in circumstances such as those at Vanduzi. It was impossible for four men carrying heavy Bergens to get in close to such a heavily-populated camp where the security was so good.

He felt they would stand a much better chance if there were only two men using light-weight packs enabling them to move far and fast. They would be able to cover a much greater distance than four men burdened with heavy packs, he added.

Rich had long been impressed with the two-man operational concept ever since reading a book on the Malayan Emergency *The Jungle is Neutral* by Spencer Chapman. He put it to his squadron commander that they should take a leaf out of Chapman's book.

By an amazing coincidence, Spencer Chapman was a name not unknown to Martin Pearse – he had been Martin's schoolteacher.

The two-man concept was not looked upon favourably in the SAS and with good reason too. Were one man injured, there was only one other available to carry him out ... and he might not be in a position to do that.

Lieutenant Chris Schollenberg, the SAS's first Silver Cross soldier, had used the two-man concept when he was in the unit and he had even carried out a one-man close-in reconnaissance. But that was all a long time ago and it had not been done in the SAS since ... although Schulie, now in the Selous Scouts, continued to use the concept with spectacular results.

Martin Pearse and Rich Stannard sat down and discussed the pros and cons of the two-man concept. Martin could see the advantages and was flexible enough to go along with the idea.

Between them, they came up with a way of using the concept and, at the same time, providing the two operators with the necessary back-up.

Rich, his partner and four others were to be choppered into the general Vanduzi area, although far enough away to prevent the enemy hearing the helicopters. Then, while most of the party set about establishing a firm base with radios, rations, water and medical kit, the two operators would move into the camp and carry out their close-in reconnaissance.

They were to take the small lighter short-range radio, *The Small Means*, so as not to be weighed down. They would pass their messages back to their collegues in the firm base who would also have the long-range radio enabling them to relay Rich's messages to Rhodesia.

If the going got difficult, the two operators could always return to the firm base for R and R and to draw more rations before starting out again.

And if, at any time they were compromised, they could simply take off, moving fairly fast, anti-tracking back to the relative safety of the base.

Rich sought out the officer who kept a store full of kit for special jobs. He wanted an extremely powerful telescope and a really good pair of binoculars.

He decided to take along a new territorial captain, known as *Jungle Jordan*. Jordan had passed selection, but had not yet got his SAS colours, as he still had to prove himself on operations. The Vanduzi visit would be his first bush trip with the SAS.

At the beginning of March, the six soldiers were choppered 14 kilometres (eight miles) from the Vanduzi main camp. The HQ element set up their firm base on the summit of a high feature and Rich Stannard and *Jungle Jordan* set out for the camp.

To keep their weight down, they had minimum rations and it took them more than a week to ease through the thick grass in the surrounding woods before getting in close to the camp.

They were now at the base of Monte Bossa mountain, and that night crept closer to the camp. They kept coming across bashas that were obviously in use, although unoccupied at the time.

Suddenly, the two SAS men heard voices and laid low, hardly daring to breathe as the voices got louder.

Then, out of the night loomed a group of ZANLA. They were carrying large plastic bags full of maize which were slung under mopani poles. And they were getting nearer. It was time for the SAS to make tracks.

Having passed a pile of rocks at the bottom of the mountain, Rich reasoned they could use them to get up on to the mountain. They had been briefed it would be too inaccessible for foot soldiers, but Rich felt that with their light packs they might just make it.

Quickly they skirted back around the mountain, scrambled over the rocks and were soon leaving the unsuspecting enemy far behind.

The vegetation was difficult underfoot with clumps of bamboo and vines slowing down their progress. It was a tortuous journey.

Occasionally, they took a breather and looked back through their nightscopes. ZANLA were still at the foot of the mountain and their numbers seemed to be swelling.

It was a devil of a climb, but the two men persevered and pushed on. By the time they reached the top, the sun was just coming up and they could see their long night's haul had not been in vain.

They had arrived in a magnificent position; had a bird's eye view of the ZANLA camp far below and could see the roads leading to and from the camp.

With the aid of their powerful telescope, the two men on the mountain could see 15 kilometres across the countryside into Chimoio town and into the FRELIMO tank training ground. Rich even spied the *Windmill Restaurant* where he had once enjoyed a meal in the last days of Portuguese rule. (He had been in Chimoio [then Vila Pery] in an undercover role to observe FRELIMO as they came in from the bush in the wake of the Lisbon coup).

The area beneath them was thickly treed, but they could monitor the movements far below without the enemy having the slightest idea they were in the area.

No sooner had the two weary men flung their packs down than they heard a commotion far below. Rich reached for his binoculars once more to see a group of ZANLA walking in single file, carrying blankets and little yellow plastic water containers from the river to their day base under the trees.

From their lofty perch, the two SAS men counted 250 ZANLA, six of them women.

They sported an assortment of dress, from a combination of khaki trousers and civilian shirts, to complete civilian outfits, light green FRELIMO uniforms with matching combat caps and even an assortment of old Portuguese camouflage. The women were smartly turned out in green T-shirts, trousers and veldskoens, and each woman wore chest webbing.

Everyone's kit was freshly laundered with creases ironed in shirts and trousers. Most carried AKs or SKSs and there were a few RPDs to be seen.

Rich zeroed in on one commander's expensive-looking watch and was most impressed. You couldn't even get watches like that in Rhodesia. And yet here was a terrorist running around the bush with one.

There were six populated areas altogether and it suddenly struck the two SAS men that instead of being on the *fringes* of the camp as they had thought, they had walked right into the *centre* of it. Still, no one knew that they were there, so there was no need to worry.

At 05h30, they saw fires in three of the six areas. Thirty minutes later the 250 ZANLA spread all over the camp got together, bringing along their maize, yellow water containers and packs. They were noisy and the two Rhodesians heard plenty of laughing and shouting.

But at 09h00 all fell quiet. ZANLA went to ground in their day base, taking their blankets with them.

Occasionally, two Toyota Landcruisers would move around the camp. The driver of a green Land-Rover turned out to be none other than ZANLA commander General Josiah Tongogara, who would normally park his vehicle under a tree out of view of Rhodesian war planes.

At night the camp came to life again. The sounds of singing, laughing and chatting drifted up to the men maintaining their lonely vigil far above. ZANLA sang their Chimurenga songs as they relaxed around blazing fires, safe in the knowledge – or so they thought – that the Rhodesians were unaware of their new camp.

Rich concluded that the countryside and the camp seemed a fairly pleasant place to be and it was no wonder that ZANLA morale was high. He relayed all his intelligence back to Rhodesia and asked for a camp attack.

If stop groups were dropped off at the day and night bases and the stores area, he felt they would account for most of the 300-400 occupants.

With the two SAS men on top of the mountain keeping watch, the Rhodesians would, in addition to the element of surprise, have a magnificent advantage and be in a very strong position to outwit the enemy. They would be able to direct ground troops ... tell them where ZANLA were ... tell if the enemy was closing in on them ...

Being so close to Chimoio town, FRELIMO would undoubtedly be swift to react and send troops to the camp, but Rich would be in an excellent position to warn of approaching armour, enabling the necessary action to be taken.

But the plan was not to be. With thousands of enemy inside Rhodesia and every security force unit working internally crying out for fireforce actions, they were killing too many inside the country to worry about those outside at this stage.

There were other voices in the security forces however, who viewed it from another angle. They felt it was far better to take on the enemy in their external bases before they infiltrated.

But a large-scale camp attack with the full back-up of a forward assembly point – fuel area, casevac set up – would have called for considerable planning. And to commit aircraft to an external camp attack would mean withdrawing them from internal operations where they were desperately needed. Rhodesia simply did not have sufficient aircraft to do everything.

Much to the dismay of Rich and *Jungle Jordan*, who could see the vulnerability of the ZANLA below them, the national planners decided against using troops to attack the camp.

They settled instead on a Hunter strike, a Canberra bombing run followed up by G-cars and K-cars and fixed-wing aircraft.

At first light on March 17, Rich and *Jungle Jordan* were up and waiting and were so high, they could see right down on top of the Rhodesian planes as they swept in for the kill.

Two Hunters screamed in angrily, dropping their bombs and rockets in among the thick trees covering ZANLA at their night base. There was only one enemy up and about that morning ... and he stood mesmerised by the planes and their descending cargoes.

Branches shredded and cracked off and massive explosions tore apart the still-sleeping camp.

John and Janet, the tame baboon early-warning sentries, were caught napping too for the element of surprise was absolute.

Then, after the initial explosions, the rudely-awakened ZANLA were up and running. Everywhere there was pandemonium.

The Canberras came in, then the G-cars ... K-cars ... the fixed-wing aircraft.

As the choppers came around a corner, the pilots were taken completely unawares as a 14,5 millimetre and two 12,7 millimetre heavy machineguns and smallarms fire opened up on them.

257

With fire now coming from areas they had been unaware of, it was becoming dangerously clear to the two SAS observers that they had been watching only a small portion of the camp. Instead of there being 300 or so ZANLA down there, there were probably more like one thousand, most blotted from view by the thick springy tree tops. Thus the two men on the mountain were totally surrounded by them. It was big odds, even for the SAS.

Then one of the fixed-wing aircraft took a hit and had to turn back to Rhodesia.

The two SAS men watched as the planes, their strikes over, returned to base in readiness for another visit to Vanduzi later that day. But the cloud base was too low over the camp and the plan had to be scrapped.

During the day, ten FRELIMO moved into the camp in a Russian Gaz truck, and three hours later it pulled out laden with ZANLA and FRELIMO.

Next morning, the SAS men watched as FRELIMO cautiously approached the camp. This time they came in an armoured personnel carrier which was followed by a Russian truck. There were infantry armed with AKs on either side of the vehicles and they were searching for landmines the Rhodesian might have left lying in wait for them.

It was an opportunity not to be missed; and Rich Stannard once again called for the Hunters.

While the jets were on their long journey from the border, thirty wounded enemy were loaded on to the truck and ferried to a holding position.

Eventually, the two Hunters swept in. This time they were aiming for the FRELIMO armoured personnel carrier and truck parked under cover of the trees. But the enemy had deployed a two-man Strela team to the top of a little rise which formed the lowest part of the mountain and as the first Hunter completed its strike and was moving up and out, a missile homed in on it and raced through the air.

The pilot in the mutually-supporting second Hunter saw the danger and screamed a warning. It was instantly heeded . . . and the first Hunter headed into the sun and managed to avoid being hit by the deadly heat-seeking missile.

Then the two Hunters returned to give the Strela team a taste of their own medicine . . . and as the Rhodesians struck, the two enemy leaped over their hill and doubled away to the safety of the thick bush.

The Hunters then eliminated the personnel carrier and some of the ground troops.

* * *

That night, a Rhodesian pilot sneaked over the mountain to drop off a resupply of batteries and rations to the two men to enable them to maintain their vigil for a few more days. With pinpoint accuracy, their provisions landed just a few metres from them.

The two SAS men hurried forward to break open the packages. They had been living on the minimum possible rations for two weeks and the resupply was badly needed. As always, the SAS caterers had done them proud and they were soon tucking into a tasty feast of still-warm sausages and juicy steaks.

Later squadron commander Martin Pearse, back in the firm base, came on the radio to warn that the radio intercepts had learned that FRELIMO, having guessed there were Rhodesian observers somewhere in the area, were being deployed to search for them.

It was time to get going . . . and the two men spent the whole night climbing down their mountain . . . and with each step he took, Rich was getting more and more disgruntled with the way things had turned out.

First he had wanted ground troops and that had been denied. Had he got his way, he knew they would have accounted for hundreds of enemy. Then, they had been told to pull out before he could direct another air strike on the camp . . . which by now was already being evacuated.

As they moved around the bottom of their mountain, the sun was already up. Rich now decided that as there was no chance of putting in another strike, they might as well pull out of the area straight away . . . and contrary to the principles of SAS *modus operandi*, he decided to move out during the day.

Off they went, hugging the side of the mountain until they came to a track.

They checked out the spoor, saw some blood-stained bandages, then skirted around for a couple of kilometres to get back on to the road.

Rich couldn't resist the temptation to look back down the road, and as he did so, he saw two ZANLA armed with an RPD watching them. For a moment nothing happened. Neither group made a move.

The SAS men were blackened-up and were so filthy from the long night's march through the long grass, the vines, and from clambering all over the rocks, that they must have resembled *comrades* themselves.

It had to be the only possible explanation why ZANLA had not already killed them. It was only when Rich and *Jungle Jordan* began whispering to each other, that the enemy became suspicious and brought forward their RPD.

Suddenly, the rounds were raining all over the place. Trees were being hit, sending showers of kindling splintering into the air. The very grass was bending as the rounds whistled past.

The two Rhodesians fled. Then *Jungle Jordan* took a hit below the knee and assuring Rich he was all right, he took off again, skirmishing backwards, with Rich trying to keep up with him.

There was just savannah vegetation all around and no cover anywhere. ZANLA were still putting long down bursts of fire. There was nowhere to hide; no opportunity to fire back . . . they just had to keep running in the direction of the firm base.

As he ran, Rich had a single thought on his mind – "Today I'm going to die. There's no ways we are going to get out of this."

There was enemy spoor all over the place and it was obvious the original two enemy had been joined by their comrades and the SAS men were being surrounded. There was only one option left. As he ran, Rich grabbed his radio handset and gave the current code word for *hot extraction*. He didn't know how many enemy had joined in the chase, but there were human tracks everywhere and he wasn't prepared to take any chances.

They were still heading towards their firm base, and from time to time, Rich helped his injured colleague along.

Two hours later, ZANLA were still in hot pursuit behind them. Then three kilometres from the firm base, they heard the sounds of a chopper approaching. Saved at last! Or were they?

Soon the chopper was hovering above them. The pilot lowered the *hot extraction* bar. They clambered on, clipped their harnesses on to the ring. Rich turned to the pilot and gave the thumbs up sign, signalling they were ready to be whisked to safety.

The chopper lifted, but almost immediately began to lose power and for one worrying moment Rich and *Jungle Jordan,* snatched from certain death, thought they were about to return to hostile countryside.

But the pilot hovered and moved forward and the two men swinging on the bar below were dragged right through the treetops. When they emerged at the other side all their kit had been ripped from them and their clothes were hanging in tatters. But they were alive, and as they flew home to safety, they marvelled at their good fortune.

Both men knew that things might have turned out very differently had *Jungle Jordan's* injury been more serious.

As far as Rich Stannard was concerned, his two-man concept, using light packs, enabling them to move far and fast, had worked. Things might not have worked out so well had ZANLA been pursuing four heavily kitted-up people. However, Rich was the first to concede that the two-man callsign would have been more successful had they not moved out during the day.

Rich and *Jungle Jordan* who had been outnumbered 1 000 to two throughout the mission and had successfully directed the war planes on to the camp, were later honoured for their bravery.

Rich was awarded the Bronze Cross of Rhodesia and *Jungle Jordan* received a Military Forces Commendation (Operational).

It was ruled that *Jungle Jordan,* surrounded by terrorists, wounded, hunted and *hot extracted* as he had been, had proved himself operationally and he was awarded his SAS colours.

Subsequent intelligence revealed that Tongogara had been injured in the leg during the first airstrike. It was the closest the Rhodesians were to come to eliminating him.

* * *

Two months later, Rich and another operator were back on the mountain directing the jets on to another 150 enemy camped below. When the survivors began to pull out, he called for another strike, which left the entire area and the buildings flattened.

The mission had been a success and Rich was delighted the two-man concept had worked better the second time around.

Attack on Beira Fuel Depot, March 23, 1979

The Mozambique National Resistance was now about to begin a new phase in the fight for the control of Mozambique.

Until now, MNR attacks had been confined to targets in small towns and rural areas, and although important installations like the Mavuze Power station had been attacked, the rebels had never hit vital strategic points in major cities, which if successfully destroyed, would deliver a telling blow to FRELIMO and have a ripple effect on the whole country.

But that approach was about to change and the war to topple Samora Machel and install a pro-Western government was to take on a new and daring aggressiveness.

The MNR and their SAS colleagues were planning a top secret and highly sensitive operation, one of the most daring ever mounted in Africa. The SAS were well used to dangerous and varied operations far from home, yet the sheer size of the main target and the audacity of the plan astounded even them.

In a bold and unprecedented show of force, the SAS and MNR were to infiltrate right to the doorstep of FRELIMO's second largest port, Beira, a very heavily-populated and well-defended city on the Mozambique coast.

They had their sights set on the most important target in Beira. And yet, they wanted more.

Having infiltrated so far, two of the most formidable fighting forces on the continent aimed to make their presence felt by attacking as many important economic and strategic targets and inflicting as much damage as humanly possible, before their time ran out.

Then, as stealthily as they had arrived, they would melt away.

The cost to FRELIMO, of such a visit, would – if all went well – be astronomical; the benefits to the rebel organisation from a propaganda point of view alone, enormous.

The major prize was the giant Munhava Oil Storage Depot, a mere two kilometres from downtown Beira, housing more than forty fuel tanks and several sheds full of 200 litre fuel drums. It represented an investment of many millions of dollars and the FRELIMO government, already in dire economic and financial straits, could ill afford such a crippling loss.

For the Rhodesians, it represented the biggest single economic target they had taken on in their war; for the MNR, it would be the first of many in a long list in their campaign to oust FRELIMO.

When the SAS and MNR studied their maps, they realised there were more than a dozen other vitally-important installations worthy of their attention. But because they were spread over such a wide area and, as the raiders would be working on a very rigid timescale, mission commander Captain Bob McKenna eventually decided on a much more feasible plan.

He was still left with an impressive list of targets all close to the fuel depot, and given the time, they aimed to blow up a transformer station which supplied Beira with electricity . . . topple an electricity pylon . . . sabotage a railway junction over which all trains travelled to and from the docks . : . set a coal dump ablaze, and sever a pipeline leading from the oil depot to the wharfs.

And while they were at it, they also intended aiding the Rhodesian war effort by destroying ZANLA's main warehouse, crammed to capacity with arms and general stores. The ZANLA warehouse was in a long row of warehouses but the MNR intelligence was good and they knew exactly which building to hit.

It would be an extremely high-risk operation and taking on a target in an urban area was an entirely different proposition to a rural attack, where the strike force could melt into the endless bush and shrub after making their hit. In an urban setting, the scales would be tipped more in favour of FRELIMO.

Small armed groups patrolled the city streets on the look-out for trouble . . . and there were known to be FRELIMO guards on duty around the fuel depot itself.

Just to make life more difficult for any would-be attacker, there was a FRELIMO trench system and 37 millimetre anti-aircraft battery a mere 800 metres from the fuel depot, which was manned around the clock by protecting troops. It was the biggest threat of all, and would have to be taken very seriously.

Then there were thousands of shanty dwellers not 300 metres from the depot who could raise the alarm even before their attack went in; and, there was the very real MiG threat.

Beira was a very long way from Rhodesia and the MNR's bases in the Mozambique hinterland, and timings would be absolutely critical.

They would have less than four hours to get into Beira from their pre-determined arrival point, do the job, and get clear of the area before the MiGs could be scrambled from Beira airport and before the thousands of locally-based FRELIMO could react.

As it was, they were expecting FRELIMO in the A/A position near the main target to open up on them while they were still attacking the fuel depot.

It was a formidable target with countless risks involved and like all major external operations far from home, and without the benefit of air support, a thousand things could go wrong.

Yet in spite of all the dangers, mission commander Bob McKenna was confident that they could pull the task off.

Apart from their own abilities, they would have the protection of an almost moonless night to cover their infiltration and exfiltration phase.

They would also have the benefit of total surprise on their side. The mission would involve a very deep penetration and long infiltration phase and as the SAS themselves very well knew, the further inland they went, the greater was the element of surprise, particularly the first time a new place was hit and the security was not all it might be.

The Rhodesian Air Force, flying low level and under radar cover, would put them down near the Pungwe River some distance from the target. Then they would march into the area. The Resistance, specially chosen for the mission because of their knowledge of the region, would again act as guides and "faces" among any locals they might encounter, while the all-white, albeit blackened-up SAS remained under cover.

Before attacking the fuel depot, they were to lay an assortment of suitcase bombs and incendiaries around the secondary targets, which were set to go off at varying intervals over the following two days.

Bob McKenna was gambling that by the time the FRELIMO anti-aircraft gunners opened up on them, the SAS and Resistance would have done their worst and would be ready to make tracks.

The Resistance was to take advantage of any buffer time to distribute resistance leaflets and badges around the blazing fuel depot.

Exfiltration would be much the same as their entry, involving a long march out and then recovery by aircraft.

Having got their entry and exit routes sorted out, the high-powered planning of the finer details of the mission and the intensive rehearsals began in earnest.

A formidable target called for a formidable team and Bob selected a group of men who had over the years proved themselves under fire on numerous operations into Mozambique. The track record of the assembled team was outstanding, and apart from men with particular specialities there were also two squadron commanders – Bob McKenna himself and Captain Colin Willis.

Planning the operation was very much a team effort and although Bob drew up the final plan and gave the orders, it had been discussed among all the officers in the team during the many long hours of exhaustive rehearsals.

Their intelligence on the fuel depot and subsidiary targets was excellent and told them most things they needed to know.

Their plans and aerial photographs showed them the entire lay-out of the main target; the only details they were unable to assess accurately was which fuel tanks were full, and which were not, and which would have been emptied by the time they got to the target.

They had a few questions about some of the structures on the aerial pictures and a visit to the experts at Salisbury's own fuel farm, under the guise of being on an anti-sabotage course, cleared up those points. The Salisbury oil men told them that some of the tanks contained tar and pitch and advised which tanks would burn best.

The Salisbury fuel farm had been virtually destroyed the previous December by a terrorist attack and having seen the terrible devastation that could be inflicted with just a couple of RPG-7 rockets and a few smallarms rounds, the operators were confident that what they had in mind for the Beira depot would cause considerably greater havoc. The psychological damage to FRELIMO alone would be grievous indeed.

They intended using a heavy mixture of RPG rockets, armour-piercing RPD machinegun fire and AK tracers at the Beira depot, and after some useful technical advice from the boffins, they worked out a plan that was designed to inflict the most damage in the shortest possible time.

Then, using a model based on their aerial photographs, they went over and over what they would do come the night – the sequence of events . . . their timings . . . the routes they would take to get to the main and subsidiary targets . . . the positions each man would take up outside the depot . . . how far they would be from the security wall . . . which fuel tanks each would shoot at first . . .

Every minor detail had to be thrashed out and their contingency plans had to cater for every possible eventuality. They had to consider what to do if compromised, what the arrangement was if they got separated or if their escape route was blocked . . . and the rendezvous procedures. Their comprehensive training included tuition from Salisbury police on the finer points of car stealing, a skill that would enable them to make a rapid escape if things got too hot.

They planned to take plenty of ammunition along in reserve in case they had to fight their way out.

Eventually, all the rehearsals, some of the most thorough of the entire war, were at an end, and every man knew exactly what he was to do and when he was to do it.

Then, their local homework over, the mission commander boarded a Canberra and carried out a night-time aerial reconnaissance over Beira to check the lighting around the main target and the surrounding area.

For lighting was crucial to the success of the operation. Too much and they would be seen: too little and they would be unable to see what they were doing.

The commander need not have worried. The lighting was perfect for their particular purpose. There was a whole battery of lights strung around the walled fuel depot, but the security people had made the rather foolish and elementary error of positioning them so that they shone *inwards.*

The target was thus completely illuminated making the saboteur's job easy for them. It was a very thoughtful gesture, Bob remarked at the time, and he had no doubt that heads would roll because of it.

Apart from a string of security lights along the nearby warehouses and shunting yards, virtually everything else in the vicinity was in total darkness. The soft glow from the city would enable them to see what they were doing and they were hoping there would be just enough starlight to aid their activities.

Bob returned home from his recce extremely excited, knowing that he could not have arranged the lighting any better himself.

Within days, the last-minute preparations had been completed and one of the most exhilirating, daring operations of the war was under way. Bob and his SAS/MNR team boarded the aircraft en route to Beira and after a long journey, they arrived on the outskirts of Munhava a few days later.

* * *

The fringes of Mozambique's second largest port lay silent and still, the quietness of the night magnifying every sound. The attack team could just make out the hazy glow from the city lights beyond the black hulks of the buildings.

The atmosphere was now thick with tension and there was a fair amount of excitement in the air. The earlier infiltration phase had gone well, and they had arrived without incident, save for a small navigational problem which had put them well behind schedule. It was an added worry and served to heighten the tension.

Beira had been built on a mangrove swamp and entry to the low-lying coastal city was through a network of muddy, black and very smelly river beds and slippery, steep hills. They were soon wading through the mud and slipping and sliding all over the hills. The heat and humidity of Beira was intense and hit them immediately. The perspiration poured off them running into their eyes and noses and making streaks in their camouflage cream as they struggled and slithered on their way.

Several men had to be hauled out of the mud with the aid of their rifles and by the time they had negotiated the mud and slime, they were all extremely tired.

It had taken them a great deal longer to get through the mud than they had expected and Bob McKenna ordered his men to take a short rest. They could not really afford another delay but Bob wanted them at peak fitness for the hard work ahead.

As they regained their strength and brushed off the mud already beginning to cake dry on their FRELIMO uniforms, Bob McKenna carefully thought things over.

Apart from millions of mosquitoes waiting to greet them, they had arrived in Beira undetected and there were no other enemies to stop their progress. He now knew that apart from a major set-back, the fuel depot was in the bag. He would worry about the pull-out phase and possible enemy reaction later.

But the delays had seriously affected their original time appreciation and they were now ninety minutes behind schedule. It meant they had only two-and-a-half hours to do their damage and get clear under cover of darkness. There was simply too much to do and too little time to do it in.

The commander signalled his men that it was time to get going again and the heavily armed group staggered to their feet, eager to be gone. The tension was now unbearable.

Then, with their rifles at the ready and the MNR contingent guiding them to their pre-arranged dispersal point, they made their way through the back streets of downtown Beira. Now that their muddy hurdle was behind them, they made rapid progress.

As they moved through the darkness and along the unlit streets with silent purpose, the commander considered which of the subsidiary targets he could afford to cancel. Time, not generosity, was the deciding factor and he finally allowed FRELIMO to keep their electricity transformer, the railway junction and coal dump and ZANLA their warehouse.

However, there would still be time for Colin Willis and his MNR/SAS crew to lay their suitcase bomb on the fuel pipeline running from the depot to the wharfs; and for another group commanded by Pete Cole to go in the opposite direction and rig up their explosives on an electricity pylon.

At the dispersal point, the commander gave the teams their final modified orders, their last word of encouragement and wished them well.

Colin Willis mumbled a reply, gathered up his men, then led his team to the east while the others headed north.

As the overall commander and the main team took up their places and sought the cover of the long grass on a small bank at the edge of a rice paddy, Pete Cole and his group peeled off towards the nearest electricity pylon.

The commander was much relieved to find that nothing had changed since his aerial reconnaissance. All the floodlights were still shining inwards, brilliantly illuminating the massive fuel tanks behind the security wall.

The guards in their pillboxes and sentries on their beats had not noticed the dark shapes of armed men as they took up their places in the blackness. So far, so good, Bob McKenna told himself.

As they lay in a line waiting for the others to join them, only their eyes moved, each man taking in the scene before him and zeroing in on the tank he was to shoot at first.

The Beira fuel farm was enormous. It had to be a good five times bigger than the one back home in Salisbury. The frontage stretched some 800 metres and the silver grey tanks, of varying sizes, were in rows as far as the eye could see.

There was not a sound, not a movement from the confines of the depot. In the eerie silence behind the security wall, the huge vulnerable tanks lay waiting their fate. It would not be long now, the operators thought as they quietly envisaged the exploding, roaring inferno that was about to erupt before them.

Some of them began to worry if they were far enough away from the target: if the tanks would blow up and if they would be engulfed by flames, for the tanks were so enormous they seemed dangerously close.

Every so often, the late-night dockland noises punctuated their thoughts. Although it was almost midnight, life in downtown Beira seemed as lively as it undoubtedly was during the day.

Only a small swampy rice field and a road separated the strike force from Beira's densely-populated shanty town, and the soldiers could clearly hear people shouting and laughing. Dogs were barking and chickens squawking. There was a fair old racket going on at the beerhall, too.

Now and then the door would swing open and the light would momentarily stream out as someone lurched away into the night. Pete Cole, scaling the nearby electricity pylon, paused for a moment and followed the progress of one of the late-night revellers until the man's silhouette merged with the darkness.

There was much activity too at the city rubbish dump further along the road. The SAS and MNR could hear the refuse trucks rolling up and down the road 100 metres behind them, emptying their loads, then leaving to make another pick-up.

They could make out the silhouette of a refuse collector as he dangled precariously from the backstep of the truck, but the man could not see them as they lay low in the long grass.

When Pete Cole's group had finished laying their explosives and setting the time delay at the pylon, they joined the main party at the fuel farm. Then they waited for Colin Willis and his team to take up their position on the opposite side of the target.

The attack was to be launched from two sides and it was imperative that both assaults go in at the same time for maximum effect in their limited time-frame.

It was due to start at 23h30, but 23h30 came and went and still the other group was not in position. Everyone silently began to wonder what was keeping Colin Willis and his crew.

Mission commander, Bob McKenna glanced at his watch once more and began to get nervous. As the troops lay waiting for the signal to come, the tension was almost unbearable. Their pulses raced and trickles of sweat gathered along their spines.

The mosquitoes whined persistently around their ears and, beyond the swampy ricefield in the shanty town, a dog barked.

Meanwhile Colin Willis and his party having had further to travel, was going as fast as caution would allow. But they faced a far greater risk of discovery and their movement had been slower.

From the dispersal point they had to travel along the entire frontage of the fuel farm, and as they had no idea where the FRELIMO guards were patrolling, it was essential to make many listening stops.

The fuel pipeline which they planned to sever with their suitcase bomb was also very close to FRELIMO's anti-aircraft battery, and their journey was of necessity particularly cautious.

Colin pulled out his wire cutters and cut an entrance through a security fence protecting the pipeline. Then he deftly tucked the suitcase bomb underneath the pipe, camouflaging it well and set the fuse.

He returned to the rest of his team and then, as cautiously as before, he led his men into their positions for the attack on the main target.

Before the attack could begin, he had to be absolutely certain that each of his men could positively identify his correct targets. For there were lethal tanks of liquid gas on their side of the fuel farm and they knew that if they accidentally hit them, someone would be picking up their pieces in Salisbury before morning.

Just to make sure they avoided the killer gas, they crept to within fifty metres of the security fence, which unlike that on the opposite side of the target was made of wire, not brick.

At 23h45, Colin called the mission commander on the radio on the opposite side of the fuel farm to report that they were now in position and ready.

As he heard Colin's voice, Bob McKenna's nervousness suddenly vanished. Relieved that all was well, he gave the order to standby. On the opposite side of the target, Colin and his team braced themselves for the signal that would come any moment.

The commander took up a kneeling position and as he pointed his RPG-7 at the nearest fuel tank, he heard a dozen safety catches click off around him.

Then he fired his first rocket and even before it struck the tank, the rest of his men were joining in, pouring a non-stop hail of RPG-7 rockets, armour-piercing machinegun fire, and coloured tracers at the tanks.

A split second later, Colin and crew on the opposite side of the fuel farm were doing the same.

Within seconds, the commander's target had begun to melt from the top like a giant slab of milk chocolate and within a minute, it had virtually disintegrated.

The heat was intense as first one then another monster tank burst uncontrollably into flames and petrol gushed out of the holes, only to ignite as the saboteurs continued raking the tanks with fire, keeping up their merciless attack.

By now the flames had consumed so much air, that a breeze had sprung up and was blowing towards the fuel depot.

Tracers were criss-crossing the night sky and there were terrific flashes of light as rockets exploded into the fuel tanks.

Some of the tanks exploded immediately, and soon, massive belching black clouds hung over the fuel farm, reflecting the reddish hue of the blaze back on to the landscape and the attackers as they lay and knelt on the now-warm soil.

As soon as the tanks began igniting, the entire area was lit up as if it were broad daylight.

Colin Willis was rather taken aback by the incredible amount of light that was thrown up so quickly, and as he glanced around and saw his men firing, he suddenly realised how vulnerable they were, silhouetted as they were like black dots in an open field just eighty metres from the security fence. They would have made perfect targets for the odd FRELIMO bold enough to take them on.

But there was such a weight of fire being directed at the fuel depot that the guards in the various pillboxes around the security fence generally kept their heads down or ran away; they never became a problem. Just to ensure they kept out of it, the strike force gave the guard towers the odd burst now and then.

There must have been a fair amount of noise too, but the operators were concentrating so much on the job, and firing so rapidly, they later could not remember hearing any.

The Rhodesian security force officers in the command Dakota over Mozambican skies were to congratulate Bob for the spectacular show the SAS and MNR put on that night.

Suddenly, the FRELIMO manning the 37 millimetre anti-aircraft guns in their trenches not 300 metres from Colin Willis and crew woke up and began firing wildly into the air. Initially they thought that the depot had been bombed.

Their high explosive shells were streaking across the night sky in every direction. Brilliant orange flashes from the flak were bursting over the city as they proceeded to give the attackers and the whole of Beira an impressive fireworks display.

The strike force meanwhile was putting on its show, the likes of which Beira had not seen before and would not forget in a hurry. They maintained the momentum of their attack and soon there were at least eight fires roaring through the fuel farm.

By now, Bob McKenna had decided that the mission had definitely been accomplished and with a final look at his watch to see how they were doing, he gave the order to pull out.

His team, attuned at all times to the word of command, quickly obeyed. They travelled down the length of the fuel farm and having got themselves in another vantage point, stopped just long enough to have a final go at the tanks. They hoped that by firing from a different angle they would be able to hit the tanks previously obscured from view.

Bob bellowed a final command, then they were on their way again, pausing only to fire warning shots over the heads of some of the shanty dwellers standing idly on the side of the road watching the fireworks. The not-so-curious, however, continued their partying in the beerhall regardless, as if such goings-on were everyday occurrences.

Across the far side of the fuel farm, behind the blazing tanks, Colin Willis had passed on the pull-out command to his team. As they began withdrawing towards the RV point, the FRELIMO gunners suddenly realised that the attack was coming from the ground and not the air and began to depress their anti-aircraft guns and fire towards Colin and his team.

For one horrifying moment, Colin and his crew had their hearts in their mouths as sheets of 37 millimetre tracer went hell for leather over their heads. They knew that if FRELIMO lowered their barrels, they would be in real trouble.

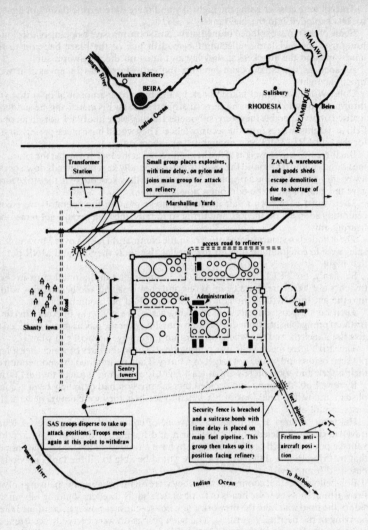

The highly successful attack on the Beira fuel farm, an audacious operation far from home and carried out by a combined force of SAS and members of the Mozambique National Resistance movement

But FRELIMO could not depress their barrels much further and as the relieved soldiers hurried on their way, FRELIMO shells whistled overhead and began exploding beyond both teams.

Other shells shot across the fuel farm and landed in the shanty town; and subsequent intelligence told that FRELIMO managed to kill 18 of their own countrymen.

Sadly for the attackers, some of the FRELIMO fire was accurate and one MNR man in Bob's party was killed and an SAS operator injured. Sadly, too, the heat was on and the operators were moving too fast to take the dead man along with them.

Bob and the main team hurried away, helping their wounded man along . . . while FRELIMO shells continued exploding ahead of them and giant flames licked the night sky behind. By now, the fuel tanks resembled melting candles on a giant birthday cake.

Back at the RV point there was little time to talk. Time was against them and they still had to struggle through the slippery mud hills and river beds before they could even begin to feel safe.

The return journey was as difficult as their earlier trip and Colin Willis fell into a muddy hole and snapped a ligament in his leg. Yet despite the hardships of the mud, they took great comfort in looking back at the enormous blazing fire and the clouds of black smoke belching up into the night sky.

As the raiders silently disappeared into the night, a muffled explosion rolled across the countryside. It was a small affair compared to the others that had rocked Beira that night, but they knew their suitcase bombs on the fuel pipeline had gone off.

Within a few hours, their night's work would be complete as the explosives on the electricity pylon would detonate and the pylon would topple over, cutting electricity to the city. But by then the men responsible for all Beira's troubles would be well on their way back to their bases. They had done a good job and there would be much to celebrate atop Gorongoza mountain and in the various SAS messes.

Next morning, the pall of black smoke that hung over the twisted heaps of charred metal was clearly visible in Umtali, 300 kilometres (186 miles) away.

It had been a difficult operation, faultlessly carried out despite the long approach and the presence of the FRELIMO anti-aircraft batteries so close to the target. Bob McKenna subsequently received the Silver Cross of Rhodesia, the country's second highest gallantry honour, which was partly awarded for the success of the mission and his conduct during such trying conditions.

The Voice of Free Africa was the first to spread the news of the attack, and within days every major newspaper in the southern hemisphere was desperately trying to get photographs of the inferno – and were prepared to pay handsomely for them, too.

Despite the widespread success of *The Voice of Free Africa* inside Mozambique, the rest of the world had known little of the Mozambique National Resistance and its aims. The successful attack on the Beira fuel depot, a turning point in their confrontation with FRELIMO, had changed all that.

FRELIMO refused to allow photographs to be taken of the blaze, which caused an estimated three million Rhodesian dollars in damages and losses.

They vainly attempted to put the blaze out and although they had a water reservoir available to them, they lacked the expertise to extinguish the fire. Adding to their initial worries, too, was the fact that the electricity supply needed to pump water to the tanks had been blown up and the pipeline down to the sea had been severed, seriously hampering their firefighting capabilities.

Most of the fuel was destined for FRELIMO but some had belonged to Malawi, and FRELIMO was finally forced to call in a team of South African firefighters together with twenty tonnes of specialised equipment to put the blaze out. By the time the South Africans got there, the fire had been raging for 36 hours. Fortunately for FRELIMO, the experts were able to extinguish it within hours.

Intercepts revealed that a British-owned fuel tanker had dropped anchor in Beira to top up some of the empty tanks on the night of the attack. The enormous fires licking the skyline so startled the captain that he wisely decided to keep going.

Had the raiders known about the ship, they would have waited until the tanks were full and caused even more havoc. Nevertheless, the fuel was not delivered – and it was a further loss to FRELIMO.

It had been the most spectacular MNR success to date. It had further fuelled tensions in the region and if Samora Machel had harboured any doubts before, he had to admit that the MNR were indeed a force to be reckoned with, both in the rural and urban area – and that nowhere was out of reach or safe from an MNR strike.

Dousing the flames of rebel action was not going to be easy.

Easter Offensive – Operation Bastille, April 13, 1979

The days of white rule were now drawing to a close and Rhodesia was gearing itself up for the first one-man-one-vote elections. After almost eighty years of white rule, power was about to be transferred to the blacks.

After the historic March 3 (1978) agreement between Ian Smith and the three internal moderate black leaders, there had been a period of transition, during which black and white cabinet ministers had worked together to guide the country towards black majority rule.

The elections, originally planned for December, 1978, had been postponed to the following April. Although three-quarters of the country was already under martial law, it had been impossible in the limited time frame to mobilise all Rhodesia's available manpower which was needed to protect voters at the polling booths.

Yet despite overtures to the external leaders, they still refused to have anything to do with the whole arrangement and had condemned it from the outset. They branded the three internal black leaders puppets and traitors – and ZANLA had included them on a special Christmas "death list".

Both ZANLA and ZIPRA pledged to intensify the armed struggle, and the internal settlement, far from bringing a ceasefire, increased the tempo of the war with a death rate of thirty-a-day.

By early 1979, the infrastructure of the tribal trust lands was in tatters. Insurgent activity had led to the closure of 900 schools together with mission hospitals, clinics and administrative centres in the rural areas. In many areas, there was virtually a total or partial breakdown of law and order.

The white farming lands and other areas where vital assets were situated were threatened and a number of important mining operations were closed down or forced to curtail production.

The economy which was also suffering from the effects of sanctions, was being attacked at strategic points. To the south, the rail lines were subjected to constant harassment, and the convoy system operated on all but a few major roads.

On the military front, the thin line of operational troops was stretched to its limits. Operational intelligence could not always be reacted to because of a lack of a sufficiently large mobile reserve of troops and helicopters, and at the same time there were increasing demands to act against bases in Mozambique and Zambia.

Rhodesian security forces were continually frustrated by the enemy's ability to rebuild its forces and make good their losses.

The whites' morale had plummeted to a new low when Joshua Nkomo's ZIPRA shot down an Air Rhodesia Viscount full of holiday-makers . . . slaughtered ten of the survivors . . . then five months later downed another plane killing everyone on board.

The country's tourism slogan had been: "Rhodesia is Super." As one South African newspaper headline commented: "Rhodesia is not so super now".

To the west a Danish airline was ferrying ZIPRA recruits from Botswana to Zambia for terror training. Some 2 670 men had been airlifted to Zambia before the Rhodesians let it be known via diplomatic channels that they were also prepared to shoot the plane down if the charter flights continued. The airlifts ceased immediately.

The blacks too continued to suffer at the hands of their fellow blacks. As always, the soft underbelly of society – the young, the pregnant, the defenceless – made excellent targets. Death came in many forms for Rhodesia's suffering civilians: an axe in the back, a bullet, torture . . .

As one commentator noted: "As so often happens in a guerilla war, civilians were the first and final losers."

Then an urban terror group dealt the Rhodesian economy a severe blow by destroying the Salisbury fuel depot containing a quarter of the country's fuel resources. Of the 28 storage tanks, 22 were completely destroyed and Ian Smith called it a "great disaster".

White emigration was rising and more than 13 500 people left the country in 1978, an increase of more than 3 000 on the previous year. But they were the official figures. Not reflected were the people who left ostensibly on holiday and never came back.

For what had started as "the chicken run" was now being called the "owl run" – a route taken by the wise.

Pressure was mounting from all sides and Rhodesians had their backs to the wall.

Now, just as black majority rule was about to become a reality, the Patriotic Front – the so-called alliance between ZANLA and ZIPRA, which was no more than a marriage of convenience maintained largely for the benefit of the OAU and various aid sponsors – threatened to disrupt the elections by force.

Then, an interesting item of intelligence came the Rhodesians' way.

It had been known for some time that ZIPRA hierarchy travelled on the Grove Road in Botswana, en route to and from their Francistown offices, and in mid-March, the Selous Scouts ambushed a ZIPRA Land-Rover and car on a lonely stretch of the road leading to the Kazangula ferry.

They had hoped to waylay top ZIPRA man, Dumiso Dabengwa, Nkomo's second-in-command, as well as Elliot Sibanda – the senior intelligence officer for all ZIPRA's intelligence and security operations from Botswana – who were travelling north to Lusaka.

While they failed to get Dabengwa, their ambush had not been in vain. They managed to capture Elliot Sibanda – codenamed *The Black Swine* – who was to prove the most important prisoner of the war. As a result of the wealth of information he gave the intelligence people, several very sophisticated operations were mounted.

The Scouts' claymore went off behind the vehicle, and, thinking the petrol tank had exploded, Sibanda stopped the car, put on the handbrake and stepped out. It was only when he saw the black smoke hanging in the air that he realised what had happened, and fled. He ran straight into a stop group and was injured.

Soon a Special Branch officer had arrived to whisk him back across the border for immediate surgery to save his life.

"Hello, *Black Swine*," the SB man said casually when he saw the injured terrorist. *The Black Swine* was flabbergasted that the Rhodesian knew his name; but the Rhodesians had been monitoring his activities for years and there wasn't much they didn't know about the top ZIPRA man.

On the plane to Matabeleland, the injured prisoner promised SB that if they sorted him out, he would "see what the story was". And when he came around from his anaesthetic, he kept his word and was only too willing to talk. It was an unbelievable tale he had to tell, too.

Former SAS intelligence officer Captain Scotty McCormack, a member of the national intelligence team, was sent for and when he heard what *The Black Swine* had to say, he headed for Salisbury and hurried straight to ComOps.

He was eventually ushered into Ian Smith's office to give him a briefing.

"Very interesting, young man," the Prime Minister said to Scotty when he had finished, "thank you very much indeed. Good afternoon."

What Elliot Sibanda had to say, was indeed riveting. A specially-convened meeting was held at ComOps and SB officers were called from Bulawayo to give a briefing. So improbable was the prisoner's story that they were hard put to convince their superiors that Sibanda was telling the truth, and they left the meeting certain no one believed them.

For what Nkomo was planning was a whole new ball game in the war that had ground on in much the same way year in, year out, and which had followed the normal revolutionary doctrine to the letter.

Unlike Robert Mugabe, who had always sent droves of men into the country, Joshua Nkomo, who had a different strategy altogether, had been holding back most of his men in their Zambian camps, committing a small fraction, a mere couple of thousand guerillas, to Rhodesia. It had become a sore point with ZANLA cadres, so much so that they bitterly referred to ZIPRA as the *matshowashowe* (shuffling walkers) because of their slow prosecution of the war.

The Rhodesians too had largely concentrated their attention on ZANLA, for that was where the main threat lay. ZIPRA, the feeling went, could be sorted out once they had dealt with ZANLA.

But Nkomo, lavishly supported by the Soviets, who eyed Rhodesia with its natural resources as a glittering African jewel, had now emerged as a key factor in the military equation and was all set to enter a new phase in the war.

Acting on the Russians' advice, Nkomo planned to adopt a more positive and meaningful approach to all their operations. Not only that, but he was going to pour thousands of conventionally trained troops – regulars, trained in classical warfare, as opposed to guerillas – into Rhodesia.

They were poised to mount a full-scale invasion.

The idea was to send his guerillas in first, sabotaging and preparing the way for the conventional forces.

They planned to have two bridgeheads across the Zambezi, one at Victoria Falls, the other at Kariba/Chirundu. If they were unable to use the bridges that were already there, or in the event of their being destroyed, they would make use of their own pontoons.

Then, conventionally trained infantry in armoured vehicles would drive into Rhodesia, taking over the airports at Victoria Falls, Wankie, Kariba and later at Salisbury. Once in control at Wankie and Kariba airports, they planned to fly in other conventional troops in Libyan transport planes.

In terms of international recognition, if they could say they controlled an area – which they undoubtedly would if they had the airfields – they would be recognised as a government.

It was to be a lightning attack and for the plan to succeed, Salisbury would have to be taken within 24 hours. Columns of armoured vehicles together with foot soldiers were to be used to capture the capital.

Rhodesian security forces were to be eliminated in their push through the country. ZIPRA also planned to crush ZANLA who were pushing across Rhodesia into Nkomo's western stronghold of Matabeleland. Mugabe's men had crossed the Plumtree rail line and definitely had the upper hand.

The Russians, who had been taking a much more active interest in ZIPRA's operational activities, including the Soviet Ambassador to Zambia, Vassily Solodovnikov, a senior KGB official, had assigned a 12-man Soviet advisory team to ZIPRA, headed by Colonel Vladimir Buchiyev, a KGB military specialist.

The SAS were subsequently tasked to eliminate the Russian advisers, but the plan never came to fruition. They knew exactly where they lived and planned to drive to the house in a captured ZIPRA Land-Rover and park under the trees. Then they were simply going to ring the doorbell, storm the building and kill everyone inside. In the end, the CIO put a stop to the plan as the Russians could always have denied the victims were military advisers. Such an incident too would be guaranteed to spark off an international uproar.

The Soviets had reorganised ZIPRA's operational boundaries and made other changes but they were appalled at the way ZIPRA had been conducting the war. Finally, a conference of the ZIPRA War Council was convened and all the front commanders were recalled from the field.

"Here is a map. You *must* know the disposition of your own forces – who you've got where, what sectors they control, what their targets are – and everything about the enemy," an adviser briefed them.

Makepesi Tshuma, the northern front region commander, was called forward to give a briefing.

"How many troops have you got?"

"I don't know," he replied.

"Show us on the map where they all are."

"I don't know."

"What area are you controlling?"

"I don't know."

"How many enemy are in your area of operation?"

"I don't know."

"Which are your temporary and permanent camps?"

"I don't know," said the deflated ZIPRA commander.

The Russians were seething. It was all quite useless: ZIPRA could never expect to achieve anything, they said.

ZIPRA commanders then spent the next three weeks learning how to plot ZIPRA deployments and security force dispositions on to maps.

Their lessons over, the entire ZIPRA high command was assembled for a meeting at which the Soviets did most of the talking, emphasising that maps had to be kept showing dispositions and targets, that reconnaissance missions were vital to operations, that security forces had to be attacked in their home bases and not merely in the bush.

The Soviets stressed that they should rely on surprise attacks rather than meeting the security forces face-to-face as they did not have enough experience to take the Rhodesians on in direct combat.

They emphasised that ZIPRA should not fight white civilians and were angry about those killings, particularly of white farmers who were growing food which might be of use to ZIPRA. White skin was not the criteria, they argued. The war was against a system of government.

They disagreed with ZIPRA Army Commander Lameck Mafella, who said ZIPRA should fight ZANLA. The Soviets' idea was that the two nationalist forces should unite, and once big enough they could free the country in six months.

Russian advisers said that ZIPRA had to change tactics in favour of much larger forces. In short, they had to get on to a more conventional footing.

The most successful idea would be a mechanised infantry role where they had infantry-fighting vehicles with foot soldiers in between. Then, they could invade . . .

Nkomo, very much in the Russian camp, did as he was bid. Acting in liaison with the OAU and the Zambian authorities, conventional training began at Mulungushi and in Boma Camp in Angola, where the mechanised infantry role with soldiers strung out in between the vehicles was practised ad nauseum.

As part of his master plan to rule Rhodesia, civilian pilots were under training in Ethiopia. Police, customs and immigration officers were being trained by the Zambians. Nkomo – and the Russians – wanted people capable of running Rhodesia when he took over.

And he certainly had the manpower for his "government-in-exile" . . . from schoolchildren, right up to university graduates, both volunteers to his cause and people abducted from Rhodesia over the years. In their drive for recruits, ZIPRA had succeeded in destroying the school system in Matabeleland.

The military statistics were indeed alarming. The Rhodesians knew that Nkomo planned to infiltrate 9 000 ZIPRA to occupy Victoria Falls, Pandametenga and Plumtree. Of ZIPRA's 20 000 trained men biding their time in Zambia, 4 000 were conventionally trained.

Although only 2 500 men were operating in Matabeleland by Easter, 1979, eight ZIPRA battalions had been regrouped at Mulungushi training camp in Zambia while a ninth – a motorised battalion – equipped with SAM-7 missiles and 14,5 A/A guns was said to be held in Livingstone in readiness to storm Victoria Falls bridge.

The feeling in some Rhodesian military circles was that ZIPRA would initially use three forces to invade. One would cross the Zambezi both up and downstream. Another would secure Victoria Falls airfield and its confines. One would block the roads both in and out of the village, while another would move in and secure the bridge. Then, thousands of reinforcements would cross the bridge.

Nkomo had boasted to the world that he would occupy Salisbury by May, 1979, and had stated that all units of ZIPRA had been ordered to paralyse the enemy with attacks on military, economic and strategic installations.

ZIPRA supporters in the Lupane region of Matabeleland had been told to prepare for a campaign of civil disobedience to coincide with the infiltration of the ZIPRA army.

Now, on the eve of black majority rule and after more than twenty long years in black nationalist politics, Nkomo, the Kenyatta-like demagogue, the father figure of Zimbabwe nationalism, was about to make his move and take Rhodesia by force.

Security force troops were immediately deployed along the border in strength to monitor crossing points and defend the country. But it was imperative that the threat be pre-empted and the guerilla tide turned. The answer was obvious.

They would have to strike at the very heart of the ZIPRA terror organisation. Nkomo would have to be *taken out* ... assassinated.

The Rhodesians' intelligence was excellent and SB had gained further information on the lay-out and security arrangements at Nkomo's house in the Zambian capital from a capture who had lunched with the ZIPRA leader in January. He had been there when a British diplomat had carried a message from Rhodesian politicians that they wanted to talk to Nkomo again.

Undercover Selous Scouts had infiltrated Zambia several months before and reccied Nkomo's house – the former residence of President Kenneth Kaunda – a sprawling light-green bungalow in a well-to-do suburb in the heart of Lusaka. Following the downing of the first Viscount, the Scouts had been tasked to eliminate Nkomo and several daring, clandestine and overt attempts on his life had been made.

Nkomo however, proved an elusive target and spent more time away than at home. Many ingenious plans were hatched by the Scouts, but they were beset with difficulties and downright bad luck, and further thwarted by Nkomo's irregular comings and goings. The operation – codenamed *Aspect* – was first on ... then off ... then on again.

The operation dragged on for several months – and then came disaster. The Selous Scouts undercover agent, Mike Broadman, was arrested and thrown in gaol just as he was about to leave the country.

It had happened just as the all-important one-man-one-vote elections were to be held and some 60 000 men called up to provide a solid web of defence to protect the voters as they went to the polling booths.

It was imperative ZIPRA's invasion plans be halted before then; crucial Nkomo be assassinated as quickly as possible.

While an intense air strike programme was carried out against ZIPRA targets, including the conventional training camp at Mulungushi, 100 kilometres (62 miles) north-east of Lusaka, Nkomo still lived. Then the SAS was called in, told what had been tried to date and tasked to prepare a parallel plan in the event of the SAS getting the job.

Their contingency planning started almost immediately and the Squadron Second-In-Command Major Dave Dodson, and Captain Martin Pearse, commander of "C" Squadron, got together to dust off several ideas.

Martin Pearse, renowned and respected in the SAS for his meticulous planning, did a lot of good work and spent many long hours at home, including an all-night session, poring over the plan, considering and weighing up the pros and cons before arriving at a feasible proposition.

The two men worked on a full military appreciation of the task – methods of entry ... the likely enemy they might meet ... the methods of exfiltration ... the risks involved ... And there were certainly plenty of those.

The Zambian Army just two kilometres away from Nkomo's house at Arakan Barracks . . . the resident armed guards at President Kaunda's house a stone's throw from the target. Then there were the police . . . the air force . . . the new beefed-up British-supplied air capabilities . . . the 150 tons of equipment and Rapier missiles . . . the locals . . . the dozen or so ZIPRA guards at Nkomo's house . . . Nkomo, too, was known to carry a pistol.

The unknown factor was the Zambian reaction to a ground strike in the heart of the capital, and with this in mind, the two men realised they would have to be flexible, have a lot of firepower, and be completely mobile themselves without having to seize anything from the Zambians.

There was only one logical course of action – they would have to drive to Lusaka in their *own* transport, and do so at night. Their plan hinged on a fleet of vehicles . . . a ferry . . . and a few tins of paint. Plus a lot of bravado.

The two officers decided the best plan would be to use Sabre Land-Rovers, the SAS's redundant pre-bush war specialist vehicle, to give them a dark-green colour scheme with yellow paint splodges, making them similar to the Zambian security force vehicles.

The Zambians did not in fact have vehicles of that same configuration, but the two men were gambling that, with the paint job, and the fact that the front of the first and the back of the last vehicles in their convoy would have Zambian number plates – none of the others would have plates – they would get away with the scheme.

They would wear their own Rhodesian Army combat camouflage uniforms, their normal NATO pattern helmets and *Black-Is-Beautiful* masks.

A large double-storey commercial ferry, *The Sea Lion,* was to take them and their vehicles to the northern shores, putting them down as soon after last light as possible. They would then follow a rough track . . . then a dirt road west of Siavonga to the main Kafue-Lusaka road.

Thereafter, the convoy would drive into Lusaka . . . assassinate Nkomo – then drive all the way back to the lakeshore again.

The biggest worry facing the SAS was what awaited them at the Kafue River bridge. They knew it was guarded, and sketches drawn by Selous Scouts undercover agents had shown a heavy army presence, with four 14,5 millimetre anti-aircraft weapons in position 300 metres on the south side of the bridge. The agent had seen a 12,7 millimetre gun there, too, but the latest reports were that it had been moved.

If they had to fight it out, it would depend on the extent of their casualties as to whether they aborted the mission or not. And if they continued to the target regardless, would the Zambian Army be waiting for them in Lusaka?

Even if they got to the capital undetected and pulled off the job, what of their return journey? Surely the Zambians would try and cut them off at Kafue bridge?

The two men had come up with an ambitious yet brilliant plan. It would be Rhodesia's own Entebbe. And it would have to be carried out with the same sort of panache as the Israeli's displayed on their most famous strike.

They knew it was well within the SAS capabilities; but would the ComOps people approve the scheme, when other less-audacious suggestions for missions had been turned down in the past?

When some of the national planners heard of it they were totally against the scheme. They felt it was an extremely high-risk operation. The Kafue bridge was guarded and they felt the Rhodesians would never get across it. They felt, too, that the intelligence on Nkomo's movements was not good enough to mount such a massive mission so far from home.

Nevertheless, the plan was accepted and the operation – codenamed *Bastille* – given the go-ahead to the utter surprise of Major Dave Dodson and Captain Martin Pearse, who were unused to a favourable response to SAS-inspired suggestions.

When it became apparent that the *Sea Lion* would take 42 men, and the attack on Nkomo's house could be done with only 16 operators, the SAS asked that they be given other targets to inflict as much damage as possible on one operation while the political climate was favourable ... to spread confusion ... and thus stretch any Zambian reaction force.

They also hoped that by taking extra men they would be able to provide a reserve element if their original escape route was blocked.

The additional troops would be able to help out in the event of a breakdown and would be able to step in should they take heavy casualties either on the infiltration, the attack or exfiltration phase.

The SAS suggested to the hierarchy that a possible target might be the Lusaka prison where the Selous Scout agent, Mike Broadman, was incarcerated. But permission was refused although the SAS could never really understand the reason why. The commander of the Selous Scouts, Lieutenant-Colonel Ron Reid-Daly, had also sought approval for a similar plan and had met the same response.

The SAS were, however, to get their extra men and two other targets – ZIPRA's main armoury to the west of Lusaka, which they shared with the Zambian army, and 'Liberation Centre', a guarded prefabricated building that housed many of the ZIPRA hierarchy as well as SWAPO and ANC insurgents. Rhodesian intelligence agencies knew of the existence of both targets, but the prisoner, *The Black Swine,* had been able to confirm the exact locations.

Everything had to be worked out in the finest detail, the least of which was ensuring their ten-year-old vehicles were serviceable. The Sabres had seen their fair share of action in the rugged terrain of the Zambezi Valley, but since the introduction of mine warfare, they had been placed virtually in mothballs. Eventually, the fleet was ready for the 200 kilometre (124 mile) trip to Lusaka.

Security was extremely tight, and as it was necessary to carry out most of the preparation for the op in Kabrit, Dave Dodson initially only briefed the vehicle commanders.

When he told them of the plan, one incredulous sergeant stood up to enquire: "Are you fuckin' mad?"

That, they joked afterwards, was precisely what one kamikazi pilot asked after *his* briefing.

As Dodson recalled: "There was general hilarity and quite a bit of excitement. Disbelief, too."

A couple of days' rehearsals got underway at Kabrit Barracks with the drivers practising four-wheel drive in preparation for the rugged trip on the dirt road north.

Then the seven vehicles and 42 men made their way to Lake Kariba, with the drivers fully testing their vehicles on the way. As most men still didn't know the exact nature of the mission, there was much speculation, with some thinking they were going to Zambia to make a snatch – to take a prisoner.

They stopped off at Karoi for a drink and a snack, and the convoy caught the attention of a couple of men at the nearby police camp.

"Hey, where you guys going?" one asked casually.

"Oh, we're off to Lusaka," quipped an uninformed trooper with a laugh ... and it was only when the convoy got to Kariba that the SAS were called into the ops tent, told not to speculate any more – and that they were indeed going to Lusaka.

The ops tent was not big enough for everyone to fit in and as one group filed in after the other to be briefed, the faces of the men coming out were a picture.

There was a distinct feeling of excitement in the air and most men were speechless. "What could you say? It was brilliant. It was the op of a lifetime and *we* were going on it," said one.

One man managed to get hold of a "Rhodesia Is Super" postcard, which he planned to leave at the house of *The Fat Man* as Nkomo became known to the SAS.

To maintain security, they kept well away from Kariba village itself and were based up at Wafa Wafa, the Selous Scouts training camp, and staying well away from other troops.

After the outline briefing, they split into their groups for their detailed orders.

Martin Pearse was to lead the main strike force to Nkomo's house – the priority target which was screened from view by a high-wire security fence covered with green hessian, with grass and vegetation woven into it. Major Dave Dodson, who was to be in overall command of the operation was to go to Nkomo's house with them.

They studied photographs taken by the Selous Scouts agent and a British film of Nkomo outside his home . . . went over and over which routes they would take to get to the house . . . where they would split up . . . who would go where . . . what they would do and when . . . and the rendezvous procedures afterwards.

Lieutenant Mac McIntosh was to take another group to attack the armoury on the west of Lusaka – while Lieutenant Rich Stannard and his team were to flatten Liberation Centre a few kilometres away from the main target.

The Sabres were painted green . . . mortar cases were packed full of plastic explosives to make demolition charges . . . and the three teams ran through their procedures until they got them down to a fine art. And while all this frenzied activity was going on Sergeant Willum Butler found a deserted landing close to Siavonga where the thirty metre (100 feet) *Sea Lion* ferry could beach unnoticed, finding a place shallow enough to allow the ferry to land right on the shore, yet not too shallow to preclude them from getting their vehicles straight on to dry land.

With him was RSM Pete Allan, who was to command a six-man beach party, which would secure the area, set up mortars, and support the beach landing by providing protection just before the ferry docked.

The party was to remain on the beach until the rest of the operators returned from Lusaka ensuring the ferry could dock again in safety and the raiders had a secure place from where they could cross back into Rhodesia. They would be missing out on the action, but they took comfort in the fact that their role was crucial to the success of the mission.

The commander then prepared report lines, code names for various landmarks on the way to Lusaka and for each particular phase of the operation. Thus when they reached a specific place and completed a task, he would simply radio the pre-arranged code word telling the ComOps planners and intelligence chiefs where they were, and if they were sticking to their original time appreciation.

Apart from being quicker, this would also be indecipherable to anyone monitoring their signals that night.

He named many of the places after characters in a television series, *The Muppet Show.* ComOps was known to the SAS as the *Muppet Show,* largely, as the SAS explained, because of their lack of positive thinking. (ComOps was not amused and would eventually order the SAS to stop calling them the *Muppet Show.*)

Two other soldiers with a sense of humour were Lieutenant Rich Stannard and his callsign second-in-command, Sergeant Billy Gardner. Rich had planned his fun back in Salisbury and taken along a little yellow duck in his kit.

He painted it green and drilled it in place on his Sabre. He didn't want it to be *too* conspicuous on the long journey north, after all.

Influenced by a recently released citizen's band trucking film entitled *Convoy*, Rich chose *Rubber Duck* for his "handle".

Then the two friends painted a pink pig on the side of Billy Gardner's Sabre. They were now set for their citizen's band trucking trip on the long night-time haul to Lusaka.

An ex-British SAS man who had worked in Zambia for some time and knew his way around the capital was to travel to Lusaka with them to act as a guide.

Eventually, the strike force was ready. All they needed now was the word. An externally-based CIO agent was to let them know when Joshua Nkomo was at home in Lusaka.

There were problems getting the vehicles on to the ferry, but eventually all seven made it. Now the freshly-painted Sabres were daubed with yellow paint splodges to add to the charade that they were Zambian army vehicles.

Everyone was tense as they headed for Zambia that night. But they got half way across the lake, and were recalled to Rhodesia. No, their radio told them, the mission was not tonight. A sense of anti-climax swept over them just as it always did when they were keyed up to the limit . . . and then had to relax to await another day.

Returning to Wafa Wafa, the commander was told that they had to take two Selous Scouts on the mission, and one, Captain Ant White, who had been involved in the Scouts' plan to eliminate Nkomo in Lusaka, was to act as their guide.

"This immediately rubbed everyone up the wrong way . . . and we tried to get rid of them. Not because they were Selous Scouts, but we objected very strongly to the General dictating to us exactly who we would take on the raid, which was most unusual : . . It was not well received, especially as a couple of blokes had to get off to make room for them," Dodson recalled.

What further rattled the SAS was that they already had a guide, the ex-British SAS man. But as the Selous Scouts had done a lot of the work, ComOps felt that they deserved to be in on the final act . . . and Ant White and a black Scout were to go along.

The black Scout was to be dressed in a Zambian army captain's uniform and his role was to do the talking at Kafue bridge or wherever they got into difficulties.

At 11h00 on April 12 – five days before the elections were to begin – the strike force and their camouflaged vehicles were back on the *Sea Lion* again, waiting for the word to come.

Some put their sleeping bags down on the top deck and had a nap under the morning sun. Would it be another case of greatcoats on, greatcoats off, they mused?

Secretly they thought that this time would be the real thing. Now, they were much more relaxed than the previous days' wait. They were with an experienced crew. They had the benefit of a perfect plan. Everyone knew what to do; knew what the alternatives were.

Then came the green light. The Rhodesian external agent had seen Nkomo go into his home and the all go was flashed to "C" Squadron waiting patiently out on the lake.

"Bastille Go," the signal read. "Have fun!"

At last! Everyone was relieved that the op was on; excited at the prospect of what lay ahead. They were within hours of driving through the streets of the Zambian capital under the full glare of the city lights. And while Rhodesians slept soundly in their beds, one of the country's two public enemies was going to be blasted to kingdom come in the heart of his friendly host nation.

There was still a bit of daylight left as *Sea Lion* approached Zambian waters and the commander decided to vary his original timings and risk landing as soon as possible rather than wait until just after last light.

His plan went without a hitch. *Sea Lion* nosed into the shore and the protection party under the command of RSM Pete Allan went ahead to set up their mortars and to secure the beachhead.

There was no one around to oppose them and once the mortars were in position, the 42 troops, who were to travel to Lusaka in their seven Sabre vehicles, drove off the ferry, with the commander leading the way.

The ferry moved back on to the lake to avoid discovery and to await the word for the pick-up.

So far, so good. It was just after 18h00. They were ahead of schedule, and as the attack on Nkomo's house was due to go in at 02h00, there was plenty of time to get to Lusaka.

They were a long way from anywhere and were not anticipating any Zambian resistance. The only thing worrying the commander at this stage was an unmarked landmine planted somewhere in the area by Rhodesian security forces.

Most men were apprehensive but silently acknowledged they were so well-armed that they would be able to deal with most problems with the possible exception of Kafue bridge.

They set off immediately. Their vehicle lights were on and the moon was shining brightly, and that helped them considerably on the dirt track.

Thirty minutes later they sent their first progress report to ComOps via the command Dakota flying somewhere over Zambia that night and carrying the SAS CO, Lieutenant-Colonel Garth Barrett. As the ComOps teleprinter clattered into life and punched out the report line, *Horny Prawn,* the military planners and intelligence chiefs back in Salisbury knew that the operators were well and truly on their way.

The dirt track was far better than the commander had expected and for the first ten kilometres, they made good time. But then the road began to deteriorate, and although Dodson had anticipated that from his aerial reconnaissance, they became disorientated.

They drove into the middle of a village and the black Selous Scout who spoke the local dialect asked the way from the locals, whose first reaction was to whip out their ZAPU membership cards, thinking their unexpected visitors were ZIPRA.

The Rhodesians put them right and the translation that came back was "Oh My God! There's going to be trouble."

But the SAS only wanted directions and the villagers were only too pleased to point the way to Lusaka. The villagers were not considered a risk and as they were unlikely to raise the alarm, they were released unharmed.

The commander was grateful for their help, and the convoy was soon on its way again, having lost about twenty minutes.

Rich Stannard thought it was about time he tried out his citizen's band trucking technique. Abandoning his *Rubber Duck* "handle" for the time being, he called up his callsign second-in-command, Sergeant Billy Gardner travelling in the Sabre behind.

"*Suicide Jockey* to *Pink Pig. Suicide Jockey* to *Pink Pig.* Do you read me? Over."
From the vehicle behind, came: "*Pink Pig* to *Suicide Jockey.*"
But the commander had heard all and promptly ordered them to cut it out before their transmission could get into full swing.

* * *

At 19h40, Siavonga police messages intercepted in Salisbury reported that the *Sea Lion* had been seen violating Zambian waters. They assumed that the Rhodesians were on their way to attack a nearby army camp.

JOC *Splinter* was immediately called in to help and troops were sent across the lake to Chipepo harbour to harass and attack a fishing camp, a decoy tactic to mislead the Zambians into thinking that was where the main attack was centred.

Meanwhile, the strike force was on its way north. But the track deteriorated further and at times it faded away completely. It was necessary to use a lot of four-wheel drive and fuel to cover the twenty kilometres (12 miles) to one of the main bus routes, which they knew by the codename *Swedish Chef*.

But the planning had been meticulous and Dave Dodson had anticipated most problems, and each vehicle carried three times the fuel needed.

By now the excitement had died down somewhat and there was very little talk. Everyone had settled down to a long hard slog on the poor track. They bounced their vehicles through the mud and where the track was washed away, they felt more like sailors than soldiers, as they put their weight on one side to stop the listing vehicles sinking into the mud.

Then came another problem.

At 21h30, an urgent message was passed to the commander that one of the vehicles had broken down. The vehicle, commanded by Lieutenant Phil Brooke, had been driven through a puddle and had spluttered to a halt in the clearing in the bush, refusing to go any further.

They were already running quite late now because of the poor state of the track and it was just about the last thing the commander wanted to hear.

Several heads went under the bonnet. There was a bit of tinkering, but the ignition coil had been burned out and not having a mechanic with them, nothing could be done to solve the problem.

There was only one answer. The vehicle would have to be left behind as would the driver and passengers, who were to have gone with Mac McIntosh and his crew to the ZIPRA armoury. They would be picked up when the others returned from the mission. In the meantime, they were to rig up the vehicle for demolition.

When Dodson reluctantly broke the news to Phil Brooke and his men, they were just about ready to cut his throat.

They asked if they could travel on the other vehicles but the commander ruled there was just no room. He couldn't risk overloading the Sabres with any further passengers only to have them break down, too.

The bitter disappointment felt by Phil Brooke and his team at that moment can only be imagined. First, they had the excitement of having been lucky enough to get on the mission, an opportunity the men of "A" and "B" Squadrons would have given their eye-teeth for. Then there was the utter frustration of getting this close only to miss out on what had to be one of the greatest adventures of the war.

It was a grim little group indeed which watched and cursed as the remaining six vehicles moved off into the gloom of the night again.

By the time they hit *Swedish Chef* – the main dirt bus route – it was 22h05 and they were already ninety minutes behind schedule.

Would they manage to stick to their timings and attack the targets by 02h00, allowing them plenty of leeway to get out of town under cover of darkness? And what of the armoury target now that they were six men short?

281

Just to add to their worries, the commander was told over his radio that there was now thought to be a Zambian Army presence on their infiltration route.

They were relieved to find the dirt bus route in good order. The going now was easy and they sped along calling off the various codewords, arriving within 200 metres of *Fozzie Bear* – the main tar road – at 00h46.

They were still running late but afforded themselves a brief stop to stretch their legs and have a smoke, while they refuelled and checked their weapons. They discussed whether or not they should call off the mission that night and try again the following night. But in the end, the commander decided he was quite happy to carry on and risk being caught in Lusaka at first light.

A couple of vehicles rolled past them in the early morning, and the soldiers thought it a bit strange. It was very different from Rhodesia where there was very little night-time traffic in the farming areas because of the fear of ambushes.

The SAS waved the late-night travellers on, and they went on their way unsuspecting.

All too soon it was time to go and give Lusaka a rude awakening. Stuart Batters had been driving the command vehicle and had done a magnificent job of driving through the hills, making Dodson prematurely greyer in the process, but getting them there as quickly as possible.

They now changed drivers and the ex-British 22 SAS guide took over the wheel. But within fifty metres the driver inadvertently jammed his rifle in the steering wheel and the vehicle veered up the verge and overturned, throwing the passengers and equipment out and bringing the column of vehicles to a grinding halt.

Fortunately, there were no serious injuries, but it had been a close shave. Their main radio was however, damaged, although they didn't realise it at the time.

They were soon on their way again, and now had a few more minutes to make up. Although there were a couple of other worrying moments, nothing came of them. A luminous sign warned of *Police Ahead,* but it was only a traffic accident and there wasn't a policeman to be seen. As they approached the Chirundu-Kafue turnoff and the main Lusaka road, their hearts were in their mouths when they saw a Zambian Army vehicle outside a beerhall. But again, there was no one to give them trouble and it was obvious the Zambian soldiers were inside having a fine old time.

Then came the biggest worry of all – the Kafue river bridge.

If there was going to be a compromise it would happen here. They were well blackened-up, but as every man knew, they would not fool anyone on close inspection.

When the bridge came into view, the commander could see that it was exactly as their photographs has shown – very long and very imposing. The troops were a bit taken aback by its sheer size and the mass of steel girders. They had imagined it to be a lot smaller.

Everyone braced himself for a punch-up. The machineguns were mounted now and the safety catches were off their rifles. Apprehension and danger were in the air and there was more than one sweaty palm.

Dodson gripped his silenced pistol and ordered his vehicle ahead. The others dropped back to two hundred metres so as not to illuminate the command Sabre with their lights, but were close enough to give fire support if necessary.

Then came the biggest surprise of the entire operation. There was nothing and no one to hinder their progress. No barricades, no weapons; not a single sentry.

Both Dave Dodson and Martin Pearse had not really believed the reports of their being vast numbers of enemy on the bridge, and they were proved correct. Nevertheless, it was a great relief to all.

The others followed Dodson over the Kafue bridge, hardly daring to believe their good luck. The last vehicle fell behind a bit, and Martin Pearse urged his driver Barry Skinner to catch up.

They now set course for Kafue town and Lusaka, stopping for a couple of minutes only to put Sergeant Mike Beal and his small callsign down two kilometres from the bridge. They were to monitor the activities and see if the Zambians put up roadblocks to prevent the raiders returning home.

If something went wrong and the convoy had to take another route, Mike Beal and his men were to walk out of the area and be picked up later. Within seconds, they had waved a farewell to Mike Beal and were on their way again, passing Kafue police station without incident.

There was far more traffic than they had been expecting, and they deliberately kept their faces averted to avoid their features being recognised in the glare of the on-coming lights. Most operators were crowded into the back of the vehicles so as not to arouse any undue suspicion.

When a vehicle pulled up behind them, the operation suddenly took on the sus-pense of a Hitchcock thriller. Not wishing to shoot the passengers and alert the Zam-bian police training camp further on, Martin Pearse stood up and waved the driver on.

The man obeyed the command and pulled out, then hit the accelerator and disap-peared without suspecting a thing. It was only afterwards when the SAS had time to analyse the events of that night, that they realised how incredible it was.

Twenty-five kilometres out of Lusaka the convoy passed a little shanty town. Lights were on and there was a string of shacks. People were milling around, while inside a building, men were gathered around a pinball machine. Again, the SAS men marvelled at how busy Lusaka was at night.

The convoy drove on. There was not long to go now. Then, suddenly, they were there.

An orange glow ahead of them warned they were approaching the Zambian capital. Some of the chaps took off their scarves and gloves for they knew that once the action began, they would be sweating and wouldn't need them any more.

Then came the street lights of the Zambian capital. It was just like any other big city with its lights on. Traffic rolled on its way, and off in the distance, they could make out the blink of traffic lights.

Suddenly, the large "Welcome to Lusaka" sign on the side of the road brought home the reality of the situation. Here they were in the heart of hostile Zambia, home to Joshua Nkomo ... not to mention the Zambian police, army and air force.

There was a smell of danger about the place and the tension in the six Sabres was unbearable. A couple of chaps who had been napping in the back of the vehicles were shaken awake.

The SAS were trying to look as nonchalant and as negroid as possible as the glare of civilian headlights threatened to expose their true identity.

Andrew Standish-White in the rear vehicle realised he had a rip in his camouflage uniform and was having to crouch lower than the others, fearful that his pink arm showing through the tear would give their game away even before it had begun.

At last, they turned right towards a roundabout leading to the city centre where a huge octagonal glass skyscraper dominated the Lusaka skyline. This was codenamed the *Muppet Show* and was the final report line that had to be sent back to Salisbury.

A few soldiers looked at the skyscraper with a professional eye and couldn't resist commenting in muted tones what a lovely target it would make. The scenario wasn't difficult to envisage. A few well-placed grenades and the glass would be cascading down on the city in no time at all. Right at that moment though, there was far more important work to do. Perhaps they would get a crack at it later?

They were minutes away from shattering the very heart of the ZIPRA war machine – the assassination of Joshua Nkomo, father figure of Zimbabwe nationalism to countless thousands.

In view of the loss of Phil Brooke's Sabre and the six troops, the commander now decided to abandon Mac McIntosh's armoury task.

To send Mac's vehicle to the armoury on its own was risky. The armoury was on the opposite side of Lusaka to the priority target, and without a back-up vehicle there could be problems. If the vehicle was waylaid, or seized up, the troops would be unable to get out of Lusaka.

While the six men on Mac's vehicle could have coped with the target, they could hardly inflict the damage that the original 12 attackers could do. They had already discussed sending another callsign to help out at the armoury, but the operators in question were reluctant to undertake the mission without a full briefing.

Much to their disgust, Mac McIntosh and his five men were told they would have to go with the main party of men to Nkomo's house, where they would go into a reserve role.

As the 36 Rhodesians drove into the heart of Lusaka, their watches showed 02h40. They had managed to make up a bit of time but they had arrived a lot later than they had expected.

Lieutenant Rich Stannard, who was to lead a team to Liberation Centre, was towards the back of the convoy and turned off to his target.

The rest of the convoy continued on through the well-illuminated city streets, heading towards Brentwood Drive and *The Fat Man's* house.

They knew that behind the green hessian screen surrounding Nkomo's rambling colonial bungalow, there would be guards on duty. There were between 15-20 weapon-wielding bodyguards in the house itself and more lived in a nearby white building; then there were two armed guards on the gates to check on callers' bona fides.

It was eerie driving through the middle of Lusaka. "There we were, fairly well gunned up – two machineguns and an RPG-7 per vehicle, each gun having 1 500 rounds in it, six or seven troops in the back, helmets on, blackened-up," the commander recalled.

"The traffic lights were working, and so to keep the convoy together and delay any suspicions of the locals drifting around, we stopped at the lights. A bloke pulled up next to us and we half waved at him and he half waved at us."

The SAS knew that only bluff could succeed in getting the party through. As the lights changed to green, the drivers slowly let out their clutches and then they were on their way to Nkomo's house, again no one suspecting a thing.

A few kilometres away across the city, the two other SAS vehicles were en route to Liberation Centre, just five minutes' ride from the huge roundabout, a journey which took them south past the railway line and a few little African stores.

At first, they drove straight past Liberation Centre, which was obscured from view by a high wall. Sergeant Major Bruce Langley spotted their error and they did a quick U-turn, travelling all the way around the building until they neared the main gate, carefully keeping out of sight of the sentries at the entrance.

Now they had to sit and wait until they heard the sounds of firing coming from *The Fat Man's* house – the signal for Rich Stannard to initiate the attack on Liberation Centre.

The main strike force, meanwhile, were closing on Nkomo's house, having taken only one wrong turning. It was exactly as they had seen it on their film and still photographs. The yard was screened from the road by the hessian covering the high fence and grass was woven into the screen.

They stopped for thirty seconds while the commander gave his final orders. Every driver knew where he was to go, every operator knew what he had to do.

Martin Pearse was to breach the 1,8 metre (six feet) security wall on President's Lane, then after all opposition was silenced, he was to lead three other men into the house to assassinate Nkomo.

At the same time he was blasting an entrance on his side, Dave Dodson and his team in one vehicle and Sergeant Major *Petrol Paul* in the other, were to breach the two main gates, then bunker bomb and rocket their side of the house, leaving the way clear for Martin Pearse to get on with the house-fighting.

Mac McIntosh and his team meanwhile would be in reserve, keeping their eyes peeled for outside interference.

Dodson gave the command, wished them well and three vehicles roared off at speed along the deserted streets, two in one direction, the remainder in the other.

It was now 02h55.

Martin Pearse's vehicle came screeching up with the intention of stopping behind the house, thereby using it as protection from the commander's arc of fire from Nyerere Road.

The plan had been for Martin to tap his driver on his helmet to stop. But a trigger-happy guard behind the security fence had already opened up. The order never came and the driver overshot slightly. Some of the shots the vehicle collected may have come from the SAS commander's Sabre on the opposite side of the target as a result.

Immediately the first guard opened up on them, Andrew Standish-White, manning the rear machinegun on Martin's vehicle, stood up and initiated for the Rhodesians, letting rip at a cluster of security huts, and emptying his first belt in record time.

There was no time to be lost and Martin Pearse leapt from his vehicle and raced to the fence to attach an explosive charge to blast an entrance to the grounds. The charge was made up in an ordinary normal garden hose and on the rush to the gate someone stood on the hook needed to attach it to the fence and valuable time was wasted attempting to sort out the problem.

Martin Pearse whipped out his wire-cutters, forced an entrance big enough to take a man wearing webbing, and within a minute he had penetrated the Bastille grounds. Inside *The Fat Man's* house, the twinkle of lights could be seen.

Then they took their first casualty. A sergeant, one of Martin Pearse's assault team, was hit in the buttocks, putting him out of action and cutting the house-fighting team down to three men.

Martin's driver/medic, Barry Skinner, had already pulled the vehicle over to the opposite side of the road. Now he dragged his casualty off the vehicle and into the ditch, and while he busied himself sorting out the sergeant's wound, the casualty opened his own drip and prepared to put it in himself. Fortunately for him, he didn't need it.

Once the enemy fire was neutralised near his entrance, Martin Pearse led his two remaining men into the garden, stepping on a guard sleeping under his blanket on the lawn. As the fence began to burn, they could see that the guards had been asleep in shell scrapes.

Martin carried a forty-round magazine on his AK-47 rifle and had six thirty-round magazines in reserve which gave him a larger magazine capacity than the normal Rhodesian issue FN. It was also easier to handle in confined spaces. He also carried five explosive hand grenades, five *Knock-Knock* charges, a 9 millimetre pistol and a spare magazine.

Meanwhile, at the opposite side of the target, Sergeant Major *Petrol Paul* and Major Dave Dodson were attempting to batter down the two locked front gates. Everything went well for *Petrol Paul*, and he crashed through his entrance just as planned, breaking the lock, the machinegunner opening up immediately.

But the angle of the commander's approach was wrong and they failed to hit the gate at full speed – and the gate, padlock and chains stayed firmly intact.

As they bounced off the gate, the commander realised there was no time for another try. He ran to the gate to blow an entrance with a *Gatecrasher*, while his team began firing to keep interference from the guards around the gate to a minimum.

But the driver had left the lights on and Dodson realised he was about to be silhouetted, making him a wonderful target.

He hesitated for about ten seconds then sprinted around the vehicle, switched the lights off himself, then returned to the gate and blew it down. Both vehicles were then half-in, half-out of the gates and every man proceeded to machinegun the house … the vehicles … servants quarters … anything they saw moving.

There was quite a bit of return fire. The commander's vehicle took a couple of strikes and the driver was hit in the back.

Once they had suppressed all opposition from the thirty or so guards there that night, everyone on the Nyerere Road side of the target began rocketing and bunker bombing the house.

Dodson dealt with Nkomo's lounge by lobbing in a bunker bomb. The lounge immediately burst into flames. There was no chance of anyone being left alive in there.

Masonry was crashing … timber was falling and the lights were blown out. Fire had quickly taken hold and everywhere, there was smoke and flames. All the SAS were hit by falling debris.

The noise was fantastic. The exploding bunker bombs, machinegunning, rocketing appeared magnified and an incredible amount of smallarms fire all added to the commotion. The commander removed his earplugs for a second and was nearly deafened. Even when he put them back, it was still noisy.

It was a spectacular sight as well. The machineguns had one tracer in three rounds, so all they could see were red sheets of tracers. The tracer provided the storm troopers with excellent light, enabling them to see the target.

Mac McIntosh and his crew, parked outside the main gates, were having a grandstand view of it all.

At the Zambian President's palace just five hundred metres away, the presidential guard began firing, their red and green tracer was criss-crossing and ricocheting across the night sky. But it was only a token show. Nothing and no one came near the raiders.

Soon the initial resistance from Nkomo's guards was subdued and the din began to subside. The dark humps of fifteen bodies lay sprawled around the grounds, the remainder keeping a low profile, discretion being the better part of valour.

"There was a real ding-dong battle going on. When the firing died down, there were some pretty big explosions," a British diplomat watching the proceedings from the safety of his bedroom window, recalled later.

Elsewhere in the capital, Zambians began to run into the streets in their underwear. At first they thought there had been a coup because the firing went on for such a long time and came from the vicinity of State House.

Martin Pearse and his assault team knew exactly which bedroom Nkomo slept in, but their original plan to throw in a bunker bomb was frustrated as the window was barred.

286

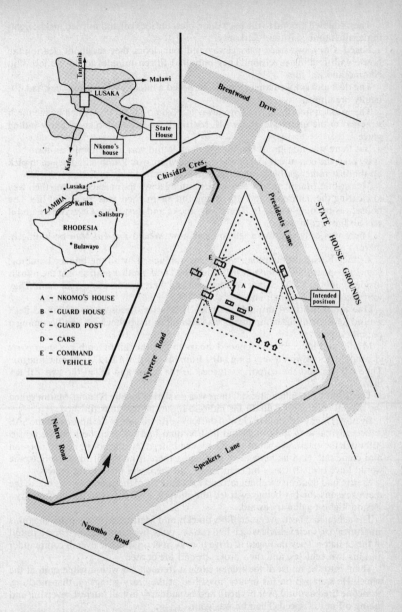

Operation *Bastille;* An apt name for the storming of Joshua Nkomo's home. The attack into the heart of the Zambian capital, was one of the most daring operations of the war

They doubled around to the back door, blew the lock off and hurried inside, fighting against time, dust and darkness.

Faced with a two-sided passageway and four doors, they set about clearing the house with chilling precision. They only had fifteen minutes to do the job, find Nkomo and kill him.

The dust and smoke hanging in the air posed a major problem and they had difficulty breathing.

The wooden floor had been torn away in Nkomo's bedroom. Aided by the torch strapped to the underside of his AK, Martin Pearse fired into every likely hiding place.

But there was no sign of Nkomo. All they found was his general's uniform.

By now, the command Dakota flying somewhere over Zambia had begun to pick up the first rather garbled and excited police reports of heavy firing.

Meanwhile, Martin and his men were scuttling down the passageways on their way to clearing the bathroom and storeroom. But again, there was no sign of life. The house was burning furiously. There was smoke and dust almost everywhere and it was all fairly confusing.

There was only one room left to clear now. Would *The Fat Man* be hiding in there?

As they burst into the room, which was untouched by all the bunker bombing, someone opened up on them from under a bed and another man shot at them from inside a cupboard. The enemy were trapped and there was no way out for them. They were fighting to the bitter end.

One round whistled through the back of Martin's trousers giving him a flesh wound and one of his companions was also hit in the buttocks. It was becoming a popular target.

Martin and his corporal grenaded the room and the third member of their party cleared the room with a very long burst from his cut-down RPD light machinegun. Then Martin and the corporal returned to the room and killed the two ZIPRA men.

The Bastille had fallen. But still there was no sign of Joshua Nkomo. Martin called the overall commander up on his radio to report he had now finished.

By now, Dave Dodson had cleared the lounge on his side of the house and the SAS reluctantly came to the conclusion that Nkomo had not even been in the house. Although the externally-based agent had seen him go into the house, he had not seen him come out. Had he been there that night, there is no doubt what the outcome would have been. It was a bitter moment, but there was no time for regrets.

Martin had done an excellent job and his handling of the operation was one of the main reasons for his being awarded the Silver Cross of Rhodesia, the country's second highest gallantry award.

The action had been over incredibly quickly and Martin and his team left the ruins and hurried to their vehicle which had two flat tyres, two casualties on it and a round in the radiator. They managed to drive it away, met up with the overall commander and his two vehicles, and then drove around the corner.

Then, into the midst of the frenzy came a Renault car with a white man at the wheel. He stamped on his brakes, mystified at the crazy goings on that morning. Someone fired a round over his head and he suddenly lost all interest, reversing and taking off at full speed. Then he was gone.

At the rendezvous point around the corner, they stopped to reorganise, while the commander grabbed a quick smoke.

They were all very pleased. The entire operation had been pulled off in 25 minutes and all their detailed planning had paid handsome dividends. It had been unnecessary to give orders during the raid, for each man knew exactly what to do at every stage.

Zambian police signals were now reporting that Lusaka was being bombed. Five minutes later, police headquarters told stations not to publish the incident over their radios.

The situation in the capital was being described by the police as "too serious". "It's the maningis (whites)," one station reported.

Another could not find its commandant to organise a reaction force ... while police elsewhere were racing around in their vehicle. But it had a blow out, overturned and three policemen were killed.

The result was that no one appeared to oppose the strike force, which by now had decided to abandon Martin Pearse's ailing Sabre.

A couple of men discussed leaving their "Rhodesia Is Super" calling card on the Sabre for Nkomo, explaining their visit had been in return for the Viscount atrocities, but in the end, good sense prevailed and they reckoned he would get the message anyway.

After stripping the vehicle of most of its equipment, they doused it with petrol then threw a white phosphorus grenade underneath. Their own engines roared into life once more and they began to pull out of town.

The blazing vehicle had come to the end of its days outside the home of the Zambian Minister of Tourism. The events in the capital that night could hardly be expected to attract visitors to the country.

They passed a number of military vehicles heading in the direction of Nkomo's suburb, but they were on the other side of the carriageway and the Zambians showed no interest in the convoy as it observed the speed limit and made its way out of town.

The vehicles turned left at the main north-south highway and then it was on to the *Muppet Show,* the roundabout with the glass skyscraper. Now for the first time since the operation had begun, the tension eased slightly and they could relax and have a proper smoke, swop accounts – and hope that everything was going well for Rich Stannard and his team at the remaining target, the Liberation Centre.

* * *

Rich Stannard and his second-in-command, Billy Gardner had decided to carry out a quick reconnaissance before mounting their attack. They were scaling a two metre-high security fence when the sounds of firing could be heard coming from Nkomo's home.

With a final push from his sergeant, Lieutenant Stannard reached the top of the fence and from his perch, quickly gave the courtyard, the military transport yard, and the buildings the once over.

There was a light on in an office directly beneath him and he reasoned it had to be the operations room – and he knew he would be in with a fair chance of finding some-one in there.

But now the Liberation Centre security guards were becoming curious about the unmistakable sounds of shooting from across the city. Rich watched as a couple of them strolled out of the steel gates and walked off down the street to investigate, totally oblivious of the two SAS men spying on them from the wall, and others lurking some-where nearby in the shadows.

Sergeant Billy Gardner took a bunker bomb from his webbing and heaved it straight into the lighted window of the enemy operations room.

A split second later the bomb found its mark and the room burst into flames. There was one almighty thunderclap and the roof lifted and flew through the air.

Both men leapt down, taking cover behind the wall. A fraction of a second later the metal whistled uncomfortably close to their heads and clattered down centimetres behind them in the street.

The sergeant had earned himself a new nickname – *Billy Bunker Bomb*.

They dashed for their vehicles and roared around the corner to the entrance. The front and rear machinegunners were poised to take on any opposition.

As the security guards had already left to investigate the sounds of firing – an action that undoubtedly saved their lives that night – the raiders met no resistance as they swung through the open gates, the twin machineguns on the two Sabres spraying a deadly hail of hot lead in all directions.

The small guardhouse, still with one man on duty, came under a withering rate of fire, and bullets carried death to the sentry.

A well-placed phosphorus grenade spread the contents of the outside toilet all over the show. ZIPRA were known to hide their arms caches and often themselves in the toilets, thinking that well-bred Rhodesians would avoid them.

At this stage, the city lights were doused and air-raid sirens whined across the city as the Zambians thought the Rhodesians were about to carry out an air raid.

But aided by the light of the still-blazing ops room, Rich Stannard and his team were able to continue raking the area with machinegun fire, spraying rounds at the buildings and parked vehicles.

Within thirty seconds, the lieutenant reckoned they had done enough damage to the entrance, and had put a stop to all possible resistance.

They ceased firing for a moment. Off in the distance, other explosions told their tale.

Positioning one vehicle at the entrance with two men on board to take care of any outside interference or any fleeing enemy, the lieutenant hurriedly split the rest of the operators into two demolition teams.

While one team destroyed all the enemy vehicles in the car park, the others were to deal with the office block.

There were three blocks of new prefabricated asbestos buildings, totalling nine offices in all, far more than they had anticipated. One block housed ZIPRA offices, another belonged to the South West Africa People's Organisation (SWAPO), and the third to the South African ANC.

The offices had not long been completed and the Rhodesian intelligence agencies had told the lieutenant that they would be empty. But the soldiers not only found them bulging with propaganda, but with desks, swivel chairs, maps on the walls, boxes and cabinets full of files, and a huge SWAPO flag gracing Liberation Centre.

Rich yanked open the filing cabinets to find an impressive amount of paperwork, all of it meticulously kept. It was obvious that strict office routine had been followed in the terror centre, and there was much that might prove useful to the Rhodesian and South African war effort.

But the pressure was really on now, and the limited time-frame precluded even a cursory search of the files. Even if they had the time, they did not have the necessary trucks to cart away such a wealth of paper work.

But destroying it was the next best thing. That way, ZIPRA, SWAPO and the ANC would not have it either.

With precision timing, the two teams quickly dealt with the offices. It was a slick operation, previously rehearsed so that they could move far and fast.

With one man at the front with an RPD for protection, the others in the demolition team followed closely behind. Second in line was the team commander – Rich Stannard or Billy Gardner. Swiftly they moved in to break a window in an office, a preliminary to sticking a two kilogram charge on the walls with *Wonder Glue*. Another man followed up to run out a long *Cordtex* ringmain . . . and the man behind him would connect it up.

It was a fluid motion and by the time the man at the back of the line had connected up the ringmain, the two team commanders had moved on to the next offices.

In the car park, the thirty-odd vehicles were being attended to by two other soldiers.

There were Land-Rovers, buses, station wagons, a truck filled with ammunition, Peugeots, Fiats, five-tonners and ten-tonners with crane attachments, and SWAPO vehicles that were about to be used to deploy trained insurgents to their drop-off point for infiltration into South West Africa (Namibia).

The two men had not expected to find so many vehicles, but had wisely taken along extra explosives, which they had made up in Kariba, and there were enough to take care of all the vehicles.

They slapped the *Wonder Glue* on to their charges, and while one man ran from vehicle to vehicle sticking the charges under the axles, on the engine block and under the differential, the other ran out a big ringmain from all the vehicles to the main initiation set.

Having finished connecting up the offices, Rich Stannard hurried to the armoury. It was located next to the burning ops room and it was imperative they deal with it before the blaze reached the vast quantities of weaponry.

Rich found a sergeant major already there. He had left his colleague in charge of the Sabre at the entrance while he went in search of a long-admired Russian pistol. But his luck was out that night and he had to be content with a holster.

By now, two other men joined them and the sergeant major remained to help place their charges in strategic positions. In addition, the enemy's own TNT was positioned where it could do the most harm.

Then the anxious voice of Major Dave Dodson waiting patiently by the round-about, came up on the radio to warn Rich Stannard and his team that they were running out of time.

By now however, the Liberation Centre task was all but finished. The sergeant major returned to take up his position in the Sabre at the entrance.

A huge ringmain led from the motor transport park; another connected the charges in the offices and the armoury . . . and a pre-cut piece of safety fuse with a five-minute burning time was to be used to blow all the targets up at once.

The voice of the commander came over the radio one more time to warn them to get out.

Suddenly, a white Peugeot car shot around the corner and unintentionally drove straight into the path of the Sabre parked at the entrance of Liberation Centre.

The car contained a member of the ZIPRA High Command, not that the Rhodesians knew that at the time.

The soldiers blasted away putting belt-after-belt of machingun fire into the car. The vehicle crashed to a halt. The windscreen was shattered. The driver's head was severed.

Above the roar of the machineguns, the other passengers could be heard screaming "Comrade, Comrade!" The SAS continued raking the enemy car until it resembled a sieve, and when the holes were later counted, there were 83.

Seconds after the machineguns opened up, Rich Stannard lit the safety fuse on the ringmain connecting the offices and armoury, and a corporal lit his fuse on the car park ringmain. Then they dashed for their own vehicles.

But Rich had just one more job to do before leaving Liberation Centre.

Sprinting to the middle of the compound, he yanked down the Zambian flag and darted off with his much-prized capture.

The ops room was still blazing furiously as they roared down the road at high speed, putting as much distance between themselves and the forthcoming blast. Down the unlit streets they raced, fighting against time to meet up with the others just beyond the roundabout.

The sirens wailed. Lusaka knew there was more to come.

At the roundabout, the men who had not long ago blasted Nkomo's personal command centre off the face of the earth, leaned back in their vehicles and chatted. Some smoked. The atmosphere was fairly relaxed. Not that they were out of the woods yet.

The commander glanced at his watch once again. Time was getting on.

The rumble of heavy vehicle movement reached them across the early morning. Was that the Zambian Army reacting? Would Rich Stannard's escape route be blocked?

But they saw no sign. Then the two speeding SAS Sabres came into sight. Rich and his men had resisted the temptation to have a quick blast at the glass skyscraper. Time had not been on their side that night.

A mere twenty minutes had elapsed since Rich Stannard and his team had fired their first shots and the overall commander was anxious to know if it had been long enough to complete their task. "What a question," the tired, but smiling lieutenant thought, but assured him all was well.

Quickly, they reorganised, spreading their kit out evenly among the five remaining vehicles.

Then they waited for the explosion.

A huge orange mushroom billowed up into the sky, followed five seconds later by an enormous thunderclap which rumbled over the capital.

"Just check that!" one impressed soldier exclaimed as Liberation Centre went up, plus all three office blocks, all the vehicles, the armoury, the security walls, nearby houses and parts of the road, the entire complex being flattened with the help of ZIPRA's own weaponry.

When the dust finally settled and the fire burned itself out, all that was left was a massive crater marking the spot where the armoury had once been.

A year later, after the war had ended, Rich Stannard drove past the spot where Liberation Centre had stood to find it being rebuilt. As he went past, he waved at the men putting the roof on the centre and they waved back. He couldn't help thinking how ironic life was sometimes.

By now the Zambians had had enough. The sirens were still wailing out their urgent messages as the civilians came streaming out of the homes, many still in their nightclothes, their suitcases and chattels stacked high on their heads, their bleary-eyed children trailing behind them.

They were frightened and confused about the events that night and ignored the Rhodesians, as they kept their heads down and bounded through the bush near the SAS. All they knew was that they had to get out of town and fast.

The men responsible for all their troubles were also leaving the capital. It was 04h00 and soon it would be light enough for them to be seen by anyone on the look-out for them.

But on the long journey south, there was no one to stop them. The nearest they got to potential trouble was when they saw police talking to the driver of the Zambian Army Land-Rover they had seen on their infiltration. But it seemed that they had nothing more serious on their mind than seeking out drunken drivers.

The Zambian Army knew that Rhodesian troops dressed in "Zambian camouflage" and driving Land-Rovers were responsible, and they talked of manning roadblocks to cut off the attackers. But it never happened.

The SAS strike force meanwhile were making their way southwards. Ahead lay the Kafue bridge – the last real obstacle. If they were prevented from crossing, they planned to destroy their vehicles, then set off on foot, sorting out their exfiltration later.

But when they stopped to pick up the small observation party monitoring the bridge, there was nothing to report. There was no one to bar the way and the only person they saw was a rather sleepy sentry. As before, they experienced a wonderful feeling of relief as they sped over the bridge. Now all they had to worry about were the Zambian MiGs and a possible army ambush group.

They hit the dirt road at 05h50 and continued on their way uneventfully passing villages. It was getting light and now and then they waved to the locals. After the rigours of the night and the effects of perspiration, most of the camouflage cream had come off, so there could be no mistaking the travellers for Zambian Army.

The astonished locals did a quick double-take and when they realised the soldiers harboured no aggressive intentions towards them, waved back at the Rhodesians.

As dawn broke over Lusaka, curious Zambians were driving to inspect the damage at Nkomo's house, and by 07h00, a large crowd had gathered outside the burned-out shell opposite the State President's home, only to be kept at bay by troops. The roof of the building had long ago fallen in.

An hour later, the SAS reached the bad dirt road. By now, most men were feeling totally exhausted and medic Bruce Langley came to their aid with large bottles of anti-fatigue tonic.

By 10h00, they cut a landing zone and called in the choppers to take out the three wounded men. The commander was glad to get rid of them as they were beginning to suffer on the bad bumpy road.

The convoy continued on its way, eventually arriving at a particularly bad stretch of road where the SAS's problems were multiplied by the already churned mud. It was here that Lieutenant Phil Brooke and his team had been abandoned with their broken-down vehicle.

"How'd it go?" they enquired eagerly, disappointed at not having made the trip themselves, but anxious to learn the outcome. The six men were told of the happenings in Lusaka a few hours before and Rich Stannard showed off his captured flag.

The SAS attempted to drive the vehicles through the mud but finally had to resort to manpower, with one man driving and the others up to their knees in mud.

The war and the Zambian MiGs were forgotten as everyone slogged it out in the ever-worsening quagmire. Rich Stannard's vehicle, *Rubber Duck*, was the only one that made it without getting stuck. *Petrol Paul's* vehicle broke down completely and the steering rod broke.

By now the men were totally exhausted, despite much guzzling of anti-fatigue tonic. The commander realised there was a chance of saving the vehicle, but they were too tired and there was the very real danger of the MiGs being scrambled to search for them.

Besides, there was still the possibility of a Zambian Army company waiting for them along their exfiltration route. They had seen no sign of them on the way in, but they were not prepared to take any chances, and the commander decided to destroy *Petrol Paul's* vehicle. But they decided against destroying Phil Brooke's Sabre and within 500 metres of towing it down the road, the engine roared into life. Knowing he could have made the trip to Lusaka after all, Phil Brooke was not impressed.

Unbeknown to the weary men, a Zambian MiG had been deployed to search for them, but when it was pointed out to the pilot he was heading the wrong way and had to go in the opposite direction, he was heard to reply: "No, no. It is *not* my job!" And with that, he returned to base.

The Zambians however had not linked the earlier sighting of the *Sea Lion* with the raid and three days later deployed the MiGs to the wrong end of the lake where they proceeded to attack a Zambian Army convoy.

Eighteen hours after *Sea Lion* had delivered them to the Zambian shore, they arrived back at the beachhead. It was midday and much had happened in those eighteen hours. Despite their exhaustion they were all excited and as they waited for the ferry to come and collect them, they told the beach party of the events in Lusaka.

The beach party had good reason to feel pleased with themselves, too. They had done a good job and reported that their only experience had been when a Zambian police boat had come roaring along. The Zambians saw them protecting the beach, then disappeared at high speed, never to be seen again.

Soon the ferry could be seen coming to take them home. The ramp came down and the vehicles drove on. The ferry cast off immediately and away they went, soon enjoying a welcoming cup of tea. The pick-up had taken place in broad daylight, but there had been no one around to stop them.

Someone had stashed six bottles of rum away for their journey home but by the time they were remembered and brought out to lace their tea, some of the men had fallen asleep. Others recall doing justice to a couple of cups of the special brew.

Then came the fantastic sight of a Rhodesian helicopter. It hovered above the ferry and lowered a crate of beers which were consumed with great delight by those troops still battling to keep awake. Then at last, the Rhodesian shore.

The troops drove off, the vehicles were resprayed, and the operators returned to Salisbury by road together with a little rubber duck which had gone all the way to Lusaka and back. The operation was finally over and they looked forward to reading about it in the following day's papers. Not of course that the press would get to know all the fascinating details of one of the most dramatic raids of the war.

Major Dave Dodson boarded a boat and hurried to Kariba where he climbed into a helicopter. He was taken to Kariba Heights and from there by car to the airport. Within two hours of arriving in Rhodesia, he was reporting back to the ComOps planners and intelligence chiefs. It had been a long worrying night for them, too, and there was much for the SAS officer to tell.

In Britain meanwhile, the Foreign Office deplored the attack, which was also condemned by the UN Secretary General, Dr Kurt Waldheim.

Nkomo, humiliated before the delegates of the Afro-Asian Peoples' Solidarity Organisation conference meeting in Lusaka – he had been attending their opening session at the time of the strike – vowed to take his revenge.

Reported to be "shaken but determined," he told hundreds of people standing outside the shell of his home: "I can assure you the Patriotic Front is going to punish these savages."

He said that he had been home at the time of the raid and had escaped through a toilet window. "I had to get out as best I could, " he explained.

At a press conference in Salisbury, General Walls commented: "I find it hilarious to think of him escaping through a lavatory window – that alone would have caused the damage." As he spoke, Rhodesian war planes were blasting ZIPRA's conventional terror camp at Mulungushi for the third time that week.

"I had to get out as best I could," - Joshua Nkomo

The Zambian ground raid had been part of a strategy to ensure the safety of voters, General Walls told the world. In the face of the Patriotic Front's threat to take Rhodesia by force, the military had to take the necessary action against those who did not take up Rhodesia's amnesty offer.

"Some of our resources have to be used offensively. We have a job to do. We can't sit back and see people killed and maimed," he said.

The SAS thought it had just been bad luck Nkomo had not been at home. It would be the nearest the Rhodesians would come to assassinating Nkomo. For it was the last attempt on his life, and the ZIPRA leader later moved to Ndola.

But was it bad luck? The SAS had not got their man for the very simple reason he had been tipped off. That was why the guard had been increased.

A voice over the telephone had told of the impending attack 12 hours before the SAS had struck. Nkomo, his number two and Dumiso Dabengwa told the ComOps hierarchy this after the war.

Even more amazing, the initial telephone call had been made from ComOps building itself where a well-placed British agent was employed. The man responsible had telephoned British officials in Lusaka, who had passed on the message to Nkomo.

The ComOps spy is alleged to have deliberately fed Prime Minister Ian Smith and security chiefs inaccurate and misleading information to further the ends of the British. According to some sources, much information he gave them was watered down. (Security chiefs eventually worked out where the spy leaks were coming from and disinformation was in turn fed to him. But unearthing a spy is a lengthy process and concrete evidence hard to get.)

Joshua Nkomo, who said in his own book that the security forces missed him by an hour, was never again seen wearing his general's uniform, which had hung in his bedroom on the night of the raid.

As a result of the ground strike, President Kenneth Kaunda imposed a curfew in the border regions. An appeal was made for all able-bodied men with military training to report for army duty in an attempt to boost Zambia's 8 000-strong army.

In the event, the ZIPRA invasion did not take place prior to the elections as initially thought. Nkomo had not however cancelled his plans. ZANLA did not cause too much trouble either and the five-day one-man-one-vote elections were enormously successful, bringing in moderate Bishop Abel Muzorewa as the country's first black Prime Minister and Minister of Defence.

Never had a white tribe worked so hard to transfer power to blacks.

Some 64,45 percent of the country's electorate had voted. What now of the black nationalists' claims that they were fighting for the country's liberation? Could the war be seen in terms of a black-white confrontation any longer?

Outgoing Prime Minister Ian Smith – soon to become Minister Without Portfolio of the new State of Zimbabwe Rhodesia – now asked the world: "What more do you want us to do?"

Operation Dinky, April 13, 1979

For more than a year, there was one subject that was guaranteed to raise temperatures at ComOps . . . and that was the Kazangula ferry, the Zambian-owned civilian craft which operated between Kazangula in Zambia and Botswana, plying the four-nation border point of Zambia/Botswana/Rhodesia and South West Africa (Namibia).

Apart from the railway through Rhodesia, the ferry was Zambia's only ground link with the south. Not only did it ferry travellers but it was a vital trade link between

South Africa and her northern neighbours, carrying much-needed commodities between the south and Zambia, Malawi, Zaire and beyond.

But, was it also being used for more sinister activities?

Was it being used as an instrument by ZIPRA to wage war against Rhodesia? Was it being used to ferry war materials? And was it being used to transport vast numbers of ZIPRA from Zambia to Botswana, thereby affording them easy and unhindered access to the south from where they moved into Rhodesia?

The security forces had been putting pressure on ZIPRA's usual entry routes across the "horn" of Rhodesia – the north-western reaches of the country – and since then ZIPRA had indeed been using the Kazangula ferry to get from Zambia to Botswana. Once in the safe haven of Botswana, they had an easy and uninterrupted journey south in ZIPRA trucks before nipping across the long arid international boundary into their support area in Matabeleland.

But the point was, did Zambia and Botswana know about it and condone the use of the *civilian* ferry to wage a *military* fight?

Available intelligence led ComOps people to believe Zambia did not want an economic confrontation. Zambia's president, Kenneth Kaunda knew that should the ferry be used to transport men and arms, the Rhodesians would destroy it. His country and those black states around him could not afford that . . . and he had apparently refused permission for ZIPRA to use the ferry.

The Botswana Government had no knowledge themselves that the ferry was being used to transport men and materials, although they were put in the picture by the Rhodesians.

The doubts still persisted however, and the Kazangula ferry had become a hotly-debated issue at ComOps for many long months. And while the hierarchy thrashed out the problem, the SAS was called in to look at the ferry as a target.

While the ComOps military planners felt that the ferry could be blown off the face of the earth with a couple of rockets from a pair of Hunters which carried no risk to life or limb, the politicians considered that a somewhat *blatant* act.

If it had to be done, they argued, it had to be done clandestinely, so that no one could prove who did it!

Captain Colin Willis, the "B" Squadron commander, was tasked to work on a feasibility study to destroy the ferry. It was to prove a frustrating experience, for no sooner had he worked out a plan than the mission was postponed.

One idea was to destroy the ferry while it was in Zambia. An eight-man SAS team had infiltrated across the Zambezi under cover of darkness to learn the size and construction, the speed and depth of the river and the number of guards.

Then, as silently as they had entered Zambia, so they slipped back across the small strip of water separating the two countries.

They returned to their base at Victoria Falls to work out a plan. This was that six men would swim to the ferry carrying explosives in submerged motor car tubes.

They would inflate the tubes under the ferry forcing the explosive charges against the craft where they would be secured. A series of time pencils set to detonate in the early hours of the morning would serve as the initiation.

It was a feasible plan, but never to be tried . . . for once again the operation was called off and they were recalled to Salisbury.

Colin Willis and his "B" Squadron operators began to think they would never get to grips with the ferry.

But while "B" Squadron were out of the picture, at least for the time being, other security forces were giving the ferry some concentrated attention.

Trackers from one of the independent companies, SAS and Selous Scout callsigns were putting up with many privations in an attempt to build up a case against ZIPRA. For weeks at a time they lurked along the banks of the Zambezi and perched precariously up trees, faithfully recording from their spy nests the makes of vehicles and number plates and the movement of men, until eventually, the evidence began to stack up.

Groups of men, seen talking to Zambian soldiers would run on to the ferry just as it left, while their Zambian friends would monitor the southern bank through their binoculars to make sure they arrived undetected.

Then Rhodesian Special Branch learned that ZIPRA had been secretly transporting landmines and brand new weapons over on the ferry in 200-litre fuel drums. The rifles were sealed in the drums, petrol was poured on the top and a lid put on. In the event of the lid being removed, all that was visible was petrol. Once in Botswana, the fuel drums and their hidden cargoes were buried in the ground outside Francistown.

It was the perfect plan. The only snag was that the Rhodesians found the cache and recovered all the weapons. Worried that the Botswana Government had found their weapons and landmines, ZIPRA changed tactics and transported their weaponry in false bottoms built into a couple of civilian trucks that regularly travelled to and fro on Kazangula ferry.

At the same time, Special Branch was monitoring all the telephone calls between ZIPRA's Lusaka office and those in Francistown in Botswana. The Lusaka office would give the Francistown representative the code word – which the Rhodesian Special Branch eavesdroppers knew – that they were sending another truck down with a hidden cargo of arms.

Eventually, definite evidence began to trickle in that in addition to the arms that were being shipped, ZIPRA personnel, intelligence agents and hierarchy, were openly using the ferry.

The Rhodesians now had all the proof they needed. Yet for the military planners it was still not a clear-cut matter. They realised only too well that to destroy the ferry would have economic and political effects throughout Africa and the repercussions had to be very carefully weighed up.

Not only would the destruction of this crucial trade link seriously affect black states, but it would also hit friends in the south – the South African exporters and hauliers.

Long and involved discussions followed with the South African authorities, but in the end, the planners decided that all the arguments against destroying the ferry were secondary to dealing with such a very definite ZIPRA threat. Particularly so, at a time when ZIPRA were planning to invade Rhodesia.

Repeated diplomatic representations to both Zambia and Botswana had failed to halt the flow of men and material. The warnings of drastic military action had fallen on deaf ears. Now it was time for action and they must suffer the consequences.

The long on/off operation was finally given the green light. A plan to plant a remote-controlled device on board the offending trucks was seriously considered, then abandoned ... and Colin Willis and his "B" Squadron men were at long last given the mission.

They had now come up with another plan, the brain-child of Captain Pete Fritz.

He suggested that instead of destroying the ferry on the Zambian side, where it carried all the risks of being guarded day and night, they should deal with it while it was on the Botswanan side of the river.

Although there was a Botswana Defence Force presence in the vicinity of the docking area, the ferry itself was not guarded.

Not only that, but the ferry was closer to Rhodesia than the Zambian docking point ... and Botswana was easier to infiltrate than Zambia. The boundary dividing Rhodesia from Botswana was merely an old dilapidated fence, a simple enough hurdle compared to the hazards of canoeing across an open river.

The beauty of the plan, too, was that the op would cause friction between Botswana and Zambia – as well as demonstrate that Rhodesia meant business.

The SAS decided to destroy the ferry with the aid of an RAD, a radio activated device, a mechanism capable of setting off a charge from a distance of up to four kilometres (2,5 miles) on the ground and 15 kilometres (nine miles) from the air. They had been experimenting with a much more sophisticated device than previous RADs and several had been made up especially to suit the needs of special forces.

Territorial officer, Lieutenant Laurie Walters had helped design the latest RAD in collaboration with colleagues at the civilian company where he worked, and Laurie with his SAS experience had advised what was needed in an operational role.

The device comprised a transmitter/radio unit, which was to remain at the side of the ground commander; and a separate receiver station, which in turn was to be connected up by wires to the actual charge itself.

The charge was to be command-detonated by pressing a button on the ground commander's transmitter unit; thus the signal setting off the explosion would pass from the transmitter ... to the separate receiver station which would be no more than 150 metres from the target ... and then on to an electric detonator set into the charge itself.

The charge was tailor-made to suit the needs of the ferry task. It consisted of a total of 110 kilograms (242 lbs) of explosive, the bulk of it being contained inside a large washing-up bowl. It was boosted with two PVC tubes which had been cut in half, then filled with explosives. Pentolite was used instead of plastic explosives; certainly not an ideal explosive for the military as a bullet could set if off, but easier to get hold of in sanctions-hit Rhodesia. It was a lot cheaper, too, specially as such a vast amount was needed.

The SAS planned that the exact method of the destruction should remain a mystery. After the ferry had blown, a self-destructing mechanism built into the RAD would be activated and the receiver would go up in a puff of smoke – leaving nothing behind to give the game away.

At the end of March, "B" Squadron moved up to Victoria Falls to await the final clearance for the mission.

As always, intelligence was the key to a successful outcome, and a reconnaissance team was sent on a night-time mission to learn the details of the nearby terrain and ensure the ferry only docked in one place.

The final plan called for the washing-up bowl containing the charges to be placed at the end of the concrete slipway in the water, which would be an ideal setting for an explosion. Surrounded by concrete and water, the blast would only have one way to go – straight up through the ferry.

But getting such a vast amount of explosives down to the water's edge was going to be a problem. Then Pete Fritz came up with another idea.

He suggested that they strap the explosives on to a bicycle. It would be far easier than man-handling them, he argued. Not only that, but bicycle tracks left in that neck of the woods were common and in no way suspicious.

His plan was accepted and a bicycle was specially modified to take the charges.

ComOps finally gave their official blessing and at 20h00 on April 12, a dozen SAS men, led by Pete Fritz, loaded the charges, their machineguns, mortars and the specially-modified bicycle on to two trucks.

Commander Colin Willis wished them well, and they moved off from their base near Victoria Falls on their way to the Rhodesia/Botswana border.

There was a good moon that night and they turned off their lights on the last stretch of their journey. Once over the crest of the final hill, they cut their engines and freewheeled down to the border.

Silently they unloaded their equipment, the washing-up bowl crammed with the charges and the all-important radio-activated device.

Four men were to remain with the vehicles to man the machineguns and mortars and provide protection for the other operators if things turned nasty.

The others helped Corporal *Mitch* strap the explosives on to the bicycle. Cautiously he set off, pushing his precious and sensitive cargo on its journey down towards the water's edge, while the others carried the ancillary equipment.

Their travels that night were taking them virtually along the border fence itself. The road was a raised embankment which ran through a marshy floodplain. As they carefully picked their way along in the moonlight, game fed near the embankment undisturbed by the silent, shadowy figures.

It was a peacefully calm night in Southern Africa. The animals quietly munched the vegetation. And the bicycle slowly rolled on its way . . .

Suddenly, the tranquility was broken by a deafening roar that stopped the soldiers dead in their tracks. For a moment the commotion had them mystified.

Then, thundering across the marsh came a stampeding herd of buffaloes. The soldiers watched in amazement as hundreds crashed on their way, splashing and clattering like a great tornado and leaving a flattened trail in their wake.

The din very soon became a muffled noise in the distance; then the herd was gone . . .

For a few moments the SAS didn't dare move. Would the noise alert the Botswana Defence Force men, thought to be on the other side of the border fence and a mere 200 metres away?

But there was no reaction; no one came to investigate, and they realised that such an event was probably a common occurrence. They breathed easy again and continued on their way uneventfully, soon arriving at a spot in the treeline next to the border fence.

There was not one Botswanan to be seen and Lieutenant Laurie Walters and Corporal Ron Bracchi stepped unnoticed through the fence separating the two countries. They began to search for a good vantage point to set up the command post from where the blast would be detonated with the transmitter/radio. They looked at every available angle and eventually settled on a suitable spot about 130 metres back from the slipway and some six metres from the fence on the Rhodesian side of the border.

They could not have found a better position. Standing, they would be able to see the ferry as it made its way over the Zambezi from the Zambian docking area. Sitting, a clump of bushes would provide reasonable cover.

Lieutenant Walters and his team of two corporals set up the radio/transmitter unit and put up a small aerial at their command post.

It was now Captain Pete Fritz's turn to cross the border and he led the rest of the party down to the slipway.

Three men kept a look-out while Lieutenant Mike Rich and Corporal *Mitch* removed the explosives from the bicycle and carefully carried them into the water. Then, ever-so-gingerly, they lowered the massive charge, complete with its washing-up bowl, in the middle of the ferry slipway.

They took the wires to an anthill twenty metres from the slipway and hid the receiver station among the reeds, but above the water.

They radioed back to the command station, then with Lieutenant Laurie Walters operating his transmitter, they carried out three trials to make sure the RAD was working properly. Each time a small light came on at the receiver station hidden among the reeds.

The circuit was working; there was no need to worry.

The wires were connected, the lid of the camouflage-painted box housing the receiver was put in place and further camouflaged with leaves to add to the deception.

Then the demolition team returned across the border fence to Rhodesia, taking the bicycle with them. Captain Fritz stayed with the small team of men in the command post . . . and the others returned to the protection party who fortunately had not been needed after all, and they all moved back a safe distance to the crest of the hill.

Finally, Friday 13th arrived bright and clear. Up in Lusaka the "C" Squadron operators had already smashed Nkomo's personal command post, flattened the Liberation Centre and shattered ZIPRA morale. Maybe the "B" Squadron men would be able to round off the SAS's run of military successes against ZIPRA that Easter weekend?

Excitement was mounting in the command post down at the border, each man longing for the time when the target would cross over to Botswana.

Although they couldn't see the ferry from their hiding place among the bushes, the sounds of shouting, banging and clinking of spanners coming from the Zambian bank indicated that all was not well with the pontoon.

If only it could be fixed for just one last trip across the Zambezi.

At about 07h00, the first vehicles began arriving at the Botswana docking area.

At Spray View private airfield at Victoria Falls, meanwhile, the SAS squadron commander was climbing aboard a Lynx. Colin Willis and the pilot were to orbit north of the ferry in Zambian airspace. By Colin's side was a transmitter/radio unit similar to the one being used by the ground troops. In the unlikely event of something going wrong down at the command post, Colin would still be able to activate the charges with his back-up transmitter.

Meanwhile, the queue of cars on the Botswanan side of the river was growing longer. The ferry had still not been fixed and the motorists were growing impatient.

One businessman in a hurry to get over to Zambia was bribing his way up to the front of the queue. Watching the transactions from the cover of the bushes, the SAS saw him pass banknotes to some of the truck drivers, and they followed his progress as he gradually edged his way nearer to the slipway.

But there was still no sign of the ferry.

Finally at 10h00, two hours behind schedule, the ferry's engines started up. The Rhodesian soldiers and the impatient drivers breathed a sigh of relief, although for very different reasons.

In the bushes by the international boundary separating Rhodesia from Botswana, the tension was mounting as the ferry came into view. It was carrying two vehicles, one a jeep with a white family of three children and their parents.

The SAS's orders had been to destroy the ferry with the minimum loss of life. But as the ferry moved closer to the docking site, the queue of cars and trucks began edging towards the slipway. The SAS realised that if they did not press their fire button at precisely the right moment, the impatient Botswanan drivers and their passengers would be on the pontoon as soon as the Zambian vehicles were off.

The ferry pulled alongside. The truck with the children in got clear of the 110 kilograms of pentolite hidden beneath them. Immediately, the column of impatient drivers who had been despairing of ever getting to Zambia that day, began moving forwards.

"*Fire!*" Pete Fritz ordered.

Lieutenant Walters switched to the correct channel and pressed the firing button. There was a momentary delay while the signal passed from the transmitter by his side to the receiver station hidden among the reeds near the slipway.

"*Fire!*" repeated an anxious Pete Fritz urgently, during the delay, concerned about the danger to the motorists ... but the message was already on its way.

As the explosion went off with devastating effect and the earth trembled, an SAS corporal had his camera at the ready to record the severing of the vital ZIPRA infiltration route.

Steel, concrete and water shot into the air as the massive explosion tore the ferry completely in half, spraying enormous chunks of debris in all directions. A piece of plate screamed over the heads of the detonation party ... and back up the crest of the hill the rest of the "B" Squadron operators saw a jet of water shoot 150 metres into the air.

One half of the ferry was blown right out of the water and landed on the bank. The rear half of the ferry remained afloat for a while before settling into a muddy, oily patch at the slipway. Everywhere there was pandemonium.

Animals were stampeding all over the place. People were screaming. Metal rained from the skies and as it clattered down, the long queue of drivers, waiting for so long to get on the ferry, suddenly thought better of the idea and roared off back down the road.

In the bushes, on the Rhodesian side of the border, Lieutenant Laurie Walters turned his transmitter switch to another channel and pressed the firing button.

Out among the reeds near the torn-apart slipway, there was a secondary explosion as the receiver station self-destructed, blowing all evidence of how the ferry had been sabotaged. No one heard it, except the SAS who had been expecting the explosion and were able to isolate the sounds. Everyone else was far too interested in getting away. Besides, their ears were still ringing from the initial blast.

Quickly the "B" Squadron men dismantled their aerial, gathered up their belongings and headed back up the hill to rejoin the rest of their party.

ZIPRA's tactic of sneaking their men and materials across into Botswana for a trouble-free journey to Rhodesia had been blown sky high. They were left with no other option but to travel across "the horn" of Rhodesia, a hazardous route dotted with Rhodesian security forces ever-eager to take them on.

As predicted, both Botswana and Zambia blamed each other for not properly looking after the ferry. Zambia blamed Botswana for allowing the Rhodesians to destroy the ferry in Botswana. Botswana countered and accused Zambia of allowing a spy to place a bomb on the ferry while it had been over in Zambian waters.

Zambia thereafter promised that the ferry would be used only for commercial purposes. But the Rhodesians did not believe them and ComOps made it clear they would blow up any replacement pontoon.

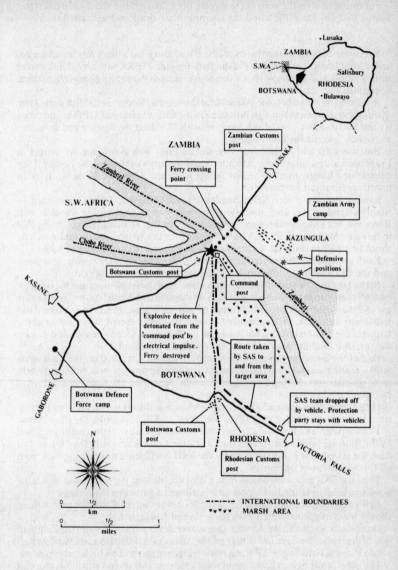

Operation *Dinky:* A four-nation border point, scene of the SAS's attack on the Kazangula ferry operating between Zambia and Botswana

303

Following hard on the heels of the successful Lusaka ground attacks as it did, it had been a bad day for ZIPRA and the countries that aided and succoured them.

* * *

Yet in one of those strange twists of fate, it had also been a black day for others not so far from home. For not only did the ferry provide ZIPRA with a vital link to and from Zambia and Botswana, but it was also crucial to the Selous Scouts clandestine operations into Zambia.

By mid-1978, it had become essential for the security forces to establish some form of transport movement through Botswana and Zambia to combat ZIPRA . . . to set up a route into Zambia . . . establish a spy network . . . collect intelligence and to be able to "snatch" people for information.

Bulawayo SB had at that time virtually no links with Botswana, no sources in Francistown, and no ready access into Botswana anywhere along the border. They complained bitterly that the Selous Scouts had ruined their whole network by an abortive raid into Francistown.

Special Branch officer Keith Samler, co-ordinating the Scouts operations in Matabeleland at the time, discussed the matter of re-establishing the link with Botswana, but Bulawayo SB were terribly indignant that he should suggest being able to do something which, firstly, had been ruined by the Scouts, and secondly, that he should be able to do what they had failed at. There was much bitter debate.

Keith approached the Selous Scouts commander, Ron Reid-Daly, with the scheme and the CO was very enthusiastic and offered men and total support.

Both of the men provided by Reid-Daly – one a territorial member and the other an ex-SAS man – went on heavy duty vehicle driving courses. Keith Samler arranged the ex-SAS man a job with a trucking company and his first assignment was a round trip to Malawi and back. He experienced no real problems except for a beating at the hands of the Zambian Army, but it was par for the course for any new white driver on the run. An African heavy vehicle driver was also recruited.

One of the Scouts involved in the transport scheme – it relied on the Kazangula ferry – made many visits to the Botswanan capital, setting up shop, bribing government officials and making well-placed contacts. He rented a flat and became part of the scenery.

His spying activities were productive and one of his drinking friends was a somewhat talkative member of the ZIPRA hierarchy . . . Elliot Sibanda, *The Black Swine*.

The transport and Botswana spying link became operative at the end of 1978, and by the time the SAS began to turn their attention to the Kazangula ferry for the last time, the system was in full swing and some good intelligence was coming back from all three undercover operatives.

Then the SAS, following orders from ComOps, blew up the ferry – and with it the Scouts carefully planned transport and intelligence gathering operations.

Keith Samler and other members of the team were incredulous that such a thing should have happened and it gave them several headaches.

One Selous Scout and the African undercover driver were held up on the Zambian side of the border for days and in the end, the African was forced to swim the Zambezi above Victoria Falls to give SB some hot intelligence gleaned on his latest trip north.

The other white Selous Scout agent was beaten up and several situations cropped up exposing everybody involved to unnecessary danger.

There were some angry men around that Easter weekend . . . and they were not all ZIPRA either. The destruction of the Kazangula ferry was to remain a hotly debated issue in some quarters just as it had before the SAS sent it on its final journey.

Operation Carpet, June 26, 1979

Nkomo's Russian advisers, who had convinced him to put his army on a much more conventional footing, had also been turning their attention to ZIPRA's intelligence department, the Department of National Security and Order (NSO), and were unimpressed by what they found.

The Soviets were highly critical of the NSO's operations and considered them to be totally ineffective. ZIPRA was told they could not hope for any success unless they developed an accurate intelligence picture.

Nkomo listened to his Russian friends once more and the NSO was given a complete overhaul. As a direct result of the Soviet's influence, the department was expected to produce much more tangible results, which were in turn expected to improve ZIPRA's overall effectiveness.

Several agents were subsequently infiltrated into Rhodesia, including two women with British passports who travelled via Botswana. Ten other women were sent to Kitwe in Zambia for counter-intelligence duties before travelling to Botswana "refugee" camps acting as "screeners" to vet potential insurgents and seek out Rhodesian Special Branch spies.

The NSO began training their own military and civil police and the first civil courses were held at the Zambian training school while military courses were held in East Germany and Russia.

The NSO intelligence officers took their duties very seriously and were hated by the ZIPRA rank and file. They saw spies behind every tree and anyone suspected of treachery was severely beaten, even tortured.

The men running the NSO had all been trained by the KGB in Moscow ... and the man in charge, Dumiso Dabengwa, was allegedly a KGB colonel.

Dabengwa, the second most important person in ZIPRA, was a personal confidante of Joshua Nkomo, briefing *The Fat Man* daily when he was in Lusaka. He even described himself as "Rhodesia's Public Enemy No. 2."

Dabengwa received his orders directly from Nkomo and was kept aware of all military operations, planning and strategy being undertaken by ZIPRA.

He ran a number of agents throughout the globe, including some whites in Europe.

Assistant Director of Intelligence Victor Mlambo also employed a number of white agents in Zambia, as well as members of communist agencies in the UK.

ZIPRA's overseas representatives based in external offices around the world sent their intelligence to NSO, which also worked closely with the intelligence department of the South African ANC, also said to have a number of influential European sympathisers.

There was liaison with Soviet and East German intelligence, and NSO was in constant contact with its own ZIPRA intelligence agents in training in Russia.

Five of the top people in the ZIPRA intelligence organisation not only worked but slept at the NSO headquarters, which housed material of immense importance. All the files, including top secret documents detailing agents and their operations, as well as ZIPRA's military operations, were kept there. Plans for urban operations and reports from the war front were filed there, too.

Thus all the intelligence vital to ZIPRA's war effort, and all the people in on the secrets, were concentrated under one roof.

From an intelligence point of view, it was clearly the most important ZIPRA building in Zambia ... and the hierarchy kept the whereabouts of the headquarters a closely-guarded secret.

It was called *The Vatican* ... a holy place because no one but key personnel was allowed in.

So important was it that the entrance was kept padlocked and the main gate was hidden from prying eyes by a hessian screen. The entire complex was surrounded by a two-metre high security fence, which was topped with three-strand barbed wire. There was also a guard system.

The ZIPRA capture *The Black Swine*, who had proved such a useful source of intelligence to the Rhodesians, had put SB in the picture about *The Vatican*. "Hey, why don't we go and take the NSO out?" he had suggested one day.

It was the first SB had heard of the place, and now they were in on the secret it was essential that action be taken.

But first they had to pinpoint *The Vatican*. Initially, all *The Black Swine* could remember was that it was in the middle of an exclusive residential area in the north of the Zambian capital where overseas diplomats and ambassadors had their official residences.

To make matters worse, it had been many months since he had been to *The Vatican* and anything might have happened in the interim. The place might have changed beyond all recognition. The NSO might even have been moved.

Many fruitless hours were spent poring over all the available maps and aerial photgraphs of Lusaka. Then, one day as he was driving an SB officer home, *The Black Swine* remembered that the NSO was in Lutuba Road, Roma Township, ten kilometres (six miles) to the north-east of the city centre.

And that was that. Another dramatic raid was about to take place. The Rhodesians were breaking all the rules ... the intelligence, the maps and the photographs were all old.

Any other country would have insisted on up-to-the-minute intelligence before contemplating such an operation so far from home.

But on the importance of the place alone, it was decided to mount an extremely daring raid to *take out* the headquarters. Once again it would mean going 200 kilometres (124 miles) into the heart of the Zambian capital with all the attendant risks.

Such a mission, far from home with an army, air force, SAM-7 and even Rapier threat, was fraught with danger. A thousand things could go wrong.

Perhaps the Zambians would be quicker to react than they had been during the Easter raid into their capital? They certainly ought to be more on their toes.

The plan was to surround the headquarters and take the intelligence VIPs by surprise. They would then fight their way into the intelligence HQ neutralising all resistance.

Then, using a loud hailer, *The Black Swine* would call out to the ZIPRA hierarchy and get them to surrender.

The first prize was to capture alive the elusive Dumiso Dabengwa, head of the NSO. Second prize was Victor Mlambo, assistant director of intelligence, and third prize, Gordon Butshe, assistant director of counter intelligence and security.

The Rhodesians were hoping against hope that they would be able to take home all three. It was strongly felt that given the chance, they would all surrender.

If they did not, they would have to be eliminated.

Either way, the inter-city raiders would not be returning home empty-handed. They planned to recover all the important intelligence documents and top secret records obtainable.

The entire complex was to be set alight and destroyed . . . and they would be off and away before the terrorists knew what had hit them, and before the element of surprise had been lost.

It would involve being on the ground for some considerable time . . . long enough for the MiGs to be scrambled and the Zambian Army to react. Speed would be of the essence.

The mission, codenamed Operation *Carpet,* was given to "C" Squadron, the squadron that had carried out the daring Operation *Bastille* on Nkomo's house. "C" squadron commander, Captain Martin Pearse, was to be the tactical commander, and the CO, Lieutenant-Colonel Garth Barrett, was to be the overall ground commander.

Once again, the all-important method of entry into the heart of Lusaka was examined and Martin drew up a long list of possibilities.

Should they use a pantechnicon? During Operation *Bastille,* Martin had noticed pantechnicons parked along the outskirts of Lusaka and it was obvious that no one would give them a second thought. Perhaps they could parachute in, take motor bikes with them, meet a pantechnicon driven by an agent, park the truck in Lusaka, travel to the target on motor bikes, then afterwards, put them back in the truck and drive out of town?

Perhaps they could hijack private transport . . . or perhaps try the Sabre trick again? An agent parked nearby in a truck could provide back-up support; then again, maybe the helicopters could pick them up after the raid?

While the headquarters was bang in the middle of a residential suburb, it did have in its favour the fact that it was on flat ground and was on an isolated plot with vacant one-acre plots on two sides. And in the end, it was decided that if it was feasible, the troops would be ferried in four Bell 205 helicopters, putting them down right next to the security fence.

The Bells would be ideal. The longhaul helicopters meant that targets once out of helicopter range were now accessible. Lusaka was now a mere two-hour hop from the border.

And the far larger load capacity of the Bells greatly assisted external operations as they could carry almost four times the load of the Alouettes.

Squadron Leader Ted Lunt, a much-admired pilot and the OC of 8 Squadron, the Bell Squadron, received a telephone call a few weeks before the operation was mounted, asking him to pop over to Kabrit to chat to SAS CO Garth Barrett and the lads as they had a few questions they wanted to put to him.

Asked if it was feasible to land troops with total surprise at first light in Roma suburb, the squadron leader said that whilst it could be done, he very much doubted ComOps, let alone the commander of the Air Force, would sanction such a hazardous raid, as the chance of losing fifty percent of their air effort seemed pretty good.

A chorus of voices assured him it had already been cleared and it merely needed 8 Squadron's approval as far as feasibility was concerned. Getting the SAS in undetected and safely out was 8 Squadron's problem; sorting out the ZIPRA intelligence headquarters was to be Martin Pearse's baby.

The squadron leader's orders were clear and simple – drop about 28 SAS at the given address, give them as much time on the ground as possible, pick them up again and get out safely to Rhodesia.

Total secrecy was clamped on the plan and for the next few weeks he pored over maps and stereo photographs deciding on the best routes in and out. He also had to plan the fuel requirements, which were critical on that operation, as the maximum load of men and equipment was to be carried by each of the four 205s that were to make the trip to Lusaka.

307

The problems facing the squadron leader and the men of 8 Squadron were enormous. They had to get in to Zambia under radar . . . and they had to avoid villages and terrorist camps that might raise the alarm.

For the squadron leader, the most worrying of all was leading in a formation in the dark with aircraft navigation lights off and having to fly at the lowest height above the ground they dared. He decided they would fly between 400 and 700 feet.

The plan was to put in an air strike on FC camp shortly before the raid on the NSO as a diversionary measure to draw attention away from Lusaka in the hope that the Zambian army and air force would rush up there. FC camp which had been bombed the previous October, now only housed a caretaker element.

Then, while everyone was scurrying to FC, the assault on the NSO would get under way. It was hoped that the noise from the camp attack would cover the approach of the noisy Bells and the attack on the intelligence headquarters.

Captain Martin Pearse, the tactical commander, had to cover every possible eventuality the SAS men on the ground would face . . . and once again he drew up a meticulous set of orders.

The first inkling the "C" Squadron men had that something was afoot was when reconnaissance parties were sent out to find an isolated spot and an old house where they could rehearse their all-important house-clearing drills.

It was like Operation *Bastille* all over again, they agreed . . . and they knew they were on to something similar.

The reconnaissance parties chose an old farmhouse some fifty kilometres (thirty miles) from Salisbury. It was on a long peninsular jutting out into Darwendale Dam and was fenced on one side. It was in the centre of a game area and more than met the requirements of being in a very secluded spot.

The area fell under the jurisdiction of National Parks Board officer Stu Hulley-Miller, who, when on call-up, was the SAS/SB liaison man. He had planned to demolish the old brick and mud farm buildings and tobacco barns anyway, so the SAS chaps would be doing him a favour.

The whole of "C" Squadron deployed to the dam, the exact mission still shrouded in secrecy.

After a couple of days of sorting out their kit, Martin gave them a full briefing and told them exactly what the task was to be.

Once again, they found it hard to believe they would be attacking a target right in the heart of Lusaka, and were more than a little amazed that they would be doing it so soon after their first visit.

Every effort was to be made to attain the mission's objective, the commander stressed.

There were five offices in two office blocks at NSO, a storeroom and an underground bunker, believed to be used for the safe-keeping of important documents rather than people.

The four-bedroomed house had bars on all the windows and there would be about eight guards who were expected to react aggressively to an attack, Martin told the men.

They split into small teams and were allocated their tasks. Three groups would fight their way into the intelligence headquarters, while two external security groups would take up defensive positions and make sure there was no interference from other enemy elements.

Working on the aerial photographs and a sketch supplied by *The Black Swine*, they virtually mapped out the entire NSO on the ground.

308

A week of very intensive rehearsals followed during which they perfected their technique of breaching the walls, getting into the building, calling the terrorists out and, in the event of their not coming, planning how they would go in and get them.

Using as a basis a British Army system of room-to-room fighting techniques, the SAS had come up with their own version, simplified here and there with short cuts evolved from various types of operations and aided by a variety of home-grown weapons.

For training, an assortment of targets would be placed inside an empty building which was sandbagged at the windows... someone would shoot to simulate fire coming down... four men would rush up to the house and take on the various targets: one man would throw a grenade in and move up to the door.

As the grenade went in, another man would move to the door and fire into the corner of the room. Another would move in, firing to light the place, firing low into corners, into cupboards, under beds and all the places where the enemy could be expected to hide.

The number two man then moved into the room and covered the first man who moved to a point where he could dominate the whole room. He would switch on the torch strapped to the underside of his AK and finish clearing the room.

The stone wall surrounding the NSO complex was to be breached in three places with a Rhodesian-manufactured charge known as *The Hulk*, which contained five kilograms of explosives, enough to blow a man-sized hole in the wall enabling the operators to get through to their target.

The Hulks were potent and had a twenty-second fuse on them, long enough for the soldiers to get clear before the damage was done.

After that, the rooms were to be bunker bombed. Martin Pearse was to throw in his bunker bomb first to initiate the house attack.

The bunker bomb concept was gone into at length during their rehearsals and they worked on the principle that, if possible, they needed to get two walls between the bomb and the operator. For the bombs were so powerful there was a very real possibility of the walls caving in.

Martin and Lieutenant Rich Stannard who was to be the 2IC on the operation were to command two of the assault groups and they had many discussions about the bunker bomb procedure. Martin was uncertain about what he would do once he had thrown in his bunker bomb. He could not decide if he was going to move right away from the wall and around to the other side of the building... or crouch down underneath it... or move back and then crouch down. Rich said he had definitely decided to move right away.

SB representatives Stu Hulley-Miller and John Grey had got the sketch of the NSO lay-out from *The Black Swine* and showed it to the SAS.

"Fine! But what are those, there? Are they windows? If not, what are they? And are there burglar screens on them?" the soldiers queried.

"What's the door like in the office? In the living quarters? What's the design of the cupboard and the cabinets in the office? Is there a spare ammo magazine anywhere?"

The SAS wanted to know every possible detail. Fortunately *The Black Swine* had a good memory and was able to explain where everything was to the best of his knowledge, giving them the inside story.

Martin went over and over the plan with his troops using air photographs and the model of the NSO. Nothing was left to chance. Every man knew his role inside out. There were to be 24 men involved in the target area; some on the actual house attack, the others in defensive positions around the NSO.

The pilots practised the run-in to the NSO, the soldiers rehearsed deplaning as the choppers came in to land ... the sequence of events ... which callsigns were to go where ... the action on the prisoners-of-war they hoped to get ... what *The Black Swine* was to say over the loud hailer ... where the two stop groups would be positioned to prevent civilians and the Zambian army approaching the target ... practised getting back in to the choppers for the lift off.

It was to be an open Rhodesian raid. There would be no blackening-up. Normal Rhodesian camouflage and steel helmets were to be worn.

Even the tame terrorist, *The Black Swine*, was to be dressed in Rhodesian camouflage and issued with a weapon to help out. AKs, lighter, easier to wield in confined spaces and with a larger magazine capacity than the FN, were to be carried.

SB officer John Grey was to go to the NSO to escort *The Black Swine* and to help the former terrorist round up captures and interrogate them.

The Quartermaster, Major Paul Simmons, had organised the manufacture of huge sausage-shaped bags, made from canvas mattress covers. These were to be used to carry the wealth of important documents they hoped to capture.

The Special Branch men had to delve into the coffers of their secret money to buy satchels for the operators to carry the bunker bombs. On ops such as this, it was essential that there was no *cuffing*, as they said in army circles ... it was essential that every man had precisely the pouches and aids he needed.

Plastic handcuffs and black hoods for the prisoners were also on their shopping list.

While some operators searched for the VIP prisoners and others cleared the offices of their paper work, others had been tasked to hunt for the underground bunker which housed a safe containing top secret papers plus some thirty thousand dollars in foreign currency.

Luckily, the squadron had among its ranks the services of a TA soldier who earned his living in civvy street as a locksmith. Les Clark had done his homework well and reckoned he would be able to pick the lock within 15 seconds.

If, for some reason, he was not able to do that, they were going to blow it open ... and if that didn't work, they planned to pull it out with a chopper.

But Les and Stu Hulley-Miller were unable to find anyone who could tell them the secret of blowing a safe effectively. Other special forces who had done it had usually gone for overkill, destroying not only the safe, but the contents as well.

In order to become safe burglars, they really needed the help of a safe expert, but could hardly walk into a shop and ask for help.

Stu chose a likely candidate, checked him out – where he lived, his background, connections, his politics – then made his approach.

Flashing his SB identity card, but omitting any mention of an SAS connection, Stu explained he had to get documents out of a safe. After verifying *his* credentials, the man agreed to help, and provided them with some safes to practise on ... and they eventually got their safe-cracking technique down to a fine art.

Using *Knock-Knock* charges, they were able to blow the lock off without destroying the safe. After that, it was merely a matter of turning the handle.

310

Finally the exhaustive rehearsals, the best the "C" Squadron operators had undertaken, were over. On the afternoon of June 25, they all moved out to Makuti airfield on the Rhodesian side of the Zambezi in readiness for the flight to Lusaka.

It was clear from things Martin said in private to some of his men that he had an uneasy feeling about the operation.

The raid was being launched early on Tuesday morning, before the NSO guards and the Zambian army were up and about and when the reaction time would be slow. Three days later, Martin was to be presented with his Silver Cross of Rhodesia, the country's second highest gallantry honour, to be awarded, in part, for his role on Operation *Bastille*.

The night before they lifted off for Lusaka, he had a quiet word with SB officer John Grey: "Wouldn't it be funny if I copped it before I got my medal?" he said.

He had already spoken to medic Sergeant Major Bruce Langley under the shade of a bluegum tree at Darwendale. Hitting his trouser pocket, Martin told him: "There's my medical kit. If I get shot ... "

That night they all slept on the airstrip underneath the choppers. John Grey for one was not getting much sleep though.

"What's the matter?" *The Black Swine* enquired. "Can't you sleep?"

"No – I'm too worried," John confided. "What if we've got the wrong place after all?"

"It'll be all right man, I'm telling you," *The Black Swine* assured him, "Okay, so it *might* have changed a bit, but I *know* I've got the right place."

John felt a bit better after that; but he still lay awake all night.

At last D-day dawned. It was June 26. The choppers had already refuelled. At 04h00, the men were shaken awake. They donned normal Rhodesian camouflage as well as balaclavas and thick jerseys, and carried gloves for later.

Apart from the command chopper, none of the others had doors and without warm clothing they would have been just too cold to move once at the target.

They had a quick cup of tea, and Martin once again ran through his orders.

"Remember," he briefed his team. "This thing is like a race ... if anything goes wrong ... If I go ... the race carries on."

Just before they left he confided in Lieutenant Rich Stannard. "You know Rich," he said, "I'm still very worried about this bunker bomb." Martin was still undecided about where exactly he would move to while waiting for the powerful bomb to go off.

In Salisbury, Air Commodore Norman Walsh and SAS Major Dave Dodson were preparing to board the command Dakota to fly straight to the target. In Thornhill air base, Gwelo, four Hunter pilots were readying themselves to fly out and drop their deadly golf bombs on FC camp. Two other Hunters, armed with air-to-air missiles, were going to act as top cover.

Then, towards 05h00, the 24 operators, pilots and crews climbed aboard the choppers and in the darkness took their leave of Makuti. Soon they had overflown the Zambezi and were en route for Lusaka.

It was going to be a very significant raid in more ways than one. Not only was it going to strike at the nerve centre of ZIPRA's intelligence centre, but the air and ground forces were to launch their attack only hours before Bishop Abel Muzorewa's black-dominated coalition government of national unity took power.

It would show ZIPRA and the world that Muzorewa, who was also Minister of Defence, meant business. He had already warned that the advent of black rule did not mean that cross-border military raids would stop if there was a threat to the nation's security.

311

The SAS were feeling extremely confident. Their intelligence was the best that was possible. The rehearsals had been exhaustive and they could not have been more prepared. They knew much more about the NSO than they had known about Nkomo's house.

It was to take the Bell 205s about one hour 45 minutes to get to the target and the route was from Makuti, across the Zambezi, well east of Lusaka to a point about fifty kilometres (thirty miles) north-east of Lusaka. Then, they were to fly across to the west of the railway line towards the vicinity of FC terrorist camp, just north of Lusaka, where the diversionary strike was to be put in by jets.

After that, their route would take them south to the outskirts of Lusaka, where it was thought the clatter of the Bells might be mistaken for diesel trains.

Squadron Leader Lunt who had the unenviable task of navigating the way through the darkness, would then look for a landmark – a school – from where they would run in and land at the NSO.

Navigation was purely on time and heading basis. The squadron leader had planned his route and timings precisely, working out how long they would travel in one direction before changing course.

When the pilots lifted off from Makuti it was pitch black and they could see absolutely nothing outside the perspex windows of the Bells.

The helicopters had to get to the target at the crack of dawn well before the five VIPs and eight guards in the NSO were awake. The attack was due to go in at 06h15.

It was still dark as the choppers began their approach to the Zambian capital and the early morning air cut keenly through the operators' uniforms and jerseys.

At first light, the helicopters descended to treetop level and tightened formation. Winds had given them problems but it was only by the grey of first light that they realised they were more north than planned. They could not pull up higher either for fear of being picked up by radar at Lusaka.

The pilots turned back towards the capital and were veering around trying to spot landmarks.

Time was running out. Fuel was getting low. It was getting lighter by the minute.

Inside the Bells, the tension was mounting. They had to be getting near the target by now surely?

Squadron Leader Lunt asked Air Commodore Norman Walsh and Major Dave Dodson on board the command Dakota and flying in Zambian airspace for the Hunters to put their strike in early to help them pinpoint FC camp.

He dare not move the formation south too early, for if they overflew the camp in error, the entire formation would be shot down.

Norman Walsh and Dave Dodson discussed the plan and it was decided to put the strike in only if the troops were going to have a reasonable amount of time at the target.

By now, it was fairly light and squadron leader Lunt had picked up his bearings. He gave a revised time over the target. It was almost twenty minutes later than originally planned.

The fuel situation was serious, affecting the flying time back to the border, but Squadron Leader Lunt suggested that the op go ahead. They would be able to give the operators extra time at the target if he could call forward the air force's one and only standby 205 with fuel to a position on the Zambezi. Alternatively, they had a Dakota already airborne with six fuel drums on board and they could be parachuted to them in the bush.

312

The original plan had been for the choppers to orbit an area away from the target while the SAS were busy with the NSO, but to conserve fuel, it was decided the choppers would sit on the ground instead with their engines idle.

The SAS would have only about forty minutes at the target and ground commander Garth Barrett radioed across to Martin Pearse's chopper to stress the strict time limitation and ask if he could still do the job. Martin, keen for the mission to continue, said it would be no problem.

The squadron leader radioed the hierarchy in the Dakota that the SAS and pilots wished to go ahead with the raid and that they were confident the task could be done.

Major Dodson and the air commodore agreed and the Bells flew straight to the target, the jet strike being put in on FC five mintes before their arrival at the NSO.

The limited time span meant the troops did not have the luxury of doing a quick assessment and sifting out what paperwork was of no use to them and what was essential. They would have to get into the house, kidnap the prisoners, find the underground bunker and bring out every piece of paperwork they came upon.

It was no longer a first light attack. The raid was to go in in broad daylight.

Amazingly, the local Zambian population waved at the Rhodesians in the Bells. The choppers were flying straight to the target in the elite Roma township. There was not one manicured lawn to be seen. Every one was unkempt and neglected.

The Bells came in low over an African school, just as planned. The soldiers readied themselves, firmly gripping their AKs. The atmosphere was electric. The SAS gunners positioned by the open doors prepared to go into action the moment they touched down or even before if the circumstances called for it. The doors of the command chopper were opened as they came in to land.

The Rhodesians could clearly see the vacant plots by the side of the NSO complex. As they came down they could see that the NSO had changed considerably since their aerial photographs had been taken.

There was now a completely new office block, something they had not catered for in their clearance drills.

There were machineguns mounted outside the walls; also not anticipated. Fortunately, the gunners, although at their posts that morning, possibly thought that the choppers belonged to the Zambian Air Force and as a result did not react. It was a lucky break for the attackers – the ZIPRA gunners could have exacted a heavy toll on the very vulnerable Rhodesians and their precious aircraft.

The armed guards, alerted by the racket from the Bell engines, began to spill into the courtyard. Others, who had been sleeping along the perimeter fence, took up their positions. There were some 24 altogether, three times more than the visitors had been expecting.

The Bells were committed to landing among them and a tremendous hail of bullets met the descending choppers. The Rhodesians opened up. The choppers were orientated at just the right angle to give the Rhodesian machinegunners full view of the building and they were firing as they came in to land. They had obviously succeeded with the surprise aspect of the mission.

The enemy guards were being killed even before the SAS had touched down.

A lone terrorist ran up an anthill on the outside of the building and opened up on them with a light machinegun. He aimed at the command chopper carrying CO Garth Barrett, John Grey, Lieutenant Stan Hornby, two medics and *The Black Swine,* and a round smashed into the perspex bubble right next to the pilot's head.

Then before the terrorist could do any more damage, his weapon jammed. It was another lucky break for the Rhodesians for they would certainly have lost the chopper and possibly the passengers had he continued firing.

The pilot virtually landed on top of the terrorist, but at the last moment, the man managed to duck away and flee down the hill.

"THERE HE IS," *The Black Swine* bellowed above the noise from the engine and the sporadic firing.

Quickly, Garth Barrett and John Grey leapt out of the chopper and killed the terrorist and then his partner, who had joined him to man the light machinegun.

The choppers landed in the vacant plots next to the NSO. It was 06h38. The initial resistance had been swiftly neutralised and there was virtually no firing as everyone leapt out into his correct position.

The choppers reported to the command Dak that the situation was looking good.

The choppers immediately lifted off to a holding area in the bush just seven minutes flying time away to refuel from the drums they were carrying. They could not go further out because of the shortage of fuel. They shut down their rotors and the aircraft were throttled back to idle, ready to lift off at a moment's notice to extract the troops, either at the conclusion of their mission or in the event of an early Zambian reaction.

The CO, Garth Barrett, had taken up his position in one of the vacant plots with the two medics and Lieutenant Stan Hornby who was to man the 60 millimetre mortar and provide protection. Barrett was to be in constant radio communication with the groups assaulting the house, all other groups, and the command Dakota.

The Command Dakota meanwhile had the task of monitoring Zambian army, air force and police networks and passing the word of any Zambian reaction to the CO.

The troops had no sooner disemplaned than they heard a wailing sound exactly like the frenzied shrieking before a charge. But it was nothing more serious than the ululating rantings of the high school children, just one block away from the firing and highly agitated at the sight of the Rhodesian choppers.

Three callsigns – Martin Pearse's, Rich Stannard's and Mike Barlow's – took up their positions on three sides of the security wall in readiness to detonate their *Hulks* and blast their way through the two-metre-high walls.

Another callsign had already made their way to the front entrance to keep it covered from any escaping guards once the house attack went in, and to protect the assault force from any outside interference.

Two others, one under the command of *Jungle Jordan* and the other commanded by *Petrol Paul*, deployed to the two approach roads to provide early warning of any interference, to keep innocent civilians away, and to take on any hostile intruders.

The Black Swine, the former top ZIPRA official, stood guard outside *The Vatican* waiting to call on his former colleagues to hand themselves over to the Rhodesians.

Quickly, the three men tasked to place the *Hulk* charges ran to the walls, stuck them in position and lit the fuses, swiftly taking cover from the impending explosion that would blast an entrance into the ZIPRA Holy of Holies.

All three breaching charges were to go off simultaneously, but only Martin Pearse's blew. They had taken the necessary precautions and kept them covered during the night but perhaps the early-morning dew had affected the igniter mechanisms. Still, it did not really matter now, the pressure was on and they had to get inside the courtyard.

Rich Stannard and his team sprinted around to the front entrance. They slapped a *Gatecrasher* charge on the padlocked main gate, stood back and blew the lock off. Rich and his team of three men hurried through.

By now, Martin Pearse's callsign had already got through the breach in the back entry route.

Mike Barlow in charge of the third assault group got his team together and they ran down to Martin's entrance.

The back entry route was lined with trees giving them a bit of cover from the building. As they stepped through the back breach, sporadic firing came from inside the courtyard. Guards were running everywhere but they were more intent in putting as much space between themselves and the visitors than trying to defend the place.

The Rhodesians quickly overcame what resistance there was and a dozen guards soon lay dead in the courtyard. Another was killed on the main road.

In the process, the raiders had taken a casualty of their own. A ricochet from a machinegun hit a corporal in the back and lodged in his stomach.

Martin Pearse grabbed him and heaved him outside the breached wall and the troops waiting there hurried him straight to the medical team.

Up the road, *Jungle Jordan* was having a small problem with one of the guards who was armed with an RPD. But the ZIPRA man was soon killed and the RPD silenced.

Inside *The Vatican* courtyard, the teams moved in.

Rich Stannard went to the side of the house near a verandah to throw in his bunker bomb and Martin Pearse moved to the side of the building to place his bomb in the guard's room.

The plan called for Martin to put his bunker bomb in first. He would then give a quick blast on his dog whistle, which was the signal for Rich and his entry team to throw in their bunker bomb at their side of the house. They would then move in and begin their house-clearing exercise.

The window in the guard's room was covered in mesh which meant that Martin had to feel his bunker bomb in rather than hurl it in, as he normally would have done.

The commander put the bunker bomb in, moved right back and around the side of the house and crouched down.

The bomb exploded ... The SAS men in position around *The Vatican* saw the asbestos roof lift off.

Then ... silence, and a sudden lull. Rich Stannard was patiently waiting for the whistle to signal the start of his bunker bombing and house-clearing phase at the front of the house.

"Callsign 39 ... What's happening?" queried Garth Barrett, the overall commander on the radio from the outside of the wall. There was no reply.

Rich Stannard was getting worried. "HAVE YOU SEEN CAPTAIN PEARSE?" he shouted to one man. The soldier said he had not.

Rich decided to find out what was happening.

Abandoning his own task for the moment, he took the other three men in his callsign and raced around to the back of the building and into the dust and mess to investigate. Martin was nowhere to be seen.

The devastating picture that met Rich clearly told what had happened. The bunker bomb, instead of simply destroying the room had not only brought down the entire side of the house where the bomb had been thrown, but the other wall too behind which Martin was crouching for protection. Although Martin had followed their rehearsals to the letter, such was the inferior quality of the building that it had not been able to withstand the force of such an explosion.

315

"START DIGGING!" Rich yelled to the soldiers.

The huge chunks of concrete were quickly heaved out of the way. Clouds of dust and smoke hung in the air.

It was a race against time. If Martin was under that lot, they had to get him out fast.

They dug deeper and deeper. Still they found no trace. Then, someone spotted Martin's radio aerial, then his helmet.

Martin's lifeless body was eased from the rubble. His premonition of disaster had not been unfounded after all.

Rich immediately radioed Garth Barrett at the command post and told him what had happened.

"Carry on as planned," came the order.

It was as Martin would have wished. The race, as he had called it, was continuing ... He was carried out through the breach in the wall and handed over to the medics.

The delay meant there was now no time for *The Black Swine* to call out the NSO hierarchy. They would just have to go in and get them.

Rich Stannard's team returned to the front of the building. Rich heaved in their bunker bomb and ran around the corner to take cover. Their bomb blew a huge hole in the dining room taking away the entire outer verandah in the process.

Even before the belching clouds of dust and smoke had settled, the four-man assault team had moved inside. They had no opposition. Swiftly, they set about clearing the house and searching for the VIPs. Aided by the torches strapped to their AKs, they fired under beds, into cupboards, anywhere ZIPRA's top men were likely to be hiding.

Ricochets and chippings screamed in all directions, as one by one the rooms were swiftly dealt with. But there was no sign of the top three ZIPRA intelligence men. Only Dumiso Dabengwa's clothes, his diaries, leather case and pigskin briefcase.

A Danish Embassy official living opposite stuck his head out of the window and began taking pictures of the breakfast-time raid. Someone sent a quick burst in his general direction and his curiosity suddenly waned. He quickly disappeared behind a wall, never to be seen again.

Inside the house and the nearby office blocks, the SAS were ransacking the place. All the drawers, briefcases, cupboards and files were emptied. Every scrap of paper was being bundled into the huge sausage-shaped bags. There were thousands of papers, a good two tons of the stuff.

When the troops had finished with one building they tossed in a bunker bomb to destroy it.

The callsign tasked to get into the underground bunker and break into the top secret safe were having no luck. They just could not find the place. They knew where it ought to be; the only trouble was the new office block had been built over it and they did not know where to start looking for the entrance hole.

Petrol Paul's road block group guarding one of the access routes to *The Vatican* could see a group of civilians gathering on a slight rise up the road.

The Zambians seemed fascinated by all the noise from the bunker bombing and grenades, but their curiosity never extended to moving down their hill for a closer look.

Then a Peugeot car roared down the road, passing the swelling crowd of interested onlookers. When it got to within 200 metres of the road block group, it screamed to a halt and the driver and passengers, all dressed in civilian clothes, leapt out.

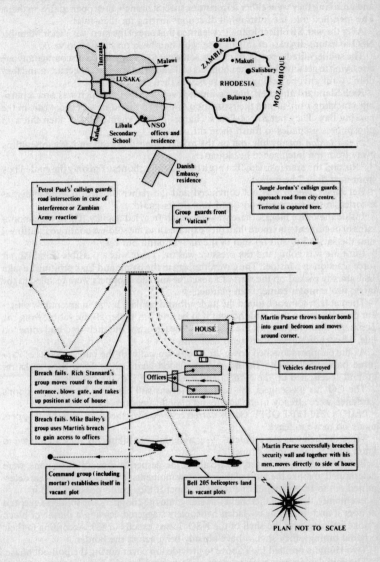

The following labels appear on the map/plan:

Tanzania

Malawi

LUSAKA

Kafue

Libala
Secondary
School

NSO
offices and
residence

Lusaka

ZAMBIA

Makuti

Salisbury

RHODESIA

MOZAMBIQUE

Bulawayo

Danish
Embassy
residence

'Petrol Paul's' callsign guards
road intersection in case of
interference or Zambian
Army reaction

Group guards front
of 'Vatican'

'Jungle Jordan's' callsign guards
approach road from city centre.
Terrorist is captured here.

Martin Pearse throws bunker bomb
into guard bedroom and moves
around corner.

HOUSE

Vehicles destroyed

Breach fails. Rich Stannard's
group moves round to the main
entrance, blows gate, and takes
up position at side of house

Offices

Breach fails. Mike Bailey's
group uses Martin's breach
to gain access to offices

Martin Pearse successfully breaches
security wall and together with his
men, moves directly to side of house

Command group (including
mortar) establishes itself in
vacant plot

Bell 205 helicopters land
in vacant plots

PLAN NOT TO SCALE

Operation *Carpet*: The attack on ZIPRA's secret intelligence headquarters in the north of the
Zambian capital

The soldiers distinctly saw one man clutching an AK climb out of the driver's seat and, thinking they were either terrorists or special branch, they opened fire on them. The men fled into the bush in all directions fearing for their lives.

After the war, SB officer John Grey learned that one of the men was Victor Mlambo, NSO assistant director of intelligence, who had been on his way to work.

The soldiers fired a couple of rockets at the car to destroy it and discourage anyone else trying to get any closer. The choppers still had to return and collect them and they didn't want anyone getting too close before then.

Rich Stannard and crew, having finished with the house, which was now a burning, crackling ruin, turned their attention to the two brand-new Peugeot cars in the parking bay. They put *Knock-Knock* charges on the engine blocks, then threw in phosphorus grenades to finish them off.

Jungle Jordan meanwhile, out on the road, managed to grab an African scuttling away from the intelligence headquarters.

"No, no," the man insisted, "I'm not a bad boy boss, honest. I'm only the garden boy from next door," he wailed.

But *Jungle Jordan* was not convinced and the rather worried-looking man was escorted to the command post and kept under guard.

Inside the office blocks, there was still much frenzied activity. There were mountains of documents, far more than they expected and the soldiers continued stuffing it into the sacks. But still no sign of the underground bunker.

But time was going and the pressure was on. There was a possible Zambian air force reaction to consider. The eavesdroppers in the command Dak orbiting Lusaka had already picked up the start of a reaction and the choppers were recalled to the target two minutes earlier than planned.

Then at last, someone found the underground bunker. It was in an entirely different place to where they had thought it to be and was under all the rubble from the perimeter wall. It contained the safe and some terrorists, but their find had come too late. They didn't have the time to deal with it.

As the choppers touched down the troops ran out with the bulging sacks of captured paperwork. While *The Black Swine* stood guard, they threw their sacks on ground sheets, tied up the corners and loaded them into the choppers.

The CO, his passengers, the capture who was still claiming he was next door's gardener, were already in the command chopper ready to take their leave.

"LIFT OFF! LIFT OFF!" Garth Barrett ordered over the radio. But the choppers made no move to leave.

What the hell was the problem? Why were they not taking off, they all wanted to know in the command chopper?

But the soldiers, while very aware about the desperate urgency to be gone, were determined to make the most of their last few moments at the NSO. They were determined not to leave behind one scrap of paper if they could possibly help it.

Eventually, the last of their haul was slung into the choppers, the soldiers squeezed in after it and up the heavy-laden helicopters staggered, leaving a plume of black smoke hanging over the shell of the NSO. It was exactly 07h30. According to their original timings, they should have already been across the border.

Two Hunters orbited high above to provide top cover during the pull-out phase.

The initial plan had been to circle right around Lusaka before heading homewards. But it was felt that the safest route out was to fly straight over the centre of the city. The Zambians would not be expecting them to take that route and would not be too keen to fire weapons with civilians around.

318

They flew over the ring of Zambian troops who had been deployed and they could clearly see armaments in the back of the trucks. The Zambians kept their heads down and no doubt their fingers crossed and did not make a move to do anything aggressive.

The Rhodesians passed the odd hotel very low and observed the occasional rather startled face peering out at them.

There could be no mistaking the Rhodesian choppers for Zambian aircraft and as they flew across the capital, both blacks and whites stopped and waved at the Rhodesian raiders.

Other Zambians were not so sure about the events that morning and scattered to the four winds.

As they flew home, the SAS dropped thousands of leaflets over the city calling for friendly relations with Zambia and stressing the raid had not been against the Zambian Government or her people but against ZIPRA.

Then the command Dakota crew gave the alert that the Zambian MiGs had definitely been scrambled to search for them. A couple of the pilots shouted to their passengers above the clatter of the engines for them to keep an eye out for them ... and they set course for home, revising their plan and asking that fuel be brought right up to the Zambezi by the fifth 205.

As the choppers flew low, carrying the soldiers southwards, the locals came out of their huts to wave at them, just as they had done to the SAS ground troops after the raid on Nkomo's house.

The route was constantly varied to take advantage of the terrain and hopefully to avoid the MiGs, and a grid reference was passed where they wanted the spare 205 to meet them with the extra fuel.

They got clear of Zambia without incident. By now fuel was extremely low and the Bells landed immediately after crossing the Zambezi, refuelling from the spare 205.

Martin, and the wounded corporal were loaded into the fifth chopper and it headed for Salisbury.

The Hunters, which had struck at FC camp that morning, were by now readying themselves to take part in a ceremonial fly-past at the opening of the country's first black-dominated parliament.

SB officer John Grey lost no time checking out his blindfolded capture. While the choppers were refuelling, he took *The Black Swine* on one side and asked him who their prisoner was. He was Alexander Brisk Vusa, the Russian-trained deputy head of intelligence. A prize indeed.

In the face of such a positive identification, Vusa had no hope of continuing with his gardener story.

"When I heard the choppers, I thought it was the Zambians," he told the SB officer. "Then I heard the firing. I can't believe you came all the way to Lusaka," he said incredulously and full of wide-eyed admiration. "I just can't believe it ... "

Since the raid on Nkomo's home, the ZIPRA hierarchy had not dared risk sleeping in the NSO any more, he said, and that was why they had not found Dabengwa and the others there. They were too scared to set up a routine pattern of movement, and used to spend as little time as possible in their offices.

They generally came to work every day at 08h00 and were all gone by nine. No one wanted to be caught out again by the Rhodesians.

They had been extremely lucky to find him at the NSO, Vusa said. He normally stayed with his girlfriend, but he had got drunk the previous night and slept if off at the NSO.

The guard had also been strengthened as a result of the Rhodesian raids on *The Fat Man's* house, and many of the new guards who had escaped that attack had transferred from Nkomo's house.

ZIPRA were obviously extremely concerned at the possibility of a raid on the NSO. However it was not until after the war that it was discovered that they had actually been *expecting* one.

Dumiso Dabengwa later claimed he had a dream about a Rhodesian raid and that was why he was not there. But other ZIPRA hierarchy told security force chiefs it was because they were *forewarned*. That was why the guard had been trebled and why there were machinegun positions.

Exactly who had tipped them off remains a mystery as there was more than one spy in the know.

If the guards had been told anything at all, they would probably have expected the Rhodesians to come by road and in the dead of night, like the last time.

In any event, despite not being able to capture the three top NSO men, despite all the problems of arriving late at the target, being low on fuel, finding more buildings than they had expected, machineguns and more guards, the op had been a total success. After the war, "C" Squadron operators rated it one of the best-rehearsed and organised operations they had taken part in.

Despite the tip-off, they had brought back a member of the ZIPRA hierarchy who would prove to be a very significant capture.

And they had returned with many tons of records representing virtually every piece of paper inside the NSO.

ZIPRA claimed that all their top secret papers had been locked in the underground bunker, but the Rhodesians found a catalogue of all the records held in the complex and there was very little missing.

The choppers had been so full of documents that one of the sausage bags fell out and landed slap bang in the middle of the courtyard of a suburban police station. A police van duly roared into Kabrit and a fairly-switched on policeman leapt out, grinned and stated: "I guess this little lot belongs to you guys!"

The sacks were piled high in the SAS briefing room and it was only when they started sifting through the pile did they realise they had an incredible assortment of blockbuster material detailing political and military strategy. The documents blew the lid off ZIPRA's secret operations.

So dynamic were they that in one of its rare revelations of details, ComOps displayed part of the massive haul to the press and openly admitted that the skilfully executed mission had probably been the most important undertaken by the security forces.

Snatches read from the documents at the press briefing revealed the bitter differences between ZAPU and its Patriotic Front partner, ZANLA, which one document claimed could "easily be wiped out."

What was *not* revealed to the press was that the NSO had a spy ring and the Rhodesians now had all the names of the agents feeding ZIPRA intelligence.

The contents of one letter sent to Nkomo by a white Rhodesian were considered high treason material and hushed up. Fortunately for him, the man – once a prominent personality in Rhodesia's public life – had fled the country thereby escaping prosecution.

He had told Nkomo – whose terrorists had shot down the two Viscounts – that Rhodesia was using a certain anti-heat seeking paint on their civilian aircraft to offset attacks from SAM-7 missiles.

A white security force deserter had also given accurate and important intelligence to Nkomo in a tape-recorded briefing.

ZAPU, the political wing, had set up a spy ring of radical European sympathisers in the UK and elsewhere with the sole object of obtaining intelligence that would prove useful to ZIPRA. Many of the spies had previously been in the Rhodesian security forces and one of their aims was to undermine the morale of the European population in Rhodesia.

"Friendly agencies" – the International Defence and Aid Fund, the British Communist Party, Amnesty International, the Palestine Liberation Organisation, the South Africa National Congress, the South African War Assistance Committee – were channelling their intelligence to ZAPU. And because of Nkomo's close ties with the KGB, it was all being fed to Moscow.

A white journalist in Rhodesia codenamed Jason was feeding Nkomo intelligence as was a British journalist, a member of the British Communist Party, who operated under the codename Alison.

They were buying up all the Rhodesian war books and literature they could lay their hands on inside Rhodesia and overseas, publications setting out the strengths of the army, air force and police reserves.

This was being analysed by Nkomo's Department of Analysis and Research and the findings fed to the military high command. ZIPRA thus had an up-to-date intelligence picture on Rhodesian security force capabilities.

The spy, Jason, had forwarded notes made at a closed "invitation only" meeting of voters at Chisipite High School, Salisbury, and addressed by the Co-Minister of Foreign Affairs, Mr P.K. van der Byl. They had also infiltrated the Scorpion organisation – for ex-Rhodesians – in England and were visiting public houses frequented by ex-Rhodesians to gain intelligence.

The documents were also to reveal that Nkomo had an agent working in Combined Operations and the incriminating piece of evidence even gave his name. Later still it was learned he was a KGB agent.

He worked in an office which gave him access to just about all the goings-on at ComOps, the most important building in the land.

The man was subsequently watched and his movements monitored, but no action was taken against him. For by the time the piece of paper giving his name had been found among the tons of captured documents, the war had all but run its course.

Papers also spoke of a "high ranking officer" in the army being on the terrorist's side, but he was not named and come the end of the war the intelligence agencies still did not know exactly who he was. Later information however, indicated that the agent was an intelligence officer, who, in his dealings with ZIPRA, passed himself off as being in the army.

Once again the raid made headlines around the world. It had come a little more than five weeks before the Commonwealth conference in Lusaka to be attended by Queen Elizabeth, who would address the summit at the Mulungushi Hall, two kilometres from the scene of the raid.

It demonstrated how powerless Zambia's own forces were in the face of an attack from any side and as the Rhodesians had clearly shown they were capable of striking right up to the conference hall's front door.

(A Sunday Mail cartoon would show Rhodesian Air Force hero, Green Leader, grinning from his Hawker Hunter and giving the Queen the thumbs up to land at Lusaka). The Royal Air Force was to work out lengthy flight plans to avoid Rhodesian air space.

But the operation had cost squadron commander Martin Pearse his life and the SAS's victory was tinged with sadness.

His death was a tremendous shock to everyone and a very bad blow for "C" Squadron. He had been such a figurehead for the younger men and seemed to inspire most of the great team spirit they had. He was held in the highest esteem too by the air force and ranked equally in ability and bravery with the SAS hierarchy.

Martin, who had come first in the Order of Merit on his officer's course, saw Operation *Carpet* as one of the culminating points of his career. Yet his overwhelming premonition of his own death did not undermine his determination.

Three days after the successful raid Martin had masterminded, and the day he had been due to get his Silver Cross of Rhodesia, he was cremated. Within a few hours of the cremation, Martin's widow accepted the award from Army Commander Lieutenant-General Sandy Maclean, at a moving ceremony attended by the entire regiment and their families.

Martin's Silver Cross was awarded "for gallantry and leadership in action above the call of duty" as were those of the two other squadron commanders, Captain Colin Willis and Captain Bob McKenna.

The event was the first for many months in which all three squadrons were out of the bush and back in Salisbury at the same time. It was also the only medals parade attended by the entire regiment.

* * *

Meanwhile, the Op *Carpet* capture was being extremely co-operative.

"You know," Alexander Brisk Vusa was telling SB officer John Grey, "there's something funny going on near JZ camp."

"Oh really?" John appeared not to take much notice but the intelligence officer in him knew he was on to something significant.

"They never used to let me in there; it was all very strange," the capture was saying.

It certainly was, John Grey thought. Vusa, as deputy head of intelligence, had made many trips to JZ terror camp to visit the NSO policemen who were undergoing their training there. He was clearly an important man, one of the hierarchy, yet not even *he* was allowed access to this mysterious area south of the camp.

Vusa had also seen heavily-laden trucks visiting the place; had seen the head of *logistics* driving towards there.

It was not only Vusa who was fascinated by JZ camp now. Could this be the place the Rhodesians had been searching for for so long? If so, they had just got themselves a lucky break.

They knew that Libyan aircraft had been making secret night-time flights from Angola and landing in Lusaka, offloading their large supplies of weapons from Russia and East Germany under cover of darkness. Such vast resupplies of weapons were clearly destined for Nkomo's conventional forces in training at Mulungushi. But where was *The Fat Man* hiding his weaponry?

(The West's apparent lack of recognition of the Muzorewa government had encouraged the Russians and East Germans to move in arms and men to train ZIPRA.)

The Zambians were doing their level best to control weapons at this stage. ZIPRA were all too fond of selling their weapons to Zambian civilians and as a result, there had been an increase in armed robberies.

The Zambians were insisting that ZIPRA weaponry be kept in the national stores where it would be issued only on requisition.

But the Rhodesians knew that ZIPRA were loath to stick to this plan. They wanted control of their own weaponry – hence the secret night-time flights from Angola.

Could they be hoarding them at the same place Vusa had just tipped them off about? It was the merest hint that something was in the air and it was too good a chance to miss.

A Canberra overflew the area south of JZ camp, fifteen kilometres (nine miles) west of Lusaka, on a reconnaissance mission and the photographic interpretation indicated there were a vast amount of weapons cached all over the bush. There were heavy vehicle tracks under practically every tree on the fifteen-acre area, and there were also bunkers and trenches.

An immediate decision was made to send the SAS in to *take out* the place as soon as possible.

The main JZ camp, a training/holding area which also included a political commissar's camp, would also be hit.

* * *

In Lusaka, the NSO people were counting their dead and wounded.

Realising that Vusa was missing, they asked themselves what he knew that could be damaging to them, and came up with the probability that he either suspected or knew of the site of the arms dump.

Nkomo was hurriedly put in the picture with the NSO hierarchy recommending that the arms be moved as soon as possible.

But there was *such* a vast quantity that to move them would have been a monumental exercise. It was the biggest arms dump in Zambia, totalling something like 100 tons. They simply could not move it quickly at such short notice. Nkomo decided against the recommendation.

It was a decision that was to cost him dearly. For even as he debated the problem, the SAS squadron commanders were being summoned to the briefing room at Kabrit where they were put in the picture about the new op.

Operation *Chicory* was to be a quickie raid, CO Garth Barrett told them. They were to fly straight to the target and would only be on the ground for three and a half hours. Speed and efficiency would be the essence of the exercise.

Fifty men drawn from all three squadrons were to mount an attack to destroy as much war material as possible ... kill terrorists ... and recover any worthwhile documents and prisoners.

The commander's brief was to keep conflict with the Zambian army to a minimum. Shooting Zambian soldiers would only detract from the political advantage gained by exposing ZIPRA's massive arms dump to the Zambian authorities.

As usual, none of the troops was told what the target was or when the op would be mounted. They were only told to prepare for a camp-type attack and get their operational kit ready. It was to be an open Rhodesian raid again without *Black-Is-Beautiful.*

They were stood down, and that week-end the commanders worked out the detailed planning of their particular phases.

The intelligence services meanwhile were having a chat to the commander of Com-Ops, General Peter Walls: "Hell, sir. Everything's happened so fast. We haven't even told CIO or the police about this op."

"Okay. It doesn't matter," the general assured them. "We'll just go ahead and do it."

* * *

At 05h00 on Sunday, July 1, the SAS were back in camp and ready for action. The operators drew their equipment and were very soon on their way to the refuelling point at Bumi Hills on the banks of Lake Kariba. The red ball on the horizon that was the sun was already coming up over the silent lake.

It was only now that the troops and the chopper pilots were briefed what the target was to be. For the "C" Squadron operators, it would be their second raid into the Lusaka area in less than a week.

They drew extra ammunition and bulk explosives from RSM Pete Allan, but it was not necessary to take much as they knew they would be able to make use of the armaments at the target. They studied the aerial photographs, rehearsed their sweepline formations along the airstrip until everyone knew exactly where he was going and what he was doing once at the target.

As it was a Sunday, they did not expect to find many ZIPRA in camp.

Canberras and Hunters would be going in ahead of the troops to bomb the camp ... to neutralise the camp and making it safe for the Bells to land.

Overall control of the ground and air operations was to be from the command Dakota with General Walls directing operations, and two Hunters would provide top cover to protect the ground troops from enemy air retaliation.

Five Bells – every serviceable one Rhodesia possessed – would take the SAS to the target. There would not be single Bell in reserve in the event of something going wrong. No other army in the world would have undertaken such an operation without a reserve machine standing by. It was against all the rules of war. Rhodesia, of course, did not have the benefit of such luxuries.

Back in the heart of Salisbury, the capture, Alexander Brisk Vusa, the man who had put them on to their hot target, had his feet up at the five-star Monomatapa Hotel with SB funds footing the bill.

He had been so co-operative that Special Branch decided to keep him there until Operation *Chicory* was over, then he would be driven to his home outside Salisbury to resume a normal life again.

He was confined to his room, not that that worried him too much. After the deprivations of a terrorist's life where the rations were bad and there was the constant threat of a security force attack, he was not about to complain about plush surroundings, a soft bed and whatever he wanted from the hotel kitchen. Later, he would give the SB extensive lectures on Soviet training and spy methods.

At the other end of the country the fifty SAS operators were climbing aboard the five Bells for their Sunday afternoon visit to Zambia. At 12h45 the pilots started up their engines, lifted off over the lake and set course for Zambia.

Almost an hour later, the Canberras and Hunters suddenly overtook the five Bells, sweeping low to make their strikes. The war planes struck, shattering the peace of that sleepy Sunday afternoon.

Large clouds of black smoke and dust billowed up in front of the approaching heliborne troops. They peered out of the choppers to get a better look. In another four minutes it would be their turn to attack.

The moment the choppers touched down in three separate dropping areas, the troops, their rifles at the ready, jumped out, deploying immediately into their sweepline formations.

324

Then they advanced towards their designated targets – the munitions caches, and the political commissar's camp. Just as their briefing had indicated, there was only a small caretaker force on duty and resistance was light.

Soon 100-high metre sheets of flames and debris were raining down all over the camp and 122 millimetre rockets were burning and zig-zagging in every direction as the SAS set about destroying the camp.

At the nearby political commissar's camp 500 tents full of personal belongings and weapons went up in smoke and there were so many tents, that at one stage, the SAS ran out of matches.

Meanwhile, Zambian Air Force MiG pilots were climbing into their planes at Lusaka and Mumbwa air bases. They knew the Rhodesians were still on the ground. They knew too that the choppers still had to return to collect them and carry them back home. But the Zambians were also aware that the Hunters would be in a top cover role, high above the SAS.

Suddenly, a Rhodesian Hunter pilot saw two silver-coloured MiGs below him in a low-level battle formation.

"Permission to shoot them down with a Sidewinder?" he radioed to callsign Dolphin 1 – General Walls – orbitting in the command Dak.

"If they show any sign of coming for you, then by all means. But if they don't, leave them," came the general's reply.

However, the MiG pilots harboured no aggressive intentions. Their radar controller was furiously trying to direct them on to target but the pilots were completely ignoring his instructions. All they did was fly from their bases to JZ camp – then fly back home again.

Then a column of Zambian armoured vehicles approached but wisely decided to keep well away from the Rhodesians.

All too soon, it approached last light and the troops moved to the landing zone to await the arrival of the choppers to take them home. Enemy RPG-7 rockets and Strelas were still exploding as the troops' own prepared charges continued to go off. As one chopper came in, it was rocked in the air by the deafening blast from a cache of Russian demolitions kit going up.

The loaded choppers lifted off, and as they did, the Zambian troops decided it was now safe enough to take on the Rhodesians with smallarms fire. But none hit home and the choppers continued on their way.

Then one hit a tree with its rotor blade. The occupants held their breath, but all was well and the chopper remained airborne.

As they headed homewards, fires were still smouldering from the 100 tons of weapons, ammunition, tents, canoes, cars, blankets and medical equipment that had gone up in smoke. What had once been the biggest ammunition dump in Zambia was now a bombed and blackened reminder of the lightning Rhodesian raid.

The long list of arms and ammunition destroyed was based on actual counts done and included 2 000 kilograms of plastic explosive, 400 anti-tank landmines and 85 assorted mines, 500 x 60 millimetre mortar bombs, 800 hand grenades, 400 x 82 millimetre bombs, 104 PPSH sub-machineguns, 1 050 SKS rifles, 600 RPG-7 rockets, 216 limpet mines, 80 AK rifles, 400 rifle grenades and 30 anti-personnel mines, 21 light machineguns, nine sub-machineguns, eight Thompson machineguns, 160 B-10 rockets, 70 x 122 millimetre rockets, 213 metres of *Cordtex* detonating cord, one 3,5 millimetre rocket launcher, seven RPDs, 726 000 rounds of smallarms ammunition, 50 compasses, 13 RPG-7 sights, two 75 millimetre recoilless rifles – plus two cars, one Land-Rover, four outboard motors, 75 Klepper canoes, several inflatable boats and 14 tons of diesel fuel.

Both operations had been enormously successful for the Rhodesians producing fantastic results, and it was unfortunate that Martin Pearse had not been there to reap the benefits of his superb efforts.

The enemy certainly had not been up and waiting for them this time. Perhaps the fact they had not told CIO or the police had something to do with it? Perhaps that was where their weakness lay? Maybe someone there was responsible for all the spy leaks?

The attack had temporarily put paid to Nkomo's plans to mount an invasion. For that 100 tons of hidden weaponry had been earmarked for not only his non-conventional forces but his conventional troops too.

The arms dump represented his total reserves. It was at that stage, his last hope for arming his battalions for conventional assaults on Rhodesia.

The arms had been the ace up his sleeve, the weapons he had been relying on for his battalions in training at Mulungushi; and now he had lost them. It would mean he would have to hold back his battalions until he got a resupply – if he got one – and he could only hope the weaponry arrived in time to deploy his forces into Rhodesia prior to a ceasefire.

Meanwhile, Nkomo was hell-bent on training as many police, customs officers, pilots, all the people for his government-in-exile, as possible. More and more men were reporting to Mulungushi and Boma for conventional training in readiness to take over Rhodesia.

The potential threat still existed . . . could the security forces do anything about the build-up in time . . . could they prevent the invasion?

Operation Bouncer

The Rhodesian public had long been conditioned to judging the success of external operations by the number of kills achieved, and this was understandable as the mission given for the initial attacks was to "kill or capture the maximum number of terrorists."

But later, the planners changed this to a multiple mission where they hoped to: prevent enemy locations from functioning as bases . . . kill or capture the enemy hierarchy; or capture or destroy enemy weapons and logistical supplies . . . kill or capture the maximum number of terrorists and gain intelligence.

While the Selous Scouts were able to capture Elliot Sibanda, *The Black Swine*, ZANLA's top men fared much better, managing to escape all Rhodesian attempts to waylay and account for them.

For months, special forces working externally on Operation *Bouncer* ops as they were known, sat in wait for vehicles driven by the ZANLA hierarchy. A number of vehicles were ambushed and a few Russians accounted for – and ZANLA's lucky streak continued, although it was certainly not for want of trying on the Rhodesians' part.

On two occasions, small SAS teams infiltrated into the heart of the Mozambican capital, Maputo, in a bid to eliminate the hierarchy. But on both occasions, the operators had no choice but to return home without the mission having been accomplished. For the ZANLA hierarchy had been tipped off too, although unlike ZIPRA, the ZANLA brass had taken the precaution of evacuating every single member of their staff before the Rhodesians arrived.

Operation Uric, September 5-8, 1979

> *"If you want to make peace, you*
> *don't talk to your friends. You*
> *talk to your enemies."*
>
> *– GENERAL MOSHE DAYAN*

Despite the success of the one-man-one-vote elections, which had brought moderate Bishop Abel Muzorewa to power, and the positive response by European and American opinion, there was still no official recognition of the new order from Britain or anywhere else.

The Rhodesians, who had long felt that their salvation lay with the Tories rather than the Socialists, were to be proved horribly wrong.

When Margaret Thatcher won the British elections, Rhodesians were elated. Had not Lord Boyd and his team already pronounced the Rhodesian April elections free and fair? Surely recognition had to follow?

Yet, even before the Tories went on to win their own election, Lord Peter Carrington, destined to play an important role in Rhodesia's history, was saying: ". . . if you are going to bring Rhodesia back to legality, it will be necessary to get the support and agreement of the international community."

The main stumbling block preventing Britain from recognising the Muzorewa Government appeared to be the Commonwealth members of the OAU. But the British premier hoped to convince them to recognise Muzorewa at the Commonwealth prime ministers' conference in Lusaka in August.

But when August came around, attitudes among many Commonwealth countries had hardened and member countries were divided between those willing to recognise the Muzorewa administration and those which were not.

Such was the intensity of the debate that it even threatened the break-up of the Commonwealth itself.

Britain finally resolved the matter by advocating an all-party conference on the Rhodesian issue. What, Rhodesians wanted to know, of all those pledges to recognise the first black prime minister elected by 64 percent of Rhodesians? Why had the Tories reneged on their pre-election promises?

The simple truth was that the west was not prepared to recognise the internal agreement in the face of such opposition from the OAU and the front line states, which recognised the PF as the only "authentic and legitimate representatives of the people of Zimbabwe."

Despite all the pledges of support, Britain also had the very real matter of British interests to consider.

British exports to black Africa were worth £2 000 million a year and half of them went to oil-rich Nigeria. On the eve of the Lusaka summit the Lagos government announced it was nationalising the entire remaining assets of British Petroleum.

The seizure of more than six billion US dollars worth of BP's operation was stimulated by an attempt to force Britain not to sell oil to Rhodesia and South Africa.

Further, Nigeria threatened to cut off the billions of US dollars worth of goods and services bought every year from Britain, if Muzorewa's government was treated as legitimate.

It was the big squeeze. And the point was taken.

After much frantic effort by the British premier, the Australian Prime Minister Malcolm Fraser, and others attending the Commonwealth conference the details for a Rhodesian settlement were finalised. Others ironed out differences among the various delegates. Eventually, everyone in Lusaka agreed there was to be an all-party conference at Lancaster House, London.

The British were to draw up a new constitution, and after an all-party agreement and ceasefire had been negotiated, they would supervise new elections monitored by Commonwealth observers.

If Rhodesians felt incensed and in a no-win situation, it was no wonder. *The Herald* asked if Mrs Thatcher was "really a Labour Prime Minister in drag" and Tory MP Julian Amery commented that the agreement to hold all-party talks was "a black day for Britain and the Conservative Party." He added: "This will bring neither peace nor honour."

Deeply disturbed by the news of the all-party talks, Pik Botha, South Africa's Foreign Minister, voiced the sentiment shared by many Rhodesians: "The Zimbabwe-Rhodesian settlement issue is beginning to look like a rugby match where the game is played until the winners lose.

However, the Salisbury government, although initially insulted by proposals for an all-party conference, failed to heed South African advice and reluctantly agreed to attend the talks.

The war had to be stopped once and for all and sanctions lifted. Apart from the tragic loss of life, and mounting pressure from all sides, they were slowly running out of money and manpower. Perhaps the conference would provide the solution.

(Between the beginning of April and the end of July alone, 3 149 war deaths had been recorded *within* the country's borders. Of those, 1 808 were insurgents, 1 161 were black civilians and 31 were white, while security force losses stood at 141. There were no figures for those killed outside the borders.)

A few days later, the Patriotic Front, who had been equally reluctant to sit around a conference table, also agreed to go to London. Machel pointed out to Mugabe that they had not yet beaten the Rhodesians on the battlefield. It was time to negotiate.

The opening session of the marathon conference, destined to drag on for three tortuous months, was due to start on September 10. Back in Africa, meanwhile, the war raged on.

* * *

As the various delegations prepared for what was to be the final conference in the 14-year quest for a political solution, the security forces were planning to strengthen the Rhodesian's hand by mounting a major pre-emptive strike into Mozambique.

Operation *Uric* was to be the biggest offensive of the war, and it heralded the beginning of a new strategy.

During the initial stages of external operations, specific orders had been given that the Rhodesians had no quarrel with the armies of Mozambique and Zambia.

Their fight was solely against ZANLA and ZIPRA forces who were using the neighbouring host countries as a springboard, and many an operation was cancelled where there was a sporting chance of getting involved with the armies of the host country and thus increasing the chances of escalation.

As the war progressed, however, intelligence produced indisputable evidence that both Zambia and Mozambique were openly assisting the ZIPRA/ZANLA war effort.

Initially, the host countries gave help secretly, but towards the end of the war, they provided intelligence, helped train recruits, supplied them with arms, ammunition and transport, assisted them carry out trans-border crossings, and helped with all logistical matters. And they allowed them to set up their headquarters in major towns and cities.

There were enemy base camps in Zambia and Mozambique where Rhodesian guerillas actually shared camp facilities including a common anti-air protection system and enemy armour. ZANLA and their FRELIMO friends and ZIPRA and their Zambian Army comrades were, in fact, one and the same.

Linked with the policy of non-aggression towards host countries, no action was allowed to be carried out against industrial or agricultural targets, strategic bridges, or any target within Zambia or Mozambique which the Rhodesian Intelligence Agency considered to be against the economy of the country.

There was considerable frustration in some military quarters when clearance was sought – and refused – for attacks on Mozambique's sugar crop or Zambia's copper mines or major bridges, thereby bringing the host countries to their knees and forcing them to boot out their nationalist guests. The possibility of world pressure was always a major consideration in the Rhodesian camp.

To the simple soldier, such a policy was inconceivable.

If the enemy were using the main host country trunk routes, why couldn't the Rhodesians destroy the bridges and prevent the easy flow of enemy logistics?

If the terrorists were storing their arms and ammunition in host country barracks and armouries, why couldn't they attack them?

Every question of that nature was always fobbed off with the usual cliché: "It's a political decision."

It took until the final year of the war before the high command and the politicians decided that in order to stop the hordes overrunning Rhodesia from four fronts simultaneously, they would have to attack host country economic targets and, where necessary, host country forces.

The flow of ZANLA into the south of the country through the Gaza Province – *The Russian Front* – had reached such grave proportions that the planning team at Com-Ops was finally able to convince the national JOC that the FRELIMO and insurgent lines of communication had to be drastically disrupted.

Of the 10 800 ZANLA in Rhodesia, some fifty percent were deployed through Gaza, and with another 17 000 trainees in the pipeline, one-third were earmarked for deployment into Rhodesia through the province. All had staged through Mapai, the FRELIMO 2 Brigade headquarters and controlling centre for ZANLA.

Until the end of 1978, security force contacts with transit groups close to the border areas were frequent and kill rates were steady, if not spectacular.

Long-range SAS operations, supported when necessary by airstrikes and aimed at disrupting supplies by paralysing vehicle movement, had taken their toll of ZANLA arms and ammunition resupplies, effectively putting a brake on aggression in the Operation *Repulse* area.

Such was the strain on ZANLA logistics that ZANLA had been issued with obsolete Eastern Bloc rifles and even World War-2 Thompson sub-machineguns.

But since 1979, financial and manpower problems had brought changes.

329

The final phase in the *cordon sanitaire* minefield programme in the Gaza Province had been delayed, thereby aiding troublefree infiltrations. Small callsigns had lacked the firepower to either take on or inflict heavy casualties on enemy forces.

And on the few occasions when sizeable numbers had been on the ground, the isolated character of their deployments had enabled FRELIMO to determine quickly where they were assigned to and instigate follow-up operations.

The nature of the terrain in the south-east made life very difficult for the security forces and once their initial ambush had been mounted, they could not stay for long in the area without being chased. Everything was on FRELIMO's side.

Then in April, enemy incursions had taken on a new dimension.

The ZANLA/FRELIMO co-operation was stronger than ever, and changes in *modus operandi* revealed the very real threat posed by the Gaza Province.

The first indication of the new approach came when a FRELIMO soldier was captured as far inland as Kezi in Matabeleland. Subsequent intelligence told that there were more than 200 FRELIMO regulars operating inside Rhodesia alongside their ZANLA comrades and they had radio communications back to Mapai. Before deploying, they had undergone a two-month guerilla warfare updating course, covering bushcraft, weapon handling and sabotage.

They were heading for Bulawayo and their tasks were to blow up the railway lines, lay landmines and engage the enemy. Their deployment – albeit under duress – was for a three month stint and they were to be paid only on their return to Mozambique.

Another 1 000 FRELIMO were in the pipeline for deployment through the Gaza Province. The aim of the joint ZANLA/FRELIMO groups was simple: to hasten the end of the war.

Most worrying for the Rhodesians was that the country's economic lines of communication to the south – the rail links to the South African border and over which the majority of the country's emergency fuel supplies travelled – were under threat. If one particular bridge had been destroyed, it would have been irreparable.

A joint political-military decision had been taken by President Samora Machel and FRELIMO commander General Sabastian Mabote, in consultation with Robert Mugabe, which not only included the deployment of FRELIMO troops alongside ZANLA into Rhodesia, but also involved the complete integration of FRELIMO and ZANLA forces in Gaza.

FRELIMO also took over command and control of ZANLA and resumed responsibility for their logistics and protection in Gaza.

Clearly, something drastic had to be done to stem the rate and scale of ZANLA infiltrations ... pre-empt the threat of combined ZANLA/FRELIMO incursions ... take the pressure off the country's economic lines of communication with South Africa ... and halt the free movement and passage of war materials to the war front.

The time had come to kick the enemy off the doorstep, take the pressure off *Repulse* and *Tangent* operational areas and redirect the enemy flow to an area where the security forces could combat it.

Operation *Uric* was conceived to do just that. Now that the country had a black Prime Minister, it was hoped there would not be such a hue and cry from critics about such aggression.

The aim of the mission was to smash the road and rail communications ... flatten the Mapai forward base, which was so vital to both FRELIMO and ZANLA ... and force FRELIMO to abandon the border areas by pushing them below Barragem.

After that, if any ZANLA or FRELIMO wanted to infiltrate into Rhodesia, they would face a very long and difficult walk through areas where there was little water.

FRELIMO and ZANLA lines of communication were to be disrupted by the demolition of five tactical bridges – the most important phase of the operation. Pre-emptive strikes were also to be mounted on selected enemy targets and ZANLA/FRELIMO bases.

Thereafter, ambushes, aerial attacks and an intensive mining programme would disrupt road and rail communications, and prevent orderly movement.

Command and control positions ... wheeled transport ... a logistics base at Mabalane ... and telecommunications were also to be hit, including a *Troposcatter* communications centre.

If all went well, there would not be a single military bridge of strategic importance left in the Gaza Province.

Apart from slowing down the seepage into Rhodesia, it would also deliver a shattering blow to the Mozambican economy.

The most important demolition task was to be the Aldeia da Barragem irrigation canal and the road and rail bridges over the dam feeding the irrigation scheme for the whole area. Four lesser bridges would also be dropped.

Pre-emptive air strikes were to be made on Barragem, Mapai and Maxaila, and helicopter-borne troops would then be dropped off for the exploitation of that phase.

By eliminating the Gaza lines of communication, bombing Mapai to break morale, and a long harassment programme around the base, the Rhodesians were hoping to take Mapai.

With the bridges destroyed, the roads mined, communications totally severed, water and supplies cut off, Mapai would have been in a very vulnerable position. The enemy would have had no option but to leave.

Then, once everyone had left, the security forces intended to move in with a small force and destroy whatever was left of Mapai.

Mapai was a very heavily-defended forward base, and ComOps knew that to mount an attack would have needed a conventional force of two battalions, artillery and tanks.

An alternative had to be found and they were gambling that the long-term harassment coupled with the other phases of *Uric* would be the key to taking Mapai.

The operation would involve 360 men drawn from the SAS, the RLI and engineers, together with the air force, which was to deploy every available aircraft. These included, eight Hunters, twelve Dakotas, six Canberras, six Lynx aircraft and twenty-eight helicopters, including the Bell 205s.

Initially, because of the on/off nature of the operation and last-minute political considerations, which were totally beyond the control of the planners, they ended up with what was to be their third plan.

As a result, the final plan was still not completed by 20h00 the night before the troops were to start moving to the various internal and external administrative bases.

D-Day was scheduled for 07h00 on Sunday, September 2, but on Saturday it was evident that the weather would not allow *Uric* to begin on time. The weather had clamped down at Chipinda Pools tactical headquarters and forward airfield and the choppers could not take off.

331

As more than two hundred men had already been deployed externally to the adminstrative area – the start point for the bridge attacks – the planners were immensely worried.

They were certain that security would be blown and the mission compromised.

What concerned them too was that if the troops in the admin area inside Mozambique got into trouble, there could be no air support to assist them or helicopters to extract them. They were a good 200 kilometres (124 miles) from the border – one of the furthest admin areas set up in the war.

The deployment of so many aircraft at the various forward airfields along the border also caused grave concern and the planners were worried that civilian Viscount passengers arriving at Buffalo Range (one of the forward airfields) would pick up the additional air movement.

To add to their worries, the lowveld locals gave the planners the sad news that when low cloud and drizzle came in, it could be expected to last for three days.

From the start of the operation, things went wrong.

At the initial briefing, the troops were told that the external administrative area would be on an island in the middle of a large swamp. "Don't worry," they were told, "no one will be able to get at you over that swamp."

When they got there, they found that the "swamp" was as dry as a bone and that a division of tanks could have crossed.

During the long wait for the weather to clear, the planners back in Rhodesia were continually getting reports that FRELIMO columns were searching for the Rhodesians. One FRELIMO platoon, however, did its best to avoid the Rhodesians' position but failed. It says much for the camouflage of the admin area and little for the enemy platoon commanders' navigation that the platoon walked straight on to the position.

By now, the cloud base had lifted and the choppers were on their way to collect the troops for the start of Operation *Uric* and the bridge-blowing phase.

Quickly, SAS Quartermaster Major Paul Simmonds radioed base and told them to hold the choppers. Eventually, the FRELIMO platoon walked to within one hundred metres of the position and were still heading towards it. The RLI sub-unit covering that part of the perimeter opened fire and after a brief exchange of fire, twenty-two out of twenty-four FRELIMO were killed. One was wounded and the other managed to escape.

RLI Major Pete Farndell was injured and subsequently casevacked. He was not to know it then, but that incident was to save his life.

The frightening thing about the encounter was that the admin area had been located. If the security forces could not hold the position, they could not continue with the operation.

They had dropped off hundreds of drums of fuel, and a vast quantity of landmines and explosives, so they could not abandon the position either.

It was now September 5, and at last the mission was about to begin. The delay had seriously affected their original time appreciations and various adjustments were made in the planning.

The air strike on Barragem, 320 kilometres (200 miles) inside Mozambique and 150 kilometres (93 miles) north-west of the capital Maputo, took place exactly on time.

Four Hunter jets swept down the fertile Limpopo Valley to attack the enemy defensive positions holding the road and rail irrigation canal bridge, the most important bridges in the south-east, feeding the irrigation for the entire area.

All aircraft were subjected to anti-air fire, but the jets scored a number of direct hits on weapons, destroyed two barrack blocks and all transport.

Exactly five minutes later, 48 SAS helicopter-borne troops were dropped within one kilometre of Barragem road and rail bridges. The choppers lifted immediately for the safety of a holding area.

A number of heavy enemy machineguns were still in action after they had landed, but the fight through the Barragem defences was fairly rapid.

The SAS were fortunately able to capture two enemy 23 millimetre anti-aircraft guns one of which they were able to use to great effect in the ground role against enemy pockets of resistance on both banks of the river, thereby reducing the pressure on the SAS.

During this action, one of the men was shot in the leg and an immediate casevac called for.

In the confusion and heat of the battle, a communications error was made and the helicopter flew over the main enemy position . . . and as the Bell came into the landing zone, an enemy RPG-7 rocket launcher was fired while the aircraft was still hovering. The rocket struck the helicopter just below the blades, severing the main rotors. The Bell plummetted to earth and almost instantly burst into flames.

Technician Alexander Wesson was killed on impact, and the pilot was pulled from the flaming wreck by an extremely brave SAS Sergeant *Flash* Smythe. This action deserved recognition, and but for an administrative blunder at the end of the war, *Flash* would have received the BCR for this and other heroic deeds.

The pilot suffered a broken elbow, lacerations and shock, but thanks to the efforts of the quick-thinking sergeant, he was lucky enough to escape death. The helicopter was burnt to the ground – a terrible waste of life and a vital aircraft.

Meanwhile, the demolition teams were busying themselves setting up their charges on the two Barragem bridges. They had an elaborate system of ropes and pulleys worked out for the team to get under the bridge spans and were literally getting stuck in with *Wonder Glue* when the man on the captured 23 millimetre gun opened up.

Suddenly, rounds were cracking over their heads breaking the sound barrier. Split seconds later, the delayed sounds of the guns being fired reached them. Then came the deafening din as the rounds exploded in the distance.

"When you hear all that without being warned and you happen to be dangling on a precarious stamp-size platform ten metres from the concrete *and* endeavouring to place 20 kilogram satchel charges at the same time, it's not conducive to either balance or steady heartbeat!" explained Lance Corporal Andrew Standish-White.

Fortunately, he was glued to the platform at that stage, so he remained suspended.

It took about five hours to prepare the bridge for demolition, and at one stage it was touch and go as to whether there would be enough light to extract the troops that night.

Preparations on the other four bridges were unopposed, and by 16h30, the demolition job was completed.

An RLI-Engineer callsign under former SAS man Joey Du Plooy had a good morning at one of the targets. They had swept through the nearby town, taken it over, sprayed thirty vehicles with rounds, drained a fuel bowser and blown up two power stations. Then Engineer Captain Charlie Small blew the bridge.

All bridges with the exception of Barragem had been totally destroyed and the rail link severed.

Unfortunately, because of the time factor, the SAS men were extracted without physically checking on the damage at their Barragem target. While the rail line was cut, it later transpired that the road bridge had not been completely destroyed and light vehicles were still able to use it.

Their extraction had been premature and, according to some planners, more explosives should have been carried in the following morning and the job done properly. Although the SAS had the detailed plans of the bridge, they found that the engineers who had built it had put far more reinforcing into the bridge than the plans indicated. As a result, the SAS did not have enough charges with them to destroy it all.

The main Gaza supply route was, therefore, still open and the attack on Barragem had been of nuisance value only. It had served only to slow things down as opposed to cutting the communications link.

By last light on D-Day, all the troops had been extracted from their tasks and were back in the admin area. One hundred and twenty SAS men and 72 RLI troops were now to go on to Mapai, the heavily-defended FRELIMO 2 Brigade headquarters and ZANLA command centre.

The initial plan for Mapai had been the long harassment by the air force, with large ambush groups totally ringing Mapai on all three major access routes. After FRELIMO/ZANLA morale had broken and the enemy had fled, the idea was that ground troops move in to Mapai and destroy whatever was left of it.

But for a number of reasons, some to do with the weather, some political, and some involving other reasons which are still controversial in many circles, the concept was changed and instead of harassing Mapai with large ambush groups, a decision was made that ground troops should attack Mapai, after the bombing and before the enemy had left.

All FRELIMO bases in the province had already been put on alert about the bridge demolitions, but in Mapai, although the A/A gunners took up their positions, no undue alarm was caused by the warning.

Next day, a complete air of nonchalance existed in the enemy complex with no thought of an attack in anybody's mind. Some units were on muster parade, others were washing and having their breakfast. Others were still in bed, while the nine Russian advisers busied themselves checking the camp routine.

Thirty minutes later, 500 and 1 000 pound bombs, and golf bombs were raining from the skies as the Rhodesian planes swept over Mapai.

The FRELIMO command element area and communications centre were demolished, and the Russian's bunker collapsed from a direct hit. Lucky to be alive, the Russians quickly pulled out of Mapai.

Scores of tents went up in smoke, a small armoury exploded, 22 FRELIMO were killed and 32 wounded. All the uninjured hurriedly took up their defensive positions.

Thirty minutes later, however, the general feeling was that it was all over.

Then, the Rhodesian jets struck again, blowing up the main fuel dump with its underground storage tank. The main radar station was knocked out, one A/A position was destroyed and more people were wounded.

The Hawker Hunters were subjected to severe ground fire, but miraculously escaped without casualties.

The 192 helicopter-borne troops were meanwhile on their way to their pre-selected dropping zones, one kilometre from Mapai.

Earlier, because there was not enough room in one of the choppers, a group of security forces had drawn straws to decide who should stay behind. Corporal Ronnie Bell drew the short straw, and watched as the others climbed into the chopper.

Then the commander, Joey du Plooy, who had taken injured Pete Farndell's place on the operation, told Gavin Hulley-Miller to change places with someone in another chopper.

Before Operation *Uric,* the security forces had rarely had to contend with an enemy who was prepared to stay and fight. The only opposition on previous large-scale camp attacks came from a trapped enemy who had no alternative other than to fight it out. For it was always the enemy's tactic to disperse the moment an aircraft was heard.

Not this time.

As one unfortunate pilot of the chopper bearing Joey du Plooy and team and their explosives, flew directly over a satellite camp, miles from the main target, the enemy opened up.

There were two distinctive bangs as what was probably an RPG-7 rocket struck the aircraft immediately behind the pilot. The chopper rolled to the right and crashed into the ground. The occupants never stood a chance as the helicopter went in. It exploded in a ball of flame on impact, killing everyone on board.

It was the worst single military disaster of the war. Killed were the commander, South African born Joey du Plooy, Captain Charlie Small, the Operation *Uric* demolitions officer; well-known national rugby star Cpl LeRoy Duberly, 2nd Lt Bruce Burns, Cpl Hugh Fry, L/Cpl Peter Fox, Tpr Jacobus Briel, Tpr Brian Eslin, Australians Tpr Stephen King and Tpr David Prosser, and Sgt Michael Jones from England.

When the corporal who had drawn the short straw heard what had happened, he went back to the landing zone in the admin area to search for the straw that had saved his life.

He couldn't find it, but really needed no reminder of how lucky he had been. Neither did Pete Farndell and Gavin Hulley-Miller, brother of SAS/SB liaison officer, Stu Hulley-Miller. Stu had seen Gavin climb into the chopper but had not seen him get out, and for the remainder of the operation, he was convinced his brother had perished in the crash.

When an RLI callsign went in to inspect the crash site, they confirmed everyone was dead and it was impossible to bring out the remains.

As a result of the helicopter casualties, a number of operational adjustments were made to the plan.

The bulk of the SAS/RLI troops were however dropped in their correct landing zones. As the sweeplines closed with the main enemy position, it was very obvious that Operation *Uric* was not going to be a cakewalk.

Many of the old hands who had seen a lot of action agreed that they had never been subjected to such intense enemy smallarms, recoilless rifle and mortar fire.

The terrain was dead flat, the vegetation consisted mainly of thick jesse bush, and the soil was sandy loam. It made command and control extremely difficult. The temperature must have been in the nineties which made fighting a hot, thirsty business.

Jet strike after jet strike was called for, and due to Rhodesia's limited resources there was a three-hour turn-around gap where aircraft had to return to New Sarum or Thornhill to refuel and rearm.

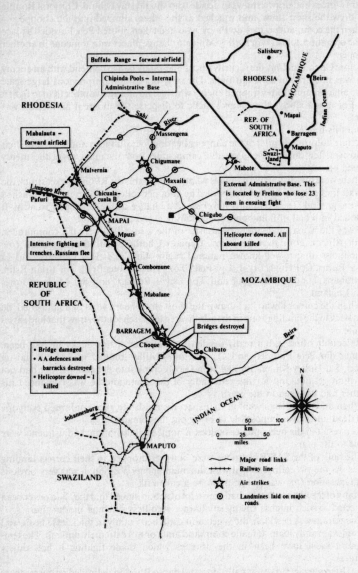

Inset map labels:
- Salisbury
- RHODESIA
- MOZAMBIQUE
- Beira
- Indian Ocean
- REP. OF SOUTH AFRICA
- Mapai
- Barragem
- Maputo
- Swaziland

Main map labels:

Buffalo Range – forward airfield

Chipinda Pools – Internal Administrative Base

RHODESIA

Sabi River

Massengena

Mabalauta – forward airfield

Chigumane

Mabote

External Administrative Base. This is located by Frelimo who lose 23 men in ensuing fight

Malvernia

Maxaila

Limpopo River

Pafuri

Chicuala-cuala B

Chigubo

MAPAI

Helicopter downed. All aboard killed

Mpuzi

Intensive fighting in trenches. Russians flee

Combomune

REPUBLIC OF SOUTH AFRICA

MOZAMBIQUE

Mabalane

BARRAGEM

Bridges destroyed

Choque

Chibuto

Beira

- Bridge damaged
- A A defences and barracks destroyed
- Helicopter downed – 1 killed

Johannesburg

INDIAN OCEAN

0   50   100
km
0   25   50
miles

N

MAPUTO

SWAZILAND

Major road links

+++++ Railway line

☆ Air strikes

⊚ Landmines laid on major roads

Operation *Uric:* Map showing major security force offensive into Gaza Province, Mozambique

336

The security forces were almost helpless during the period when all the aircraft returned to base. Rhodesia simply did not have the air support to provide a cab-rank facility over the target.

On their approach to Mapai, the SAS had discovered a series of early-warning stations built on platforms in the trees and connected by landline to the FRELIMO central command post in Mapai. It was a fascinating find and explained how FRELIMO had been able to monitor Rhodesian helicopter movements so accurately and for so long.

The SAS ended up against a two kilometre maze of typically Russian designed interconnecting zig-zag trench works, which put the attackers in an extremely difficult situation.

No sooner had they cleared one area than the enemy would pop up behind them.

Meanwhile, the jets continued to put in strike after strike and the ground troops couldn't quite believe the amount of fire being directed at the aircraft. There were 37 millimetre and 23 millimetre guns, and there had to be about twenty of them spread over half a kilometre.

The Canberras were forced to do a restrike from 21 000 feet, as it was unsafe to go any lower. And as they flew over Mapai, every one of the twenty heavy weapons, opened up on them.

The Rhodesian ground troops had problems of their own and were having 122 millimetre rockets and heavy mortars fired at them. The enemy anti-aircraft fire was equally effective in the ground role, too. Some said they could hear the secondary weapon on a tank firing, although later intelligence was that there were no tanks in Mapai at the time.

In any event, the heaviest support weapons the ground troops had were 60 millimetre mortars, which were no match for the heavy weaponry they were encountering.

The Rhodesians' attack was a very light infantry assault against a large well-defended conventional position, which would have been no problem had most of the enemy left, as had been anticipated. Except in this case, they had not.

Progress was extremely slow and it was soon evident that Mapai could only be taken with very heavy security force casualties.

The position was far better defended than they had imagined . . . the Rhodesians were ill-equipped . . . and it appeared pointless to continue.

Visibility in some cases was restricted to about ten metres and contacts were taking place at point blank range.

For the first time in the history of the war, the Rhodesians had been stopped dead in their tracks.

General Walls was airborne in the command Dakota and after a discussion with senior officers, he took the unenviable decision to withdraw from Mapai without physically taking the position.

Controversy still rages about whether or not the attack could have been pressed home and Mapai taken.

According to a captured FRELIMO man who was in Mapai at the time of the attack, it subsequently became general knowledge in the area that had the Rhodesians remained in Mapai for another two days, Mapai would have been taken as FRELIMO had very little food or water and were exceptionally tired.

The SAS were prepared to stick it out in the trenches, but had the unit lost thirty or so men, it would have had a dramatic effect on Rhodesia's counter-insurgency operations.

While the enemy had no manpower shortages, the security forces certainly had.

In view of all the enemy ground fire, the choppers could not return to uplift the 200-odd troops manning ambush positions and sweeplines around Mapai and they were faced with a ten kilometre (six mile) walk to a pick-up point.

The Rhodesians simply could not afford to lose another precious helicopter and more men.

A long straggly line of soldiers set off for the pick-up point and it became a race against time to get them all back to Rhodesia before dark. By late afternoon, the helicopters had arrived to begin picking up the weary disappointed troops.

The long line of choppers skimmed the treetops and made their way homewards through the dusk.

The entire area appeared to be teeming with enemy and the helicopters were subjected to ground fire throughout their flight, coming under heavy fire as they overflew a FRELIMO Mobile column. It was a most frightening exercise for passengers and crews alike. Eventually, all the troops were returned to the admin area.

Fortunately, the air strike schedule had gone almost to plan. During the two-day period, air strikes were put in on 14 enemy strongholds in Gaza. Much damage was caused including the destruction of the telecommunications and radar links at Malvernia. It was a truly magnificent effort by *The Blues*.

The mining programme had gone fairly well, despite adjustments having to be made, and by D-Day plus two, most of the roads had been mined and enemy transport had begun to hit the landmines.

As a result of withdrawing from Mapai and because of the increasing anxiety over the admin area being located, it was decided to terminate *Uric*.

In analysing the operation, the Rhodesians learnt many lessons.

They had underestimated the enemy. They were outgunned by enemy support weapons. Their air support was almost ineffectual against enemy troops, dug in with overhead cover. With Rhodesia's limited resources, they were virtually helpless when the aircraft returned to base to re-arm and refuel.

The weather had been against them but that had just been bad luck. In view of political considerations, the plans were changed too often at the last minute and as a result, the end plan was too rushed and not as thorough as it should have been.

They had not stuck to their original aim of disrupting the Gaza lines of communications. It had been changed to that of destroying Mapai. The destruction of the bridges almost became secondary, and they did not go back to finish off the Barragem bridge demolition.

There was much heated argument and harsh words behind closed doors at ComOps among several personalities as to where the responsibility lay for getting the planners to change their aim. One man denied the aim had been changed. The matter was never resolved and the controversy still rages. The author, therefore, can only give as accurate an account as possible after hearing most views.

However, the anger was nothing to that being felt across the border. The Mozambican economy had been dealt a serious blow and was reeling.

The attacks against the country's already shaky transport system had hit Mozambique where it hurt most – in the breadbasket. Even before the raids, food shortages and lack of transport were major problems. Now, the position was worse.

Gaza provided eighty percent of the nation's food. While the SAS did not break the dam at Aldeia da Barragem, they damaged one of the four sluice gates, which meant that 25 percent less water was available to irrigate the new rice crop.

For a country with a critical food shortage, it was a drastic blow. Yet had the security forces succeeded it destroying Aldaia da Barragem bridge completely, the damage would have been catastrophic.

The blow to the economy only served as an urgent reminder to Machel of the desperate need for a peaceful settlement.

Meanwhile, in London, the final battle of words was about to begin ...

Operation Norah, September 12, 1979

By now, the joint SAS/MNR callsign was working exceptionally well. Together, the two forces had notched up a string of successes and SAS officer Lieutenant Andrew Sanders, who had commanded numerous combined operations, was most enthusiastic about the rebels' role in Mozambique.

What FRELIMO thought of such team work is not known, but the cost to FRELIMO of such a liaison was becoming astronomical. The increasing numbers of blasts rocking the country were being taken very seriously and FRELIMO had been forced to re-introduce the death penalty for treason, sabotage and terrorism.

Yet, hated and harassed though they were by FRELIMO, the rebels' popularity with civilians was continuing to grow and had a great deal to do with many of their successes.

In September, that popularity was again put to the test when a 32-strong combined SAS/MNR group arrived a few kilometres from the towering Xilvuo Mountain where their latest target lay. Their deployment had been from Lake Alexander, an isolated spot a few kilometres from the Mozambican border, especially chosen to cover the SAS's involvement with the MNR. It had taken the Bells two lifts to get all 32 heavily-laden operators to their LZ deep inside Mozambique.

It took a further two days of hard marching for the group to reach the target area 165 kilometres (102 miles) inside Mozambique.

At the top of the mountain was one of FRELIMO's vitally important tropospheric scatter stations – a highly-sophisticated radio transmission and telecommunications centre. The Monte Xilvuo station was part of a communications chain linking major FRELIMO bases around the country – the key between FRELIMO in the north, south and central areas of Mozambique.

Cutting that chain would not only seriously disrupt FRELIMO communications, it would also force them to switch from using the tropospheric scatter communications which were difficult to monitor, to a system which was far easier for the Rhodesians to intercept.

Such was the importance of the centre that it was well-fortified, and there were reports that the platoon of protecting troops quartered in a three-storey barrack block had the benefit of anti-aircraft guns. Not only that, but the troops also had the ability to call in the tanks from the FRELIMO base at Dondo, five kilometres away.

But having arrived just short of the mountain, on the main road leading to Beira, the SAS and MNR could go no further.

There were civilians ahead and a few kilometres further on stretched the Pungwe River which twisted and turned on its way down to the Indian Ocean. And where there was water, there were bound to be locals who could report them to FRELIMO.

The SAS/MNR were deep inside Mozambique, were without immediate air support, and had no wish to tangle with tanks. It was time for the men of the Mozambique National Resistance to come into their own.

Leaving the SAS in the cover of the bush, they walked off into the nearby villages to liaise with the civilians and were able to persuade a couple of men to escort their party through the civilian population, across the river, and guide them to the foot of the mountains.

But for the MNR and their good relations with the locals, the SAS doubted if they would have reached the target that night, if at all. For the bush was extremely thick and there was only one crossing point over the river.

By last light, the 32 men had eased their way through the population, negotiated the river, and were at the bottom of the mountain.

Then, they began their long hard climb to the top, an agonising journey, made worse by their packs, which even by SAS standards were extremely heavy.

Five hours later and a good three-quarters of the way to the top, they hit the tar road which wound on its way to the *Troposcatter*. It was already midnight and time was against them.

A reconnaissance party reported that the *Troposcatter* was surrounded by a security fence and there was a sentry on duty at a guard hut, although he was fast asleep.

Time was now the enemy and they decided against taking a devious route in favour of sticking to the road – then walking in through the front gate!

The entrance was locked, but good old *Freddie* FRELIMO had done them a favour and lost the key – and the gate was wired up with the padlock still in position. Now all they had to do was cut the wire holding the gate in place and tiptoe past the snoring guard.

No one saw them nip through the entrance and ease around the back of the target where they cut a hole in the fence for their escape down the mountain.

The commander had picked up a number of twin-barrelled 23 millimetre anti-aircraft guns with his night binoculars, and, getting the operators to sit outside the fence, he, the mission 2IC Dave Berry and a couple of others silently moved around the target assessing which of the weapons could pose a problem for them.

There was certainly an impressive amount of firepower protecting the *Troposcatter*, but only one of the four 23 millimetre guns was in a position to give them any serious trouble. It was near their escape route and Dave Berry was given the job of destroying it.

They gathered up the other men, then quickly led them into position around the telecommunications centre.

Dave Berry and his RPD gunner moved up to the 23 millimetre gun, which was nicely sandbagged, and no doubt protected a couple of sleeping gunners. Two other men were to take on another gun position where the gunners were tucked up asleep under a bivvy.

The commander was to launch the attack by throwing a bunker bomb into the control room. That would be the signal for the men to open up on their specific targets.

Soon, everyone was in position and only FRELIMO was unaware of the trouble that was about to erupt.

Suddenly, the silence was shattered and all hell broke loose as the main group's bunker bomb exploded in the control room.

Within seconds, the roar of rapid shooting had added to the commotion of the attack. Fires were burning, smoke was billowing and a vivid display of streaming tracer lit the early morning.

Then the RPG-7 gunners were on their feet. There were a couple of huge bangs and flashes, and the first of their rockets left their launchers to punch holes into the various communications positions.

The minute the signal came and the firing started, Dave Berry threw a bunker bomb into the gun pit, then ran for cover. But nothing happened, and he ran forward to try again, this time with a white phosphorus grenade.

As he closed in on the gun position, he saw a sleepy gunner clamber out from behind the sandbags and climb on to the seat of his gun.

Dave pulled the pin on the grenade and threw it towards the gunner. The canister arched through the air towards the gun pit, but even before it hit home, Dave had accounted for the gunner with his AK. As the grenade exploded and white smoke billowed out of the pit, the gunner, who by now lay slumped over the seat, was thrown forward on to the barrel.

Dave Berry's RPD gunner immediately offloaded his belt into both man and gun and Dave finished off the remainder of his magazine on the FRELIMO man. By now, the grenade had set the sandbags alight and a fire was raging in the gunpit.

Over in the other gun position, another bunker bomb had also failed to go off. As the two SAS men responsible ran for cover, the FRELIMO gunners opened up, hitting one man in the head and the other in the foot.

The SAS returned fire and all fell silent in the gun pit. The two SAS men examined their wounds, but fortunately they were not serious.

For the next ten minutes, the SAS and the MNR kept up the attack, pouring a fierce amount of firepower into the targets. And despite all the din, the FRELIMO in their three-storey barrack block, kept their doors tightly bolted.

But now the attackers were rapidly losing the fight against time. They had to be on their way and off the mountain before first light and before reaction troops and the tanks could be deployed.

The damage to the *Troposcatter* was far from complete but it was enough to upset FRELIMO and would cost them the equivalent of ten thousand Rhodesian dollars to repair.

The commander shouted the ceasefire and the operators gathered their equipment and deftly withdrew around the side of the destroyed control room and past the still-burning gun pit.

They consolidated, then stepped through the escape hole in the security fence and out into the thick bush once more, setting off down the mountainside as fast as they could. But the bush was extremely thick and the going hard; and they couldn't see a thing. The only way was to slide down the mountain, continually saying where they were for the benefit of the men behind.

Above them, the telecommunications centre crackled and burned. Now that the commotion had died down, FRELIMO were venturing out of their barracks and beginning to get themselves organised.

The attackers had been battling through the bush for about an hour when a loud explosion rocked the mountainside ... and Dave Berry knew that the fire he had started in the gunpit had finally spread to his unexploded bunker bomb.

By now, FRELIMO were firing down the mountainside with everything they had. But they didn't know where the troublemakers were and their searching fire was going all over the mountain. Streams of tracers flew through the darkness over the attackers' heads, to be followed by the explosions as the 23 millimetre shells went off.

It was an impressive and fascinating sight against the blackness of the night. But it was pretty terrifying, too, and it gave the saboteurs plenty of incentive to get moving.

Suddenly, they were out of the undergrowth and at the bottom in a small clearing, hitting the tar road at about 04h00. It would be daylight soon and they knew they had to be out of the area and across the main Beira road by then. Only then could they feel safe and relax.

They decided to stick to the road in the hope of gaining a few vital minutes. It was something they wouldn't normally do as they had no idea if FRELIMO were waiting in ambush at the bottom of the road.

But time was now totally against them and the pressure very much on.

They raced down the tar and could hear the rumble of vehicles crunching along the main Beira road. Was it military transport bearing FRELIMO reaction troops? Would they be cut off almost 200 kilometres (125 miles) inside hostile territory with no means of transport except their feet?

They hurried down the mountain, hoping against hope that it was just civilian traffic after all.

The 23 millimetre shells continued to search for the elusive attackers, now nearing the flatlands close to the road.

Suddenly, a very loud voice rang out across the night and challenged them in Portuguese.

"HOLTA!" its owner ordered from the bush just 25 metres away, uncertain if the shadowy shapes clattering down the mountainside were friends or foes.

Then, without waiting for a reply, the FRELIMO group waiting in ambush near the bottom of the mountain opened up with smallarms fire and a 12,7 millimetre machinegun mounted on a vehicle.

The SAS and MNR fled for their lives, leaping over small rises and running blindly to the right – while yet another group ran up an embankment to the left.

The volume of fire that came down was tremendous and the SAS were big enough to admit that it was all fairly frightening.

Then Dave Berry on the right of the road crashed to his knees and his Bergen pinned his head to the ground. He staggered to his feet and took off again, finishing his journey with a record-breaking long jump, landing in a shallow riverbed on top of 13 other lads who had already beaten him to it.

A tremendous feeling of relief swept over him. But where the hell was the commander and all the others?

The first thing he did was check that they had the *Big Means* with them. They did, and again he experienced an overwhelming sense of relief. At least now they could communicate with the outside world.

They lay low for 15 minutes with FRELIMO keeping up their barrage. Dave tried to make radio contact with the mission commander and the others, but there was no reply. He shouted to them but couldn't make himself heard above the roar of FRELIMO guns, and knew that even if they shouted back, he wouldn't be able to hear them anyway.

Those who had run to the left of the road were pinned down between the FRELIMO ambush group at the bottom of the mountain and the reaction team firing from the top. Soon the ambushers dispersed and the trapped men darted across the mountain road to join the main SAS/MNR group to the right.

Five men crossed over and three went for cover near each other. When Bob Jones, Paul Schofield and an MNR man saw each other, they thought they were part of the main group, but when they looked around, they realised their little party was completely alone.

Everyone else had gone. Where to, they hadn't a clue. They called out a few times, but there was no reply.

The three men decided to cross the main Beira road at the foot of the mountain as soon as possible and get into open country, for they knew that to be caught on the wrong side of the road would be disastrous. They had to get a move on before a reaction force could follow up with tanks.

* * *

The other SAS/MNR groups meanwhile were still lying low at the bottom of the mountain with angry FRELIMO still firing at them.

Then, as if in answer to their prayers, a funny thing happened.

FRELIMO at the top of the mountain opened up on the FRELIMO ambush group at the bottom . . . and the ambushers began firing back at their own men up the mountain. A real ding-dong battle raged between both FRELIMO groups, and for a few moments, the focus was taken off the SAS and MNR.

But now the sun was coming up and Dave Berry's 14-man group knew they had to get going. They gathered up their packs and quickly moved off the mountain, walking under the high canopy of tracers and smallarms rounds coming from both ends of the mountain and arching high above them.

As they neared the Beira road, they were very apprehensive, remembering all the traffic they had heard earlier. They managed to cross over uneventfully, but almost immediately heard the sound of tanks approaching.

It was yet another incentive to get going and they quickened their pace. Once back at the river, they refilled their water bottles, for they had no way of knowing how long they would have to stay in the area before recovery.

They were all dog-tired by now, but there could be no relaxing; they set off once more, with the pace as fast as before.

It was now almost 05h00 and fairly light.

As Dave Berry and his 13 SAS and MNR men approached an African kraal they could see people lying outside their huts. But the Africans kept their heads down and pretended they were asleep . . . and the column of men snaked around the prostrate figures uneventfully and continued on their way.

Eventually, they got well clear of the civilian population and reached their crash rendezvous. But there was still no sign of the 18 missing men.

They lost no time in rigging up their radio to tell the officer co-ordinating the operation back in Rhodesia what had happened . . . and he immediately got airborne with an instruction to the Lynx pilot to get across the border as quickly as possible.

The Hunters had been put on standby, too, which was always a comforting thought to ground troops in a spot of bother. The choppers were involved in another pick-up, but would be with them soon.

Two hours later, the Lynx arrived overhead and as soon as the airborne commander began talking to Dave Berry over the radio, mission commander Andrew Sanders came on the air. It was the first time Dave Berry had heard from the commander since the ambush, and the good news was that he and another group were only two kilometres away from them.

A roll call accounted for everyone bar one MNR man and two SAS troopies, Bob Jones and Paul Schofield. There was no way of knowing, either, if the three missing men had stayed together or if each was running around Mozambique on his own.

There was now very heavy vehicle movement in the area and the general feeling was that if the three men had not been killed, they would almost certainly have been captured ... and if so, they were as good as dead anyway.

But Dave Berry and his party had their own worries. They were caught in a triangle of roads. They could hear FRELIMO military vehicles and tanks deploying on all sides, and dropping troops to cut them off.

Dave called for immediate jet support and the Hunters were soon with them, dropping off their deadly payloads. Then, as the jets' time overhead ran out, they returned to base.

Eventually, the helicopters could be heard coming to take the first load of men to safety. Unfortunately for those left behind to await the second lift, the Lynx, which could have given support if need be, had returned to Rhodesia to refuel – while all around their triangle of roads were enemy tanks and troops.

They had no idea how many FRELIMO tanks had been neutralised by the Hunters and the atmosphere was electric as they sat with their rifles ready waiting for FRELIMO to flush them out of their bush hideaway.

But FRELIMO never came, and the SAS and MNR neither knew nor cared why. After a worrying ninety minutes without air cover, the Lynx appeared overhead again and shortly afterwards, the Bells arrived to take them home.

Even before the choppers had touched down, the operators had thrown in their kit. The Bells struggled up but at fifty feet, could go no higher. Dave Berry threw a couple of Bergens out and the choppers lifted. The operators had quite a bit of adrenalin to replace that night and readily admit to consuming large quantities of vodka.

But the fate of the two SAS troopies, Bob Jones and Paul Schofield, plus the MNR man, was still unknown.

The two troopies had only six months' operational experience behind them and were still very much new boys by SAS standards. If they had not already been killed or captured, would they know what to do? The longer they were on their own, the bigger the odds against them, and some of the older hands, now safely back in Rhodesia, feared the worst.

* * *

The three missing men, however, were still very much alive. Having crossed the Beira road, they realised that a reaction force would probably be deployed to both their north and south. Forcing themselves to think clearly, they reckoned they had only one day to attract the attention of the choppers or spotter planes. After that they would be caught between both reaction forces.

Their position was critical. They were deep inside hostile territory, had just contributed to an attack on a vital FRELIMO telecommunications centre, and were not the most welcome characters. They had no communications to call for help, and water would not be easy to come by.

As they began to walk northwards away from the road, tanks began arriving and there was a lot of movement on the road.

Then one tank closed on the three men and they ran for their lives. But after two minutes it broke off its advance and the little party slowed to a brisk walk, their hearts pumping, the adrenalin flow easing slightly as the pressure lessened.

They walked until dawn then crossed a river. The water was a godsend; they needed it badly for the long walk ahead of them.

They had decided the best plan was either to head north and walk 100 kilometres (62 miles) to the MNR's Gorongoza mountain base where they could call for help, or head west to the eastern highlands and home. The second plan meant a trek of almost 200 kilometres (124 miles). Both alternatives were daunting.

They had little food left and although they replenished their water, they knew it would have to be conserved until they reached the next river source, sixty kilometres (37 miles) to the north.

They were by now feeling the first effects of fatigue and felt physically drained. By early morning, they had walked about twelve kilometres (seven miles) away from the target, walking due north and using their standard issue wrist compasses for their bearings.

Then, to their utter relief, came the welcoming whirr of rotor blades and a few moments later, a Rhodesian chopper appeared in the skies.

But their green smoke grenades and phosphorus failed to attract the pilot's attention, and the trio felt only frustration as the chopper, which represented life itself to them, flew off, and the bush fell silent once again.

The whirr of the rotors generally meant uplift and it was the most loved sound by any operational soldier. But this time the rules had changed and the sight and sound of the choppers seemed only there to tantalise.

If the two SAS men were worried, it was nothing to that of the MNR operator. For he knew no mercy would be shown to him if caught by FRELIMO. He would be beheaded.

They were now between two major roads and could see FRELIMO sweeplines . . . and they wondered who or what would arrive first – the *Freds* or the choppers. They knew they had to move to survive.

Another chopper came in but again the pilot failed to see them. Then another put down 400 metres away from them to refuel from its inner drums. They were saved at last!

The three stranded men ran towards the waiting chopper, but the going was hard through the thick grass. They could see the Bell sitting waiting for them, but they got to within eighty metres when it slowly lifted, banked to the north and then was gone.

A feeling of despair set in, and, as they set off to find some open ground so they could be seen by the choppers, morale was low.

Now, they forced themselves to think like the *Freds*. What would they do? What would they use? The three men acknowledged FRELIMO were capable of very fast and thorough follow-up.

From their position atop Monte Xilvuo, FRELIMO would be in an ideal spot to see all the open spaces and helicopter movement. Then the three men began to think of the smoke and phosphorus they had thrown and if the *Freds* had seen it.

Now they realised they were in a no-win situation. They wanted to attract attention to themselves, but certainly not FRELIMO attention.

They moved off again, slowly this time, taking more care over their anti-tracking techniques.

Eventually, they found an ideal spot and decided to lay low and wait for an aircraft rather than walk to Gorongoza or home. They had to give the pilots a sporting chance of finding them.

Tiredness swept over them and they wondered if they would have the energy to move away if a FRELIMO sweepline came. But they knew their minds would carry their bodies through bad times, and they would move if they had to. It was something they had learned on their selection, but had only fully appreciated once with the troops.

The MNR operator began his customary afternoon prayer session and made a small offering of powder on the ground to appease the spirits. It did nothing to soothe SAS nerves.

Soon after 13h00, two Lynx aircraft came overhead, traversing the area for about twenty minutes and coming close to their position. Having used all their smoke grenades, they desperately began signalling their position with their heliograph.

But again they were not seen. Then they lit a fire. But still no reaction. Eventually the Lynx, by now low on fuel, disappeared from sight.

The three men were desperately disappointed. Their means of escape had been so close – and yet so far.

At 15h00, the Lynx was back again and the three men felt it was probably their last chance of recovery. After that they would be on their own and they would have to begin walking to get clear of the area.

For twenty frustrating minutes, their heliograph and fire gave out their urgent calls for help, but to no avail.

Suddenly, the Lynx's wings tipped left, then right. They had been seen and they knew that a chopper would be with them soon. The three men were ecstatic.

What happened next, they found out later. The Lynx pilot lost them, and with the chopper on its way for recovery, the Lynx pilot and passenger still could not see them and were close to calling the Bell away. For by now there was no one for them to uplift.

Then the passenger, Sergeant Major Karl Lutz, picked up their fire and registered their heliograph ... and the helicopter pilot came in with the usual Rhodesian Air Force precision. The LZ was only just big enough for the Bell to hover above them at six feet.

The three men scrambled up into the chopper, climbed out of the LZ and headed home.

There was no energy left for a celebration and the three men slept soundly that night. It had been a worrying experience – and FRELIMO would not be the only ones to remember their visit to the Mozambican mountain!

Beira Revisited, September 18, 1979

Within six months of their daring and highly successful attack on the fuel depot, the MNR and SAS were planning to slip back into Beira again. This time, their visit was to take them right into the heart of the FRELIMO stronghold, not merely the fringes.

It would call for a certain amount of bravado, but at that stage of the war, that was one quality the operators did not lack.

Top of their hit list this time was FRELIMO's stategically important telephone exchange, the main telecommunications link between FRELIMO's major operational areas in central Mozambique and FRELIMO's command centre in Maputo, the capital.

Entry to the telecommunications complex was to be as surreptitious as possible, not only to ensure they achieved their aim, but so that they still had the element of surprise on their side to take on another target.

Although there was a guard on duty at the front of the telecommunications complex, intelligence said he generally hung around the steps of the post office and even slept some of the time. The SAS/MNR team would have to get into the building without alerting him or waking the two Cuban telecommunications experts who slept in the centre.

Their entry was to be through the metal gates at the back of the centre but as there would be no time to pick the lock holding the padlock and chain in place, they would have to use bolt-cutters.

The operators would slip through, piece the chain together with a length of wire, then with Pete Cole and Les Clark picking the inside locks, make their way to the most important rooms housing equipment which, if destroyed, would cause the most damage to the FRELIMO telecommunications network.

They knew exactly which equipment to lay their time-delayed charges around, having gleaned their knowledge from advanced demolition courses over the years. A recent visit to Salisbury's telecommunications centre on the pretext of doing another demolition course had also enabled them to update their knowledge.

Their charges, set to go off during the exfiltration phase, would partially demolish the building. The most important rooms were on the first floor and once destroyed, the floors above would collapse like a pack of cards. The SAS and MNR planned to leave enough thermite and fire bombs around to reduce what was left of the building to a pile of ashes.

After setting their time delays, they were to turn their attention to the prison on the opposite side of the road, where hundreds of political prisoners were kept in appalling, almost Dickensian, conditions.

According to some of the horror stories coming out of Beira, the prisoners would stick their arms through metal bars and plead with passers-by for help. The MNR and SAS now planned to answer the prisoners' cries for help and they were to attack the prison, eliminate the guards and release the prisoners, just as the remarkable Andre Matangaidze, the MNR leader, had done at Gorongoza the year before.

While the main party, commanded by Captain Colin Willis, was doing that, two other groups would be lurking around the docks intent on doing more damage, for the other major targets earmarked for destruction were two dredgers, the *Matola* and the *Pungoe*, and the drydocks.

If all went according to plan and the dredgers were put out of the action, the harbour would silt up very rapidly preventing large shipping getting into Beira. This would greatly aid Rhodesia's war effort by preventing Russian resupply ships bringing ZANLA munitions and arms into the harbour ... while the destruction of the drydocks would further hamper the use of Beira as an economically viable port by anyone wanting to bring ships in for repair.

Having missed the chance of attacking one of ZANLA's warehouses on their first trip to Beira, they hoped to be more successful the second time around. This time, a ZANLA warehouse right on the dockside was to get a visit from a group of demolition experts.

The mission was planned for late one Sunday night in September when the docks and the city were reported to be as quiet as a grave. The few FRELIMO who did patrol the city did so in small groups, and were armed with AKs and just a few rounds.

But Sunday night came and went and the hand-picked SAS and MNR men were still on their way to Beira. The infiltration phase had been a lot harder than they had anticipated and it was Monday night by the time the black shapes of the Beira skyline loomed into sight.

The feeling was that Monday was as dead as Sunday and the various commanders decided that the mission should go ahead.

The original plan too was that they sneak into Beira after 23h00, but Colin Willis and the ten operators in the main party arrived on the outskirts of the city much earlier and a decision was made to get into town without delay, destroy the telephone exchange, storm the prison and release the prisoners. The two other groups meanwhile, were to get on with their tasks and set up their charges on FRELIMO's precious dredgers and drydocks, and around ZANLA's warehouse.

Two men were left behind in the mangrove swamps to watch their route out, and on Colin's signal, the other eight operators came out of the black mud and the slime of the mangrove swamps, changed into clean, crisp FRELIMO uniforms and began moving down the streets of Beira, bold as brass and looking for all the world like a FRELIMO patrol about its business.

Most sported the usual array of communist weapons and their side pockets concealed holsters containing silenced pistols, in case they had to extract themselves from a situation quickly and quietly.

Colin and Lieutenant Mike Rich had silenced American AR40 rifles, which had the ability to fire at an extremely rapid rate. They were to take on any FRELIMO men who looked like raising the alarm, swiftly pumping them with dozens of rounds to ensure their permanent silence.

They felt very conspicuous and a little apprehensive. Yet each man was quietly confident that he was with a highly trained and capable team.

As they made their way down the city streets, they constantly reminded themselves to act naturally and walk casually. But their nerves were taut and many felt that their bodies must have looked the same. Although they were well blackened-up, the SAS men in the party were very conscious that their European features would not pass close inspection.

They kept their heads slightly lowered and hugged the shadows, but every pair of eyes was on the look-out for trouble and every finger was curled around a trigger.

Now and then, the odd pedestrian passed within a few paces of them and the soldiers felt as if they were on the stage with every Mozambican eye riveted on them. But none of the passers-by even bothered to give them a second glance, and the saboteurs knew they were doing well.

They turned into a main street and headed straight towards the city centre.

The scene that confronted them was not at all conducive to steady heartbeat.

The quiet grave-like atmosphere they had been expecting had given way to a veritable hub of activity and the thought flashed through one man's mind that it resembled Salisbury's main thoroughfare, Jameson Avenue, on a Saturday morning.

The city was well lit and there were people strolling about and waiting for buses. Other groups were gathered on the street corners, idly chatting and passing the night away.

The restaurants and pavement cafes were still open and business appeared to be booming as the late-night customers crowded around the metal tables, smoking and leisurely sipping at their bottomless coffee cups.

Cars rolled on their way and occasionally, buses swung around corners at break-neck speed, their impatient hooters blaring out their urgent warnings and adding to the city sounds.

It was blatantly obvious that even though the Portuguese had left, their lifestyle for a late-night social life had lingered on.

And there in the thick of it all were eight MNR and SAS operators with sabotage clearly in mind. Undaunted by the unexpected turn of events and the increased risk of compromise, the MNR/SAS team continued to brave it out, snaking their way around pedestrians and crossing streets, just as a normal FRELIMO patrol would do.

None of the Mozambicans suspected a thing as the soldiers marched on their way, silently ticking off the various landmarks en route to the telephone exchange.

Yet Colin Willis, concerned though he was by all the people milling around, was still confident that as long as they could continue the bluff, they could achieve the mission.

Then, 300 metres from the target, the commander suddenly saw a FRELIMO guard at about the same time that he saw them.

He had been slovenly lounging in the shadows against a building, but the moment he saw Colin and his team, he leapt to attention and started gathering civilians around him checking their passes. It was obvious he was convinced the uniformed men bearing down on him was some sort of high-ranking FRELIMO party.

He nervously allowed them to ease past him unopposed and they rounded the last corner without him guessing their true identity. They offered up a silent prayer and continued on their way.

But their relief was very short-lived. If they had been taken aback by the sight of so many people around the city centre that night, it was nothing to the consternation they felt when they caught their first glimpse of the target.

Instead of the one guard they were expecting to find on duty at the telecommunications centre, there were nearer ten heavily armed FRELIMO patrolling the building.

To further complicate matters, there was a bus stop near the back gate where they planned to cut their entry – and there were dozens of people milling around the gate and lounging in the shadows waiting for their transport home.

Colin needed time to think things over carefully. There could be no panic decisions, no hasty actions.

Quickly, he led the way across the road, then nipped down a dark alley where they would not be silhouetted by the street lights.

Then they based up in the grounds of a partially constructed building while Colin took stock of the situation and contemplated what to do for the best.

The odds against success were stacking up rapidly, but there was no cause for despair yet. The mission was still possible. But the commander realised there was not the slightest chance of them pulling the job off while so many people were around. Even if they were to storm the exchange and kill everyone in sight, by the time they had spread their charges around the building, the alarm would have been raised and their escape route would be blocked.

Colin decided that they would just have to bide their time. They would sit it out for a few hours until the FRELIMO patrols and the pedestrian traffic died down. Then, if it wasn't too late, they could carry out their task and still get away before daylight.

Then, another crisis. Their arrival in the shadows had not gone unnoticed. For as they debated what to do, a night watchman stood in the grounds of the construction site and wondered why a heavily armed bunch of men should be sitting in such a gloomy spot for no apparent reason. Eventually, his curiosity got the better of him, and Pete Cole suddenly saw a movement as the man sauntered off towards the FRELIMO guards on duty outside the telephone exchange.

Expecting trouble, they prepared themselves for a fight. But nothing happened and they lessened their grips on their rifles.

But within twenty minutes, Colin had been forced to change his plans again. A group of FRELIMO, armed with at least one machinegun suddenly stepped into the little alley and began walking straight towards them.

It was clear that the night watchman had finally convinced them that something was not quite right. It was equally clear that the MNR/SAS's little game was up; that they had been compromised and they would not be attacking the telephone exchange and prison that night.

But there was no time for regrets – or finesse.

There were walls on three sides of them and FRELIMO was advancing down the fourth side. They were trapped and would have to fight their way out.

Colin quickly gave a whispered command to his callsign to get ready to pull out and prepare to cover both himself and Mike Rich.

Colin and Mike stepped from the shadows and approached the FRELIMO patrol, their silenced 22 rifles hanging loosely in their blackened hands, the deadpan look on their faces telling the lie that they were friendly forces.

Their bravado and acting abilities did them great credit that night, for by the time the FRELIMO group finally got close to them, they appeared totally offguard. But the mission could not go ahead and the two SAS men knew what must be done if they were to get away unscathed.

As the FRELIMO patrol commander and his second-in-command got to within a few paces of them, Colin and Mike swiftly lifted up their rifles. There was an immediate *sss, sss, sss* sound as each offloaded an entire magazine of silenced 22 ammunition into them, and the lifeless bodies of the two FRELIMO men crumpled to earth with a thud.

Thereafter things happened fast. For it was time for the SAS and MNR to get going.

As they hurried away, the four FRELIMO survivors darted for cover around the back of the buildings and began firing at the fleeing attackers with machineguns and AKs. But generally, their firing following the typical FRELIMO pattern and was aimed not so much at their assailants, as above their heads.

Nevertheless, Colin and party were quick to dodge away and with Pete Cole and Nick Wilson bringing up the rear and covering them, they nimbly scaled the wall.

As one giant of an operator leapt over the wall, his landing was cushioned by a somewhat startled pedestrian who had the misfortune and incredible bad timing to walk by just as the hulk set sail through the air.

Then they all thundered away, running through a muddy swampline and back on to the main street in the same direction they had come. Pete Cole had to stop on a traffic island to let a bus screech by, but otherwise they were still in a reasonable semblance of order.

With the commander setting the pace, they dashed across streets and darted around civilians, shooting at various FRELIMO people on the way.

Despite all the commotion, the town seemed to be carrying on much the same as before. None of the civilians made any attempt to dive for cover, the customers in the pavement cafes continued sipping their coffees, and no one seemed startled as eight heavily armed men clattered by.

As they ran up one road, another restaurant came in sight. For Nick Wilson, carrying a pile of MNR pamphlets, it was a golden opportunity.

The look of sheer horror on the faces of the Portuguese restaurant manager and his customers can only be imagined as a man suddenly appeared in the open doorway, said a brisk "Here" in English, then threw in a bundle of MNR pamphlets. Then, leaving them to read all about the exploits of the rebels, the SAS men raced away.

Then it was back to the muddy mangrove swamps to rendezvous with the others. In view of the compromise, the operators waiting in the docks for the command to destroy ZANLA's warehouse were told to abort their task, so once again, ZANLA's luck held and they got to keep their precious stores.

They successfully exfiltrated without any further encounters with FRELIMO, but they were all bitterly disappointed.

At the subsequent debrief, the commander stated that he was quite convinced there had been a security leak. But nothing so sinister had happened this time. The MNR had been conducting an extensive and successful suitcase bombing campaign in the urban areas at that time and it had so worried FRELIMO they had tightened security and increased the guard at all key installations.

For the SAS and MNR it had been bad luck. Yet FRELIMO did not get everything their own way that night. The other phases of the mission went ahead as planned and the dredgers and drydocks were successfully blasted with limpet mines, putting them out of commission for many months.

The assault team responsible for putting the charges and limpets under the dredgers had a narrow escape when a 42 kilogram charge prematurely detonated while they were a few minutes away, creating severe underwater shock. Although stunned and exhausted, they persevered and laid six limpet mines on the two dredgers in strong underwater currents.

The next morning, the crew of the dredger, the *Pungoe,* were on deck watching in wide-eyed amazement as the *Matola* sank, when, to their horror two more limpets rocked Beira – and the next they knew they were up to their knees in water as their own ship started to sink under them. As punishment for their lack of vigilance, they were made to help salvage the *Matola.*

The Cubans unsuccessfully tried to salvage the uninsured *Matola* and in the end a South African marine salvage team had to be called in to repair the Dutch-built dredger and to remove 800 tons of silt, but it was a good six months before FRELIMO got the use of her again.

FRELIMO didn't have enough money to salvage the *Pungoe* and at the time of writing, the wreck of the dredger still lies buried in mud at the bottom of the harbour, where it continues to be a hazard to shipping.

But for an unexpected breeze which sprang up at the change of tide, the dredgers would have swung into the main channel, blocking shipping and closing the port. As it was, they swung away from the main channel, and the port was only partially closed.

A third dredger which had not been in the harbour that night was brought in to continue the dredging programme, but FRELIMO were so worried that she would meet the same fate as the other two, they posted armed guards and never tied her up in the same place twice.

But with the loss of the *Matola* and the *Pungoe,* the port began to silt up very rapidly and one vessel touched the bottom of the harbour. The marine insurers then viewed Beira as a risky port, and a surcharge was imposed on cargoes, which had a ripple effect on both Mozambique and neighbouring Malawi.

It had not been an entirely wasted trip after all ...

Monte Cassino Reconnaissance, September-October, 1979.

Inspector Winston Hart of the national intelligence team, whose job had been to keep abreast of ZANLA camps in what had become known as the Chimoio Circle, had got wind the area was now in use again.

Repeated security force attacks had left previous Chimoio camps decimated and after SAS Lieutenant Rich Stannard had called in the jets to flatten several new camps which had sprung up, the area had gone quiet again.

But now, recent captured documents and prisoners told that another large base had been established and there were three separate camps. Such was the importance of the New Chimoio that ZANLA commanders Josiah Tongogara and Rex Nhongo slept there, and captured documents indicated that New Chimoio was the most important ZANLA camp in Mozambique.

If it could be located and destroyed, it would drastically curtail the ZANLA seepage into the *Thrasher* operational area. Incursions were taking place countrywide and the Rhodesians were still desperately trying to halt the flow at source.

But while the national intelligence team was beginning to build up an accurate picture of the layout and personalities involved, the exact location of the New Chimoio remained a mystery.

Captured terrorists could only give a vague indication of where it was.

"We walked from Vanduzi then across the railway line ... travelled in a truck for half an hour. Then we went to the power lines, walked up them for another half an hour or so and ... ," that was as close as Winston Hart and his team got.

The Rhodesians knew the new camp was bounded by certain rivers ... was on the side of a hill ... and on the east side of the Chimoio-Tete road. But it was all rather sketchy.

They didn't want to put up a photographic-reconnaissance plane either. Spirit mediums attached to ZANLA bases had the knack of using them to trick ZANLA with their talents, to the frustration of the Rhodesian war effort.

"Ah!" they would say when they heard the high flying planes, "I think we might be attacked." The rank and file would be impressed with their amazing prophetic magical powers – and the camp would be quickly vacated.

Then there were John and Janet, the two tame baboons, used in an early-warning role, to consider. The Rhodesians certainly didn't want a couple of frenzied animals giving the game away.

The latest information was that there were 2 000 ZANLA in the New Chimoio and a decision was made to send an SAS reconnaissance team into the area to try and pin-point the camp.

The team was also to spring an ambush on a path on the outskirts of the suspected camp in the hope of getting to grips with one of the Toyota Landcruisers which invariably carried the elusive ZANLA hierarchy.

Lieutenant Andrew Sanders of "A" Squadron was to command the team and, in addition to the 11 SAS operators, there would also be four members of the Mozambique National Resistance movement with them.

Judging by the old Portuguese maps available to them, they were going into a heavily populated area and the four MNR could prove useful for wheedling intelligence from locals.

"A" Squadron commander, Rob Johnstone decided to set up a radio relay station for the op, something seldom used by the SAS.

Operating in-depth into hostile territory as they did, their lifeline with home and help was the heavy HF radio enabling them to have communications over vast distances. But an antenna had to be set up ... and that took time.

Rob Johnstone felt that were things to go wrong and it became a mobile war, the callsign might not have time to rig up an antenna.

The answer was to use the lighter, short-range radio with a ground-to-air capability which had a fixed aerial. With a relay station in position on a hill inside Rhodesia near the border, the reconnaissance team could send their messages to the relay team ... and they would pass it back to the squadron commander based at Grand Reef airstrip.

Bruce Langley, Hennie Pretorius, Barry Deacon and Rob Hepple were to man the relay station on a mountain in Rhodesia, 15 kilometres (nine miles) or so from the intended ambush position.

Andrew Sanders, the mission 2IC, Dave Berry and their team, plus the MNR chaps, were choppered into Mozambique a good 45 minutes before last light, and set off walking immediately.

There was very little moon that night and progress was slow. At 23h00 the light was so bad they were forced to call a halt. They bedded down for the night and next day got an early start, striking out for a range of hills they had to cross to reach a path on the fringe of the new camp, where they would mount their ambush.

But first, the team had to work their way through a heavily built-up area, and progress was at a snail's pace. Then they crossed a new and well-used road not marked on their maps and arrived at the foothills of the mountain range.

Having scaled a large hill, the commander decided to remain there for the rest of the day rather than cross the range to the path where they planned to spring their ambush.

The area was far too busy for their liking, and it would be dicey to move around during the day.

Later, twenty armed ZANLA suddenly appeared below one of the early-warning groups. Some were prodding the road for landmines, others were walking behind them in extended line searching the bush.

Having heard the Rhodesian choppers the previous day, it was only natural that ZANLA would be expecting landmines to have been laid in the night. But the SAS were a bit taken aback to find them doing it just there.

It could only mean that the suspected camp was probably a lot closer to the border than the intelligence team imagined.

The operators decided to observe the road for a further day before making a plan of action. The MNR suggested they speak to the locals and within a couple of hours they were back to report that the New Chimoio terror camp was about five kilometres away.

At 08h00 next day, a ten-man ZANLA clearance patrol walked up the ridge – straight into one of the early-warning positions. The SAS had no choice but to open up and by the end of the action, two enemy lay dead and the others beat a hasty retreat.

Almost immediately, heavy weapons on a nearby mountain were brought to bear on the attackers.

That was it, the SAS thought; the whole scene had been blown. The enemy knew their exact position and there was no hope of remaining in the area for an ambush now.

The commander and his 2IC had a quick discussion and decided to move down to the road. There was a chance the team might still get something in the way of a target, and as long as there was that chance, they would try and do the best they could.

They knew they really ought to be pulling out. ZANLA might decide to follow-up. The commander realised it was going to be very dicey. They didn't know exactly how many people were in the enemy camp; didn't know what the odds were ...

Quickly, the SAS and MNR moved down the hill, going towards the camp, not away from it. Suddenly the unmistakable sound of vehicles starting up came from the direction of the camp.

It was an opportunity not to be missed, but not knowing how many vehicles there were, it was worrying, too, considering the size of their callsign and the fact that they only had one RPG-7 among them. The RPG-7 man would just have to make his first shot count; but he was an expert and hadn't let them down yet.

An hour later they had arrived at the road. The two commanders did a quick reconnaissance and found the best available ambush position possible.

Andrew Sanders and Dave Berry showed each man exactly where he must go and told Dave Bradley manning the RPG-7 rocket launcher where his position was; then the team moved back from the road.

The troops quickly put claymores out on their flanks and one to the rear to cover them. Then began the wait.

A civilian who had been buying clothes in the terror camp wandered into their ambush and was captured. He would prove a useful gift for their SB friends.

About ninety minutes later, the sound of vehicles could be heard crunching nearer to the killing ground.

Immediately, everyone took off for his fire position, sinking low, pressing his body flush to the ground, heart beating a little faster as it always did in the final moments before an attack.

Five minutes later, two Toyota Landcruisers came roaring along the road.

As the vehicles entered the killing ground, the second one attempted to overtake the first. But by then, Dave Bradley had already stepped out on to the road with his RPG-7 rocket launcher.

There was a distinctive *whoosh* as his rocket struck the engine and radiator of the first vehicle. The vehicle, which had been doing about forty kilometres (25 miles) an hour, came to a dead stop and reared back.

An escort perched on the customary 200-litre fuel drum at the back shot into the air and took off down the road as fast as his legs could carry him. He was to be the only lucky one that day.

The first Landcruiser and its fuel drums burst into flames.

There were three bodies in the front and another five in the back. So intense was the heat from the fuel fire, and so fiercely were the bodies burning, that the ambushers were unable to get near to carry out a search of either bodies or vehicle.

The RPD gunners had by now killed the driver and occupants of the second Landcruiser . . . and the drum of petrol on the back had burst into flames.

One man managed to leap out, fleeing down the road for his life. A tracer followed him and he fell, mortally wounded.

Within seconds it was all over. The two ZANLA vehicles were engulfed in flames. And 14 enemy lay dead.

Dave Berry got to within twenty metres of the second vehicle to try and capture documents or weaponry, but was driven back by the flames. He thought he saw the body of a white man lying across the seat, but couldn't be sure.

Everyone collected up his kit and withdrew in double-quick time.

The commander called up the SAS relay team on their mountain with a request to send in the choppers post haste. The message was passed on to "A" Squadron commander, Rob Johnstone, who got into a Lynx to orbit the area while his men withdrew.

Back inside Mozambique, the fifteen ambushers were hurrying towards the border in search of a suitable landing zone for the choppers. Within a kilometre they had found an open piece of ground. They ought to have continued on and found another LZ further from the ambush site, but the team had got on to what had to be the highest piece of ground in the area and it would be ideal.

They cleared the area and took up all-round defensive positions. Then they laid low in the long grass and waited for the choppers to arrive for the pick-up.

Suddenly, the soldiers on the east of the landing zone saw men approaching. They were only 100 metres away from them.

"Psst . . . psst!" It was the usual hissed warning to the rest of the callsign that told of trouble. Everyone was alert and waiting. Every finger on a trigger.

A team of women trackers was also closing in on them. Dave Berry began inching his way up to the soldiers on the east. As he did so, the enemy suddenly opened fire. The SAS returned the fire and six ZANLA went down.

Then the two sides fought it out. ZANLA – their numbers soon boosted by new arrivals – put down an intensive volume of fire and began to encircle the 15 soldiers with mortars, rifle grenades, heavy weapons and smallarms. The battle lasted for ten minutes; but for those involved, it felt more like an hour.

It was clear the Rhodesians couldn't take on all the opposition. The commander yelled at his men to withdraw, and his troops, attuned at all times to what he had to say, took off after him as he led his pack through the long grass. It had become a running battle and the callsign was under very heavy fire.

Back inside Rhodesia on the hill overlooking Mozambique, the relay team could see the clouds of dust as they followed the progress of the ZANLA mortars pursuing the fleeing ambushers across the countryside.

When squadron commander Rob Johnstone appeared overhead in the Lynx, the firing momentarily let up.

The four choppers would be with them in a couple of minutes, he reported. But one of the pilots refused to take his chopper down as long as there was firing on the ground.

"You'll get there and take the bloody choppers in," Rob Johnstone radioed from the Lynx, concerned for the safety of his men.

"Is there any firing?" enquired the pilot, a bit later, equally as concerned about the fate of his aircraft.

"No," Rob Johnstone lied.

With the prisoner, there were now 16 men who had to be snatched to safety. The choppers were flying with minimum fuel in an effort to pick everyone up and avoid two lifts. Even if kit was jettisoned, the choppers would be hard pressed to get the extra passenger back to the border.

But the capture absconded during the running punch-up and the problem was solved.

The soldiers had been running for about one kilometre, through maize fields ... through a ZANLA training ground ... hotly pursued by an angry, determined enemy. And still the operators hadn't found a suitable landing zone. Then came the sound of the choppers and the relief of knowing that they were all but safe.

With a bit of coaxing and a couple more white lies from the "A" Squadron commander in the Lynx, the pilots swooped down for the rescue ... and were not amused to find the battle still raging.

ZANLA were 150 metres away from the callsign and still firing at the ambushers. Even before the choppers touched down, the soldiers had tossed in their packs.

A couple of helicopters struggled to lift off. Batteries, rations and a few packs were jettisoned. The choppers lifted. Suddenly, the technicians spotted a bunch of ZANLA and blasted them with their twin Brownings ... while the troops fired from the hip cowboy fashion, through the open door.

The smoke from the battle still hung in the air as the aircraft turned and set course for home. It had been a close thing and the team had been lucky they had taken no casualties. But for the timely arrival of *The Blues*, it might have been very different.

Intercepts revealed that three Russian advisers had been killed in the ambush. One was believed to be a general.

The intelligence team couldn't quite understand what a ZANLA sweepline had been doing so far from the camp site, and a Selous Scouts team under John Gardner, formerly of the SAS, was put in for a close-in recce – and the Scouts also had to be hot extracted.

In the end, despite the possibility of alerting ZANLA, an aerial photographic reconnaissance was flown and although only a portion of the camp could be seen through the cloud cover, it revealed five very heavily defended camps with anti-aircraft guns dug into solid rock in the hills overlooking the tree-covered plains. The Rhodesians would later learn that the Soviets had advised ZANLA in their defences.

The camp was dominated by a huge flat-topped feature, nicknamed *Monte Cassino* by the security forces, after one of the fiercest, most gruelling World War-II battles for the impregnable German-held natural defensive position and monastery in Italy and involving troops from twenty allied countries, including South Africa.

It was obvious that *Monte Cassino* would have to be taken in order to occupy the New Chimoio.

The SAS and MNR had been bang in the middle of the enormous New Chimoio, surrounded by thousands of hostile enemy. The new path they had come across had been gouged into the bush by hundreds of enemy feet.

After Rich Stannard had called in the jets, the camp had moved west across the Tete-Chimoio road and thus nearer to Rhodesia. It was now only about twenty kilometres (12 miles) from the border.

The Rhodesians were worried that after the two security force compromises, the camp would be moved. But ZANLA had moved in so much equipment and got themselves so well dug in, it was virtually impossible for them to resite the camp.

Instead, ZANLA decided to stay and fight it out. According to captures, they had indeed been alerted by the aerial reconnaissance, and extra ammunition was brought in.

A major external operation codenamed *Miracle* was subsequently launched against the New Chimoio under the command of Captain Richard Pomford, of the Selous Scouts.

The feeling in the Rhodesian camp was, if the biggest ZANLA complex in Mozambique could be smashed, it would serve to weaken Mugabe's bargaining position in the Lancaster House conference in London.

The operation followed hard on the heels of *Uric*, where one of the lessons learned was that the security forces needed a properly constituted battle group consisting of mobile infantry, armoured cars and artillery.

Not wanting to repeat the mistakes of *Uric*, Captain Pomford's forces consisted of such a group. His vehicles were armed with 14,5 millimetre and 12,7 millimetre heavy machineguns and he was supported by a squadron of armoured cars and a battery of 25 pounders belonging to the artillery. The operation was also supported by maximum air support.

The battle lasted two days and progress against this extremely well-sited enemy defensive position was slow.

In the past, the early base camp attacks had almost been a cakewalk. Now the Rhodesians were up against conventionally sited battalion positions whose resistance was determined. And unlike the normal enemy they had encountered over the years, who ran away, these ZANLA were prepared to hold their ground.

The enemy machinegun and mortar fire was well controlled and accurate. By night, mutually supporting heavy machineguns would fire tracers at a target, and where the tracer arcs met, they would then mortar that target. This made matters most unpleasant for Captain Pomford and his men.

When *Monte Cassino* was eventually taken, a grand total of 11 enemy bodies were located and minimal amount of enemy equipment recovered. Valuable documents were recovered, as were John and Janet, the two tame baboons.

Assuming the enemy had carried their dead away with them, the results were still far from spectacular.

The camp was an incredible 64 kilometres (forty miles) square, far larger than they had been led to believe from the aerial pictures. It had housed 12 000, although a few thousand only had been there at the time the attack went in. There were so many people there that they had burned fully-grown trees, not merely logs, for their cooking fires.

Shoes and clothes lay in heaps as the wearers ran out of them in their haste to escape. Plates of mealie-meal porridge lay scattered in their trenches.

When a bomb run was put in on the camp, the elusive Rex Nhongo and his driver jumped into Nhongo's green Landcruiser and bolted. The driver panicked and crashed into a tree, whereupon the occupants leapt out and ran away. ZANLA commander Josiah Tungamirai, seen hiding in his vehicle under the trees, also managed to get away with his life.

RLI stop groups were able to account for an untold number of retreating ZANLA.

An extremely sophisticated and vast trench system had been established in all of the three camps in New Chimoio. Even on the top of *Monte Cassino*, bunkers had been built into rocky ground and camouflaged by aloes.

The only Mozambican army involvement came in the night when six T34 tanks clanked towards the camp to bombard the troops on *Monte Cassino*. But they were beaten back by artillery fire from the Rhodesians' rear base inside Mozambique. They returned next day, but by then the security forces had gone home.

In terms of costs, the air weaponry expended alone made such attacks a very expensive business.

The Rhodesians had now reached the situation where large groups of men, supported by air and support weapons, would capture a feature in host country territory, only to be forced to give it up almost immediately it had been won.

The casualty rate – several men had been lost – together with the expenditure in ammunition, was, from the planning viewpoint, making this type of operation non-cost-effective.

Camp attacks were no longer a cakewalk.

Operation Cheese, October 12, 1979

Rhodesia now began to turn her attention to hitting the Zambian economy and putting the big squeeze on President Kenneth Kaunda.

While Kaunda had been forced to reopen his border with Rhodesia the previous October to import maize from the south to feed his starving nation, the border was still not as fully open as Rhodesia would have liked.

How could they make Kaunda more reliant on Rhodesia when he still had the ability to import and export via the all-important Tazara (TanZam) rail link to the Tanzanian port of Dar es Salaam? The track was Zambia's lifeline to the port, moving 25 000 tons of cargo a month into Zambia, and carrying forty percent of the country's foreign trade, including copper, upon which Zambia's national economy hinged.

If Rhodesia wanted to force Kaunda to use the southern communications routes more fully, they would have to cut his rail links to the north. They would have to destroy the biggest stretch of track that they could.

Rhodesia's intelligence gatherers and military strategists – tasked with studying where the vulnerabilities lay in neighbouring countries and the impact of destroying such targets – had long ago realised the significance of the Tazara line.

Crucial to the success of the line was the giant Chambeshi rail bridge straddling the Chambeshi River in north-eastern Zambia, the longest bridge on the rail track. There was a major road bridge 600 metres away and that too was vitally-important to the Zambian economy, and used to export cement and petroleum products to Burundi.

All this information had been filed in a dossier until the time was right. In August, 1978, the file was reopened. The SAS began making their appreciations on destroying the two bridges, and an explosives expert had worked out how many charges it would take to drop both of them.

But it was ruled the time was not right, and it was not Rhodesian policy to attack economic targets in neighbouring countries; *only* terrorist ones.

The demolition calculations were filed away and the frustrated SAS commanders kept hoping that perhaps one day they would get a crack at the bridges.

Then in early September, 1979, a few days before the start of the Lancaster House Conference, the green light was finally given. Fortunately, the homework had already been done; the calculations were taken out, dusted off – and Operation *Cheese* got underway.

The logistics of mounting such an attack were formidable, with distance the major problem.

The two targets were 320 kilometres (200 miles) from the Rhodesian border, 750 kilometres (470 miles) from Kabrit Barracks. It was to be the furthest north that ground troops had operated during the entire war and the problems were enormous.

All they needed was for one man to be seriously injured or for them to be dropped in the wrong place and they would have a major crisis on their hands. The enormous distances involved meant that there was no way anyone in Rhodesia would be able to help them. The distances were even beyond the capabilities of the long-haul Bell 205s.

They would be totally on their own, without help or the prospect of getting any, hundreds of kilometres inside hostile territory.

The mission posed a number of important questions. What was the situation regarding the local population in the area? Where were they, and how many were there ... and how close did they live to the bridge? Was the bridge guarded? And where was the nearest police post?

How would they get to the target? How would they be able to spread their charges around the bridges without the Zambians raising the alarm?

And the biggest worry of all – how would they make good their escape once the bridges were blown?

For once the big bang went off and the alarm was raised, it was still a very long way back to the border.

The defences at the bridge and the situation of the locals were of prime importance, and, as they had no intelligence available on the area, an agent, based externally, was dispatched to drive through the area and carry out a reconnaissance.

He reported that there was a small police guard post near the bridges and that locals lived near the riverbanks along the entire length of Chambeshi.

In outline, Operation *Cheese* promised to be fairly straightforward.

Being so far from home, it was out of the question to drive to the target as they had in Operation *Bastille,* or be choppered in as in Operation *Carpet.* The decision was therefore made for them. They had to make a parachute drop by night.

A four-man freefall team was to jump in first, carry out a reconnaissance of the two bridges and check out the defences. The remaining 12 men would parachute in, using static line chutes and bring in the explosives, boats and other equipment. Then the whole force of 16 men would travel upriver to the bridges.

It was crucial for the pathfinder/reconnaissance team to know exactly where they were being dropped. But how could they find the most suitable spot to land in?

Mission commander Major Dave Dodson briefed SAS/SB liaison man Stu Hulley-Miller. "I need a place where there is no population, near a recognisable feature, near a river. I've got to go downstream, so I want to be upstream ... "

Stu went off to find out everything he could about the area, a task which meant an on-site inspection.

Pilot Jack Malloch was called in to help and late one night, Stu and Jack flew off from Salisbury and headed across the border en route for north-east Zambia.

It was cold and windy and the chill night air blew in through the open door of Jack's DC-7, but he had come prepared and laid on coffee, *Coke* and sandwiches.

It took three hours of flying by a roundabout, devious route to get to the river itself. Now, they had to find a suitable spot where the pathfinder team could be dropped. But try as they may, they could find nowhere. The trouble was they could not really see any recognisable features because of haze near the ground.

They had no option. They would just have to turn around and go home.

On the next trip, mission commander Dave Dodson went along to see if he could help pinpoint a position. It was still a difficult job, but they knew they could not go home again without finding a dropping zone.

Jack Malloch kept circling, searching . . . and eventually it dawned on them how to solve their problem.

As they flew over the Chambeshi, they could see that the moon cast a reflection on the water, and, with that to aid them, they were able to recognise various features.

Using the reflection from the water as a guide, they were at last able to find a DZ – a sparsely populated area near the river forty kilometres (25 miles) south-west of the two bridges, but unfortunately downstream from the targets.

Back home at Darwendale Dam, they carried out their trials. It was a bright moonlit night, as the plane, bearing the soldiers, approached the dam. As always, the rehearsals were realistic and they were wearing the kit and equipment they would wear on the night of their deployment – and it was extremely heavy.

Below, Stu Hulley-Miller was in a boat, just in case he was needed to fish anyone out of the water.

The dispatchers could see the reflection on the water. The paras dropped to earth and the wind blew. Luckily, despite the strong wind, Stu did not have to go fishing that night. All but Bob McKenna landed on the shore.

Aerial photographic interpretation of the bridges had already been done to enable the demolition calculations to be worked out, but another photographic run was made to get an up-to-date picture of the targets.

They would be going for overkill, taking fifty percent more explosives than they really needed. Having gone that far, they were not about to take any chances.

The main party was to take a ton of explosives, an inflatable rubber boat with an outboard motor and several new canoes. It was quite a cargo to haul along, and much time had to be spent packing and rearranging loads as well as on the practice drops.

Once at the Chambeshi River, every boat would have a specific task and it was essential that equipment be precisely loaded into the correct canoes to aid the actions at the different targets. Many days and nights were to be spent at Darwendale Dam, practising canoe and inflatable boat techniques, formations and relative speeds.

It was crucial that the bridges were not only blown, but blown effectively and to do that they needed to lay some of their many charges below water level. The soldiers moved out to a bridge on the Hunyani River, outside Salisbury to rehearse positioning the charges.

They also needed to test a new item of equipment, essential to the demolition task. In addition to the many charges they were to spread around the bridges, they were also to use an experimental device, a demolition net, which was to be used on the rail bridge alone – the major prize of the mission.

There were to be three 100 kilogram charges submerged on one side of the centre pier – the thickest of the three rail piers – and the demolition net would be on the opposite side of the pier.

The idea was that the net would detonate a micro-second before the three charges, blowing water away from the pier and creating an air bubble. This would make the charges more effective. For when they detonated, there would no longer be the enormous water resistance on the far side of the pier.

While not a new concept in military circles, it was the first time it had been used by the Rhodesians.

Spreading the many charges all over the spans and piers was going to be a time-consuming business and the longer they stayed at the bridges, the greater the risks of interference from the Zambians.

Much careful thought went into their escape plans and they felt it feasible to parachute in a take-apart Land-Rover, but trials proved it to be an impractical idea.

In the end they decided that the best plan was to hijack a vehicle to make their getaway. And it had to be big enough to take all 16 operators as well as their kit, canoes and boat.

It meant that once the bridges had blown they would have to drive through Chambeshi town itself and another town called Mpika.

The maps they had were not good and while they felt Chambeshi town would probably be a small place, they were not sure about Mpika, or whether or not there were police there.

In the event of them getting clear of the two towns, they were then to travel cross-country until they got within helicopter range of Rhodesia where they would call in the choppers to carry them back home.

Their escape hinged on their finding a suitable vehicle. They hoped they would be able to capture one in the early hours of the morning. If not, they would have a severe problem.

Finally, the order came for the rehearsals and preparations to cease, and the operation to begin.

On September 12, the 16 men moved out to their staging area at Fylde, a secret military airfield near Hartley, 150 kilometres (93 miles) from the capital.

The four freefallers, faces black with camo cream and led by Major Dodson, climbed into their DC-7 and headed north into the night.

There was a heavy haze over the Chambeshi that night and they were unable to find their DZ, and had no choice but to turn around and head back home.

Everyone was disappointed. They had been keyed up to the limit for danger; now, instead they had to relax and unwind again.

As they climbed into their trucks and made their way back to Salisbury, they consoled themselves with the thought that they would soon be back at the airfield for another attempt.

But they had to wait until the next moon phase.

The mission commander was in some ways relieved. The extra time the delay gave them meant they were able to polish their plans, sort out a lot of small problems, which perhaps would not prove so small with the targets so far from home.

On October 3, it was all systems go again and at 22h00, the freefall team once more climbed into the DC-7 and took off for Zambia.

Once in the area of the bridges, the heavily-laden freefallers staggered to their feet. They had so much kit on they looked like hunchbacks.

But pilot Jack Malloch, and dispatcher Frank Hales, were struggling to find the DZ. Twenty minutes later they still had not located it and the freefallers were still standing, weighed down by their unbearably heavy packs.

Eventually, the commander had had enough.

That was it, he said. They were not jumping. They all lumbered back to their seats.

Suddenly the "GO, GO, GO" rang out through the plane as Jack and Frank finally recognised the DZ.

The four freefallers struggled from their seats and moved towards the door.

361

This time there was no postponement and at almost midnight, the team, plus their box of canoes and other equipment fell into the night from 13 000 feet above ground level.

For just under a minute they fell until their chutes opened, and for another couple of minutes they drove their canopies to the DZ.

As they floated down, they looked around in the light cast from the moon to see if everything had gone to plan.

It was with horror they realised that one of the chutes was missing. It had obviously had a malfunction and its load had to be lying smashed on the ground. They could only hope that it was equipment and not a freefaller.

It was with much relief they learned it was equipment and not a team member. But it meant that somewhere out in the bush were two canoes, plus a spare, which they were relying on to get them to the bridges to carry out their reconnaissance. It was a serious problem.

The HF radio was also missing. Fortunately, the commander had taken the precaution of getting one of the freefallers to carry a spare.

For all that night and half the next day they searched for the canoes, but without success. In the end the commander decided the time had come to abandon the hunt.

It was bad luck but the commander decided to carry on. They would just have to walk to the bridges. It would take a considerable time to walk to the river and get back to the DZ and it would drastically alter their original timings. But better that than abort the mission.

The commander radioed the SAS HQ in Rhodesia to tell of their contingency plans. The main body of men, who would be joining them in a few days, would now have to bring in replacement canoes.

Two-and-a-half days later, the four weary men arrived at a wide tributary that came in from the west and joined up with the Chambeshi.

Leaving one man to guard their kit and clothing, Major Dodson, Lieutenant Phil Brooke and Lance Corporal Andy Standish-White stripped off, and with just a silenced .22 pistol between them, the three naked men swam to the bridges.

There was no one around and the three men were fairly relaxed as they swam under the two monster bridges. The commander made a mental note of the two-metre-high ledge inside the rail bridge ... they could use that to rest their explosives on.

From bank-to-bank, the channel was 400 metres wide, sufficient to handle the annual floods during the wet season. But at that time it was only 200 metres wide and four metres deep.

Their measurements of the bridge confirmed exactly what the aerial photographic interpreters had told them. They knew that there was no need to change the plan; that there would be more than enough explosives coming in.

They confirmed the presence of a guard at the bridge, swam back across the river and away they went. The recce had gone well. Now for the real thing.

Four days after setting off at the start of their trek, they arrived back at their DZ. They had walked 100 kilometres (62 miles) and would be able to rest up while awaiting the arrival of the 12 men in the main party who would be bringing in the explosives and canoes.

At 01h00 on October 8, the rest of the operators arrived without incident, parachuting into Zambia from 1 000 feet above ground level.

From then until sun-up, all 16 men busied themselves, digging pits to hide the parachutes and packing material. Then they hid the explosives and boats in the bush, posted sentries and tried to sleep.

All was quiet. It was the usual sultry October day in the bush.

In the early afternoon the sentries noticed smoke from a bushfire in the distance. But it was too far away to threaten them.

The men continued to doze in the heat of the day.

Suddenly, at 15h00, the situation changed dramatically and the alarmed sentries hurriedly ran to shake everyone awake.

A new fire had flared up and it was sweeping nearer to them. It was already only a 100 metres or so from them and their massive cache of explosives and equipment.

Dave and his 2IC, Bob McKenna, had a hurried discussion. While they were whispering about what they should do, they heard several men shouting at each other from the direction of the fire.

The soldiers' first thoughts were that they had somehow been discovered ... hundreds of kilometres behind enemy lines with no means of escape but their feet. Quickly, they spread out into their positions and prepared for a fight.

Then a sentry spotted the source of the voices. It was a group of African hunters who had obviously started the fire to flush out game.

They were not directly a threat to the soldiers as they only carried spears, but they *could* report them to the authorities.

The hunters were unaware they were within 100 metres of 16 heavily armed Rhodesian soldiers, and, as long as they remained unaware the SAS would not harm them.

But right now, the fire was a much bigger problem. As they hid and watched, the fire crept dangerously closer to them and their cache of high explosives.

It was imperative they stop it before it reached the explosives. They would have to act fast and without being seen. But luck was on their side that day.

A buck suddenly broke from the smoking bush and the hunters gave chase – away from the soldiers.

As soon as they were out of sight, the 16 men turned firefighters as, for an hour, they cleared firebreaks and battled the flames. With one final concerted effort, they managed to stop the fire just twenty metres from their cache.

Hot and tired but much-relieved, they sank into what cover still remained, hoping that the few hours left until dark would be uneventful. And apart from one incident, when a hunter came wandering back, it was.

The African was studying the ground intently and the men lying low in the bushes could not work out what he was doing until he bent down and picked up a rat the fire had killed. The hunting had obviously not been very successful.

As it started to get dark, they began the night's work. They had to ferry their ton of charges 400 metres to the river's edge, as well as their boat, outboard motor, six canoes, petrol for the motor and personal equipment – and for a couple of hours they went back and forth humping everything down to the river.

Even with 16 men sharing the work, they were tired enough to need a thirty-minute rest before assembling and loading the boats.

The plan called for six canoes to carry two men each plus as much equipment as they could carry – and the boat with its outboard motor was to carry four men, plus the bulk of the explosives.

It was midnight by the time they were ready to start upriver. It was the night of October 8 and according to their original timings, they should have been halfway to the bridges by now.

The aerial photographic interpreters had told them that from the ripples on the river, they must expect a six-knot current. As the loss of the canoes had prevented the reconnaissance party being able to assess accurately the state of the river, they did not know for sure what the river was like.

They were soon to find out.

The current was very much against them and was far stronger than the six knots they had been anticipating. It was more like 15 knots. And just to make life interesting there were hippos, rocks and rapids in great abundance. Even the 15 horse-power (11 kilowatt) outboard motor on the inflatable Zodiac MK 111 boat, which was bringing up the rear, was severely strained in the rapids.

The four freefallers were beginning to realise that even had they had the canoes for the reconnaissance, it would still have taken them four days to get to the target and back again. It had long ago dawned on them that the mission was not going to be as easy as they had originally thought. First the loss of the canoes . . . then the long walk . . . and now this. It was the final straw. But each man was confident that as long as they could negotiate the river, the mission was still on.

The chaps in the canoes envied those in the boat because they were riding and not paddling . . . while the four men in the boat envied them for the relative ease with which they were manoeuvring their canoes through the rapids. Yet Bob McKenna and his team in the boat could guarantee they were having more problems than the canoeists.

The boat was sitting very low in the water because of all the kit and explosives it was carrying . . . and Bob and his passengers kept being swept on to the sides of the river with the trees hanging over them and the propeller crashing on to the rocks.

It was becoming apparent to all that their original time appreciation was far too ambitious and that they would not make the target by the next day. Instead, they were to spend the next couple of nights battling upriver in their overloaded craft. And the days were spent lying low in what grass and vegetation there was in the gullies close to the river's edge, and keeping out of the way of the locals living near the banks.

As they struggled upriver, they seemed to be making no progress. So strong was the current and so fiercely were they battling against it that at times they thought they would never make it.

At one set of rapids, the men in the boat lost control completely and were washed spinning and bouncing off the rocks for several hundred metres back downstream, nearly swamping in the process.

Once more they tried negotiating the same set of rapids. Again they were unsuccessful.

"Goodbye charge one and two," Bob McKenna said at last, as 150 kilograms of explosives were heaved over the side of the boat.

Bob was annoyed at having to jettison the explosives as it would mean that one less pier could be destroyed on the rail bridge. But he had no alternative; they had to get past the rapids if they wanted to reach the target.

Fortunately, because they had brought more than enough explosives along they would still be able to destroy the centre pier on the rail bridge, the one it was essential to drop to render the bridge useless. Even without the jettisoned explosives, they barely made it past the rapids.

Then another problem. One of the jerry cans containing fuel had somehow taken in water and when they hooked the jerry can on to the fuel pipe, water got into the carburettor and it stopped working completely.

As Dave Dodson and the others in the six canoes battled through the night on their way upriver, Bob and his crew and the bulk of the explosives were being washed downstream. Eventually, they managed to paddle into the bank, but Bob and his team knew that if they could not get the motor going, they and the explosives would never reach the target and the op would have to be aborted.

The commander meanwhile was continuing on his way, unaware of the latest crisis to befall the mission.

Luckily, SAS men are versatile as well as determined, and NCO Vossy Vosloo was able to dissemble the motor by the light of a shielded flash-light, clean out the water and put the motor back together again. But it was only by draining the fuel off the top of the jerry can that they could gather enough to complete the journey.

They were back in business, except now, they were ninety minutes behind the others. However they managed to catch up on their timings during that night's journey.

At last, on the night of the 10th, they neared the two bridges. They were close enough to hear trains rumbling over the Tazara rail bridge, and could hear road traffic travelling over the nearby road bridge.

They found an exceptionally thick clump of trees just a few kilometres from the bridges and lay up for the day.

Again and again they discussed exactly what they would have to do at the bridges. They went through their approach procedures ... remembered they had to check for guards ... discussed where they would place the charges ... how they would go about capturing a vehicle for their escape.

There were dozens and dozens of details and contingency plans to go over. Eventually they all knew what to expect and what to do should anything untoward happen.

Darkness fell and the blackened-up men waited in the trees for a few hours. Then the 12 men in the six canoes finally set off for the bridges, leaving the motor boat party behind to follow later with the explosives.

They planned to reach the bridge at about 22h00 to allow the locals plenty of time to get to sleep and the traffic time to diminish. They estimated the task would take about four hours.

Two canoes went towards the riverbank where the four passengers were to check the area for police and guards. Two other canoes were to go right up to the centre rail bridge pier and put a rope around it to enable the outboard motor party to hold the boat against the current while they laid their charges.

The third couple of canoe teams were tasked to fix three hooks on to the centre pier to support the three 100 kilogram charges that the boat party would attach to them.

Suddenly – dramatically – there was a single, brilliant almost supernatural flash of lightning. It lit up the entire area and illuminated the massive silver-painted girder rail bridge in every detail, giving the saboteurs still travelling towards it their first awe-inspiring glimpse of the target.

To the soldiers, it was the most fantastic sight – a vivid picture burned into their eyeballs that they would remember long after other details of the mission had faded from their memories.

To anyone who might have been around to watch, the Salisbury saboteurs were clearly visible, as if on a stage. But there was no reaction and the canoeists continued on their way.

When the motor-boat party reached the bridge, they saw that the operators in the canoes had done their job exactly as they were meant to do. The centre pier had a rope around it and the hook points were ready and waiting for the charges.

The boat party grabbed the rope and pulled the boat against the pier, then started to wrestle the first of the charges over the side on to its hook.

The three charges were attached to the hooks then eased below the water level, with the detonating cord leads remaining above the surface.

Next, they had to tussle with the demolition net, the experimental explosive device which had to be placed on the opposite side of the pier to the three charges.

It proved quite a battle weighting it, getting it down to its proper position flush against the pier, then having to anchor it in place against the current. But eventually the job was finished.

They hooked up the *Cordtex* leads from the three charges, leaving them to be connected later to the ringmain.

Suddenly, their concentration was interrupted by the sound of firing on the river-bank. They listened intently, momentarily pausing in their tasks.

Up on the bank, a policeman armed with a shotgun had appeared on the scene and challenged Phil Brooke and Frank Booth. Sadly, for him, his weapon was no match for the silenced AKs waiting for him, and although he managed to get away, he died in the bush.

Commander Dave Dodson, meanwhile, sat on the bank under the railway bridge gathering reports from the various groups.

His men were now climbing all over the two bridges positioning their many charges to ensure maximum destruction. Lieutenant Phil Brooke and his callsign, having finished their initial task of checking the area for police and guards, now turned their attention to sorting out the details for the great escape.

Phil and his team had come prepared for setting up a roadblock, essential in the plan to hijack a vehicle to take them south. The roadblock team had done their home-work and taken along exact duplicates of Zambian police and roadblock signs. And as planned, vehicles slowed as they approached the signs, stopped, then were waved on by the Rhodesians.

There was a lot more traffic than they had anticipated and the roadblock party had got themselves quite a job, although they had not yet found the perfect get-away truck capable of carrying 16 men.

There was now activity all over and under the bridges. Vehicles were being stopped and waved on; people were crawling over both bridges laying their charges; others were taking the boats apart. And the commander sat below by the radio accepting reports, checking everything was going as planned with the precision they had rehearsed so many times beforehand.

Finally, the ringmain on the road bridge was hooked up and a lead was run down to join up with the rail bridge ringmain, ensuring that both bridges dropped simultaneously.

Time was getting on and the commander told Phil Brooke to select a suitable vehicle. Before long, traffic began piling up at the roadblock and at one time, six vehicles had come to a halt and Phil was frantically trying to signal them on.

Finally, a twenty-ton chemical fertiliser truck came in sight and Phil knew it would be perfect for what they were planning.

The truck stopped at the roadblock and the European driver and his black co-driver were taken into custody and the truck was pulled to the side of the road. Break-down signs were hurriedly placed front and back, and the police roadblock signs were removed.

They hoped that all subsequent traffic would see the breakdown signs and proceed without stopping. But events were not quite so straightforward.

As soon as the breakdown signs were out, another truck drew alongside and insisted on helping.

This driver, an Irishman, was also taken into custody and his truck pulled to the side of the road in front of the fertiliser truck.

But the complications were not over yet.

A truck that had already gone through the roadblock turned back 15 minutes later when the European driver suddenly realised that the fertiliser truck was not following him any more.

Bob McKenna meanwhile, having finished helping with the explosives on the road bridge took a couple of men up top to see if they could help.

They arrived to see two trucks pulled over and the two drivers and co-drivers in custody, the *other* truck returning to the bridge – and a *fourth* approaching from the opposite direction. Any minute now, there was going to be a traffic jam.

As the driver of the fourth truck approached the bridge, he could see men carrying AKs. Realising that the situation called for discretion rather than valour, he was easily persuaded to go through the roadblock and pass on up the road.

But the driver of the returning truck was not so easily convinced. He was adamant. He was not going anywhere without the fertiliser truck and its driver.

It was then that Phil Brooke and his team learned that both the trucks had been travelling in convoy – and that the drivers were brothers.

The SAS had no way of knowing that because of the situation in Zambia at that time, it was the practise for truck drivers travelling in convoy to stop and help one another if one appeared to be having trouble with the police or bandits; or if there were more mundane problems like breakdowns.

And try as they might, the soldiers could not convince the returning driver to continue of his way, so they had no choice but to take him into custody, too.

There were, it turned out, only six European truck drivers in the whole of Zambia – and the SAS had captured half of them.

But yet another complication. In addition to the three white drivers and two co-drivers, they had got themselves another prisoner – a 10-year-old white boy.

He was the nephew of one of the drivers and had been taken along for the ride as a special birthday treat. It proved to be a birthday like no other he was likely to have.

He had little to say for himself but his eyes were like saucers, and the look on his face was one of pure excitement rather than fright.

The white drivers, however, were not so thrilled with the turn of events that night. They were convinced they were going to be done away with.

The African co-drivers, meanwhile, sat around and shrugged their shoulders and accepted the situation as if being detained by blackened-up armed Rhodesians was an everyday occurrence.

Down under the bridge, the commander was furious.

"What the *hell* do you think you're doing?" he demanded to know when he got the roadblock party's progress report.

He was certainly not expecting such a crowd of prisoners. They were all shepherded under the bridge near him, and while one man stood guard over them, the rest of the soldiers got on with their tasks.

The group which had been dismantling the boat and canoes began carrying them up to the road . . . and the final charges were laid on the rail bridge, while up on the road bridge, the soldiers were turning their attention to the fertiliser truck.

All the fertiliser bags in the centre of the open truck were jettisoned and the outside ones left nicely in place.

Thus they shaped themselves a small fort; they could hide in the centre and make their getaway without being seen.

While this was going on, several lorries drove over the bridge, accepted there was a breakdown of some sort and kept going. The soldiers had no trouble waving them through their little traffic jam, although there were a couple of times when they had to insist by gesticulating with the muzzles of their AKs.

The commander, meanwhile, was trying to decide about the prisoners. It would cause all sorts of problems to take them back to Rhodesia, he knew. On the other hand, if he released them, they would lose no time raising the alarm. And with distance being the main consideration on this op, the SAS might well be located before they got to the border.

His categoric order from ComOps was that it had to be a strictly clandestine mission. No one in Zambia must know who was responsible for blowing the bridges. But he realised the Zambians would have little trouble deciding where the blame lay.

The SAS would simply have to take the prisoners with them and worry about the complications later. They probably would not be that keen but would be given some alternatives.

Two men were now hooking up the final aspects of the ringmains on the bridges, while the prisoners, most of the SAS men, their canoes, boat, the motor and other bits and pieces were loaded into the centre of the fortified truck. The back of the truck was fairly bristling with weapons.

The two captured brothers climbed into the cab and one took up his position behind the wheel. Dave Dodson got in beside them with his silenced pistol and the brothers quickly got the message ...

The truck was moved to the southern end of the bridge ready for the getaway.

All that remained was to light the fuses on the ringmain linking the two bridges.

They had built in a 15-minute time delay, giving them long enough to get well clear of the bridges. They had tripled up on the initiation, so there was little chance of things going wrong.

The initiation party lit the safety fuses and sprinted across from the northern side of the bridge to join the rest of their colleagues in the back of the truck.

It was now 02h15 and Dave Dodson ordered the driver to get a move on. The very nervous driver did exactly what he was told.

The driver and his equally-worried brother kept asking the commander to assure them they would not be harmed.

As long as they kept driving southwards, and fast, they would be safe, he told them.

Then the driver began to worry about the fate of his truck, a precious item indeed, as trucks were virtually unobtainable in Zambia. It had cost him 48 000 Zambia kwacha, had under 10 000 kilometres (6 215 miles) on the clock, which for Africa was not much. It hadn't been paid for, either.

The driver's brother, whose haulage truck was now parked near the road bridge, wondered if his truck would be blown up in the forthcoming blast.

The SAS commander was purposely vague about the information he gave them and the other prisoners in case anything went wrong and they were recovered by the Zambian authorities.

The two drivers and all on board remained tense as the truck sped southwards in the early morning. As they approached the little town of Chambeshi, the brothers, without much prompting, told the SAS commander what lay ahead of them.

The truck, with its cargo of 16 heavily armed Rhodesian SAS men and six prisoners, drove into town.

The brothers had warned of a little police station but there were no lights on at the station and no sign of life at all. They drove on and reached the outskirts of Chambeshi uneventfully.

The SAS breathed slightly easier, while the two brothers continued to worry about their precious trucks.

The little boy in the back still had eyes the size of saucers, as he ogled the blackened-up soldiers and their weapons. He was enjoying his unconventional birthday treat.

Just to make him feel more at ease, Bob McKenna gave him some imported tinned chocolates he had been carrying around for years. He had brought them back from a trip to America and they were probably older than the boy himself.

Twenty kilometres (12 miles) from the target, the driver was ordered to stop while a couple of men leapt from the back to cut the telephone wires from the bridges, the police station, and all points south.

Just as they finished cutting the lines, they saw a huge orange flash, as their explosives went off . . . and soon the sound of the blast came rumbling across the Zambian countryside.

The 16 soldiers were elated at their night's work. The operation had been a big strain and they had worked so hard that when the big bang came they could hardly believe it. It would have been a spectacular sight, they knew. Sadly, there could be no going back to check out the damage, for now time was short and the pressure was really on.

They were well aware that some of the truck drivers who had already crossed the bridge may have reported the roadblock activities to other police stations on the way down south . . . and they still had Mpika to drive through before they could consider themselves even slightly safe.

They had to get past that at least before daylight dawned.

Their maps told them that the main road did not go through Mpika but was deviated around it. However, the mission commander was apprehensive about the accuracy of the maps, the state of the road, and whether they could pick the right one.

The soldiers in the back were alert and expecting trouble.

Surely by now the word would have gone out about the events at the Chambeshi River a few hours earlier? As always, trigger fingers tightened on their AKs.

Up front, the commander was learning all about Mpika from the driver. It had apparently developed into a railway repair workshop for the Tazara rail line, something the Rhodesian planners had not known. It was double the size the soldiers had thought it was.

Luckily, the driver picked the by-pass road avoiding Mpika itself.

Then it was a matter of trucking southwards, as far and as fast as they could, until it started getting light.

There was still a surprising amount of traffic on the road but none of the drivers gave any trouble. They had no way of knowing, of course, that the ordinary-looking fertiliser truck hid six prisoners and sixteen alert soldiers who had just shattered Zambia's economy.

As daylight began to dawn, they started looking for dirt roads leading off the main road, so they could hide up somewhere for the day. They hoped to find one just north of a town called Selenje, which would take them into the Luangwa National Park and south; and they found it just before sun-up.

They stopped and changed drivers, and Bob McKenna climbed into the front to help the commander with the map-reading. It was getting light and the sun caught them driving through what was virtually a huge African tribal trust land.

For ninety minutes they drove through the densely-populated area and were seen by thousands of locals.

Dave Dodson and Bob McKenna were still blackened-up and did not know whether the locals suspected them or not. But the Zambians gave the lone fertiliser truck and the people in the cab a friendly wave and a smile as the travellers continued on their way.

The Rhodesians waved back and commented how unbelievable it all was. Between the two of them, they worked out where they were and eventually made it in to the area of the national park.

While they were heading southwards, Rhodesian Air Force Canberras were flying over Chambeshi to view the damage.

A message flashed over the *Big Means* to the operators inside their fort in the back of the fertiliser truck. "The bridges are jacked – they're gone," it said. Next to the explosion, that little message was one of the highlights of the mission. With one hundred percent success guaranteed, morale was extremely high.

They had been driving down dirt roads for hours and were now fairly confident that without an intensive air effort they would not be spotted. But again they were wrong.

As they drove over a hill, what should loom before them, right in the middle of a desolate wildlife area, but a large power station.

The only good thing about it was that it had helped to confirm their location, but otherwise it spelt trouble. For, as with all power stations, there were bound to be guards.

Immediately, they pulled off the road into a side track and stopped for a brew while Dave Dodson and Bob McKenna decided what to do.

Now they had a dilemma. They had no idea how big the power station was or how many people were in it. If they were unable to kill everyone there, those who survived would undoubtedly give the alarm and the hunt would be on. Worse still, their location would be known to Zambian security forces.

Unbeknown to the SAS men, the power station guards had already spotted them, and while the soldiers were having their tea and deciding their next move, the guards had already climbed into their Land-Rover and were following up tracks.

Towards 10h00, the soldiers and their prisoners heard the sound of a vehicle. They immediately deployed into an ambush position and waited.

The Land-Rover came to a halt close to them and half a dozen uniformed Africans got out.

A blackened-up SAS soldier called out to them, trying to beckon them forward with the idea of capturing them without too much trouble.

But the guards decided that something was not quite right. They abandoned their Land-Rover and took to their heels as fast as they could. Those SAS who could, opened fire, and apart from two who got away, that was the end of the power station security guards.

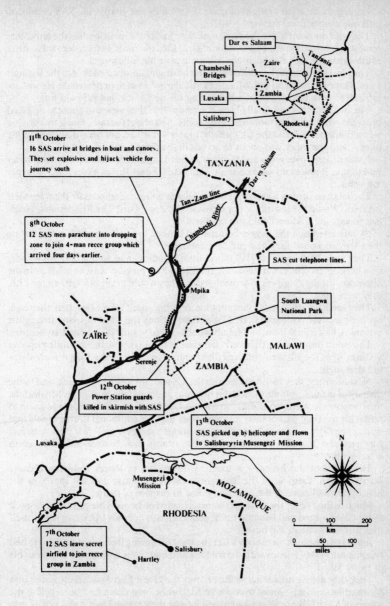

11th October
16 SAS arrive at bridges in boat and canoes. They set explosives and hijack vehicle for journey south

8th October
12 SAS men parachute into dropping zone to join 4-man recce group which arrived four days earlier.

SAS cut telephone lines.

South Luangwa National Park

12th October
Power Station guards killed in skirmish with SAS

13th October
SAS picked up by helicopter and flown to Salisbury via Musengezi Mission

7th October
12 SAS leave secret airfield to join recce group in Zambia

Dar es Salaam
Chambeshi Bridges
Lusaka
Salisbury
Zaire
Tanzania
Zambia
Rhodesia
Mozambique

TANZANIA
Dar es Salaam
Tan-Zam line
Chambeshi River
Mpika
ZAÏRE
Serenje
ZAMBIA
MALAWI
Lusaka
Musengezi Mission
MOZAMBIQUE
RHODESIA
Salisbury
Hartley

N

0   100   200
km
0   50   100
miles

Operation *Cheese:* The bridge-blowing season begins

371

Having made a fair amount of noise dispatching the guards, the SAS decided to pull out further from the area.

They did not want to use the same road they had come in on, and, as the only other road wound down to the power station itself, Dodson and his men decided to drive southwards through the bush and escape a possible follow-up.

They hid the guards' Land-Rover in the bush and climbed back into the fertiliser truck. Dave Dodson and Bob McKenna told the owner of their new route. He was not impressed with the idea of bundu-bashing his new truck, not yet paid for.

The two brothers had finally been convinced that they were not going to be killed but were now becoming more and more concerned about the fate of their trucks. One was abandoned back at the Chambeshi bridge – if it had not been destroyed in the blast – and the other was about to go bundu-bashing.

It was ordered over rocks and through gullies. It knocked down trees and the driver had to take it places no sane person would take a Land-Rover, never mind a twenty ton truck.

The anxious drivers wanted to know who was going to compensate them for their troubles. Would the insurance pay or who? The Zambians? The Rhodesians? Needless to say, the soldiers could not tell them.

By late afternoon the terrain became too broken to continue any further. But by then they reckoned they had gone far enough.

They were 200 kilometres (124 miles) from Rhodesia and within range of Rhodesian helicopters. The exhausted soldiers radioed for a pick-up but it was too late in the afternoon for the choppers to come that day. They would arrive at 08h00 on the 13th, they were told.

They spent what was left of that afternoon cutting an LZ for the choppers, then took up their tactical positions, shared what little rations they had to spare among the prisoners, had a final brew, and finally went to sleep, posting their customary sentries.

They were thoroughly exhausted after their many days of walking, battling upriver to the bridges, the job itself and their flight southwards. No one had any trouble sleeping that night.

Next morning, they finished clearing the LZ with the help of the truck, and to the dismay of the unfortunate owner. But time was short and the trees huge. Meanwhile, the choppers flew from Salisbury to Mount Darwin, then to Musengezi Mission to refuel for the final part of their journey. They took on additional drums of fuel and during the flight northwards to collect the bridge saboteurs and their prisoners, fuel was pumped into the choppers from the drums, which were kicked to earth when empty.

The moment the helicopters touched down, the prisoners suddenly became worried again. Despite all the assurances to the contrary, they felt that now the helicopters had arrived, the time had come to dispose of them.

Much to their relief, the prisoners were all loaded on board. One driver bid farewell to his dust-covered and battered truck, pleased it was only his truck and not himself that was left to lie in the bush.

Judging by the look on the boy's face, he was still having the time of his life. He had become the best of friends with the soldiers and had never entertained any thoughts of being killed.

They flew across the Luangwa River, over the Great East Road, then across into Mozambique, flying almost over where Macombe base camp had been before the waters of Lake Cabora Bassa had wiped it from their maps. Then it was across into Rhodesia, landing at Musengezi Mission, for refuelling.

As they flew home, the SAS men thought about the mission. A lot had gone wrong, the op seemed jinxed at times, but the aim had been achieved.

As they approached Kabrit Barracks, the prisoners were hooded to prevent them passing on information later about what they had seen.

The operators had a quick debrief, got cleaned up and left for home, tired but satisfied at a job well done.

As Bob McKenna loaded the prisoners into the truck for the last leg of their journey, one of the European brothers reached out and took his hand.

"Shit, man! Thanks a lot for taking care of us," he said. "If you're ever in the area again, call in and have a few beers," the grateful man added in all sincerity.

The doors closed shut; the truck rolled out of Kabrit and the prisoners were taken to a *safe house* outside Salisbury, where they became guests of Special Branch.

They stayed at the secret house for many weeks and were given every comfort. The boy even got a private tutor as he was missing so much schooling.

Special Branch were worried that the Zambians would think the prisoners had taken part in the raid voluntarily and might kill or imprison them when they returned home.

To complicate matters further, the boy's mother was a British citizen. Thus his capture not only involved Rhodesia and Zambia, but internationalised the matter further, and so not to alarm his mother too much, word of his safety was flashed to her via the British Consulate in South Africa.

After many lengthy negotiations, the British finally got guarantees for the prisoners' safety and they were returned to Zambia. The Zambians, however, lost no time in imprisoning the captives. The boy was spared, but it would be a long time before he forgot his birthday adventure.

Zambia would not forget the events of that night in a hurry either. Zambian President Kenneth Kaunda described the actions of that night as "economically crippling sabotage".

As a result, 18 000 tons of goods, including much-needed maize to make up the harvest shortfall and bound for Zambia were immediately stranded at Dar es Salaam.

By severing Zambia's lifeline to the Tanzanian port, the country's copper exports and directly-related foreign exchange earnings were to suffer. At the time the SAS blew the bridges, there were already 10 000 tons of copper waiting to be shipped to world markets.

The Works and Supply Minister, Mr Haswell Mwale, appealed to the country's hard-pressed road haulage companies to help shift the stranded goods. But the scarcity of lorries compounded the problem and those few that did exist were fully committed.

Observers believed that Zambia's hopes for self-sufficiency in food production for the following year were destroyed with the bridges. Relief supplies of maize were needed because poor rains and late deliveries of fertiliser had stunted the previous year's crop.

Engineers estimated it would take about six months to rebuild the rail bridge and three to fix the road bridge. The Zambians said it would cost six million kwacha to repair the bridges and went with the begging bowl to the European Economic Community.

Dropping the Chambeshi bridges had delivered Kenneth Kaunda's head on a platter. He would now have no choice but to deal with the south and a regime he was committed to overthrow.

The End Of The Line, October 13, 1979

While Dave Dodson and his team were battling the current on the Chambeshi River, other SAS teams, intent on a similar mission in Mozambique, were completing their demolition trials and perfecting their bridge-blowing techniques.

Destined for the Tete Province, they planned to cut three bridges on the all-important rail track which ran from the east coast up to the railhead at Moatize, Mozambique's largest coal mine.

With three Mozambican bridges destroyed, neighbouring Zambia would also be denied access to the east coast port of Beira, thereby increasing the pressure on Zambia to open the border with Rhodesia.

Not only that, but it had become far too risky of late for ZANLA to move men and arms by road to the Tete area, from where they would ultimately find their way into the *Hurricane* operational area and beyond. The main road northwards ran close to the Rhodesian border and anything travelling on it was extremely vulnerable to SAS and MNR ambushes.

The rail line was a much safer proposition altogether – or so they thought.

It had been ten months since Mac McIntosh and his team had destroyed the Mecito rail bridge – and the valuable train – on the track, and while the line had not yet been repaired, it was still in use.

FRELIMO were merely operating a shuttle service – moving one train up to the severed track, offloading goods and passengers and then transferring them to another train on the other side.

The damage had thus been an inconvenience only – and the Rhodesians had learned a very valuable lesson from FRELIMO's ingenuity.

Now the Rhodesians planned to extend the damage one downed bridge could do, by dumping three major bridges in a row, thereby putting an end to the bridges . . . the track . . . and FRELIMO's ability to run a shuttle service.

FRELIMO had already demonstrated that they were incapable of repairing one bridge. Three, hopefully, would take forever.

The three bridges earmarked for destruction were from the northerly one to the southerly bridge 100 kilometres (62 miles) apart. The mission was to see the introduction of unique demolition devices – one was a large nylon mesh demolition net to be strung under the decking of two of the bridges enabling the operators to attach explosives to the top of the abutments. The other devices were enormous custom-made charges.

It was going to take six 100 kilogram charges of pentolite explosive to blow the incredibly thick piers at the northerly bridge – the biggest of the three targets – and the monster explosives had been cast into huge moulds . . . 200-litre fuel drums sliced down the centre which were then encased in nylon mesh.

The charges were to be hung on to the bridge by hooks set in wooden blocks which were to be attached to the piers by the powerful *Wonder Glue.*

The operators practised their demolition drills on a bridge on the outskirts of Salisbury . . . lowering the demolition net under the bridge, pulling it up tight and clambering inside to spread out their charges, just as they would come the real thing.

Finally, all the rehearsals were over and demolition commander Lieutenant Pete Cole was satisfied that their timings were perfect; that every man knew his job; knew what to do in the event of someone being injured and the team having to be changed.

Their convoy moved off to Mtoko and only now were the troops told their specific targets. Pete Cole and his team were to get the biggest bridge in the north, Mike Rich was to be in charge of the centre demolition and Rich Stannard, the third. Two Dakotas were to drop the three demolition teams close to their respective targets just before last light. The troops were to move in, secure the bridges, deal with any opposition, then carry out a reconnaissance . . . and next morning, the Bells would bring in the explosives and the bridges would be blown in broad daylight.

The weather was still hot and sunny when they took off for Mozambique. But as they climbed and turned away from Mtoko it became increasingly hazy, making visibility on the ground poor.

Not for Rhodesian Dakota pilots the sophisticated navigational aids of other air forces. They had to rely on their ability to map-read their way to a target, and that meant they had to see the ground clearly.

Eventually, the visibility became so bad that it was even difficult to see rivers and roads. The men in the Daks were straining their eyes to pick up features and stay on their correct flight path. The Number Two pilot even lost sight of the aircraft in front.

Just as it was approaching drop time, they were forced to agree that they would have to abort. There would be no drop that evening. The bridges would stand for another night.

Luckily, there was no great urgency and as the sky in the distance turned a deep gold slashed with scarlet, the Dakotas turned and headed back to Rhodesia.

Next afternoon, the visibility was good and the mission on. The Dakotas flew high level and followed the same flight path as the normal scheduled commercial run from Salisbury to the Malawian capital . . . a devious tactic to convince anyone below that they were on their way to Blantyre.

The SAS could see the lights of Blantyre 150 kilometres (93 miles) away. But at Matarara, they turned left and headed north into the fading light.

Captain Colin Willis was to supervise the drop at the centre and northerly bridges from one Dakota: Pete Cole that at the southerly target from the second Dakota. Twenty-five minutes from drop time, Pete popped through to the cargo bay to see the troops in his Dakota. They were sorting out their equipment and his wave was answered by a number of sickly grins.

Both aircraft located the rail line without any difficulty and turned in for the drop at the same time. They descended to 500 feet and even from the rather ponderous Dakotas, the ground below them seemed to rush past at a fast pace.

A few kraals flashed beneath them . . . and as one Dakota approached the centre target, the pilot reached up to the button that controlled the dispatch lights above the exit door of the aircraft and held his hand there. Colin Willis standing behind him, could see the spot where he wanted the troops to be dropped off racing towards him and gave the pilot the usual thumbs-up sign.

The pilot pressed the red light button and both men knew that the troops would be standing in the door. Then the pilot pressed the green button and away they went. There was no turning back for the SAS stick now. Soon, another demolition team would be dropped off at their bridge.

Meanwhile, the other Dakota was turning in to make its drop at the last bridge and the third party of bridge-blowers dropped in to their target. As the Dakota continued on its flight path, Pete Cole, standing behind the pilot, managed to catch a glimpse of the bridge off to the starboard. It looked exactly as they had expected. Good, he thought. It ought to be an easy one.

All three drops had gone well and the teams had reported landing safely near their targets. Both Dakotas turned for home, and soon Colin and Pete in their respective planes could see the two rows of landing lights burning ahead and guiding them into the airstrip at Mtoko.

They landed and climbed out into the darkness and were suddenly blasted by the wind from the engines and the noise as the two aircraft turned and took off again into the night. The SAS men hurried to the ops tent and were soon discussing the drop over a welcome cup of tea, and mulling over what was going to happen the following day.

Then they turned in for the night and must have mentally blown the three bridges at least six times before they fell asleep. All too soon, the guard was shaking them awake. Now it was time to go and blow them for real.

It was still dark, but there were already signs of dawn in the greying sky to the east. They gathered up their rifles and equipment and went out on to the airstrip, stopping only at a bowser just long enough to splash water on their faces.

Pete headed for a Bell bearing the 600 kilograms of explosives to the northerly bridge; Colin, who was to remain airborne throughout the operation, made for a Lynx.

* * *

Across the border, the three SAS demolition teams were already moving into position.

At the northerly target, there was an exchange of fire with a couple of FRELIMO and the enemy ran off. The SAS got into extended line and advanced towards the bridge. There was another exchange with FRELIMO occupying bunkers near the bridge and again the enemy fled.

But the SAS did not pursue the matter this time. All they wanted was the bridge.

They fired a few mortar bombs near an African village just sixty metres from the bridge, merely to show the locals what was what, and to chase them away. The SAS were not blackened-up and it must have been obvious even to the most unsophisticated person, that such heavily armed white men were not friendly forces.

But the villagers accepted the situation and continued fetching and carrying their water from the riverbed regardless of the goings-on at the bridge.

Soon the three choppers had arrived at their respective targets to drop off their load of explosives.

Sergeant *Small Bez* was waiting to greet Pete Cole at the northerly bridge. The sergeant had it all buttoned up and told where he had positioned his troops to protect the demolition party while they fixed their charges.

Pete chalked a cross on the piers where he wanted the explosives attached and although he knew the 600 kilogram charges would rip the rail lines from the track, he was taking no chances. He sent a sergeant to set up separate charges to cut the rails.

Eventually, the monster charges were attached to the bridge, the ringmain was run out and the track ready to be cut.

Everyone moved away to take cover and the six-man demolition team moved along the river and around a bend, hugging the high banks for protection.

Just then the Lynx pilot came up on the radio to tell them to delay the demolition – he was bringing in Commander Colin Willis who wanted to get into a good position to see the fireworks.

Once the Lynx was circling safely in the distance, Pete and *Small Bez* lit the fuses and hurried to join the others around the bend in the river.

Then Pete gave the okay to blow the rails. There was a brief wait, then a massive explosion followed by some very speedy pieces of steel screaming overhead, cything their way through the thick bush. There was another short wait, then came an explosion twenty times bigger than the first.

There she goes, they thought. Everywhere there were smiling faces. Some of the men still had their hands pressed over their ears.

"LOOK UP!" some bellowed instinctively.

They all looked for the enormous pieces of concrete raining down from the skies, drenching the countryside and crashing all around them into the bush, followed a few seconds later by the patter of hundreds of smaller pieces.

Pete and *Small Bez* hurried back around the bend to see the damage. But all they could see was dust.

"It's okay," Colin assured them from the orbiting Lynx "No need to worry; it's gone!"

And as the dust started to settle, they began to see that for themselves. Two piers and three spans were down, and the demolition team lost no time in congratulating each other.

Time was on their side and there was still the chance to use two reserve 48 kilogram charges to blow the abutments. They began to climb over the rubble, eager to get the bridge down as soon as possible.

Suddenly, the trooper up front, dropped his explosives and hurtled past the others at high speed.

"What's going on ... ?" Pete began to say, amazed at the strange turn of events. Then he realised they were all being stung by thousands of angry bees, sent wild with frenzy by the shock wave of the explosion, which had blown away their nest under the bridge.

Soon, everyone was in hot pursuit of the first man and running as fast as he could away from the bridge.

They splashed in a nearby waterhole and furiously tried to beat the bees off one another. When that failed to work, they crawled under some low thorn bushes and covered their heads as best they could.

When it seemed as if the bees had finally had enough, the SAS gingerly emerged from the bushes to assess the damage – to themselves this time, not the bridge.

All six men in the demolition team had been stung. Two were in a very sorry state indeed and the medic immediately set about treating them.

Then they attempted approaching the bridge from all angles in a bid to blow out the abutments. But all they succeeded in doing was getting stung again.

They couldn't even get close enough to recover the first charge the trooper had dropped in the initial panic. They tried subduing the bees with smoke grenades and Lieutenant Angus Hyland-Smith even tried draping a mosquito net over his head to protect him as he tried to reach the charge.

But it was no use. The bees were painfully persistent. As Pete Cole photographed what remained of the bridge, he couldn't help thinking how frustrating it was to be driven off by a swarm of bees.

Now time was running out. The choppers would be coming for them soon and they would have to think of another plan.

They moved to a two-storey lookout post near the bridge and tried to destroy their charge with an RPG-7 rocket. They managed to damage the charge but not detonate it. However, the back-blast from the launcher blew the roof off the lookout post as an unexpected bonus.

Meanwhile at the other two bridges, everything had gone according to plan and both bridges were successfully demolished.

The three bridge-blowing parties met up again at a staging area inside Mozambique, rigged up all their unnecessary kit and unused charges for demolition, and, when the choppers lifted for home, they could see the dust as the explosion went off. But it was a small affair, a tiny puff compared to the earlier ones that day.

The two severely stung soldiers had to be admitted to hospital, and one was hospitalised for several days to recover from the wounds from the SAS's only attackers on the operation. The bees had proved to be far better fighters than either ZANLA or FRELIMO. They had fought the SAS time after time and did not give in, eventually forcing the Rhodesians to withdraw licking their wounds.

As for the SAS, they had now downed five bridges in two days. It would prove invaluable experience for the bigger stuff yet to come. For the bridge-blowing season was far from over.

Hero of the Highest Order

In June, 1978, former SAS officer Chris Schollenberg, then a Selous Scout, became the first holder of the country's highest bravery award, the Grand Cross of Valour, equivalent to the Victoria Cross and the American Congressional Medal of Honour.

There was only one other GCV ever awarded and that too went to an SAS officer. Unfortunately, his identity cannot be revealed and the part of his citation recorded here tells only some of the story.

He was the most decorated soldier in the Rhodesian security forces and the only person to get the hat-trick – the Bronze Cross of Rhodesia, the Silver Cross and the top gallantry honour, the GCV. Naturally too, he held the SAS's own coveted Wings on Chest honour awarded to outstanding operators.

His citation reads, in part: "His leadership and performance on operations has been of the highest order, his devotion to duty has been extremely outstanding. And his contribution to the war effort has been incalculable ...

"His extreme devotation to duty, performance on operations and general conduct have contributed greatly to the successes this unit has achieved."

Operation Tepid, October, 1979

The situation in Zambia had now changed drastically, and intelligence was continuing to come in about the training of regular conventional terrorists and the formation of conventional battalions and brigades.

There were thus two distinct brands of ZIPRA who were entirely different from each other – the unconventional, irregular guerrillas, and the regulars trained in classical warfare.

Early in the year during a helicopter extraction, a number of choppers were fired at from a location about sixty kilometres (37 miles) south-west of Chirundu. The area was marked by the pilots and later a photographic reconnaissance mission was flown by a Canberra from 5 Squadron.

Interpreting the photographs proved a very difficult task. Unfortunately, when the sortie was flown, the haze was so bad that the 3-D effect essential for a clear and accurate interpretation was lost. The photographs therefore appeared totally flat, making it difficult to pick up areas of dense jesse bush, ideal for affording the enemy cover.

The fact that it was October and the height of the dry season did not help either. Everything was brown anyway, and from the air the jesse tended to blend in closely with the colour of the ground.

The area under scrutiny was around Lusuto, 21 kilometres (13 miles) north-west of Siavonga on the Zambian side of Lake Kariba and seventy kilometres (43 miles) from Kariba. The Rhodesians were particularly interested in two ridges astride a large salt pan. And after many long hours of studying the photographs, the interpreters eventually fathomed out the story.

On the low ground to the north and south of two ridges and in the pan area itself and near the waterlines, there were areas of dense vegetation and very thick jesse bush.

There was also some vegetation and tree cover on the smaller, the most western, of the two ridges.

On the other ridge, the bigger of the two, the eastern side was covered with sparse vegetation. However, it was so open that it was the most unlikely spot for the enemy to be based up in. ZIPRA normally chose areas of dense tree cover to protect them from Rhodesia's eyes in the sky.

There was no evidence either of track patterns worn in the ground by people walking from one spot to another.

But then came a stroke of luck. The interpreters began to pick up signs of trenches, and from the number and the way they were sited, it became apparent that this very sparsely vegetated area, a very unlikely hide-out indeed, had to be the position of a conventionally-trained ZIPRA battalion, the first the Rhodesians had pinpointed.

ZIPRA had learned their lessons well and there were no give-away tracks leading from one trench to another – the occupants had very wisely walked on rocky areas and made use of extremely hard soil.

And to make life even more difficult for the interpreters, ZIPRA had taken the precaution of camouflaging the bottom of the trenches with soil of the same colour as the surrounding area so there were no differences in soil colouration. Loose stone had also been used to break up outlines.

But having at long last located one of the elusive enemy battalion positions, the Rhodesians were unable to assess how many people were holed up there, and what weaponry they had.

Even if there was a full battalion of several hundred troops, numbers did not really mean that much to the Rhodesians. After all, a mere 200 SAS and RLI troops had attacked 10 000-plus at Chimoio-1, and it had been a walk over as the enemy was not inclined to stand and fight.

To take on a conventional enemy would need heavy support weapons and transporting them was a problem. At least in Mozambique the Rhodesians could drive to the enemy positions. This was not the case in Zambia where the Zambezi separated the two countries. The Rhodesians were entirely reliant on what they could carry across the river in choppers, or by para drop.

Rhodesia simply did not have the necessary resources to attack ZIPRA conventional battalions.

Rhodesia had already learned several severe lessons about attacking enemy base camp positions which were well-sited and protected, and they were extremely loath to get involved in another major external operation which would end up in much the same way as *Uric* and *Miracle*.

But something clearly had to be done to blunt the threat on the northern border.

ComOps decided the best plan would be to disrupt the positions by double ambushing the roads on the low ground leading to and from the suspected battalion positions to stop anyone going in and coming out . . . to cut it off in the middle . . . and hope it would be abandoned.

A bombing run was planned, after which two 16-man SAS fighting patrols would be inserted to watch for any reaction . . . block the routes in and out . . . sweep the area . . . and, if the opportunity presented itself, return with a suitable capture to provide the Rhodesians with a useful source of intelligence. In the likelihood of trouble, the groups were strong enough to fight off any opposition.

Bob McKenna's "C" Squadron got the job and travelled to Kariba to prepare for the op – and on the morning of October 18, under cover of a Hunter and Canberra bombing run, the two separate groups were put down in the area.

One group, under the command of Lieutenant Rich Stannard, was dropped about 12 kilometres to the north-east of the main ridge and the other, under Lieutenant Phil Brooke, the same distance away to the south-east of the same ridge.

After the air strike, a Dakota circled the area then flew up one ridge and down the other, dropping incendiaries out of the door from 200 feet in the hope of burning the place out, thus making any ZIPRA there more vulnerable.

As it was, many of the incendiaries failed to go off, and although the pilot reported seeing trenches, he could not see anyone in them.

The two SAS fighting patrols could see no reaction either. There was not a single shot fired in retaliation at the jets or the Dakota. In fact, they saw no movement whatsoever, and in the light of such a negative response, a third Hunter strike was cancelled.

Bob McKenna, too, circling in a Lynx, silently registered the mission as a *lemon* . . . a pointless exercise. It was obvious the position had been abandoned.

The two patrols were equally convinced that any enemy who might have been there earlier had already vacated the area.

Nevertheless, Bob decided the two teams should remain where they were and they hid in the bush hoping it might still be possible to get a capture.

They stayed for the rest of the day with Rich Stannard and his team on the north-east seeing no sign of any enemy.

Phil Brooke and his group set up an ambush and they had hardly taken up their positions than one of the early-warning groups came on the radio to warn of a twenty-man enemy sweepline advancing towards the main killer group. The SAS had no option but to engage them. One ZIPRA was killed and the remainder took flight.

That night, Bob McKenna radioed each of the two groups to press on and sweep towards the top of the ridge. They were to rendezvous at first light then move into the camp and see what, if anything, was going on there. After that, the choppers would come in and take them back to Kariba.

The bush on the approaches to both sides of the ridge turned out to be incredibly thick and both patrol commanders came to the conclusion that the only way to reach the ridge was to walk on the track. It was a dicey move in any circumstances, but the lack of moon and the nature of the terrain left them with no option.

However, they took the normal precaution of putting out a scout section in front to lead the way, with the rest of the men walking close behind.

The incredible heat of the Zambezi Valley at that time of the year, coupled with the walk, resulted in one very severe case of heat fatigue in Phil Brooke's group. The man could barely walk and he was left behind with a three-man escort while the remaining 12 men continued moving ever-so-carefully towards the suspected camp at the top of the huge ridge.

Rich Stannard and his team meanwhile were doing the same from the opposite direction. It was a very still night in the valley. There was not a sound to be heard. Quietly, stealthily, the two groups closed in through the darkness.

Suddenly, Phil Brooke's group heard the distinctive sound of an AK being put from safe to fire. Then a burst of red tracer arched four metres over their heads.

"Inanda?" ("Who is it?") a harsh urgent voice demanded of Phil and his group.

There could be no replying to the ZIPRA ambush patrol lurking on the side of the track, and the callsign immediately went to ground and tried to move away.

For a few moments nothing happened. Then it dawned on the enemy that the shadowy figures were not comrades as they had at first thought, and a burst of machinegun fire shattered the night.

Lance Corporal John McLaurin went down in the initial burst, severely wounded in the stomach by a stray shot.

"Open Fire," the SAS commander shouted to his men. There were eight RPD light machineguns among the 12 Rhodesians and with the constant heavy rate of fire the SAS was putting down, it was obviously too much for the ZIPRA ambushers.

They must have thought they had taken on a far larger group, and after a short firefight, they took off for the bush, leaving their weapons, spare magazines and blankets, and dragging a wounded colleague with them. Next morning, Phil and his men would inspect the ambush scene to find the six ZIPRA men had opened up 25 metres from the track. There was blood spoor and from the orderly manner in which they had left their belongings, it was obvious they had been well organised.

After the firefight, the SAS pulled back 200 metres from the track, doing their best to keep their seriously injured patient quiet.

Further injuries had been averted but by the narrowest of margins. The patrol had good reason to be thankful for those few precious moments of hesitation when the enemy had mistaken them for ZIPRA.

Immediately, the troop medic set to work putting up a drip and giving John McLaurin morphine; and a signal was sent to "C" Squadron in Kariba requesting an urgent casualty evacuation.

But the weather was poor and the moon phase was such that no helicopter support was immediately available ... and the callsign stayed in the same spot for the rest of the night without anyone really getting any sleep.

John McLaurin was wounded at midnight and the unfortunate young soldier eventually died five hours later.

Rich Stannard and his team meanwhile had been pressing on through the night towards the ridge. He had planned to travel all night, but in the early hours he had an uneasy feeling and decided they ought to snatch a couple of hours sleep.

381

That morning, after the casevac chopper had arrived on the far side of the ridge to collect the body of John McLaurin and casevac the heat fatigue case, Phil Brooke and his callsign, now convinced ZIPRA had abandoned the position after the previous night's contact, were choppered forward closer to the main camp area.

The ridge had a steep gradient with a number of false crests and just as they reached what they thought was the top, so another rise would appear before them. They pressed on up and were almost at the top when all hell was let loose and they were in hot water again.

For waiting to greet them was a fusillade of very effective and heavy enemy fire, which was controlled, accurate and supplemented by mortars carrying out searching fire.

But, initially, because of ZIPRA's excellent trench system, which was superbly camouflaged and because ZIPRA discipline was so good, Phil thought Rich Stannard and his team were unintentionally firing at them from the opposite side of the ridge.

He immediately reached for his radio and quizzed Rich about the matter. No, replied Rich, it wasn't them; they couldn't even hear shooting; it had to be coming from the enemy.

The SAS fired back, but as soon as they so much as showed themselves over the ridge, they were met by a hail of bullets. Phil and a corporal looked over the ridge, and Phil got a nick in the buttocks for his trouble and the corporal was shot in the arm.

Phil and his team were up against rifle fire, recoilless rifles, mortars, 12,7 millimetre and 14,5 millimetre heavy weapons and were thoroughly pinned down.

The enemy's aggressiveness and determination to destroy them came as quite a shock. There was no doubt in anyone's mind that they faced a much higher calibre of enemy than they had previously encountered in Zambia.

Phil contacted base and called for immediate jet support. Bob McKenna scrambled the Hunters from Thornhill air base, Gwelo, then immediately got airborne himself in a Lynx with pilot Trevor Jew at the controls . . . and the two men made their way across the Zambezi to the target area as quickly as possible.

They hoped to provide some support until the jets arrived, after which they would be able to give the Hunter pilots instructions on exactly where to make their strikes.

Meanwhile, unbeknown to Phil Brooke and his men, a ZIPRA assault platoon was forming up behind them awaiting the word to advance.

Subsequent intelligence revealed that ZIPRA were planning to draw the SAS nearer to them until just the right moment when they could sort them out properly.

But the SAS ended up in dead ground and the enemy could not winkle them out . . . and ZIPRA had dispatched a platoon behind them with the task of annihilating every member of the callsign.

Rich Stannard and his group were moving as fast as they could from the opposite direction to try and neutralise ZIPRA and take some of the weight of fire off Phil and his party, enabling them to get away. The vegetation was still bad and they were walking on a low ridge and not the high one as they had been instructed. Had they followed their original plan, they too would have got into a position where they were pinned down.

There were a few old African kraals dotted here and there on their way and although they didn't see any enemy, that familiar feeling of danger was there.

At the very moment the ZIPRA assault platoon was readying themselves to advance on Phil's callsign, the sound of a Rhodesian Lynx aircraft could be heard overhead.

Bob McKenna and pilot Trevor Jew had arrived in the area slightly ahead of the jets, and as they approached the ridges, Bob spoke to Phil Brooke on the radio asking him for a sitrep.

"There are between 12 and 20 enemy shooting at us with mortars and recoilless rifles," the patrol commander reported.

As the Lynx got closer, the two men in the plane could see a recoilless rifle firing at Phil's callsign and they agreed that if conditions were suitable, they would give the callsign a hand by dropping off their Frantan and firing rockets on the ridges.

"Confirm the number of enemy?" Bob radioed Phil again.

"Twenty maximum," came the reply.

"Okay. We'll see what we can do," the squadron commander said as the Lynx, with its deadly payload, got closer. "But if there are more than twenty, I'll be bloody cheesed off."

During the air strikes the day before, the enemy had not fired a single shot and that said much for their fire discipline. This time, however, they had no intention of holding their fire.

For the pinned-down SAS men, the Lynx had arrived in the nick of time. The ZIPRA holed up in the labyrinth of trenches, and those closing in on them, suddenly decided to turn their attentions away from the SAS men on the ground and concentrate on the plane and its two occupants.

Bob told the pilot to turn in and put a strike on the recoilless rifle position and, as they turned for the dive, the sky was suddenly filled with bullets. The Lynx was met with a merciless hail of 12,7 millimetre and 14,5 millimetre anti-aircraft rounds and the trenches erupted with the muzzle flashes from a hundred enemy rifles.

Phil Brooke and his men suddenly learned that there was an anti-aircraft position just fifty metres from them. The bush was so thick that they had not seen it. And by now, Rich Stannard and his team, racing to the rescue, were so close to the action that they were able to hear the terrorists cocking their weapons.

"Bloody hell!" cursed the normally-calm "C" Squadron commander, as sheets of red tracer streamed past the cockpit.

The pilot immediately aborted his strike without firing anything and turned away, the safety of his plane, his passenger and himself now of overriding importance.

As he did so, an armour-piercing incendiary tracer from a 14,5 millimetre weapon smashed into the control panel between Bob and the pilot, then glanced off and came to rest in the front engine.

The cockpit immediately filled with smoke and neither man could see the other.

Shrapnel went into the pilot's legs and other bits pinged into the plane. A flash of flame burned the hair on the SAS man's legs and he silently cursed himself for not exchanging his shorts for the regulation pair of long trousers SAS men were supposed to wear on operations.

But that was the very least of his worries at that precise moment. Both men knew that were their engine and fuel to catch alight or their bombs and rockets ignite, they could be blown to smithereens in an exploding ball of flame.

Had the enemy held their fire for another five seconds, there is no doubt that the plane would have been shot from the sky.

The two SAS callsigns on the ground could hear the pilot's calls for help as he tussled with the stricken plane.

"MAYDAY! MAYDAY!" he yelled into his radio mouthpiece. "Get the hell out of here," he instructed Bob McKenna.

But Bob had no intention of baling out and leaving the pilot to his fate.

"Negative, I'll stay," he replied adamantly.

Back in Kariba, Sergeant Major *Petrol Paul* who was running "C" Squadron's tactical headquarters, could hear the drama being played out over his radio.

"Hell! We've lost another squadron commander," thought the sergeant major who had been with Martin Pearse when he was killed.

Bob meanwhile was opening the window in the Lynx to get rid of the smoke, and, as the cockpit cleared, they discovered they were not on fire after all.

But now they noticed the pilot had not fastened his parachute and while Trevor Jew did up his harness, Bob had to take over flying the plane.

Fortunately, it was not a new experience for him as the SAS squadron commanders often practised flying with the pilots' guidance, for just such emergencies as these. This time though, his knees were trembling so much with the shock and intensity of the attack, he had difficulty controlling the rudder.

As the Lynx pulled away, Bob quickly called up Rich Stannard briefing him not to go up the ridge to Phil Brooke's aid.

"They've got mutually-supporting anti-aircraft positions and trenches," he warned. "Move off and be prepared for pick-up."

Bob and the pilot were still unsure if the outside of the Lynx was on fire or not but were taking no chances and jettisoned their bombs and rockets.

The two men finally settled down and realised that they would probably get back to Rhodesia in one piece, and as they flew back to base, they ran through their emergency procedures and did their normal checks. These revealed that the automatic controls affecting the hydraulics were not working.

They tried to work the handcrank, the emergency facility that controlled the hydraulics, but hot hydraulic fluid sprayed all over the cockpit and they gave that up as a bad idea. It meant that the flaps would not be working when they needed them and the wheels would not go down.

The pilot somehow managed to get the struggling aircraft back across the border, alerting Kariba military and civilian airstrip he was on his way and about to make an emergency landing.

On the way, the front engine packed in, and, left only with the back one, they limped over the lake.

Crash crews and ambulances were already waiting for them as they came into Kariba airport. Trevor Jew orbitted the airfield and asked Bob yet again if he wanted to parachute out. But the SAS commander decided to stay where he was.

Then Trevor Jew made his approach run, switching off his remaining engine to glide in for a crash-landing. He had decided to head for the tarmac instead of the grass as he felt it would give him more control in the forthcoming skid.

Bob held the passenger door open as the plane came down. They could not predict how the landing would go and had no intention of getting trapped in the cockpit.

The fire crew hurtled down the airstrip after them as the crippled plane headed for the tar.

It was a magnificent landing. The pilot put the Lynx gently down on its belly and as it skidded along the tarmac, sparks from the friction shot in every direction.

The moment the plane stopped moving, there was a race to see who could get out of the plane first. The pilot tried to climb over Bob, but Bob being nearer the door and equally as motivated, swung his feet out and was on the tarmac first.

Then the two men sprinted as far and as fast away from the Lynx as they could just in case a spark ignited the fuel. The crash crew was swift to react and when Bob and Trevor turned around again, it was to see the plane covered in foam to reduce the possibility of fire and an explosion.

The Lynx was not badly damaged by the landing, and more harm was done hauling it off the tar than had been inflicted on crashing it.

Miraculously, the two men had come through it all unscathed. "C" Squadron had not lost another commander and the air force still had the services of one of its brilliant young pilots. But they were badly shaken.

Bob brushed himself down, swore, and immediately hurried to the radio room to report being shot down.

"There are 200-odd guys out there shooting at us," he briefed SAS HQ in Salisbury. "They are well dug in with recoilless rifles, mortars and heavy A/A weapons. Assess we need at least another 150 troops to attack the position. Alternatively, a nuke!"

"We'll send you another squadron," came the reply from Salisbury.

"You'd better send a lot more than that," commented the squadron commander, not at all impressed.

Meanwhile, the Rhodesian jets which had been flying high altitude during the battle with the Lynx had screamed into the pan and dropped their cargoes. It was indeed a comforting sight for the SAS boys still on the ground to see the familiar shapes of the Hunters once more.

Several strikes were put in and occasionally the enemy could be seen changing fire position, each movement appeared to be a disciplined drill.

Phil Brooke and his lads had very wisely conducted a swift tactical withdrawal; the position had hardly been abandoned as they had originally thought! Enemy 82 millimetre mortar bombs were dropping behind them.

They pulled back ten kilometres (six miles) until they found a good landing zone for the chopper and were picked up and taken back to Kariba.

Rich Stannard and his group had also withdrawn and were preparing for pick up. He silently earmarked an open spot for the helicopter landing zone, and as they moved towards it, saw three men sitting under a rocky outcrop.

The SAS immediately carried out a flanking attack and when it was all over, two enemy lay dead and the third had a round through his femur.

Remembering his earlier instructions, Rich decided to spare the man. It was to prove a wise decision.

Initial interrogation revealed that the capture was none other than the camp logistics officer. Rich bandaged some of his flesh wounds, and medic Bruce Langley put up a drip. They called for an immediate casevac chopper and Rich lost no time signalling the good news to Bob McKenna.

"Oh! and by the way," he said, "I've got your capture for you!"

Bob could hardly believe it. At least that part of the mission had gone according to plan.

A chopper was dispatched across the lake and the capture was whisked back to Rhodesia to be delivered to an eagerly-awaiting SB officer.

The prisoner revealed that the enemy were conventionally trained, and that there were some 200 men who were prepared to remain dug into their trenches and stand and fight, and not run away as was the normal enemy reaction.

The captured man's condition worsened during the night and he was flown to Kariba Hospital where his right leg was amputated. The next day, feeling much better, he spilled the beans to SB officer Pete Dewe, of the national intelligence team, who had been called from Salisbury to interview him.

He said the enemy were from the First Battalion of ZIPRA's First Brigade and they had moved into that particular piece of Zambian territory five weeks earlier from Mulungushi. It was to serve as their forward base until such time as the word came to cross the border in force into Rhodesia.

They did not have a full complement of men yet and said that at the time of his capture there were 244 there. Another 100 reinforcements were expected.

They had followed their orders to the letter during the initial air strikes and had held their fire hoping that the Rhodesians would think the place abandoned and not return.

Nevertheless, they had been prepared for a confrontation and laid landmines on each of the two access roads. He was adamant that no amount of bombings or anything else would budge ZIPRA.

The ZIPRA batallion commander had reminded his men that they were conventional soldiers and trained to hold their position. They were well fortified with an assortment of light and heavy weapons giving them more than a fighting chance in the event of attack.

They had a good communications system with eleven two-way radios distributed throughout the camp. One radio linked the enemy to the regional commander based in nearby Lusoto, who in turn had direct contact with Lusaka.

The camp, which was spread between the two ridges and the pan itself, was a conventionally prepared full-scale linear defensive position according to the Russian chapter.

The place was obviously far bigger than the Rhodesians had first thought and it was clear they could not tolerate such a force sitting biding their time, waiting to pounce on Rhodesia. The initial plan of merely disrupting the enemy by ambushing was scrapped. Now an attack was to be mounted.

Back at ComOps, Lieutenant-General Peter Walls ordered his RLI commandos to move to Kariba as quickly as possible to reinforce the SAS. As it so happened, a sub-unit of 2 Commando, RLI, under Major Pete Hean, had arrived at Kariba within a couple of hours of Bob's crash landing to start border control operations. The rest of the RLI contingent was to come from 3 Commando and were flown to Kariba before first light. Men of "A" and "B" Squadrons of the SAS, who had been stood down for the weekend, were rounded up as they prepared to spend a rare Saturday night in the capital.

The Hunters and Canberras, meanwhile, were being bombed up.

The COs of the SAS and RLI had sat in on the interrogation of the wounded captive. The questions had now been answered and Operation *Tepid* was about to begin.

* * *

As there were more RLI troops than SAS and they formed the assault groups, overall command of the operation was to be by Lieutenant-Colonel Ian Bate of the RLI, with Lieutenant-Colonel Garth Barrett of the SAS providing the alternative command function. Both were to use the airborne method of command from a Lynx aircraft.

Major Pete Hean and Major Don Price were to command the RLI contingent. Pete and forty men from 2 Commando were to attack the eastern ridge, the biggest one where Phil Brooke had run into all his trouble and where it was assessed the greatest concentration of enemy were. Don Price, together with 32 men from 3 Commando would attack the western ridge.

The SAS ground forces, tasked with sweeping through the camp after the ridges were taken, were to be commanded by Major Rob Johnstone.

There were four RLI mortars in direct support of the two RLI groups; and a smaller SAS mortar team to support the SAS. All told, there were six 81 millimetre mortars, the most the Rhodesians could scrape up at such short notice.

While the Rhodesians would not have the heavy artillery support as in other major externals, there would be two Hunters in direct support of the ground troops for the duration of the op.

The troops were told that the enemy would stand and fight. However, the thinking was that as there was no longer any secrecy about the position, there was a very good chance ZIPRA may well have vacated the camp.

A callsign headed by Phil Brooke, was taken back to the area on Saturday October 19 and placed on a hill to watch the camp and keep "C" Squadron commander up to date with comings and goings. Rain delayed the operation, but by the following day the weather had cleared and the mission was on.

Trooping started early and five Bell 205s were to be used to ferry the security forces across the lake.

Five waves delivered Pete Hean and the forty men of 2 Commando to the eastern ridge; and there were four waves needed to get Don Price and his 32 men from 3 Commando to the western side of the pan.

Both groups were dropped about three kilometres to the north from the top of their respective ridges without attracting any opposition from the enemy.

At 10h00, the Canberras would carry out a bombing run on the main ridge only ... followed two hours later by simultaneous ground attacks on both ridges.

In ideal conditions, the attack ought to be mounted the moment air support lifted, but in this case, the bombing run had to be made over the heads of Pete Hean and his troops, and it was impossible for them to get from their landing position to their predetermined starting line at the top of the ridge in time to mount their attack.

The planners felt that the air strike might serve to soften the target up a bit, so that, hopefully, by the time the assault went in, the ZIPRA men would have vacated their trenches.

As it was, the air strike was ineffective and, as it did not appear to inflict a single casualty or serve to warn them off, the enemy just sat tight and waited.

The two assault groups then began moving forward towards their respective ridges in readiness for the noon attack.

At 11h00 the choppers flew in to drop off the RLI and SAS mortar teams three kilometres from the target.

Ideally, mortars need to be out of sight, out of range and not affected by direct fire. Unfortunately, this time, their landing zones were on a forward slope and in full sight of the enemy positions and, as they touched down the familiar sound of enemy mortar crumps could be heard ranging in on the helicopters. The enemy had correctly assessed possible LZs and had previously zeroed in their mortars.

As the Rhodesians ran to unload their bombs and set up their own mortars, they came under very effective and intensive enemy mortar bombardment and 75 millimetre recoilless rifle fire. There were also a fair amount of RPG-7 rockets directed towards them.

It was accurate fire and quite worrying. It came as something of a shock, too, as they had been told they would be well out of range of enemy mortars. Later, they moved back slightly, but that did not work either and the enemy bombs continued to land among them.

To be effective, the mortars needed to be mobile – to fire and move all the time. However, the mortar bombs were dropped off at the mortar base-plate position throughout the day and that was where they were to remain. To carry 400 ten-pound bombs around the bush was an impossibility.

"A" and "B" Squadrons were dropped in shortly after the mortar teams had collected their share of the hot stuff and as each wave of troops arrived, so the enemy turned their collective attention to them.

The SAS took up their positions on high ground domineering the enemy camp in readiness to sweep down through the bush of the central pan area once the RLI had taken their two ridges.

"C" Squadron, who had already tangled with the camp residents, had dug their own trenches along the access road, to take on any Zambian Army contingent that decided to interfere.

By noon, the 72 RLI assault troops were in position on the two ridges for the attack, having encountered no opposition during their advance.

Pete Hean and his forty men were to have the advantage of being in a dominating position overlooking open terrain for their assault; but Don Price and his 32 troops would be assaulting uphill through the bush.

Then the attack went in – and the moment Pete Hean and his men stuck their noses over the edge of the main ridge, two 14,5 millimetre heavy machineguns – one on each of the two ridges – opened up on them, putting down such extremely good and accurate fire that it had the forty men from 2 Commando thoroughly pinned down.

The RLI were right on the crest of the ridge and in full view of the enemy. They could see right down into the enemy position. They could see the weapons positions ... the trenches ... virtually the whites of the ZIPRA men's eyes.

The Rhodesians were in good cover and were behind large rocks and crevices and the enemy rounds were chipping away bits of the rock. Every so often when the firing died down, the RLI would get up and have a look and the enemy would start up again.

When the 14,5 millimetre gunners took a breather, ZIPRA hidden from view in the gully, between the high point where the RLI were and the main ridge, kept up the attack. They started sending smallarms fire up the ridge then began lobbing up light mortar bombs at them.

From the outset, it was very apparent that the Rhodesians were up against a vast assortment of military hardware – and an opposition whose discipline and determination were outstanding.

There was a lull during which Don Price and his group of 32 men over on their hill carried on moving up their ridge. Suddenly, there was a roar from the heaviest smallarms fire the Rhodesians had heard for a long time – and Trooper Andy Houghton went down, fatally injured.

Like the other group of RLI on the neighbouring ridge, Don Price and his men had been stopped dead in their tracks. They regrouped but were out of the battle. It was impossible to attack as they simply did not know where the enemy were among the vegetation.

By now, Pete Hean had called for mortar support with the idea of putting down pre-paratory bombardment and covering fire on to the enemy position enabling his group to advance.

But the RLI mortars were completely ineffective and of no help whatsoever to Major Hean and his men. The mortar commander was using the incorrect range tables . . . and he was not searching for the enemy properly.

Sergeant Major Pete Allan commanding the nearby SAS mortars volunteered his services and his mortars, but, as the SAS mortars were only there to protect the SAS in the event of their getting into trouble, his offer was not taken up. As a result, the RLI mortars were unusable and the SAS mortar team – who had the correct range tables and a wealth of experience – sat around idle all day.

When it became obvious the RLI mortars would be of no help, Pete Hean called in the Hunters to try and neutralise the two 14,5 millimetre positions and to stop the light mortar attacks. But the strikes were ineffective and the moment the RLI made the slightest move forward, so the enemy weapons started again.

The day wore on and whenever the Hunters were overhead, Pete called for an air-strike, but they were unable to neutralise the enemy. The camouflage in the trenches was so good that the extremely vulnerable pilots could not positively identify the enemy gunners, and the strikes were off-target.

Pete Hean realised he had to establish a secure starting point for his attack. His problem area was the little gully where the ZIPRA light mortars were positioned.

He sent 16 men down from their high point into the gully, where, taking advantage of the small amount of cover, they cleared several trenches. But within half an hour, he had pulled them back – eight men had flesh wounds.

Pete and his men now felt very vulnerable. They were on a high rocky ridge and didn't even have entrenching tools to dig themselves into a reasonable position.

Everything was on ZIPRA's side. They had a very well-sited defensive position, were extremely well dug in and were well fortified with the heavy weapons positioned in such a way that if one was threatened, two others would provide covering fire.

The numerically inferior attackers on the other hand were exposed and without the benefit of support weapons. Apart from the air strikes, which were ineffective, all the RLI had were rifles and hand-held 60 millimetre mortars, certainly no match for ZIPRA's heavy weapons.

It was obvious that with the enemy in trenches and the RLI in the open, there was no way they would be able to winkle them out without some other assistance. It was clear too, that, even with adequate covering fire, enabling the RLI to move in, the enemy had no intention of vacating their trenches during daylight hours when they were vulnerable to air strikes and whatever fire the ground troops planned for them.

Pete Hean called for a casevac chopper for his eight men and asked that it bring in a 14,5 millimetre from Kariba. He felt it might just do the trick. As the RLI dominated the position, he hoped that, with their own 14,5, they would be able to put down effective fire on the ZIPRA 14,5 on the main ridge below.

As a troop commander talked in Squadron Leader Ted Lunt, OC of the Bell Squadron, the commander mistook his chopper for another Bell and ended up talking the squadron leader straight in over the enemy position.

ZIPRA stared in amazement as a lone helicopter flew low level just above their major support weapons positions.

It was only when the squadron leader pulled away that the amazed ZIPRA decided to have a go at him . . . and a trail of angry tracer followed him along the ridge.

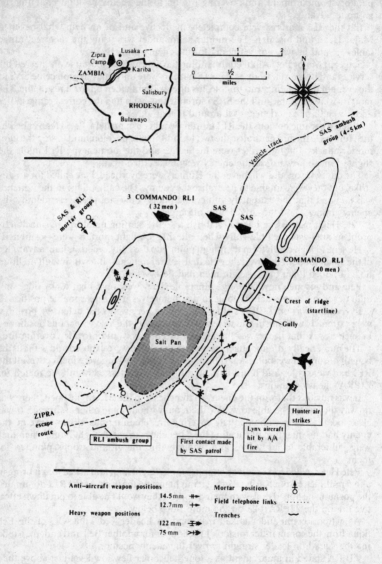

Operation *Tepid:* Map showing the security forces' clash with one of ZIPRA's conventional battalions

390

Then, while the casevacs were being loaded on to the chopper, two pilots came in to try and eliminate the main 14,5 position for the final time that day.

The sun was just starting to go down, and Pete Hean was talking to the first pilot trying to indicate the exact position of the heavy weapon. He dropped mortar smoke down on to the position, then gave the pilot a correction to bring him on to the right spot.

"Hang on," said the first pilot. "I'll send my No. 2 in first; watch for the tracer coming up and follow him in. The No. 2 will strike where we think it is: I'll see exactly where the trouble is and strike on it."

The No. 2 Hunter turned in – and before he was half way down his dive, the 14,5s on both ridges opened up on it.

The first pilot was hanging back 15 or so seconds behind and coming from a different angle.

"Okay! I've got the bugger," he said referring to the heavy weapon gunner on the main ridge.

Pete Hean watched through his binoculars and saw him turn in for the attack. The enemy was firing as the pilot came down. Then he let his front 30 millimetre Aden cannons go.

It was a pinpoint strike and the dust and stones flew everywhere as the weapon pit erupted and the weapon was momentarily silenced.

The enemy gunner shook his head, grabbed hold of the 14,5 and swung it around again, firing up at the aircraft as it pulled away. The red tracer followed it up as the pilot flew off into the sunset, but none made its mark.

Unfortunately for the Rhodesians, the ZIPRA gunner was so well protected, that short of getting it between the eyes, he was safe.

It was clear they were not going to take the position that day, and the RLI men on both ridges pulled back for the night, leaving small patrols on top to give early-warning.

The enemy had undoubtedly won that round. It was the first time in Zambia that terrorists were determined to hold a position against an equally-determined attack. They were well-disciplined, knew how to use their weapons and were fairly happy about their defences.

It seemed to SAS CO Garth Barrett, who took over the command at the end of the day, that the Rhodesians either had to accept they were there for a long time . . . or they could expect them to pull out during the night.

Earlier in the day, an SAS group from "C" Squadron had been placed on a possible escape route to the north-east, and from the air Garth Barrett selected the only other available enemy withdrawal route to the south-west, placing a twenty-man RLI ambush group on that track.

* * *

In the ZIPRA camp, the enemy's resolve was not all it might have been.

They had been subjected to relentless Rhodesian air strikes for hours. What was more worrying was they did not know if they would get a resupply of ammunition from Lusaka in time to hold the position. The battalion commander held regular meetings with his men during the night and eventually settled on a plan.

Dead on the stroke of midnight, he gave the word and ZIPRA mounted a bombardment on the Rhodesian SAS position – and the war was on again.

The dull thuds of enemy mortars could be heard in the distance ... and no one hoped more than the men in the SAS/RLI mortar lines that the bombs did not land anywhere near them. They were sitting and sleeping among piles of their own mortar bombs and equipment.

Suddenly, there was an orange flash. Every Rhodesian eye followed it as it whistled through the night before smashing just short of their position and sending giant pieces of shrapnel among the SAS. It was a 122 millimetre rocket – a rocket the size of a man.

There was a brief respite, then another orange flash sped across the pan. This time, the rocket hit a tree a few hundred metres from the main SAS position in the hills. But there was no danger to the men.

Then the harassment started again. ZIPRA mortar fire was very accurate and an RLI chap in the mortar lines had the shrapnel in his sleeping bag to prove it.

The bombardment, planned to cover ZIPRA's withdrawal, had been worked out so that once the troops pulled out, the artillery teams would follow.

ZIPRA's morale was at an extremely low ebb. They were carrying their wounded and their heavy weapons and were more than a little nervous.

The RLI ambush party positioned on the south-west escape route peered through the darkness as 150 enemy headed their way with much clanking and rattling of their heavy weapons.

The young subby in command decided against taking on the terrorists. He felt they would have taken casualties against such superior odds. His party, he was to argue later, mainly comprised cooks and bottle-washers and as they had no heavy weapons or claymores to defend themselves, they were not keen to tackle 150 enemy of that calibre. Also, the enemy were spread out in little groups which made an ambush more difficult.

It was "with astonishment" that everyone learned the enemy had made an orderly withdrawal during the night. There were some extremely harsh words said about the matter both then and later at the debrief.

At first light, the SAS came from their high ground and swept down into the valley floor; while the RLI swept the two ridges. Unfortunately, because of ZIPRA's withdrawal, the RLI never got the opportunity of using their own 14,5 against the enemy.

Lieutenant Andrew Sanders felt that the SAS sweepline moving down into the pan was advancing too slowly and he made his way up front – straight into the tripwire strung across the thick bush. It set off two Pom-Z fragmentation anti-personnel mines either side of the wire spraying shrapnel in all directions.

Both the lieutenant and Sergeant Steve Kluzniak, bore the brunt of the blast and were injured ... and the column came to a grinding halt.

The atmosphere was now quite tense. Cautiously, they eased forward, aware that there may be more tripwires waiting for them and possibly anti-personnel mines sown in the narrow tracks. There were two more wires strung across the thick undergrowth. They skirted around them, eventually reaching a main track that led into the start of the camp.

The entire area was littered with piles of broken wood and dozens of ammunition boxes and gun chests. They could clearly see a turn-around point where vehicles had brought in the munitions.

The security forces found endless kilometres of wire that linked the headquarters post in a corner of the pan to the positions all over the ridges. ZIPRA were so well organised that they had field telephones in every platoon headquarters.

The Rhodesians were to take home the ZIPRA 14,5s, but the enemy had taken the precaution of removing the breach blocks. They were, therefore unusable.

They found trenches with overhead cover, foxholes, and many positions contained steel helmets and gas masks.

* * *

To the north meanwhile, follow-up operations were continuing.

Rich Stannard and his callsign were also joining in the search for the missing ZIPRA men. Suddenly, the eagle eyes of the lieutenant settled on a helmet sticking out from under a mound of grass and bushes. He yanked it out, then unearthed a veritable cache of helmets, packs and documents, which told of ZIPRA tactics and training and were to prove an invaluable insight into just how organised the conventional battalion had been.

They were able to account for several enemy and were responsible for most of the kills on the follow-up operation. Apart from a few kills, the other groups failed to track down the rest of ZIPRA and the operation wound down a couple of days later.

The mission had been bad news for the Rhodesians. They had grossly underestimated the enemy and had the living daylights shot out of them. They had been outgunned and outranged and had been unable to take the position.

They had run into problems in Mozambique. Now, for the first time, they were in serious trouble in Zambia.

There were said to be nine other defensive positions along the Zambian border, but the Op *Tepid* camp was the only one attacked. They eventually found the others, but by then it was too late. The war was over.

Operation Dice, November, 1979

The Special Air Service together with their Air Force friends were now planning to deliver a decisive blow to ZANLA and their host country. It would not only make ZANLA suffer, but it was also designed to bring Mozambique to her knees.

Their mission – codenamed *Manacle* – would be presented as a *fait accompli* to Samora Machel who would be forced into a corner. The military planners hoped that by crippling his country, he would, in exchange for economic survival, abandon ZANLA and kick Mugabe and his men out for good. Alternatively, they wanted him to force Mugabe to stay talking at the Lancaster House conference.

In a series of slick moves, the SAS and Air Force were to sweep down Mozambique flattening key road, rail and river bridges of economic, strategic and tactical importance; bridges that were not only crucial to ZANLA's infiltration routes into Rhodesia, but vital to Mozambique's economy.

The Tete Bridge had been on the hit list, but at the eleventh hour, just as SAS commander Major Dave Dodson and his team of saboteurs were about to set sail down river with their load of explosives, the mission was called off. It had suddenly been learned that the Tete Bridge was just too important to drop. The International Monetary Fund had financed its building and it was felt that if the Rhodesians destroyed it, they would not be looked upon favourably should international recognition follow the all-party elections everyone in London was talking about.

Planning continued for the destruction of the other bridges, however, and was at an advanced stage. The demolition charges had been made and all the detailed tasks had been drawn up. The troops had been recalled to Salisbury and were poised for the op.

Then, suddenly, the ComOps planners changed the priority. The main threat was not so much Mugabe's ZANLA who could be contained for now, but Nkomo's ZIPRA.

Joshua Nkomo had suddenly woken up to the fact that if the Lancaster House talks were to produce a ceasefire, eighty percent of his troops were *outside* the country, whereas eighty percent of Mugabe's were *inside*.

Nkomo had never been interested in pushing in droves of men just for the sake of it. He was more interested in building up and training his conventional army. Then, when the time was right, he would fully arm his battalions, consolidate his conventional forces into a highly trained army and invade Rhodesia with Russian and Cuban backing.

But the SAS's highly successful Operation *Chicory* on Nkomo's massive arms cache near Lusaka had hit him hard and seriously delayed his plans. He had lost those arms and had been unable to replace them.

The repeated bombings at Mulungushi conventional training camp, while they did not kill vast numbers, had also disrupted his plans.

Before Nkomo could mobilise his battalions, arm them and put his invasion plans into effect, Lancaster House happened and he realised he had seriously miscalculated. Now, it was imperative he get as many of his troops into Rhodesia before a ceasefire to vote, and influence the elections by getting others to vote.

Should the elections not go the way he wanted, he would still have the bulk of his men in Rhodesia to continue the war. He also had to get his men out of Zambia in the event of a ceasefire and Kaunda changing his stance and agreeing to disarm his ZIPRA friends.

Three thousand ZIPRA had already crossed the border in a last-ditch bid to have as many men as possible pop up out of the bush when a ceasefire was announced and to prepare the way for the conventional forces.

Intelligence now revealed that despite previous setbacks, Nkomo's conventional army was finally going to do their bounced river crossing over the Zambezi in the push to take Rhodesia by force, by sending in motorised infantry battalions under the umbrella of Russian-supplied MiG fighters.

ZIPRA planned on taking over the main airfields, and the invasion force of conventional and guerilla forces hoped to have taken Salisbury within 24 hours of infiltrating.

As if to confirm this, the Rhodesians had picked up a sudden increase in aircraft movement into Angola and Zambia, which subsequent intelligence proved were airlifts of armoured personnel carriers and artillery.

There were two essential prerequisites for the ZIPRA military potential to be realised. First, they had to establish a bridgehead on the Rhodesian bank of the Zambezi; second, they needed the air support for it to be maintained.

The major fronts where the bounced river crossing was going to take place were at Victoria Falls and Kariba, and there was a vague possibility of ZIPRA using the area east of Chirundu.

Nkomo's plans for a large-scale conventional infiltration was the biggest threat Rhodesia had faced, and the Rhodesian planners ruled, that, as a matter of great urgency, Operation *Manacle* be put in cold storage until the ZIPRA plan was blunted.

ComOps knew there were between 18 000 and 25 000 ZIPRA amassing in Zambia, most of them trained in conventional warfare. Nkomo had been training his conventional infantry motorised battalions at Mulungushi camp to the north of Kabwe and was ferrying troops down to an assembly point known as CGT-2 some fifty kilometres (31 miles) to the north-east of Lusaka on the Great North Road.

Conventional terrorists under training in Angola and possibly others in Ethiopia were also going to make their way to CGT-2, plus every other guerilla in Zambia.

It was this large concentration of enemy in one camp who were capable of launching a conventional attack on Rhodesia which was causing such concern at ComOps.

At the same time, by marshalling his forces at one camp for the first time in ZIPRA's history, it meant that if the camp was attacked, they could disrupt ZIPRA's war machine and destroy it once and for all.

According to intelligence, there were more than 4 000 ZIPRA at CGT-2 at any one time. ZIPRA were moving their men from CGT-2 down to a series of prepared forward deployment bases, each manned by conventional troops, along the length of the Rhodesian border overlooking the Zambezi River and Lake Kariba.

Their function was to monitor the river and when their particular crossing point was secure, they would signal ZIPRA headquarters in Lusaka; then Lusaka would send a message to CGT-2 and men would be bundled into trucks and ferried to whichever forward base could form a bridgehead from where they could infiltrate into Rhodesia.

Then, groups of 100-plus would enter Rhodesia, some of them caching their weapons and equipment and walking into the villages to create a presence for the voting and prepare the way for the conventional forces.

When ComOps learned of this build-up at CGT-2 and the movement down to the border, it was decided that security forces had to get into Zambia without delay to smash ZIPRA and limit their ability to mount a conventional attack. They were to bomb CGT-2 off the face of the earth with every available aircraft; and hit all other known terrorist positions.

It was critical too, that ZIPRA's access and supply routes be cut immediately.

The Special Air Service, and in some instances the RLI and Selous Scouts, had to infiltrate deep into Zambia and sit across ZIPRA routes, ambush their vehicles and stop the large deployments southwards. If the routes were made inaccessible to vehicles and ZIPRA had to walk and carry their equipment, then it was felt they would probably not bother.

Other units would have to go back to the old border control duties to hit ZIPRA as they crossed the border.

Operation *Dice*, the last major external operation of the war, was about to begin.

The whole SAS Regiment which had been regrouped in Salisbury and which was busy preparing for Op *Manacle* was sent to Kariba from where it would stage its attacks against ZIPRA.

However, while ComOps was determined to halt the hordes of ZIPRA about to come thundering across the border, they initially imposed strict limitations on the SAS's *modus operandi.*

It was obvious both to the military planners and the SAS that the only way to stem the terrorist tide was to destroy the Zambian communications network by cutting the road and rail bridges, thereby preventing them using their heavy vehicles and forcing them to either walk or to go by a circuituous, time-consuming route.

It was not a new thought and the planners had raised the issue on numerous occasions over the years. But permission had always been denied for political reasons. There were sound economic reasons – Rhodesia exported and imported on those very routes – and it was not government policy to attack strategic targets in Zambia.

At the start of Op *Dice,* that necessary permission was still not forthcoming from the politicians and the SAS's task was solely to monitor and ambush the road, which the planners and the SAS all knew was a total waste of time.

It did not take much to realise that ambushing was a very limited project and would probably account for a few hundred enemy only. Then, having hit one convoy, the Zambian Army would be alerted, the news passed back to ZIPRA in Lusaka and on to CGT-2 – and the terrorists would be stopped using that particular route. Roads would be guarded, the element of surprise lost, and the security forces would not achieve their aim.

It was a situation that worried the CO, the squadron commanders and the planners, and while they attempted to convince the politicos to take on ZIPRA more aggressively by blowing the bridges, "A" and "B" Squadrons were deployed across the border to make the roads untenable for ZIPRA, while "C" Squadron was held in reserve for anything untoward that may happen.

The CO, meanwhile, took the precaution of moving all the explosives intended for Operation *Manacle* to Kariba in the event of the go-ahead being given.

Lieutenant Pete Cole worked through the night preparing demolition kits and carrying out procedures normally done on site. By morning, he had the first three demolition kits ready. Now all they needed was the green light.

* * *

Lieutenant Mike Rich and his team of 15 operators from "B" Squadron were on their way to ambush a road south-east of Lusaka on the Kafue-Chirundu road, and early on November 13 they were choppered their regulation distance away from the road.

Six hours later they had found a suitable spot on the side of a hill where they could base up for the rest of the day before beginning their work. They checked out the area and after leaving one man on guard, the others settled down in their usual circle formation.

There was very little cover . . . just thin vegetation and a few trees. 16 SAS men kitted up in *Black-Is-Beautiful,* with their regalia of war sprawled around it. Soon, all but the guard were sleeping soundly.

Then the sentry began to hear shuffling and scuffling. Gradually, the scuffling developed into a series of muffled shouts and screams as eight men on one side of the circle streaked out of their sleeping bags – and stranger yet, began tearing their clothes off!

Soon, everyone on the other half of the circle was awake. Each man had grabbed his rifle and was gazing nervously into the distance, trying to work out what all the pandemonium was about.

Then, the eight stark-naked men streaked up the hill.

Eventually, the commander and his fully-dressed men managed to herd the naked ones together to establish that a massive army of red nipping ants had infested the area they had chosen to sleep in, leaving a legacy of huge red welts on their victims.

396

Red soldier ants were some of the meanest little creatures in the bush and, as any operator will tell you, something worth tearing one's trousers off for.

There was then the ridiculous situation of 16 fully-grown very tough SAS soldiers, half of them naked, cowering part way up the hill gazing down at the mound of discarded clothes, weapons and kit, and nobody brave enough to go down and rescue them.

While ZIPRA and ZANLA did not worry SAS men, an army of aggressive ants was a different matter entirely.

Eventually, the eight naked chaps regained their composure and were assured their clothes were free from ants. Everyone gathered up his kit and away they all went, getting a slightly earlier start than they had planned.

It was the beginning of what was to turn out to be an incident-filled week. Thereafter, it would be the Zambians and ZIPRA who would feel the pinch.

Mike Rich had hoped to spring his ambush in some of the ravines and rivers which went across the tar road shown on his map, but they could not be located in the area he wanted to use. It meant he had to rely on springing his ambush by using a bank of claymores, which would be set off by his demolition expert. There would also be two RPG-7 rocket launchers and the normal good smattering of RPDs right throughout the 12-man ambush party, while in the observation position high above the road was Sergeant *Small Bez* and his team manning the 60 millimetre mortar.

At last light on November 15, they were in their position along the side of the road, and at 20h15 *Small Bez,* up on his hill, came on the radio to report seeing lights.

As the vehicle came up the hill, the demolition man pressed the button to set off the claymores and rip the vehicle to shreds. Everyone else kept his head down to avoid the expected blast. But nothing happened.

Lieutenant Mike Rich banged the demolition man on the shoulder to indicate that he should fire once more and the claymore operator quickly went through a series of tests on the exploder. Realising that something was wrong, the commander initiated the contact himself by firing at the vehicle.

By now the two handpicked RPG-7 operators up the road had also realised that the claymores were not going to work and both fired rockets at the target.

Unbelievable as it seemed, one rocket went straight under the Land-Rover – while the other went sailing straight over it. Thus, the double knock-out blow had failed, as had the magical claymores.

As most of the callsign had been keeping their heads down to protect themselves from the claymore blast, only a few rounds were fired.

For the occupants of the Land-Rover, their luck was in that night and they were able to make good their escape. But they must have been startled to see a couple of RPG-7 rockets flying at them through the night.

The ambushers learnt later that the Land-Rover contained a couple of Zambian Army officers and one had been slightly wounded. The SAS had been briefed not to take on Zambian Army personnel, so perhaps it was fortunate that things had gone wrong. But there were red faces all around at the time.

* * *

Meanwhile, back in Rhodesia, the go-ahead had been given to drop the bridges.

It was a bold decision and would have a dramatic effect on Zambia. By destroying the bridges, Rhodesia hoped not only to stop the ZIPRA hordes, but also to put enough pressure on Zambian President Kenneth Kaunda to convince Nkomo to stay talking at the Lancaster House conference – and to make sure he helped the London talks towards a successful conclusion.

In view of previous SAS activity, Zambia was particularly vulnerable to such pressure at that time.

By the severing of the Tazara rail link a few weeks earlier, Kaunda had effectively been robbed of his export and import route to the north and beyond. The line had not yet been repaired although the Zambians were still sending goods in both directions up to the Chambeshi bridge, unloading them on to trucks and taking them in a roundabout route to the other side.

That only left him the southern route to South Africa over which the vast majority of all Zambian imports and exports travelled – and that ran through Rhodesia over the Victoria Falls bridge.

Thus Kaunda's sole economic lifeline ran through Rhodesia – and Kaunda needed that route to feed his people.

Rhodesia, however, had no immediate plans to cut Zambia's rail line with the south. They were very aware that to do so would have a direct effect on the entire Zambian economy. The idea was not so much to cripple Zambia but to show her that her southern neighbour meant business.

By dumping the other Zambian bridges to stop ZIPRA's movement southwards, the Rhodesians would prove that they could, if they chose to, also sever the rail line south of Lusaka. They were hoping to get their point across before resorting to such a drastic measure. Routes that were not cut were to be heavily landmined.

While the Zambians were loath to take on the security forces in strength, intelligence indicated that the Zambians would not hesitate to engage small groups or enemy aircraft.

The Zambians had become very concerned by the apparent ease with which Rhodesians were able to locate and strike at ZIPRA targets in Zambia. The SAS's sabotage of the Chambeshi bridges had made them aware the Rhodesians planned to go in for more strategic targets and additional guards had been placed on major bridges and trunk routes to prevent a repetition of the Chambeshi incident.

"B" Squadron's unsuccessful ambush on the Zambian Army Land-Rover had taken place near three bridges and now that the Zambian Army knew there was a Rhodesian presence in the area, there was every likelihood they would dispatch guards to protect those bridges.

It was imperative the Rhodesians destroy the bridges before the Zambians had time to react.

Their destruction would hamper ZIPRA movement southwards and to Chirundu as well as isolate Chirundu, where there was a border bridge. Nkomo would thus be unable to move his heavy troop-carrying vehicles down to the border and across the bridge . . . or even down to the border where his men could debuss and walk across. It also meant that the access road to Kariba Dam wall dividing Zambia from Rhodesia would be cut.

Lieutenant Mike Rich and his ambushers were instructed to get moving down the road and use their left-over mines and explosives to blow a culvert and make the road unusable. After that, they were to head towards the northerly bridge, to await the rest of "B" Squadron.

Leaving *Small Bez* and his 60 millimetre mortar team behind in the hills to give early-warning of the Zambian Army, they blew the culvert and cracked the road, but the damage was not sufficient to stop ZIPRA or anyone else using it. Then they doubled along the road for a couple of hours until they reached their bridge . . . and early next morning, November 16, Operation *Dice* got under way in earnest.

It was now an open Rhodesian raid and the SAS men kitting-up in Kariba to link up with the blackened-up ambushers wore Rhodesian camouflage and no *Black-Is-Beautiful.*

Four Bell 205s flew out from Kariba in close formation taking the "B" Squadron operators, a heavy cargo of explosives and two 20 millimetre cannons and crews to the road snaking through the Zambian mountain pass.

The plan was to secure the area quickly, blow the bridges and be away before the Zambians knew what had hit them. The two 20 millimetre cannon crews – one commanded by Sergeant Major Johnny Masson and the other under Colour Sergeant Nick Breytenbach – were to provide protection in the hills on either side of the three bridges.

Johnny Masson and his team linked up with *Small Bez* on the Chirundu side of the road – the side where the Zambian Army were most likely to react – and, after dropping off a load of explosives to Lieutenant Mike Rich at his bridge on the Kafue side of the road, the choppers put Nick Breytenbach and crew and their 20 millimetre down further along the road to stop any interference from that access.

Another chopper peeled off to put Squadron Commander Colin Willis and his team down close to the centre bridge . . . while the last chopper continued to bridge number three to drop Pete Cole and his crew.

As Colin and his men came in to land at their centre bridge, a white Land-Rover went screaming past beneath them. The worried passengers stared at the chopper and heavily armed white soldiers with the biggest eyeballs the SAS had seen. But Colin decided to spare them. He felt the priority was to get on with the task – and he let the Land-Rover and its passengers continue unharmed.

But as the Land-Rover roared on its way through the mountain pass to get clear of the Rhodesian choppers, Lieutenant Pete Cole and his team still en route to their bridge, began to take a keen interest in the speeding vehicle.

Time was short, but the passengers appeared to be dressed like ZIPRA and it was too good an opportunity to miss.

Getting the pilot to put down in a field instead of on the bridge as planned, Pete Cole tasked one man with a machinegun and another with an FN to prepare to engage the vehicle. As the chopper came in to land, the two soldiers leapt out and hurried forward to take up their ambush positions.

The others quickly yanked the explosives out of the chopper and as it lifted and set course for Rhodesia, the two ambushers opened up on the Land-Rover. Then the entire callsign joined in and took on the vehicle and its passengers.

Although injured, the driver managed with superhuman effort to stumble out of the door and run down the road. A hail of angry bullets pursued him.

Within a couple of minutes, it was all over. The driver lay dead on the side of the road, and the lifeless body of the passenger lay peppered with rounds and slumped in the bullet-riddled Land-Rover.

The SAS didn't think that anyone had survived, but subsequent intelligence revealed that two ZIPRA had the good sense to flee as the vehicle sped along the pass into the ambush . . . and one had been wounded as he headed for the sanctuary of the nearby Zambian Army post.

The injured terrorist turned out to be none other than the ZIPRA battalion commander of the Operation *Tepid* position who had been making his way back to the camp site to see if it could be used again. It was his second encounter with the SAS and he knew he was lucky to have survived.

Hidden behind the seats of the Land-Rover was an assortment of weapons, maps and documents listing names of terrorists en route to Rhodesia, and a crossing point previously unknown to the Rhodesians.

Meanwhile, the Zambian Army with their usual lack of haste, were on their way to the scene of the previous day's ambush. They came in three armoured vehicles and five trucks and were not the most welcome visitors to have stumbling into a demolition task.

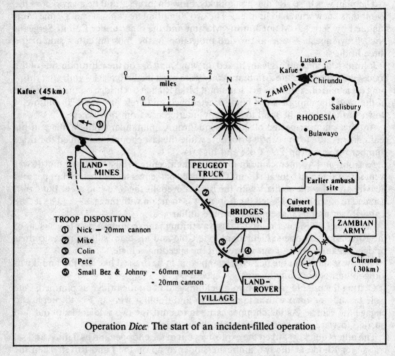

Operation *Dice:* The start of an incident-filled operation

Colin Willis gave the SAS men manning the 20 millimetre cannon and 60 millimetre mortar in the mountains the go ahead to open up on them and they proceeded to keep the Zambians at bay from their hillside perch . . . while further along the mountain pass the three demolition teams got on with the business of destroying the bridges.

The demolition commanders quickly made an appreciation of their targets and the explosives and initiation sets were moved into a safe place under the bridges.

Then the six-man demolition crews quickly and efficiently went through their various drills, which they had down to an incredibly fine art, enabling them to smash the bridges in record time.

While all this feverish activity was taking place, a white Peugeot pick-up came roaring along the road and was about to drive into the blast. The driver was flagged down and his truck commandeered.

The demolition commanders lit the safety fuses and took cover. One after the other, the three bridges were demolished as ZIPRA and their host nation were dealt their first body blow.

The damage was assessed, photographs were taken, kit packed up and the abandoned ZIPRA Land-Rover set ablaze.

Colin Willis and Pete Cole and their teams headed south towards the foothills to get out of the reach of an immediate reaction force and find a suitable LZ for their helicopter recovery ... while Lieutenant Mike Rich and his callsign were tasked to mine the access road on his side of the mountain pass.

All their equipment was loaded on to the commandeered truck and it was used to ferry a team down to an old detour road under construction, which the Zambians might well decide to rebuild now that the three bridges had been dumped. It was just the place to plant a couple of landmines in case they did.

On the way, they cut the telephone lines to isolate the area even further and a couple of well-placed RPG-7 rockets destroyed a building which looked like an electricity sub-station. Closer inspection revealed it to contain only a few telephone wires, but in any event, it was not much use to anyone after they had finished with it.

They picked up the 20 millimetre cannon and crew on their side of the mountain pass using the vehicle, and they all returned to the blown bridge to await uplift, listening to the SAS men still on the mountains fighting a duel with the Zambian Army.

After the panic and urgency to get to the bridges, and the excitement of getting them down in just twenty minutes, they now faced a long idle wait for the choppers to collect them. When they finally arrived, there were only three; the fourth had run into difficulties back in Rhodesia, and the teams in the mountains would have to stay where they were and continue engaging the Zambian Army for a few more hours.

It had been an eventful day. But there was still one more incident to come.

As one of the choppers touched down at Kariba, its mission complete and its passengers safely delivered to Rhodesian shores, a cable connecting the tail rotor blade suddenly severed ... and as the SAS stepped on to the tarmac, the pilot casually informed them that had they been airborne for another ninety seconds, they would have crashed.

Back in the Zambian mountains, the SAS had won their clash with the Zambians, forcing them to abandon their armoured vehicles. By the time reinforcements had arrived, the SAS's 20 millimetre cannon had destroyed two of the three armoured vehicles and they were blazing away merrily.

The SAS cannon crew then opened up on the reinforcements in their trucks and on their commander in the Land-Rover at the front of the column. The startled Zambian troops sat nonplussed on the back of their open trucks and wondered where the trouble was coming from.

Then the enemy commander leapt from his Land-Rover, ran to the back of the truck, and belted his men with a huge stick. That finally provoked some reaction and they all scurried for cover.

Nine hours after being dropped off, the choppers came in to pluck the SAS men from their hill. They loaded up their cannon, threw in their kit and set course for Kariba. There were other tasks to do and preparations had to be made.

* * *

A couple of days later, "B" Squadron gathered for another briefing.

This time, Colin Willis told them the mission was to destroy a bridge on the Great North Road, seventy kilometres (43 miles) south of Lusaka.

At 07h00 they flew off over the lake to Zambia, over the endless trees and the scatterings of African huts, until about 07h20, they saw the Great North Road snaking before them in the distance.

Having dropped off the first five-man protection party, the choppers continued on to put down the demolition team and a second protection party. But as they circled the bridge, thirty Zambian Army soldiers guarding the target opened up on the Rhodesians with smallarms fire. The SAS machinegunner returned fire from the second chopper.

As the choppers continued circling the bridge and the gunners gave the Zambians the occasional burst, Colin silently debated what they should do for the best.

He knew that if they went down, they would not only take casualties, but as they would have to take on the Zambian Army, it could well spark off an international incident. On the other hand, if they *didn't* go down, the bridge would stay intact and ZIPRA would continue to travel southwards across it.

Eventually, the pilot made up his mind. They would have to abort the mission and go home, he decided. "No," Colin Willis pointed out. They couldn't afford to do that. They had to stop the road being used.

Quickly, Colin studied his map. There was a bridge twenty kilometres (12 miles) further north over the Kaleya River. Couldn't they just pop up there and see what the story was, he suggested?

The pilot agreed ... and the two men were delighted to find much better pickings altogether. It was a much bigger bridge and, as a bonus, was unguarded.

The protection group put down earlier, was collected ... and before long, the demolition team and their mound of explosives were deposited next to Kaleya road bridge.

Within moments, they had slipped on their skin-tight rubber gloves necessary to prepare the *Wonder Glue* to attach the charges to the bridge. Another surgical operation was about to be performed to cut ZIPRA's access routes to the south.

A rail gang working on repairs 300 metres south of the road bridge stood and watched in wide-eyed amazement as the demolition team scurried back and forth under the bridge.

Someone waved the muzzle of a rifle at them, but it made not the slightest difference and they made no attempt to move away.

A Zambian police patrol put in an appearance and fired ten rounds of automatic fire at the saboteurs. The SAS protection party returned fire – and the Zambians sped off again.

By now, all the activity at the bridge had attracted a crowd of onlookers, who, unperturbed by the exchanges between the Rhodesians and Zambians, seemed equally fascinated at the strange goings-on that morning.

They, too, appeared a friendly lot and even though warning shots were fired above them, they were reluctant to move away.

Once the charges were laid, Pete Cole lit the fuses and raced across the bridge to join the rest of the SAS in the back of the railway gang's truck. Then they drove off to a safe spot while the bridge blew.

With some ten million US dollars worth of communications damage caused by the SAS, Kenneth Kaunda of Zambia might well wonder when the Rhodesians would strike again

Within twenty minutes of arriving, there was a deafening roar, the earth shook and the Kaleya bridge was downed. Three spans and two piers crashed into the riverbed, raising a cloud of smoke and dust high into the sky.

As they reversed their borrowed truck to inspect the damage, they noticed that the crowd of onlookers had swelled considerably.

It was time for the 16 men to head home again. But the choppers had returned to Rhodesia to refuel and as the turn-around time was ninety minutes, the SAS were ready to pull out even before the choppers had arrived back in Kariba.

There was only one option left. They would just have to hijack the rail gang's truck to make their escape. The railway workers were in no position to protest and with a wave to the rail crew and the mesmerised locals, the smiling SAS men were soon on their way trucking southwards, stopping on the way while one man leapt out to cut the telephone wires.

Sixty kilometres (37 miles) from Kaleya bridge, they abandoned the truck, dumping it in a small dam where it could be recovered without much effort.

They radioed for pick-up and the Bells were soon with them . . . and in no time at all they were off home again, exhilarated by their success although very tired, especially those who had been up most of the night preparing the charges.

There was just one moment of crisis that day. As one chopper came in to land at the airstrip a terrific crunching vibrated through the plane as the bearings on the rotor blade broke up. Had they been airborne, the chopper would have spiralled into the ground and they would all have been killed.

It was the second lucky escape for some SAS men that week and they quickly debussed, hardly daring to believe their good fortune.

Four-and-a-half hours after leaving Kariba the bridge-blowers were back in Rhodesia, the day's action over and another bridge rendered useless to frustrate ZIPRA's push southwards and further enrage Kenneth Kaunda.

* * *

Meanwhile Captain Bob McKenna and Lieutenant Phil Brooke of "C" Squadron had returned to New Sarum, boarded a light aircraft and after a circuitous journey, entered Zambian airspace.

They were looking for a suitable road and rail target north of Lusaka for the next phase of the bridge demolition programme.

While the SAS had been forbidden to drop rail bridges south of Lusaka, the northern rail line – the Tazara link – was considered expendable. By dropping the Chambeshi the month before, the Rhodesians had already declared an open policy on the line. Besides, dropping another portion would make the Zambians' shuttle service even more complicated to organise.

403

The two SAS men flew low along the rail line studying it with their binoculars. There was a parallel road three kilometres from the line and where there was a rail bridge there was a corresponding road bridge over the river.

They noticed that most of the rail bridges had a small tented camp near one end belonging to the railway police and militia who guarded the bridge.

They were looking for a spot where the choppers would be able to land virtually on the bridge, or very close by; a bridge where the piers were accessible and not submerged in water, and a target where the nearby military presence was relatively small so that they could deal with it. Ideally, they needed a road and rail bridge that were close enough to be demolished virtually at the same time; and where the Rhodesian troops could support each other.

It was a tall order, but they eventually managed to find a pair of bridges 150 kilometres (93 miles) east of Lusaka, which, except for a small police camp, fitted their requirements.

Back in Kariba, the commander was forced to make a quick change of plan when he learned that one of the choppers had become unserviceable. It was a setback, but the job could still go ahead. It meant they would have eight men less and would not be able to take such a vast quantity of explosives.

The three Bells with a total of twenty SAS operators on board plus two Lynx aircraft took off from Kariba and were soon overflying Zambia and waving at the civilians below, who now, used to such frequent comings and goings, usually waved back.

Within an hour, they were at the target. The choppers peeled off to their respective bridges; the passengers and their explosives were offloaded and the Bells pulled away, putting down in the bush twenty kilometres (12 miles) away, but keeping their turbines running in readiness for the call to recover the troops.

As the SAS approached the rail bridge with their load of explosives, they came under automatic smallarms fire from Zambian police hidden in the bush. The operators were far too busy to take on properly the troublesome police. So Bob McKenna gave the necessary target indications to the Lynx pilots orbiting the bridges and they swooped in low to deal with the enemy.

One of the piers of the rail bridge was on the far side of the river bank and it meant that operators had to walk over the exposed rail line carrying the charges on their shoulders, then humping them down the steep bank where they could be set up.

Sergeant Major Bruce Langley coolly led the way across the exposed bridge, a box of explosives on his shoulders and a complete disregard for the potential danger he was in from the enemy fire ... and his gallantry that day was largely responsible for the Bronze Cross of Rhodesia he was subsequently awarded.

The planes had soon sorted out the Zambians, either by silencing them permanently or scaring them away.

Over at the road bridge, things were going well. In keeping with the policy of not killing civilians, they were stopping all traffic to prevent it being on the bridge when it was blown, and by the time the bridge was wired up, there were forty cars lined up on either side with the drivers and passengers being treated to a grandstand view of the whole operation.

The road bridge was the first to go and the demolition completely wrecked several of the piers and spans, spraying chunks of concrete and dust everywhere and leaving the frustrated motorists no alternative but to turn around and storm back the way they had come.

The rail bridge was not completely demolished due to the thickness and the extremely heavy reinforcing of the piers and because they had been unable to take sufficient explosives. However, traffic was unable to travel over it and the Zambians had to knock the remains of the bridge down in order for it to be rebuilt.

From start to finish, the demolition had taken just three hours, and they were so fast that Bob McKenna and his Sergeant Major were able to join "B" Squadron that afternoon to help blow another major road bridge, the essence being to get as many bridges down as soon as possible before the guard could be strengthened.

Bridge number seven was about to be dumped.

* * *

The SAS's new target was the Chongwe River bridge, a mere 35 kilometres (21 miles) from Lusaka, the first major bridge ZIPRA would have to cross after leaving CGT-2 assembly area on their way southwards.

An aerial photographic reconnaissance showed that there was a Zambian Army national service defence force training camp a few metres from the bridge and that the target was also guarded by a platoon of soldiers.

This particular bridge was not going to be so easy and they were apprehensive about what would happen. Not only did they have to worry about the bridge defenders but, as the bridge was so close to Lusaka, there was a very real possibility of air force jets being scrambled.

Timings would be critical and a decision was made to call in the heavies of the Rhodesian Air Force to support them in case of Zambian Air Force interference; or to destroy the bridge if it were so heavily guarded that the ground troops could not land.

The thirty-man assault team was split into a six-man demolition squad – four men to lay the charges and two to cover their movements and provide protection.

There would be one road block team on the side of the road near the Zambian Army camp . . . and another, including a 20 millimetre cannon crew, were to be on the opposite side of the river.

There was no sign of the Zambian Army when the bulk of the SAS troops were put down, but, as the fifth and last chopper bearing the demolition team flew in, they saw six Zambians near an army ambulance and opened fire on them.

The chopper landed, the SAS yanked their explosives from the Bell and hurried to the bridge, keeping their heads well down. The chopper lifted immediately, then was gone.

Now and then the Zambian bridge defenders clashed with the SAS, but most were far more interested in getting away.

Nick Breytenbach quickly got the cannon sorted out and began firing the high explosive rounds into the army camp to keep the Zambians out of the fracas.

Rounds cracked over the heads of the demolition team as they went through their time-tested drills, while yet others thumped into the riverbank.

Meanwhile, inside the Zambian Army base the bugler was hitting the panic button . . . and blasting away at full volume in Seventh Cavalry fashion to warn of the dangers without.

But as soon as the first couple of SAS cannon shells exploded in the camp, his urgent signals trailed off dramatically . . . and all that could be heard after that was the continuous wailing of sirens.

And at no stage during the proceedings did anyone venture out of the camp to aid their bridge-defender colleagues.

The original plan had been for the stop group nearest the Army base to straddle the road to halt traffic driving into the demolition. But it was impossible to do that as they were being fired at by those Zambians still trying to defend the bridge and most of the SAS were taking cover in a trench running parallel with the road.

At about the same time two strapping SAS men were running along the road to check that a Zambian soldier they had shot was down for good, a huge Mercedes car came screeching along the road.

At the sight of the two aggressive weapon-brandishing white soldiers charging towards them, the petrified driver took the only possible course available.

He did an immediate left-turn and careered through the bush heading straight for an African village, which, because of all the activity at the bridge, had been hurriedly vacated leaving only chickens, pigs and dogs in residence.

The Mercedes came to a rest against a sturdy pole with a sickening crunch – but not before all four doors were flung open and the nattily-dressed pin-striped occupants shot off into the bush in all directions Keystone Cop fashion, and hard on the heels of all the squawking, flapping farmyard creatures.

Five minutes before detonation time, a Toyota Landcruiser doing about 130 kilometres (80 miles)-an-hour came screeching past the SAS lying in the trenches on the side of the road.

Warning shots failed to stop the driver, and having broken through their roadblock he continued on his way at high speed straight towards the RPD gunner, protecting the demolition team.

Having been briefed that anyone who broke through the roadblock was up to no good, the gunner opened up, and the driver, a Swiss national, Mr Max Zhiler, crashed into the side of the road.

He was very badly shot up and the soldiers raced to pull him from the vehicle before it caught fire. They planned to take him back to Rhodesia for treatment, but it was obvious he was beyond help and they could only make him as comfortable as possible before he died.

Twenty-four minutes after being dropped off, Pete Cole and Bob McKenna were lighting the fuses on the eight 48 kilogram charges. Then everyone pulled back a safe distance from the bridge to await the blast.

As they did so, two Zambian Air Force MiGs cruised high over the bridge.

The Rhodesians could hear their transmissions. No, the pilots told their base adamantly, they couldn't see anything. No, they stressed, they didn't believe there was anything going on at the bridge.

They did not descend to check out their statements and did not interfere in any way with the ground troops. When the SAS radioed for the Hunters to intercept the MiGs, the Zambians picked up the signal and quickly disappeared.

Suddenly, there was a blinding flash and some of the troops still moving away, stumbled forward as the shock wave hit them. Micro-seconds later, a deafening explosion tore across the Zambian countryside as almost 400 kilograms of TNT ripped the Chongwe River Bridge apart.

The operators turned to see the bridge erupt and the concrete and dust build up into a dark mushroom of nuclear proportions.

When the dust and debris finally settled, they saw that the bridge was a complete ruin and three of the five spans had been blown away.

If by now the SAS were beginning to feel the strain of all their activity, it was nothing to that felt by Kenneth Kaunda. Bridges were dropping all around him and he was forced to call for a general mobilisation.

Supporting Kaunda's call, the Government-owned *Zambia Daily Mail* acknowledged that the country could not meet the demand for weapons to fight the invaders.

"We cannot wait. The enemy is already on our soil . . . for this reason is it necessary to revive the production of spears and poisonous arrows and make them available to the people."

A ComOps spokesman laughed when told of the newspaper's suggestion. "If any of our lads come down with arrow poisoning, we'll complain to the Red Cross," he said.

General Walls's last stand

Signals monitored in Rhodesia warned all Zambian Army units to be vigilant and in a conversation between one police station and its headquarters in Lusaka, the situation was described as "double critical".

The Zambians were certainly getting nervous. When an Australian TV journalist, Tony Joyce, went to film the wrecked Chongwe bridge, he was shot in the head by Zambian security forces, and died from his injuries in a London hospital.

A Zambian driver, his truck and valuable cargo of maize plunged over the gorge and the last reports were that he was seriously injured as he attempted to drive over the bridge, which, unbeknown to him, was no longer there.

* * *

Further north on the same road were Lieutenant Dale Scott and 15 men from "A" Squadron. They had arrived a few days earlier and after an ambush phase, "A" Squadron commander Major Rob Johnstone back in Kariba, came up on the radio to ask if they could destroy two small bridges that afternoon.

"A" Squadron was only too willing to oblige, and morale went up immediately. It was always nice to keep themselves occupied and they all welcomed the chance to blow the bridges.

The choppers brought in the explosives and a 12-man RLI callsign to help with the bridge demolitions. The RLI were to go to one bridge; the SAS to the other and they all set off to their targets carrying their mass of explosives.

The bridges were about two kilometres apart. Soon the commander gave the word to light the safety fuses. There was one blinding flash followed by an almighty bang as 400 kilograms of explosives tore the first tiny bridge apart. Then a couple of seconds later, there was a repeat performance and the second bridge was dumped.

Morale was very high as they climbed a nearby hill and settled down for the night. They awoke to hear the sound of a bus speeding below them. It was overloaded with Africans and the driver had his foot flat on the accelerator as he headed straight towards the gaping chasm where once the bridge had been.

Fortunately for him he saw the dust still hanging in the air, and at the last minute he managed to bring his bus to a halt just as the front wheels were a quarter of the way into space.

He clambered out through the back window and then shouted a warning to his passengers and everyone hurriedly debussed before their combined weight forced the vehicle into the riverbed.

Later, when it seemed they would have to wait for the choppers to collect them, the SAS decided to use the time to spring an ambush and part of the team split into two groups – one with five men, the other with six. Dale Scott was to command one, Dave Berry the other, each group acting as early-warning for the other.

Dave and team had hardly got things organised on their side of the road when they saw lights approaching. Then the voice of the commander came up on the radio.

"Take it out," was all he said, and the ambushers felt that familiar surge of adrenalin as they hurried to a little embankment.

As the vehicle drew level, the butterflies suddenly vanished and the operators focused all their attention on the job at hand.

The man on the RPG-7 fired, but the headlights dazzled him and the rocket skimmed right under the vehicle. The RPD gunner immediately *took out* the driver and the vehicle crashed into the bank right in front of the ambushers who poured lead into the rear of the vehicle at a terrific rate. By then, the RPG-7 man had reloaded and put his second rocket into the cab. The vehicle immediately burst into flames.

By the time the shooting died down, ten of the 18 passengers lay dead, but it was difficult to establish if they were ZIPRA or Zambian Army. The SAS withdrew and spent a good part of the night listening to the rounds and grenades exploding in the blazing vehicle.

Another group demolished one more bridge north of Kariba – and that made ten bridges down altogether. In addition, the SAS had in the space of five days planted sixty landmines in Zambia.

The giant CGT-2 terror camp was also successfully bombed. Now the pressure was on and the Zambian Government was in a complete uproar.

Of the main bridges, only Chirundu and Victoria Falls were left intact, and it did not take much imagination on the Zambians' part to work out who administered the mortgage on their security.

Not only was Zambia affected, but Malawi too. By demolishing the Chongwe River bridge, the SAS had put a halt to Malawi's rice trade and also stopped Zambian exports via Beira in Mozambique. There were no road links to Tanzania either.

Thus the SAS had destroyed all Zambia's economic arteries with Tanzania, Malawi and Mozambique.

The Zambian President had definitely had enough, and subsequent intelligence revealed that he forced Nkomo to stay at the London conference, insisting on a successful conclusion.

The SAS, however, were not finished yet.

While the bridges were blowing, SAS Major Dave Dodson and his group were preparing for the next phase of aggression – the destruction of the massive Ndola Oil Refinery, the *only* one in Zambia.

They had done their homework and knew all there was to know about the layout of the refinery and the dangers they were likely to encounter in such a heavily-populated Copperbelt town.

Dave and eleven saboteurs were going to parachute into Zaire in the evening, bury their chutes and infiltrate into Zambia, walking the twenty kilometres (12 miles) to Ndola to get them there before dark.

The plan was to meet up with a civilian contact man, then, under cover of darkness, destroy the oil refinery using rockets and explosives.

Once their mission was accomplished, their only means of escape would have been to head back to the safety of Zaire and hide up in the jungle until things cooled down.

It would have been the final straw for Zambia. First ten bridges down; then their sole oil refinery ablaze. For the Rhodesians, it was going to be the icing on the cake.

Then on November 22, came an urgent flash from ComOps. All offensive action had to cease and all callsigns deployed in Zambia had to be withdrawn immediately. The only exception was if ZIPRA was caught crossing. All other action had to be cleared first by General Walls in London.

The Rhodesian offensive had received wide international press coverage, particularly the incidents involving the death of the Swiss national, Mr Max Zhiler, and the Zambians' shooting of Australian journalist, Tony Joyce. The impact on Zambian and Malawian trade was made much of too.

Finally, the British brought pressure to bear on the Rhodesian delegation at the Lancaster House conference and the hierarchy ordered that the operation be called off before it could be taken to its ultimate conclusion.

But by then, the SAS's brilliantly-contrived surgical operation had destroyed the secondary access bridges to the border and they had largely achieved the aim and stopped a vast majority of ZIPRA entering Rhodesia.

There was thus no way, without a very complicated manoeuvre, that any conventional force could have got into Rhodesia.

The threat had been blunted. The destruction of the massive arms cache outside Lusaka by the SAS and the dropping of the access bridges had kept ZIPRA at bay.

The ZIPRA threat now became secondary to that posed by Mugabe whose forces were flooding across the border. It was therefore essential to get the RLI and the helicopters out of Zambia and western Rhodesia to deal with the new ZANLA threat during a very critical period internally.

By prolonging the Lancaster House proceedings, ZANLA had been able to organise and consolidate the internal party and push men into the country in time for the ceasefire. An estimated 8 000 poured across the frontier into the *Thrasher* area alone.

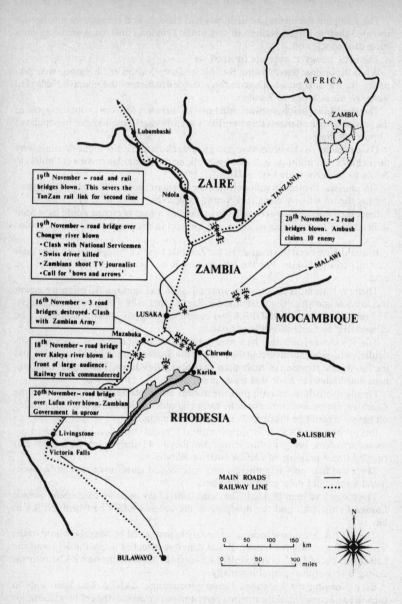

19th November – road and rail bridges blown. This severs the TanZam rail link for second time

19th November – road bridge over Chongwe river blown.
· Clash with National Servicemen
· Swiss driver killed
· Zambians shoot TV journalist
· Call for 'bows and arrows'

20th November – 2 road bridges blown. Ambush claims 10 enemy

16th November – 3 road bridges destroyed. Clash with Zambian Army

18th November – road bridge over Kaleya river blown in front of large audience. Railway truck commandeered

20th November – road bridge over Lufua river blown. Zambian Government in uproar

AFRICA

ZAMBIA

Lubumbashi

ZAIRE

Ndola

TANZANIA

ZAMBIA

MALAWI

LUSAKA

MOCAMBIQUE

Mazabuka

Chirundu

Kariba

RHODESIA

SALISBURY

Livingstone

Victoria Falls

BULAWAYO

MAIN ROADS
RAILWAY LINE

0   50   100 150 km
0   50   100 miles

N

Operation *Dice:* Map showing the bridges dropped by the SAS to halt ZIPRA's Russian-backed armoured invasion of Rhodesia

410

The Zambians would never know how close they came to losing their precious oil. The SAS saboteurs tasked with the oil refinery job were just half an hour from leaving for Zaire when the word came to end the hostilities.

Spirits were high and they knew the job was more or less in the bag. Then Dave Dodson came in to tell them the mission was off.

The rest of his party thought he had to be joking. Normally when a job was cancelled they got more notice. But it was no joke and the excitement that went with such a daring operation gave way to bitter disappointment.

In Kariba too, the troops could hardly believe it was all over. They had all looked upon the Lancaster House conference as another Geneva, another charade in a far-away place. Now, just when they were getting stuck in to the big stuff, they were told to stop.

After they had finished with Zambia, they would have swept into Mozambique to continue the postponed Op *Manacle*, which, but for the sudden ZIPRA threat, they would have already done and which would have left Mozambique in a very sorry state indeed.

The SAS had inflicted some ten million US dollars' worth of communications damage on Zambia and the unit's operations had a direct bearing on political developments over in London.

Apart from the economic pressure being brought to bear on Kaunda, Samora Machel could see what was happening in Zambia and didn't need a crystal ball to work out that he was next. Indeed, a spy at ComOps level told him that the detailed planning had already been done.

Mozambique's shaky economy simply could not afford that to happen. Apart from the poor state of the economy, the Rhodesian war was taking its toll (between 1976-1979 the war had inflicted on Mozambique damage estimated at forty-four million US dollars), and the Mozambique National Resistance movement, which was aided and abetted by the SAS, was growing and improving.

If anything, Mozambique was even more vulnerable when it came to the destruction of bridges than Zambia. The river and bridges were far bigger than those in Zambia, making repair work extremely difficult to carry out. It would have taken years, not months – as in Zambia's case – to put right.

Over in London, Mugabe had been proving difficult. He was against signing an agreement as it stood and was all set to fly to America to drum up support for continuing the war. He planned to go to the United Nations to get moral and financial support. He needed a forum where he could could publicly and immediately state why he was not prepared to go along with the Lancaster House agreement.

He was hoping that what he had to say would have a dramatic effect on all the politicos inside black Africa as well as the OAU. He hoped that this would be enough to put Machel back into a corner and force him to carry on assisting him.

But Machel had other ideas and lost no time in spelling out his terms. If Mugabe did not sign, he would kick ZANLA out of Mozambique and they would no longer have that country as a launching pad.

Machel's new attitude must have taken some soul-searching. But he had no choice. Without dropping one Mozambican bridge, the Rhodesians had achieved their aim of forcing Machel to consider abandoning ZANLA.

For Robert Mugabe, there were no options left either. He could not afford to upset Machel and it was totally unacceptable to lose the support of his host and his platform. ZANLA would be disarmed, held in custody as refugees and in three months at the outside, Mugabe would have no army left.

Both Nkomo and Mugabe heeded their hosts' wishes and stayed at the conference table to sign the ceasefire.

Dropping a few bridges and the threat of dropping others had finally set the wheels in motion for a ceasefire and the end of the fiercest war on the sub-continent.

A month later, Robert Mugabe, Joshua Nkomo and Bishop Abel Muzorewa signed a ceasefire agreement. It was December 21, seven years to the day since terrorists attacked Altena Farm, north of Centenary, and the war had begun in earnest.

External raids had already been scaled down and eventually suspended in the light of the changing political climate. Only the SAS continued to work externally with the Mozambique National Resistance.

The Commonwealth monitoring force – including British Special Air Service soldiers wearing the uniforms of other units – had begun to arrive to supervise the winding down of hostilities.

Even before the ceasefire, the British Governor Lord Soames had taken up residence in Salisbury, with Foreign Secretary Lord Carrington wishing him a "Good on you". He would need it. With his arrival, Rhodesia's decade-and-a-half of rebellion against the Crown, one of the most defiant acts in modern political history, was over.

Sanctions were to be lifted and the Rhodesian albatross was about to slip from Britain's neck ...

After the End – Or Was It?

The Op That Never Was

An uneasy peace now hung over the country. The British were in control and the final chapter of the Rhodesian saga was all but over.

For the first time since the bush war had begun, most of the enemy and all the hierarchy were inside the country. And this time, they were all in legally.

Since the start of the somewhat shaky ceasefire, they had poured across from Mozambique and Zambia and although almost 22 000 terrorists had entered the various assembly points around the country in accordance with the Lancaster House Agreement, they were not all guerillas.

Such gentlemanly agreements made around conference tables might work in London, but it was all very different in the bush . . . and thousands of *mujibas* had reported to the assembly points as a showpiece, leaving a high proportion of *real* terrorists free to roam the countryside, have a presence in every kraal, and intimidate voters.

Their respective political wings were recognised, and party officials bought and rented offices and houses in the capital and suburbs. Electioneering began immediately and was both bloody and intense.

The international press, too, representing everybody from *Pravda* to *The London Times,* poured into the country to record the rallies, the intrigues, the occasional bombings that rocked the capital – and the passing of an era. (Many of the Soviet and eastern European journalists were intelligence agents and the British had arranged for their visas to expire the day after the election results were announced.)

The official observers, there to determine if the elections were free and fair, began a round of facility trips to the assembly areas and places of interest.

In the sixteen assembly points and thirty-nine interim rendezvous points, 450 members of the ceasefire monitoring force kept an eye on the ZANLA and ZIPRA men, while around the capital, Australian, British, Nigerian, and Fijian forces could be seen hurrying about their business in distinctive British Army Land-Rovers, with large white crosses on the sides, and specially flown to Salisbury for the exercise.

Behind the scenes, too, there was much to keep the security forces occupied.

Shortly after the signing of the December 21 ceasefire agreement, the various Rhodesian security force unit commanders and other officers were summoned together and told quite categorically that there was no chance of Robert Mugabe winning the election.

At a specially convened conference at the air force cricket pavilion in Salisbury, a member of the military hierarchy told the large assembled audience that Mugabe could not, and would not, win.

In answer to several questions, he made it perfectly clear that the use of military force would prevent any unexpected election victory for Mugabe.

The unit commanders were then tasked to assure their troops that Mugabe would never come to power ... and this they did to buoy up morale and keep confidence at an acceptable level during that extremely sensitive period in the country's history.

A special committee comprising high-ranking army, air force personnel and intelligence officers was then set up to plan the organisation and details of a *coup de main* (an attack achieving complete surprise), and they met in different houses and flats around the city.

The mission was divided into two phases – Operation *Hectic* and Operation *Quartz*. Operation *Hectic* was the covert action against selected personnel; *Quartz* the elimination of major targets in Salisbury as well as others dotted around the countryside.

For the military plan to succeed, Robert Mugabe, the most hated and feared man in white Rhodesia, had to be assassinated.

Special forces had always hoped to eliminate him in Mozambique, but Mugabe had proved a slippery target. (There was even talk of assassinating him in London while at the Lancaster House talks, but the scheme was quickly abandoned.)

Now that he was inside the country they might have better luck. But although several schemes were hatched, it almost seemed as if the plot was jinxed from the outset.

One plan involved eliminating him with a radio-activated explosive device as he returned from an election rally at Fort Victoria. But someone miscalculated, the explosion missed his vehicle – and Mugabe escaped with his life.

On another occasion, special forces planned to rid themselves of him while he was on a visit to Bulawayo. A Selous Scout, hidden in an ambulance, was to kill him as he arrived at Bulawayo airport. If, for some reason, that plan didn't work, the SAS were to ambush him as he drove to address supporters in a city stadium.

As insurance, there was a third plan. A Selous Scout, posing as one of the vast press corps, was to eliminate him with a radio-activated device built into a microphone and already in position on the dias.

But the plan was not to succeed. Robert Mugabe set out for Bulawayo ... got right to the steps of the plane – then he turned on his heels and cancelled his trip. Even his bodyguard had been till then unaware of his change of heart.

It was almost as if a well-placed source in high places had put him one step ahead of them.

Indeed, when a man now suspected of being in the pay of a foreign country, heard what was being planned in Bulawayo, he went "bananas" as he had no prior knowledge of it, claims one source.

When Operation *Hectic* (against certain individuals) began to go sour, two senior members of the security forces, one the SAS CO, Lieutenant-Colonel Garth Barrett, sought an interview with the man. "We suspected the man of stuffing up *Hectic*. He was putting impossible conditions on the mission. We knew the various places Mugabe was sleeping – but he said he was not to be killed in Salisbury – then it was Bulawayo. There was another plan to kill him on the road to Gwelo, but he didn't allow that either," said Barrett.

* * *

SAS operators, meanwhile, were keeping track of former terrorists who had moved into the city, watching their many houses and offices and monitoring their movements and routines.

"A" Squadron spent many long weeks in a detailed surveillance and reconnaissance, and a special slush fund had to be set up to finance the operation.

As it was essential that the surveillance teams did not use the same vehicles all the time, Stu Hulley-Miller, the SAS/SB liaison officer, visited South Africa and spent thirty-six thousand rand on 12 Datsuns, vehicles which would not warrant a second glance in Rhodesia. He spent a further ninety-six thousand rand on sophisticated radio communications.

The surveillance teams exchanged their usual camouflage uniforms for civilian clothing, and operated from a number of rented flats and houses around the capital.

Meanwhile, other plans were afoot to blunt a possible Mugabe win.

The initial conference at the cricket pavilion was followed by a second orders group held in the operations rooms of Combined Operations and attended by all commanding officers. The commanders of the country's main units – Garth Barrett of the SAS, Charlie Aust of the RLI, and Pat Armstrong of the Selous Scouts – sat next to each other to hear a ComOps brigadier deliver his orders.

Outline directives were issued on a military plan *(Quartz)* which was to come into effect on the initiation of a particular codeword, and then the entire orders group dealt with the plan.

With thousands of former terrorists conveniently massed in their assembly points, security force units were to attack and eliminate terrorists in several assembly areas; while a number of other assembly points were to be bombed, with security force personnel directing the jets on to target from their observation positions.

Essential to the success of the operation was the SAS's part in the plot.

Their mission involved the assassination of Robert Mugabe, his vice-president, Simon Muzenda, senior commander Rex Nhongo, and hundreds of ZANLA in separate buildings around the capital.

(By now, the charismatic ZANLA military leader Josiah Tongogara had been killed in a "car accident" in Mozambique. Rhodesian intelligence sources are convinced that despite all evidence to the contrary, the accident was rigged and Tongogara was assassinated. He was felt to be too pragmatic and there were some who wanted him out of the way. "Friends" helped them achieve this objective.)

SAS "A" Squadron operators were to eliminate the ZANLA leader at his home in Quorn Avenue, Mount Pleasant ... as well as supporters in two houses in the Belvedere South area of Salisbury.

"B" Squadron was to kill vice-president Simon Muzenda at his home in Enterprise Road, Highlands ... as well as 100 ZANLA men at the nearby Medical Arts Centre, the ZANU administrative headquarters.

"C" Squadron had been tasked with the biggest target – the University of Rhodesia's audio-visual centre where 200 ZANLA and ZIPRA men were housed in a military headquarters together with their senior officers, Rex Nhongo (ZANLA), Dumiso Dabengwa (ZIPRA) and Lookout Musika (ZIPRA).

While the "A" and "B" Squadron operators were to kill everyone at their assorted *ZANLA* houses around the capital, there was to be a slightly different plan at the "C" Squadron target, the only building which housed both *ZANLA* and *ZIPRA.*

The word was going to be quietly passed to the ZIPRA men in the centre about the forthcoming attack. Then, as soon as they were given the opportunity of surrendering, they were to make their way outside to a holding area.

Those who did not take up the offer – and it was expected every ZANLA would remain to fight it out – would be killed.

"C" Squadron commander Bob McKenna and his men knew that ZANLA would be heavily armed, but it didn't worry them unduly. No one would have survived the SAS raid.

For when they opened up on the university building, they were to do so with eight Russian T55 tanks – each with a 100 millimetre main armament, 12,7 millimetre heavy machinegun and a 7,62 millimetre co-axial machinegun. Then, there was a 20 millimetre cannon, RPG-7 rocket launchers and automatic rifles.

It was to be the most fire support the SAS had ever had available to them in their entire history, and the results were guaranteed to inflict total overkill.

In the highly unlikely event of a few enemy escaping with their lives, they would be reduced to jibbering idiots just from the shock, noise, smoke, flame and the psychological value of having tanks used against them.

After the tanks had done their worst, the SAS would storm the building, killing everyone left in sight.

The tanks – originally destined for Uganda before surreptitiously finding their way to Rhodesia – were kept at Inkomo Barracks, 25 kilometres (14 miles) from Salisbury, where "C" Squadron underwent extensive familiarisation courses. The SAS developed a good rapport with the *tankees* who were to operate the T55s during the attack on the building.

At the "A" and "B" Squadron targets, the SAS would have Eland 90 armoured cars – manned by crews from the Armoured Car Regiment – each sporting its main 90 millimetre gun.

They would also have top secret sanctions-busting 106 millimetre recoilless antitank rifles which were to be used for the first time . . . as well as 20 millimetre cannons, 12,7 millimetre heavy machineguns, RPD light machineguns and rifles.

The heavy weapons would have soon punched the buildings to pieces and after a few shots from the 106 millimetre recoilless rifles, the "A" and "B" Squadron targets in Mount Pleasant, Belvedere and Enterprise Road, would be reduced to rubble.

If there was anything left standing, they would sweep through the ruins and kill any survivors.

Rehearsals for the operation were intensive and thorough, and as the targets were in the capital, the reconnaissance of the buildings was the best available. They were able to walk past them every day, either under the guise of being civilians or dressed as *Wombles* (Police Reservists), checking out the access routes, guard systems, the position of neighbouring houses, and to look for suitable arcs of fire.

They were also able to drive past in convoys on their way to and from manning strategic points around the capital in the run-up to the election.

The heavily armed and helmetted troops soon became familiar sights around the city. They were there in their Eland 90 armoured cars, Sabres and troop-carrying vehicles as civilians went to work each morning; and there when they returned home.

Officially, their presence was to boost white confidence, yet it also provided the SAS with the perfect cover, enabling them to drive past their targets without arousing suspicion, update their intelligence and work out their timings for the attack.

From their positions on street intersections and junctions, the SAS would be able to get to their respective targets within minutes of the codeword being received.

In the case of "C" Squadron, they would be able to throw a cordon around the university building within two minutes, using their Sabres and troop-carrying vehicles.

Two minutes later, the tanks would arrive to close off the cordon and, using a loud hailer, Bob McKenna would give the residents at the university centre the opportunity of surrendering.

Those who decided to run away would be quickly cut down ... and those who preferred a fight would be blasted to kingdom come with the full wrath of eight tanks, a 20 millimetre cannon, rockets and assorted weaponry.

The initial barrage would last a full two minutes after which the front tank would breach the two-metre-high security wall around the hostel. The front mudguards had been removed to prevent bricks getting caught up and slowing down their advance.

The tank would then reverse, leaving the way clear for Lieutenants Rich Stannard, Phil Brooke and Mike Rich and their house-clearing teams to spill through the breach and storm the building.

Wearing full body armour, the teams would hasten to their appointed floors in the centre and systematically set about clearing the corridors and rooms.

Initially, they would use the Rhodesian version of the British stun grenade to frighten and disorientate ZANLA. The grenades were similar to those used by 22 SAS for their highly successful attack on the Iranian Embassy in London, and the Rhodesian copies had been specially made for the mission by one of the army's demolition experts, himself an ex-SAS member.

Then, once their grenades had done their job, the storm troopers would follow up with AK fire.

As the three groups cleared each of their allocated rooms with precision timing, they would hang sheets out of the windows to indicate their progress to overall commander Bob McKenna waiting below.

The three commanders inside the building would be in radio contact with the commander and he would organise extra ammunition and dispatch replacements for those who might be wounded.

The tanks, meanwhile, would have pulled back into a forming-up area.

By this stage, "A" and "B" Squadrons would be storming whatever was left standing of their targets and neutralising all opposition, including the Number One target, Robert Mugabe, and the Number Two, Simon Muzenda.

The "C" squadron target would have taken the longest to neutralise, but the entire operation would have been all over bar the shouting by the time most civilians got out of bed.

The intelligence on their targets was extremely detailed and in the case of the three-storey university building and the Medical Arts Centre in Enterprise Road, they had been provided with the complete floor plans. They knew who slept in each bed, what weapons each man had and knew where all the RPG-7 rocket launchers and machineguns were kept.

Exhaustive battle preparations and house-clearing drills for all the targets were carried out at Kabrit Barracks.

Every imaginable contingency was practised, from starting and extinguishing fires, sorting out casualties, to the communications they would use in the buildings during the raid.

Finally, all the rehearsals were over and everyone was 100 percent certain of his role in the forthcoming attack. The eight tanks were put on low-loaders, covered and moved under the cloak of darkness to KG VI Barracks, in readiness for the attack. The Armoured Car Regiment with their armoured cars moved out to live at the SAS barracks during this time.

The mission was one of the most-detailed and well-planned operations of the war. The plan and the timings were perfect. The rehearsals could not have been better and the fire support was the best available.

Other members of the security forces were in observation positions overlooking the assembly points ready to call in the jets. The planes had been bombed up; the crews were on standby.

Everyone was keyed up and raring to go. Now all they needed was the codeword.

Each evening, the SAS storm-troopers were told that the mission would take place the following day . . . but as each morning came and went, there was still no word.

The RLI, meanwhile, who were initially tasked to attack two assembly areas on the initiation of the codeword, were recalled to Salisbury. It was now five days before the elections and the battalion was deployed around Salisbury instead of taking on the assembly areas.

The morale and the level of confidence in the RLI was extremely high. While only the RLI CO, Lieutenant-Colonel Charlie Aust and his adjutant knew of the plan to eliminate the ZANLA leaders, most of the RLI felt that, having mobilised such a large force so close to the election, that there was going to be some sort of military action.

And right until the last moment, almost everyone else involved in the scheme thought the same.

* * *

Meanwhile, at lunchtime on Sunday, March 2, two days before the election results were to be announced, four SAS men were waiting at Kabrit Barracks for the all-clear to carry out their particular role in a contingency plan only.

Robert Mugabe and every one of his 28 members of the ZANU Central Committee had flown out to Maputo for the weekend – and a Mozambican jet was due to bring them back to Salisbury on Sunday afternoon.

Salisbury's civilian airport was right next door to Kabrit Barracks and the four operators were ideally placed to follow their orders and shoot the plane down with Strela as it began its approach to the runway. They had done a target study and knew that almost no one would have been left alive in the plane. However, while eager to get to grips with ZANU personalities, some of the SAS operators involved were against the scheme as there was a possibility of hitting the pilot and crew. There was a resistance against following the order and much debate.

But then, as the Mozambican plane crossed the border to the Eastern Highlands, the SAS was told that the contingency plan was off.

"It was a categoric 'No'. After consultation with the intelligence people, the military said it was impossible," the SAS CO explained.

* * *

Two days later, the SAS were still positioned on strategic corners, just minutes away from their targets – and still waiting for the codeword to eliminate Mugabe and his men.

But as it got closer to 09h00 and the announcement of the results, most of them realised that the codeword – kept a closely-guarded secret – would never come. Having been assured that everything would turn out all right, they then began to think that perhaps Mugabe had lost the election after all; that there was no need for any military plan.

But things were not all right and when they switched their army radios into the local radio frequency, it was to hear that Robert Mugabe had not only won the election, but that his victory was both crushing and absolute.

He had taken 57 of the 100 parliamentary seats and the unthinkable had come to pass. Robert Mugabe, the arch enemy, was to become the new Prime Minister of an independent and internationally recognised Zimbabwe.

The reaction among the security forces and the country's whites was one of paralysing shock, then disbelief, then dismay.

The hardened SAS operators were disgusted that they had been duped. All that work; all those rehearsals ... Then, nothing. More than once, the SAS had Robert Mugabe in their sights during the run-up to the election. But they were unable to make their move until the word came.

Some stunned soldiers got from their vehicles and wandered around aimlessly, trying to work out what had gone wrong.

In the RLI ranks, it was much the same story. As they manned key intersections in their vehicles, each soldier sat wondering what the next chap was thinking.

Many wept, others maintained a stiff upper lip although the shock and dismay were clearly visible on their faces.

In the Selous Scouts ops room, hysterical laughter greeted the news that Robert Mugabe had won the election. No one could believe it.

The pilots on standby to deal with the assembly areas were seen to throw their helmets on to the tarmac in sheer frustration.

Most whites stayed in their homes. Those who heard the news over their office radios didn't get much work done that day. Their whole futures were at stake and serious thought had to be given to that.

There was much panic and many women took their children out of school. Others packed and began heading south to the border. Some businesses shut up shop and the staff went home. Estate agents were inundated with telephone calls from people wanting to put their houses on the market.

Grim little groups huddled in cafes, hardly touching their drinks ... while in many government offices, work began immediately on shredding secret documents, photographs of terrorist atrocities, whatever could be incriminating in the new order of things.

In town, young blacks rode around on the back of flatbed trucks yelling Mugabe slogans. They danced in Manica Road, outside the ZANU offices, prancing and strutting like roosters, Mugabe's election symbol. Here and there, crowing could be heard.

Overhead, the helicopters circled around to remind people that looting would not be tolerated ... and General Walls appealed for calm. A special noon edition of *The Herald* announcing the "Massive Win for Mugabe" sold out.

Both the RLI and SAS were ordered to continue manning the street corners – and to smile to instil confidence in the white population.

They obeyed their orders – and in defiant mood, they flapped their arms and squawked as the busloads of cheering Mugabe supporters drove by. For a moment, the black youths were nonplussed at such a reaction. It helped to relieve the tension, but underneath it all, the troops were bitterly disappointed.

419

Occasionally, a car would draw up and a weeping driver would ask the soldiers what they were going to do about Mugabe's win. But they were unable to explain that their well-laid plans had gone astray; that the codeword had never come.

The British, too, were said to be taken aback that nothing had happened. They knew that the security forces had a military plan and were fully expecting it to take place. A high-ranking member of the British contingent was to ask a leading Rhodesian politician why the plan had not gone ahead. The politician, also assured that everything would be "all right", was unable to tell them.

Perhaps there was some truth in the theory that Nkomo, when told of the military plan, had stated that he could not be seen to be taking the country from white officers, and that he would be hard-pressed to sell the idea to the west? If true, there would have been little point in continuing the exercise. No need to change the course of history. (The plan had been for Nkomo to head a coalition government.)

Perhaps if the earlier plans on Mugabe's life had worked; if he had not been tipped off . . . ?

But, perhaps things had gone too far and it was all too late anyway . . . ?

And what had happened to the top secret plans to rig the elections? Special Branch Task Force were to have switched ballot boxes during a period when the boxes were unguarded. But at the last minute someone put a stop to the plan.

And had the spy at ComOps tipped off Mugabe and his men about the operation anyway? And if he had, would their defences have been any match for tanks, recoilless rifles and machineguns? The only way they could have survived was by not being in the buildings that morning. And there are reports that they were not.

But was it necessary to wait until the dawn of a British-supervised Independence? From the time of the troops' initial briefing, it was always envisaged that they would make their move long before then. For the longer they waited and the surveillance was maintained on the key personalities, so the risks of compromise increased.

But perhaps it was never meant to be after all? A member of the ComOps planning team says that although the possibility of a *coup* was discussed, the idea was quickly abandoned, for the wrath of the world would have been down on Rhodesia's shoulders. "We discussed it for 15 minutes," he said.

Perhaps then, the "coup" was merely to keep the security forces busy and out of mischief? Who knows . . . ?

* * *

The head of CIO, Ken Flower, had meanwhile summoned SB officers to ComOps, to tell them that the possibility of Mugabe winning the election had not been foreseen. Asked if it was still possible to "do something", he said no, they had to accept the situation.

The special slush fund set up to finance various aspects of the operation still had several thousands of dollars left in the kitty. But no one wanted to know anything about it anymore. In those traumatic days, there was much back-pedalling. Eventually, it helped some of the SB officers to get out of the country. No one wanted to know about them either.

Later, two members of the ComOps hierarchy visited Kabrit to offer the soldiers honeyed words of comfort and reassurance. But the SAS men were not impressed, and although the hierarchy handled the situation with great aplomb, it was not the best of meetings.

As for the RLI, they closed ranks and withdrew into themselves until late October when the unit disbanded and the colours were laid in the vaults of Salisbury's Anglican Cathedral.

Shortly after the election, the RLI CO, Lieutenant-Colonel Charlie Aust, walked on to the parade square where the whole battalion was formed up, faced the 600 men whom he had personally assured a few weeks earlier that Mugabe would not come to power, and said:

"Guys, I'm sorry. It's a cock-up."

There seemed nobody to whom the RLI CO could turn to for guidance during those particularly sensitive days following the election.

Charlie Aust personally took steps to remove all the battalion treasures out of the country and went to see a member of the hierarchy who had been closely associated with the RLI over the years. As the RLI CO walked into the man's office he was writing a letter, and did not look up or stop writing the entire three minutes that Charlie Aust was there.

The RLI commander said he sought the officer's advice in getting the RLI statue out of the country. He was promptly told not to be a fool.

"I've lived through the trauma of moving from Northern Rhodesia when the Federation broke up and I know all about this sort of thing. Don't try and be clever." He then told the RLI CO to clear out of his office.

It was an unhappy period and there was a great deal of distrust in many quarters.

Fortunately for the RLI, they were able to smuggle their statue, a tribute to their war dead, out to the safety of South Africa.

The Selous Scouts were virtually disbanded overnight and their very name became a dirty word in the new order. Unlike the RLI, there was no formal disbandment or parade where they could lay up their standard.

Even after the election, there were some who thought there was still time to stage a *coup*, but despite frantic efforts on the part of some determined special force officers, nothing came of the plan. It was over before it had begun. And that was that.

Later, a feasibility study on the possibility of staging a *coup* in Zimbabwe was conducted elsewhere in Africa, but the recommendation was that it was all too late.

General Walls is reported to have said that with the control Robert Mugabe's party had in the country, a military *coup* against the Mugabe government would not have lasted more than 48 hours. Many farmers and people in the rural areas would have been killed and it would have been a chaotic state of affairs.

The security forces were, it was true, thin on the ground at that stage and if they could not have held the country, there's no doubt there would have been much bloodshed. And the war would have continued.

Intimidation aside, Robert Mugabe did enjoy massive popular support. The 250 000 people who greeted him in Salisbury when he returned from exile was proof of that (although they did turn up to see Joshua Nkomo, too). It would be hard to argue that they had all been intimidated.

Granted advance intelligence of the election results, General Walls had cabled Margaret Thatcher urging her to declare the election null and void because of massive intimidation. His plea made not the slightest difference. (There are claims that the Foreign Office deliberately held up his request in Nairobi so that Mrs Thatcher did not receive it before the results were announced – thus protecting her from having to make a decision.)

In the light of reports from election supervisors and observers, who found the elections to be as fair and free as possible in the circumstances, she did not feel there were any grounds to declare the election invalid.

Whitehall sources considered the General's plea to have been a non-starter anyway. Mrs Thatcher would have had to cut across the opinion of Commonwealth observers and impose British rule on the country, an action which most certainly would have been opposed by the Commonwealth and the nationalist parties.

Thus it was that one era came to an end, and another began ...

The British mopped brows, shook off the African dust ... and Robert Mugabe and his election symbol came home to roost.

The Great Con Job

During the election, one of the observers approached a top British official and asked how his government had ever managed to get all the mutually antagonistic factions together during the initial negotiations and keep them on track.

"Frankly, it has been an enormous con job," the man replied.

American politician Dr Richard T. McCormack, who visited Rhodesia during the elections reveals this in his analysis on the Rhodesian debacle published in the States. Dr McCormack, later Assistant Secretary of State for Economic and Business Affairs, added that the title of his work should really have been *"The Great Con Job"*.

McCormack – CIO view his report as extremely accurate – says that to understand what the British official meant, it was necessary to step back in time to the immediate period after the April 1979 election. At that time, Nigeria threatened to cut off the billions of dollars in British goods and services bought every year if Mrs Thatcher and her government carried out campaign pledges to drop sanctions and recognise Rhodesia.

For an economy the size and condition of Great Britain's, such retaliation along with threats that the Commonwealth itself might break up over the issue, provided the critical arguments for liberal members of the British foreign service to undermine the new Muzorewa government. They were assisted by equally liberal members of the Carter Administration who felt, on principle, that Muzorewa and his alliance with the whites should not be permitted to continue.

And in the background, the Soviet Ambassador to Zambia, Vassily Solodovnikov, stepped up arms deliveries in the weeks after the April election to reinforce the arguments of the Western liberals that any attempt to consolidate the Muzorewa position would be countered by an intensified war.

The decision was thus eventually reached in Britain to opt for new elections. The problem then became how to persuade Muzorewa and the whites to step down and permit those elections to take place under British auspices.

The critical task, says Dr McCormack, "was to convince each involved party that he stood to gain by new elections and a new constitution."

Thus, Muzorewa was told by the highest officials in Great Britain that the British objective was to give him more power – to free him from excessive white influence – and enable him to be the dominant factor in his nation.

For this reason, he trusted the British and threw away his bird in the hand, with the hope of obtaining two in the bush at the Lancaster House conference.

General Walls, Commander of Combined Operations, was assured that Great Britain would never permit the Marxist Mugabe to come to power in Rhodesia – that the British were just as repelled by Mugabe's philosophy and ruthless operating methods as were the white Rhodesians.

"To reinforce the feeling that Great Britain had forgiven the white Rhodesians for their rebellion, great efforts were made to bring General Walls closer to the British socially and personally during the weeks of the conference."

(General Walls points out however, that he rejected every invitation placed his way. The only person he was willing to meet – and the suggestion came from him, not the British – was the Queen Mother, Colonel-In-Chief of various elements of the Rhodesian security forces.)

Gradually, top white Rhodesian leaders were persuaded that new elections were necessary and their essential interests would be safeguarded.

It was clear the Rhodesians were slowly but steadily running out of money and manpower. By June, 1979, top Rhodesian Treasury officials believed the war might not be sustainable for more than a year without risking a fatal collapse of morale and the economy.

The white population figure had already dropped by almost a third from its peak of a quarter of a million and many of those emigrating were valuable specialists and technicians.

The terrorists morale, too, was not high. Bishop Muzorewa's election and the immediate strongly positive response by large segments of American and European opinion had discouraged them. That, and their high casualty rate, brought matters to a very tense state in high guerrilla councils. They, too, had some reasons to seek another less painful route to power.

Finally, the British got everyone around the conference table. Dr McCormack says the actual process of negotiation at Lancaster House was assisted by superb work on the part of the British intelligence agencies, who were reported to have bugged almost every conversation held by many of the principals through the conference. If this is true, the British government was aware exactly how far each side could be pushed at any given moment.

(Such tactics were, of course, denied but that was only to be expected, writes the author. The British were on their home territory and who was to stop them? It is understood too that they had cameras hidden in electric light fittings above the Rhodesians' telex machine. Rhodesian CIO men acknowledge that the British intelligence service's handling of the Rhodesian issue was thoroughly professional. They inserted their M16 man into Maputo in 1977 and he was on first name terms with both Mugabe and Machel. The man was to tell CIO that ZANLA's intelligence was good. What he really meant was that the British intelligence was good. It probably explained why Rhodesian security force attempts to eliminate Mugabe failed.)

Dr McCormack says that top white Rhodesian leaders were told that a British objective was a coalition government headed by Nkomo but containing both the whites and Muzorewa. The whites were assured that as Nkomo headed the minority Matabele tribe, he would never be able to govern without the help and co-operation of both the whites and Muzorewa's Shona followers.

Under this plan, Mugabe was to be the odd man out. If he was to be offered anything, it would be a subordinate role in the new cabinet. In the event of his refusing and returning to the fighting, it was strongly hinted that Nkomo and the Rhodesian security forces would be given a free hand to deal roughly with Mugabe's forces.

Nkomo went along with the plan and as a demonstration of good faith brought part of his army into the assembly points. He did, however, keep some 10 000 of his best forces in Zambia as insurance.

The British assured Mugabe they would protect him and his forces from any Rhodesian security force retaliation. But Mugabe did not trust the British and it was necessary to bring great diplomatic pressures on Machel to force Mugabe to co-operate.

As for the South Africans, the British assured them they would never tolerate Mugabe coming to power in Rhodesia. The elections were necessary to isolate Mugabe in the eyes of Africa, and give the confrontation states a graceful way of withdrawing their support of Mugabe.

The word was quietly passed around about the Nkomo strategy and it was bought by all parties except Muzorewa, says Dr McCormack. Muzorewa was to be given either the powerless figurehead Presidency or the Vice Prime Ministership.

As everybody involved knew that Mugabe would do dangerously well in the elections if he were to intimidate the voters in the TTLs, the British assured the whites, Muzorewa and the South Africans that they would strictly police the elections and disqualify Mugabe if he attempted to intimidate voters.

These pledges were accepted at face value and each party went into the elections believing his main objective would be achieved ...

Nkomo felt he was the concensus choice for Prime Minister. Muzorewa believed that Mrs Thatcher wanted to increase his power. The whites believed that the British would ensure their safety in the new Nkomo coalition – and that, as a result, the war would end.

And Mugabe calculated that his terrorist network and his strong tribal base might bring him close to power.

Ironically, says Dr McCormack, he was the most reluctant participant of all and felt that the British, Rhodesians, South Africans, Nkomoites and Muzorewa people might gang up on him. But pressure from Mozambique, coupled with his faith in his terrorist network, finally brought him along.

Why did the British choose Nkomo to be their candidate for the prime minister-ship? While it was true he had received almost one billion US dollars worth of Soviet arms (to be repaid after he came to power) he had also taken money from a host of non-communist sources in the course of his long revolutionary career.

It was felt he was not a Marxist at heart. Many compared him to Kenyatta in outlook and potential as a unifying leader.

The problem facing the British though was, how could Muzorewa, who was expected to get the most votes, be persuaded to play second fiddle to Nkomo, who was rightly projected to get only about twenty seats?

Dr McCormack states: "To get Muzorewa to accept second position to Nkomo, it would be necessary to apply pressure. It would, of course, be considerably easier if Muzorewa were to do less well than expected in the actual voting. If Mugabe were to pick up a good piece of the Shona vote and leave up to 25 seats or so, it would make it much easier to persuade Muzorewa to accept the secondary position."

Dr McCormack says the British did nothing to stop the rampant intimidation by the various parties. Mugabe maimed and terrorised his competition out of the vast Shona tribal trust areas to give his own campaign a free hand. Nkomo kept Mugabe's and Muzorewa's people out of his Matabele areas and only in the urban areas was there a semblance of free and fair campaigning on the part of all groups.

"There were a number of reasons why the British did nothing to stop the intimidation by Mugabe. It would have required firmness and muscle beyond that at their disposal. Or it would have required them to disqualify whole sections of Rhodesia from the election process."

This would have incurred the anger of rich Nigeria and other black Commonwealth members, which might have applied economic reprisals on Britain.

Dr McCormack writes that it served British purposes to let Mugabe do reasonably well. It would be much harder to bring Muzorewa into a coalition as number two if he did too well in the elections. It ensured that Muzorewa would not get a runaway victory.

The ultimate results shocked and confounded everybody including the British and Rhodesian intelligence services. Nobody expected Mugabe to do as well as he did, or Muzorewa as poorly as he did. Why, asks Dr McCormack, did it happen?

The intimidation factor was pervasive and overpowering in the rural areas where most voters lived, he explained. (It was also rife in the urban areas, including the capital.)

Many young educated black Rhodesians from urban areas resented the power position of the whites and were impatient with Muzorewa's gradualist approach. They identified with the men with the guns, muscle and radicalism.

Muzorewa was not in power long enough to keep election promises to end the war and improve the lives of the people. He may have relied too heavily on his own narrow sub-tribal base when choosing people for jobs in his government.

Many Shonas became convinced by Mugabe's argument that since he had started up the war, only he could end the fighting and bring peace.

"The British Governor, Lord Soames, appeared to be a fairly weak person and generally allowed his own instincts about intimidation to be overruled by stronger and more disciplined Foreign Office advisers who were felt to be more tolerant of Mugabe's penchant for intimidation and violence," Dr McCormack says.

In the end, however, the British Foreign Office may have outsmarted itself. By permitting the intimidation to complete the process of Muzorewa's destruction, they lost control of events and the ability to pressure moderation by balancing one faction against the other in a broad based coalition government. They also paved the road to absolute power along which Mugabe and his brand of Marxism are now slowly but surely riding.

"For Rhodesia, it was a sad and fatal miscalculation."

Dr McCormack said that although limited sections of the electorate voted in conditions approaching free and fair elections, there were vast stretches of the country populated by millions where the campaigning process was a caricature of democratic procedures as people understand them in the west.

The real problem, he said, was that due to intimidation, millions of people lived in regions where it proved impossible for a legitimate campaign to be conducted by more than a single party. At Fort Victoria, for instance, where more than one million people lived, the British election administrator openly admitted that no party other than that represented by Mr Mugabe was permitted to campaign.

Nkomo's and Muzorewa's election workers had met violent deaths when they attempted to organise a campaign in the non-urban areas, and eventually all parties other than Mr Mugabe's were forced to withdraw from the entire area.

The pattern was much the same in other tribal areas, particularly along the Mozambique border. It was, however, only the beginning of intimidation practised on the voters, says Dr McCormack. People were not only forced to vote but were warned that Mugabe's men had the means to know how they voted. In at least one instance, young girls were taken to the polling booths and their parents told the girls would be taken to Mozambique to help with the war, if Mugabe lost the election.

One of Nkomo's parliamentary candidates was killed by a Mugabe supporter by having hot coals poured down his throat, stated Dr McCormack.

"For an American to grasp fully what has happened in large parts of Rhodesia during this election campaign, one may think of·an election held forty years ago in an ethnic neighbourhood largely dominated by the Mafia.

"Although a cop may be stationed near the polls on election day to keep the lines of voters orderly, his presence is simply incapable of mitigating the impact of the pervasive sinister forces which have been at work in the neighbourhood for months prior to the election.

"Nobody but the Mafia candidate was permitted to campaign. Nobody was permitted to canvass, or make speeches, or distribute literature, or organize the workers ... except the Mafia candidate. Any infractions were sternly dealt with.

"And on election day, the Mafia representatives made the rounds and said: 'All of you will go to the polls today and vote for our man. In case you get any strange ideas about voting for anyone else, you should know that we have paid off one of the election officials to stand behind the voting machine and let us know how each of you vote. Now, our man is going to win. But in case he doesn't, we intend to trash (kill) the whole damn neighbourhood.'

"The picture I have presented here is obviously overdrawn – but not by much. Godfather Mugabe has made an offer to the Shona people of many primitive areas of the country they simply cannot refuse."

Dr McCormack said none of the parties was totally above reproach, and this included undisciplined elements of the security forces who were involved in scattered incidents of attempted intimidation.

"But it is absolutely clear from available statistics that Mr Mugabe's intimidatory tactics dwarfed those of other candidates in terms of scale, sheer brutality and effectiveness."

Take Mugabe's main campaign argument – he had brought them the war and only he could end it. Otherwise it was back to the bush and the killing.

When Mugabe's escort officer in one assembly point was asked what would happen if Mugabe lost the election, he responded that every voter in the region knew what would happen. Asked to be more specific, he merely repeated himself, that every voter knew what would happen. "Of course, he meant that Mugabe would start up the war again, together with its killing and disruption," Dr McCormack said.

There were more subtle forms of intimidation too – such as Mugabe men pretending to take notes of people going in and out of the polling areas, crowing in the distance (Mugabe's election symbol was the rooster) and making it very clear that Godfather Mugabe's presence was all pervasive and all watching.

"Some individuals expressed the pious hope that the people would react against all this terror by voting against Mr Mugabe at the polls. By the time the voters arrived at the polls, they were thoroughly cowed ... "

Intimidation undoubtedly played a significant part in the large voter turnout (94 percent), states Dr McCormack.

"It was obvious that the ordinary citizens of the war-weary land were desperately tired of death and disruption involved in the conflict. Many people would undoubtedly have voted for Atilla the Hun if he offered the prospect of an end to the conflict, regardless of the long term impact of such a victory. These people were not thinking in long term contexts. They were worried about physical survival through the next weeks and months."

Dr McCormack says the British Foreign Office carefully chose their own parliamentary delegates and officials from those who would certify the election as fair and free. British personnel privately stated before polling began that the elections would be declared free and fair and *that would be that.* It seemed very likely too that some of the members of the Commonwealth delegations were also hand-picked to include people who would co-operate, although there were exceptions.

One German observer declared: "If this election is fair and free, then I am a Chinaman." One New Zealand observer stated privately: "This process offends every democratic bone in my body." Delegates from Freedom House (a conservative non-governmental think tank) were also deeply distressed at the intimidation.

"But these were isolated voices, muffled by the vast chorus of those orchestrated to sing another tune. From a detached point of view, it was, in fact, a superbly managed operation," writes Dr McCormack.

One British official complained that criticism by some observers "wasn't constructive in the least." But Dr McCormack says that some of the older retired British officials who had been called back into service to assist with the election process were clearly uncomfortable over what was happening.

"They knew that it was an exercise in real politik; that important British interests were involved; that British prestige and interests required that this election process be judged legitimate and a 'success' and they went along with it.

"But the day the results were announced, the old colonials knew that the thing had misfired. That Mugabe had outfoxed them. That their chosen instrument, Nkomo, had been defeated and that their whole plan lay in shambles."

The task then became to put the best face on the situation and try to make the best of things.

After Robert Mugabe's crushing victory was announced to a stunned audience of foreign observers and visiting journalists, one British official left the briefing room, turned to a senior Rhodesian official and said: "Well, at least now you have got us Brits off your back." The stunned Rhodesian was barely able to contain a physical response to such fatuity.

Summing up, Dr McCormack says that his analysis was not intended for the purpose of pointing a hostile finger at British Rhodesian policy and operations. All nations act on their interests and British diplomats can hardly be faulted for placing British interests over those of moderate Rhodesians.

"And, let there be no mistake, very important British interests were at stake in Rhodesia . . . And, in fairness, it must be said that British diplomacy intended to bring out of the Rhodesian tangle a solution that would end the war and establish a stable coalition government, whose various factions would balance off against each other to prevent a one-party dictatorship. Unfortunately, a tragic miscalculation was made."

* * *

The most violent and savage election campaign in recent world history was over. Within days, the bulk of the 700 visiting journalists had left and Rhodesia had disappeared from the front pages of the world . . . and by the end of the year, many whites, including members of the security forces, had left the country.

Would it be the last election, asked Dr McCormack? Would it follow the familiar African pattern of one man, one vote, one time?

* * *

For seven long years, Rhodesians had waged what is recognised as the most tactically-brilliant and determined counter-insurgency campaign of modern times. It had been fought against almost insuperable odds and with a record that was unsurpassed in both skill and bravery, according to military historian Michael Evans.

*And yet it could only ever be a holding action until such time as a political solution could be found to end the conflict.

While the insurgents were not winning and while the Rhodesians were prepared to strike offensively at enemy concentrations "to hell and back if necessary", the Rhodesian military always conceded that a military victory was an impossibility.

That the odds were certainly stacked against the Rhodesians there can be no doubt. *They were in an impossible strategic position with an operational area of 3 200 kilometres (2 000 miles) rugged, exposed border terrain. They were diplomatically isolated; had economic sanctions to contend with; often had to make do with obsolescent equipment; did not possess conventional military hardware; had severe manpower restrictions as opposed to the enemy who had unlimited reserves . . . . and they faced increasing white emigration (12 000 in 1978).

Rhodesians responded to the intense political, military, psychological, economic and international pressure with great resilience and as one military analyst commented: "If in the end the fight against Chimurenga was lost, it was not for want of effort, skill and idealism but because the costs became too great and the odds too overwhelming."

The price of peace had indeed been high and grevious. *White Rhodesian casualties have been calculated as being proportionately ten times more that those suffered by the Americans in Viet Nam and half of Britain's losses during the Second World War.

The red soil of Africa had been stained a deeper hue with the blood of more than 27 500 black and white Rhodesian lives (insurgents, servicemen and civilians). Some 275 000 had been wounded and injured with 1,5m refugees, homeless and displaced people.

For thousands of others too – the orphaned, widowed and bereaved on both sides – the mark of war would never be erased.

At the time of writing, the Rhodesian-Zimbabwean bush-war is assessed as being *the most bitter struggle ever fought in sub-Saharan Africa. Those involved in it would hope it was the last, but without a much-needed crystal ball, particularly essential in a turbulant Africa, no one is making any guarantees.

Certainly when the first shots in the Chimurenga war were fired, no one could have predicted the scale and intensity of the coming conflict, or guessed how long the fight would last.

*Michael Evans   428

No one in his wildest dreams could have foretold that the Portuguese, who had effected some measure of control over anti-Rhodesian terrorists, would lose control of neighbouring Mozambique or that the entire eastern and south-eastern flanks would become totally vulnerable, enabling insurgents to pour across in their thousands.

Rhodesian Special Branch had, through their excellent network of ground agents, kept abreast of terrorism in the early days of the war. But once the conflict was taken into the population, it was an entirely different matter. It became obvious that the tide of events that began at the end of 1972 could only be solved by political means.

That it took the two nationalisms and two races so long to find a political accommodation was tragic.

Every political opportunity missed was in fact one more option lost to the Rhodesians, who never controlled the rate, the intensity and scale of the war.

"The illusion that having educated the peasantry in many cases to University standard and induced them to enter the Western capitalist system they could be denied political power or a share of it was indeed facile thinking," one intelligence source commented.

According to the same source, the blame for the war rested with "the whole fabric of Rhodesian society brought up to believe by continued and slanted propaganda that Rhodesia was different. No heed was paid to the lessons of Indo-China, Viet Nam, Algeria, Malaya, Angola and Mozambique.

"We almost had the same attitude as the Americans when they went into Viet Nam. It was as if to them there had been no previous colonial war in Indo-China and if there had been, then it was the French Army who lost. And the Americans attitude was that they were not colonials; their cause was to bolster up a weak and corrupt government against communism.

"The idea of black terrorists standing up to the highly trained Rhodesian Army was in any case preposterous. It appeared that no one had heard of Mao's concept of the fish swimming in an ocean of people; of the terrorists strangling the life of the country by dominating the rural areas; of an army winning battle after battle but losing the people and thus the war."

The principals involved in the decision-making, only listened and reacted to what they wanted to hear and in essence were as events showed, not prepared to change believing that they had numerous options open to them and controlled the situation, but their attitude was 'Canute'-like in its miscalculation, the source added.

The Rhodesian intelligence organisation ultimately fed information into the system, which was sometimes read and digested and filtered out, but was often countered by the "Administration", who had served the needs of the blacks for years but who failed to perceive the change in their political aspirations.

"The military would find that fighting guerillas on the floor of the Zambezi Valley was a different proposition from combating them when they merged in a sea of people and thus they were fighting the tip of the iceberg, that part of the problem that was visible.

"By banning all black political leaders and the organisations that they represented and not replacing them with an alternative in the form of political advancement in step with other black aspirations in the educational, social, political and public service fields, the only other outlet left open to blacks was violence." (From 1976, there was a gradual slowing down in the economy and black youths who would normally have been absorbed into the economy turned to terrorism as a source of income. This factor was to give terrorism a tremendous boost.)

Even after the Portuguese collapse, there was according to the same intelligence source, a mindless optimism that prevailed in all sections of government that "something would turn up".

The Victoria Falls bridge conference and the release of Nkomo, Sithole and Mugabe – following pressure from South Africa – was designed to break that impasse. The events which took place at the conference showed that another option had been cast aside, and the war expanded in magnitude drawing into the whirlpool more and more manpower and finance.

Introducing the traditional and accepted leaders of black political thought and aspirations back into the terrorist fold at a time when FRELIMO was taking over in Mozambique, merely led to an escalation in the war.

Then in 1976 came the Kissinger diplomatic shuttle, and Ian Smith, again under pressure from South Africa, conceded majority rule. The subsequent Geneva Conference came to nothing, but for white Rhodesia, there could be no going back from that stand. "Many times I sat down and thought of the treachery and betrayal by our friends and not our enemies," Smith commented much later.

By 1978 the need to bring about a political settlement after the unsuccessful Kissinger negotiations became a critical factor. Despite attempts to divide the PF leaders by embracing Nkomo, he elected to continue his alliance with Mugabe.

The only option left was to gain broad black support with the internal settlement. But it was too late. The ZANLA cadres were too deep in the popular sea to be defeated politically.

When power was eventually handed over to Bishop Muzorewa's black majority rule government, he had only one option left to him and that was to stop the war. Despite efforts to sell the internal settlement, the country had been subjected to such a degree of negative propaganda that the effect of the internal settlement was a shock to the system.

Then came the British and the Lancaster House Conference – and the rest is well-recorded. The ZANLA cadres deep-seated in the population delivered Zimbabwe to Mugabe, not by the bullet but by the ballot, according to historian Michael Evans.

As one senior Army commander told the author: "If history is to be accurately recorded, the world must be told that a very fine Army which had never been defeated on the battlefield, collapsed in virtual ignominy – albeit kept tightly within the ranks that remained – through defeat in the council chamber."

*According to one military commentator, the passing of Rhodesia and the coming of Zimbabwe marked the real end of the British Empire.

"In one of the quirks of history, it was ironic that Lord Peter Carrington should have presided over the foundation of black power in Zimbabwe in 1979 when his namesake, Major-General Sir Frederick Carrington, had presided over the foundation of white power in Rhodesia in the 1890s. Symbolically, what one Carrington gave, another took away," said Michael Evans.

"Thus when in April, 1980, the Chimurenga flag went up and the Union Jack came down, it was, in truth, the last imperial sunset."

The guns had fallen silent and the war was over. Yet there was still one more secret operation that the SAS had to carry out. This time, however. it would take them southwards and not to the north or east as in the past.

Their mission: to get their memorial plinth bearing the names of the war dead out of the clutches of the new order. It would certainly mean very little to the men the soldiers had been fighting during the long bitter years of war.

Other Rhodesian memorials had been hauled from their stands and it seemed certain that with the passing of time, the SAS plinth would go the same way.

As always, top secrecy was clamped on the operation and the 25-ton plinth was spirited away from Kabrit Barracks, loaded on to an Army truck, then camouflaged with a tarpaulin. Not long afterwards, the truck and its secret cargo crossed the border into South Africa where it now stands in the peaceful gardens of a MOTH ex-servicemen's home outside Durban.

For those who dared and died, the final battle had been won.

* * *

On December 31, 1980, the Rhodesian SAS disbanded. A telegram from 22 SAS in Britain paid tribute to the operators:

"Farewell to a much admired sister unit. Your professionalism and fighting expertise has always been second to none throughout the history of the Rhodesian SAS. C Sqn still remains vacant in 22 SAS orbat."

At a ceremony on December 13, the last official function of the unit, the last CO, the most decorated member of the security forces, had this to say:

"We will leave here not only in sorrow but filled with pride, dignity and honour in ourselves and in 1 SAS. We have much to be grateful for.

"I am eternally grateful to those men who served with the unit before we did; to those among us who have lost loved ones: to those who were wounded: to those friends, and there are many of them, who have stood by us: to those wives and families who stood behind us: to those who have fought with such courage beside us, and especially to those who gave their lives for Rhodesia and the unit.

"We have not let them down and we will not forget them.

"I know that in the years to come, we can, with the greatest pride say: 'I served with the Rhodesian SAS.'

"May God bless you and thank God we did our duty."

ROLL OF HONOUR

MALAYA
Sgt O.H. Ernst, 13 June 1951
Cpl J.B. Davies, 25 June 1951
Cpl V.E. Visagie, 23 April 1952

RHODESIA, ZAMBIA, MOZAMBIQUE
WO2 R. Bouch, MCM, 12 October 1966
C/Sgt J. Wright, MCM, 12 October 1966
C/Sgt M.P. Cahill, MCM, 12 October 1966
Tpr M. Mullin, 26 March 1968
Sgt F.L. Wilmot, 19 January 1973
Tpr J.P.G. Mendes, 22 August 1973
Sgt A. Rabie, MLM, 16 September 1973
Tpr M.J. Morris, 31 January 1974
Tpr N. Willis, 14 February 1974
L/Cpl K.R. Smith, 8 June 1974
Tpr J.G. Walsh, 3 September 1974
Tpr W.R. Walton, 14 March 1975
Cpl K. Storie, 2 September 1975
Tpr E. Lotringer, 31 October 1976
2/Lt B. Burrell, 16 December 1976
Tpr E. Van Staden, 16 December 1976
L/Cpl G.J. Nel, 22 December 1976
Tpr S.D. Seymour, 22 December 1976
Capt R.S.S. Warraker, SCR, 12 January 1977
Sgt A. Chait, MLM, 24 March 1977
Tpr F.J. Nel, 23 November 1977
Sgt R.L. Biederman, 6 December 1977
Tpr C.M. Meddows-Taylor, 20 January 1978
Lt N.J. Theron, BCR, 20 January 1978
Tpr C.T. Vermaak, 20 January 1978
Cpl A.W. Lynch, 6 September 1978
L/Cpl S.M.G. Donnelly, 21 September 1978
L/Cpl J.D. Collett, 19 October 1978
L/Cpl M. Taylor, 17 December 1978
Sgt C.G. Cripps, 11 January 1979
L/Cpl N.E.S. Barber, 7 February 1979
Tpr G.R. Macmillan, 7 February 1979
Cpl R.J. Slingsby, 11 April 1979
Tpr S.G. Hartley, 6 June 1979
Tpr R.J.S. Hickman, 7 June 1979
Capt M.F. Pearse, SCR, 26 June 1979
Tpr G.V.M. Maguire, 1 August 1979
L/Cpl D.J. McLaurin, 19 October 1979
Trooper H.J. Mollentz, Sergeants Ian Suttil, Robert Hutchinson,
        and Lance Corporal Jim Park

CHRONOLOGY OF MILITARY AND POLITICAL EVENTS

1888   Rudd Concession granted to Rhodes by Matabele king, Lobengula, gave him mineral rights of Mashonaland.

1889   The Charter to British South Africa Company to exploit Rudd Concession received Royal assent.

1890   The Pioneer Column runs up the Union Jack in Salisbury in the name of Queen Victoria.

1891   Order-in-Council in London declares Mashonaland and Matabeleland British Protectorates.

1895   Mashonaland and Matabeleland renamed Rhodesia.

1896   Matabele and Mashona uprisings. 244 settlers murdered. Matabele uprising quelled in October and the Mashona uprising in the following year.

1914-   Twenty-five percent of the total European population of Rhodesia served in
1918   the First World War. A native regiment of 456 African troops was also raised.

1919   Privy Council in London decides Rhodesia belongs to the Crown.

1922   Referendum rejects Union with South Africa and decides in favour of "responsible government".

1923   Southern Rhodesia annexed as a British Colony with internal self-government.

1939-   Restraints brought in to *stop* too many Rhodesians leaving the country
1945   to fight for Britain, to protect the functioning of essential services.
        Rhodesians with SAS founder David Stirling in Western Desert.

1951   One hundred Far East Volunteers (C Squadron, Special Air Service) go to Malaya to fight with the British, gaining valuable experience of counter-insurgency warfare.

1953   Referendum approves Federation with Northern Rhodesia (Zambia) and Nyasaland (Malawi).

1957   Joshua Nkomo becomes President of African National Council.

1959   African National Congress parties in each of component territories of Federation begin a deliberate campaign of rioting and intimidation. In Southern Rhodesia the party was banned and the leadership placed behind bars, but the rioting, intimidation continued, however, and gangs of political thugs roamed the townships, while in the rural areas, crops were burned and cattle maimed. Southern Rhodesian Special Branch officers round up 500 agitators.

1961   New Constitution, negotiated between the Southern Rhodesian and the British Governments, widens the franchise to bring Africans on to the B voting roll, which meant that for the first time, Rhodesian blacks would sit in Parliament. At first the Nationalists approved the plan; then changed their minds.
        C Squadron, Special Air Service resurrected.
        The Rhodesian Light Infantry formed.

433

ZAPU (The Zimbabwe African People's Union) formed with Joshua Nkomo, Rev. Ndabaningi Sithole and Herbert Chitepo the principal office bearers.

1962   Rhodesian Front (RF) party formed.

The SAS move to Northern Rhodesia.

ZAPU banned.

First armed terrorist infiltration. Captured insurgents found in possession of three Lanchester sub-machineguns and two Enfield revolvers.

1963   Zimbabwe African National Union (ZANU) formed by ZAPU members dissatisfied with Nkomo's leadership. First squad of ZANLA (ZANU's military wing) recruits sent to China for terrorist training. Nkomo forms People's Caretaker Council (PCC) to continue activities of banned ZAPU.

November – SAS move to Salisbury. December – Federation of Rhodesia and Nyasaland officially dissolved.

1964   ZANLA "Crocodile Gang" stab and kill first white – Mr Petrus Oberholtzer – in first act of war since 1897. This act recognised as forerunner of terrorist war.

Ian Smith becomes Prime Minister.

ZANU and PCC banned. Nationalists – Joshua Nkomo, Rev Ndabaningi Sithole, Robert Mugabe – detained.

Southern Rhodesia to be known as "Rhodesia".

1964-   Rhodesians felt independence ought to be granted on same terms as had been
1965   to former Federal partners. Britain told PM if they wanted independence under 1961 Constitution, it had to be accepted by the people as a whole. A white referendum voted 10–1 in favour of independence. African chiefs and headmen also gave it their unanimous support. However, new British Premier, Harold Wilson refused to accept this as a valid indication of African opinion. Rhodesia made further changes; but Nkomo, leader of ZAPU and Sithole, head of ZANU, told Wilson they were unwilling to accept independence unless preceded by majority rule.

1965   February. Visiting British Secretary for Commonwealth Relations, Mr Arthur Bottomley stresses that while the British Government favoured a peaceful transition to "majority rule" (as provided in the 1961 Constitution), it would not advocate an immediate hand-over to majority rule.

October. Independence based on 1961 Constitution not acceptable to Britain.

November 11, 1965. The rebellion begins as Rhodesia severs ties with Britain and declares Unilateral Declaration of Independence based on 1961 Constitution as amended as necessary to suit a fully independent Sovereign State. Britain imposes selective sanctions and Wilson states UDI will end in months, if not weeks. He was wrong. It would take 14 years.

1966   UN imposes selective sanctions. Wilson and Smith meet on HMS *Tiger* – a Royal Naval cruiser anchored off Gibraltar – in search of the all-elusive settlement. The talks fail.

April 28. Seven insurgents die in battle at Sinoia with Rhodesian security forces. The Nationalists marked this as the start of the armed struggle.

May. ZANU terrorists murder Mr and Mrs Johannes Hendrik Viljoen. They were the first whites to be killed by Communist-trained and armed terrorists.

Wilson states there would be no independence in Rhodesia before African majority rule (NIBMAR).

SAS undertake their first clandestine operation into Zambia.

1967   ZIPRA and ANC (South Africa) involved in large battle with Rhodesians at Wankie. South African Police sent to assist Rhodesian Forces.

1968   October. Wilson-Smith talks aboard HMS *Fearless* in Gibraltar collapse.

November. The Appellate Division of the High Court of Rhodesia rules that the Government now the *de jure* Government.

November 11. New flag raised in Rhodesia.

FRELIMO, fighting the Portuguese troops open Tete Province in Mozambique.

1969   ZANU meet FRELIMO to ask for access to Rhodesia through Tete.

Rev Ndabaningi Sithole, leader of ZANU, sentenced to six years' imprisonment for plotting to assassinate Ian Smith. His denouncement of the armed struggle during the trial would ultimately cost him the ZANU leadership.

Voters decide in favour of adopting new Constitution and of becoming a Republic.

1970   The country's 80-year link with the Crown severed and Rhodesia becomes a Republic. New Constitution comes into effect. Rhodesia's first President sworn in. The use of the prefix "Royal" for the Royal Rhodesia Regiment and the Royal Rhodesian Air Force suspended.

Conservatives win British general election and new Foreign Secretary, Sir Alec Douglas-Home, attempts to find a solution to the Rhodesian problem.

FRELIMO cross the Zambezi, opening up Mozambique from the river down to the Rhodesian border.

1971   Smith accepts the Lord Home settlement proposals. Bishop Abel Muzorewa forms the African National Council to oppose them.

December. First two ZANLA insurgents cross into Rhodesia from Tete.

1972   Pearce Commission finds settlement proposals unacceptable to Rhodesian blacks.

Armaments are carried through Tete to Rhodesia and 60 terrorists infiltrate in preparation for the war.

December 21. Attack on Altena Farm in north-east Rhodesia – and the war begins in earnest.

JOC *Hurricane* Operational Zone established, dealing with the north-eastern part of the country.

1973   Rhodesia closes border with Zambia. Under pressure from South Africa, it is re-opened, but Kenneth Kaunda of Zambia keeps his side of the border closed.

Air Rhodesia acquire three sanction-busting Boeing 707 jets from an undisclosed source.

SAS carry out first external airborne operation since the counter-insurgency days of the Malayan Emergency.

Terrorists abduct 295 African pupils and staff of St Albert's Mission in north-eastern border. All but eight soon rescued.

The Selous Scouts Regiment formed.

Bishop Abel Muzorewa starts negotiations with Ian Smith.

1974   February. Ministry of Defence changes role from defensive to offensive. Call-up widened to include white males in the 25-38 age bracket. National Service intake doubled.

April 25. Left wing *coup d'etat* in Portugal leads to Independence in the African colonies of Angola and Mozambique. Overnight it opened up an additional 1 100 kilometres (683 miles) of hostile rugged frontier to guard against increasing insurgent infiltration. Rhodesia now has 3 000 kilometres (1 864 miles) of hostile border and only a 200 kilometre (125 mile) friendly stretch with South Africa.

September. The 145 kilometre (90 mile)-long Rutenga-Beitbridge rail link completed 21 months ahead of schedule.

November. At a meeting in Que Que prison, Rev Ndabaningi Sithole, leader of ZANU, was suspended for the denunciation of the armed struggle in 1969. Robert Mugabe, the man who was to replace him abstained from voting. They did not have a quorum and he felt it was unconstitutional; and that nothing could be served by unseating a man in prison.

Detente exercise drafted in Lusaka following talks between Kenneth Kaunda, John Vorster and the giant conglomerate Lonrho, with interests in Africa.

Following pressure from South Africa, Rhodesia releases detained Nationalist leaders in return for an end to the war, but the ceasefire fails to take effect. Within days of the ceasefire announcement, four South African policemen are gunned down in cold blood.

Releasing the traditional and accepted leaders of black political thought into the terrorist fold, would ultimately lead to an escalation of the war.

1975   March. Black Nationalist Herbert Chitepo, who masterminded ZANLA's 1972 offensive campaign, assassinated in Lusaka. ZANLA leaders and personnel arrested and Josiah Tongogara imprisoned. As a result, the war slows down. ZANLA move to Mozambique to begin operations from there. Only ZIPRA now operates from Zambia.

Robert Mugabe appointed leader of ZANU.

July. Rhodesian Government announces dusk to dawn curfew along one-kilometre-wide strip stretching 500 kilometres (310 miles) along Mozambican border.

August. Similar curfew announced along 640 kilometres (400 miles) of Botswana border.

South African forces withdraw from Rhodesia.

Victoria Falls Constitutional Conference talks fail.

December. Negotiations between Smith and Nkomo, Father of Zimbabwean nationalism begin but soon run into difficulties.

1976   ZANLA resumes war on three fronts – Tete, Manica and Gaza.

February. Operation *Thrasher* (Eastern Highlands) opens.

May. Operation *Repulse* (the south-east through which the vital South African rail link passed) opens.

August. Operation *Tangent* (the length of the Botswanan border, and including Victoria Falls and Wankie areas) opens.

March. Mozambican President, Samora Machel closes border with Rhodesia in retaliation for Rhodesian raids and declares full-scale war on her white-ruled neighbour. Rhodesia loses outlet for 25-30 percent of her exports and 2 300 Rhodesia Railway wagons are trapped in Mozambique. Britain forks out £15 000 000 of British taxpayer's money in compensation to Mozambique.

"It is quite unbelievable and grotesque that a Marxist and terrorist regime should be financed by the British Government in order to destroy a section of what was part of the British Empire," Rhodesian Defence Minister, P.K. van der Byl commented.

Fortunately, following the Portuguese coup, Rhodesia had the foresight to speed up the Rutenga rail line to South Africa to help offset the loss of the link to eastern ports.

April. Four South African tourists (Janos Sziliagyi, Gavin Adcock, Julius Mojzes and Vonda Hope) killed on Fort Victoria-Beitbridge road.

August 9. South Africa's Foreign Minister, Dr Hilgard Muller, states he supports majority rule in Rhodesia.

South Africa withdraws 26 of its 40 helicopters on loan to Rhodesia; 50 pilots and technicians also recalled.

September. Kissinger and Vorster persuade Smith to accept principle of majority rule. There was to be no going back from this stance which marked the beginning of the end of white-ruled Rhodesia.

Kenneth Kaunda of Zambia releases detained ZANU leaders.

Patriotic Front (PF), created to bring together the two terror groups as a joint negotiating power for Geneva Conference. It was merely a "marriage" of convenience, however.

Geneva Conference opens to negotiate the transfer to black rule only to adjourn inconclusively nine weeks later.

December 5. ZIPRA insurgent, Albert Sumbe Ncube ambushed and killed the 71-year-old former Roman Catholic Bishop of Bulawayo, the Rt Rev Adolf Schmitt, as well as a priest and a nun, on a lonely dirt road. The murders coincided with the ill-fated Geneva Conference and the only survivor of the massacre, Sister Ermenfriend Knauer, accepted an offer of a Rhodesian farmer to fly her to Geneva to give evidence of the attack to any interested parties. But then her Mother General refused to let her go. Commented the farmer: "I would remind the Mother General of my favourite quotation, 'All that is necessary for the triumph of evil is that good men do nothing'."

December. 27 African tea estate workers killed by terrorists in Honde Valley.

1977   The war escalates. The security forces lose about one man a day. The SF/terrorist kill ratio falls from one-ten to one-seven. While the two terror groups did not have any shortage of manpower, Rhodesia did.

Defence budget upped 44 percent and war now costing almost one million Rhodesian dollars a day.

Compulsory National Service extended to two years. Whites in the 38-50 age category called up and all military deferments cancelled irrespective of the economic implications.

400 African pupils abducted by ZIPRA across Botswana border. Despite pleas by parents, less than 100 children return. The remainder were flown to Zambia for military training.

February. Seven white missionaries murdered at Musami by 12 insurgents. The British government refuse Rhodesia's request to set up inquiry into killings.

March. Combined Operations (ComOps) formed with former SAS Commanding Officer, Lieutenant-General Peter Walls as Commander.

July. Twelve RF rebels launch new party – Rhodesian Action Party.

August. Terror comes to town. A 30kg ZANLA bomb explodes in Woolworths store in Salisbury, killing 11 people and injuring 76.

Operation *Grapple* (Midlands) opens, marking saturation of entire country by insurgents.

British Foreign Secretary, Dr David Owen and the American Ambassador to the UN, Andrew Young, arrive in Salisbury with Anglo-American proposals for a settlement. Ian Smith rejects them and begins long negotiations with internal moderate leaders, Bishop Abel Muzorewa, Rev Ndabaningi Sithole and Senator Chief Jeremiah Chirau to form a Transitional Government to precede majority rule.

November. Special Air Service, Rhodesian Light Infantry and Air Force mount a massive pre-emptive raid on Chimoio and Tembue terrorist bases in east and northern Mozambique, killing thousands. It is the biggest, most successful operation of the war.

1978   Government launch a "safe return" programme for nationalists wishing to return to Rhodesia in peace.

Ian Smith and the three internal black leaders sign the March 3 Agreement to form the Transitional Government.

UN Security Council debate resolves any internal settlement to be "illegal and unacceptable".

April. Nine black Government Ministers sworn in to serve on Ministerial Council of Transitional Government.

April. Mass release of political detainees.

The first ZANLA women combatants under their own command, enter Rhodesia.

June. Former SAS officer, Captain Chris Schollenberg, becomes the first holder of the country's highest bravery award, the Grand Cross of Valour, equivalent to the Victoria Cross and the American Congressional Medal of Honour.

June. C Squadron becomes 1 Special Air Service Regiment (Rhodesia).

June. ZANLA murder nine British missionaries and four young children.

including a three-week-old baby, at Elim Mission. It was the worst massacre of whites since the war began.

June. Operation *Splinter* (Lake Kariba) opens.

August. Ian Smith holds secret talks with Joshua Nkomo.

September. Nkomo's ZIPRA down Air Rhodesia Viscount; then slaughter 10 of the survivors. The other eight flee into the bush to survive.

Martial law proclaimed in selected areas of Rhodesia.

October. Africans in 18-25 age group now liable for call up.

October. Zambia opens border after six-year closure and the southern rail route. Zambia needed food from Rhodesia and South Africa to feed her nation. 1 SAS move to their own barracks, named Kabrit after the SAS pioneers' first camp in the Western Desert.

Eleven sanctions-busting Bell 205 helicopters, the Viet Nam workhorse, ideal for counter-insurgency work, with a far greater range capability and bigger load capacity than the Alouette IIIs, arrive in Rhodesia. However, not all were used in an operational role. One was stripped down for spares and accidents claimed others. By the following June, only five were flying.

November. The Transitional Government decides to form a coalition Government of National Unity to create a period of political stability after advent of black rule.

December. Fuel storage tanks severely damaged by fire after terror attack.

1979   January. Areas of martial law extended.

February. Second Viscount shot down. All 59 people aboard killed and Nkomo claims responsibility.

Four white abductees released in Mozambique.

First integration in Government schools.

March. Nkomo's ZIPRA shoot down two Zambian Air Force jets in Zambia.

The SAS begin training and operating with the Mozambique National Resistance (MNR).

European men in the 50-59 age group called up for duties in urban areas.

SAS visit Lusaka again ... and again ... and again ...

Muzorewa wins elections. British Conservative peers find elections free and fair but international recognition is withheld.

Bishop Muzorewa as PM designate appeals to US for recognition.

Terrorist war enters final conventional phase. Events have come a long way since the Lanchester sub-machineguns and Enfield revolvers of the 1960s era.

June. First black-dominated Government installed.

US President turns down immediate lifting of sanctions.

July. PM leaves for visit to US and meets American President.

August 1. Commonwealth Summit in Lusaka. August 2. Nigerian Government announces it will nationalise British BP interests in country. British Premier, Margaret Thatcher agrees to convene constitutional all-party conference on Rhodesian issue.

African apprentices now liable for call-up.

September. Security Forces mount major offensive into Gaza Province of Mozambique.

September 10. Lancaster House Conference starts in London.

SAS destroy ten Zambian bridges in Zambia in five days to thwart ZIPRA invasion. Zambian President mobilizes Zambia for full scale war situation against Zimbabwe Rhodesia.

December 12. British Governor, Lord Soames arrives in Salisbury. The rebellion against the Crown is over. Legality is restored and sanctions removed.

Agreement on new Constitution signed.

December 21, seven years to the day since the war began in earnest, a settlement agreement is signed and a ceasefire takes effect.

1980   March. Robert Mugabe and his election cockerel symbol come home to roost. He becomes Prime Minister of an internationally recognised independent Zimbabwe in April.

ABBREVIATIONS AND GLOSSARY OF TERMS

A/A: Anti-aircraft.

AK: Kalashnikov or AK-47, the true assault weapon of most revolutions; also used by Rhodesian Special Forces on cross-border operations.

Alpha Bomb: One kilogram bomb which bounced before exploding in the air.

Ammo: Ammunition.

ANC: African National Congress (South Africa).

ANC: African National Council (Rhodesia).

AP: Anti-personnel landmine.

Baobab: African tree with extremely thick trunk and angular branches, often known as the Upside Down Tree as the branches resemble roots.

Bazooka: Name used by terrorists for RPG-7 rocket launcher.

Big Means: TR-48, the high frequency long-range radio, main lifeline back to Tactical Headquarters and Salisbury, used throughout the Army. The SAS almost exclusively used Morse as it was more accurate on very deep-penetration operations.

Biltong: Dried meat cut into thin strips (in America, Jerky).

Black-Is-Beautiful: Black camouflage cream.

Blues: Army term for the Air Force.

BSAP: British South Africa Police.

Buffalo Beans: (Mucuna coriacea Bak.) One of the Security Forces most dreaded enemies! When ripe, gives off clouds of fine hairs which are highly irritating.

Bundu: Bush.

Bunker Bomb: One kilogram Rhodesian custom-made bomb with a four-six second hand-grenade fuse.

Callsign: A group of operators, each group with its own radio identification number.

Casevac/casevacked: Casualty evacuation.

Camo: Camouflage.

Chimurenga: A Shona word for "War of Liberation".

CIO: Central Intelligence Organisation, umbrella organisation of all intelligence.

COIN: Counter Insurgency.

CO: Commanding Officer.

ComOps: Combined Operations, nerve-centre of the Rhodesian war machine, which co-ordinated the various arms of the Security Forces.

Cordtex: Instantaneous detonating cord.

Dak: Dakota.

DZ: Dropping Zone.

Fire Force: Highly mobile troops generally ferried by helicopters direct to contact with the terrorists. Each flight of troop-carrying helicopters was escorted by a helicopter gunship.

FN: (Fabrique Nationale) Belgian designed semi-automatic and automatic NATO weapon on general issue to Rhodesian Security Forces.

FRELIMO: (The Front for the Liberation of Mozambique) which became the ruling party of Mozambique.

Fred/Freddie: Nickname for FRELIMO.

Frontline States: Tanzania, Zambia, Mozambique, Botswana and Angola.

G-Car: Troop-carrying Alouette helicopter with twin machineguns.

Gatecrasher: Rhodesian-manufactured charge designed to blow locks off gates.

H-Hour: Time attack due to start.

Hot Extraction: To be pulled from a dangerous situation. A true hot extraction was to be winched into helicopter using hot extraction harness worn by SAS troops.

Hot Pursuit: Cross-border pursuit of the enemy.

Hulk: Rhodesian-manufactured charge, powerful enough to blow man-size hole in a wall.

Indaba: Traditional meeting of African chiefs.

Jesse: Thick thorn type bush.

JOC: Joint Operational Command, local military headquarters where uniformed Police, the Army, the Air Force and Special Branch co-operated and worked in harmony to pool their intelligence.

K-Car: (Kill-car.) Alouette with 20 millimetre cannon, and often carrying airborne commander.

Knock-Knocks: Rhodesian-manufactured charges designed to open door locks.

Kopje: Hill.

Kraals: African villages.

Lemon: Military operation that came to nothing.

LUP: Lay-Up Position.

Lynx: Cessna 337.

LZ: Landing Zone.

Maningi's/Mabuno: Derogatory name for whites.

MNR: Mozambique National Resistance, dedicated to the overthrow of FRELIMO.

Mujibas: Unemployed youths who acted as the eyes, ears and runners for terrorists.

NCO: Non-Commissioned Officer.

Ndebele: Tribe indigenous to the western part of Rhodesia.

NS: National Service.

O Group: Orders Group.

OAU: Organisation of African Unity.

OC: Officer Commanding.

2IC: Second-In-Command.

Op: Operation.

ParaDak: Dakota bearing paratroopers.

PE: Plastic explosive.

PF: Patriotic Front, so-called alliance between Robert Mugabe's ZANU and Joshua Nkomo's ZAPU.

PJI: Parachute Jumping Instructor.

QM: Quartermaster.

Rafting-up: Linking boats side-by-side to form raft effect.

RAR: Rhodesian African Rifles.

Ratpacks: Rations.

Recce: Reconnaissance.

Ringmain: Device for connecting up several explosive charges, enabling them to detonate simultaneously. Normally *Cordtex.*

RF: Ian Smith's Rhodesian Front party.

RLI: Rhodesian Light Infantry.

RPD: Portable light machinegun.

RPG-7: Rocket launcher.

R and R: Rest and Recreation.

RV: Rendezvous.

SAS: Special Air Service.

SB: Special Branch.

Shabeen: A place where liquor is sold illegally.

Shrike: British exploder mechanism used in demolitions.

Shona: Tribe indigenous to central and eastern Rhodesia.

Sitrep: Situation Report.

SKS: (Simonov) 7,62 millimetre semi-automatic carbine.

Small Means: Short-range VHF radio, mainly used in ground to air communications.

Stag: Guard duty.

Strela (or SAM-7): Soviet manufactured heat-seeking missile.

Sunray: Leader.

SWAPO: South West Africa People's Organisation.

TA, TF: Territorial Army, Territorial Force.

Terr: Nickname for terrorist.

TTL: Tribal Trust Land.

UANC: United African National Council (formerly ANC) of Bishop Abel Muzorewa.

UDI: Unilateral Declaration of Independence.

WO: Warrant Officer.

Wombles: Police Reservists.

ZANU: Zimbabwe African National Union of Robert Mugabe, the political wing.

ZANLA: Zimbabwe African National Liberation Army, ZANU's military wing. Training was mainly Chinese orientated, and essentially Maoist in character.

ZAPU: Zimbabwe African People's Union of Joshua Nkomo, the political wing.

ZIPRA: Zimbabwe People's Revolutionary Army, ZAPU's military wing. Training was Russian-influenced.

BIBLIOGRAPHY

The following sources were found useful:

Anderson, Dennis, *Rhodesia: A Case of Diminishing Options* (1980)
Cowies, Virginia, *The Phantom Major,* (Collins, 1958)
Evans, Michael, *Fighting Against Chimurenga: An Analysis of Counter-Insurgency In Rhodesia 1972-79* (Salisbury, The Historical Association of Zimbabwe, 1981)
Farran, Roy, *Operation Tombola,* (Collins, 1960)
Geraghty, Tony, *Who Dares Wins,* (Arms and Armour Press, 1980)
Lovatt, John, *Contact,* (Galaxie Press, 1977)
Martin, David and Johnson, Phyllis, *The Struggle for Zimbabwe,* (Faber, 1981)
McCormack, Dr Richard, *The Rhodesian Debacle,* (1980)
Moorcraft, Paul, *A Short Thousand Years,* (Khenty Press, 1979)
Nkomo, Joshua, *Nkomo, The Story of My Life,* (Metheun London, 1984)
Padbury, Dave, *Political Consequences of Chosen Strategies in the Rhodesian Insurgency,* (1980)
Pincher, Chapman, *Inside Story,* (Sidgwick and Jackson, 1978)
Salt, Beryl, *The Valiant Years,* (Galaxie Press, 1878)
Shay, Reg and Chris Vermaak, *The Silent War, The Fight for Southern Africa,* (Galaxie Press, 1971)
Reid-Daly, Ron, *Selous Scouts, Top Secret War* as told to Peter Stiff, (Galago Press, 1982)
RAF At War, (Ian Allan Ltd in conjunction with the RAF Benevolent Fund, 1983)
Venter, Al J. *The Zambezi Salient: Conflict in Southern Africa* (Howard Timmins, Cape Town, 1974)
Warner, Phillip, *The Special Air Service,* (Kimber, 1971)
Wigglesworth, Tom, *Perhaps Tomorrow,* (Galaxie Press, 1980)

Natal Mercury, Durban
The Daily News, Durban
The Rhodesia Herald
Zambia Daily Mail
The Citizen, Johannesburg
Rhodesian Ministry of Information
The Times, London

INDEX

447

448